Dedication

First and foremost, I would like to thank my parents for being a great support throughout my career and while writing this book.

Heartfelt gratitude goes to my wife and my sisters for their patience and endurance in supporting me to take up and accomplish this challenge.

I would also like to acknowledge the efforts of the employees at CADArtifex for their dedication to editing the contents of this book.

Contents at a Glance

FreeCAD 0.20
A Power Guide for Beginners and Intermediate Users

CADArtifex

A premium provider of learning products and solutions
www.cadartifex.com

FreeCAD 0.20: A Power Guide for Beginners and Intermediate Users
Author: Sandeep Dogra
Email: info@cadartifex.com

Published by
CADArtifex
www.cadartifex.com

NOTICE TO THE READER

The publisher and the author make no representations or warranties concerning the accuracy or completeness of the contents of this work/text and specifically disclaim all warranties, including without limitation warranties of fitness for a particular purpose. The publisher does not guarantee any of the products described in the text nor has performed any independent analysis in connection with any of the product information contained in the text. No warranty may be created or extended by sales or promotional materials. This work is sold with the understanding that the publisher is not engaged in rendering legal, accounting, or other professional services. Neither the publisher nor the author shall be liable for damages arising here from. Further, readers should be aware that Internet websites listed or referenced in this work may have changed or may have been removed in the time between the writing and the publishing of this work.

Examination Copies

Textbooks received as examination copies in any form such as paperback or eBook are for review only and may not be made available for the use of the student. These files may not be transferred to any other party. The resale of examination copies is prohibited.

Electronic Files

The electronic file/eBook in any form of this textbook is licensed to the original user only and may not be transferred to any other party.

Disclaimer

The author has made sincere efforts to ensure the accuracy of the material described herein, however, the author makes no warranty, expressed or implied, concerning the quality, accuracy, or freedom from error of this document or the products it describes.

www.cadartifex.com

Table of Contents

Chapter 4. Creating Datum Geometries .... 147 - 194

Chapter 7. Mirroring and Patterning Features .... 285 - 316

Chapter 8. Creating Holes and Dress-up Features .... 317 - 356

Chapter 9. Creating Assemblies .... 357 - 392

Preface

FreeCAD is an open-source parametric 3D CAD software, the development of which is completely open-source (LGPL license). FreeCAD was primarily developed for mechanical engineering and product design. However, with its clear and simple user interface, and powerful engineering toolkits, it is now widely used across all engineering disciplines such as mechanical, architecture, finite element analysis (FEA), automobile, 3D printing, and so on. FreeCAD is maintained and developed by a community of passionate developers, users, moderators, and translators, who voluntarily come together to make FreeCAD a free and powerful tool. It is developed by everyone, for everyone.

FreeCAD is a feature-based, fully parametric 3D CAD modeling, Finite Element Analysis (FEA), manufacturing (CAM/CNC), reverse engineering, and documentation software that enables every industry to design real-life products of any size right from the point of conception of an idea to its production. It provides a wide range of powerful tools that lets you create, export, and edit full-precision real-world 3D solid models. It can generate various drawing views of models to create 2D drawings for production, export them for 3D printing or CNC machining, perform Finite Element Analyses (FEA), etc. In addition, FreeCAD allows you to export design data, validate designs, publish 2D drawings, study robot movements, produce machine instructions (G-code) for CNC machines, and so on.

FreeCAD 0.20: A Power Guide for Beginners and Intermediate Users textbook has been designed for instructor-led courses as well as self-paced learning. It is intended to help engineers and designers interested in learning FreeCAD to create 3D mechanical designs. This textbook is an excellent guide for new FreeCAD users and a great teaching aid for classroom training. It consists of 10 chapters and a total of 446 pages covering major workbenches of FreeCAD such as **Sketcher**, **Part Design**, **A2plus**, and **TechDraw**. The textbook teaches you to use FreeCAD mechanical design software for building parametric 3D solid components and assemblies as well as creating 2D drawings.

This textbook not only focuses on the usage of the tools/commands of FreeCAD but also the concept of design. Every chapter in this textbook contains tutorials that provide users with step-by-step instructions for creating mechanical designs and drawings with ease. Moreover, every chapter ends with hands-on test drives that allow users to experience the user-friendly and powerful technical capabilities of FreeCAD.

Who Should Read This Textbook

This textbook is written to benefit a wide range of FreeCAD users, varying from beginners to advanced users as well as FreeCAD instructors. The easy-to-follow chapters of this textbook allow easy comprehension of different design techniques, FreeCAD tools, and design principles.

What Is Covered in This Textbook

FreeCAD 0.20: A Power Guide for Beginners and Intermediate Users textbook is designed to help you learn everything you need to know to start using FreeCAD with straightforward, step-by-step tutorials. This textbook covers the following topics:

Chapter 1, "Introduction to FreeCAD," introduces system requirements for installing FreeCAD, different FreeCAD workbenches, user interface components, and methods to invoke shortcut menus. It also explains how to customize the Toolbar Area, change the position of toolbars, edit background color, identify FreeCAD documents, export documents to other CAD formats, save a document, and open an existing document.

Chapter 2, "Creating and Editing Sketches with FreeCAD," discusses how to invoke the Sketcher Workbench within the Part Design Workbench. It explains how to specify the units as well as the grids and snap settings. This chapter also introduces methods for drawing lines, arcs, circles, ellipses, elliptical arcs, hyperbolic arcs, parabolic arcs, B-splines, polylines, rectangles, polygons, and slots by using the respective sketching tools. Additionally, this chapter elaborates on creating fillets, trimming sketch entities, extending sketch entities, creating construction sketch entities, applying geometric and dimensional constraints, editing and modifying dimensions, and different states of a sketch.

Chapter 3, "Creating Base Feature of a 3D Solid Model," introduces how to create pad and revolution features. It also explains various methods for navigating a model, displaying standard views, and changing the display style of a model, in addition to the application of Navigation Cube.

Chapter 4, "Creating Datum Geometries," introduces various methods for creating additional datum planes, axes, and points by using the respective tools.

Chapter 5, "Creating Pocket and Groove Features," discusses how to create pocket and groove features by removing the material from the model. The chapter also describes methods for projecting external geometries into the sketch, displaying a section view and an earlier state of a model, reordering features, deleting and editing features, and defining display properties to the model. Further, it explains how to tag the degrees of freedom of assembly components and move a component along its free and fixed degrees of freedom.

Chapter 6, "Creating Pipe, Loft, and Helix Features," explains how to create additive pipe features, multi-section additive pipe features, subtractive pipe features, additive loft features, and subtractive loft features, in addition to additive and subtractive helix features.

Chapter 7, "Mirroring and Patterning Features," introduces how to mirror features of a model about a mirroring plane. It also discusses creating a linear pattern, a polar pattern, and a multi-transform pattern.

Chapter 8, "Creating Holes and Dress-up Features," discusses how to create standard or customized holes such as counterbore and countersink as per standard specifications. It also discusses the methods for creating different types of dress-up features: fillet, chamfer, thickness (shell), and angular draft for applying treatment to the existing edges and faces of a model.

Chapter 9, "*Creating Assemblies*," introduces methods for creating assemblies by using the Top-down assembly approach and the Bottom-up assembly approach. It also discusses methods for installing the A2plus workbench, inserting components, and applying different types of constraints for assembling components. Further, it explains how to tag the degrees of freedom of assembly components and move a component along its free and fixed degrees of freedom.

Chapter 10, "*Creating 2D Drawings*," discusses how to invoke the TechDraw Workspace for creating a 2D drawing of a part or an assembly. It also explains how to insert a drawing sheet, edit the title block text of a sheet, create an independent 2D projection view, modify the scale of a view, create multiple linked 2D projection views of a model, and display hidden lines on the views. This chapter also elaborates on creating a section view and a detail view, in addition to applying dimensions and exporting a drawing as DXF and SVG files.

Icons/Terms used in this Textbook
The following icons and terms are used in this textbook:

Note
Note: Notes highlight information requiring special attention.

Tip
Tip: Tips provide additional advice, which increases the efficiency of the users.

Menu
A menu is a list in which a set of tools are grouped, see Figure 1.

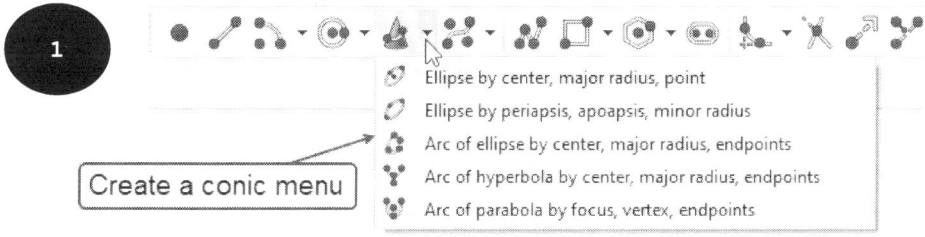

Drop-down List
A drop-down list is a list in which a set of options are grouped, see Figure 2.

Check Box
A check box allows you to turn on or off the uses of a particular option, see Figure 2.

Field
A Field allows you to enter a new value, or modify an existing value, as per your requirement, see Figure 2.

Button

A Button appears as a 3D icon and is used for confirming or discarding an action, see Figure 2.

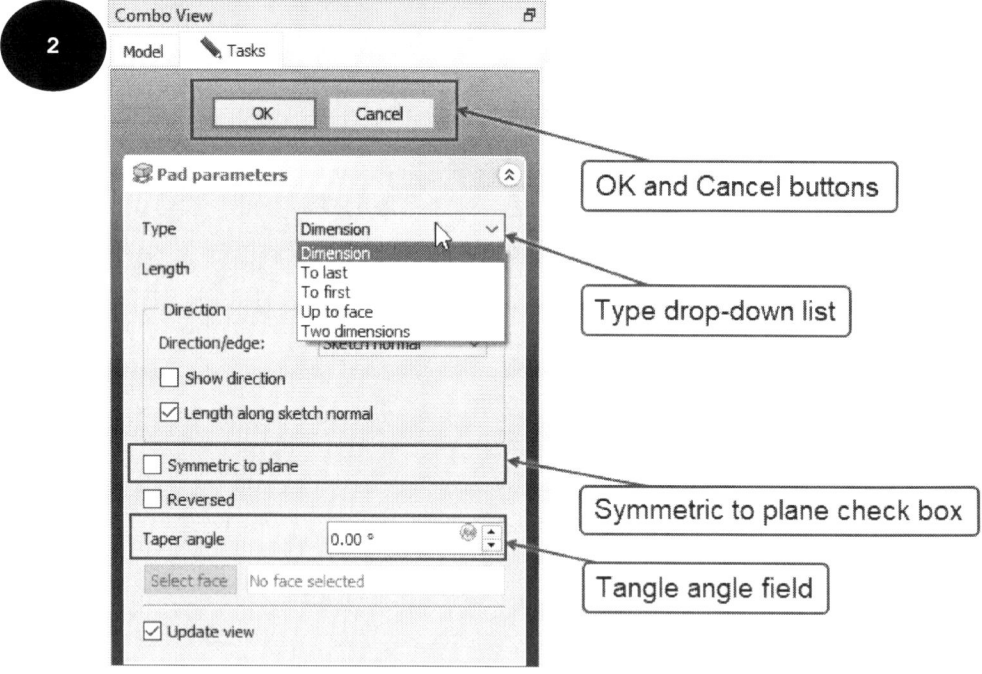

How to Download Online Resources

Students and faculty members can download all parts/models used in the illustrations, Tutorials, and Hands-on Test Drives (exercises) of the textbook. In addition, faculty can also download PowerPoint Presentations (PPTs) of each chapter of the textbook.

To download the free online teaching and learning resources of the textbook, log on to our website (*cadartifex.com/login*) by using your username and password. If you are a new user, you need to first register (*cadartifex.com/register*) to download the online resources of the textbook.

How to Contact the Author

We value your feedback and suggestions. You can email us at *info@cadartifex.com*. You can also log on to our website *www.cadartifex.com* to provide your feedback regarding the textbook as well as download the free learning resources.

We would like to express our sincere gratitude to you for purchasing the **FreeCAD 0.20: A Power Guide for Beginners and Intermediate Users** textbook. We hope that the information and concepts introduced in this textbook help you to accomplish your professional goals.

Introduction to FreeCAD

This chapter discusses the following topics:

- Installing FreeCAD
- Getting Started with FreeCAD
- Starting a New Document
- Working with Workbenches
- Invoking Different Workbenches
- Exploring the User-Interface Components
- Invoking a Shortcut Menu
- Customizing the Toolbar Area
- Defining the Position of Toolbars
- Changing the Background Color
- Identifying FreeCAD Documents
- Exporting Documents to Other CAD Formats
- Saving a Document
- Opening a Document

Welcome to the world of 3D parametric Computer-Aided Design (CAD) with FreeCAD. FreeCAD is an open-source parametric 3D CAD software, the development of which is completely open-source (LGPL license). FreeCAD was primarily developed for mechanical engineering and product design. However, with its clear and simple user interface, and powerful engineering toolkits, it is now widely used across all engineering disciplines such as mechanical, architecture, finite element analysis (FEA), automobile, 3D printing, and so on. FreeCAD is maintained and developed by a community of passionate developers, users, moderators, and translators, who voluntarily come together to make FreeCAD a free and powerful tool. It is developed by everyone, for everyone.

FreeCAD is a feature-based, fully parametric 3D CAD modeling, Finite Element Analysis (FEA), manufacturing (CAM/CNC), reverse engineering, and documentation software that enables every industry to design real-life products of any size right from the point of conception of an idea to its production. It provides a wide range of powerful tools that lets you create, export, and edit full-precision real-world 3D solid models. It can generate various drawing views of models to create 2D drawings for production, export them for 3D printing or CNC machining, perform Finite Element Analyses (FEA), etc. In addition, FreeCAD allows you to export design data, validate designs, publish 2D drawings, study robot movements, produce machine instructions (G-code) for CNC machines, and so on.

Installing FreeCAD

If FreeCAD is not installed on your system, you must install it first. However, before starting the installation of FreeCAD, you must assess the system requirements and ensure that you have a system that can run FreeCAD correctly. The following are the system requirements for the installation of FreeCAD.

1. Operating Systems: Windows 7/8/10/11, macOS 10.12 or later, or a Linux distribution.
2. Processor: 64-bit processor (multi-core processor with a clock speed of 2GHz or higher recommended).
3. RAM: 4 GB RAM minimum (8 GB or more recommended).
4. Graphics Card: OpenGL-compatible graphics card (Dedicated graphics card with OpenGL 4.0 support or higher recommended).
5. Hard Drive Space: A minimum of 1GB of free disk space is required after installation (SSD with at least 10GB of free disk space recommended).

Note: FreeCAD is an open-source parametric 3D CAD software available for free download and installation. To download FreeCAD, visit the FreeCAD website at *freecad.org/downloads.php*

Getting Started with FreeCAD

When you have FreeCAD installed on your system, launch it by double-clicking the FreeCAD icon available on your desktop. After loading all the required files, the startup user interface of FreeCAD appears, see Figure 1.1.

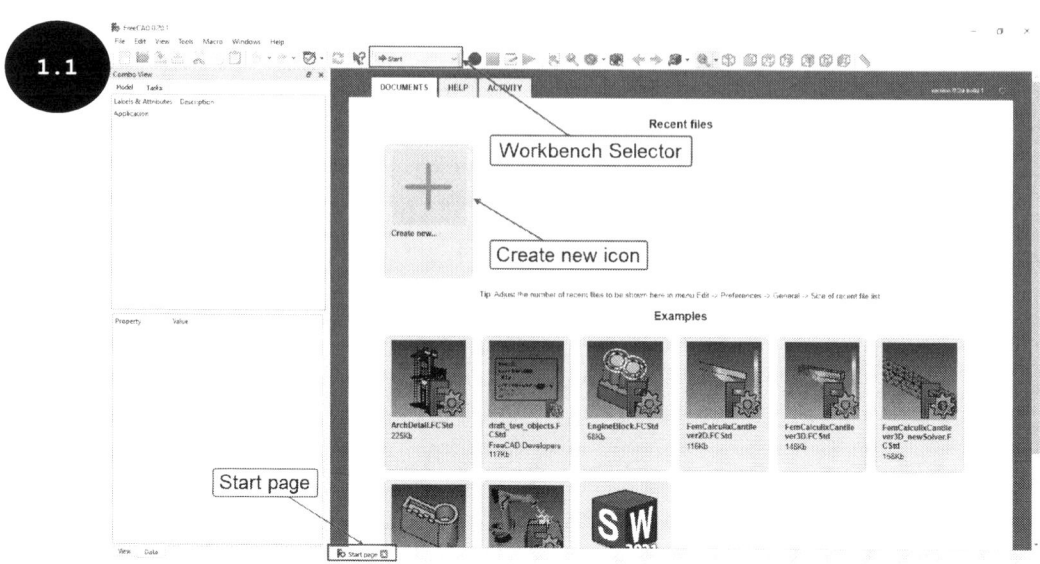

Note that every time you start FreeCAD, the **Start** workbench is invoked with the display of the **Start** page, by default, refer to Figure 1.1. The **Start** page acts as a welcome screen that displays recently opened documents, example files, help documentation, the latest activity in FreeCAD, and so on in their respective tabs (**DOCUMENTS, HELP,** and **ACTIVITY**). By default, the **DOCUMENTS** tab is activated on the **Start** page. As a result, the recently opened documents and example files appear on the screen. To access the help documents for different workbenches of FreeCAD, activate the **HELP** tab of the **Start** page. You can also access recent commits or activities related to FreeCAD by activating the **ACTIVITY** tab of the **Start** page.

Starting a New Document

In FreeCAD, you need to start a new empty document for creating a 3D solid part, an assembly, or a 2D drawing. For doing so, click on the **Create new** icon on the **Start** page of the startup user interface of FreeCAD (refer to Figure 1.1) or press the CTRL + N keys. A new empty document gets invoked with the default name "**unnamed: 1**" in a separate tab and it becomes active by default, see Figure 1.2.

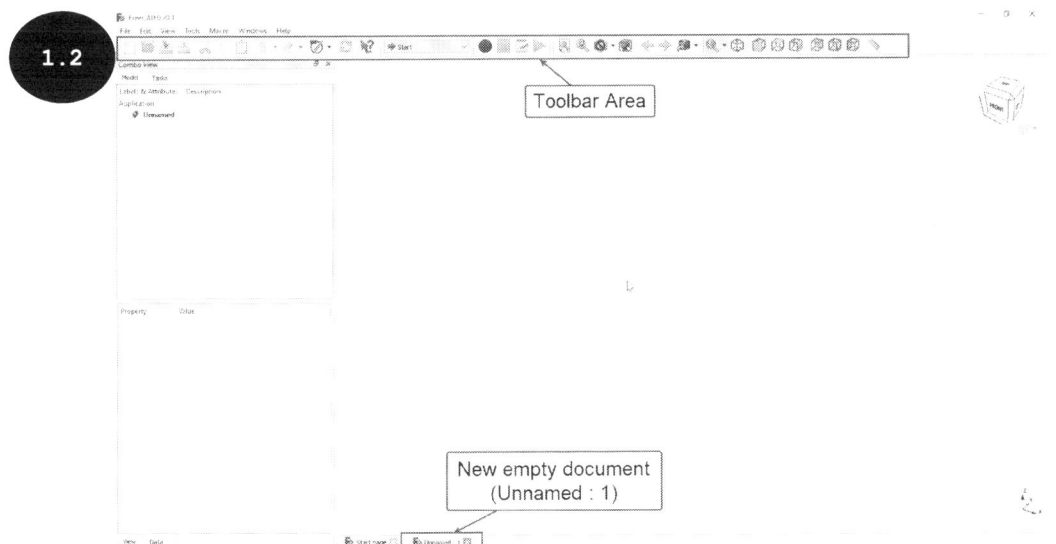

Alternatively, to invoke a new empty document, click on the **New** tool in the **File** toolbar (see Figure 1.3) or click on the **File > New** in the **Standard Menu**, see Figure 1.4.

Note that the availability of toolbars in the **Toolbar Area** of a document depends upon the activated workbench, refer to Figure 1.2. By default, when you launch FreeCAD, the **Start** workbench is activated. To create a 3D solid part, an assembly, or a 2D drawing in the currently activated document, you need to invoke the respective workbench (**Part Design**, **A2plus**, or **TechDraw**) by using the **Workbench Selector**.

Working with Workbenches

Workbenches are defined as task-oriented environments in which different tools and commands are organized according to design objectives. For example, the **Part Design** workbench contains various tools and commands for creating 3D solid designs (parts and assemblies). You will learn about creating 3D solid parts and assemblies in later chapters. Similarly, the **TechDraw** workbench contains tools and commands for creating 2D drawings. You can switch between different workbenches within a document. The method for invoking different workbenches of FreeCAD is discussed next.

Invoking Different Workbenches

In FreeCAD, after starting a new document, you can invoke the desired workbench to create a 3D solid part, an assembly, or a 2D drawing by using the **Workbench Selector**, see Figure 1.5.

To invoke the **Part Design** workbench to create a 3D solid part, invoke the **Workbench Selector** in the **Workbench** toolbar (see Figure 1.5) and then select the **Part Design** workbench. The **Part Design** workbench gets invoked, see Figure 1.6.

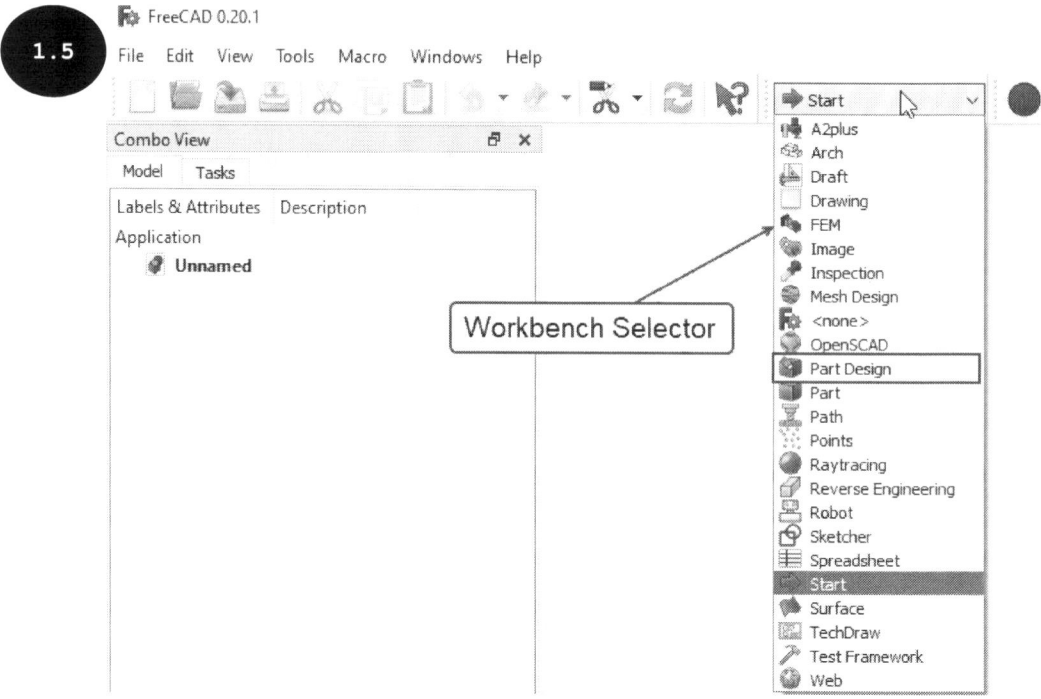

Similar to invoking the **Part Design** workbench, you can invoke other FreeCAD workbenches such as **Sketcher**, **Drawing**, and **TechDraw** using the **Workbench Selector**, as required.

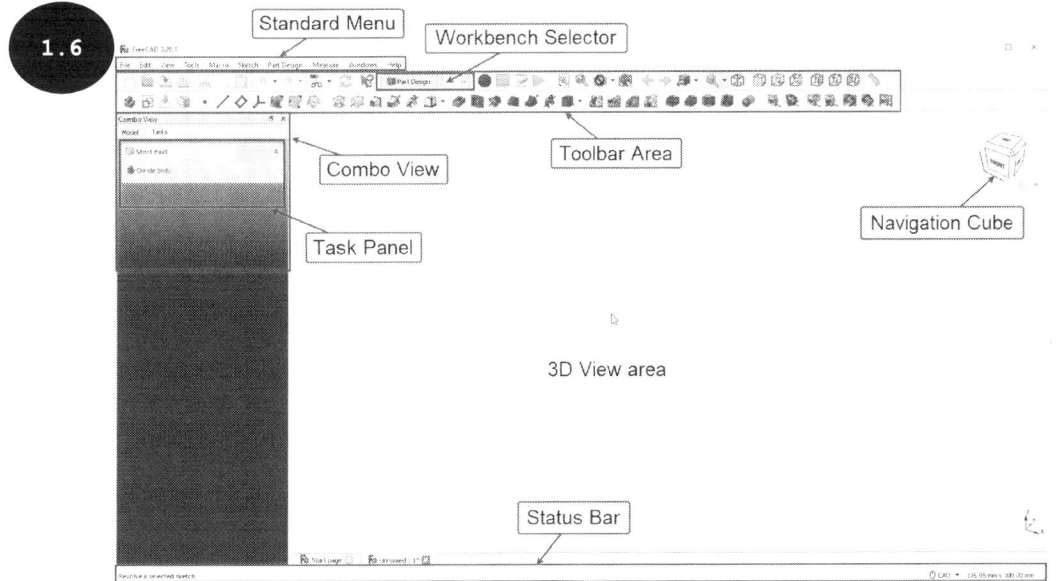

Exploring the User-Interface Components

The various user-interface components of the **Part Design** workbench such as the **Toolbar Area**, **Workbench Selector**, **Standard Menu**, **Status Bar**, **Combo View**, **Navigation Cube**, **Task Panel**, and **3D View** are discussed next.

Toolbar Area

The **Toolbar Area** contains different toolbars that provide access to various tools specific to each workbench. For example, the **Part Design** workbench contains toolbars with different tools specific to creating 3D solid models, see Figure 1.7. Similarly, the **TechDraw** workbench contains toolbars with different tools specific to creating 2D drawings for production, see Figure 1.8. In later chapters, you will learn about creating 3D solid models and 2D drawings.

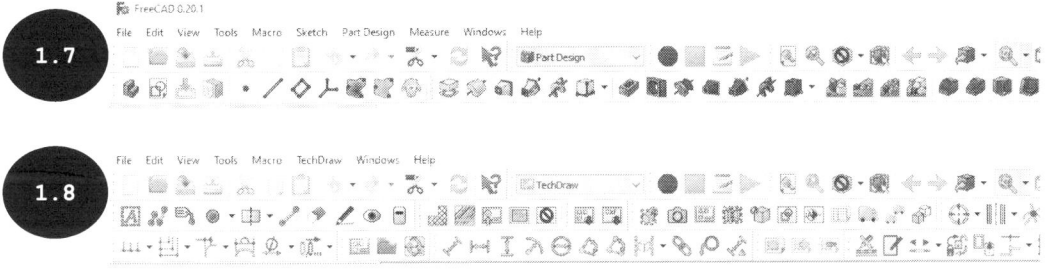

Standard Menu

The **Standard Menu** contains different sets of menus such as **File**, **Edit**, **View**, and **Tools** at the top of the **Toolbar Area**, see Figure 1.9. These menus contain basic tools and commands to operate the program.

Workbench Selector

The **Workbench Selector** provides a list of available workbenches, see Figure 1.10. You can select the required workbench in the **Workbench Selector** for activating a specific task-oriented environment to meet a particular design objective.

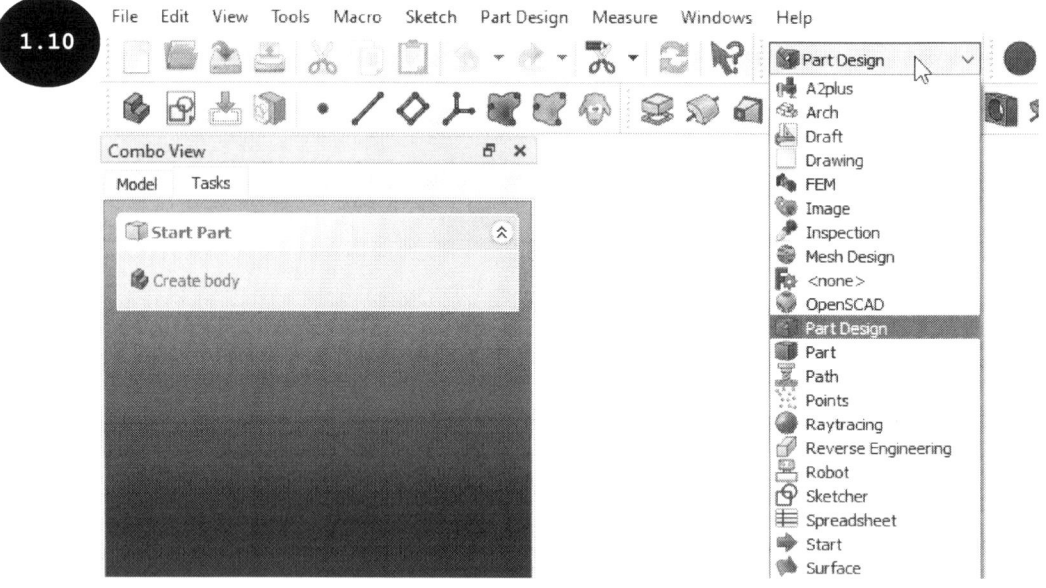

Combo View

The **Combo View** is located on the left side of the 3D View area, by default, see Figure 1.11. It is composed of two sections: the upper section and the lower section.

Upper Section of the Combo View

The upper section of the **Combo View** contains two tabs: **Model** and **Tasks**, see Figure 1.11. The **Model** tab displays the **Tree View**, which keeps a record of all features of a design created in the current document, including 2D sketches, bodies, and datum geometries.

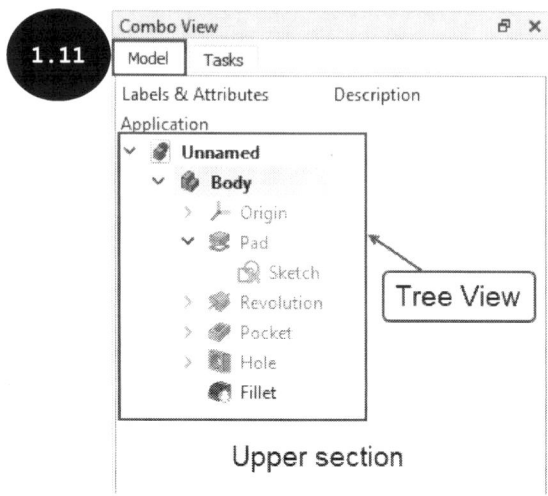

Upper section

The **Tasks** tab displays the **Task Panel**, which allows you to choose different actions depending on the selected geometry in the 3D View area (see Figure 1.12) or specify parameters depending on the active tool, see Figure 1.13. Figure 1.12 shows the **Task Panel** when a face of a model is selected in the 3D View area and Figure 1.13 shows the **Task Panel** when the **Pad** tool is activated.

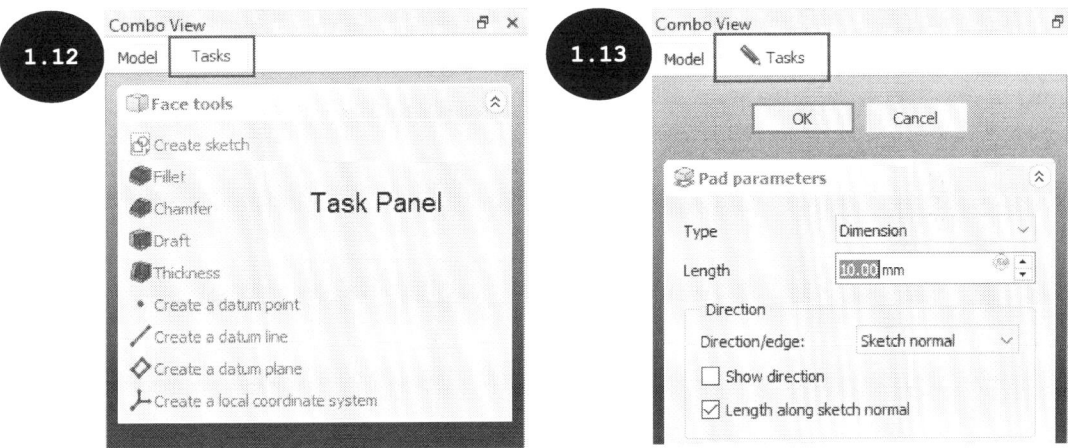

Lower Section of the Combo View

The lower section of the **Combo View** displays the **Property Editor** with **View** and **Data** tabs at its bottom depending on the geometry or feature selected, see Figure 1.14. The **View** tab displays the visualization properties of the selected geometry or feature, and the **Data** tab displays the parametric properties of the selected geometry or feature. You can also edit some of these properties if needed.

Note that the lower section appears only when the **Model** tab is activated in **Combo View** and a geometry or a feature of a model is selected in the 3D View area or the **Tree View**. Figure 1.14 shows the **Property Editor** when a hole feature is selected in the **Tree View**. You will learn about creating different features of a model in later chapters.

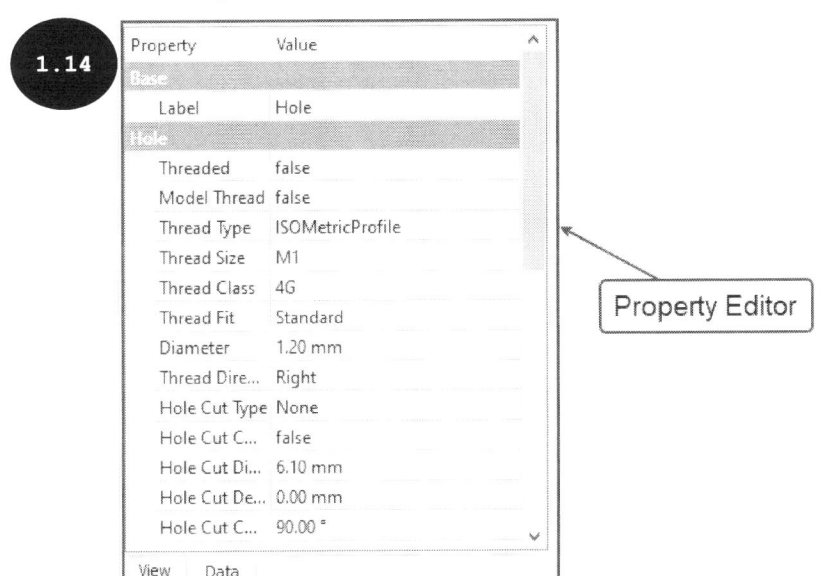

Navigation Cube

The **Navigation Cube** is in the upper right corner of the 3D View area by default, see Figure 1.15. It provides visual information about the current view orientation of a model in the 3D View area. You can also use the **Navigation Cube** to switch between various standard views of a model. You will learn about various components of the **Navigation Cube** and methods for navigating a 3D model by using it in later chapters.

Status Bar

The **Status Bar** is located at the bottom of the 3D View area. It provides some information based on the active tool as well as displays tooltips.

Invoking a Shortcut Menu

A shortcut menu is displayed when you right-click on the geometry of a model, the empty area, or an item in the **Tree View** or **Toolbar**. It allows quick access to the most used tools or options. Note that the availability of options in the shortcut menu depends on the workbench and the item/geometry selected to invoke the shortcut menu. Figure 1.16 shows a shortcut menu that appears when you right-click on the empty area in the 3D View area of the **Part Design** workbench. Figure 1.17 shows a shortcut menu that appears when you right-click on a feature in **Tree View**.

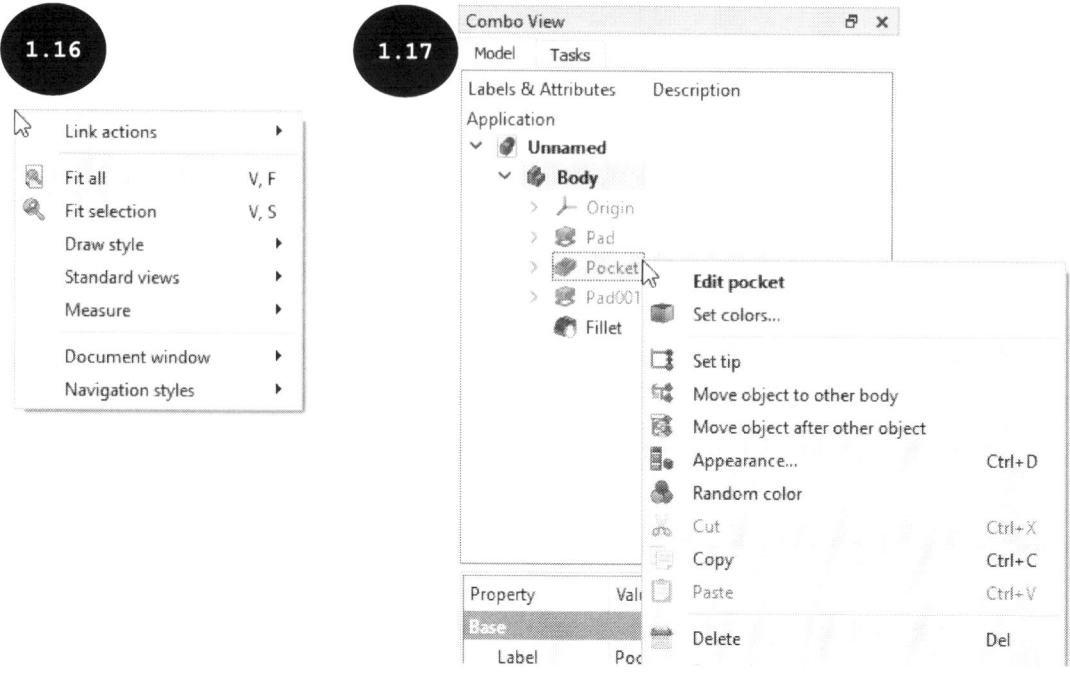

Customizing the Toolbar Area

In FreeCAD, you can customize to add or remove toolbars in the **Toolbar Area** of the active workbench. For doing so, right-click anywhere on the **Toolbar Area** (on a tool of a toolbar or an empty area), see Figure 1.18. A shortcut menu appears with the display of all the available toolbars of the active workbench.

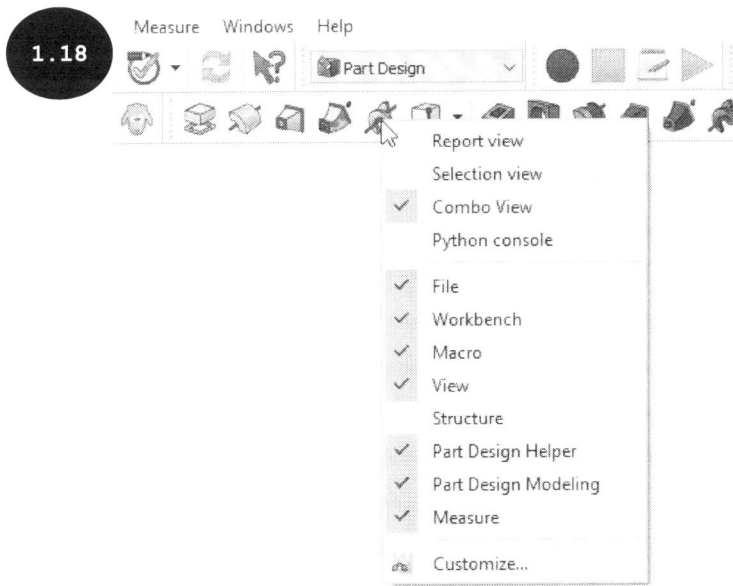

Note that in this shortcut menu, a tick mark in front of the toolbars indicates that these toolbars are already added in the **Toolbar Area**. Click on the required toolbar in the shortcut menu to be added or removed in the **Toolbar Area**.

Defining the Position of Toolbars

In FreeCAD, you can drag the toolbars to define their position in the **Toolbar Area**, as required. For doing so, move the cursor on the vertical dots in front of the first tool on the toolbar, see Figure 1.19. The cursor changes to move cursor, see Figure 1.20. Next, drag the toolbar to define its new position on the **Toolbar Area** or anywhere on the 3D View area by pressing and holding the left mouse button. After the toolbar position is defined, release the left mouse button. You can also dock the toolbars to the left or right side of the 3D View area by dragging and dropping them.

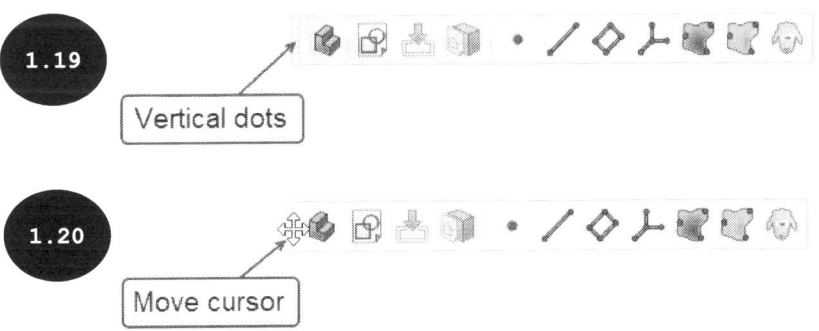

Changing the Background Color

In FreeCAD, you can change the background color of the 3D View area. The method to change the background color is discussed below:

1. Click on **Edit** > **Preferences** in the **Standard Menu**, see Figure 1.21. The **Preferences** dialog box appears.

2. Click on the **Display** section in the left panel of the **Preferences** dialog box and then click on the **Colors** tab, see Figure 1.22. The options related to defining color for selections, the background of the 3D View area, and **Tree View** items appear in the dialog box.

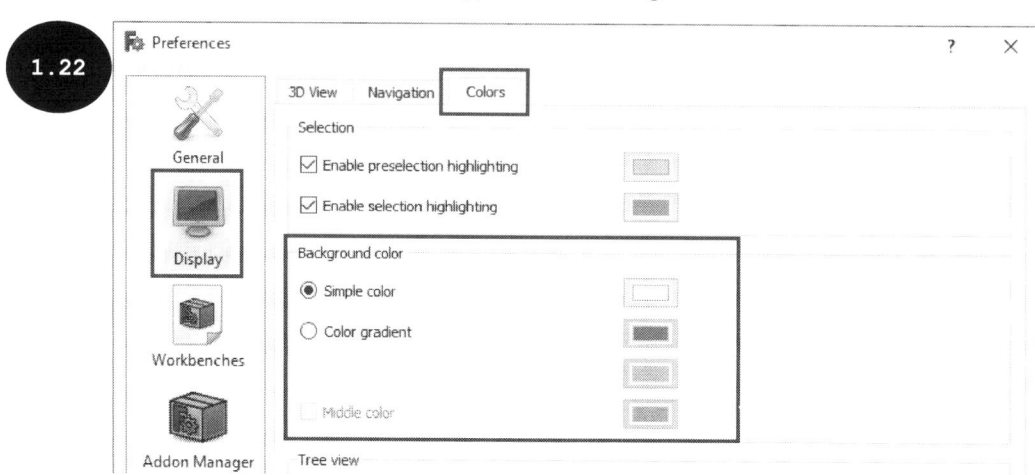

3. Define a color or a color gradient for the background by selecting the required option (**Simple color** or **Color gradient**) in the **Background color** area of the dialog box, respectively.

4. After defining the background color, click on the **Apply** button and then the **OK** button in the dialog box to confirm the change made and exit the dialog box.

Identifying FreeCAD Documents

Documents created in different workbenches like **Sketcher**, **Part Design**, **Arch**, **A2plus**, **Drawing**, and **TechDraw** of FreeCAD have the same native file extension that is *.FCStd*. It means, when you save a FreeCAD document, it will be saved with *.FCStd* file extension.

Exporting Documents to Other CAD Formats

FreeCAD allows you to export FreeCAD documents or files such as parts and assemblies to other CAD formats or neutral file formats such as STEP, STL, IGES, and SAT. The method for exporting a document to another CAD format or a neutral file format is discussed below:

1. Select a body in the **Tree View** of the **Combo View** in an active workbench to be exported, see Figure 1.23.

2. Click on **File > Export** in the **Standard Menu** (see Figure 1.24) or press the CTRL + E keys. The **Export file** dialog box appears.

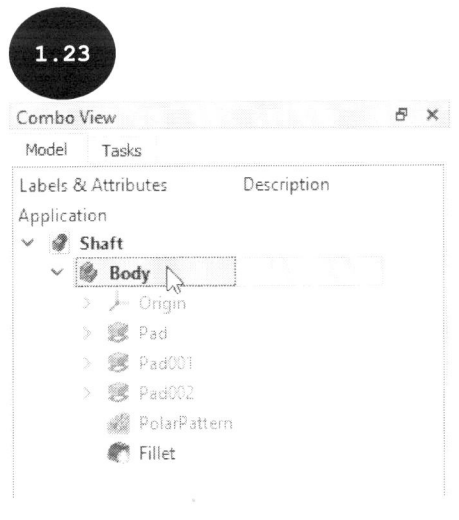

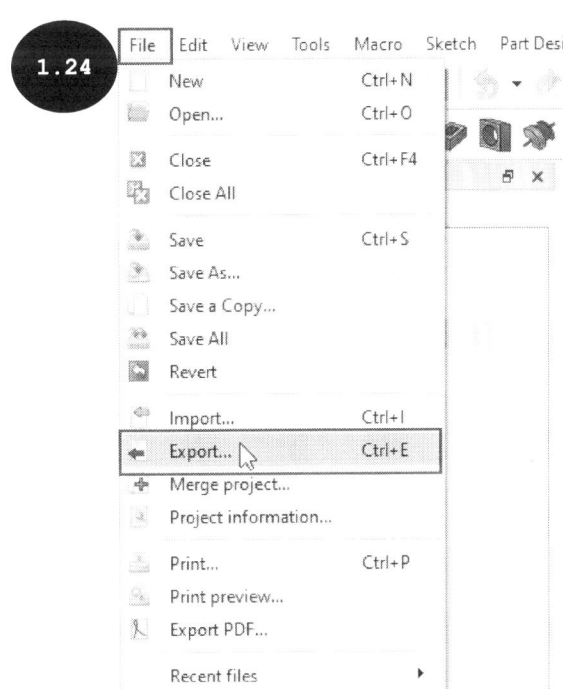

3. In the **Save as type** drop-down list of the **Export file** dialog box, select the required file format such as **3D Manufacturing Format** (*.3mf), **Autodesk DWG 2D** (*.dwg), **Alias Mesh** (*.obj), **Inventor V2.1**(*.iv), **Open CAD Format** (*.oca), **STEP with colors** (*.step *.stp), **STL Mesh** (*.stl *.ast), and **Technical Drawing** (*.svg *.dxf *.pdf).

4. Specify the name of the file or object in the **File name** field of the dialog box. Next, browse to the required location and then click on the **Save** button in the **Export file** dialog box. The FreeCAD model or object gets exported to the selected CAD format.

Saving a Document

After creating a design (Part, Assembly, or 2D Drawing), you need to save it in the required location. The method for saving a design document is discussed below:

1. Click on the **Save** tool in the **File** toolbar (see Figure 1.25) or press the CTRL + S keys. The **Save FreeCAD Document** dialog box appears.

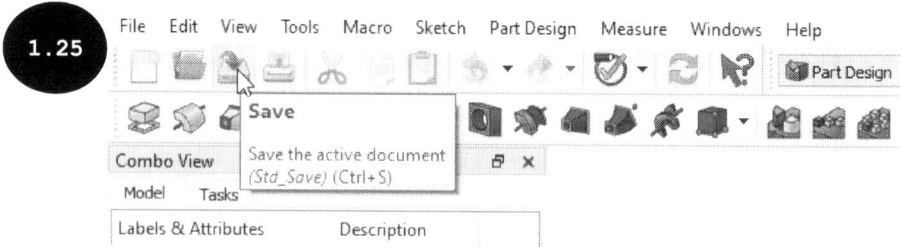

2. Enter the name of the document in the **File name** field of the dialog box and then browse to the required location in the local drive of your system where you want to save the design document.

3. Click on the **Save** button in the dialog box. The design document gets saved at the specified location with the native file extension (*.FCStd).

Note: After saving a design document, you can close it by clicking on **File > Close** in the **Standard Menu** or click on the cross mark in its tab at the lower left corner of the 3D View area.

Tip: It is also possible to save a copy of a design document with a different name. For doing so, click on **File > Save As** or **Save a Copy** in the **Standard Menu**. The **Save FreeCAD Document** dialog box appears. In this dialog box, specify a new name and location for saving the design document and then click on the **Save** button. A copy of the design file gets saved.

Opening a Document

In FreeCAD, you can open an existing native FreeCAD document (.*.*FCStd*) or a document created in another CAD application. The method for opening a document is discussed below:

1. Click on the **Open** tool in the **File** toolbar (see Figure 1.26) or press the CTRL + O keys. The **Open document** dialog box appears.

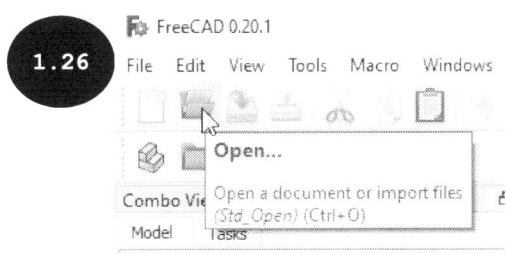

2. In the **Open document** dialog box, browse to the required location where the required document to be opened is saved.

By default, the **Supported formats** (*.FCStd *.3ds *.FCMacro ......) file extension is selected in the drop-down list of the **Open document** dialog box. As a result, all the supported FreeCAD documents including FCStd (native FreeCAD), STEP, STL, IGES, and SAT files appear in the dialog box. You can also select a specific file extension in the drop-down list depending on the document to be opened in FreeCAD.

3. Select the document to be opened in the dialog box and then click on the **Open** button. The selected document gets opened as a new document in a separate tab of FreeCAD and becomes active by default.

Note: You can also import a file such as STEP, STL, IGES, SAT, etc. into a currently active document of FreeCAD. For doing so, click on **File > Import** in the **Standard Menu** (see Figure 1.27) or press the CTRL + I key. The **Import file** dialog box appears. The **Supported formats** (*.3ds *.FCMacro *.FCMat ....) file extension is selected in this dialog box. As a result, all the support documents that can be imported into FreeCAD appear in the dialog box. Browse to the required location and then select a file to be imported into the currently active document of FreeCAD. Next, click on the **Open** button in the dialog box. The select file gets imported into the currently active document of FreeCAD as a new body.

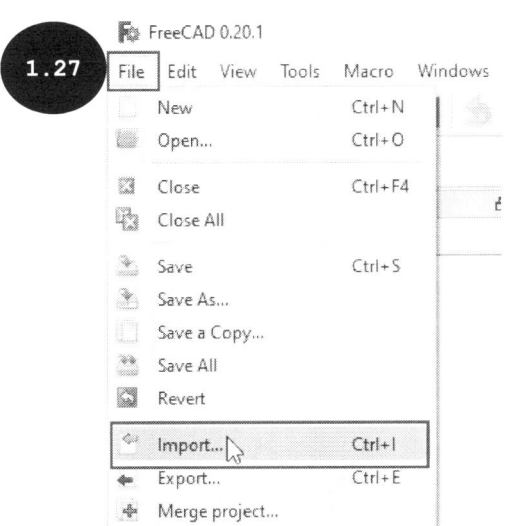

Summary

In this chapter, you have learned about the system requirements for installing FreeCAD, how to start a new document, the different FreeCAD workbenches, user-interface components, and shortcut menus. It also explained the methods to customize the Toolbar Area, specify the position of toolbars, change the background color, identify FreeCAD documents, export documents to other CAD formats, save a document, and open an existing document.

Questions

Complete and verify the following sentences:

- FreeCAD is an _____ 3D CAD software available for free download and installation.

- In FreeCAD, the _____ are defined as task-oriented environments in which different tools and commands are organized according to design objectives.

- The _____ keeps a record of all features of a design created in the current document, including 2D sketches, bodies, and datum geometries.

- The _____ is in the upper right corner of the 3D View area and is used to switch between various standard views of a model.

- The _____ is the native file extension of FreeCAD documents.

- The _____ tool is used for importing a file such as STEP, STL, IGES, and SAT into a currently active document of FreeCAD.

- The _____ tool is used for opening an existing FreeCAD document (*.FCStd) or a document created in another CAD application.

- In FreeCAD, you can customize to add or remove toolbars in the **Toolbar Area** of the active workbench. (True/False)

- You cannot change the position of the toolbars. (True/False)

CHAPTER

2

Creating and Editing Sketches with FreeCAD

In this chapter, the following topics will be discussed:

- Starting a New Document
- Invoking the Part Design Workbench
- Invoking the Sketcher Workbench
- Working with the Selection of Planes
- Specifying Units
- Specifying Grids and Snap Settings
- Drawing a Line
- Drawing an Arc
- Drawing a Circle
- Drawing an Ellipse
- Drawing an Elliptical Arc
- Drawing a Hyperbolic Arc
- Drawing a Parabolic Arc
- Drawing a B-Spline
- Drawing a Polyline
- Drawing a Rectangle
- Drawing Polygons
- Drawing a Slot
- Creating a Fillet
- Trimming Sketch Entities
- Extending Sketch Entities
- Creating Construction Sketch Entities
- Applying Geometric Constraints
- Applying Dimensional Constraints
- Editing and Modifying Dimensions
- Working with Different States of a Sketch
- Exiting the Sketcher Workbench

FreeCAD is an open-source, feature-based, free parametric 3D modeling design, and automation software. Before you start creating 3D models in FreeCAD, you need to understand that to design a 3D model using this software, you need to create all its features one by one, see Figures 2.1 and 2.2. The features are divided into two main categories: sketch-based features and placed features. A feature created by using a sketch is known as a sketch-based feature, whereas a feature created on an existing feature without using a sketch is known as a placed feature. Of the two categories, the sketch-based feature is the first feature of any real-world component to be designed. Therefore, it is important to focus first on drawing a sketch.

Figure 2.1 shows a component consisting of a pad feature and a chamfer. Of these two features, the pad feature is created by using a sketch, refer to Figure 2.2. Therefore, this feature is known as a sketch-based feature. On the other hand, since no sketch is used in creating the chamfer, this feature is known as a placed feature. Figure 2.2 depicts the process of creating the model.

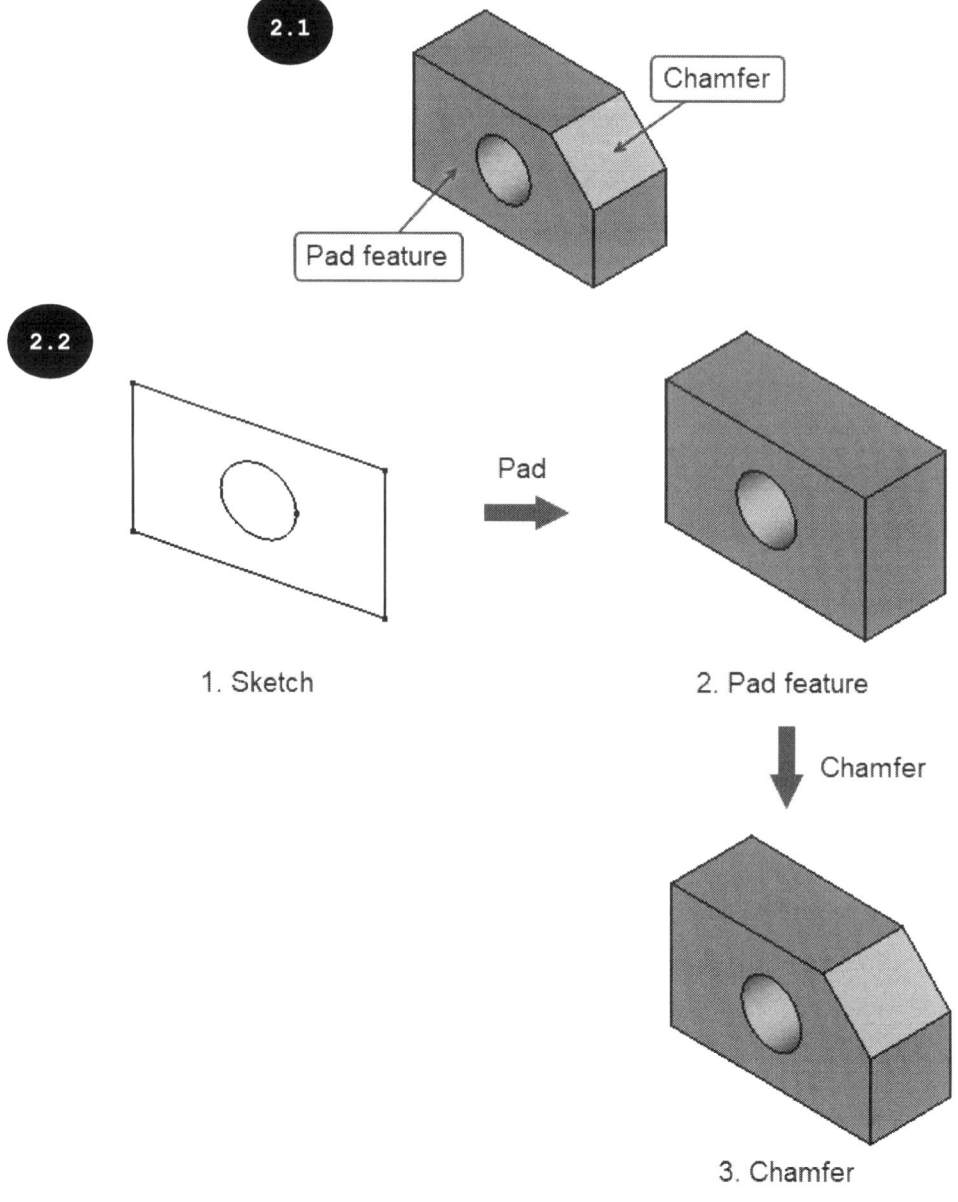

2.1

Chamfer

Pad feature

2.2

1. Sketch

Pad

2. Pad feature

Chamfer

3. Chamfer

As the first feature of any component is sketch-based, first you need to learn how to create sketches in the **Sketcher** workbench. In FreeCAD, the **Sketcher** workbench can be invoked independently or within the **Part Design** workbench. Before you learn about invoking the **Sketcher** workspace, it is important that you first understand how to start a new document in FreeCAD.

Starting a New Document

Start FreeCAD by double-clicking on the **FreeCAD 0.20** icon on your desktop. After loading all the required files, the startup user interface of FreeCAD appears, see Figure 2.3. Every time you start FreeCAD, the **Start** workbench is invoked with the **Start** page, by default, see Figure 2.3. The **Start** page acts as a welcome screen that displays recently opened documents, example files, help documentation, the latest activity in FreeCAD, and so on in their respective tabs (**DOCUMENTS**, **HELP**, and **ACTIVITY**). By default, the **DOCUMENTS** tab is activated on the **Start** page. As a result, the recently opened documents and example files appear on the screen. Various components such as the **Toolbar Area**, **Workbench Selector**, **Standard Menu**, **Status Bar**, and **Combo View** of the startup user interface of FreeCAD have been discussed in Chapter 1.

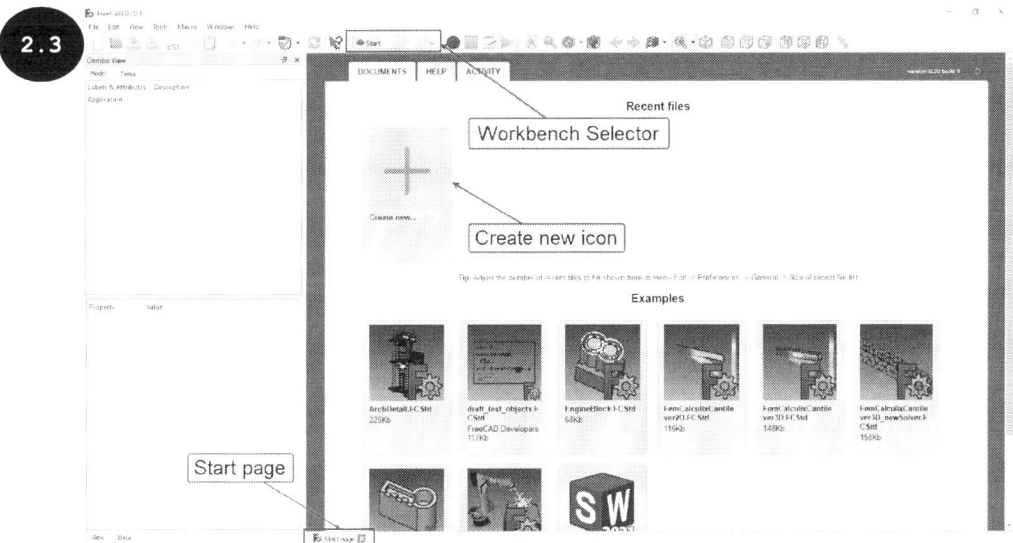

In the startup user interface of FreeCAD, click on the **New** tool in the **File** toolbar (see Figure 2.4) or **File > New** in the **Standard Menu**, see Figure 2.5. A new empty document gets invoked with the default name "**unnamed: 1**" in a separate tab and it becomes active by default, see Figure 2.6. Alternatively, you can click on the **Create new** icon on the **Start** page (refer to Figure 2.3) or press CTRL + N keys for invoking a new empty document. Figure 2.6 shows a new empty document opened with the default name "**unnamed: 1**" in FreeCAD.

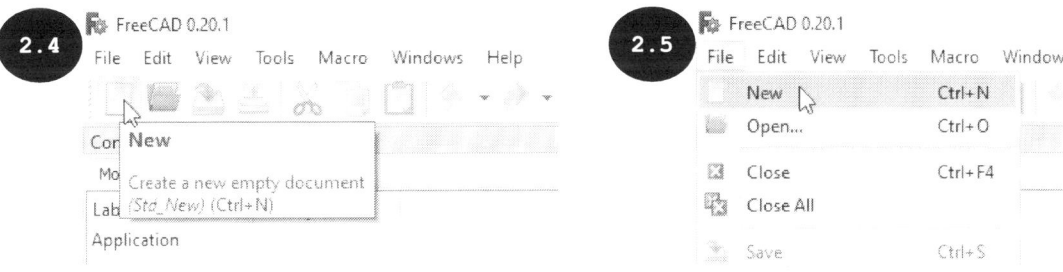

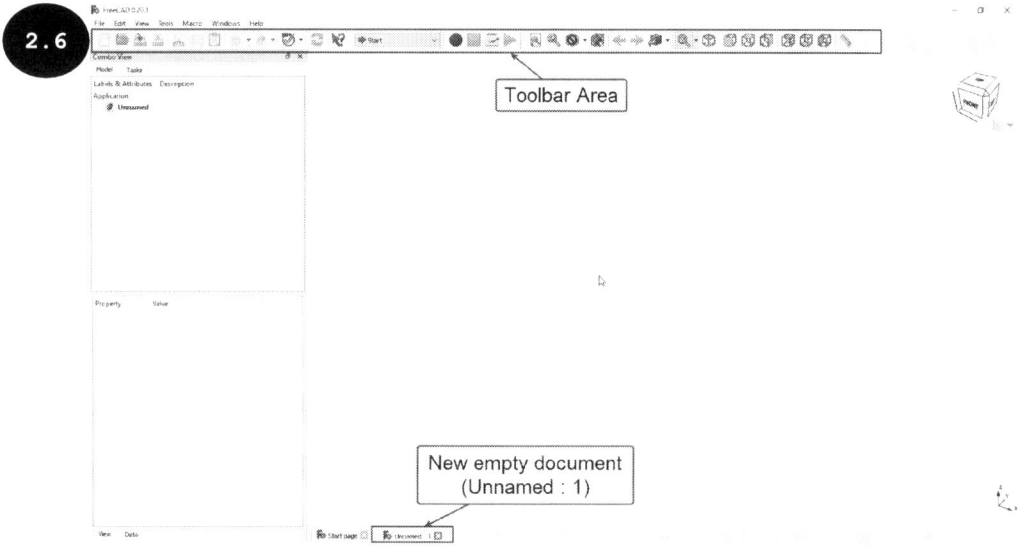

2.6

Toolbar Area

New empty document
(Unnamed : 1)

Note: The availability of toolbars in the **Toolbar Area** of a new document depends upon the activated workbench. You can switch among different workbenches within a document. The methods for invoking the Part Design and Sketcher workspaces are discussed next.

Invoking the Part Design Workbench

To invoke the **Part Design** workbench for creating a 3D solid mechanical part, invoke the **Workbench Selector** in the **Workbench** toolbar and then select the **Part Design** workbench, see Figure 2.7. The **Part Design** workbench gets invoked, see Figure 2.8.

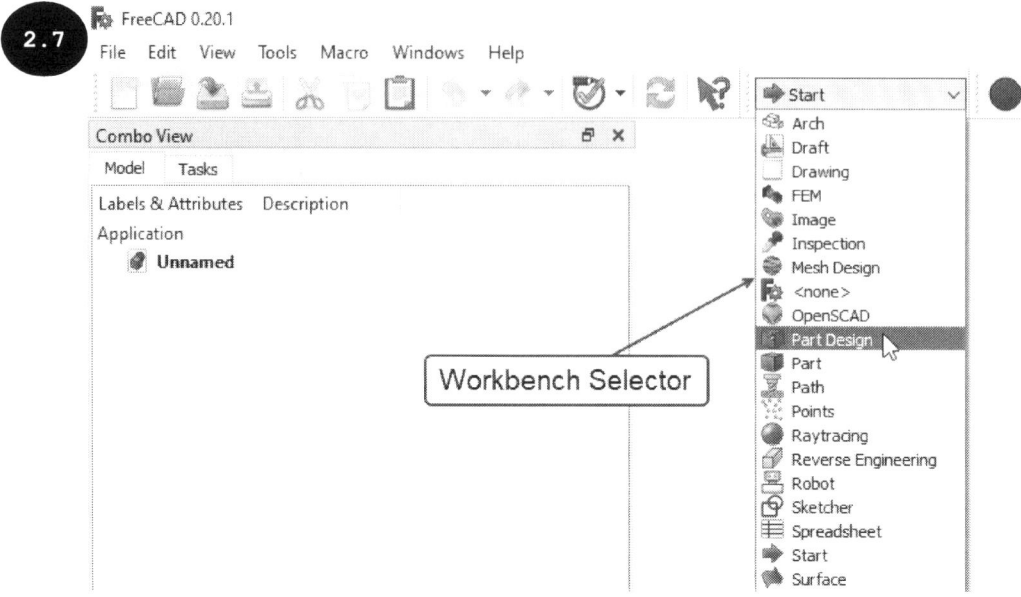

2.7

Workbench Selector

Note: Similar to invoking the **Part Design** workbench, you can invoke the **Sketcher** workbench for creating 2D sketches by selecting the **Sketcher** workbench in the **Workbench Selector**, refer to Figure 2.7. Moreover, the **Sketcher** workbench can also be invoked within the **Part Design** workbench and the method for the same is discussed next.

Invoking the Sketcher Workbench

The method for invoking the **Sketcher** workbench within the **Part Design** workbench for creating a 2D sketch of a feature is discussed below:

1. Click on the **Create sketch** tool in the **Part Design Helper** toolbar (see Figure 2.9) or click on Sketch > Create sketch in the **Standard Menu** (see Figure 2.10). The three default planes, which are mutually perpendicular to each other appear in the 3D View area, see Figure 2.11. Also, the **Task Panel** appears in the **Tasks** tab of the **Combo View** and displays the name of three default planes, see Figure 2.12.

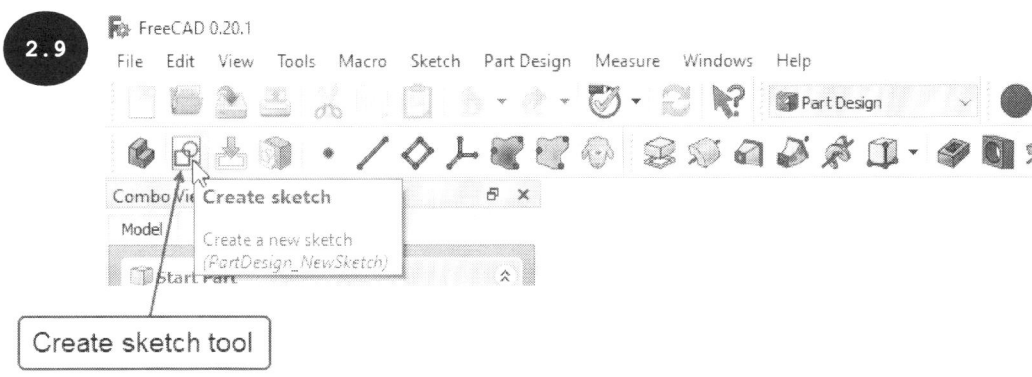

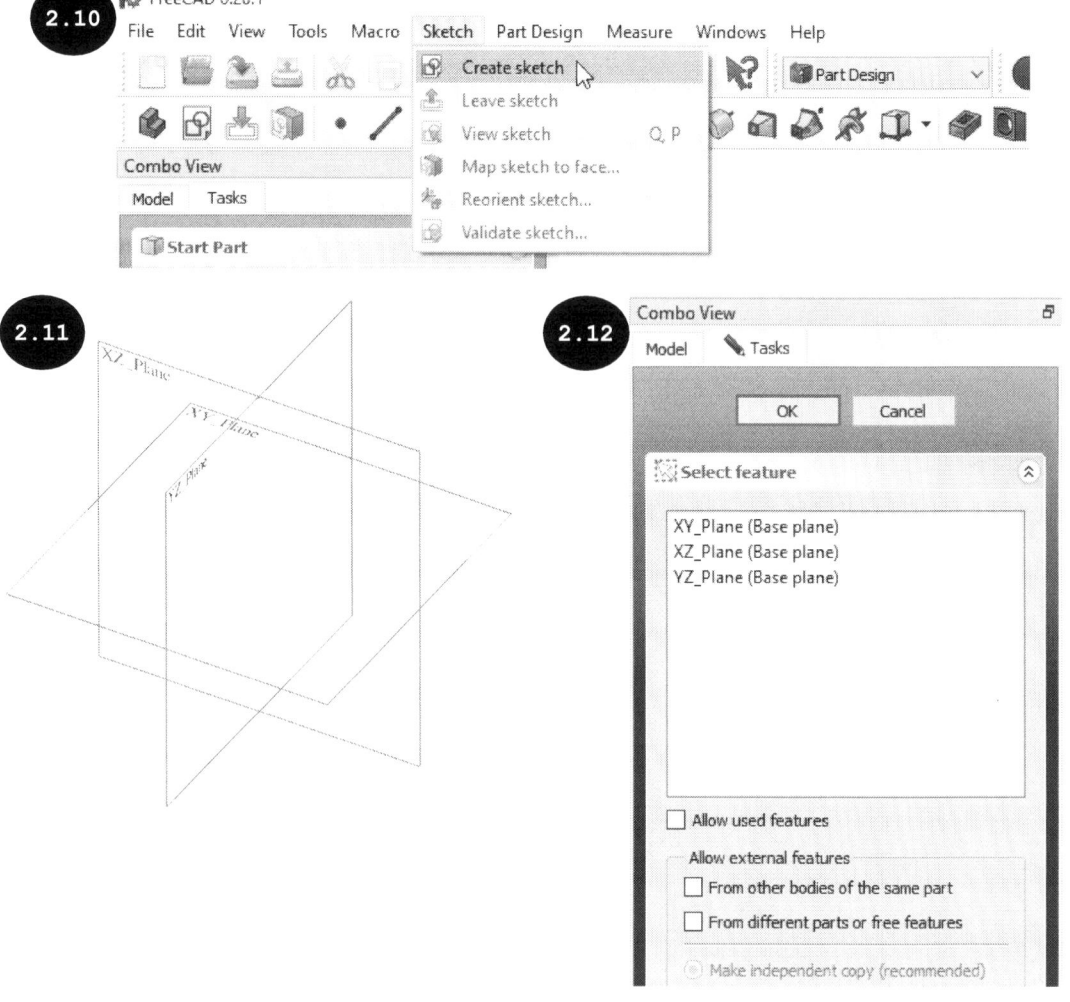

2. Select a plane as the sketching plane for creating a sketch in either the 3D View area or the **Task Panel**. The selected plane gets highlighted in the 3D View area.

3. After selecting a plane, click on the **OK** button in the **Task Panel**. The Sketch editing mode of the **Sketcher** workbench gets invoked, see Figure 2.13. Also, the selected plane becomes the sketching plane for drawing the sketch and it is oriented normal to the viewing direction so that you can easily create a sketch.

Note: In the Sketch editing mode of the **Sketcher** workbench, a point with two perpendicular axes appears at the center of the 3D View area. It represents the origin (0,0) of the sketching plane.

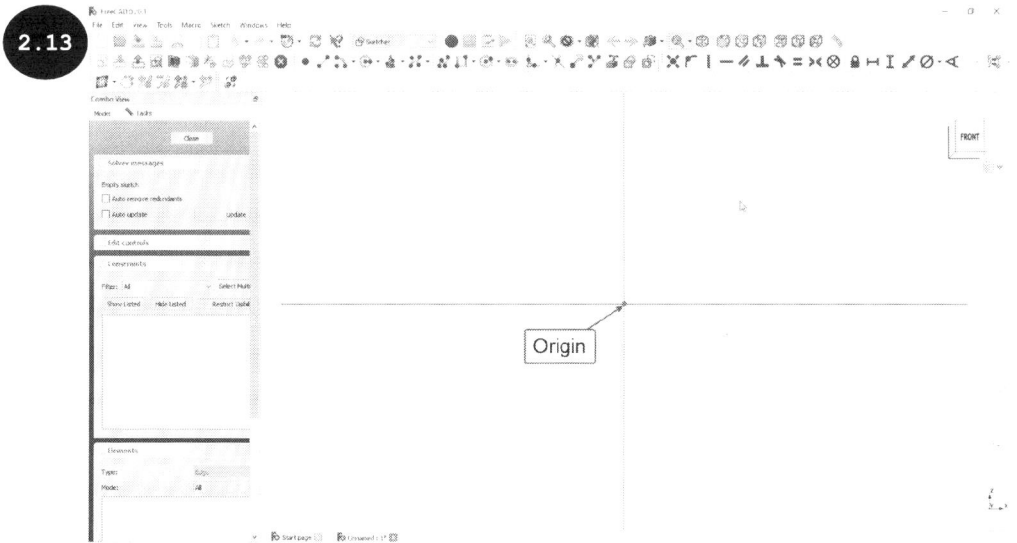

In the Sketch editing mode of the **Sketcher** workbench, you can start creating a sketch of a feature by using the sketching tools. However, before you start drawing a sketch, it is important to understand the selection of correct sketching planes, the procedure for setting the unit of measurement, and grid settings.

Working with the Selection of Planes

As discussed earlier, to invoke the Sketch editing mode of the **Sketcher** workbench for creating a sketch, you need to select a plane as the sketching plane. The selection of the correct plane is very important in defining the right orientation of the model. Figure 2.14 shows the isometric view of a model having a length of 200 mm, width of 100 mm, and height of 40 mm. To create this model with the same orientation, you can select the Top plane as the sketching plane and then draw a rectangular sketch of 200 mm X 100 mm. Later, in the **Part Design** workbench, you can extrude this sketch to a depth of 40 mm for creating a 3D solid model. You will learn about creating a 3D solid model in later chapters. However, if you select the Front plane as the sketching plane for creating this model, you must draw a rectangular sketch of 200 mm X 40 mm. Likewise, if you select the Right plane as the sketching plane, you must draw a rectangular sketch of 100 mm X 40 mm.

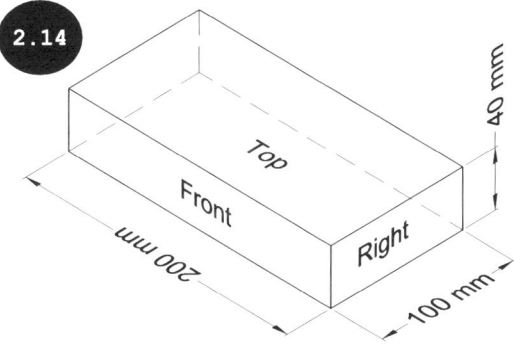

Specifying Units

In FreeCAD, you can define the default units at any point of your design for any document, as required. The method for specifying units is discussed below:

1. Click on **Edit > Preferences** in the **Standard Menu**, see Figure 2.15. The **Preferences** dialog box appears, refer to Figure 2.16.

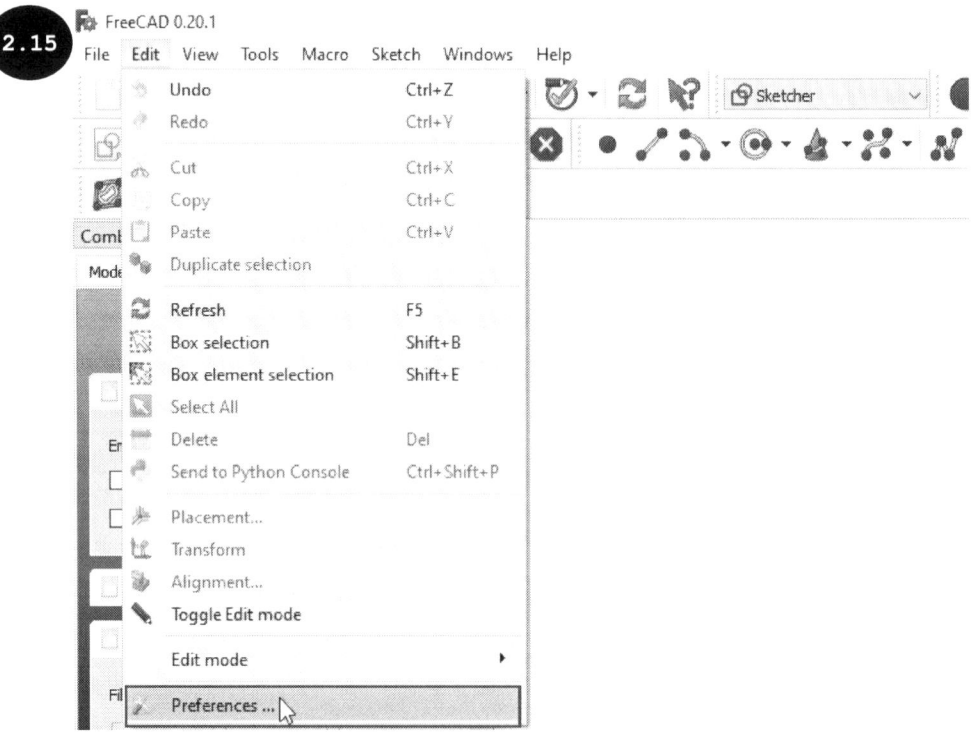

2. Ensure that the **General** section is selected in the left panel of the dialog box and then click on the **Units** tab, see Figure 2.16. The options to define unit settings appear in the dialog box.

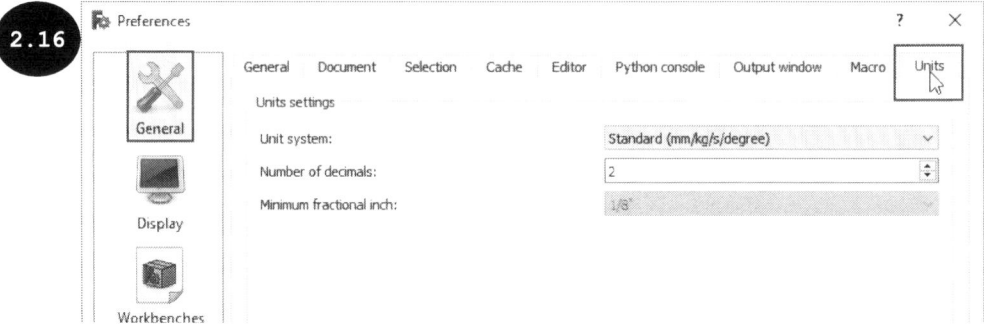

3. In the **Unit system** drop-down list of the **Units** tab, select the required predefined unit system as the default unit system for documents. For example, to set the metric unit system, select the **Standard (mm/kg/s/degree)** unit system. In this unit system, length is measured in millimeters, mass is calculated in kilograms, time is represented in seconds, and angle is measured in degrees.

4. In the **Number of decimals** field, specify the required number of unit decimals, as required.

5. After defining the unit settings in the **Units** tab, click on the **Apply** button and then the **OK** button in the dialog box. The units get defined, and the dialog box gets closed.

Specifying Grids and Snap Settings

Grids help you specify points in the 3D View area for creating sketch entities and act as reference lines. By default, the display of grids is turned off. You can turn on the display of grids in the 3D View area and the snap mode to snap the movement of the cursor on grid lines. The methods to turn on the display of grids and snap mode are discussed below:

1. Invoke the **Preferences** dialog box by clicking on **Edit > Preferences** in the **Standard Menu**, refer to Figure 2.15.

2. Click on the **Sketcher** section in the left panel of the **Preferences** dialog box, see Figure 2.17. The different options related to the **Sketcher** workbench appear on the right panel of the dialog box in their respective tabs (**General**, **Display**, and **Colors**).

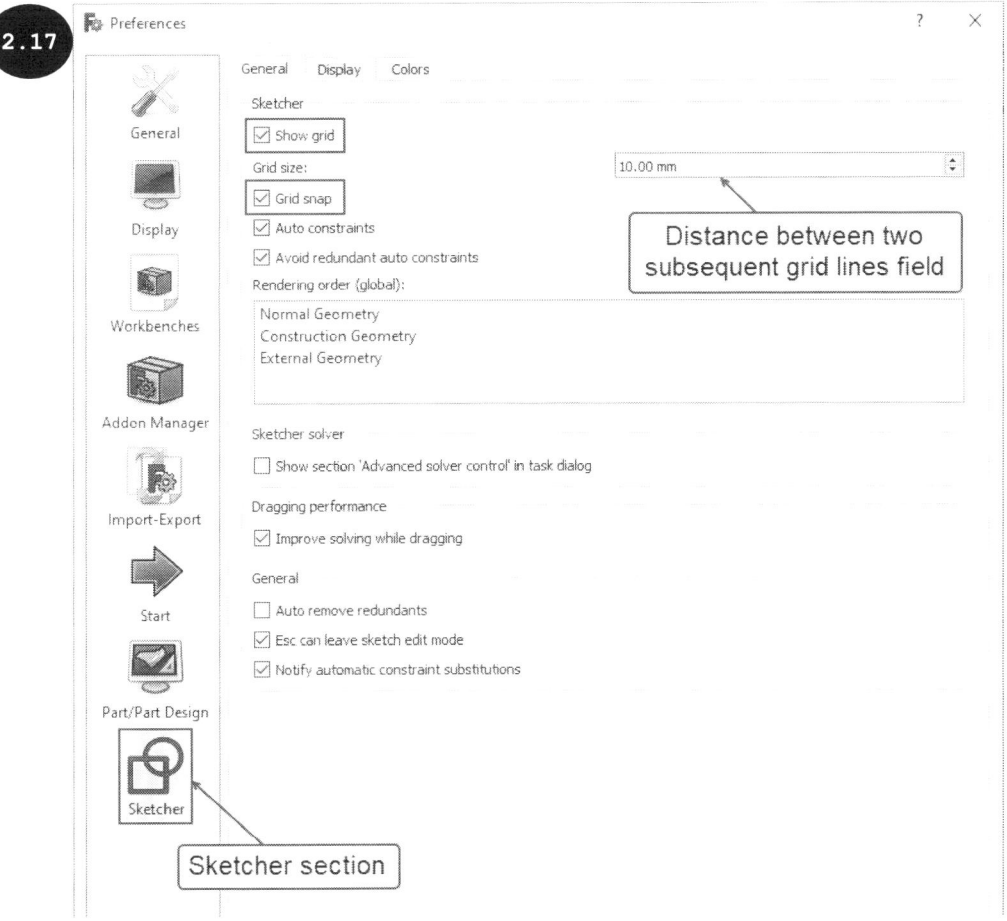

3. Select the **Show grid** check box in the **General** tab of the dialog box to turn on the display of grids in the 3D View area, refer to Figure 2.17.

Tip: To turn off the display of grids in the 3D View area, you need to ensure that the **Show grid** check box is cleared in the dialog box.

4. Specify the required distance between two subsequent grid lines in the **Distance between two subsequent grid lines** field of the **General** tab, refer to Figure 2.17.

   Now, you can turn on snap mode.

5. Select the **Grid snap** check box in the **General** tab of the dialog box to turn on the snap mode for snapping the movement of the cursor on grid lines, refer to Figure 2.17.

6. After specifying the grid and snap settings in the dialog box, click on the **Apply** button and then the **OK** button in the dialog box to accept the changes made and exit the **Preferences** dialog box. Figure 2.18 shows the 3D View area with the display of grids turned on.

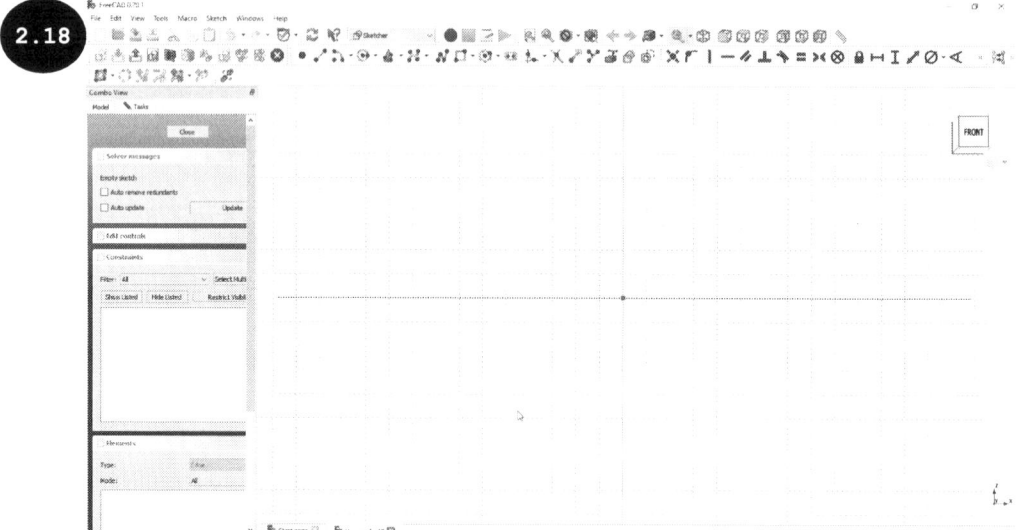

Drawing a Line

A line is defined as the shortest distance between two points. The method for drawing a line is discussed below:

1. Click on the **Create line** tool in the **Sketcher geometries** toolbar, see Figure 2.19. The **Create line** tool gets activated and the appearance of the cursor changes to a cross mark with the display of a red line icon, see Figure 2.20. Also, the coordinates of the current location appear near the cursor.

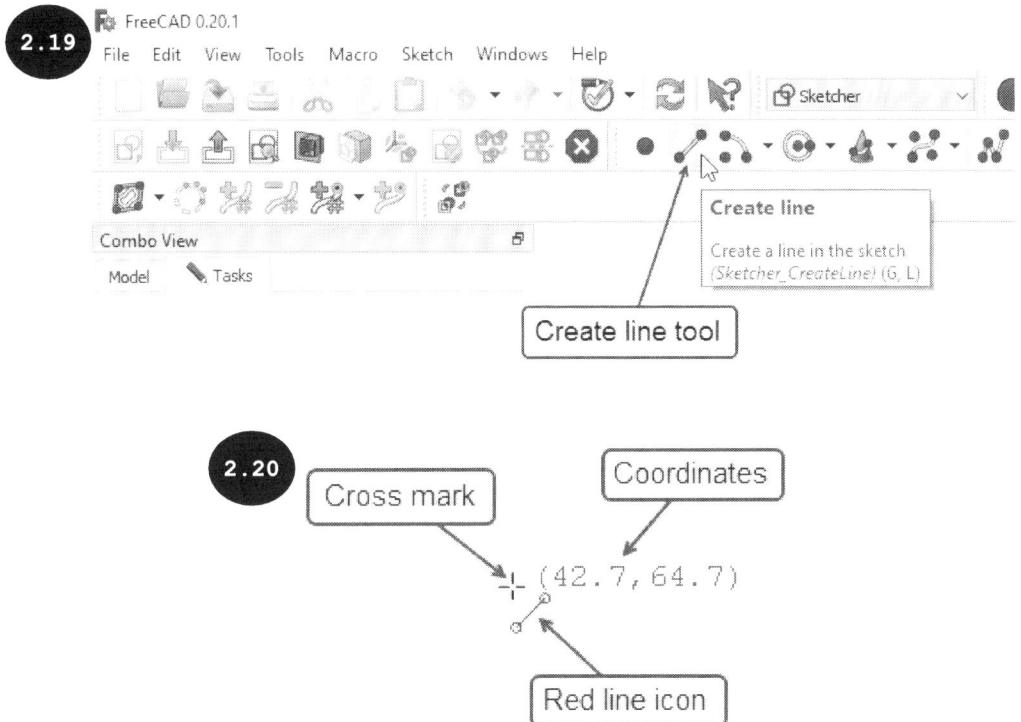

2. Click to specify a start point and an endpoint of a line one by one in the 3D view area. A line is drawn between the specified points, see Figure 2.21. Note that the **Create line** tool remains activated and you can continue creating multiple lines one after the other by specifying points in the drawing area.

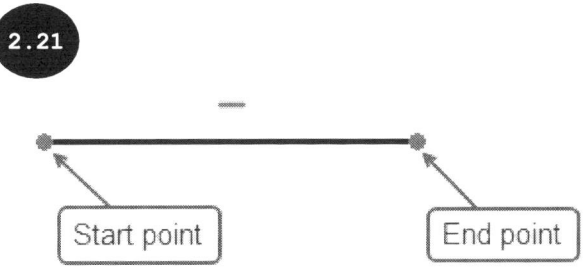

Note: When you move the cursor horizontally or vertically after specifying the start point of the line, the symbol of horizontal — or vertical | constraint appears near the line. The symbol of constraint indicates that if you click the left mouse button to specify the endpoint of the line, the corresponding constraint will be applied. You will learn more about constraints later in this chapter.

3. After creating one or more lines, press the ESC key or right-click in the 3D View area to exit the **Create line** tool.

Drawing an Arc

You can draw an arc by using the **Center and end points** and **End points and rim point** tools. You can access these tools in the **Create arc** menu of the **Sketcher geometries** toolbar, see Figure 2.22. To invoke this menu, click on the down arrow next to the active arc tool in the **Sketcher geometries** toolbar. The tools for drawing an arc are discussed next.

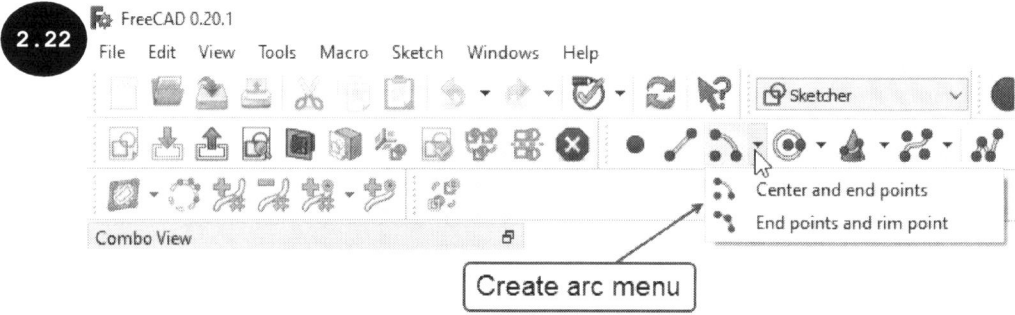

Center and end points Tool

The **Center and end points** tool is used for drawing an arc by first specifying its center point, and then the start angle and end angle points along the arc radius by clicking the left mouse button in the 3D View area, see Figure 2.23. After drawing an arc by using the **Center and end points** tool, press the ESC key or right-click on the 3D View area to exit the tool.

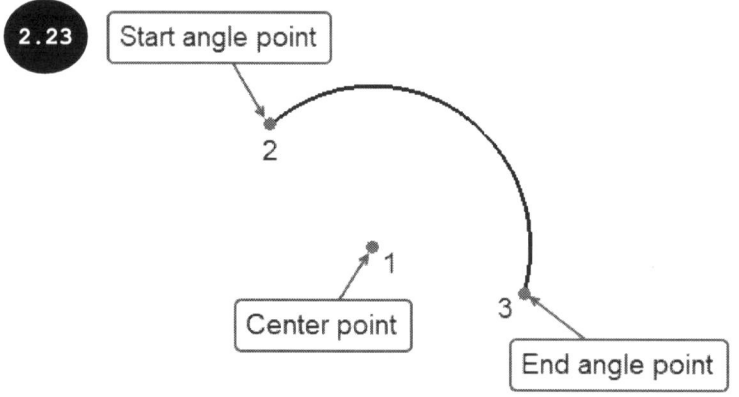

Note: In this textbook, some of the figures are numbered for your reference only, see Figure 2.23. These numbers represent the sequence of points specified in the 3D View area for creating an object by clicking the left mouse button.

End points and rim point Tool

The **End points and rim point** tool is used for drawing an arc by first specifying its start point, and then the endpoint and a point on the arc by clicking the left mouse button in the 3D View area, see Figure 2.24. After creating an arc, press the ESC key or right-click on the 3D View area to exit the tool.

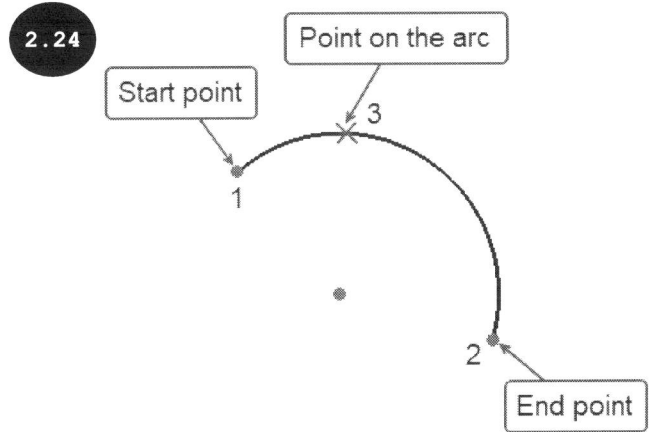

Drawing a Circle

In FreeCAD, you can draw a circle by using the **Center and rim point** and **3 rim points** tools. You can access these tools in the **Create circle** menu of the **Sketcher geometries** toolbar, see Figure 2.25. To invoke this menu, click on the down arrow next to the active circle tool in the **Sketcher geometries** toolbar. The tools for drawing a circle are discussed next.

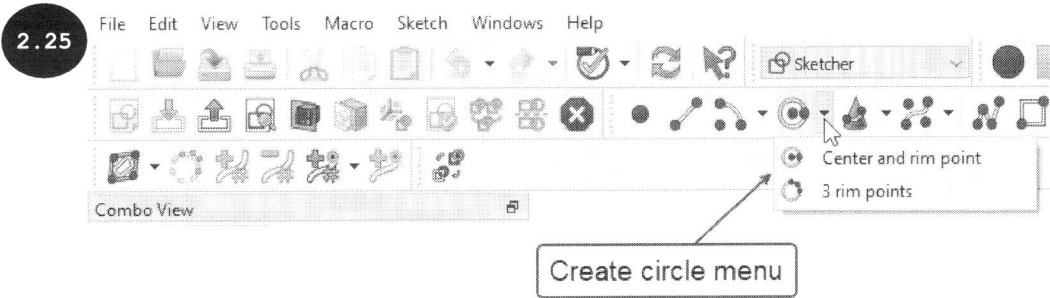

Center and rim point Tool

The **Center and rim point** tool is used for drawing a circle by first specifying its center point and then a point on its circumference by clicking the left mouse button in the 3D View area, see Figure 2.26. After creating a circle, press the ESC key or right-click on the 3D View area to exit the tool.

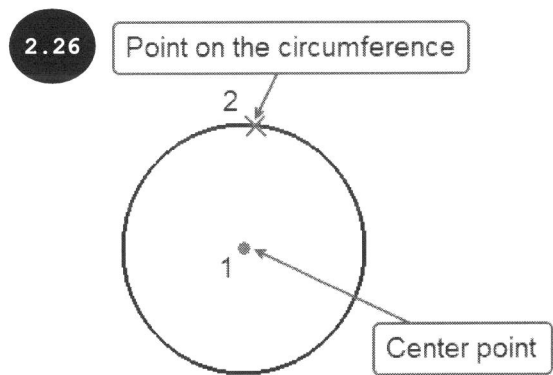

3 rim points Tool

The **3 rim points** tool is used for drawing a circle by specifying three points on its circumference by clicking the left mouse button in the 3D View area one by one, see Figure 2.27. After creating a circle, press the ESC key or right-click on the 3D View area to exit the tool.

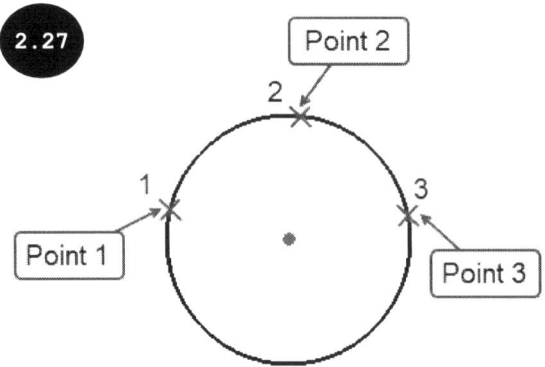

Drawing an Ellipse

An ellipse is drawn by defining its major axis and minor axis, see Figure 2.28. You can draw an ellipse by using the **Ellipse by center, major radius, point** and **Ellipse by periapsis, apoapsis, minor radius** tools. You can access these tools in the **Create conic** menu of the **Sketcher geometries** toolbar, see Figure 2.29. To invoke this menu, click on the down arrow next to the active conic tool in the **Sketcher geometries** toolbar. The tools for drawing an ellipse are discussed next.

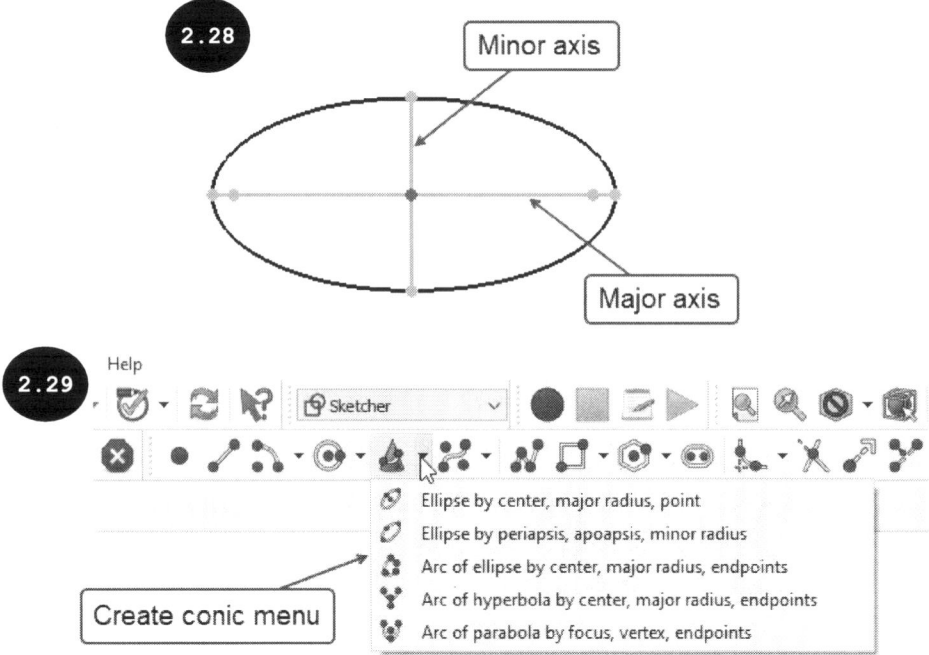

Ellipse by center, major radius, point Tool

The **Ellipse by center, major radius, point** tool is used for drawing an ellipse by first specifying its center, and then an endpoint of the major axis and a point to define the minor axis by clicking the left mouse button one by one in the 3D View area, see Figure 2.30. After creating an ellipse, press the ESC key or right-click on the 3D View area to exit the tool.

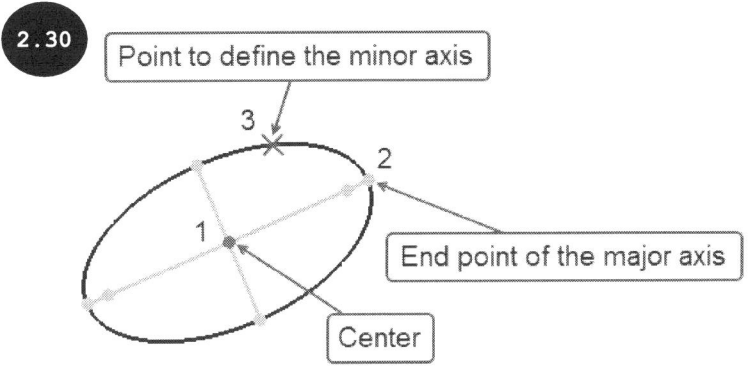

Note: In this textbook, some of the figures are numbered for your reference only, refer to Figure 2.30. These numbers represent the sequence of points specified in the 3D View area by clicking the left mouse button.

Ellipse by periapsis, apoapsis, minor radius Tool

The **Ellipse by periapsis, apoapsis, minor radius** tool is used for drawing an ellipse by specifying three points in the 3D View area, see Figure 2.31. The first point defines the periapsis (first endpoint of the major axis), the second point defines the apoapsis (second endpoint of the major axis), and the third point defines the minor axis of the ellipse, see Figure 2.31. After creating an ellipse, press the ESC key or right-click on the 3D View area to exit the tool.

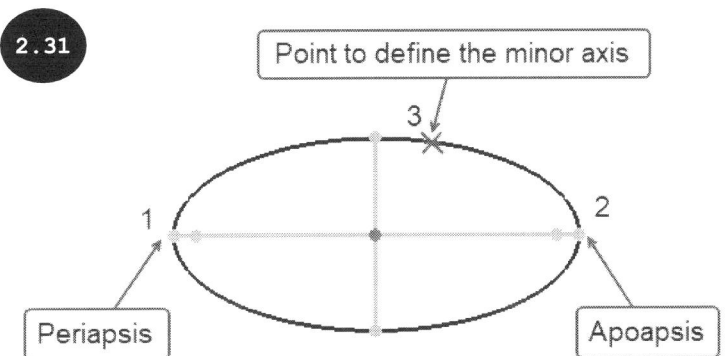

Drawing an Elliptical Arc

You can draw an elliptical arc by using the **Arc of ellipse by center, major radius, endpoints** tool. The method for drawing an elliptical arc is discussed below:

1. Invoke the **Create conic** menu and then click on the **Arc of ellipse by center, major radius, endpoints** tool, see Figure 2.32.

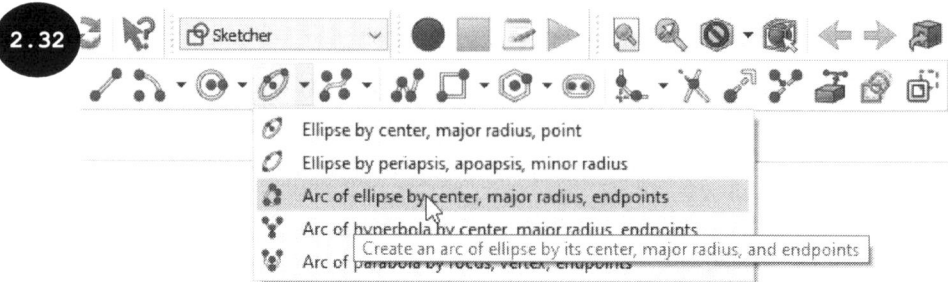

2. Click to specify the center point of the elliptical arc in the 3D View area and then a point to define its major axis, refer to Figure 2.33.

3. After defining the center and the major axis, move the cursor to a distance in the 3D View area. The preview of an imaginary ellipse appears. Next, click to specify the start point and then the endpoint of the elliptical arc in the 3D View area, see Figure 2.33. The elliptical arc is created.

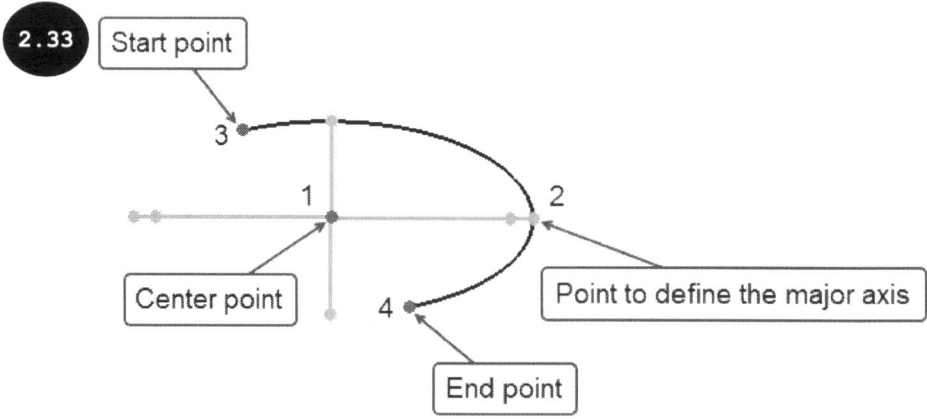

4. Press the ESC key or right-click in the 3D View area to exit the tool.

Drawing a Hyperbolic Arc

In FreeCAD, you can draw a hyperbolic arc by using the **Arc of hyperbola by center, major radius, endpoints** tool. The method for drawing a hyperbolic arc is discussed below:

1. Invoke the **Create conic** menu and then click on the **Arc of hyperbola by center, major radius, endpoints** tool, see Figure 2.34.

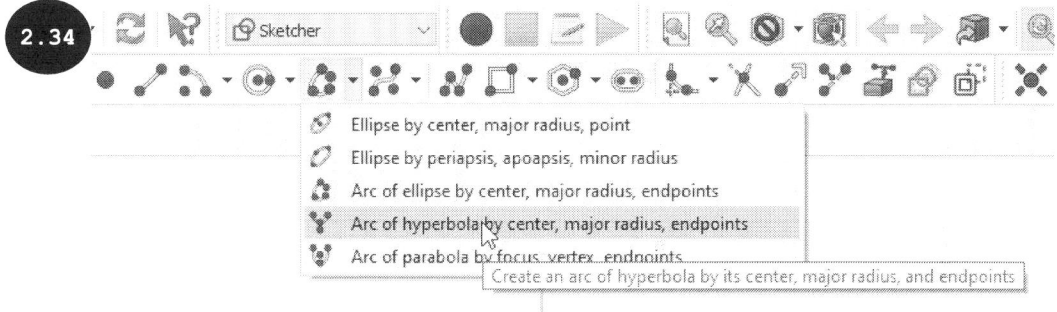

2. Click to specify the center point of the major axis of the hyperbola in the 3D View area and then a point to define its major axis, refer to Figure 2.35.

3. After defining the center point and the major axis, move the cursor to a distance in the 3D View area. The preview of an imaginary hyperbola appears. Next, click to specify the start point and then the endpoint of the hyperbolic arc in the 3D View area, see Figure 2.35. The hyperbolic arc is created.

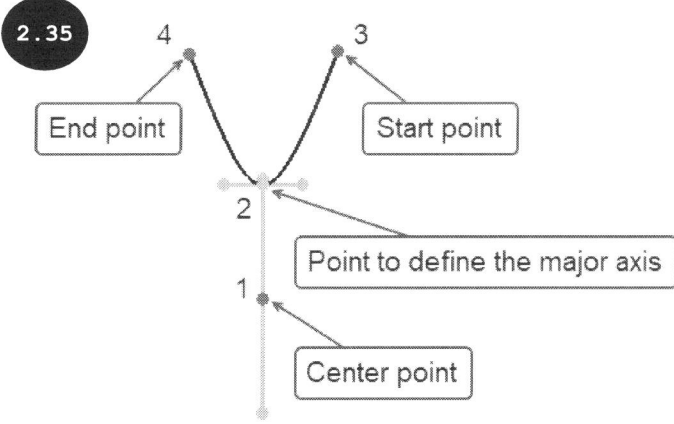

4. Press the ESC key or right-click in the 3D View area to exit the tool.

Drawing a Parabolic Arc

A parabola is a symmetrical plane curve formed by the intersection of a cone and a plane parallel to its side. In FreeCAD, you can draw a parabolic arc by using the **Arc of parabola by focus, vertex, endpoints** tool. The method for drawing a parabolic arc is discussed below:

1. Invoke the **Create conic** menu and then click on the **Arc of parabola by focus, vertex, endpoints** tool, see Figure 2.36.

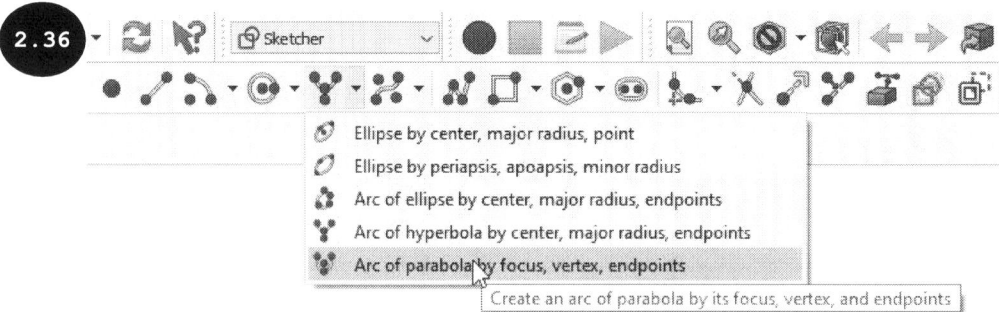

2. Click to specify the focus point and then an apex point of the parabola in the 3D View area, refer to Figure 2.37.

3. After defining the focus and apex points, move the cursor to a distance in the 3D View area. The preview of an imaginary parabola appears. Next, click to specify the start point and then the endpoint of the parabolic arc in the 3D View area, see Figure 2.37. The parabolic arc is created.

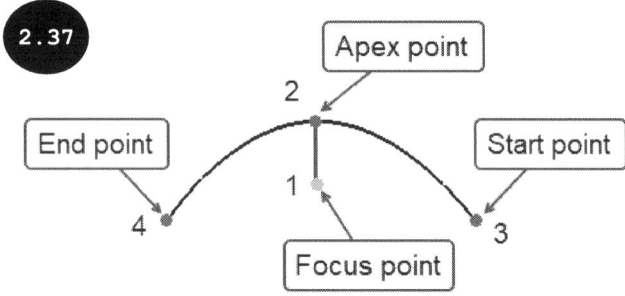

4. Press the ESC key or right-click in the 3D View area to exit the tool.

Drawing a B-Spline

A B-spline is defined as a curve having a high degree of smoothness and is used for creating free-form features. You can draw a B-spline by specifying two or more control points in the 3D View area. The different tools for drawing a B-spline are available in the **Create B-spline** menu of the **Sketcher geometries** toolbar (see Figure 2.38) and the same are discussed next.

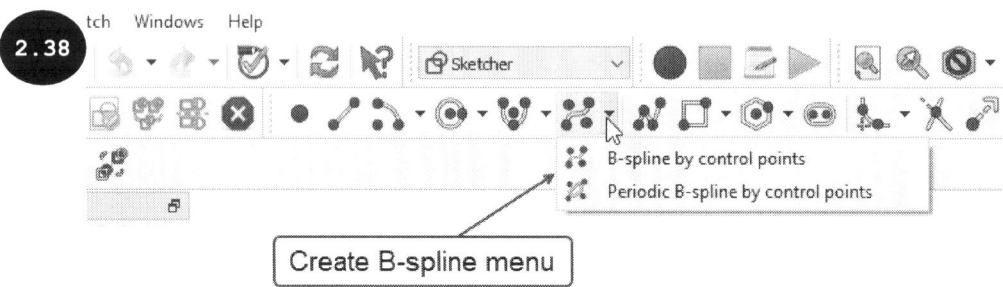

B-spline by control points Tool

The **B-spline by control points** tool is used for drawing a B-spline by specifying two or more control points in the 3D View area by clicking the left mouse button, see Figure 2.39. This figure shows a B-spline drawn by specifying 4 control points. The method for drawing a B-spline is discussed below:

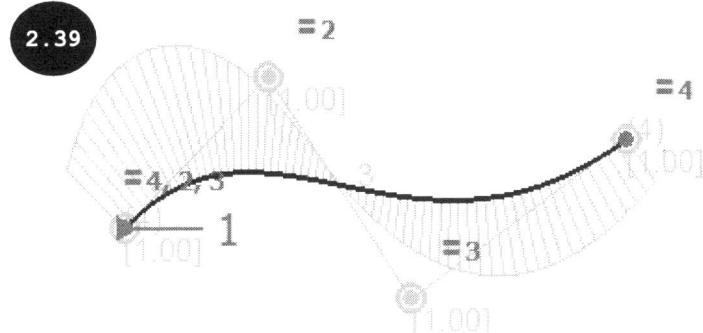

1. Invoke the **Create B-spline** menu and then click on the **B-spline by control points** tool, refer to Figure 2.38.

2. Click to specify control points by clicking the left mouse button in the 3D View area one by one. Notice that all the specified control points are connected through straight lines, see Figure 2.40.

3. After specifying the control points, right-click in the 3D View area or press the ESC key. A smooth B-Spline is drawn such that it passes near the specified control points, see Figure 2.41.

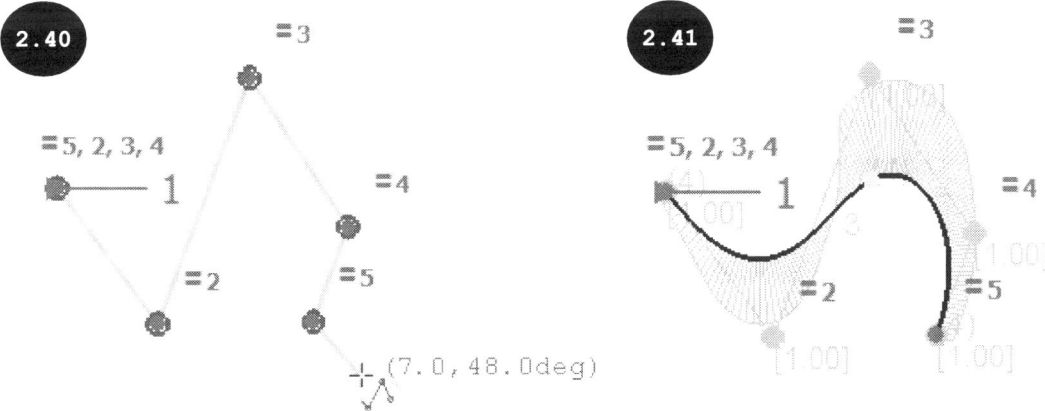

4. Press the ESC key or right-click in the 3D View area again to exit the tool.

Note: The specified control points are connected through control polygons (green straight lines), see Figure 2.41. Also, the green number (digit) at the center of the spline represents its degree. In Figure 2.41, the 3-digit number is displayed at the center of the spline as its degree. You can increase or decrease the degree of a spline. For doing so, select the spline in the 3D View area and then click on the **Increases B-spline degree** or **Decreases B-spline degree** tool in the **Sketcher B-spline tools** toolbar, respectively, see Figure 2.42.

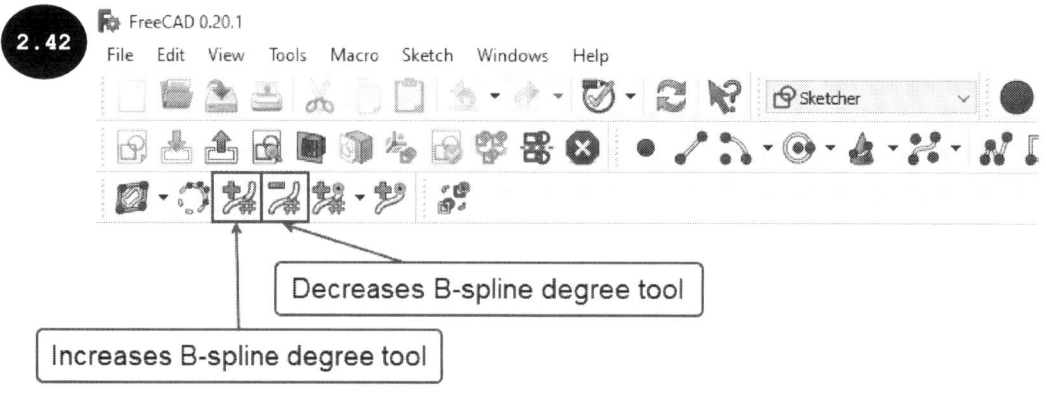

Decreases B-spline degree tool

Increases B-spline degree tool

Tip: You can edit or modify a spline by dragging its control points in the 3D View area.

Periodic B-spline by control points Tool

The **Periodic B-spline by control points** tool is used for drawing a closed (periodic) B-spline by specifying three or more control points in the 3D View area, see Figure 2.43. The method for creating a closed B-spline is discussed below:

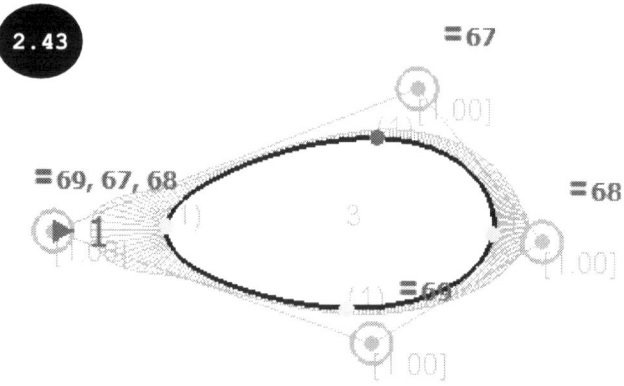

1.   Invoke the **Create B-spline** menu and then click on the **Periodic B-spline by control points** tool, see Figure 2.44.

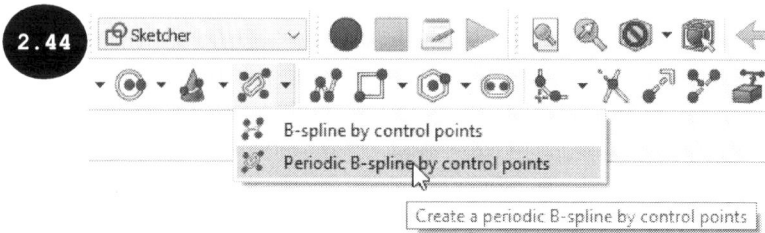

2.   Click to specify three or more control points by clicking the left mouse button in the 3D View area. All the specified control points are connected through straight lines in the 3D View area.

3. After specifying the control points, right-click in the 3D View area or press the ESC key. A periodic (closed) B-Spline is drawn such that its end control point coincides or merges with the start control point of the spline, automatically, refer to Figure 2.43. In this figure, a periodic (closed) B-Spline is drawn by specifying 4 control points in the 3D View area.

4. Press the ESC key or right-click in the 3D View area again to exit the tool.

Drawing a Polyline

A polyline consists of one or more than one line or arc segments, see Figure 2.45. In FreeCAD, you can draw a polyline consisting of a series of perpendicular or tangentially connected lines, arcs, or a combination of line and arc segments. The method for drawing a polyline is discussed below:

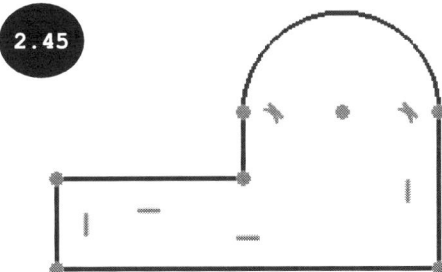

1. Click on the **Create polyline** tool in the **Sketcher geometries** toolbar, see Figure 2.46. The **Create polyline** tool gets activated and the appearance of the cursor changes to cross mark with the display of a red polyline icon. Also, the coordinates of the current location appear near the cursor.

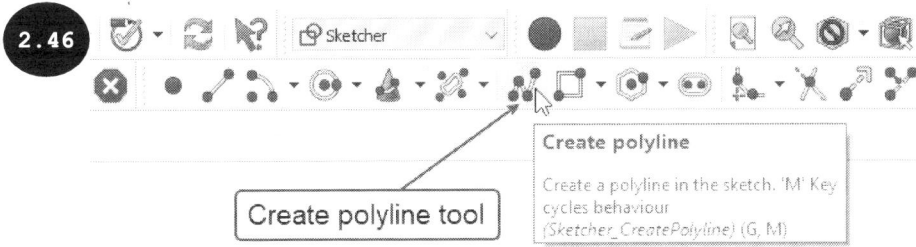

2. Click to specify a start point and then an endpoint of the first line segment of a polyline in the 3D view area. The first line segment of a polyline is drawn between the specified points, see Figure 2.47. Also, a rubber band line segment appears with one of its ends fixed or attached at the last specified endpoint and the other end attached to the cursor, see Figure 2.47.

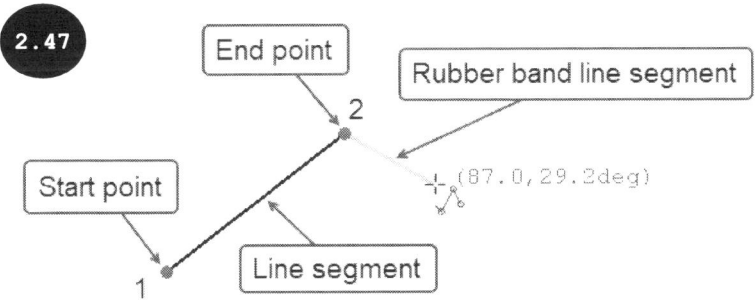

Note that the first segment of a polyline is always a line segment. After creating the first line segment of a polyline, you can create a perpendicular or tangentially connected line or arc segment as the second segment of the polyline. You can cycle through all six different polyline modes (segments) including the default polyline mode by repeatedly pressing the M key in sequential order, as given below:

i.   The default polyline mode is a line segment that is connected to its previous segment.
ii.   The first polyline mode is a line segment that is perpendicular to its previous segment.
iii. The second polyline mode is a line segment that is tangent to its previous segment.
iv.   The third polyline mode is an arc segment that is tangent to its previous polyline segment.
v.   The fourth polyline mode is an arc segment that is normal to the left of its previous segment.
vi.   The fifth polyline mode is an arc segment that is normal to the right of its previous segment.

3.   After creating the first line segment of a polyline, press the M key to invoke the required polyline mode, see Figure 2.48. This figure shows an arc mode invoked as the second polyline segment which is tangent to its previous segment. As discussed earlier, you can cycle through six different polyline modes by pressing the M key.

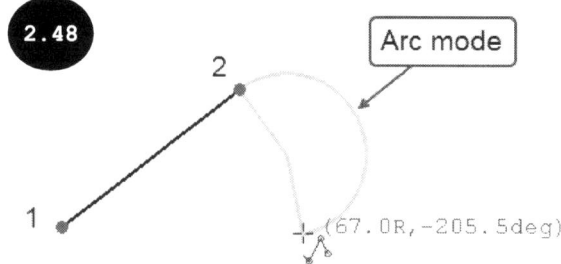

4.   Click the left mouse button in the 3D View area for creating the respective second polyline segment, see Figure 2.49. In this figure, a tangent arc segment is created as the second segment.

5.   After creating the second polyline segment, press the M key again for invoking the required polyline mode and then click the left mouse button in the 3D View area for creating the respective third polyline segment. Similarly, you can create a polyline with a series of connected lines and arc segments one after another by clicking the left mouse button in the 3D View area. After creating all the segments of a polyline, press the ESC key or right-click in the 3D View area. A polyline with multiple lines and arc segments gets created, see Figure 2.50.

6.   Press the ESC key or right-click in the 3D View area to exit the tool.

Tip: To create a closed polyline like the one shown in Figure 2.50, you need to specify the endpoint of the last segment to the start point of the first segment such that both the points get coincident with each other.

Note: As mentioned earlier, some of the figures are numbered for your reference only, refer to Figures 2.47 through 2.50. These numbers represent the sequence of points specified in the 3D View area by clicking the left mouse button.

Drawing a Rectangle

In FreeCAD, you can draw a rectangle by using the **Rectangle**, **Centered rectangle**, and **Rounded rectangle** tools. You can access these tools in the **Create rectangle** menu of the **Sketcher geometries** toolbar, see Figure 2.51. The tools for drawing a rectangle are discussed next.

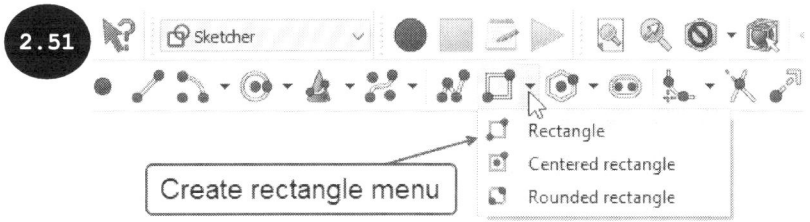

Rectangle Tool

The **Rectangle** tool is used for drawing a rectangle by specifying its two diagonally opposite corners in the 3D View, see Figure 2.52. The method for creating a rectangle by using this tool is discussed below:

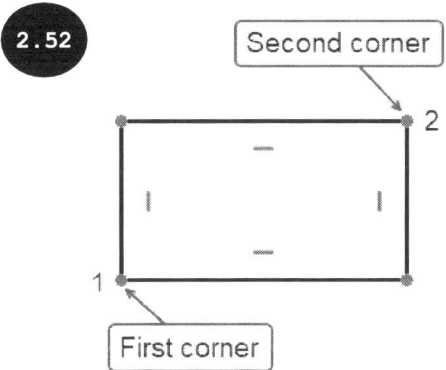

1. Invoke the **Create rectangle** menu in the **Sketcher geometries** toolbar and then click on the **Rectangle** tool, refer to Figure 2.51. The **Rectangle** tool gets activated and the appearance of the cursor changes to a cross mark with the display of a red rectangle icon. Also, the coordinates of the current location appear near the cursor.

2. Click to specify two diagonally opposite corners of a rectangle one by one in the 3D View area, refer to Figure 2.52. Note that the first corner defines the position of the rectangle, and the second corner defines its length and width.

3. After creating a rectangle, the **Rectangle** tool remains active. Press the ESC key or right-click in the 3D View area to exit the tool.

Centered rectangle Tool

The **Centered rectangle** tool is used for drawing a rectangle by specifying its center and a corner point in the 3D View, see Figure 2.53. The method for creating a rectangle by using this tool is discussed below:

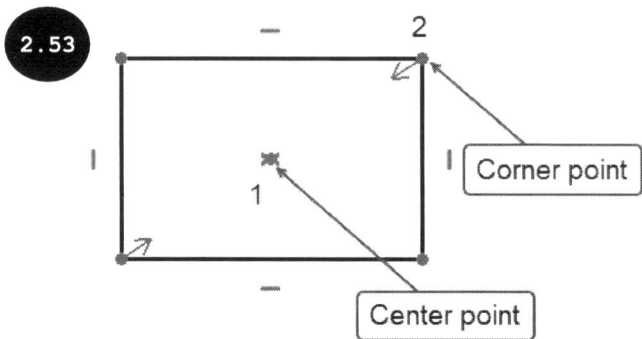

1. Invoke the **Create rectangle** menu in the **Sketcher geometries** toolbar and then click on the **Centered rectangle** tool, refer to Figure 2.54.

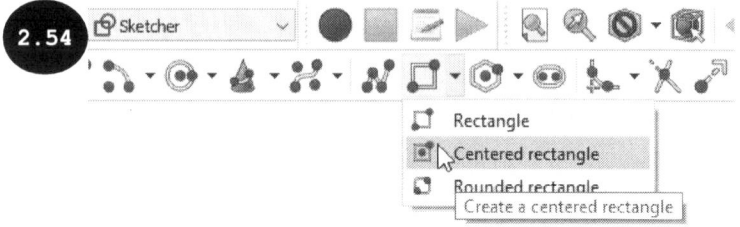

2. Click to specify the center point and then a corner of a rectangle in the 3D View area, refer to Figure 2.53. A rectangle gets drawn. Next, right-click to exit the tool.

Rounded rectangle Tool

The **Rounded rectangle** tool is used for drawing a rectangle with filleted or rounded corners by specifying its two diagonally opposite corners, see Figure 2.55. The method for drawing a rectangle with rounded corners is discussed below:

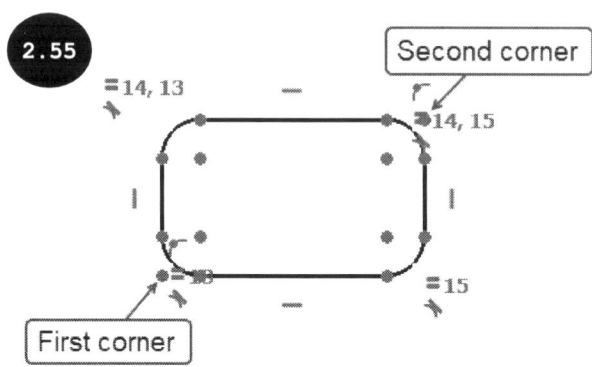

1. Invoke the **Create rectangle** menu in the Sketcher geometries toolbar and then click on the **Rounded rectangle** tool, refer to Figure 2.56.

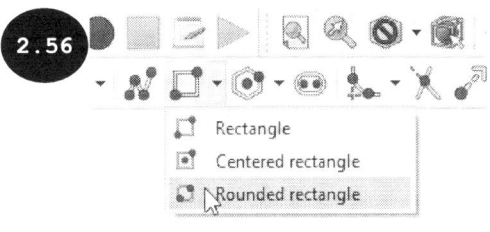

2. Click to specify two diagonally opposite corners of a rectangle one by one in the 3D View area, refer to Figure 2.55. A rectangle with rounded corners gets created. Next, right-click to exit the tool.

Drawing Polygons

In FreeCAD, you can draw different types of polygons such as triangular, square, pentagon, hexagon, heptagon, etc. by using their respective tools available in the **Create regular polygon** menu of the **Sketcher geometries** toolbar, see Figure 2.57. The tools for drawing polygons are discussed next.

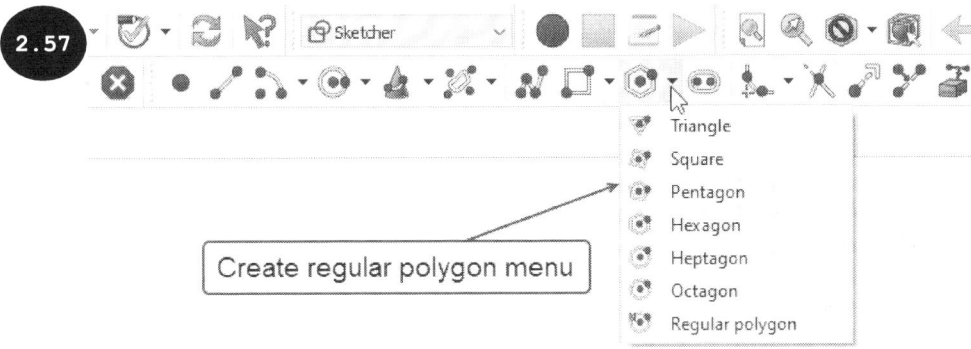

Create regular polygon menu

Triangle Tool

The **Triangle** tool is used for drawing an equilateral triangle by specifying its center and a corner, inside an imaginary construction circle, see Figure 2.58. The method for drawing an equilateral triangle is discussed below:

1. Invoke the **Create regular polygon** menu in the **Sketcher geometries** toolbar and then click on the **Triangle** tool, see Figure 2.59. The **Triangle** tool gets activated.

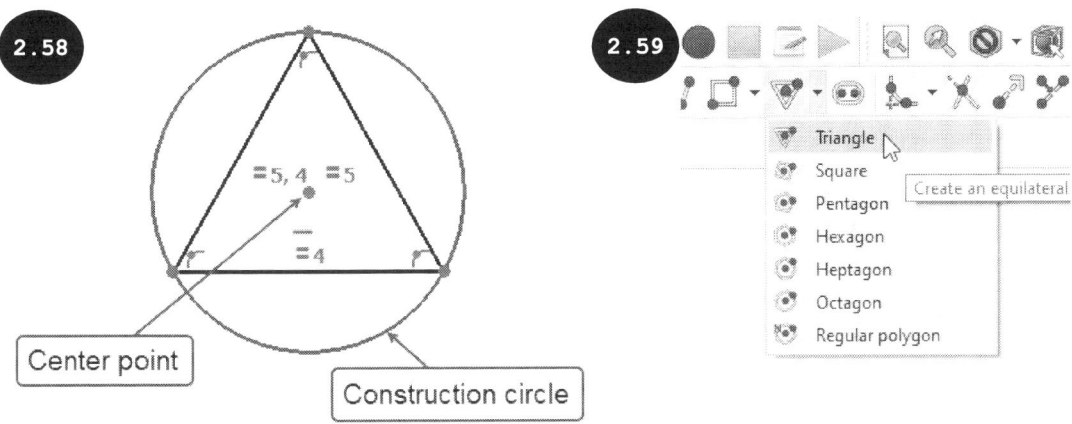

Center point

Construction circle

2.   Click to specify the center point of a triangle or an imaginary construction circle in the 3D View area, refer to Figure 2.58. The center point is defined and as you move the cursor, the preview of an equilateral triangle appears such that one of its vertices is attached to the cursor.

3.   Click to define the position of one of the vertices of the triangle in the 3D View area. An equilateral triangle is drawn inside an imaginary construction circle such that its vertices touch the construction circle, refer to Figure 2.58. Next, press the ESC key or right-click in the 3D View area to exit the tool.

Note: The construction entities of a sketch are visible only while creating or editing the sketch in the **Sketcher** workbench.

Square Tool

The **Square** tool is used for drawing a square which is a four-sided polygon by specifying its center and a corner, inside an imaginary construction circle, see Figure 2.60. The method for drawing a square is discussed below:

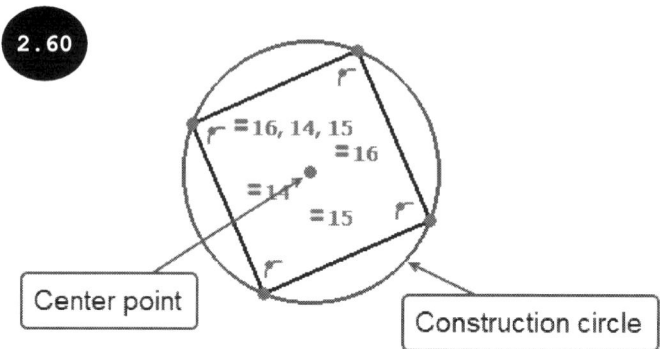

1.   Invoke the **Create regular polygon** menu in the **Sketcher geometries** toolbar and then click on the **Square** tool, see Figure 2.61. The **Square** tool gets activated.

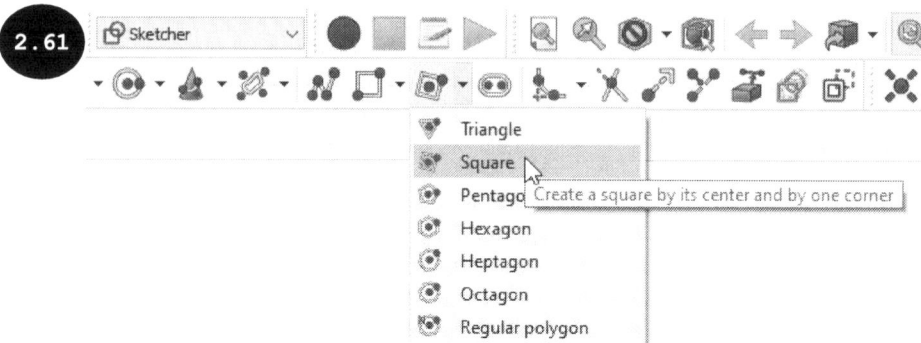

2.   Click to specify the center point of a square in the 3D View area. The center point is defined and as you move the cursor, the preview of a square appears such that one of its vertices is attached to the cursor.

3. Click to define the position of one of the vertices of the square in the 3D View area. A square is drawn inside an imaginary construction circle such that its vertices touch the construction circle, refer to Figure 2.60. Next, press the ESC key or right-click in the 3D View area to exit the tool.

Pentagon Tool

The **Pentagon** tool is used for drawing a pentagon, inside an imaginary construction circle, see Figure 2.62. The method for drawing a pentagon is discussed below:

1. Invoke the **Create regular polygon** menu in the **Sketcher geometries** toolbar and then click on the **Pentagon** tool, see Figure 2.63. The **Pentagon** tool gets activated.

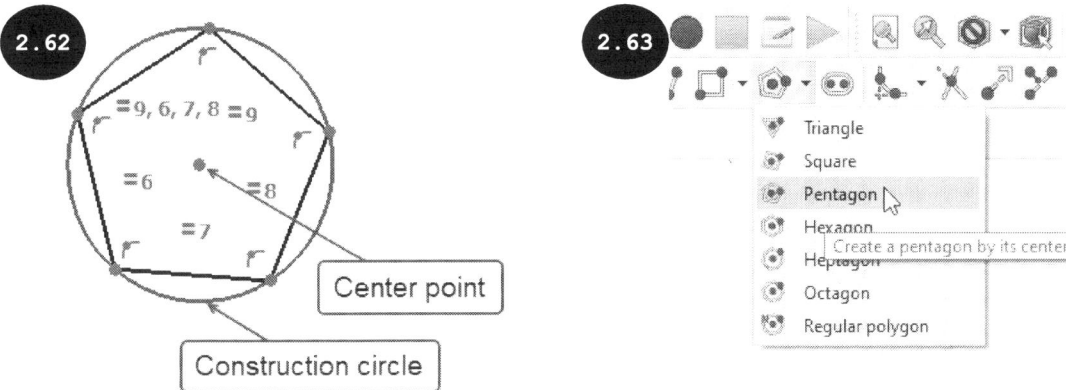

2. Click to specify the center point of a pentagon in the 3D View area. The center point is defined, and the preview of a pentagon appears such that one of its vertices is attached to the cursor.

3. Click to define the position of a vertex in the 3D View area. A pentagon is drawn inside an imaginary construction circle such that its vertices touch the construction circle, refer to Figure 2.62. Next, press the ESC key or right-click in the 3D View area to exit the tool.

Hexagon Tool

The **Hexagon** tool is used for drawing a hexagon, inside an imaginary construction circle, see Figure 2.64. The method for drawing a hexagon is discussed below:

1. Invoke the **Create regular polygon** menu in the **Sketcher geometries** toolbar and then click on the **Hexagon** tool, see Figure 2.65. The **Hexagon** tool gets activated.

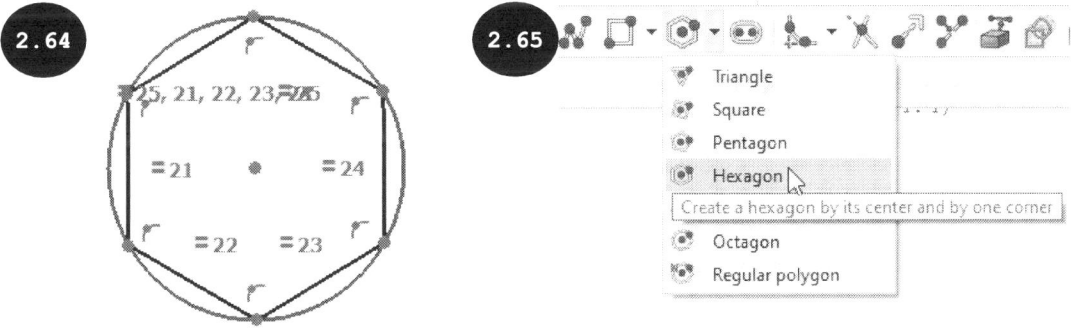

2. Click to specify the center point of a hexagon in the 3D View area. The center point is defined, and as you move the cursor, the preview of a hexagon appears such that one of its vertices is attached to the cursor.

3. Click to define the position of a vertex in the 3D View area. A hexagon is drawn inside an imaginary construction circle such that its vertices touch the construction circle. Next, press the ESC key or right-click in the 3D View area to exit the tool.

Heptagon Tool

The **Heptagon** tool is used for drawing a heptagon which is a seven-sided polygon, inside an imaginary construction circle, see Figure 2.66. The method for drawing a heptagon is discussed below:

1. Invoke the **Create regular polygon** menu and then click on the **Heptagon** tool, see Figure 2.67.

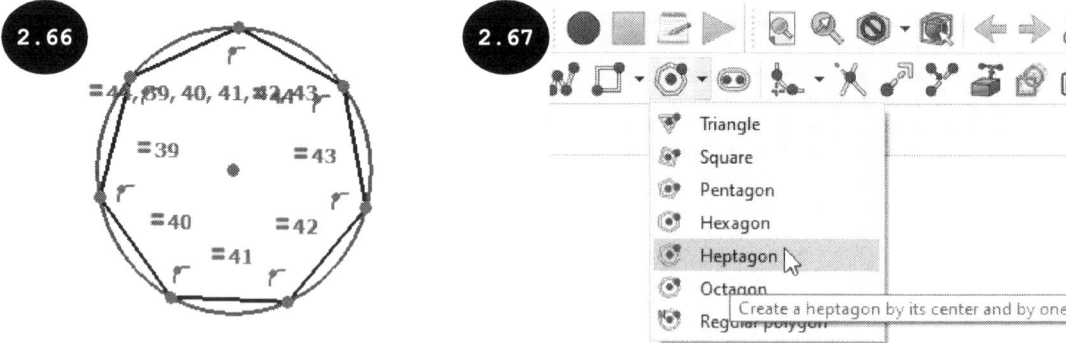

2. Click to specify the center point of a heptagon in the 3D View area. The center point is defined, and the preview of a heptagon appears such that one of its vertices is attached to the cursor.

3. Click to define the position of a vertex in the 3D View area. A heptagon is drawn inside an imaginary construction circle such that its vertices touch the construction circle. Next, press the ESC key or right-click in the 3D View area to exit the tool.

Octagon Tool

The **Octagon** tool is used for drawing an octagon which is an eight-sided polygon, inside an imaginary construction circle, see Figure 2.68. The method for drawing an octagon is discussed below:

1. Invoke the **Create regular polygon** menu and then click on the **Octagon** tool, see Figure 2.69.

2. Click to specify the center point of an octagon in the 3D View area. The center point is defined, and the preview of an octagon appears such that one of its vertices is attached to the cursor.

3. Click to define the position of a vertex in the 3D View area. An octagon is drawn inside an imaginary construction circle such that its vertices touch the construction circle. Next, press the ESC key or right-click in the 3D View area to exit the tool.

Regular Polygon Tool

The **Regular Polygon** tool is used for drawing a polygon with the number of sides ranging from 3 to 99, inside an imaginary construction circle. The method for drawing a polygon is discussed below:

1. Invoke the **Create regular polygon** menu and then click on the **Regular Polygon** tool, see Figure 2.70. The **Create array** pop-up box appears, see Figure 2.71.

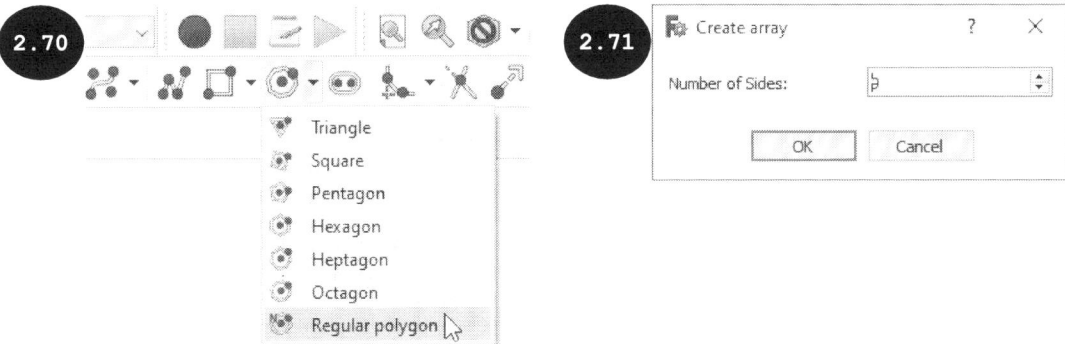

2. Enter the required number of polygon sides to be created in the pop-up box and then click on the OK button. Note that you can create a polygon of sides in the range between 3 and 99.

3. Click to specify the center point of a polygon in the 3D View area. The center point is defined and the preview of a polygon with the specified number of sides appears in the 3D View area.

4. Click to define a vertex of a polygon in the 3D View area. A polygon of specified sides is drawn inside an imaginary construction circle. Next, press the ESC key or right-click in the 3D View area to exit the tool.

Drawing a Slot

In FreeCAD, you can draw a straight slot by specifying the center points of its two semicircles in the 3D View area, see Figure 2.72. The method for drawing a straight slot is discussed below:

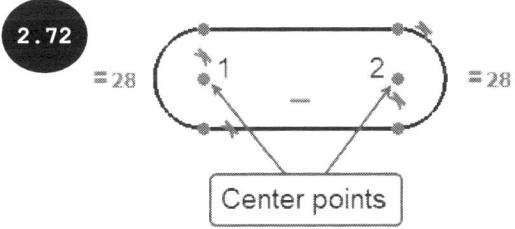

1.   Click on the **Create slot** tool in the **Sketcher geometries** toolbar, see Figure 2.73.

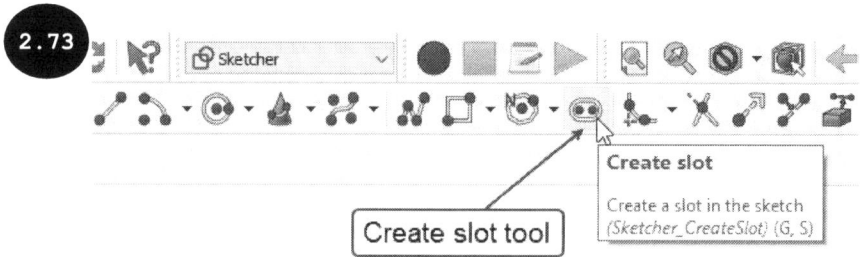

2.   Click to specify the center of one of the semi-circles of the slot in the 3D View area. The preview of a straight slot appears such that the center point of its other semicircle is attached to the circle, see Figure 2.74.

3.   Click to specify the center point of the other semicircle of the slot in the 3D View area. A straight slot gets drawn, see Figure 2.75. Next, press the ESC key to exit the tool.

Creating a Fillet

A fillet is created at the intersection of two lines by removing the sharp corner with a tangent arc of constant radius, see Figure 2.76.

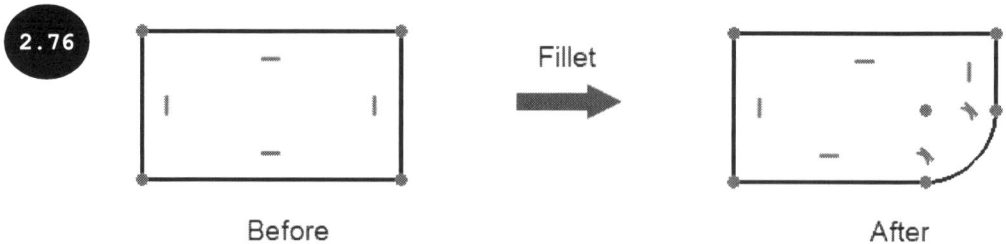

In FreeCAD, you can create a fillet by using the **Sketch fillet** and **Constraint-preserving sketch fillet** tools. You can access both these tools in the **Create fillet** menu of the **Sketcher geometries** toolbar, see Figure 2.77. The tools for creating a fillet are discussed next.

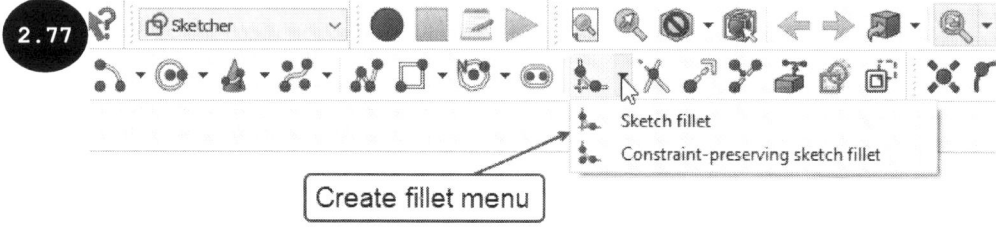

Sketch fillet Tool

The **Sketch fillet** tool is used for creating a fillet between two lines that are joined or intersected at a common point. The method for creating a fillet by using the **Sketch fillet** tool is discussed below:

1. Invoke the **Create fillet** menu in the **Sketcher geometries** toolbar (refer to Figure 2.77) and then click on the **Sketch fillet** tool.

2. Select two joined or intersected line entities one by one in the 3D View area, see Figure 2.78. A fillet of constant radius is created between the selected line entities, see Figure 2.79.

Note: By default, the radius of a fillet is defined based on the distance you click on the first line entity for selecting it from the intersection point with the second line entity. You can control or change the fillet radius by applying the radius dimension. You will learn about applying dimensions later in this chapter.

Tip: Instead of selecting two joined or intersected line entities, you can also select a corner (vertex) created at the intersection of two lines for creating a fillet.

Constraint-preserving sketch fillet Tool

The **Constraint-preserving sketch fillet** tool is used for creating a fillet between two intersecting line entities such that a virtual intersection point is created at the corner to maintain or preserve the already applied constraints and dimensions, see Figure 2.80. The method for creating a fillet by using this tool is the same as discussed earlier by using the **Sketch fillet** tool.

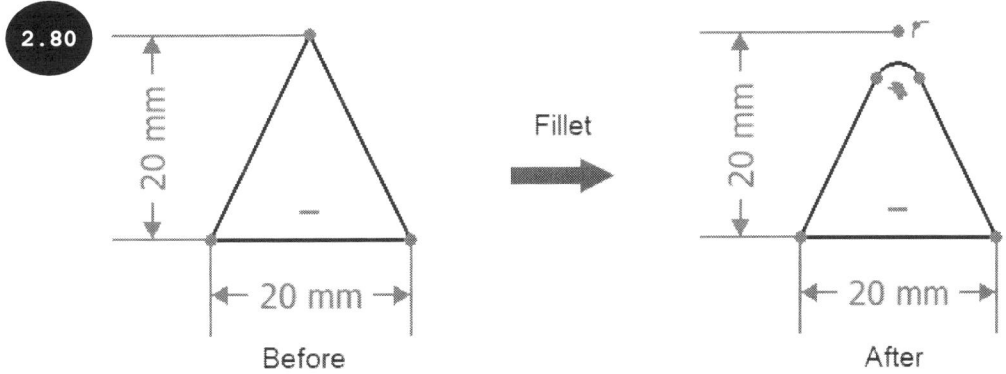

Trimming Sketch Entities

In FreeCAD, you can trim unwanted sketch entities (lines, circles, or arcs) to their nearest intersection by using the **Trim edge** tool. The method for trimming sketch entities is discussed below:

1. Click on the **Trim edge** tool in the **Sketcher geometries** toolbar, see Figure 2.81. The **Trim edge** tool gets activated and the appearance of the cursor changes to a cross mark with the display of a red trim icon.

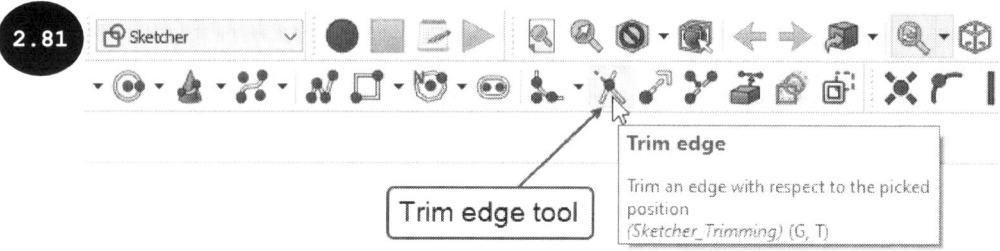

2. Click on a portion of a sketch entity (line, circle, or arc) to be trimmed, see Figure 2.82. The selected portion of the entity gets trimmed from its nearest intersection with the other entity, see Figure 2.83. Also, the **Trim edge** tool remains activated, and you can continue trimming unwanted portions of other sketch entities to their nearest intersection by clicking the left mouse button.

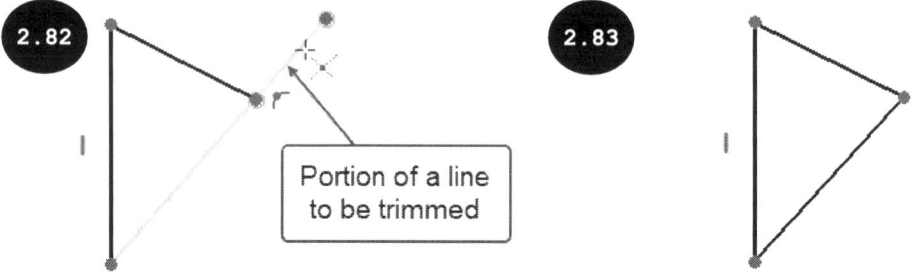

3. After trimming the sketch entities, press the ESC key or right-click to exit the tool.

Extending Sketch Entities

In FreeCAD, you can extend sketch entities up to the nearest intersection by using the **Extend edge** tool. The method for extending a sketch entity is discussed below:

1. Click on the **Extend edge** tool in the **Sketcher geometries** toolbar, see Figure 2.84. The **Extend edge** tool gets activated and the appearance of the cursor changes to a cross mark with the display of a red extend icon.

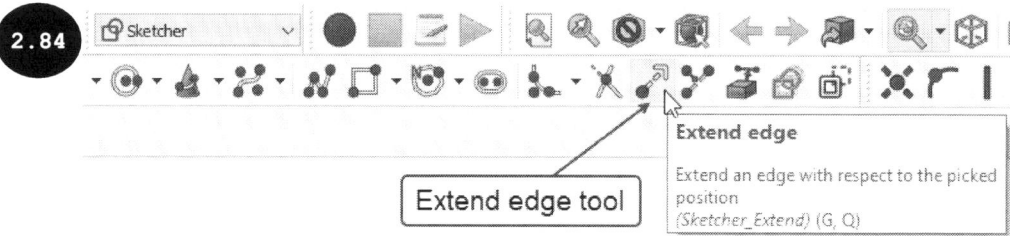

2. Click on a sketch entity (line or arc) to be extended in the 3D View area, see Figure 2.85. Next, move the cursor toward the direction to be extended in the 3D View area. Note that as you move the cursor, the preview of an extended entity appears such that it follows the cursor, see Figure 2.86.

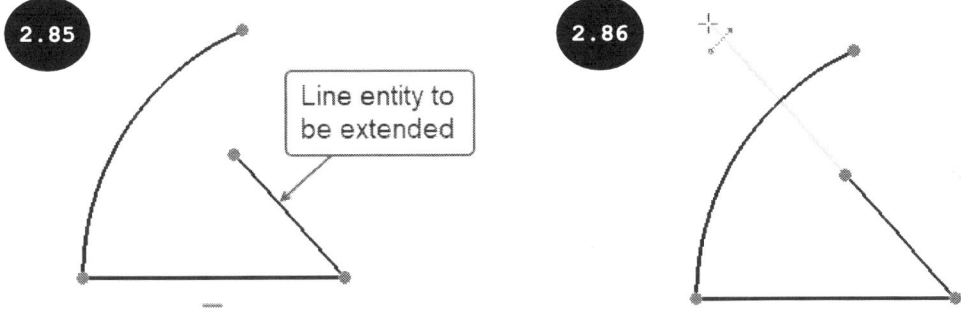

3. Click anywhere in the 3D View area as the endpoint of the resultant extended entity. The selected entity gets extended up to the specified endpoint in the 3D View area, see Figure 2.87.

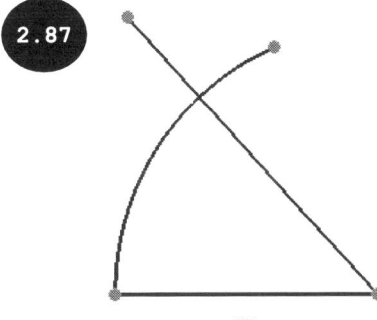

Note: In FreeCAD, you can also extend the selected sketch entity up to another intersecting sketch entity in the 3D View area. For doing so, after selecting an entity (line or arc) to be extended, move the cursor over another entity (a line, an arc, an ellipse, an elliptical arc, or a point) up to which you want to extend the selected entity and then click the left mouse button when it gets highlighted. The selected entity gets extended up to the selected sketch entity in the 3D View area.

Creating Construction Sketch Entities

In FreeCAD, you can toggle the creation of solid sketch entities to the construction sketch entities and vice-versa by using the **Toggle construction geometry** tool, see Figure 2.88. By default, this tool is deactivated in the **Sketcher geometries** toolbar. As a result, you can create solid sketch entities by using the sketching tools available in the **Sketcher geometries** toolbar.

To create construction sketch entities, click on the **Toggle construction geometry** tool in the **Sketcher geometries** toolbar, refer to Figure 2.88. The construction mode gets activated. Now, the sketch entities you create in the drawing area by using the sketching tools will act as construction entities and can only be used as references. Note that the construction entities are shown in blue color in the 3D View area.

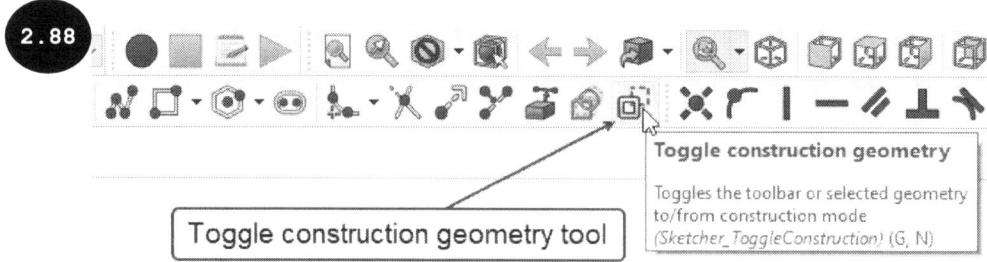

Note: The **Toggle construction geometry** tool is a toggle tool. As a result, for creating regular solid sketch entities, you need to click on this tool again to deactivate the construction mode.

Applying Geometric Constraints

Geometric constraints are used to restrict or limit some degrees of freedom of a sketch entity. You can apply a geometric constraint on a sketch entity, between sketch entities, or between a sketch point and the origin. Some of the geometric constraints such as horizontal, vertical, and coincident are applied automatically while drawing sketch entities. For example, while drawing a line, if you move the cursor horizontally toward left or right, an icon of horizontal constraint appears near the cursor, see Figure 2.89. This indicates that if you now specify the endpoint of the line, the horizontal constraint will be applied to the line and the movement of the line will be locked or restricted along the horizontal axis. Likewise, if you move the cursor vertically upward or downward, an icon of vertical constraint appears near the cursor, see Figure 2.90. This indicates that if you now specify the endpoint of the line, the vertical constraint will be applied to the line, and the movement of the line will be locked or restricted along the vertical axis.

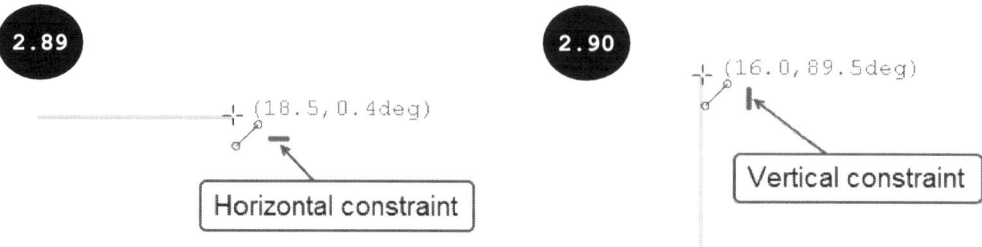

In FreeCAD, you can apply geometric constraints by using the constraints tools available in the **Sketcher constraints** toolbar, see Figure 2.91. The various types of geometric constraints are discussed next.

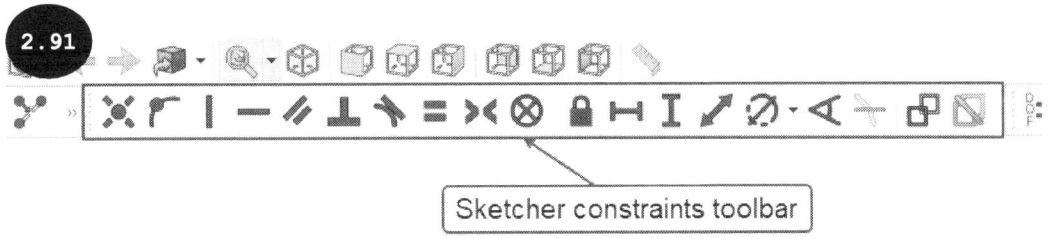

Sketcher constraints toolbar

> **Note:** In FreeCAD, you can change the position of a toolbar anywhere in the Toolbar area, which is docked at the top of the screen, by default. For doing so, press and hold the cursor over a toolbar to be moved and then drag and drop it to the new location in the Toolbar area, as required. You can also dock a toolbar to the left, right, or bottom of the screen by dragging and dropping it.

Coincident Constraint

A coincident constraint is used for making two sketch points or a sketch point and the origin coincident with each other. For doing so, click on the **Constrain coincident** tool in the **Sketcher constraints** toolbar (see Figure 2.92) or press the C key. The **Constrain coincident** tool gets activated and the appearance of the cursor changes to a cross mark with the display of a red coincident constraint icon.

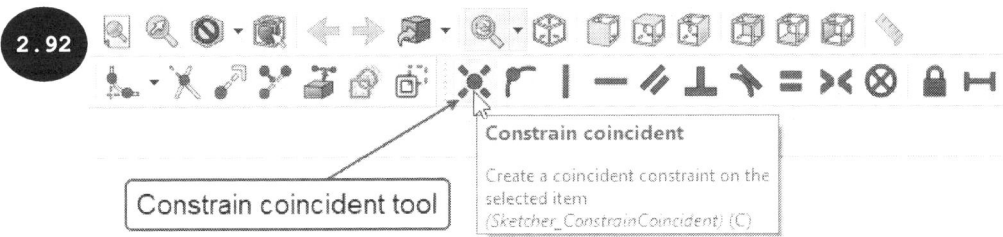

Constrain coincident

Create a coincident constraint on the selected item
(Sketcher_ConstrainCoincident) (C)

Constrain coincident tool

After activating the **Constrain coincident** tool, select two sketch points one by one in the 3D View area, see Figure 2.93. The coincident constraint gets applied, and the selected points become coincident with each other.

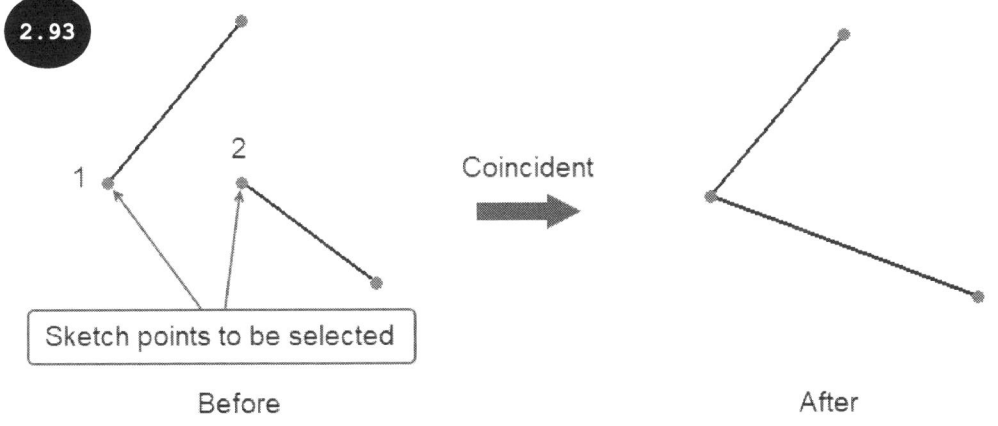

Sketch points to be selected

Coincident

Before   After

Point On Object Constraint

A point on object constraint is used for making a sketch point coincident with another sketch entity such as a line, arc, or axis. For doing so, click on the **Constrain point onto object** tool in the **Sketcher constraints** toolbar. Next, select a sketch point and then a line, an arc, or an axis in the 3D View area one by one, see Figure 2.94. The point on object constraint gets applied, and the first selected point coincides with the second selected sketch entity.

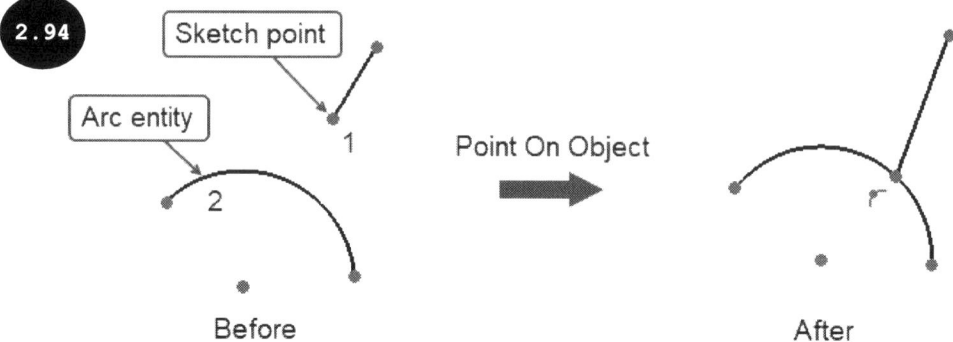

Before   After

Vertical Constraint

A vertical constraint is used for changing the orientation of a line entity to vertical and forcing it to remain vertical. For doing so, click on the **Constrain vertically** tool in the **Sketcher constraints** toolbar or press the **V** key and then select a line entity in the 3D View area. The vertical constraint gets applied and the orientation of the selected line changes to vertical, see Figure 2.95.

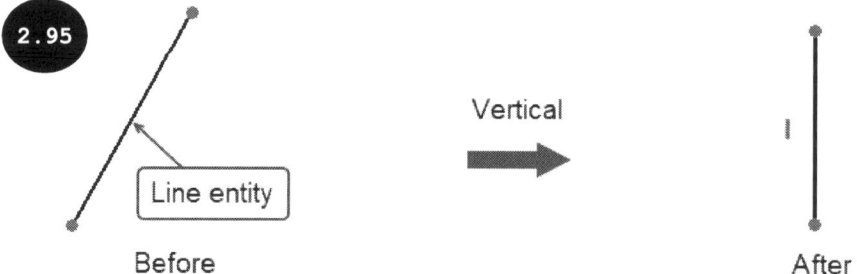

Before   After

Horizontal Constraint

A horizontal constraint is used for changing the orientation of a line entity to horizontal and forcing it to remain horizontal. For doing so, click on the **Constrain horizontally** tool in the **Sketcher constraints** toolbar or press the **H** key and then select a line entity. The horizontal constraint gets applied and the orientation of the selected line changes to horizontal, see Figure 2.96.

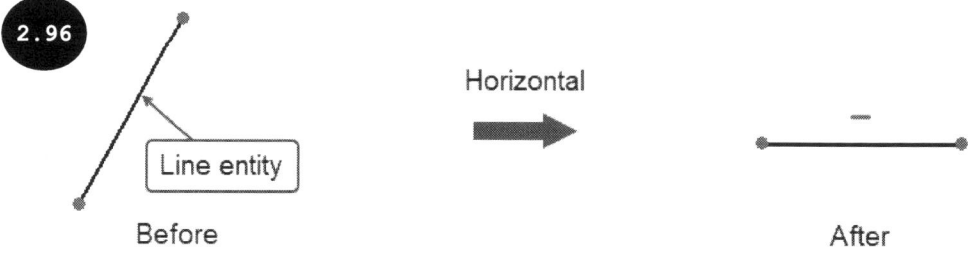

Before   After

Parallel Constraint

A parallel constraint is used for making two lines parallel to one another. For doing so, click on the **Constrain parallel** tool in the **Sketcher constraints** toolbar or press the **P** key. Next, select two lines one by one in the 3D View area. The parallel constraint gets applied, and the selected lines become parallel to each other, see Figure 2.97.

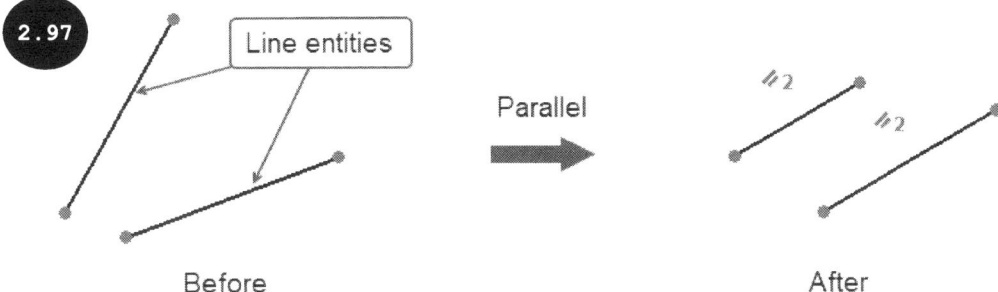

Perpendicular Constraint

A perpendicular constraint is used for making two lines perpendicular to one another. You can also make a line and a circle, an arc, or an ellipse perpendicular at their intersection by using this constraint. For doing so, click on the **Constrain perpendicular** tool in the **Sketcher constraints** toolbar or press the **N** key. Next, select two lines or a line and a circle/arc/ellipse one by one in the 3D View area. The perpendicular constraint gets applied, and the selected entities become perpendicular to each other, see Figures 2.98 and 2.99. In Figure 2.98, the perpendicular constraint is applied between two lines. In Figure 2.99, the perpendicular constraint is applied between a line and a circle entity.

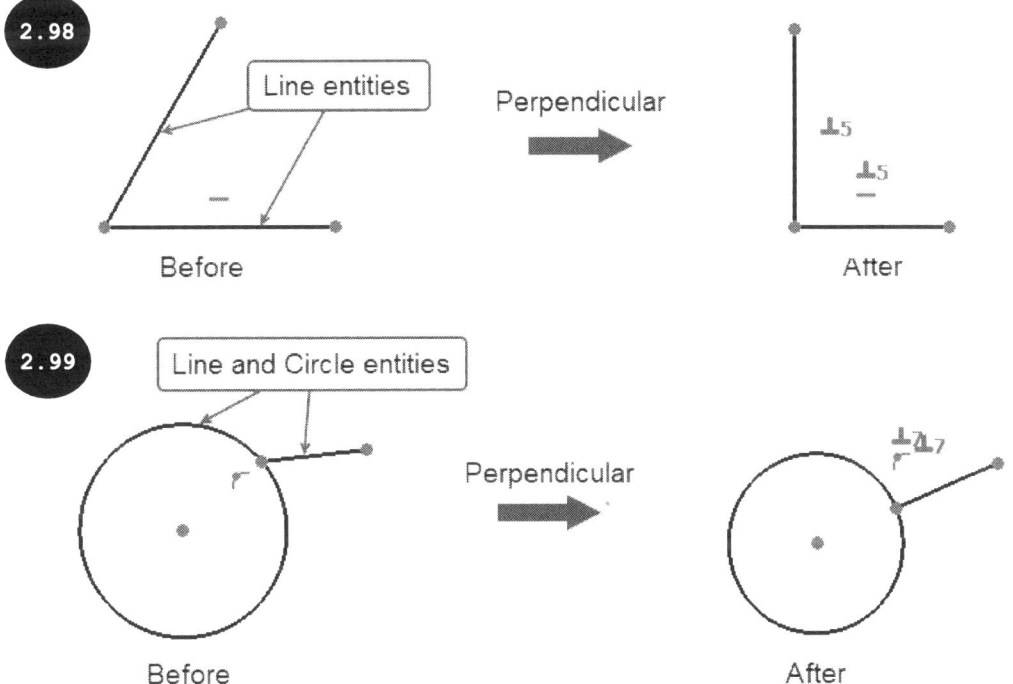

Tangent Constraint ➚

A tangent constraint is used for making two sketch entities such as a circle and a line tangent to each other. You can also make two circles, two arcs, two ellipses, or a combination of these sketch entities tangent to each other. To apply a tangent constraint, click on the **Constrain tangent** tool ➚ in the **Sketcher constraints** toolbar or press the **T** key. Next, select two sketch entities one by one in the 3D View area. The tangent constraint gets applied, and the selected entities become tangent to each other, see Figure 2.100.

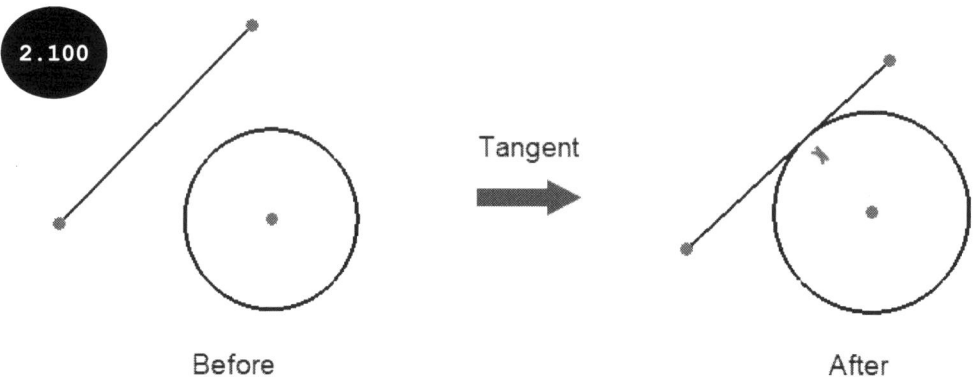

2.100

Tangent

Before   After

Equal Constraint ≡

An equal constraint is used for making two sketch entities (lines, arcs, or circles) equal. To apply an equal constraint, click on the **Constrain equal** tool ≡ in the **Sketcher constraints** toolbar or press the **E** key. Next, select two sketch entities (lines, arcs, or circles) one by one in the 3D View area. The equal constraint gets applied, and the selected entities become equal, see Figure 2.101. In this figure, the equal constraint is applied between two lines. Note that on applying an equal constraint, the length of line entities and the radii of arc or circle entities become equal.

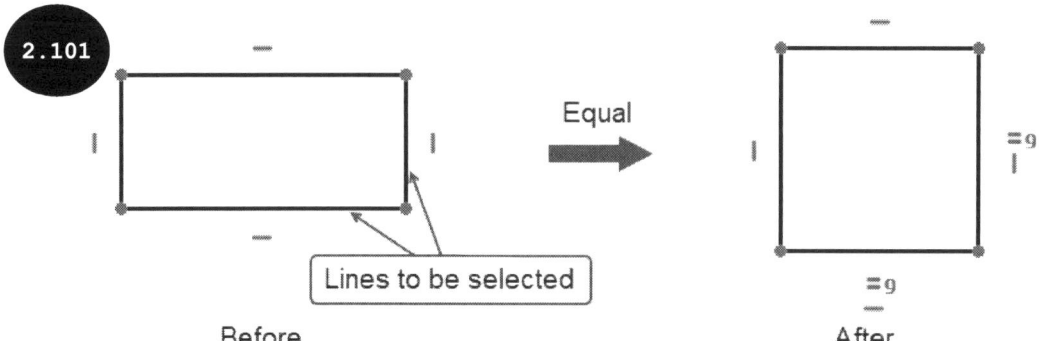

2.101

Equal

Lines to be selected

Before   After

Symmetric Constraint ⋈

A symmetric constraint is used for making two points symmetric about a line or another point. To apply a symmetric constraint, click on the **Constrain symmetrical** tool ⋈ in the **Sketcher constraints** toolbar or press the **S** key. Next, select two points one by one in the 3D View area, refer to Figure 2.102. After selecting two points, select a line or a third point. The symmetric constraint gets applied, and the first selected two points become symmetric about the line or the third selected point, see Figure 2.102. In this figure, the symmetric constraint is applied between two points and a line entity.

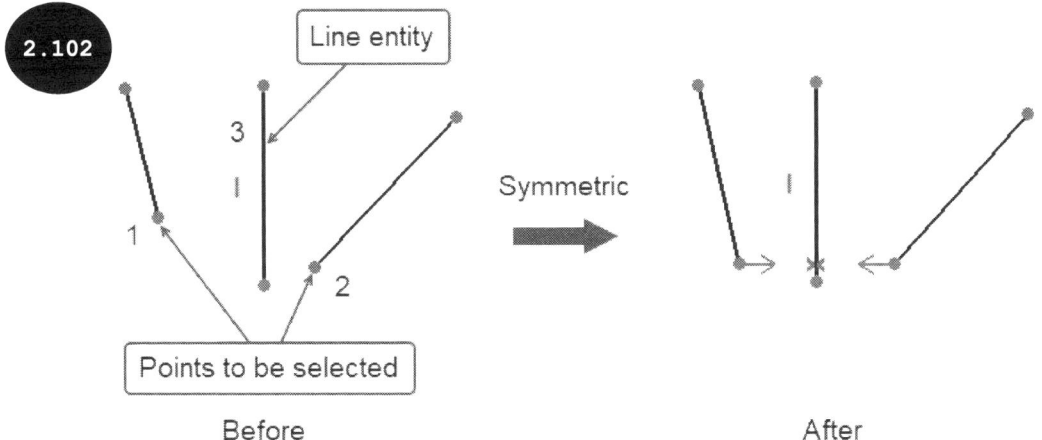

Before   After

Block Constraint ⊗

A block constraint is used for blocking or fixing the current position and size of a sketch entity and making it fully constrained. It is a very useful constraint to fix the current position of a B-spline in the 3D View area. To apply a block constraint, click on the **Constrain block** tool ⊗ in the **Sketcher constraints** toolbar and then select a sketch entity like a B-Spline to be fixed in the 3D View area. The block constraint gets applied such that its current position and size cannot be changed.

Applying Dimensional Constraints

Once a sketch has been drawn and required geometric constraints are applied, you must apply dimension constraints using the dimension tools. As FreeCAD is a parametric software, the parameters of sketch entities such as the length and angle are controlled or driven by dimension values. When you modify a dimension value, the respective sketch entity also gets modified, accordingly. The various dimension tools are available in the **Sketcher constraints** toolbar (see Figure 2.103) and are discussed next.

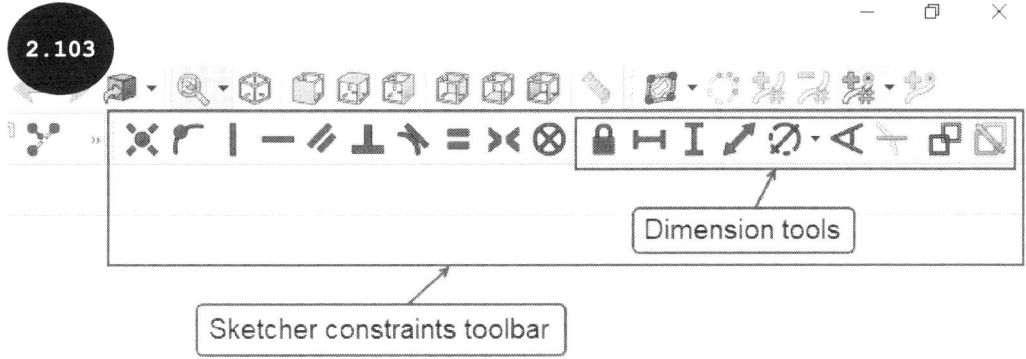

Lock Dimensional Constraint 🔒

A lock dimensional constraint is used for locking a sketch point by applying horizontal and vertical dimensions to it concerning the origin. The method for applying a lock dimensional constraint is discussed below:

1. Click on the **Constrain lock** tool in the **Sketcher constraints** toolbar, see Figure 2.104. The **Constrain lock** tool gets activated.

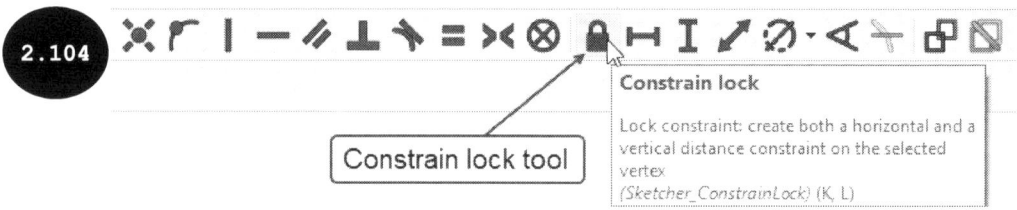

2. Select a sketch point in the 3D View area, see Figure 2.105. The horizontal and vertical dimensions get applied to the selected point concerning the origin, see Figure 2.106. Also, the tool remains active, and you can continue selecting other sketch points one by one for applying dimensions.

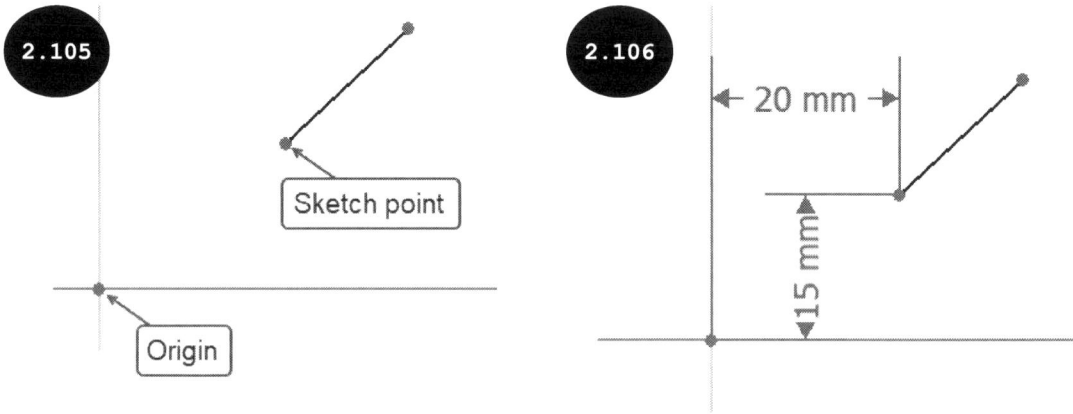

3. Press the ESC key or right-click in the 3D View area to exit the tool.

> **Note:** You can edit or change the current value of a dimension at any point in time, as required. For doing so, double-click on the dimension to be edited in the 3D View area. The **Insert length** pop-up dialog box appears with the display of the current dimension value in its **Length** field, see Figure 2.107. Enter a new dimension value in the **Length** field of this pop-up dialog box. You can also specify a name for the dimension in the **Name** field of the pop-up dialog box. It is an optional field. If you want to apply the selected dimension as a reference dimension only, then you can select the **Reference** check box in this pop-up dialog box. After entering a new dimension value for the selected dimension, click on the **OK** button to accept the change made and exit the pop-up dialog box.

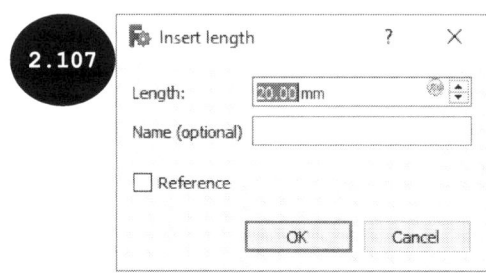

Horizontal Dimensional Constraint ⊢⊣

A horizontal dimensional constraint is used for applying the horizontal dimension to a sketch line or between two points, see Figures 2.108 and 2.109. The method for applying a horizontal dimension is discussed below:

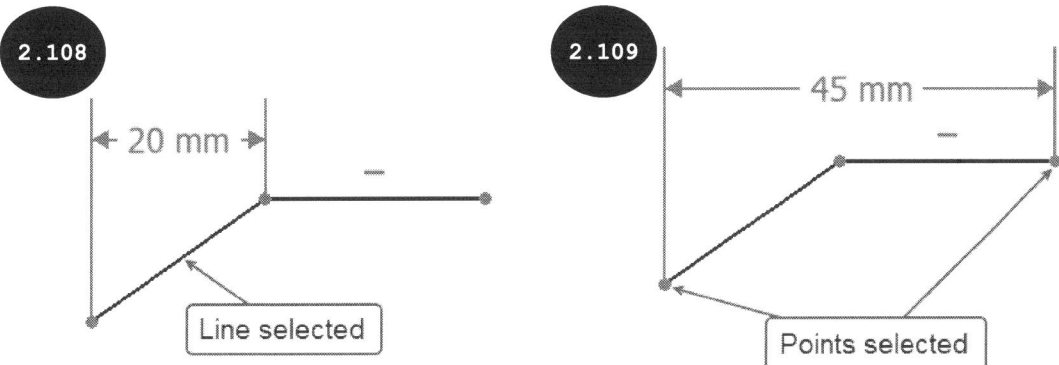

1. Click on the **Constrain horizontal distance** tool ⊢⊣ in the **Sketcher constraints** toolbar, see Figure 2.110. The appearance of the cursor changes to a cross mark with the display of a red horizontal dimensional constraint icon.

2. Select a line entity or two sketch points in the 3D View area. The **Insert length** pop-up dialog box appears with the display of the current dimension value of the selected line entity or points, see Figure 2.111.

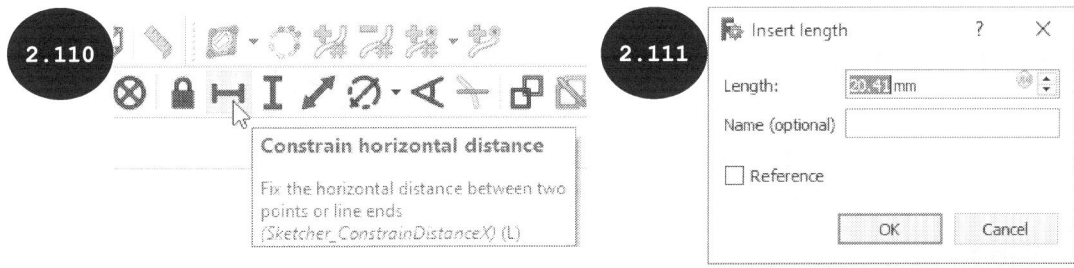

3. Enter a new dimension value in the **Length** field of the pop-up dialog box. Next, click on the **OK** button for accepting the change made and to exit the pop-up dialog box. The horizontal dimension of the specified dimension value gets applied. Note that the tool remains active, and you can continue applying other horizontal dimensions one by one.

4. Press the ESC key or right-click to exit the tool.

Vertical Dimensional Constraint ⊥

A vertical dimensional constraint is used for applying the vertical dimension to a sketch line or between two points, see Figures 2.112 and 2.113. You can apply a vertical dimensional constraint to a line or between two sketch points by using the **Constrain vertical distance** tool ⊥ of the **Sketcher constraints** toolbar in a manner similar to applying a horizontal dimension constraint, as discussed above.

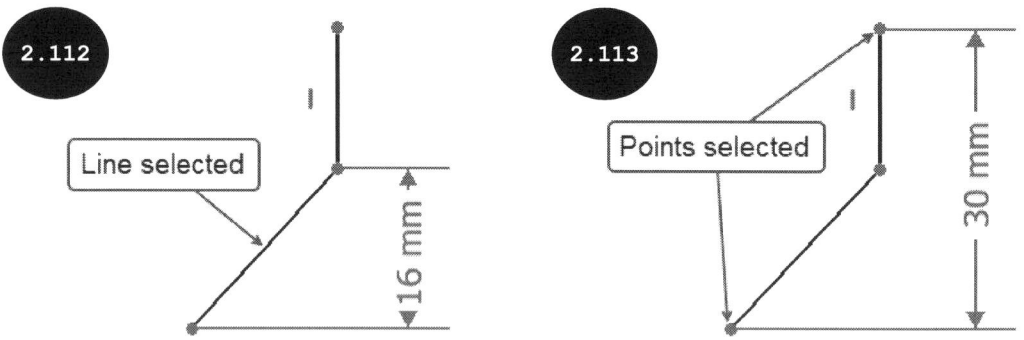

Distance Dimensional Constraint ✏

A distance dimensional constraint is used for applying a horizontal, a vertical, or an aligned dimension to a linear sketch entity (line), between two points, or a point and a line, see Figures 2.114 through 2.116. The method for applying a distance dimensional constraint is discussed below:

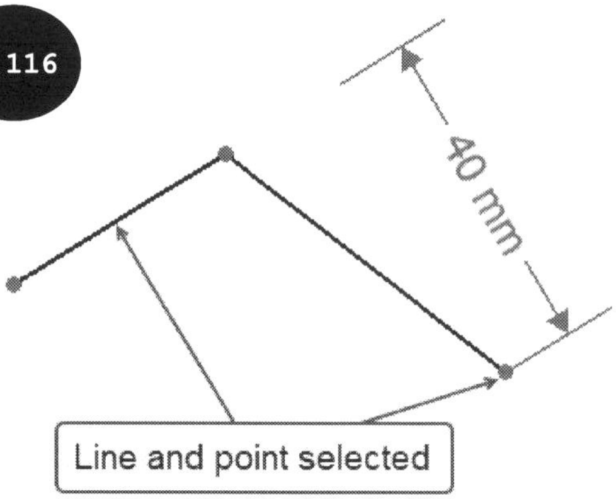

1. Click on the **Constrain distance** tool ✏ in the **Sketcher constraints** toolbar.

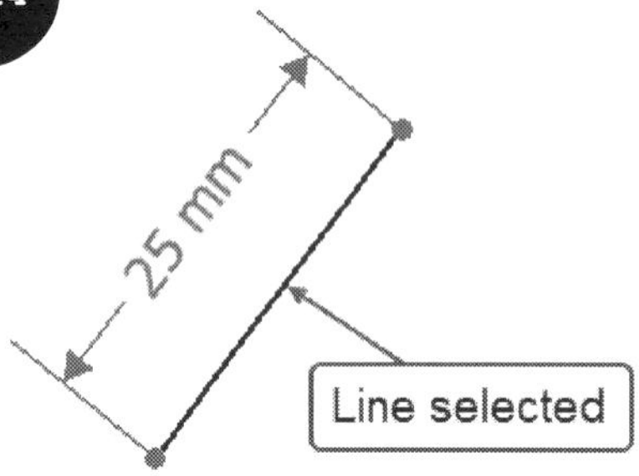

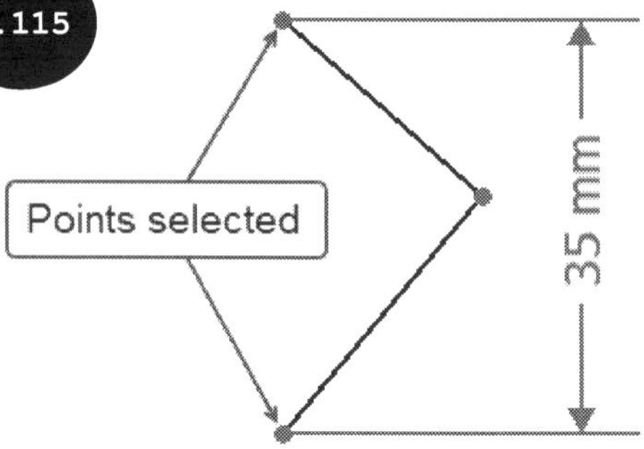

2. Select a linear sketch entity (line), two points, or a line and a point in the 3D View area. The **Insert length** pop-up dialog box appears with the display of a current dimension value of the selected sketch entity or entities.

3. Enter a new dimension value in the **Length** field of the pop-up dialog box, as required, and then click on the **OK** button to accept the change made, and to exit the pop-up dialog box. A distance dimension of the specified dimension value gets applied to the selected sketch entity or entities. Note that the tool remains active, and you can continue applying other dimensions one by one.

4. Press the ESC key or right-click in the 3D View area to exit the tool.

Radius Dimensional Constraint ⊘

A radius dimensional constraint is used for applying a radius dimension to an arc or a circle, see Figures 2.117 and 2.118. The method for applying a radius dimensional constraint is discussed below:

1. Click on the **Constrain radius** tool ⊘ in the **Sketcher constraints** toolbar, see Figure 2.119.

2. Select an arc or a circle in the 3D View area. The **Insert radius** pop-up dialog box appears with the display of the current radius value of the selected entity.

3. Enter a new radius value in the **Radius** field of the pop-up dialog box and then click on the **OK** button to accept the change made and exit the pop-up dialog box. A radius dimension of the specified radius value gets applied to the selected entity. Note that the tool remains active, and you can continue applying other radius dimensions one by one.

4. Press the ESC key or right-click in the 3D View area to exit the tool.

Diameter Dimensional Constraint ⊘

A diameter dimensional constraint is used for applying a diameter dimension to a circle or an arc, see Figures 2.120 and 2.121. You can apply a diameter dimensional constraint to a circle or an arc by using the **Constrain diameter** tool ⊘ of the **Sketcher constraints** toolbar (refer to Figure 2.119) in a manner similar to applying a radius dimensional constraint.

Note: The **Constrain auto radius/diameter** tool in the **Sketcher constraints** toolbar (see Figure 2.122) is used for applying a radial or a diameter dimensional constraint depending upon a sketch entity (circle or arc) selected. If you select a circle, then the diameter dimensional constraint will be applied, whereas if you select an arc, then the radial constraint will be applied by using the Constrain auto radius/diameter tool.

Angle Dimensional Constraint ◁

An angle dimensional constraint is used for applying an angular dimension between two lines, an arc, an individual line entity concerning the X-axis, or at the intersection of two curves, see Figures 2.123 through 2.126. The method for applying an angle dimensional constraint is discussed below:

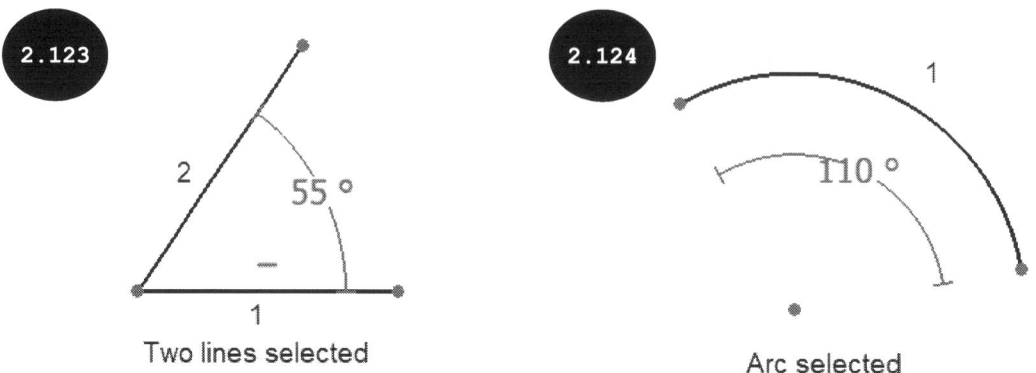

Two lines selected   Arc selected

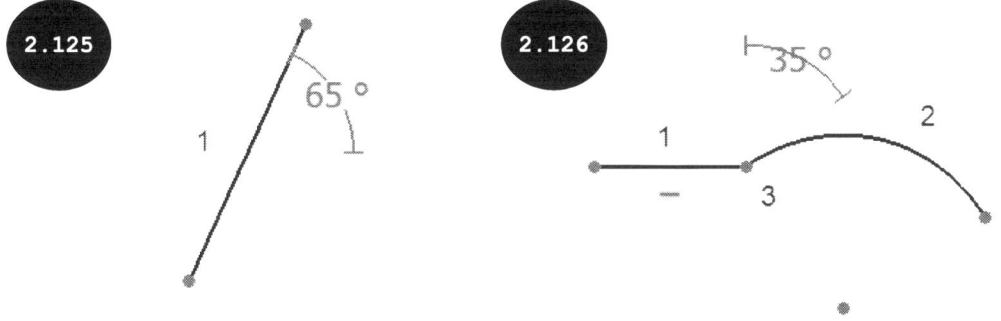

Line selected   Two curves and intersection point selected

1. Select two lines (refer to Figure 2.123), an arc (refer to Figure 2.124), a line (refer to Figure 2.125), or three sketch entities (refer to Figure 2.126) in the 3D View area before invoking the tool.

2. After selecting one or more entities, click on the **Constrain angle** tool ⊲ in the **Sketcher constraints** toolbar or press the K+ A keys. The **Insert angle** pop-up dialog box appears with the display of a current angle value.

3. Enter a new angle value in the **Angle** field of the pop-up dialog box and then click on the **OK** button for accepting the change made, and to exit the pop-up dialog box. An angle dimension of the specified angle value gets applied to the selected entity. Next, press the ESC key or right-click in the 3D View area to exit the tool.

Editing and Modifying Dimensions

After applying dimensions, you may need to modify them due to changes in the design, revisions in the design, and so on. To modify an already applied dimension, double-click on the dimension value (length, angle, radius, or diameter) to be modified in the 3D View area. The respective pop-up dialog box appears, refer to Figure 2.127. In this pop-up dialog box, enter a new dimension value and then click on the **OK** button. The selected dimension value gets modified. Also, the respective length, angle, radius, or diameter of the entity gets changed in the 3D View area, accordingly.

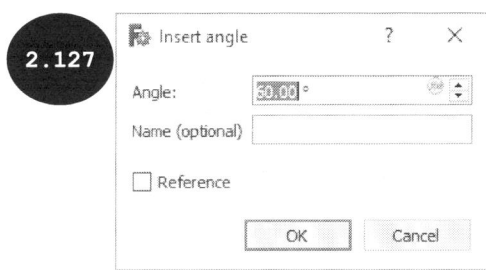

Working with Different States of a Sketch

In FreeCAD, a 2D sketch can be either under constrained, fully constrained, or over constrained. All these states of a sketch are discussed next.

Under Constrained Sketch

An under constrained sketch is a sketch, whose all degrees of freedom are not fixed. This means that the entities of the sketch can change their shape, size, and position upon being dragged. Figure 2.128 shows a rectangular sketch in which the length of the rectangle is defined as 50 mm. However, the width and the position of the rectangle concerning the origin are not defined. This means that the width and position of the rectangle can be changed by dragging the respective entities of the rectangle.

Note: The status of a sketch appears in the **Solver messages** sub-windows of the **Task Panel** that appears in the **Tasks** tab of the **Combo View**, see Figure 2.129.

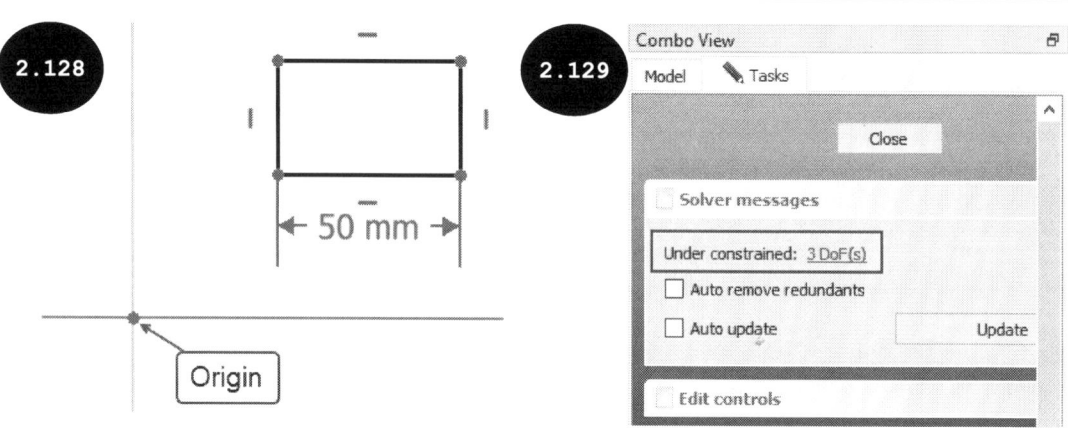

Fully Constrained Sketch

A fully constrained sketch is a sketch, whose all degrees of freedom are fixed by applying the required geometrical and dimensional constraints. This means that the entities of the sketch cannot change their shape, size, and position by being dragged. Figure 2.130 shows a rectangular sketch in which the length, width, and position of the sketch are defined.

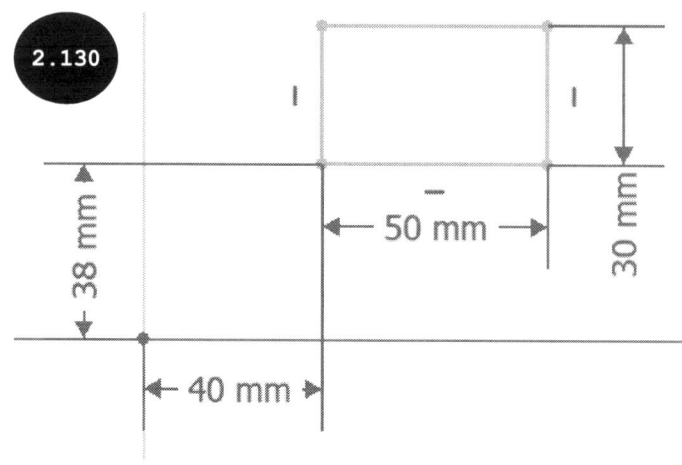

Note: The sketch shown in Figure 2.130 is fully constrained as all its entities are dimensioned. Also, the required geometrical constraints have been applied such that the horizontal and vertical constraints are applied to horizontal and vertical line entities, respectively. Note that these constraints are applied automatically to the entities while they are being drawn.

Over Constrained Sketch

An over constrained sketch is a sketch that is over-defined by applying an extra geometrical or dimensional constraint. Figure 2.131 shows an over constrained line entity. Note that in this figure, on applying a vertical constraint to the line entity, it becomes an over constrained entity.

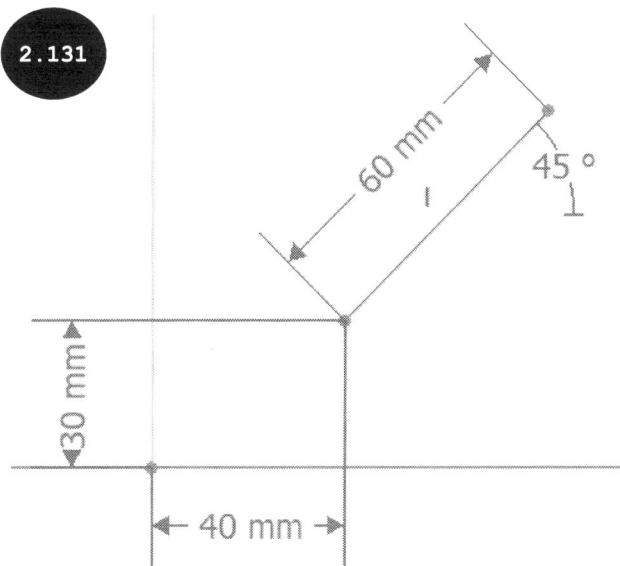

Note: In FreeCAD, when you apply an extra dimension to a fully constrained sketch, the **Dimensional constraint** pop-up window appears (refer to Figure 2.132), informing that the applying dimension is invalid. Click on the **OK** button in this window. The invalid dimension will not be applied, and the sketch does not become an over constrained sketch. Similarly, when you apply a geometric constraint that is impossible to be applied to an entity due to other applied geometrical constraints on it, then the **Impossible constraint** pop-up window appears, refer to Figure 2.133. Click on the **OK** button in this window. The extra geometric constraint will not be applied, and the sketch does not become an over constrained sketch.

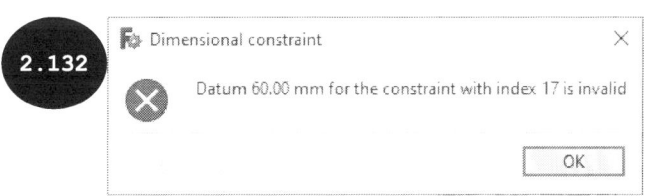

Exiting the Sketcher Workbench

After creating a sketch, you need to exit the Sketch editing mode of the **Sketcher** workbench and switch back to the **Part Design** workbench, where you can create a 3D solid feature by using the sketch. You will learn about creating 3D solid features in later chapters. To exit the Sketch editing mode of the **Sketcher** workbench, click on the **Leave sketch** tool 🔼 in the **Sketcher** toolbar, see Figure 2.134.

Tutorial 1

Create the sketch shown in Figure 2.135 and make it fully constrained by applying all the required geometric constraints and dimensions. The model shown in this figure is for your reference only. You will learn about creating 3D models in later chapters. All dimensions are in mm.

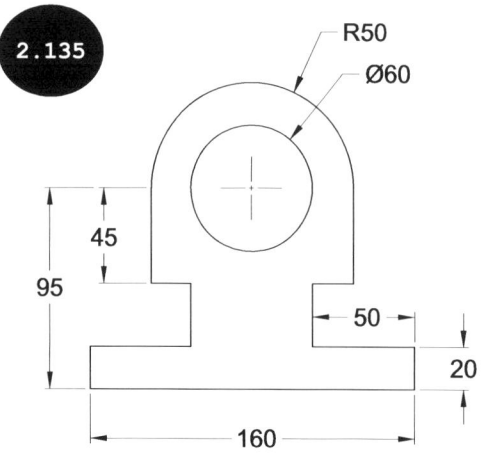

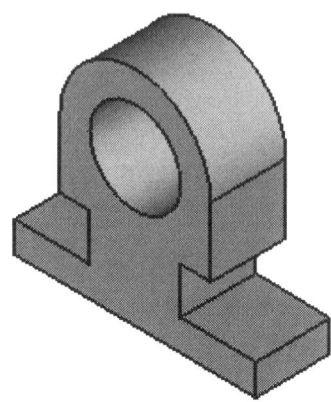

Section 1: Starting FreeCAD and a New Empty Document

1. Start FreeCAD by double-clicking on the **FreeCAD 0.20** icon on your desktop. The startup user interface of FreeCAD appears, see Figure 2.136.

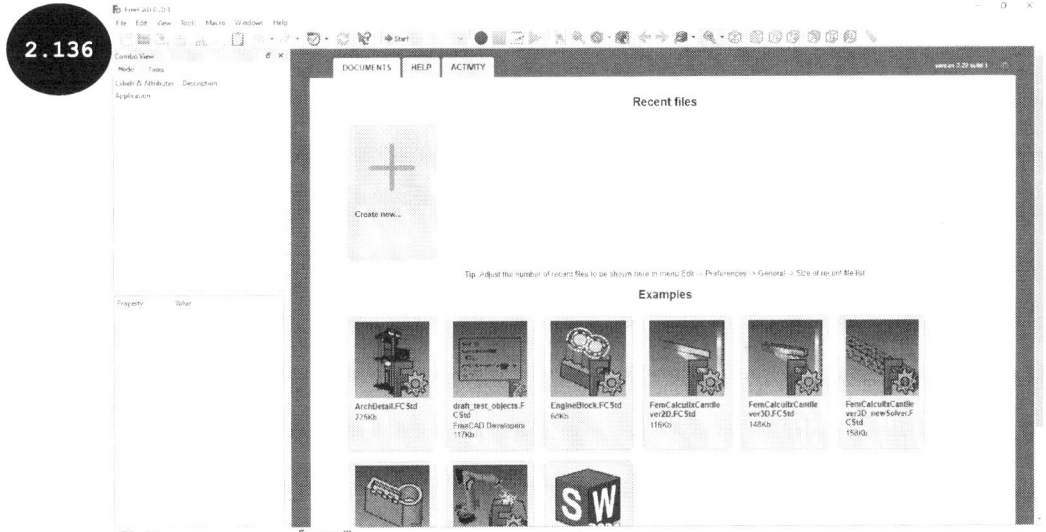

Note: Every time you start FreeCAD, the **Start** workbench is invoked with the display of the **Start** page, by default. The **Start** page acts as a welcome screen that displays recently opened documents, example files, help documentation, the latest activity in FreeCAD, and so on in their respective tabs (**DOCUMENTS, HELP,** and **ACTIVITY**).

2. Click on the **New** tool in the **File** toolbar (see Figure 2.137) or press the **CTRL + N** keys. A new empty document gets invoked with the default name "**unnamed: 1**" and it becomes active by default.

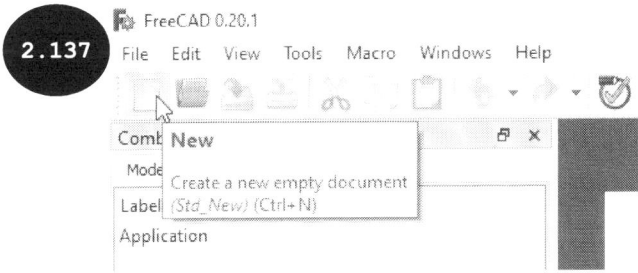

Section 2: Invoking the Sketcher Workbench

Now, you can invoke the **Sketcher** workbench within the **Part Design** workbench for creating a sketch of the base feature. In FreeCAD, the **Sketcher** workbench can be invoked independently or within the **Part Design** workbench.

1. Invoke the **Workbench Selector** in the **Workbench** toolbar and then select the **Part Design** workbench, see Figure 2.138. The **Part Design** workbench gets invoked.

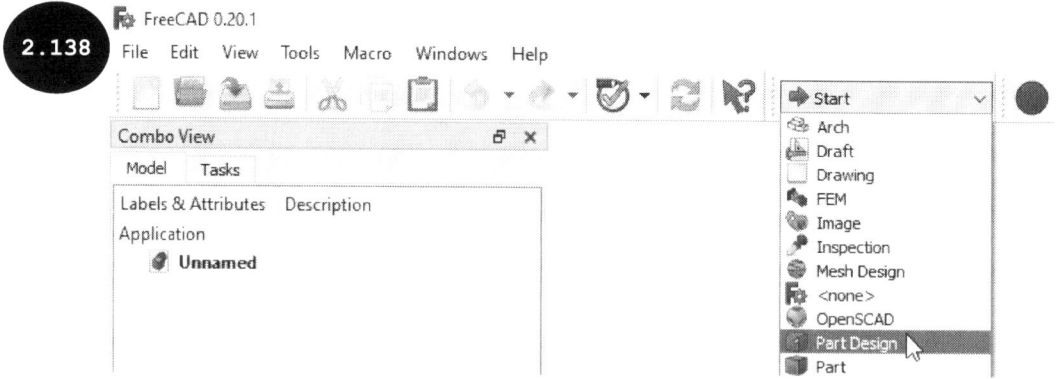

Now, you can invoke the **Sketcher** workbench for creating a sketch.

2. Click on the **Create sketch** tool in the **Part Design Helper** toolbar, see Figure 2.139. The three default planes appear in the 3D View area. Also, the **Task Panel** appears in the **Tasks** tab of **Combo View** and displays the names of the three default planes, see Figure 2.140.

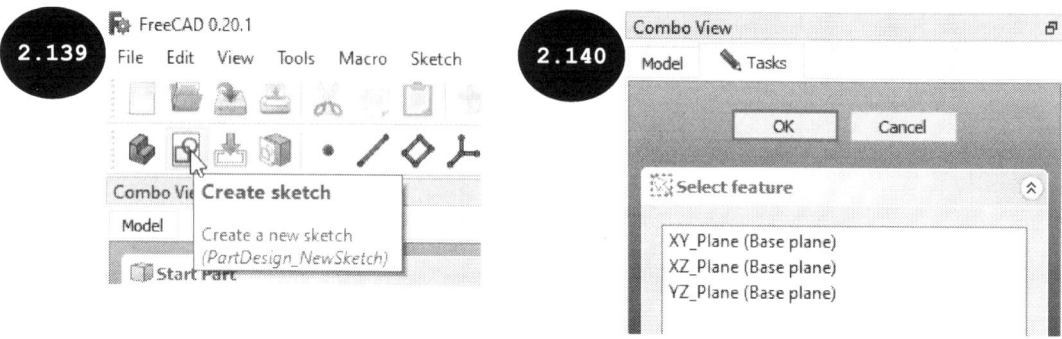

3. Select the **XZ_Plane** as the sketching plane in the 3D View area for creating the sketch. The Sketch editing mode of the **Sketcher** workbench gets invoked, see Figure 2.141. Also, the selected plane becomes the sketching plane for drawing the sketch and it is oriented normal to the viewing direction.

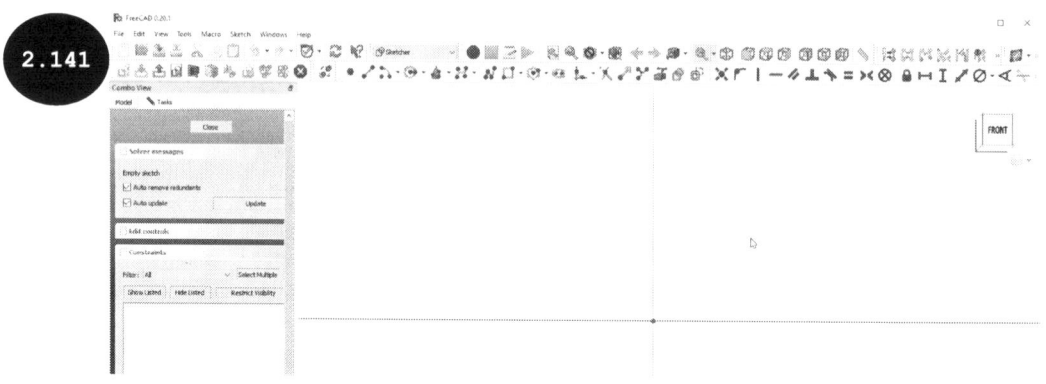

Tip: Alternatively, you can select the **XZ_Plane** in the **Task Panel** and then click on the **OK** button for invoking the Sketch editing mode of the **Sketcher** workbench.

Section 3: Specifying Units, Grids, and Snap Settings

Now, you need to specify units, grids, and snap settings for creating the sketch.

1. Click on **Edit > Preferences** in the **Standard Menu**, see Figure 2.142. The **Preferences** dialog box appears.

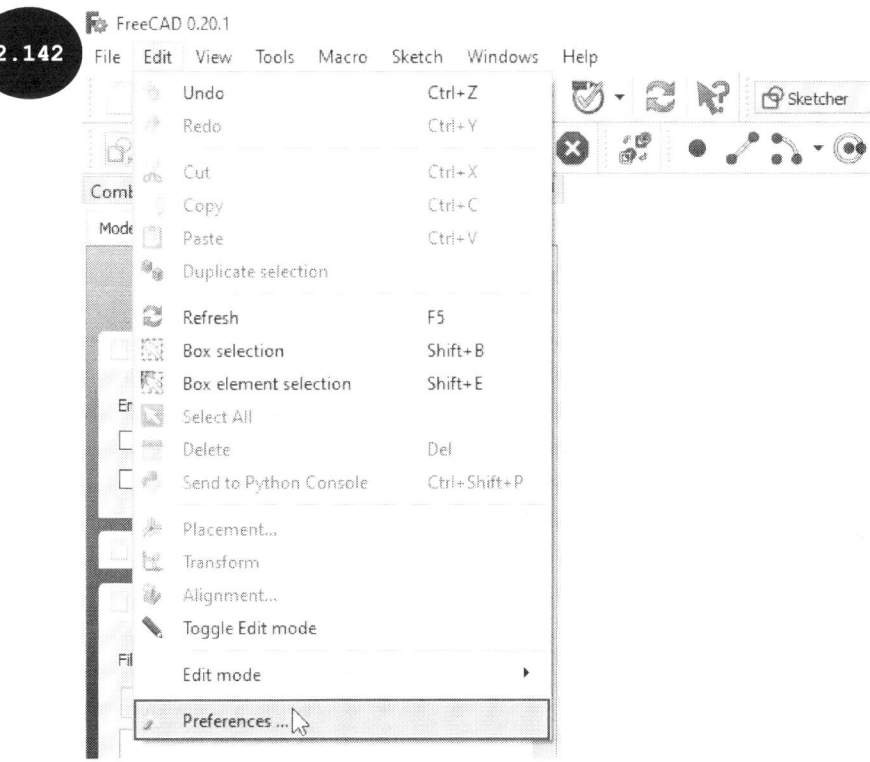

2. Ensure that the **General** section is selected in the left panel of the **Preferences** dialog box and then click on the **Units** tab, see Figure 2.143.

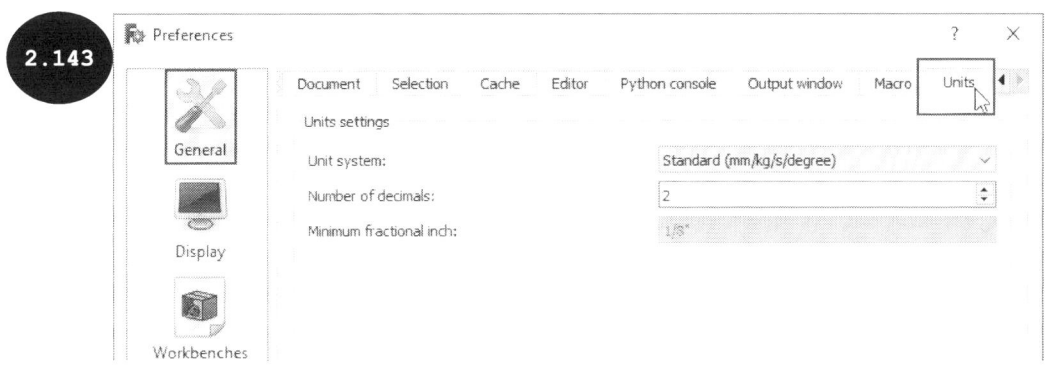

Tip: You may need to click on the arrow ▶ at the upper right corner of the **Preferences** dialog box for displaying the **Units** tab.

3. Ensure that the **Standard (mm/kg/s/degree)** option is selected in the **Unit system** drop-down list of the dialog box. In this unit system, length is measured in millimeters, mass is calculated in kilograms, time is represented in seconds, and angle is measured in degrees.

4. Click on the **Apply** button in the **Preferences** dialog box. The selected unit system is defined.

    Now, you need to define the grid and snap settings in the **Preferences** dialog box.

5. Click on the **Sketcher** section in the left panel of the **Preferences** dialog box. Next, select the **Show grid** check box to turn on the display of grids in the 3D View area, see Figure 2.144.

6. Enter **5 mm** in the **Distance between two subsequent grid lines** field of the dialog box as the distance between two grid lines in the 3D View area, see Figure 2.144.

7. Select the **Grid snap** check box in the dialog box to turn on the snap mode for snapping the movement of the cursor on grid lines in the 3D View area, see Figure 2.144.

8. Ensure that the **Auto remove redundants** check box is selected in the **General** area of the dialog box for automatically removing the redundant constraints from the sketch, see Figure 2.144.

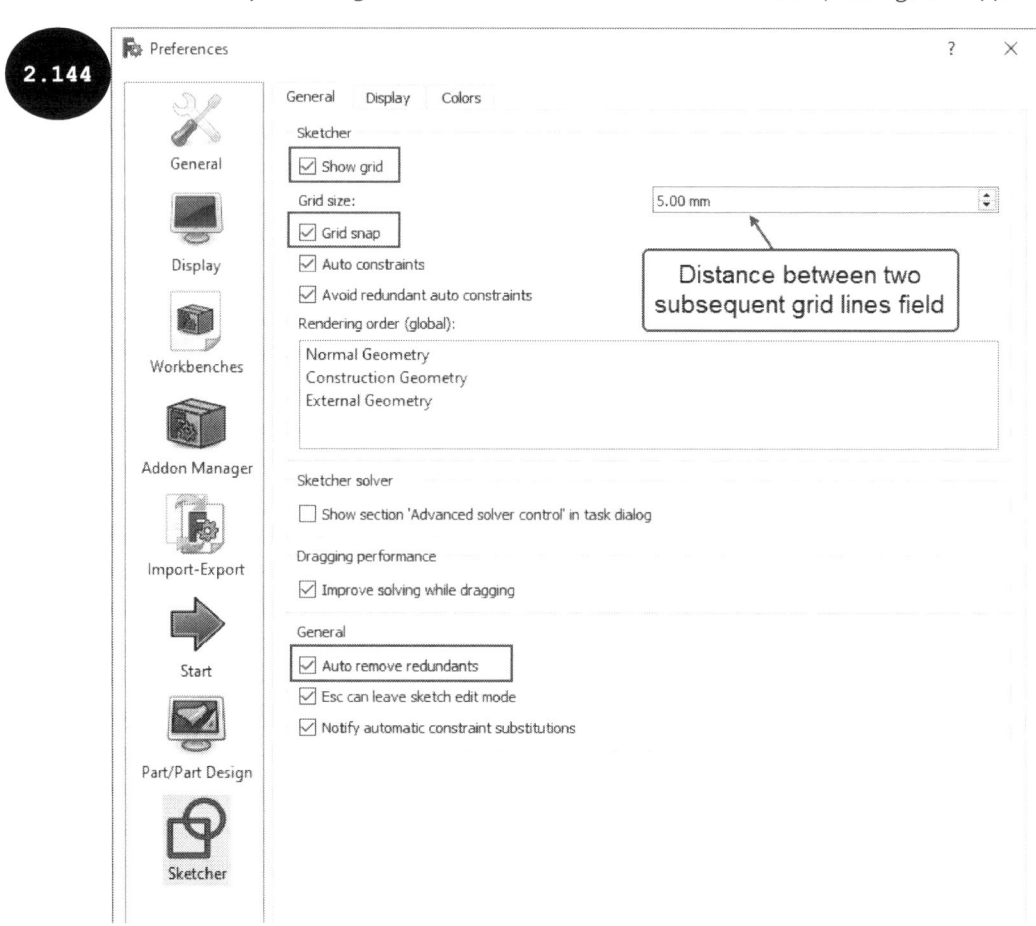

9. After specifying the required unit, grid, and snap settings in the dialog box, click on the **Apply** button and then the **OK** button in the dialog box to accept the changes made and exit the **Preferences** dialog box. The grids appear in the 3D View area, see Figure 2.145.

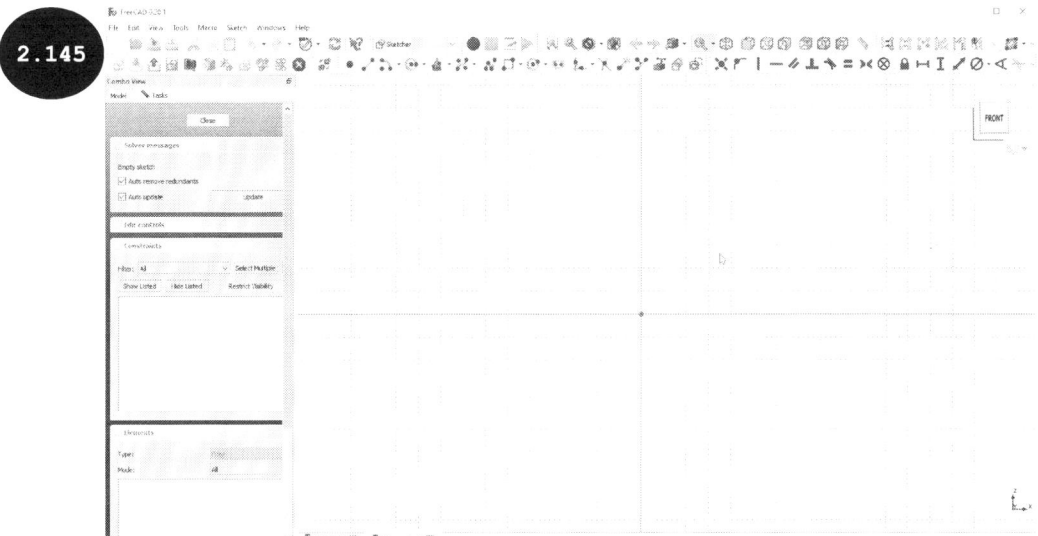

Section 4: Drawing the Sketch

1. Invoke the **Create circle** menu in the **Sketcher geometries** toolbar and then click on the **Center and rim point** tool, see Figure 2.146. The **Center and rim point** tool gets activated.

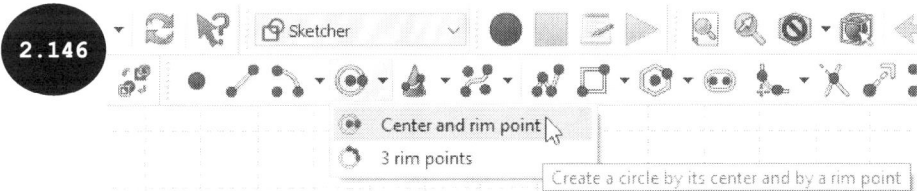

2. Click to specify the center point of the circle at the origin in the drawing area, refer to Figure 2.147.

3. Move the cursor horizontally toward the right and then click to specify a point when the radius of the circle appears as 30 mm near the cursor, see Figure 2.147. A circle of radius 30 mm is drawn. Next, press the **ESC** key or right-click in the 3D View area to exit the tool.

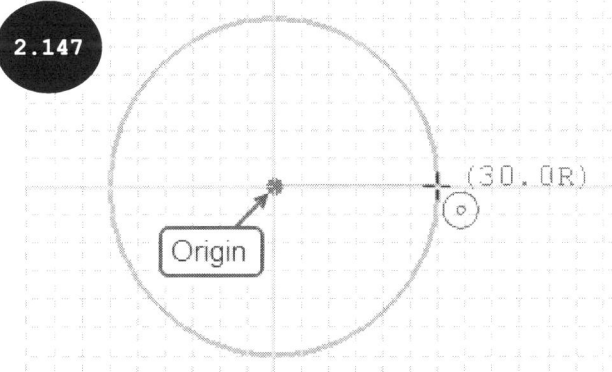

Now, you need to create an arc of the sketch.

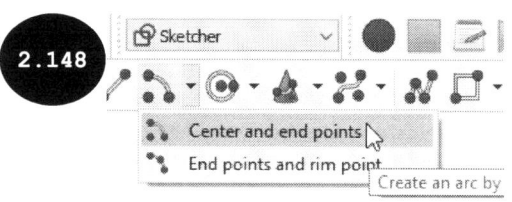

4. Invoke the **Create arc** menu in the **Sketcher geometries** toolbar and then click on the **Center and end points** tool, see Figure 2.148. The **Center and end points** tool gets activated.

5. Click to specify the center point of the arc at the origin in the 3D View area.

6. Move the cursor horizontally toward the right. The preview of an imaginary circle appears, see Figure 2.149. Next, click to specify the start point of the arc when the radius of the imaginary circle appears as 50 mm and the start angle value appears as 0 degrees near the cursor, see Figure 2.149.

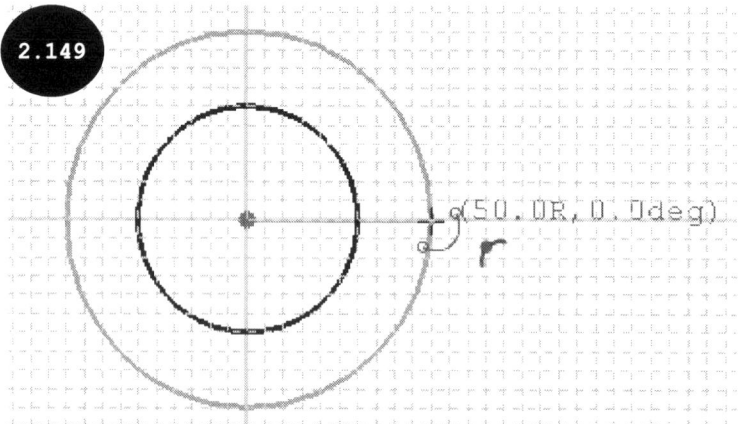

7. Move the cursor in the anti-clockwise direction in the 3D View area and then click to specify the endpoint of the arc when the angle value appears as 180 degrees near the cursor, see Figure 2.150. An arc is drawn. Next, right-click in the 3D View area or press the ESC key to exit the tool.

Now, you need to draw a continuous chain of line entities of the sketch.

8. Click on the **Create polyline** tool in the **Sketcher geometries** toolbar, see Figure 2.151. The **Create polyline** tool gets activated.

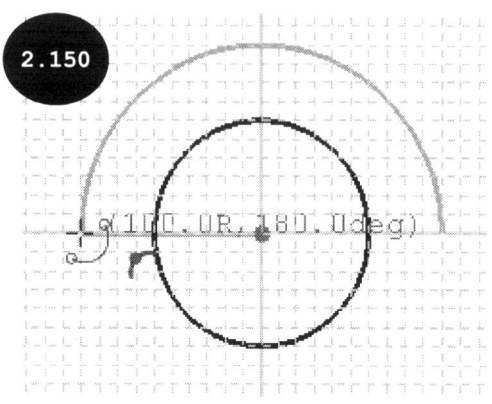

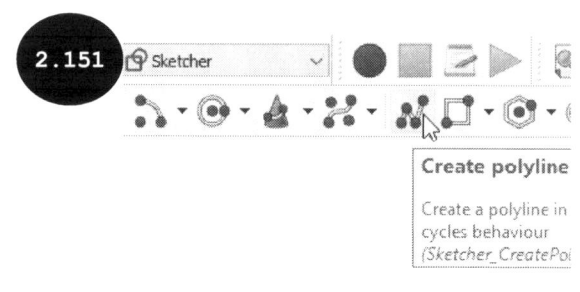

9. Click to specify the start point of the first line segment at the endpoint of the previously drawn arc, see Figure 2.152.

10. Move the cursor vertically downward and then click to specify the endpoint of the line when the length of the line appears as 45 mm, see Figure 2.153. The first line segment of length 45 mm is drawn. Also, a rubber band line segment appears attached to the cursor and the **Create polyline** tool remains active.

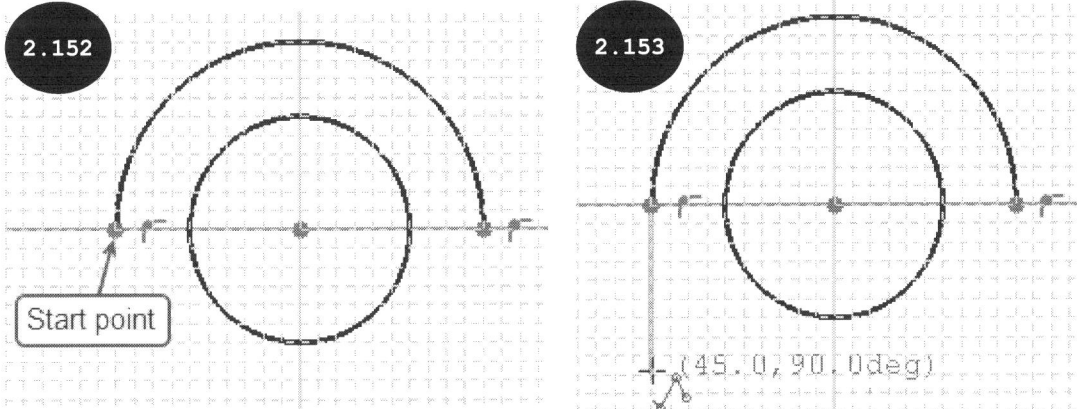

11. Move the cursor horizontally toward the right and then click to specify the endpoint of the second line segment when the length of the line appears as 20 mm, see Figure 2.154.

12. Move the cursor vertically downward and then click the left mouse button when the length of the third line segment appears as 30 mm, see Figure 2.155.

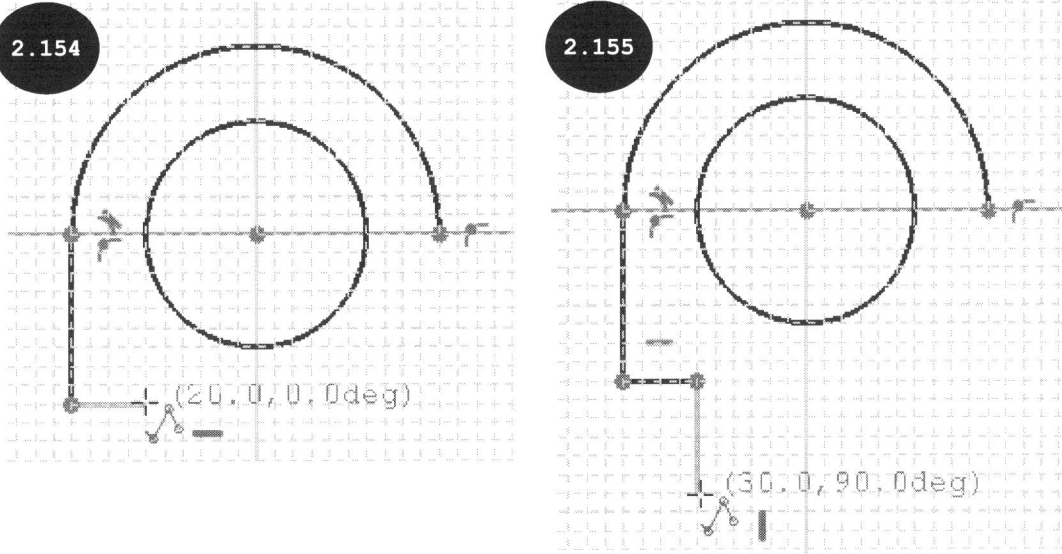

13. Move the cursor horizontally toward the left and click when the length of the fourth line segment appears as 50 mm, see Figure 2.156.

14. Move the cursor vertically downward and click when the length of the fifth line segment appears as 20 mm, see Figure 2.157.

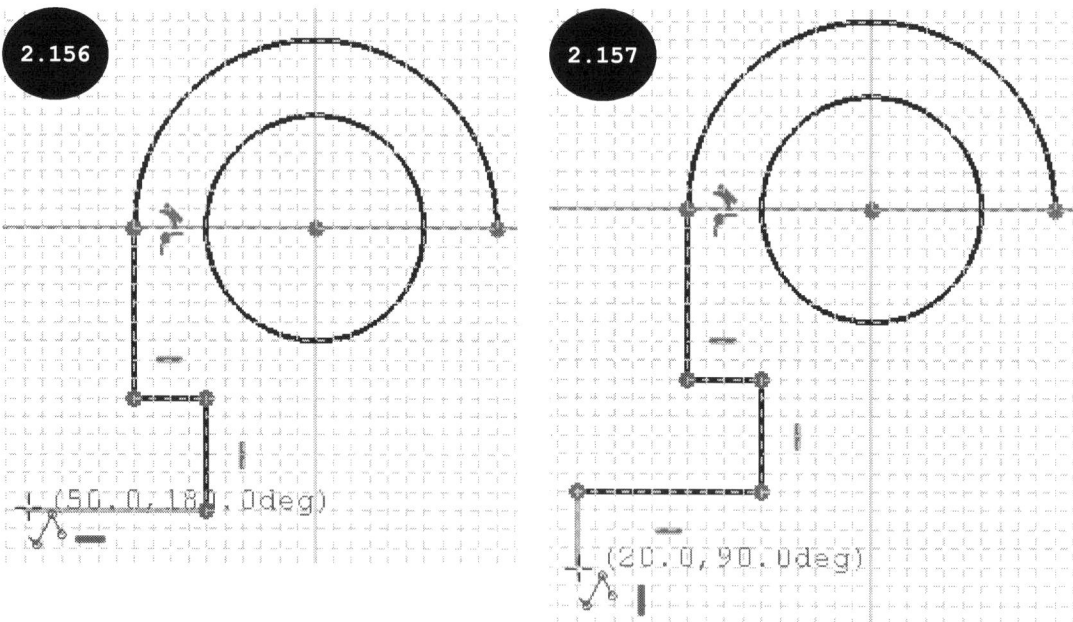

15. Move the cursor horizontally toward the right and click when the length of the sixth line segment appears as 160 mm, see Figure 2.158.

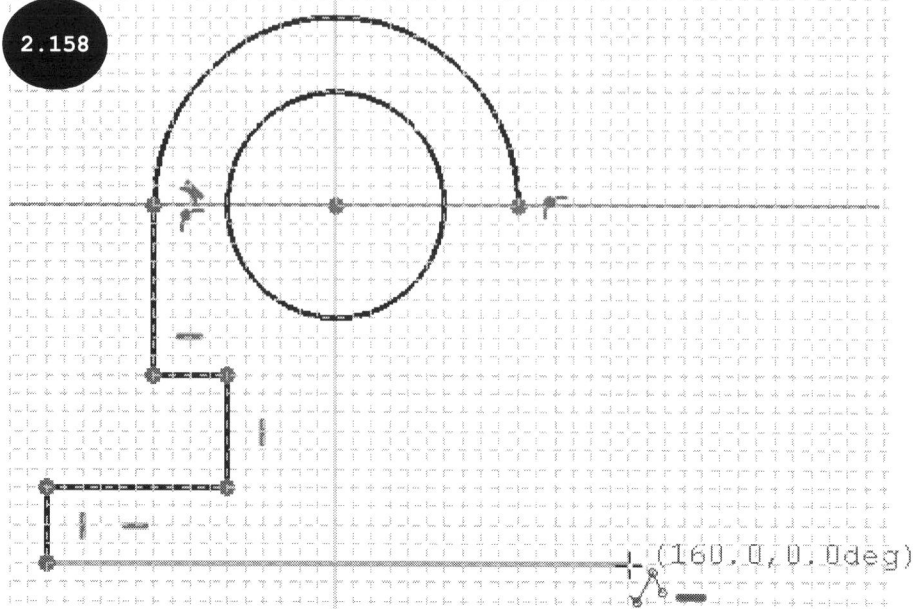

Note: You can zoom in or zoom out the drawing display area by scrolling the middle mouse button up or down, respectively. You will learn more about navigating a sketch or a model in later chapters.

16. Similarly, continue drawing the remaining line segments of the sketch one after the other by specifying points in the 3D View area, see Figure 2.159. Note that the endpoint of the last (eleventh) line segment is specified on the start point of the arc. Also, a rubber band line segment remains attached to the cursor.

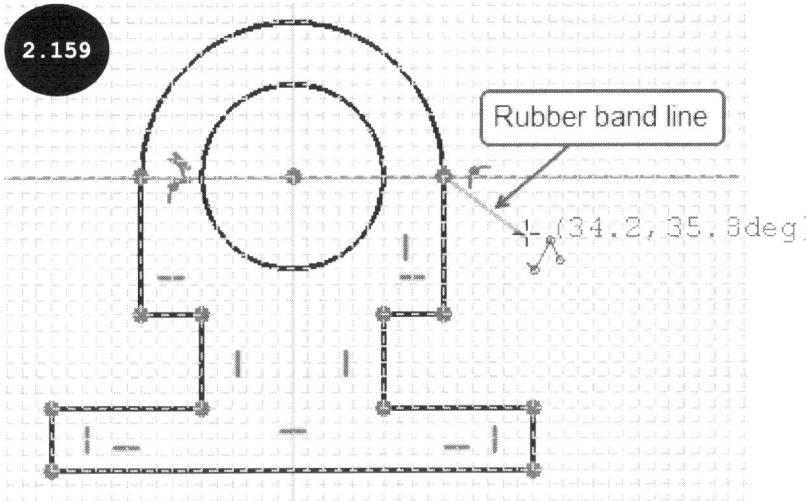

2.159

Rubber band line

(34.2, 35.8deg)

17. Right-click in the 3D View area to end the creation of a continuous chain of lines. Next, right-click again in the 3D View area or press the ESC key to exit the **Create polyline** tool.

Section 5: Applying Geometric Constraints

Now, you need to make the sketch fully constrained by applying the required constraints.

1. Click on the **Constrain equal** tool in the **Sketcher constraints** toolbar (see Figure 2.160) or press the **E** key for applying equal constraints between lines of equal length.

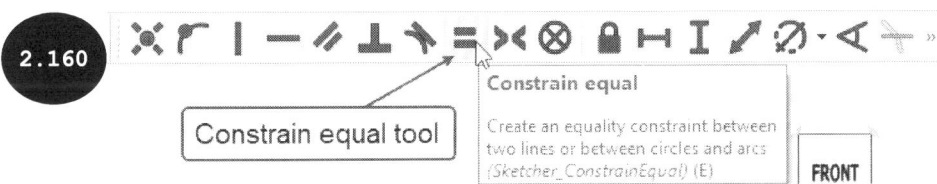

2.160

Constrain equal tool

Constrain equal

Create an equality constraint between two lines or between circles and arcs *(Sketcher_ConstrainEqual)* (E)

FRONT

2. Select the first line segment (1) and the eleventh line segment (11) of the sketch one by one, refer to Figure 2.161. An equal constraint gets applied between the selected lines. Also, the **Constrain equal** tool remains active.

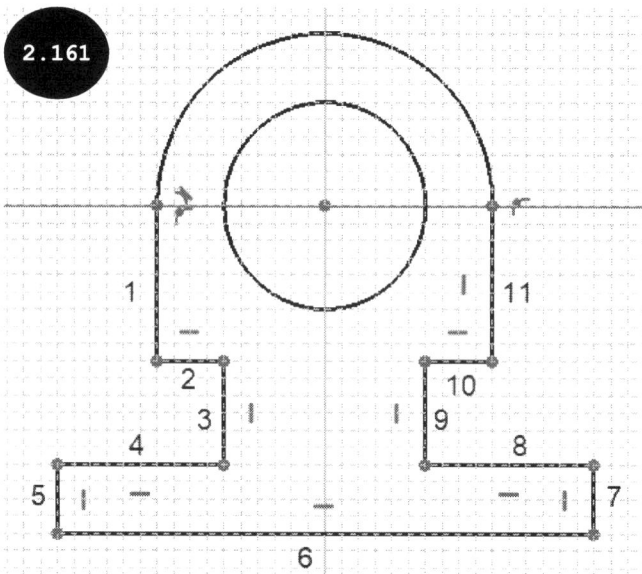

2.161

Note: In Figure 2.161, the line segments are labeled 1 to 11 for your reference only.

3. Select the second line segment (2) and the tenth line segment (10) of the sketch one by one, refer to Figure 2.161. An equal constraint gets applied between the selected lines. Also, the **Constrain equal** tool remains active.

4. Select the third line segment (3) and the ninth line segment (9) of the sketch one by one, refer to Figure 2.161. An equal constraint gets applied between the selected lines.

5. Select the fourth line segment (4) and the eighth line segment (8) of the sketch one by one, refer to Figure 2.161. An equal constraint gets applied between the selected lines.

6. After applying the equal constraint between lines of equal length, press the ESC key or right-click in the 3D View area to exit the **Constrain equal** tool.

Section 6: Applying Dimensions

Now, you need to apply the required dimensions to make the sketch fully defined.

1. Click on the **Constrain auto radius/diameter** tool in the **Sketcher constraints** toolbar, see Figure 2.162. The **Constrain auto radius/diameter** tool gets activated.

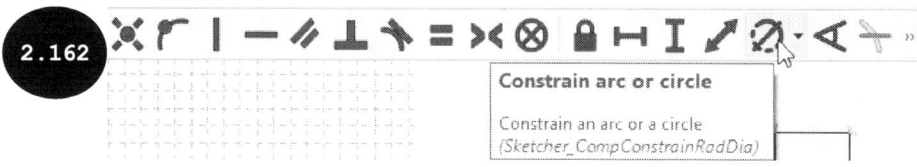

2.162

Constrain arc or circle

Constrain an arc or a circle
(Sketcher_CompConstrainRadDia)

2. Select the circle of the sketch in the 3D View area. The **Insert diameter** pop-up dialog box appears with the display of its current diameter value, see Figure 2.163.

3. Ensure that the diameter of the circle is entered as **60 mm** in the **Diameter** field of the dialog box.

4. Click on the **OK** button in the pop-up dialog box. A diameter dimension gets applied to the selected circle, see Figure 2.164. The **Constrain auto radius/diameter** tool remains active.

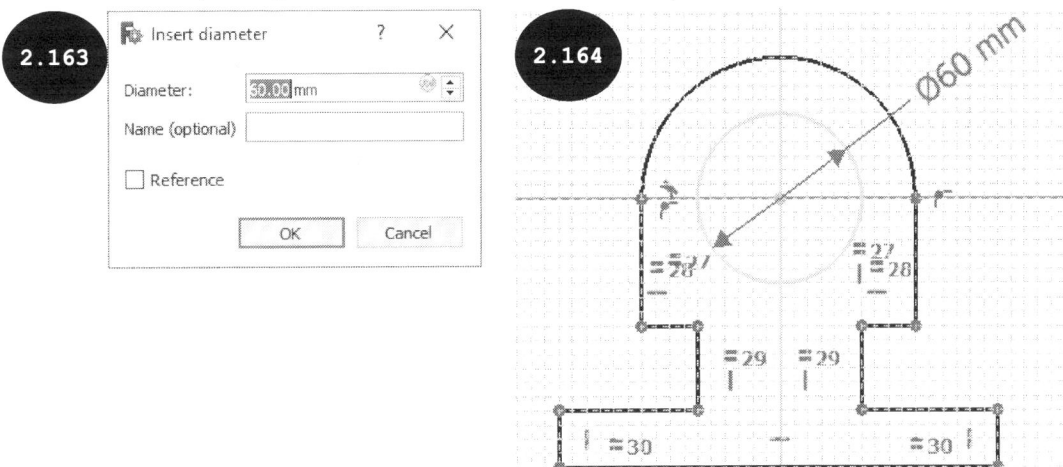

5. Select the arc of the sketch in the 3D View area. The **Insert radius** pop-up dialog box appears with the display of its current radius value, see Figure 2.165.

6. Ensure that the radius of the arc is entered as **50 mm** in the **Radius** field of the dialog box.

7. Click on the **OK** button in the pop-up dialog box. The radius dimension gets applied to the arc, see Figure 2.166. Next, press the ESC key or right-click to exit the tool.

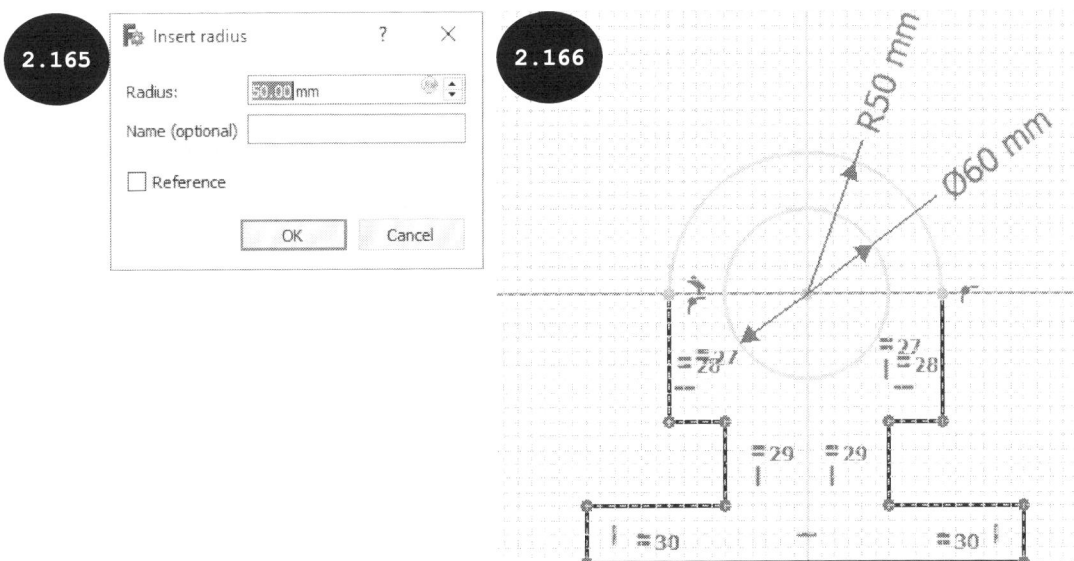

Tip: You can change the position of applied dimensions in the drawing area by dragging and dropping them to the required location in the 3D View area.

Now, you need to apply horizontal dimensions to the sketch entities.

8. Click on the **Constrain horizontal distance** tool in the **Sketcher constraints** toolbar, see Figure 2.167.

9. Select the bottom-most horizontal line of the sketch measuring a length of 160 mm. The **Insert length** pop-up dialog box appears with the display of its current dimension value.

10. Ensure that the length of the line is entered as **160 mm** in the pop-up dialog box.

11. Click on the **OK** button in the pop-up dialog box. The horizontal dimension of 160 mm gets applied to the selected line, refer to Figure 2.168. Also, the **Constrain horizontal distance** tool remains active.

12. Similarly, apply the horizontal dimension to the other horizontal line entity of length 50 mm, refer to Figure 2.168. Next, right-click in the 3D View area to exit the tool.

Now, you need to apply vertical dimensions to the sketch entities.

13. Click on the **Constrain vertical distance** tool in the **Sketcher constraints** toolbar and then apply all the vertical dimensions to the sketch, refer to Figure 2.168.

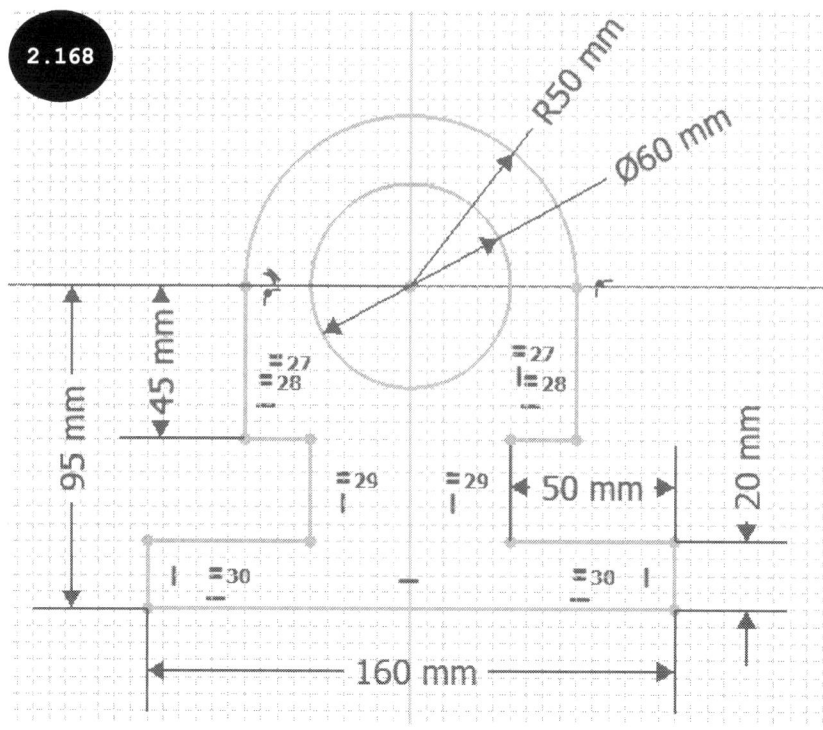

14. After applying all the vertical dimensions, right-click to exit the **Constrain vertical distance** tool. Figure 2.168 shows the fully constrained sketch after applying all geometric constraints and dimensions. Also, the position of dimensions is arranged by dragging and dropping them in the 3D View area.

Tip: In Figure 2.168, the vertical dimensions 20 mm and 45 mm are applied by selecting their respective vertical lines, whereas the vertical dimension 95 mm is applied by selecting the origin and an endpoint of the bottom-most horizontal line of the sketch.

After creating a sketch, you need to exit the Sketch editing mode of the **Sketcher** workbench.

15. Click on the **Leave sketch** tool 🔼 in the **Sketcher** toolbar to exit the Sketch editing mode of the **Sketcher** workbench and switch back to the **Part Design** workbench, see Figure 2.169.

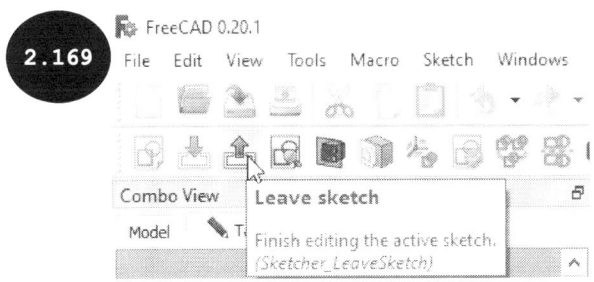

Section 7: Saving the Sketch

Now, you can save the sketch.

1. Click on the **Save** tool in the **File** toolbar (see Figure 2.170) or press the CTRL + S keys. The **Save FreeCAD Document** dialog box appears.

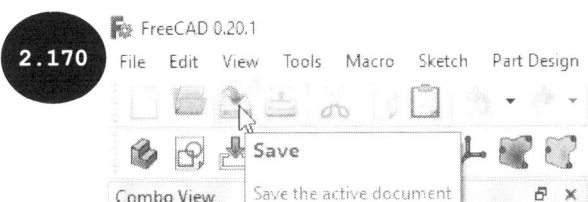

2. Browse to the local drive of your system and then create a folder with the name **FreeCAD**. Next, create another folder with the name **Chapter 2** inside the **FreeCAD** folder and then double-click to access it to save the files of Chapter 2 inside this folder.

3. Enter **Ch02-Tutorial 1** in the **File name** field of the dialog box.

4. Click on the **Save** button in the dialog box. The sketch gets saved with the name **Ch02-Tutorial 1** at the specified location (> *FreeCAD* > *Chapter 02*).

5. Click on **File** > **Close** in the **Standard Menu** to close the current document.

Tutorial 2

Create the sketch shown in Figure 2.171 and make it fully constrained by applying all geometric constraints and dimensions. The model shown in this figure is for your reference only. You will learn how to create 3D models in the later chapters. All dimensions are in inches.

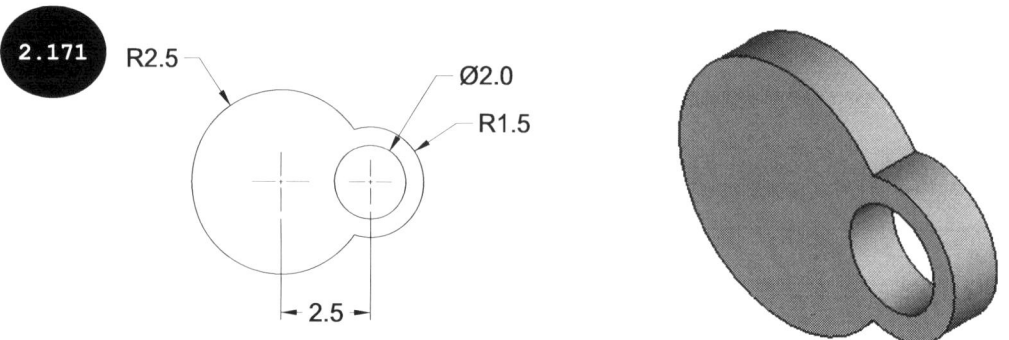

Section 1: Invoking a New Empty Document

1. Start FreeCAD by double-clicking on the **FreeCAD 0.20** icon on your desktop. The startup user interface of FreeCAD appears.

2. Click on the **New** tool in the **File** toolbar, see Figure 2.172. A new empty document gets invoked with the default name "**unnamed: 1**".

Section 2: Invoking the Sketcher Workbench

Now, you will invoke the **Sketcher** workbench within the **Part Design** workbench.

1. Invoke the **Workbench Selector** in the **Workbench** toolbar and then select the **Part Design** workbench, see Figure 2.173. The **Part Design** workbench gets invoked.

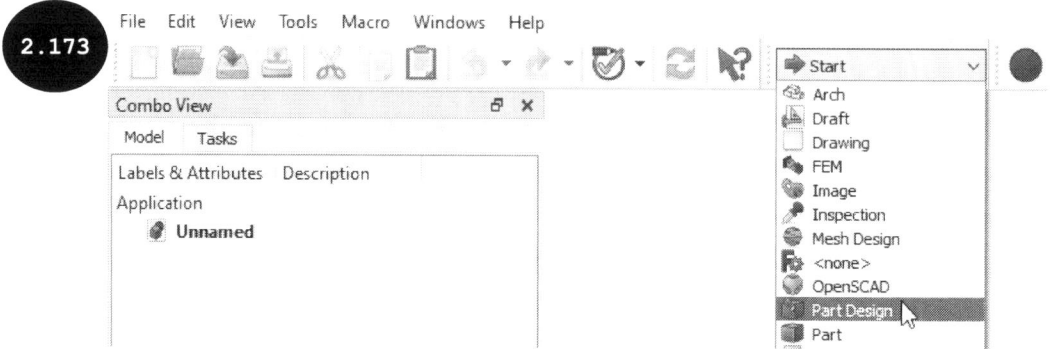

Now, you can invoke the **Sketcher** workbench for creating a sketch.

2. Click on the **Create sketch** tool in the **Part Design Helper** toolbar, see Figure 2.174. The three default planes, which are mutually perpendicular to each other appear. Also, the **Task Panel** appears in the **Combo View** and displays the names of the three default planes, see Figure 2.175.

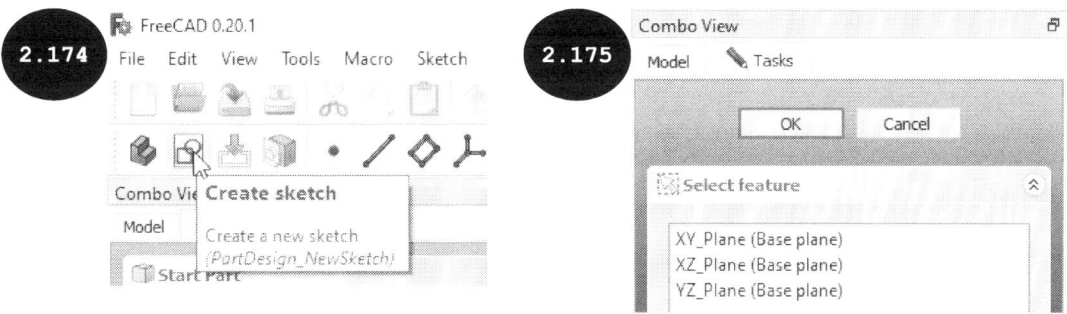

3. Select the **XZ_Plane** as the sketching plane in the 3D View area. The Sketch editing mode of the **Sketcher** workbench gets invoked. Also, the selected plane becomes the sketching plane for drawing the sketch and it is oriented normal to the viewing direction.

Tip: Alternatively, you can select the **XZ_Plane** in the **Task Panel** and then click on the **OK** button for invoking the Sketch editing mode of the **Sketcher** workbench.

Section 3: Specifying the Units
Now, you need to specify units of measurement for creating the sketch.

1. Click on **Edit > Preferences** in the **Standard Menu**, see Figure 2.176. The **Preferences** dialog box appears.

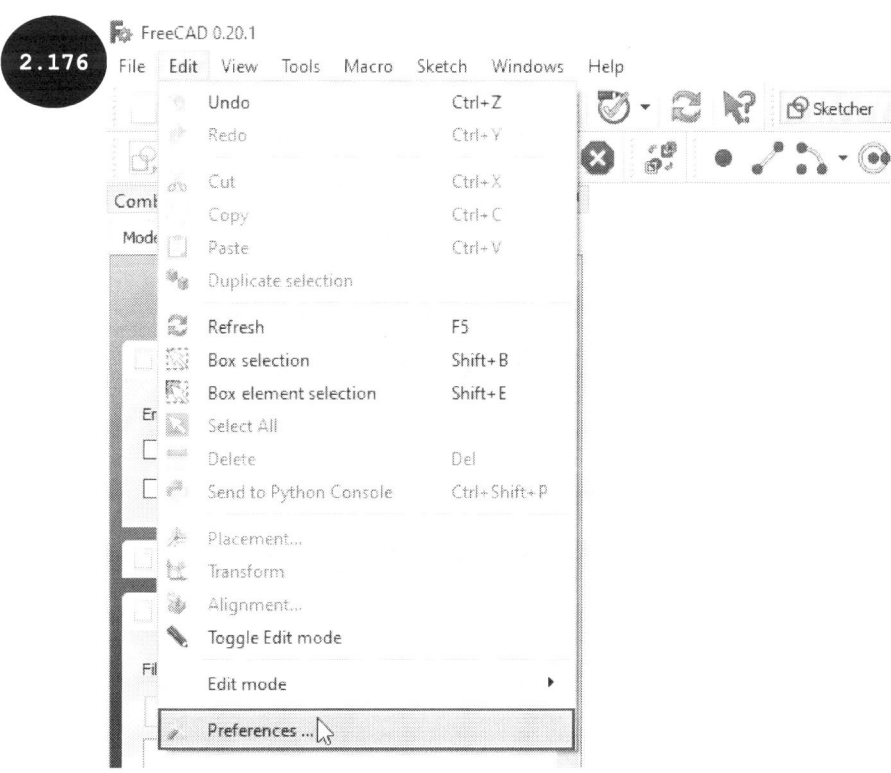

2. Ensure that the **General** section is selected in the left panel of the **Preferences** dialog box and then click on the **Units** tab. The options to define units appear in the dialog box, see Figure 2.177.

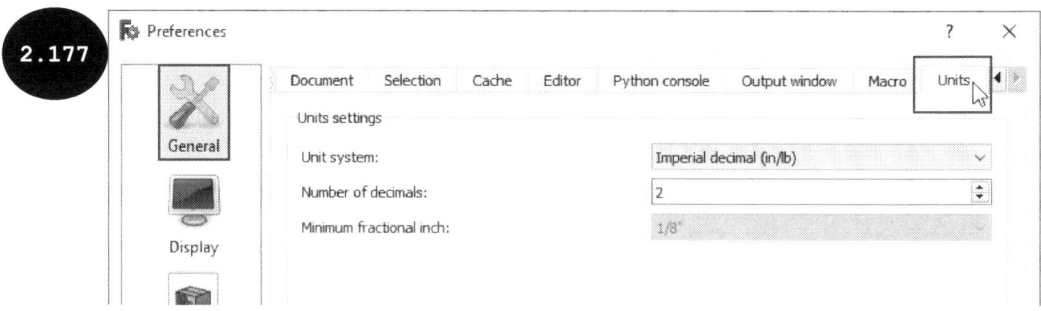

3. Select the **Imperial decimal (in/lb)** option in the **Unit system** drop-down list of the dialog box as the unit system. In this unit system, length is measured in inches and mass is calculated in pounds (lb).

4. Ensure that **2** is specified in the **Number of decimals** field of the dialog box as the number of digits after the decimal point of measurements.

5. Click on the **Apply** button in the **Preferences** dialog box. The selected unit system is defined, and the dialog box remains open.

    Now, you need to ensure that the display of grids and the snap mode are turned off in the 3D View area for creating the sketch entities by specifying points arbitrarily in the 3D View area.

Note: As FreeCAD is a parametric software, you can turn off the snap mode and create the sketch entities by specifying points arbitrarily in the 3D View area. After creating the sketch, you can apply the required constraints and dimensions to make the sketch fully constrained.

6. Click on the **Sketcher** section in the left panel of the **Preferences** dialog box. The different options related to the **Sketcher** workbench appear on the right panel of the dialog box.

7. Clear the **Show grid** and **Grid snap** check boxes in the right panel of the dialog box to turn off the display of grids and the snap mode in the 3D View area, see Figure 2.178.

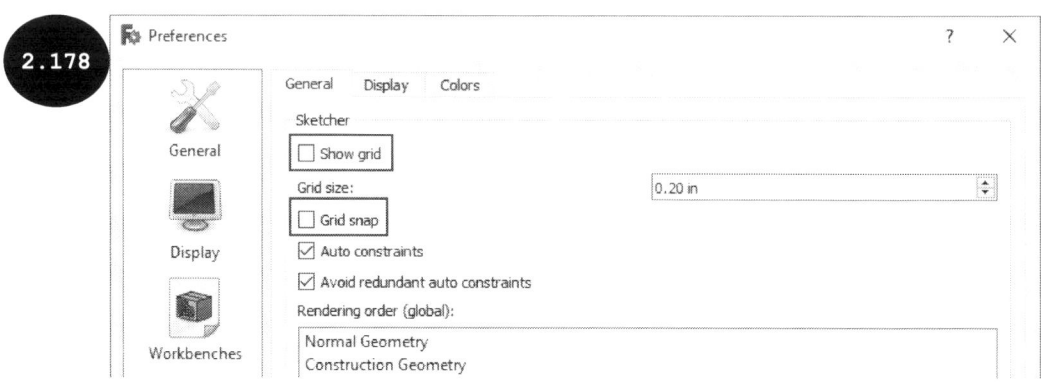

8. Click on the **Apply** button and then the **OK** button in the dialog box to accept the changes made and exit the **Preferences** dialog box.

Section 4: Drawing the Sketch

Now, you can draw the sketch entities by specifying points arbitrarily in the 3D View area.

1. Invoke the **Create circle** menu in the **Sketcher geometries** toolbar and then click on the **Center and rim point** tool, see Figure 2.179. The **Center and rim point** tool gets activated.

2. Click to specify the center point of the circle at the origin in the 3D View area, refer to Figure 2.180.

3. Move the cursor horizontally toward the right and then click to create a circle of any radius, see Figure 2.180. A circle gets created and the **Center and rim point** tool remains active.

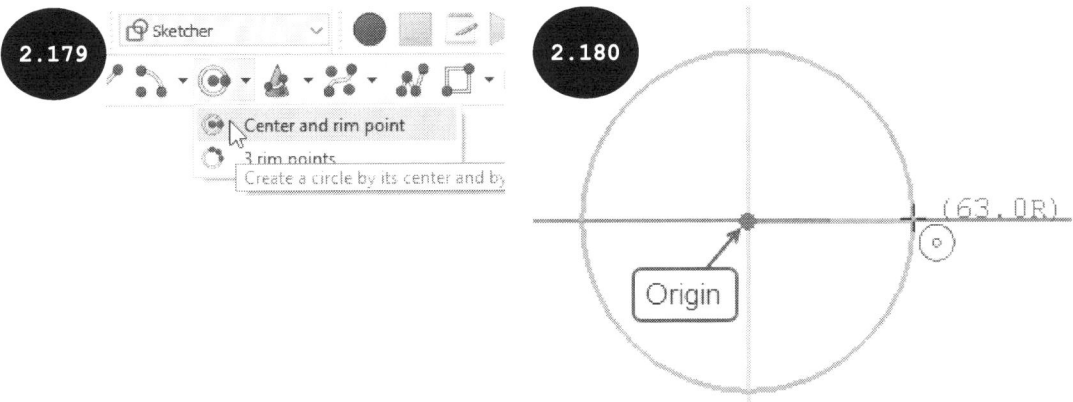

Now, you need to create two more circles on the right quadrant of the previously created circle.

4. Move the cursor toward the right quadrant of the previously created circle and then click to specify the center point when the circle gets highlighted, see Figure 2.181.

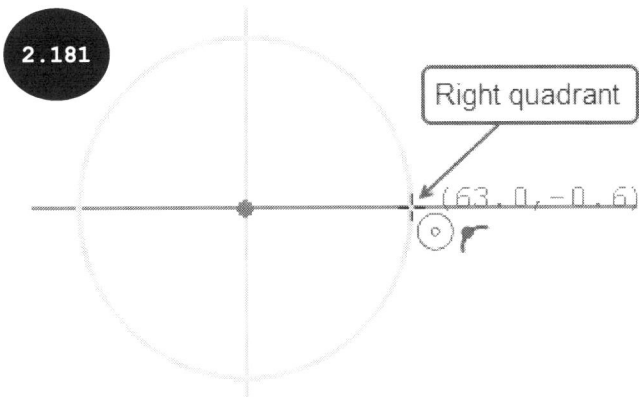

5. Move the cursor horizontally toward the right and then click to create a circle of any radius like the one shown in Figure 2.182. A circle gets created and the **Center and rim point** tool remains active.

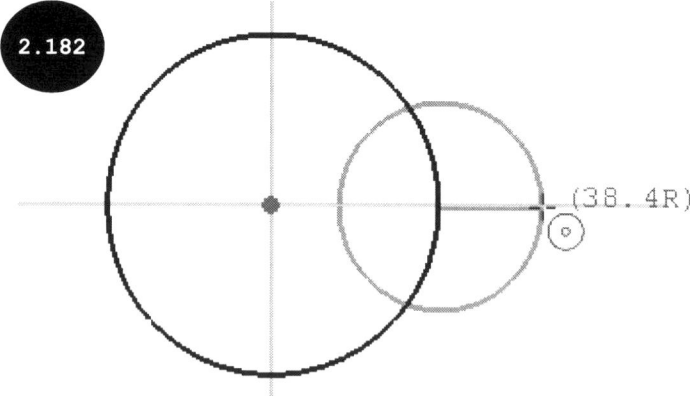

6.   Move the cursor to the center point of the previously created circle and then click to specify the center point of another circle when the cursor snaps to it.

7.   Move the cursor horizontally toward the right and click to create a circle of any radius inside the previously created circle, see Figure 2.183. Another circle gets created.

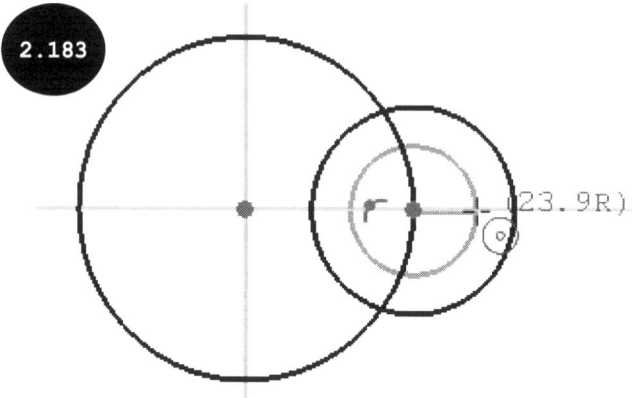

8.   Right-click in the 3D View area to exit the **Center and rim point** tool.

Section 5: Trimming Sketch Entities

Now, you need to trim the unwanted sketch entities to their nearest intersection.

1.   Click on the **Trim edge** tool in the **Sketcher geometries** toolbar, see Figure 2.184. The **Trim edge** tool gets activated and the appearance of the cursor changes to cross mark with the display of a red trim icon.

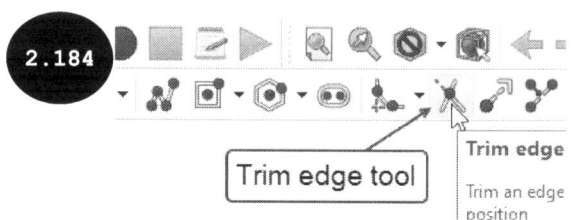

2.   Move the cursor over the left portion of the outer circle, see Figure 2.185. Next, click the left mouse button when it gets highlighted. The selected portion of the circle gets trimmed to its nearest intersection, see Figure 2.186. Also, the **Trim edge** tool remains active.

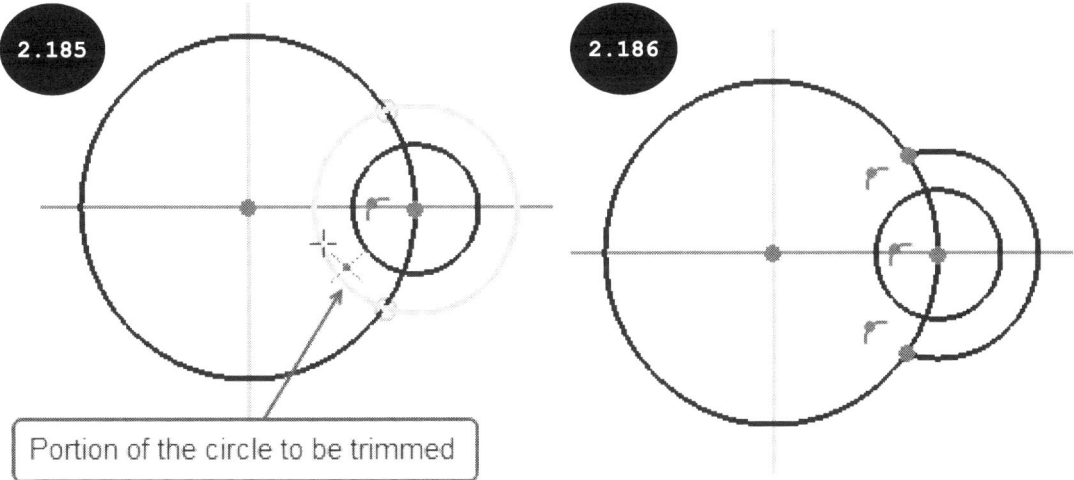

Portion of the circle to be trimmed

3. Similarly, click on the other unwanted entities of the sketch one by one to trim them. Figure 2.187 shows the sketch after trimming all the unwanted entities of the sketch.

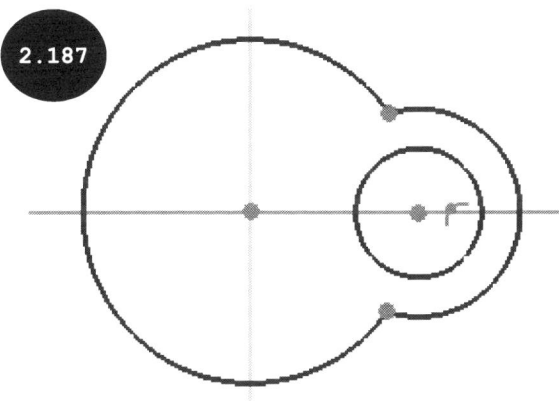

4. Right-click in the 3D View area to exit the **Trim edge** tool.

Section 6: Applying Dimensions

Now, you need to apply the required dimensions to make the sketch fully defined.

1. Click on the **Constrain auto radius/diameter** tool in the **Sketcher constraints** toolbar, see Figure 2.188. The **Constrain auto radius/diameter** tool gets activated.

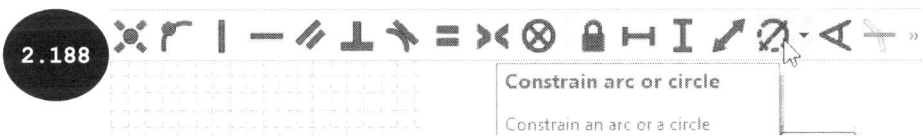

Constrain arc or circle

Constrain an arc or a circle

2. Select the left arc of the sketch. The **Insert radius** pop-up dialog box appears with the display of its current radius value.

3. Enter **2.5** inches in the **Radius** field of the dialog box and then click on the **OK** button in the pop-up dialog box. A radius dimension gets applied to the selected arc, see Figure 2.189. The **Constrain auto radius/diameter** tool remains active.

4. Select the right arc of the sketch. The **Insert radius** pop-up dialog box appears.

5. Enter **1.5** inches in the **Radius** field of the dialog box and then click on the **OK** button. A radius dimension gets applied to the selected arc, see Figure 2.190. The **Constrain auto radius/diameter** tool remains active.

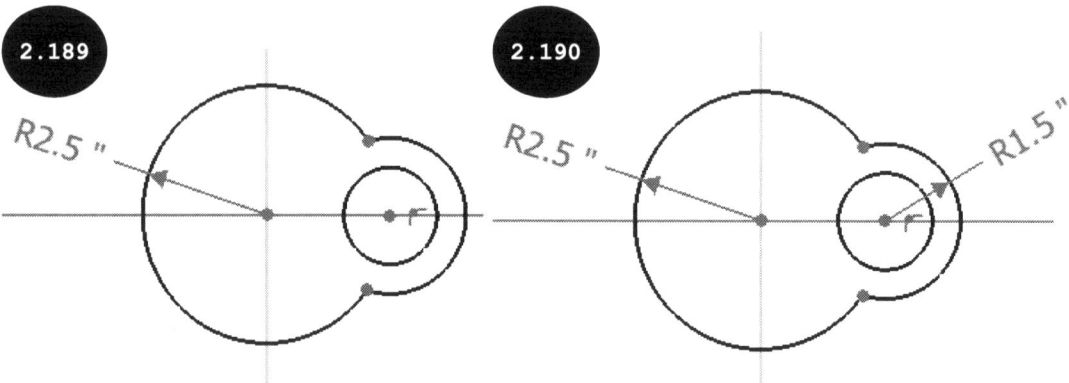

6. Select the inner circle of the sketch. The **Insert diameter** pop-up dialog box appears.

7. Enter **2** inches in the **Diameter** field of the dialog box and then click on the **OK** button. A diameter dimension gets applied to the selected circle, see Figure 2.191. Next, right-click to exit the **Constrain auto radius/diameter** tool.

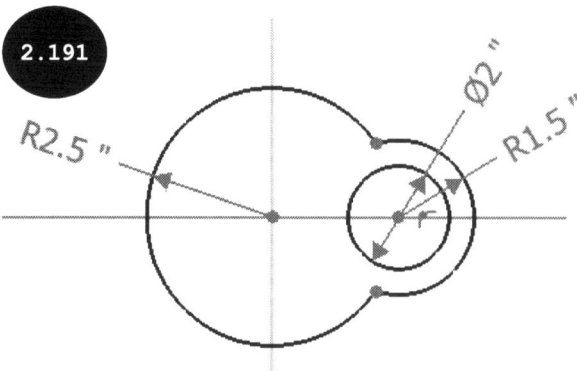

Tip: You can change the position of applied dimensions in the drawing area by dragging and dropping them to the required location in the 3D View area.

Section 7: Applying Geometric Constraints

After applying the dimensions, if the sketch is not fully constrained then you need to apply the required geometric constraints to make it a fully constrained sketch.

1. Click on the **Constrain horizontally** tool in the **Sketcher constraints** toolbar (see Figure 2.192) or press the H key for applying a horizontal constraint.

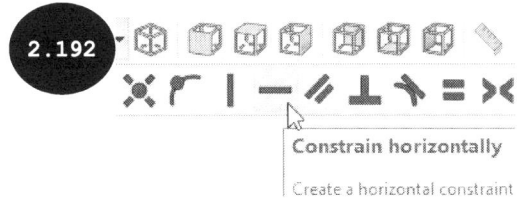

Constrain horizontally
Create a horizontal constraint

2. Select the origin and then the center point of the right circle of the sketch one by one for making them horizontally aligned to each other, see Figure 2.193. The horizontal constraint gets applied, and the sketch becomes fully constrained, see Figure 2.194. Next, right-click in the 3D View area to exit the tool.

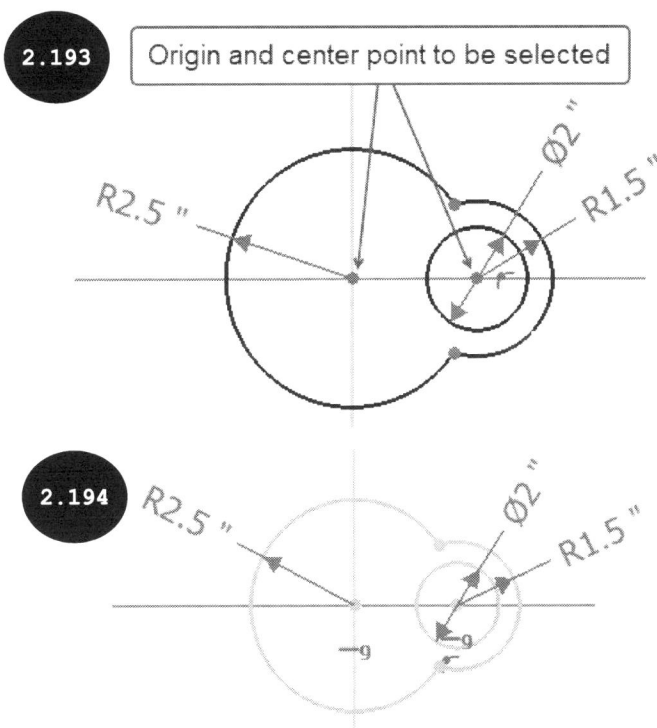

2.193 Origin and center point to be selected

After creating a sketch, you need to exit the Sketch editing mode of the **Sketcher** workbench.

3. Click on the **Leave sketch** tool in the **Sketcher** toolbar to exit the Sketch editing mode of the **Sketcher** workbench (see Figure 2.195) and switch back to the **Part Design** workbench.

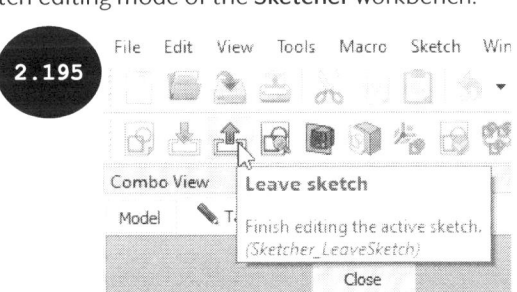

Leave sketch
Finish editing the active sketch.
(Sketcher_LeaveSketch)

Section 8: Saving the Sketch

1. Click on the **Save** tool in the **File** toolbar or press the CTRL + S keys. The **Save FreeCAD Document** dialog box appears.

2. Browse to the **FreeCAD > Chapter 2** folders in the local drive of your system. You need to create these folders if not created earlier.

3. Enter **Ch02-Tutorial 2** in the **File name** field of the dialog box and then click on the **Save** button. The sketch gets saved with the name **Ch02-Tutorial 2** at the specified location.

Hands-on Test Drive 1

Create a sketch of the model shown in Figure 2.196 and make it fully constrained. The model shown in this figure is for your reference only. All dimensions are in mm.

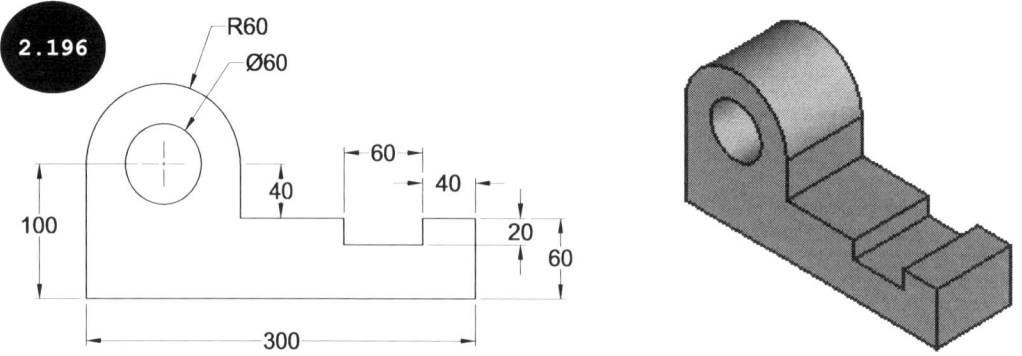

Hands-on Test Drive 2

Create a sketch of the model shown in Figure 2.197 and make it fully constrained. The model shown in this figure is for your reference only. All dimensions are in inches (in).

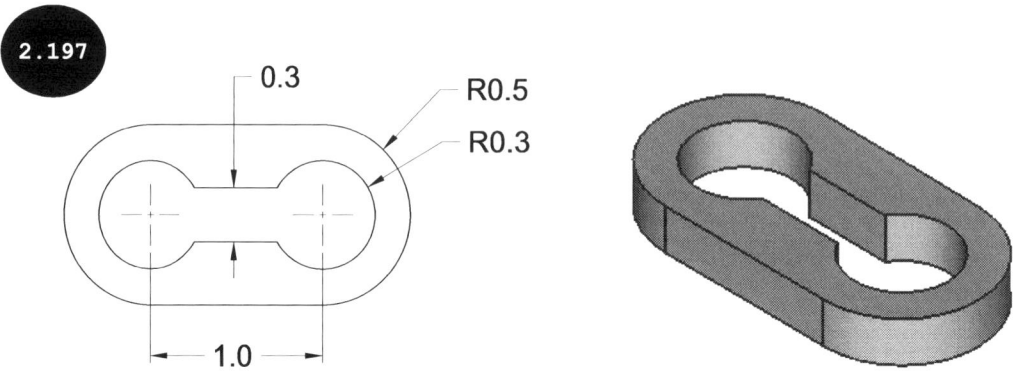

Hands-on Test Drive 3

Create a sketch of the model shown in Figure 2.198 and make it fully constrained. The model shown in this figure is for your reference only. All dimensions are in mm.

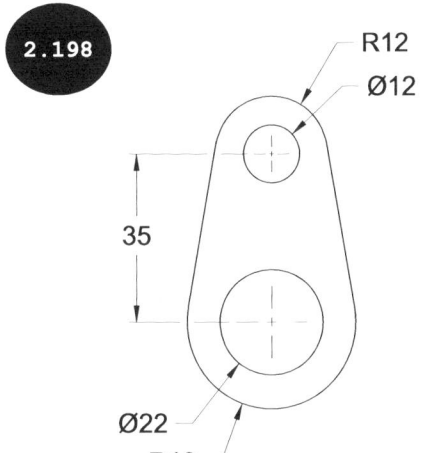

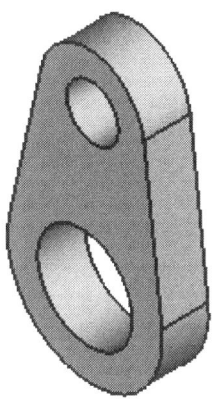

Summary

This chapter discussed how to invoke the **Sketcher Workbench** within the **Part Design** workbench by selecting a sketching plane for creating a sketch. It explained how to specify units as well as the grids and snap settings. This chapter discussed different methods for drawing lines, arcs, circles, ellipses, elliptical arcs, hyperbolic arcs, parabolic arcs, B-splines, polylines, rectangles, polygons, and slots by using the respective sketching tools. Methods for creating fillets, trimming sketch entities, extending sketch entities, and creating construction sketch entities have also been discussed in this chapter. Besides, it also discussed the application of geometric and dimensional constraints, editing and modifying dimensions, and different states of a sketch.

Questions

Complete and verify the following sentences:

- Features are divided into two main categories: _____ and _____.

- Every time you start FreeCAD, the _____ workbench is invoked with **Start** page, by default.

- The _____ tool is used for drawing a circle by specifying three points on its circumference.

- The _____ key is used for cycling through all six different polyline modes (segments).

- The _____ tool is used for drawing a polygon with the number of sides ranging from _____ to _____.

- The _____ tool is used for creating a fillet between two sketch entities.

- _____ help you specify points in the 3D View area for creating sketch entities and act as reference lines.

- The _____ constraint is used for making two sketch entities such as a circle and a line tangent to each other.

- In FreeCAD, a 2D sketch can be either _____, _____, and _____.

- The availability of toolbars in the Toolbar Area of a new document depends upon the activated workbench. (True/False)

- A fully constrained sketch is a sketch, whose all degrees of freedom are fixed. (True/False)

- You cannot apply a reference dimension to a sketch entity. (True/False)

Creating Base Feature of a 3D Solid Model

This chapter discusses the following topics:

- Creating a Pad Feature
- Creating a Revolution Feature
- Navigating a 3D Model in the 3D View Area
- Displaying Standard Views of a Model
- Working with Navigation Cube
- Changing the Display Style of a Model

Once a sketch has been created and fully constrained, you can convert it into a 3D solid feature in the Part Design workbench, see Figure 3.1. In this figure, the display of dimensions and constraints of the sketch is turned off for the clarity of the image.

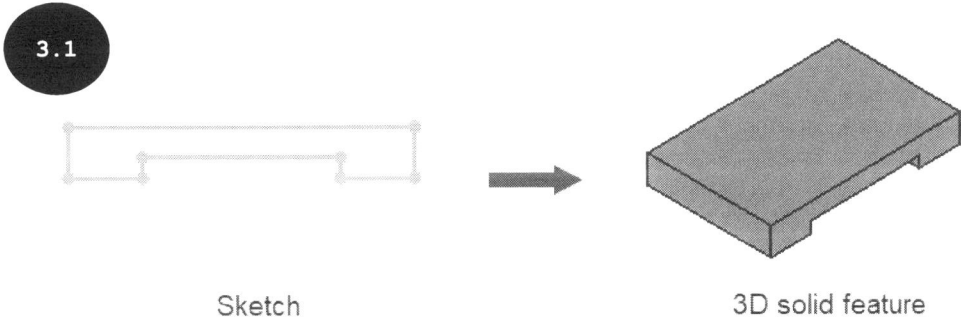

3.1

Sketch   3D solid feature

In the Part Design workbench, you can convert a sketch into a 3D solid feature by using the feature modeling tools available in the **Part Design Modeling** toolbar, see Figure 3.2. Note that to create a complete 3D solid model, you need to create all its features one by one using the feature modeling tools, see Figure 3.3. The first created feature of a model is known as the base feature or the parent feature of the model.

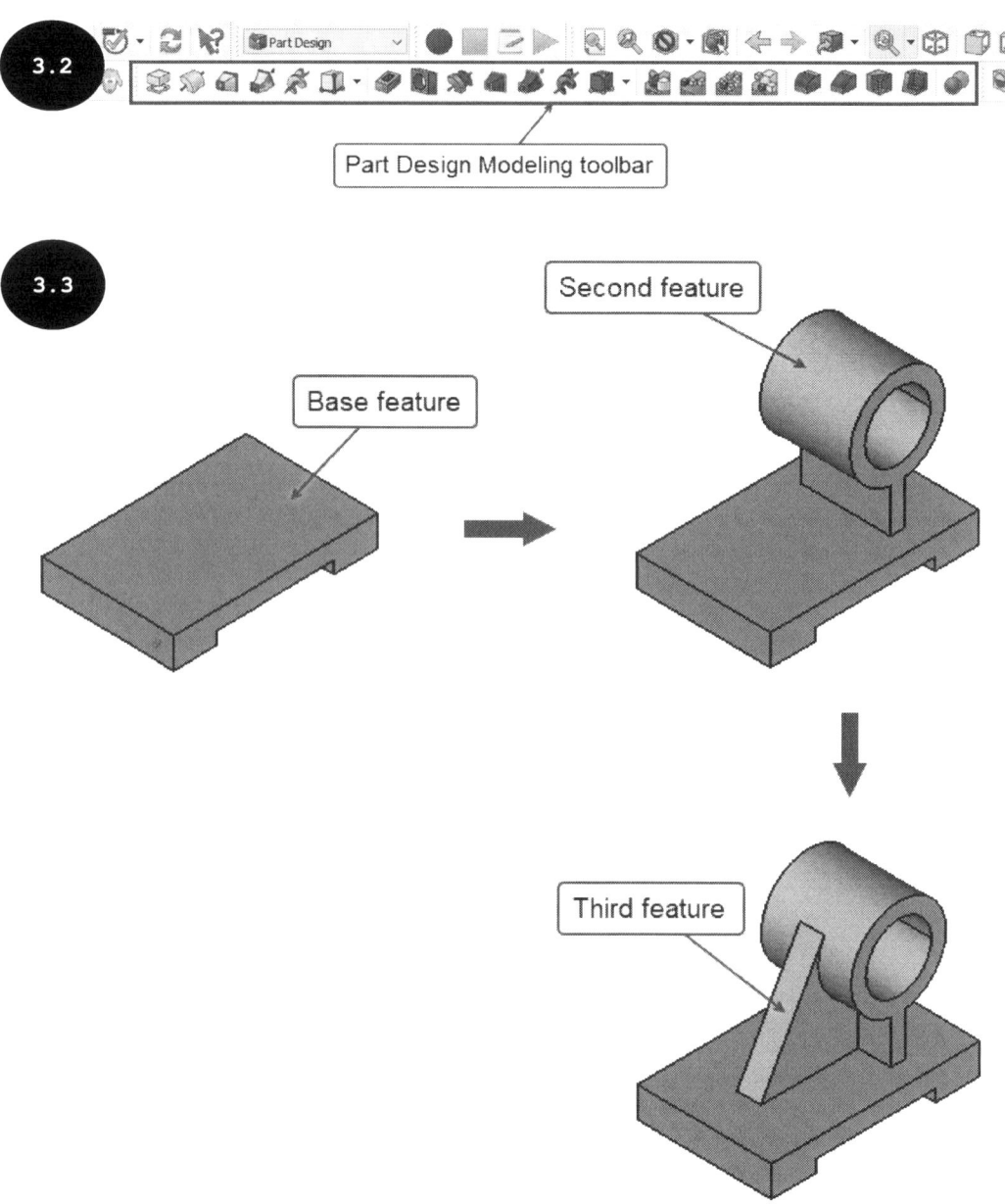

In FreeCAD, you can create the base feature of a model by using various feature modeling tools such as **Pad, Revolution, Additive loft, Additive pipe**, and **Additive helix**. In this chapter, you will learn how to create a base feature of a model using the **Pad** and **Revolution** tools. The other tools will be discussed in later chapters.

Creating a Pad Feature

A pad feature is created by extruding a sketch normal to the sketching plane, see Figure 3.4. In FreeCAD, you can create a pad feature by using the **Pad** tool.

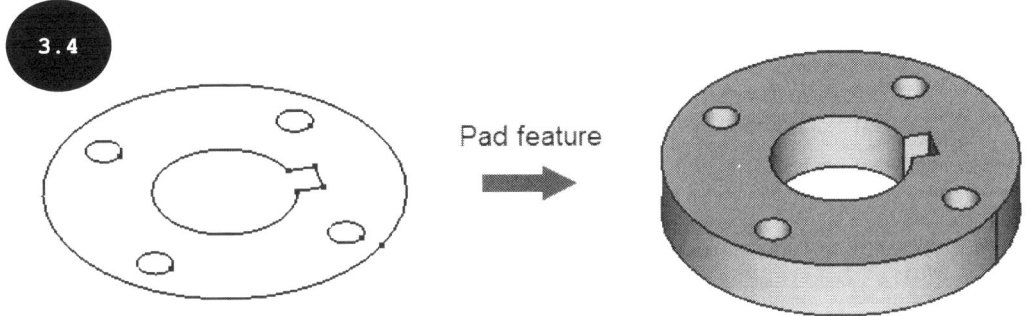

Note: The sketch of a pad feature should be closed. A closed sketch can have single or multiple enclosed profiles. Figure 3.4 shows a sketch that has six closed profiles.

1. After creating a closed sketch of a pad feature, exit the **Sketcher** workbench and switch back to the **Part Design** workbench. You can exit the Sketcher workbench by clicking on the **Leave sketch** tool in the **Sketcher** toolbar, see Figure 3.5.

2. In the **Part Design** workbench, click on the **Pad** tool in the **Part Design Modeling** toolbar, see Figure 3.6. The preview of a pad feature appears in the 3D View area with default parameters since the sketch to be extruded gets selected automatically. Also, the **Pad parameters** sub-window appears in the **Task Panel** of the **Tasks** tab in **Combo View**, see Figure 3.7.

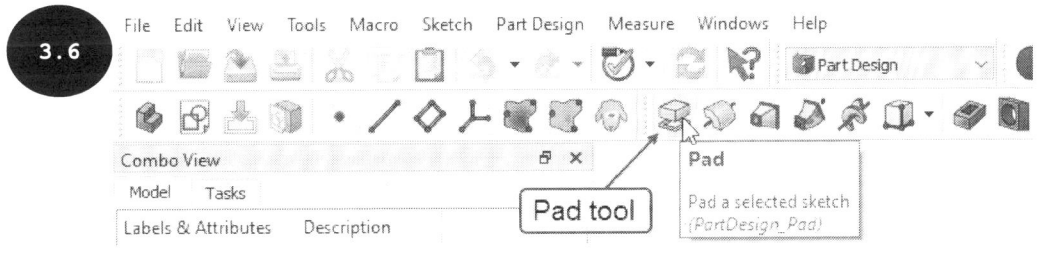

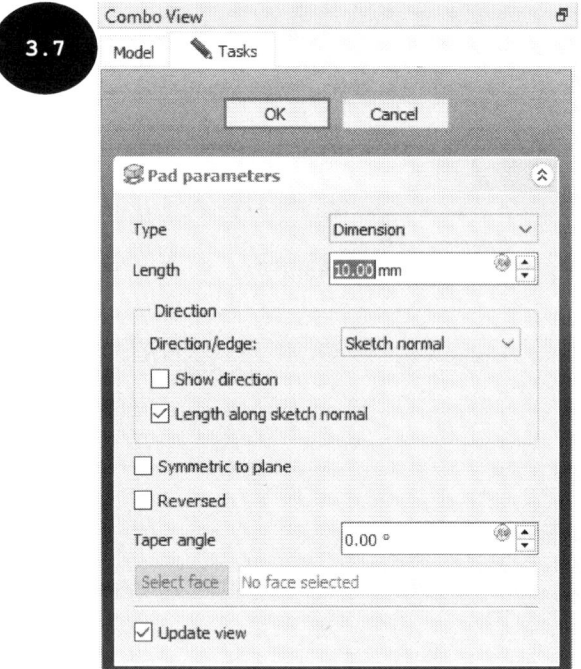

Note: If only one closed sketch is available in the 3D View area, then on invoking the **Pad** tool, it will be selected automatically as the sketch to be extruded and the preview of the pad feature appears. However, if two or more closed sketches are available in the 3D View area, then on invoking the **Pad** tool, you need to select a sketch to be extruded, manually. You can select a sketch to be extruded in the 3D View area or in the **Select feature** sub-window that will be appeared in the **Task Panel**.

The options in the **Pad parameters** sub-window of the **Task Panel** (refer to Figure 3.7) are used for specifying the required parameters to create a pad feature and the same are discussed below:

Type: The **Type** drop-down list is used for selecting an option to define the length of the pad feature, see Figure 3.8. The various options available in this drop-down list are discussed below:

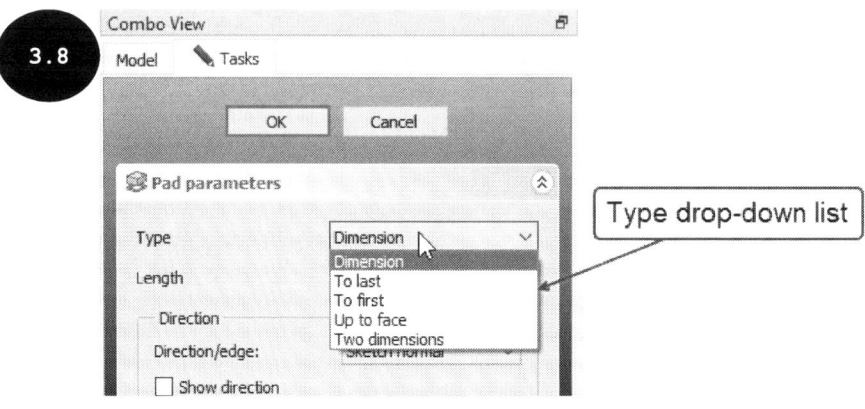

Dimension: The **Dimension** option in the **Type** drop-down list is used for extruding the sketch of a pad feature on one side of the sketching plane by specifying its length value in the **Length** field of the **Pad parameters** sub-window, see Figures 3.9 and 3.10. You can also reverse the direction of extrusion to the other side of the sketching plane by selecting the **Reversed** check box in the **Pad parameters** sub-window.

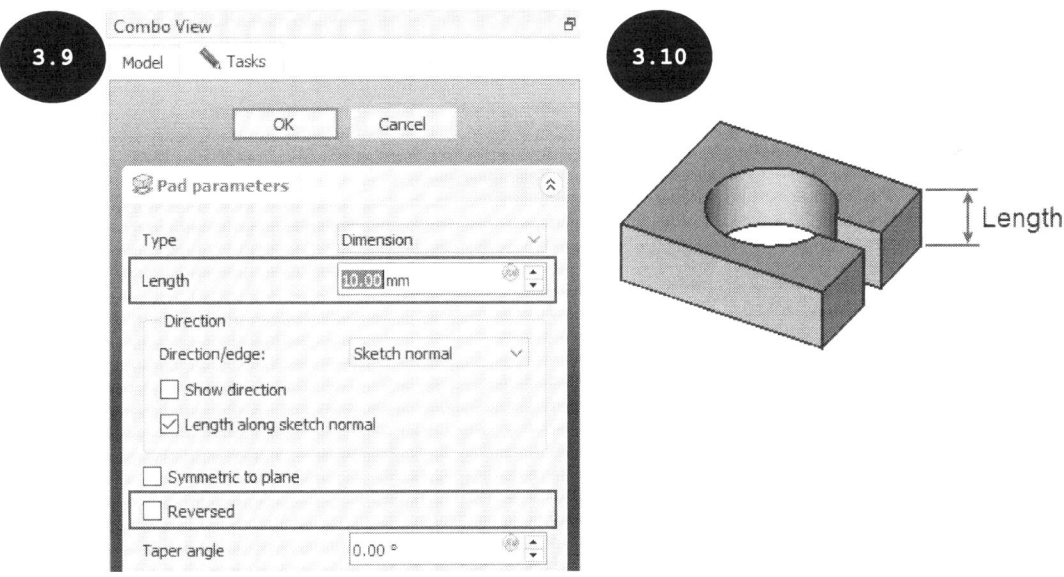

To last: The **To last** option is used for extruding the sketch up to its last intersection with a face of an existing feature of the model along the direction of extrusion. Figure 3.11 shows a sketch (circle) and the preview of a resultant pad feature extruded up to its last intersection.

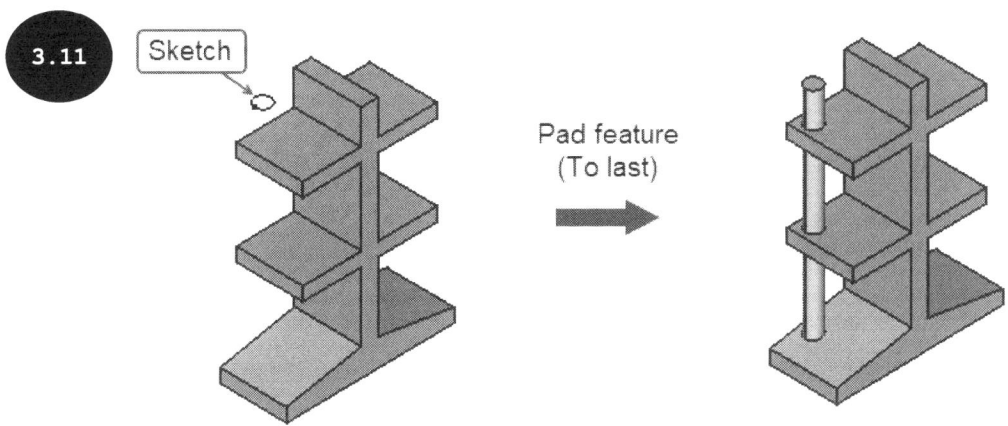

Note: The **To last** option can be used while creating second or further features of a model where the sketch of the pad feature can extrude up to its last intersecting face of an existing feature. This option cannot be used while creating a base feature of a model. You will learn how to build a multi-feature model in the later chapters.

Tip: To extrude a sketch up to its last intersecting face of an existing feature, you may need to reverse the direction of extrusion to the other side of the sketching plane by selecting the **Reversed** check box in the **Pad parameters** sub-window of the **Task Panel**.

To first: The **To first** option is used for extruding the sketch up to its first or nearest intersecting face of an existing feature along the direction of extrusion. Figure 3.12 shows a sketch (circle) and the preview of a resultant pad feature extruded up to its first intersection.

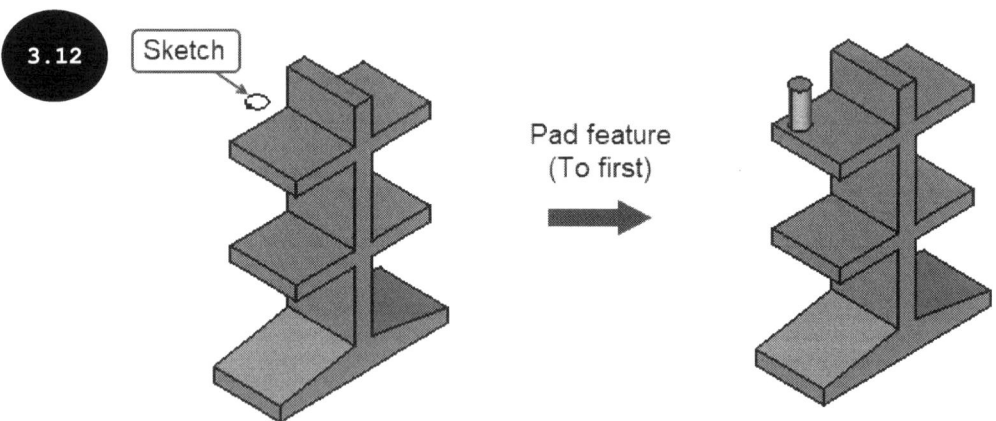

Up to face: The **Up to face** option is used for extruding the sketch up to a selected face of an existing feature or a plane. When you select this option, the **Select face** button and a field appear in the **Pad parameters** sub-window of the **Task Panel** (see Figure 3.13) and are activated, by default. Consequently, you can select a face of an existing feature or a plane up to which you would like to extrude the sketch of the pad feature, see Figure 3.14.

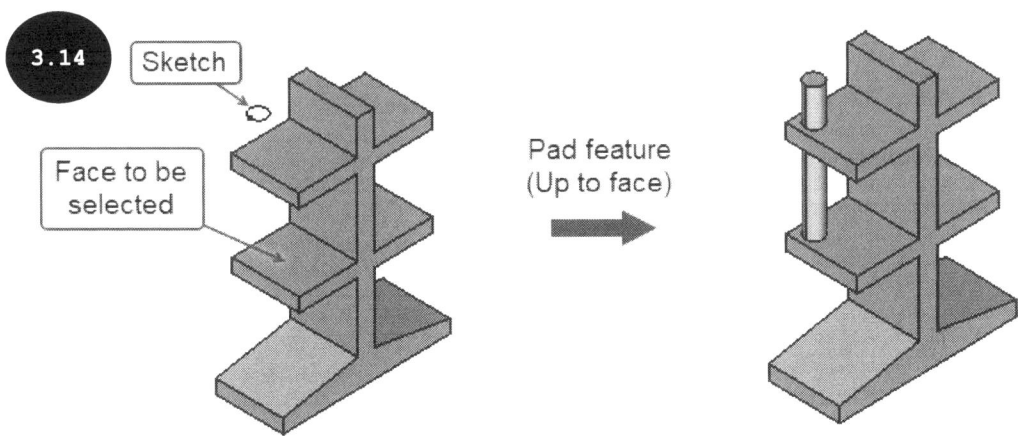

3.14   Sketch

Face to be selected

Pad feature (Up to face)

Tip: If you want to replace an already selected face/plane with another face/plane for extruding the sketch, click on the **Select face** button in the **Pad parameters** sub-window and then select a new face/plane of the model up to which you want to extrude the sketch.

Note: The **To last**, **To first**, and **Up to face** options work while creating second or further features of a model. You cannot use these options while creating a base feature of a model. You will learn how to build a multi-feature model in the later chapters.

Two dimensions: The **Two dimensions** option is used for extruding the sketch asymmetrically on both sides of the sketching plane with different extrusion lengths, see Figure 3.15. When the **Two dimensions** option is selected in the **Type** drop-down list, the **Length** and **2nd length** fields are enabled in the **Pad parameters** sub-window, see Figure 3.16. In these fields, you can specify different extrusion lengths on both sides (first and second) of the sketching plane, respectively. You can also switch between the extrusion directions (first and second) by selecting the **Reversed** check box in the **Pad parameters** sub-window.

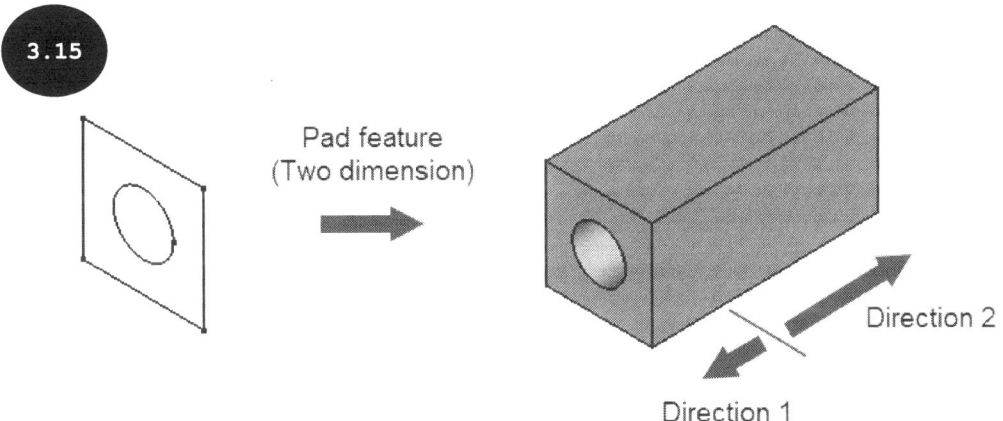

3.15

Pad feature (Two dimension)

Direction 2

Direction 1

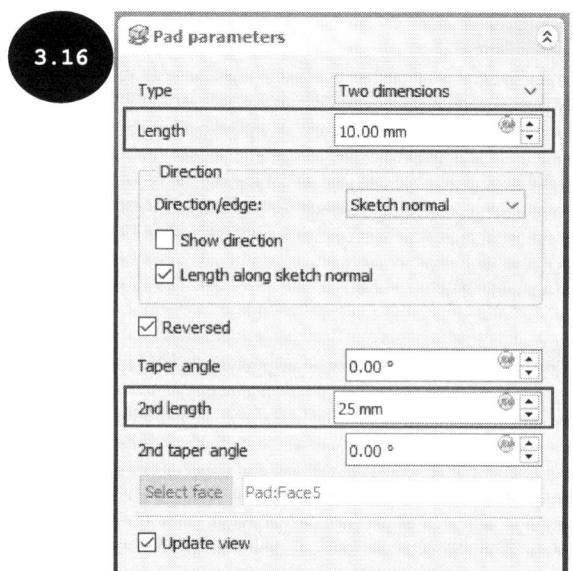

Offset to face: The Offset to face field is used for defining the termination or end of extrusion at an offset distance from a face of a model, see Figure 3.17. Note that the **Offset to face** field is enabled in the **Pad parameters** sub-window when the **To last**, **To first**, or **Up to face** option is selected in the **Type** drop-down list for creating a pad feature, as discussed earlier.

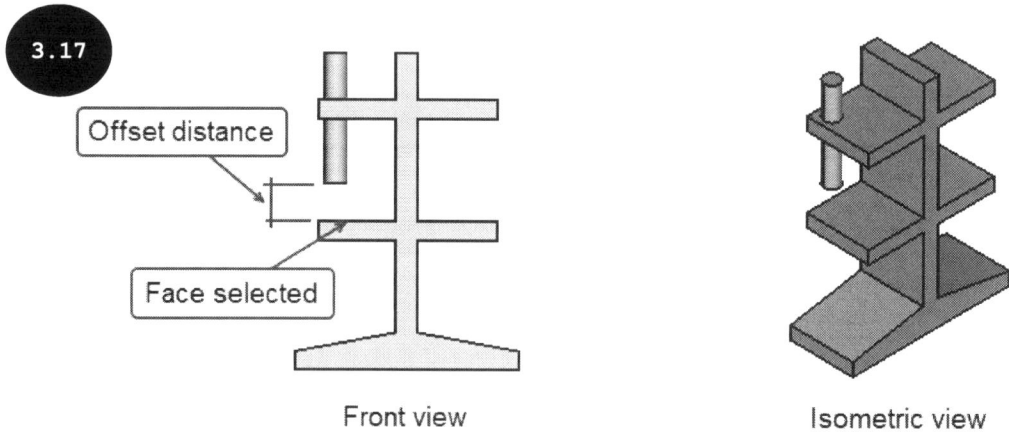

Front view   Isometric view

Note: By default, the 0 offset value is entered in the **Offset to face** field. Consequently, the end of extrusion is defined exactly on the face/plane of a model depending upon whether the **To last**, **To first**, or **Up to face** option is selected in the **Type** drop-down list.

Direction/edge: The options in the **Direction/edge** drop-down list of the **Direction** area are used for defining a direction of extrusion of the pad feature, see Figure 3.18. The options in this drop-down list are discussed below:

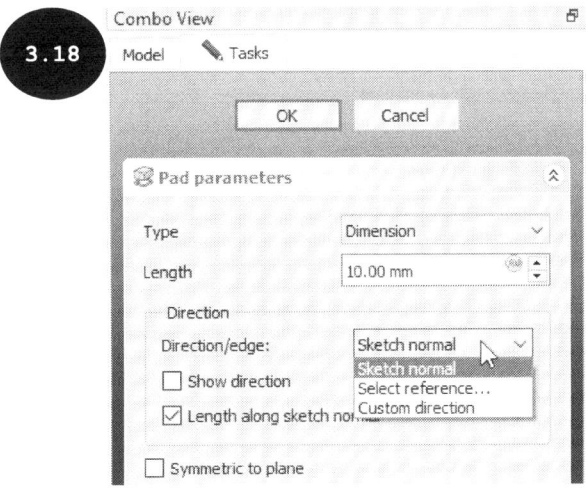

Sketch normal: By default, the **Sketch normal** option is selected in the **Direction/edge** drop-down list. Consequently, the default direction of extrusion of a pad feature is defined as normal to the sketching plane.

Select reference: The **Select reference** option is used for defining the direction of extrusion of a pad feature along a selected direction reference, see Figure 3.19. For doing so, select the **Select reference** option in the **Direction/edge** drop-down list and then select a linear sketch entity (line) or a linear edge of an existing feature as the direction reference in the 3D View area. The preview of a pad feature appears along the selected direction reference, see Figure 3.19.

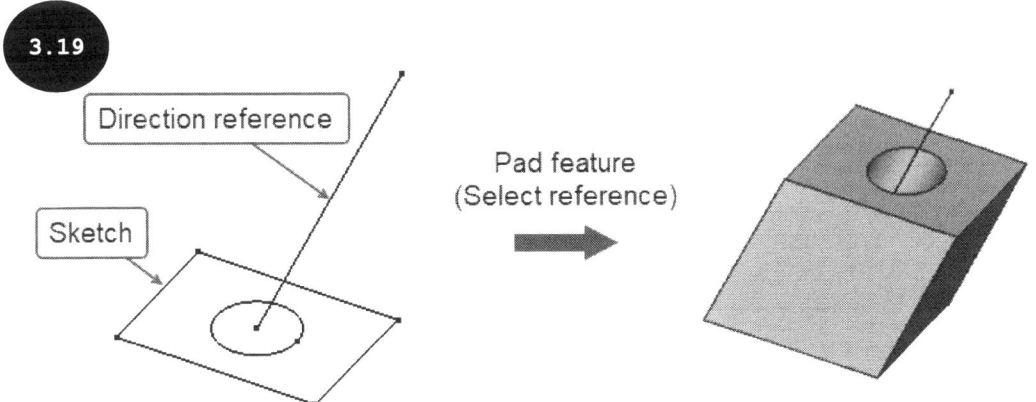

Custom direction: The **Custom direction** option is used for defining the direction of extrusion of a pad feature by specifying X, Y, and Z vector values. For doing so, select the **Custom direction** option in the **Direction/edge** drop-down list and then enter X, Y, and Z vector values in the respective **x**, **y**, and **z** fields that appear in the **Pad parameters** sub-window of the **Task Panel**, see Figure 3.20.

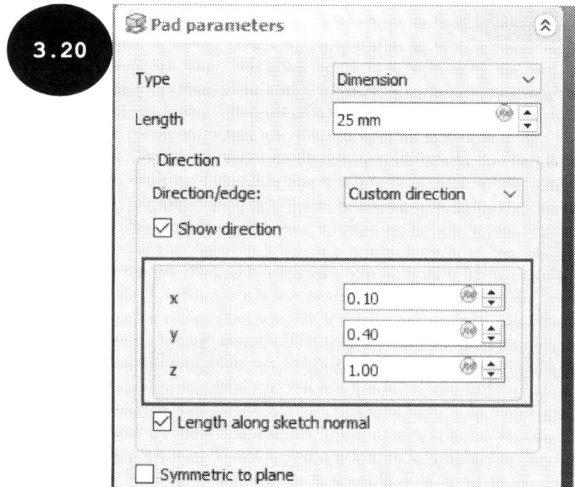

Length along sketch normal: When the Length along sketch normal check box is selected in the **Direction** area of the **Pad parameters** sub-window, the extrusion length of the pad feature is measured along the normal direction to the sketching plane, see Figure 3.21. However, when this check box is cleared, the extrusion length is measured along the specified custom direction of the pad feature, see Figure 3.22.

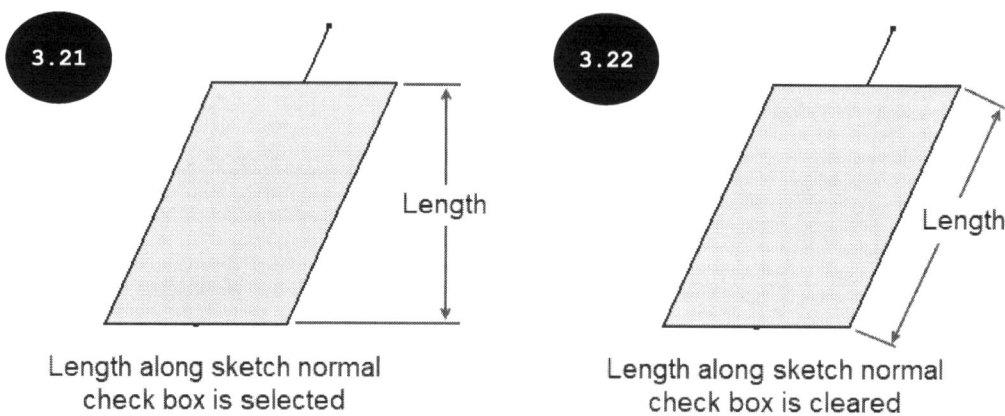

Length along sketch normal
check box is selected

Length along sketch normal
check box is cleared

Symmetric to plane: The Symmetric to plane check box is used for extruding the sketch of a pad feature symmetrically on both sides of the sketching plane. On selecting the **Symmetric to plane** check box, the extrusion length of the pad feature specified in the **Length** field gets divided equally into both sides of the sketching plane and creates a symmetrical pad feature. For example, if the extrusion length is specified as 100 mm, then the resultant pad feature will be created by adding 50 mm of material to each side of the sketching plane. Note that this check box is available only when the **Dimension** option is selected in the **Type** drop-down list of the **Pad parameters** sub-window for creating a pad feature.

Reversed: The Reversed check box is used for reversing the direction of the extrusion of a pad feature to the other side of the sketching plane.

Taper angle: The Taper angle field is used for specifying a taper or draft angle along the direction of extrusion for creating a tapered pad feature. By default, the **0** draft angle is entered in this field. Therefore, the resultant pad feature is created without having any tapering in it. You can enter the required draft angle in the **Taper angle** field. Note that a negative draft angle adds taper in the inward direction of the sketch (see Figure 3.23), whereas a positive draft angle adds draft in the outward direction of the sketch (see Figure 3.24), or vice-versa depending upon whether the **Reversed** check box is selected or cleared, respectively.

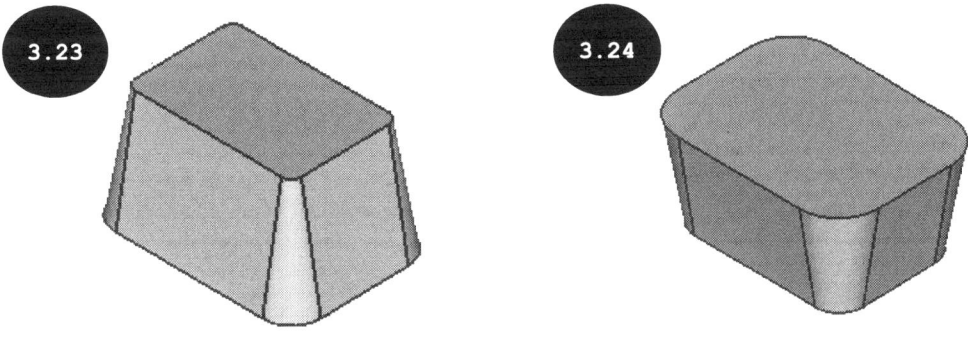

Note: The Taper angle field is available in the **Pad parameters** sub-window of the **Task Panel** when the **Dimension** or **Two dimensions** option is selected in the **Type** drop-down list.

2nd taper angle: The 2nd Taper angle field is used for specifying a taper or draft angle along the second direction of extrusion, see Figure 3.25. Note that this field is available in the **Pad parameters** sub-window of the **Task Panel** only when the **Two dimensions** option is selected in the **Type** drop-down list. Also, a negative draft angle value adds taper in the inward direction of the sketch, whereas a positive draft angle adds draft in the outward direction of the sketch.

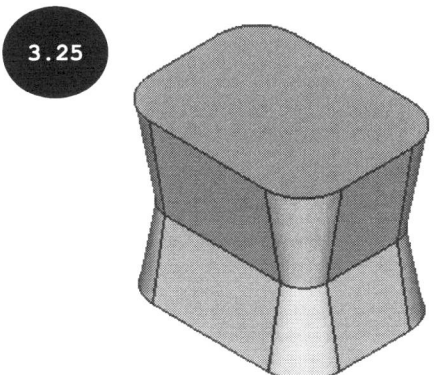

Update view: By default, the **Update view** check box is selected in the **Pad parameters** sub-window of the **Task Panel**. Therefore, the pad feature being created gets updated in real-time in the 3D View area by specifying or editing its parameters in the **Pad parameters** sub-window of the **Task Panel**.

3. Specify the required parameters in the **Pad parameters** sub-window of the **Task Panel** for creating a pad feature, as discussed above.

4. Click on the **OK** button in the **Task Panel** of the **Tasks** tab, see Figure 3.26. The pad feature of specified parameters gets created in the 3D View area. Also, its default name gets added under the **Body** node of the **Tree View** in the **Model** tab, see Figure 3.27. You can click on the **Model** tab of the **Combo View** to display the **Tree View**.

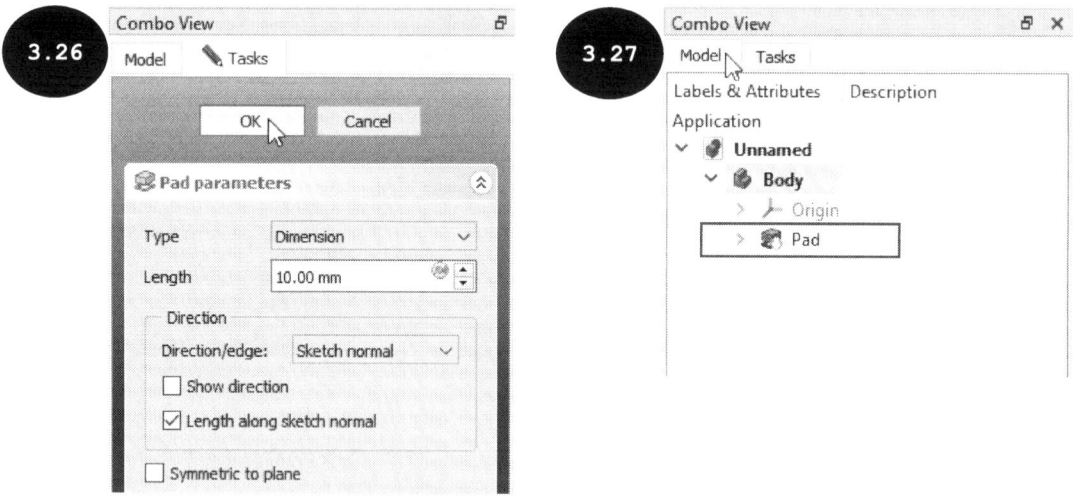

Creating a Revolution Feature

A revolution feature is created by revolving a closed sketch around an axis, see Figure 3.28. In this figure, the sketch revolved 270 degrees around an axis for creating a revolution feature. In FreeCAD, you can create a revolution feature by using the **Revolution** tool. The method for creating a revolution feature is discussed below:

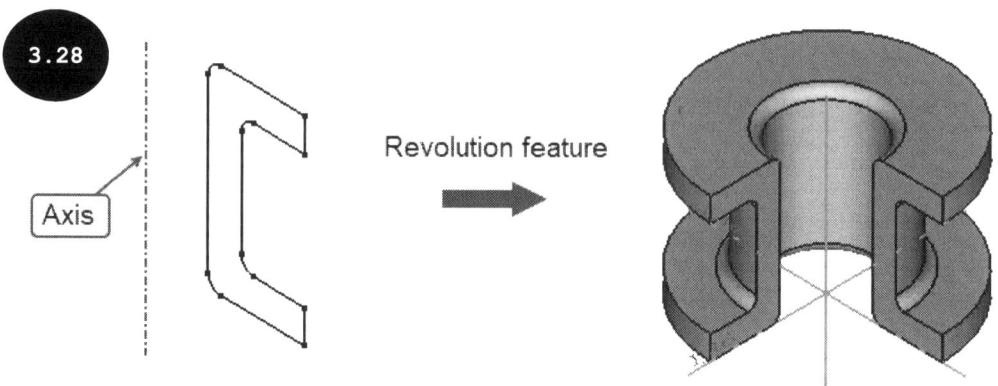

1. After creating a sketch of a revolution feature, exit the **Sketcher** workbench and switch back to the **Part Design** workbench by clicking on the **Leave sketch** tool 🔩 in the **Sketcher** toolbar. Note that the sketch of a revolution feature should be closed and on either side of its axis of revolution.

2. Click on the **Revolution** tool in the **Part Design Modeling** toolbar, see Figure 3.29. The preview of a revolution feature appears by revolving the sketch around its vertical axis in the 3D View area, see Figure 3.30. It is because the **Vertical sketch axis** option is selected, by default in the **Axis** drop-down list of the **Revolution parameters** sub-window that appears in the **Task Panel**, see Figure 3.31.

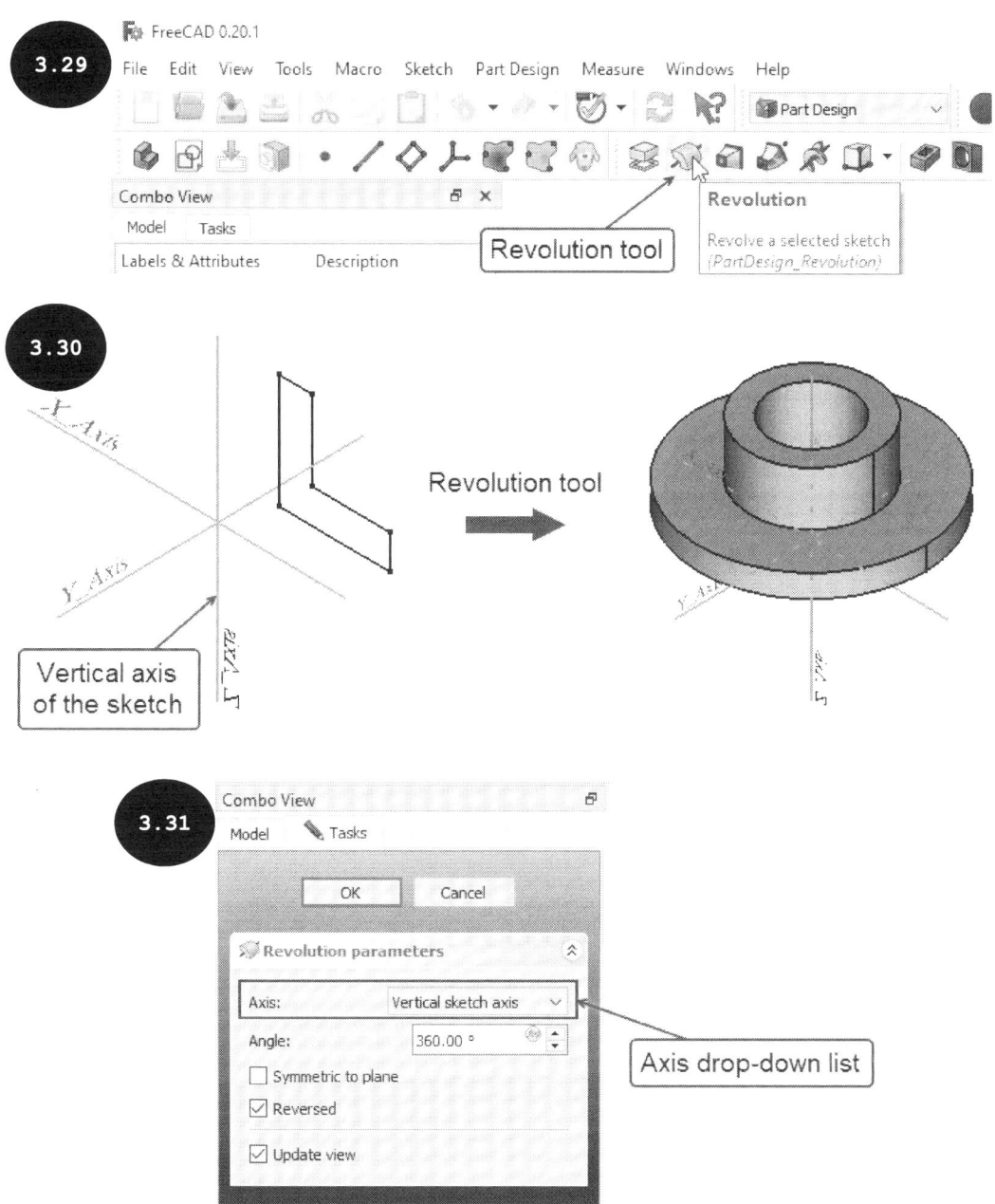

Note: If the sketch of the revolution feature is not on either side of its vertical axis, then on invoking the **Revolution** tool, an error will occur, and a preview of the revolution feature does not appear in the 3D View area. It is because the sketch cannot be revolved around the vertical axis that intersects with it. In this case, you need to define an axis of revolution for the sketch other than its vertical axis by selecting the required option in the **Axis** drop-down list of the **Revolution parameters** sub-window.

The options in the **Revolution parameters** sub-window of the **Task Panel** (refer to Figure 3.31) are used for specifying the required parameters to create a revolution feature and the same are discussed below:

Axis: The Axis drop-down list is used for selecting an option to define the axis of revolution of the revolution feature (see Figure 3.32) and the options are discussed below:

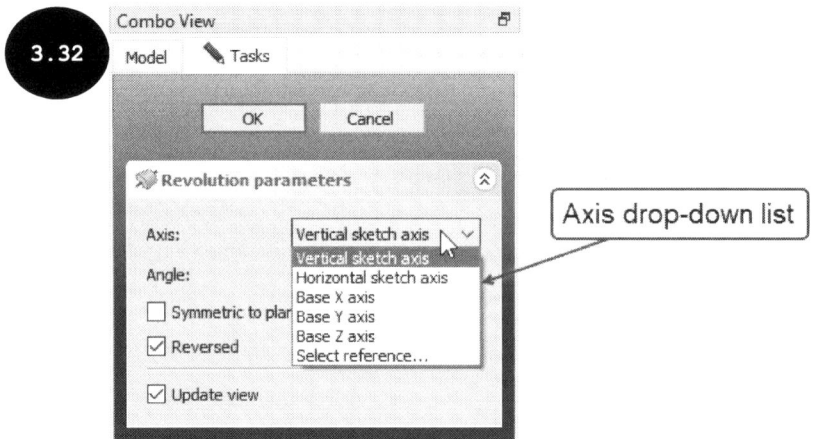

Vertical sketch axis: The **Vertical sketch axis** option is used for revolving the sketch around its vertical axis. A vertical axis of a sketch is an imaginary axis that is vertical to the sketch on its sketching plane.

Horizontal sketch axis: The Horizontal sketch axis option is used for revolving the sketch around its horizontal axis. A horizontal axis of a sketch is an imaginary axis that is horizontal to the sketch on its sketching plane.

Base X axis: The **Base X axis** option is used for revolving the sketch around the default X axis of the model, see Figure 3.33.

Base Y axis: The **Base Y axis** option is used for revolving the sketch around the default Y axis of the model, see Figure 3.33.

Base Z axis: The **Base Z axis** option is used for revolving the sketch around the default Z axis of the model, see Figure 3.33.

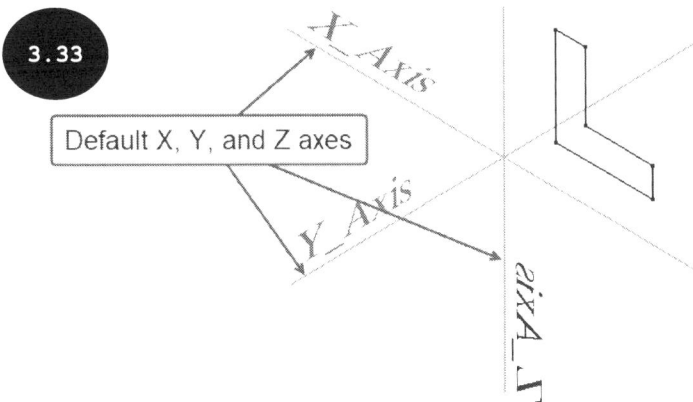

Default X, Y, and Z axes

Select reference: The **Select reference** option is used for selecting a linear sketch entity (line) of an existing sketch, an axis, or a linear edge of an existing feature as the axis of revolution for creating a revolution feature.

Angle: The Angle field in the **Revolution parameters** sub-window of the **Task Panel** is used for specifying the required angle value for revolving the sketch around the axis.

Symmetric to plane: On selecting the **Symmetric to plane** check box, the sketch revolves symmetrically on both sides of the sketching plane, around the axis of revolution, see Figure 3.34. Note that when this check box is selected, the angle value specified in the **Angle** field is divided equally into both sides of the sketching plane and creates a symmetrical revolution feature.

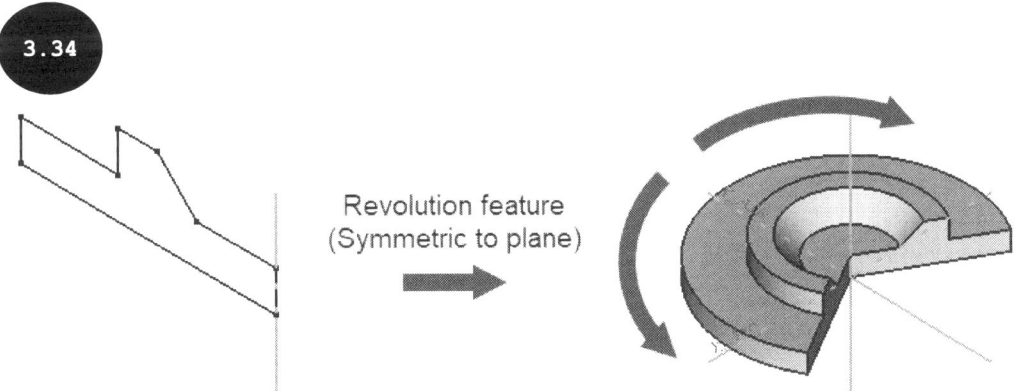

Revolution feature
(Symmetric to plane)

Reversed: The Reversed check box is used for reversing the direction of revolution to the other side of the sketching plane.

Update view: By default, the **Update view** check box is selected in the **Revolution parameters** sub-window of the **Task Panel**. As a result, the revolution feature being created gets updated in real-time in the 3D View area by specifying or editing its parameters.

3.   Specify the required option in the **Axis** drop-down list of the **Revolution parameters** sub-window for defining the axis of revolution of the revolution feature.

4.   Enter the required angle of revolution in the **Angle** field of the **Revolution parameters** sub-window.

5.   Specify other parameters for creating a revolution feature and then click on the **OK** button in the **Task Panel** of the **Tasks** tab, see Figure 3.35. The revolution feature of specified parameters gets created in the 3D View area. Also, its default name gets added under the **Body** node of the **Tree View** in the **Model** tab. You can click on the **Model** tab of the **Combo View** to display the **Tree View**.

Navigating a 3D Model in the 3D View Area

In FreeCAD, you can navigate a model by using mouse buttons depending upon the active navigation style. A navigation style controls mouse shortcuts for panning, zooming, and rotating a model in the 3D View area. FreeCAD supports multiple navigation styles for navigating a model such as CAD, Revit, Blender, Touchpad, OpenSCAD, and TinkerCAD. The methods for selecting a navigation style and navigating a 3D model in the 3D View area are discussed next.

Selecting a Navigation Style

In FreeCAD, you can select a navigation style that controls the navigation settings by using the **Preferences** dialog box. The method for selecting a navigation style is discussed below:

1.   Click on **Edit > Preferences** in the **Standard Menu**, see Figure 3.36. The **Preferences** dialog box appears.

2.   Select the **Display** section in the left panel of the **Preferences** dialog box and then click on the **Navigation** tab, see Figure 3.37. The options to control the navigation settings appear in the dialog box.

3.36

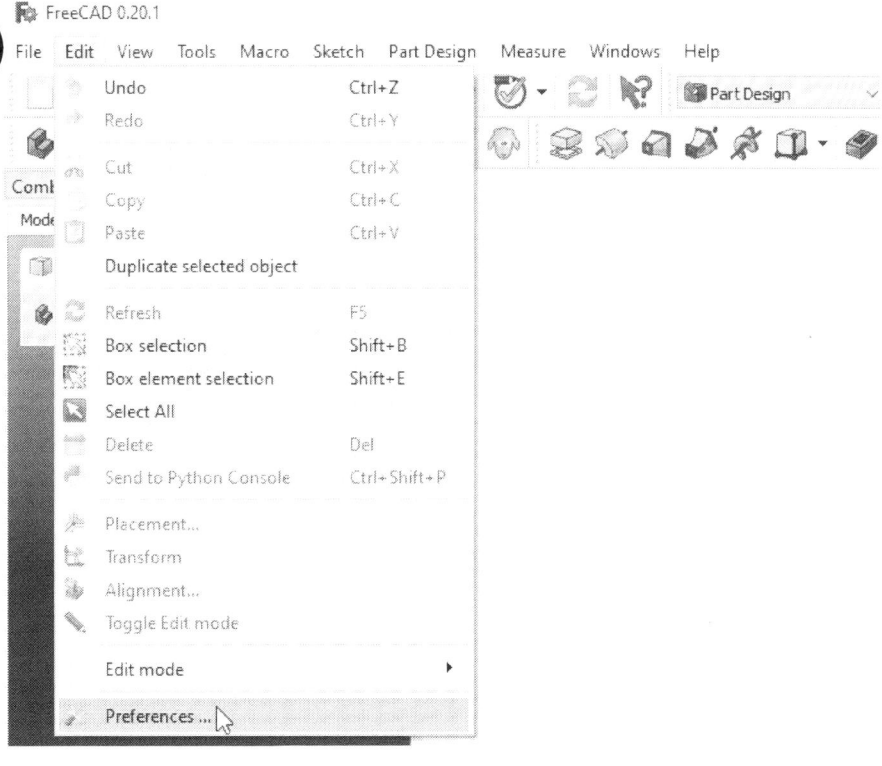

3.37

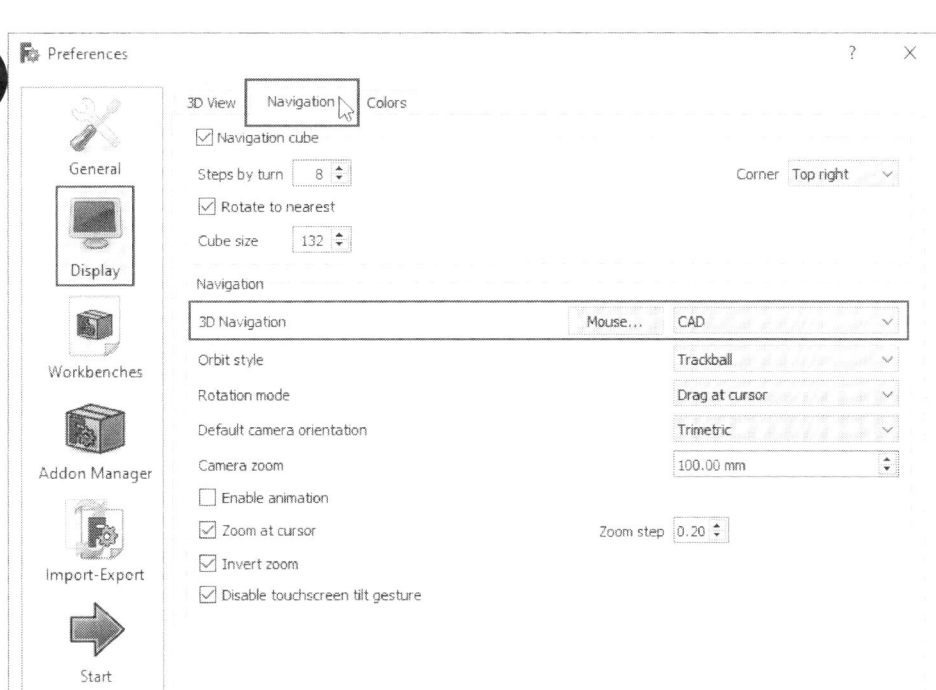

3. In the **3D Navigation** drop-down list of the dialog box, select the required navigation style, see Figure 3.38. By default, the **CAD** navigation style is selected.

Figure 3.38

Note that depending upon the navigation style selected in the **3D Navigation** drop-down list, you can navigate a model by using the respective mouse configuration. Some of the navigation styles and the respective mouse configurations are given in the below table:

	Selection	Panning	Zooming	Rotation
OpenInventor	Press CTRL and left mouse button + drag	Press the middle mouse button + drag	Scroll the middle mouse button	Press left mouse button + drag
CAD	Press the left mouse button + drag	Press the middle mouse button + drag	Scroll the middle mouse button or hold the middle and then click the left/right mouse button once	Press the middle and left or middle and right buttons + drag
Revit	Press the left mouse button + drag	Press the middle mouse button + drag	Scroll the middle mouse button	Press SHIFT and the middle mouse button + drag

	Selection	Panning ✥	Zooming ⊛	Rotation ⟲
Blender	Press the left mouse button + drag	Press SHIFT and the middle mouse button + drag	Scroll the middle mouse button	Press the middle mouse button + drag
Touchpad	Press the left mouse button + drag	Press SHIFT button + move mouse	Press CTRL and SHIFT buttons + move mouse	Press the ALT button + move mouse
OpenSCAD	Press the left mouse button + drag	Press the right mouse button + drag	Press the middle mouse button or SHIFT and the right mouse button + drag	Press the left mouse button + drag
TinkerCAD	Press the left mouse button + drag	Press the middle mouse button + drag	Scroll the middle mouse button	Press the right mouse button + drag

Tip: After selecting a navigation style, you can view its mouse configuration for selection, panning, zooming, and rotation by click on the **Mouse** button available in front of the **3D Navigation** drop-down list in the dialog box.

Note: If needed, you can also define an orbit style and a rotation mode by selecting the required option in the **Orbit style** and **Rotation mode** drop-down lists in the **Navigation** tab of the **Preferences** dialog box, respectively.

4.   After selecting the required navigation style, click on the **Apply** button and then on the **OK** button in the **Preferences** dialog box.

Tip: Alternatively, to select a navigation style, right-click on an empty area in the 3D View area and then move the cursor over the **Navigation styles** option in the shortcut menu that appears, see Figure 3.39. A cascading menu appears with the display of all the navigation styles. You can select the required navigation style in this cascading menu.

Note: In this textbook, the default **CAD** navigation style is used for panning, zooming, and rotating a model.

Now, you can navigate a model as per the navigation style specified in the **Preferences** dialog box. The method for navigating a model using the **CAD** navigation style is discussed next.

Pan

To pan or move a model in the 3D View area, press and hold the middle mouse button and then drag the cursor.

Zoom

To zoom into or out of the view of a model dynamically, scroll the middle mouse button up or down, respectively. On scrolling the middle mouse button up, the view gets enlarged, whereas on scrolling the middle mouse button down, the view gets reduced.

Alternatively, press and hold the middle mouse button and then click the right or left mouse button. Next, drag the cursor upward or downward in the 3D View area to enlarge or reduce the view of a model, respectively.

Rotate

To rotate a model in the 3D view area, press and hold the middle mouse button and right or left mouse button and then drag the cursor.

Fit All

You can fit all objects/bodies available in the current document completely inside the 3D View area (screen) by using the **Fit all** tool. This tool is available in the **View** toolbar, see Figure 3.40.

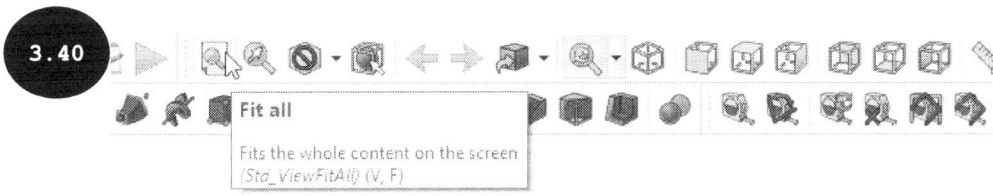

Fit selection

You can fit a selected geometry or object of the document completely in the 3D View area by using the **Fit selection** tool. This tool is available in the **View** toolbar, see Figure 3.41.

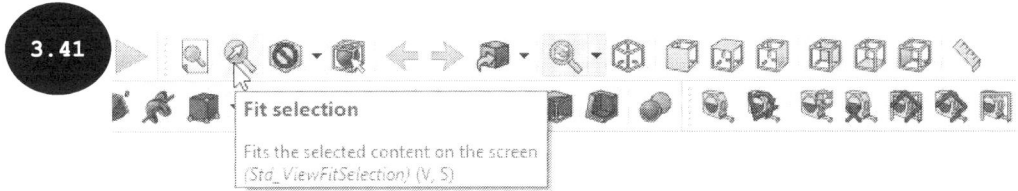

Displaying Standard Views of a Model

In FreeCAD, you can display a 3D model in various standard views such as Front, Top, Right, Rear, Bottom, and Isometric by using the respective tools available in the **View** toolbar, see Figure 3.42.

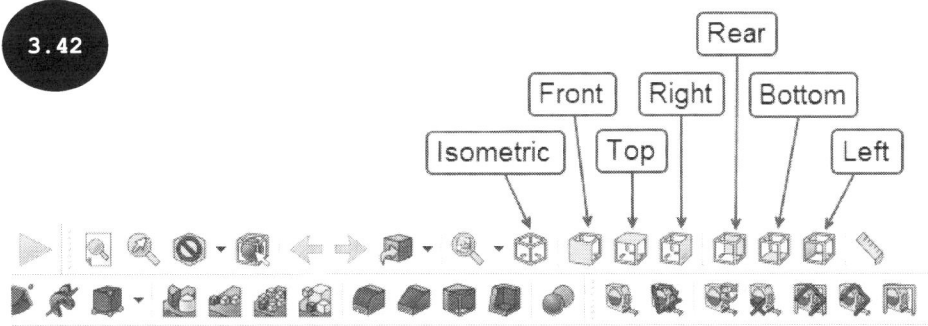

You can also access these tools to switch among different standard views such as Front, Top, Right, Rear, Bottom, and Isometric by clicking on the **View > Standard views** in the **Standard Menu**, see Figure 3.43. The tools are discussed next.

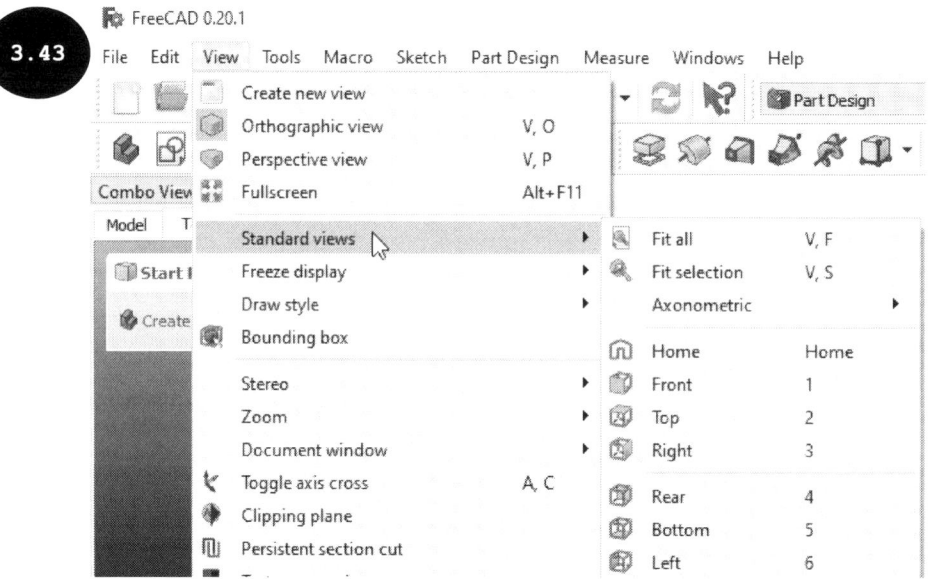

Home Tool

The Home tool is used to switch the view orientation of a model to the default home view, which is the trimetric view, by default.

Note: To change the default home view, click on **Edit > Preferences** in the **Standard Menu** and then click on the **Display** section in the left panel of the **Preferences** dialog box that appears. Next, click on the **Navigation** tab and then select the required home view in the **Default camera orientation** drop-down list, see Figure 3.44. After selecting the required home view, click on the **Apply** button and then the **OK** button in the dialog box.

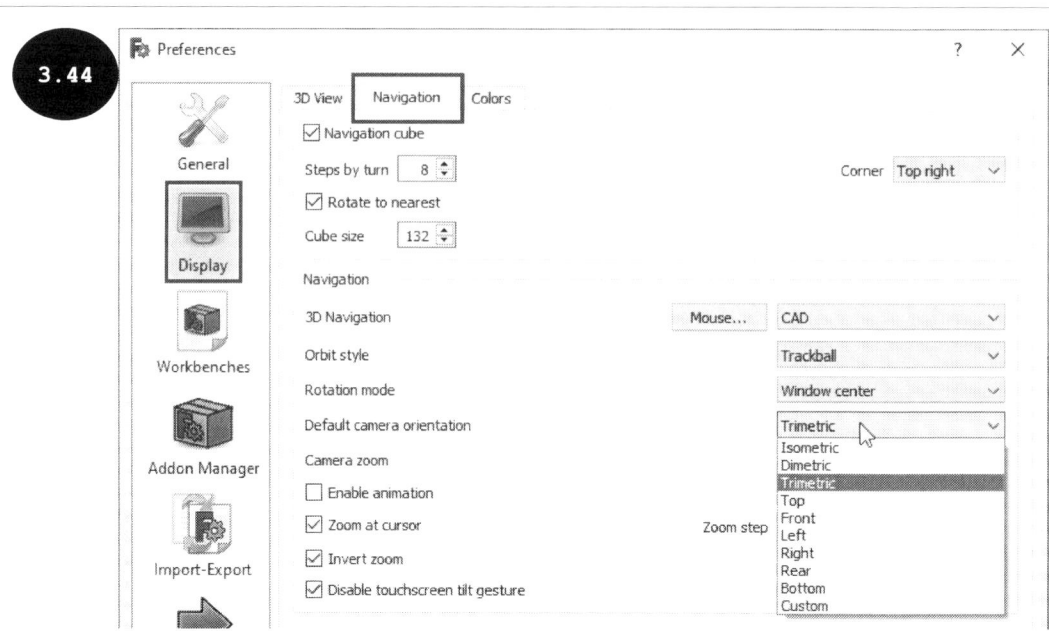

Front, Top, Right, Rear, Bottom, and Left Tools

The Front, Top, Right, Rear, Bottom, and Left tools are used to switch the view orientation of a model to the respective predefined standard view: Front, Top, Right, Rear, Bottom, and Left.

Isometric, Dimetric, and Trimetric Tools

The Isometric, Dimetric, and Trimetric tools are used to switch the view orientation of a model to the isometric, dimetric, and trimetric view, respectively. To access these tools, click on View > Standard views > Axonometric in the Standard Menu, see Figure 3.45.

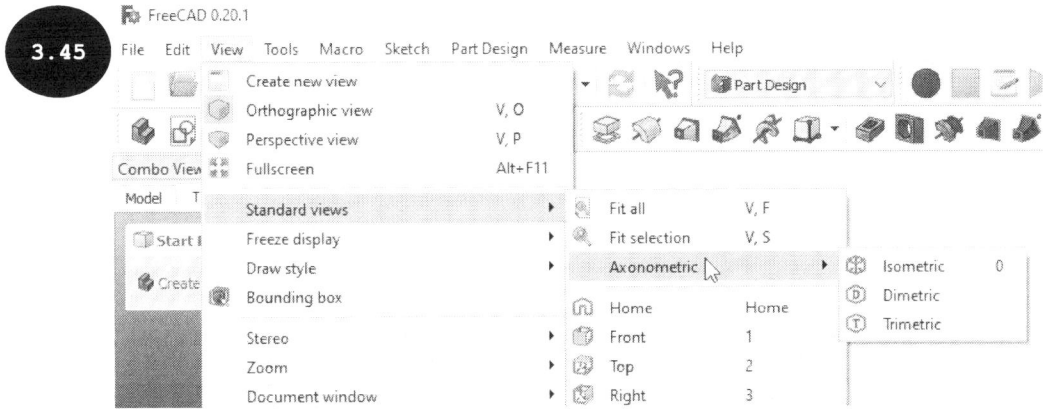

Working with Navigation Cube

By default, the Navigation Cube is available at the upper right corner of the 3D View area, see Figure 3.46. It provides visual information about the current view orientation of a model in the 3D View area. You can also use the Navigation Cube to switch between various standard views of a model. Various components of the Navigation Cube are discussed next.

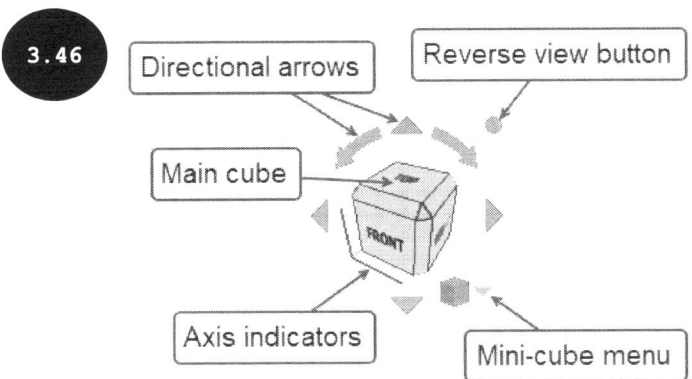

Main cube

The Main cube has 6 square faces, 12 rectangular edge faces, and 8 triangular corner faces. You can click on any of them to reorient the view orientation of the model normal to the selected face of the Main cube.

Directional arrows

The **Navigation Cube** consists of a total of 6 direction arrows. Out of which, 4 are triangular arrowheads and 2 are curved arrows. On clicking a triangular arrowhead, the view orientation of a model rotates 45 degrees around a line normal to the direction of the selected arrow. Similarly, on clicking a curved arrow, the view orientation of a model rotates 45 degrees around the view direction.

Reverse view button

The **Reverse view button** is used to rotate the view orientation of a model 180 degrees around the vertical axis of the view.

Mini-cube menu

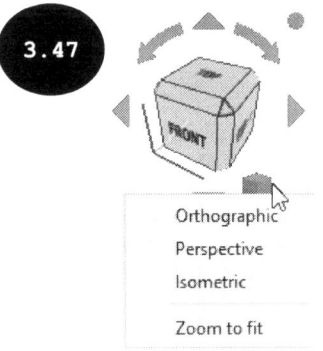

The **Mini-cube menu** is provided with additional options to control the view orientation of a model. To invoke the **Mini-cube menu**, click on the small cube icon available at the bottom right corner of the **Navigation Cube**, see Figure 3.47. The options are discussed next.

Orthographic

The **Orthographic** option is used to change the view of a model to an orthographic view.

Perspective

The **Perspective** option is used to change the view of a model to a perspective view.

Isometric

The **Isometric** option is used to change the view of a model to an isometric view.

Zoom to fit

The **Zoom to fit** option is used to fit all the objects available in the 3D View area completely inside the screen.

 As discussed, the **Navigation Cube** is available at the upper right corner of the 3D View area, by default. However, you can change its default location by pressing and holding the left mouse button on the **Main cube** and then dragging it to a new location on the screen.

Alternatively, invoke the **Preferences** dialog box and then click on the **Display** section on the left panel of the dialog box. Next, click on the **Navigation** tab and then select the required option in the **Corner** drop-down list of the dialog box to define a default location of the **Navigation Cube** on the screen, see Figure 3.48. You can also define other navigation settings by using the options available in this dialog box.

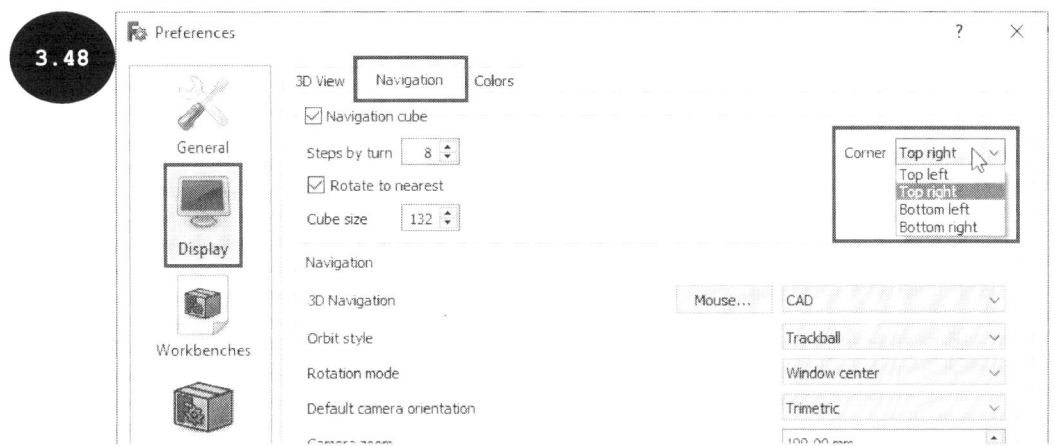

Changing the Display Style of a Model

You can change the display style of a model to Points, Wireframe, Hidden line, No shading, Shaded, and Flat lines. You can access these tools to change the display style of a model in the **Draw style** menu of the **View** toolbar, see Figure 3.49.

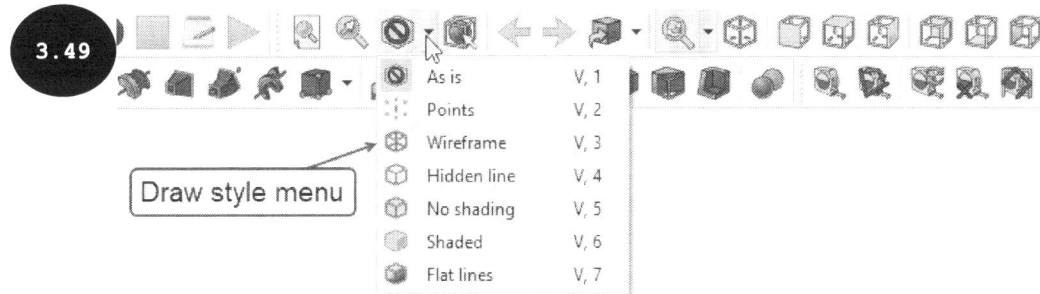

Alternatively, click on **View > Draw style** in the **Standard Menu** to access tools for changing the display style of a model, see Figure 3.50.

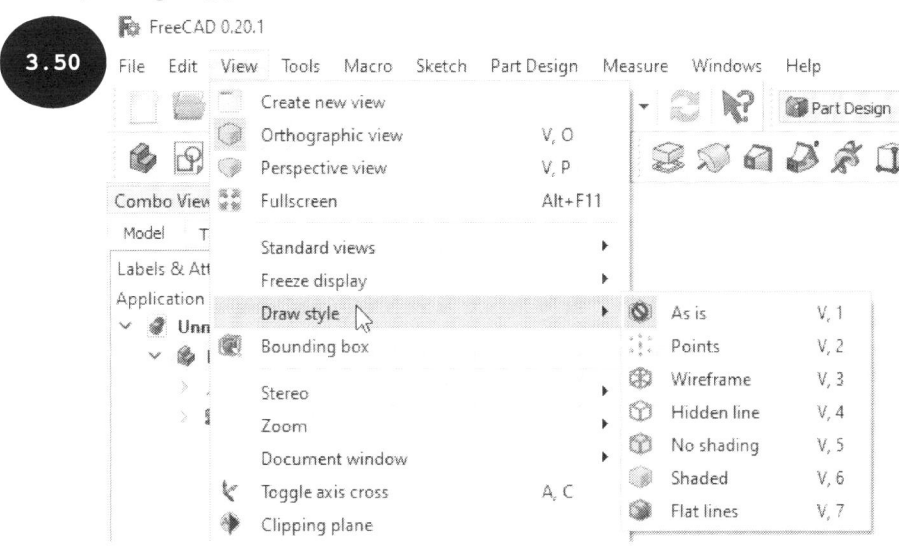

You can also right-click on an empty area in the 3D View area and then move the cursor to the **Draw style** option in the shortcut menu that appears for accessing these tools, see Figure 3.51.

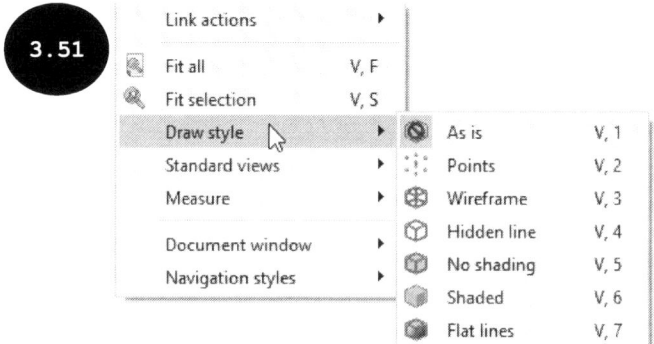

The tools used for changing the display style of a model are discussed next.

As is

The **As is** tool is used for displaying a model in the 'As is' display style. In this style, the model is displayed in its default or custom-specified display mode.

Note: To define a display mode for a model, click on the **Model** tab in the **Combo View** and then select the **Body** node in the **Tree View** that appears, see Figure 3.52. The **Property Editor** appears in its lower section with **View** and **Data** tabs, see Figure 3.53. Click on the **View** tab for displaying the visualization properties of the selected body, see Figure 3.53. Next, click on the **Display Mode** field of the **View** tab. An arrow appears in this field. Click on this arrow and then select the required display mode in the drop-down list that appears. The selected display mode gets defined as the 'As is' display style of the model.

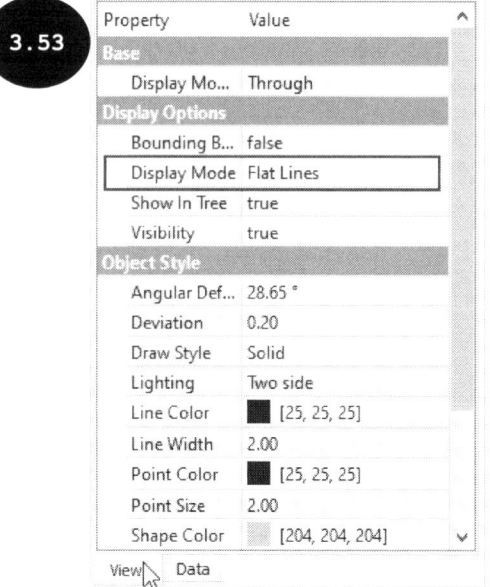

Points

The **Points** tool is used for displaying a model in the 'Points' display style. In this display style, the vertices of a model are displayed in a solid color (dots), while the edges and faces of the model become invisible, see Figure 3.54.

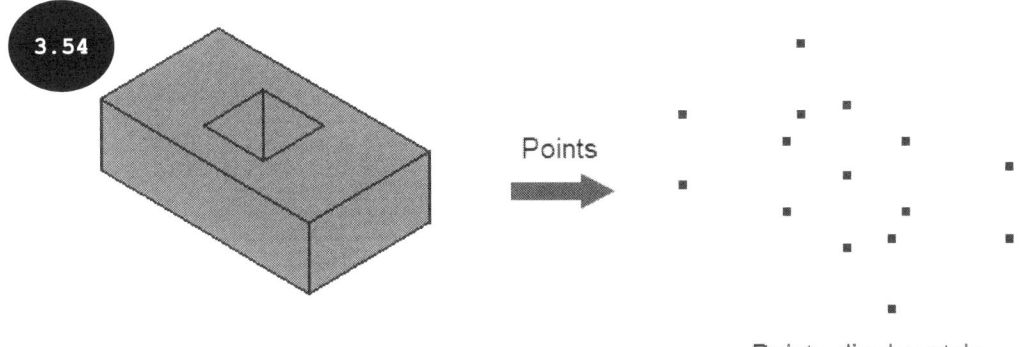

Wireframe

The **Wireframe** tool is used for displaying a model in the 'Wireframe' display style. In this style, all the edges and vertices of a model are displayed in a solid color, while the faces of the model become invisible, see Figure 3.55.

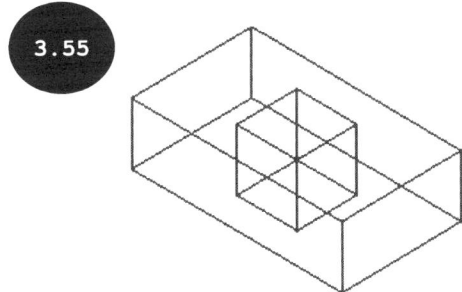

Hidden line

The **Hidden line** tool is used for displaying a model in the 'Hidden line' display style. In this style, the faces of the model are displayed in triangular meshes, while the hidden edges of the model become invisible, see Figure 3.56.

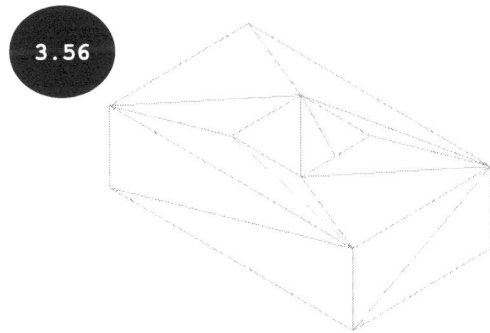

No shading

The **No shading** tool is used for displaying a model in the 'No shading' display style. In this style, the faces, edges, and vertices are displayed in a solid color, see Figure 3.57.

Shaded

The **Shaded** tool is used for displaying a model in the 'Shaded' display style. In this style, the faces of a model are illuminated depending upon their orientation in the 3D View area, while the edges and vertices of the model become invisible, see Figure 3.58. In this figure, the model is displayed in trimetric view orientation.

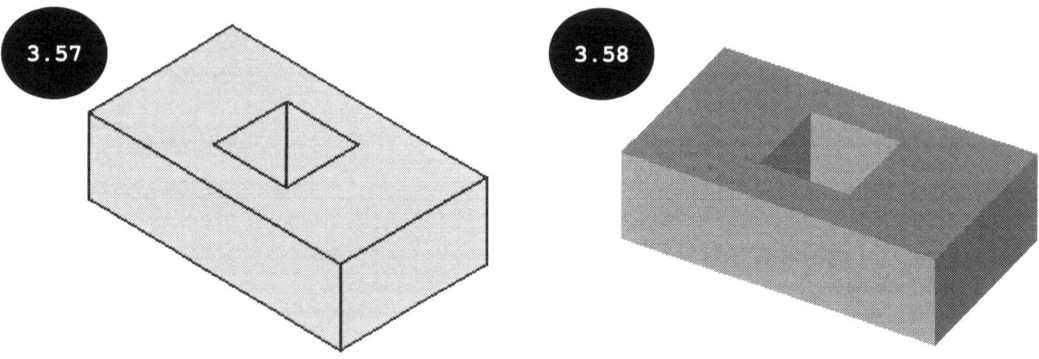

Flat lines

The **Flat lines** tool is used for displaying a model in the 'Flat lines' display style. In this style, the edges and vertices of a model are displayed in a solid color, while the faces of the model are illuminated depending upon their orientation in the 3D View area, see Figure 3.59.

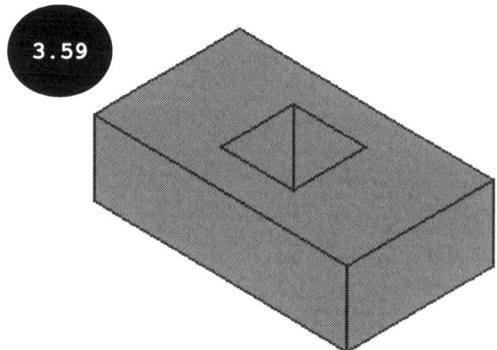

Tutorial 1

Create a sketch of the model shown in Figure 3.60 and then extrude it to a depth of 16 mm symmetrically about the sketching plane. All dimensions are in mm.

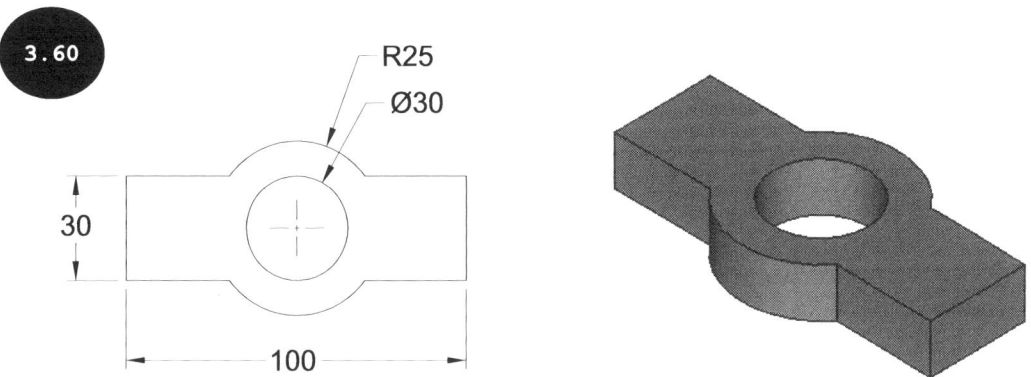

Section 1: Starting FreeCAD and a New Empty Document

1. Start FreeCAD by double-clicking on the **FreeCAD 0.20** icon on your desktop. The startup user interface of FreeCAD appears, see Figure 3.61.

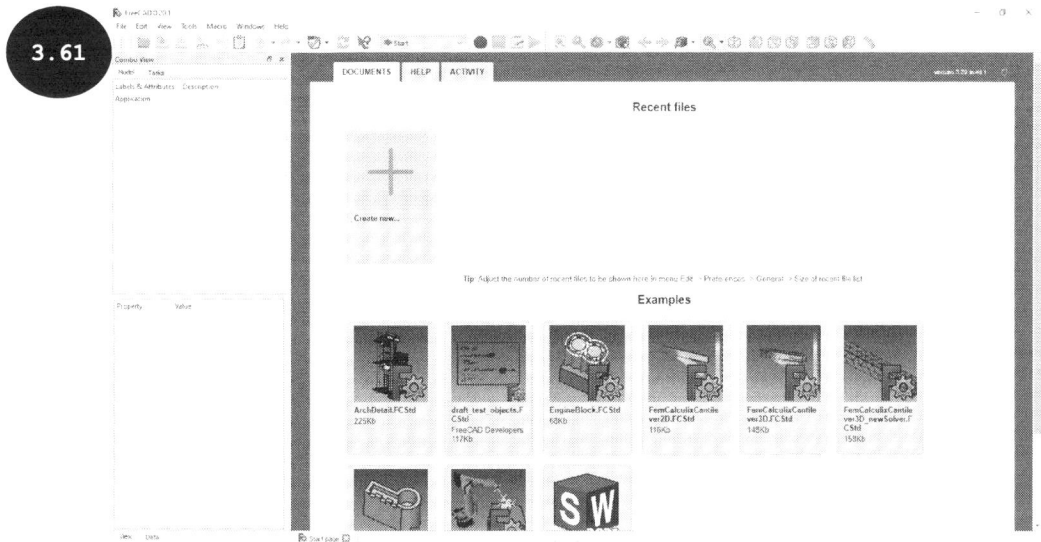

Note: Every time you start FreeCAD, the **Start** workbench is invoked with the display of the **Start** page, by default. The **Start** page act as a welcome screen that displays recently opened documents, example files, help documentation, the latest activity in FreeCAD, and so on in their respective tabs (**DOCUMENTS, HELP**, and **ACTIVITY**).

2. Click on the **New** tool in the **File** toolbar (see Figure 3.62) or press the **CTRL + N** keys. A new empty document gets invoked with the default name "**unnamed: 1**" and it becomes active by default.

Section 2: Invoking the Part Design Workbench

Now, you can invoke the **Part Design** workbench for creating a 3D solid model.

1. Invoke the **Workbench Selector** in the **Workbench** toolbar and then select the **Part Design** workbench, see Figure 3.63. The **Part Design** workbench gets invoked.

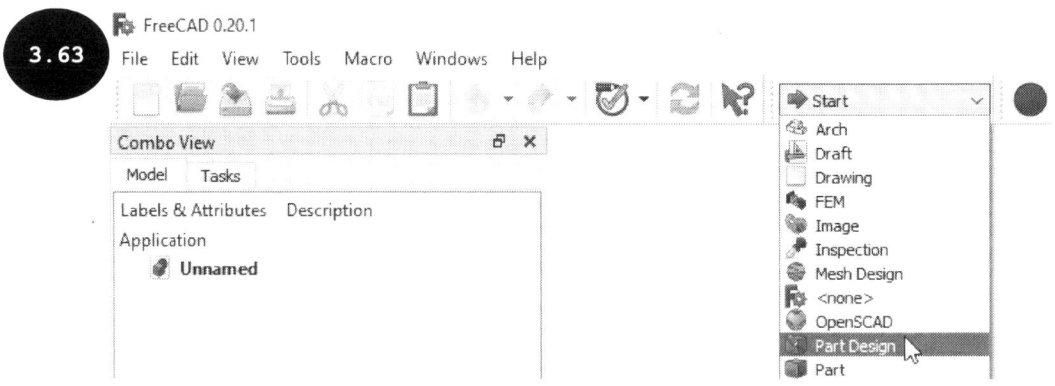

Section 3: Invoking the Sketcher Workbench

Now, you need to invoke the **Sketcher** workbench for creating a sketch of the base feature.

1. Click on the **Create sketch** tool in the **Part Design Helper** toolbar, see Figure 3.64. The three default planes appear in the 3D View area. Also, the **Task Panel** appears in the **Tasks** tab of the **Combo View** and displays the name of the three default planes, see Figure 3.65.

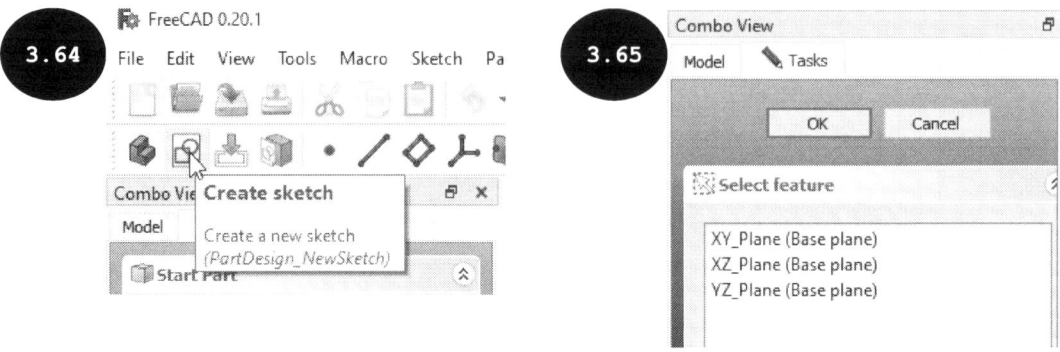

2. Select the **XY_Plane** as the sketching plane in the 3D View area for creating the sketch. The Sketch editing mode of the **Sketcher** workbench gets invoked, see Figure 3.66. Note that the selected plane becomes the sketching plane for drawing the sketch and it is oriented normal to the viewing direction.

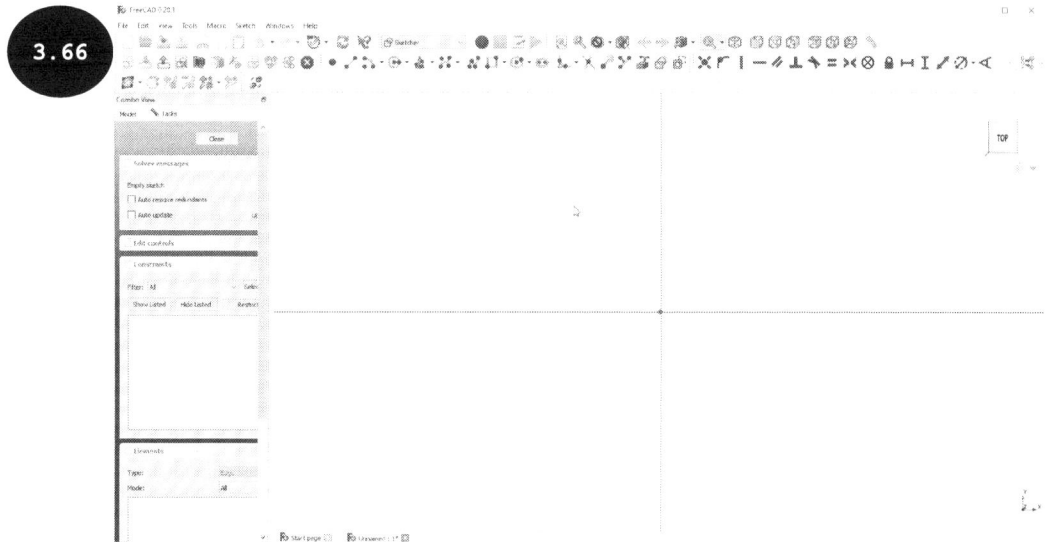

Section 4: Specifying Units, Grids, and Snap Settings

Now, you need to specify millimeters (mm) as the measurement unit for the document. Also, you need to turn off the display of grids and snap mode for creating the sketch by specifying points arbitrarily in the 3D View area.

1. Click on **Edit > Preferences** in the **Standard Menu**, see Figure 3.67. The **Preferences** dialog box appears.

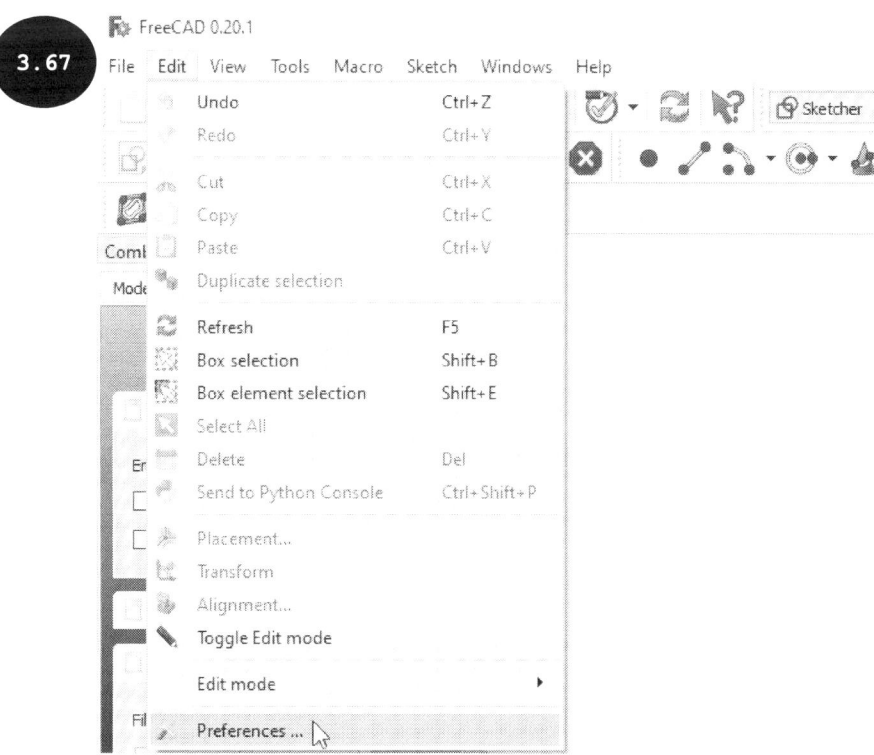

2.   Ensure that the **General** section is selected in the left panel of the **Preferences** dialog box and then click on the **Units** tab, see Figure 3.68.

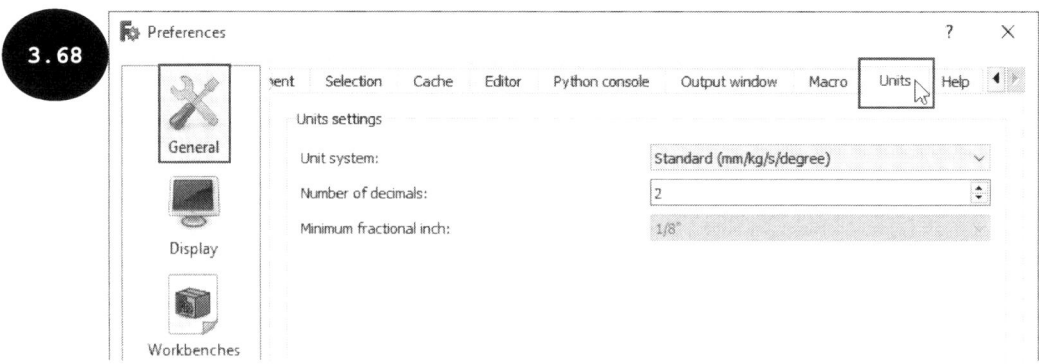

3.68

Tip: You may need to click on the arrow ▶ at the upper right corner of the **Preferences** dialog box for displaying the **Units** tab.

3.   Ensure that the **Standard (mm/kg/s/degree)** option is selected in the **Unit system** drop-down list of the dialog box. In this unit system, the length is measured in millimeters, the mass is calculated in kilograms, the time is represented in seconds, and the angle is measured in degrees.

4.   Ensure that the **2** is specified in the **Number of decimals** field of the dialog box as the number of digits after the decimal point of measurements.

5.   Click on the **Apply** button in the **Preferences** dialog box. The selected unit system is defined.

Now, you need to ensure that the display of grids and the snap mode are turned off in the 3D View area for creating a sketch by specifying points arbitrarily in the 3D View area.

Note: As FreeCAD is a parametric software, you can turn off the snap mode and create the sketch entities by specifying points arbitrarily in the 3D View area. After creating the sketch, you can apply the required constraints and dimensions to make the sketch fully constrained.

6.   Click on the **Sketcher** section in the left panel of the **Preferences** dialog box. The different options related to the **Sketcher** workbench appear on the right panel of the dialog box.

7.   Ensure that the **Show grid** and **Grid snap** check boxes are cleared in the right panel of the dialog box to turn off the display of grids and the snap mode in the 3D View area, see Figure 3.69.

8.   Ensure that the **Auto remove redundants** check box is selected in the **General** area of the dialog box for automatically removing the redundant constraints from the sketch, see Figure 3.69.

9.   Click on the **Apply** button and then the **OK** button in the dialog box to accept the changes made and exit the **Preferences** dialog box.

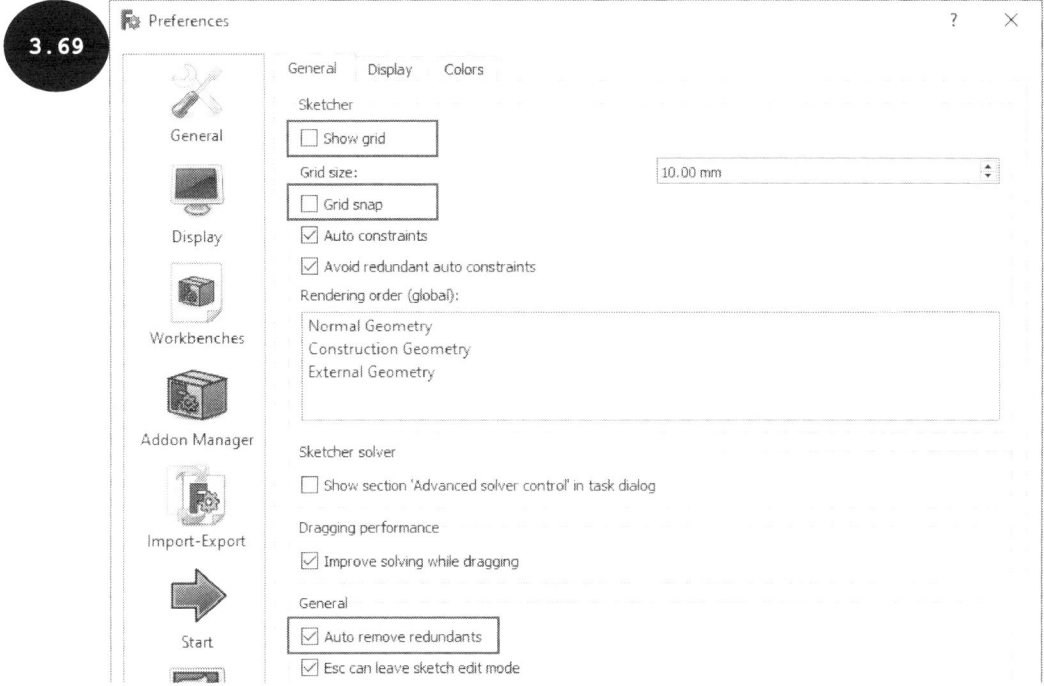

3.69

Section 5: Creating the Sketch

Now, you can create a sketch of the pad feature by specifying points arbitrarily in the 3D View area.

1. Invoke the **Create rectangle** menu in the **Sketcher geometries** toolbar and then click on the **Centered rectangle** tool, see Figure 3.70.

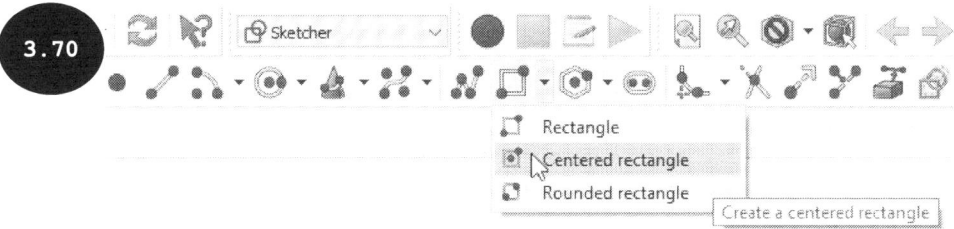

3.70

2. Click to specify the center of the rectangle at the origin in the 3D View area, refer to Figure 3.71.

3. Move the cursor towards the right and then click to specify a corner of the rectangle when its half-length and width values appear close to 50 mm and 15 mm near the cursor respectively, see Figure 3.71. A rectangle gets created.

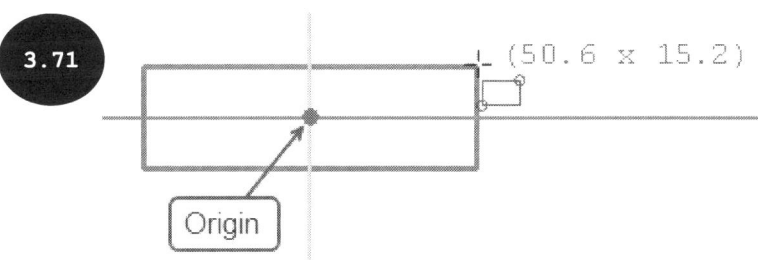

3.71

4.   Press ESC or right-click to exit the **Centered rectangle** tool.

Now, you need to create two circles.

5.   Invoke the **Create circle** menu in the **Sketcher geometries** toolbar and then click on the **Center and rim point** tool, see Figure 3.72. The **Center and rim point** tool gets activated.

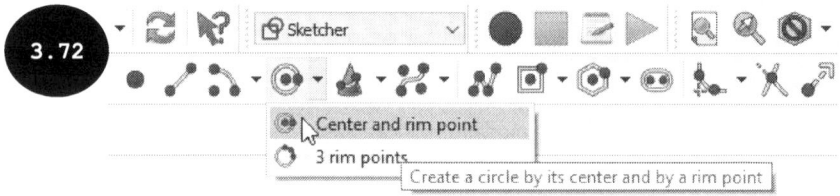

3.72

6.   Click to specify the center point of the circle at the origin, refer to Figure 3.73.

7.   Move the cursor horizontally toward the right and then click to specify a point when the radius of the circle appears close to 25 mm near the cursor, see Figure 3.73. A circle gets drawn. Also, the **Center and rim point** tool remains active.

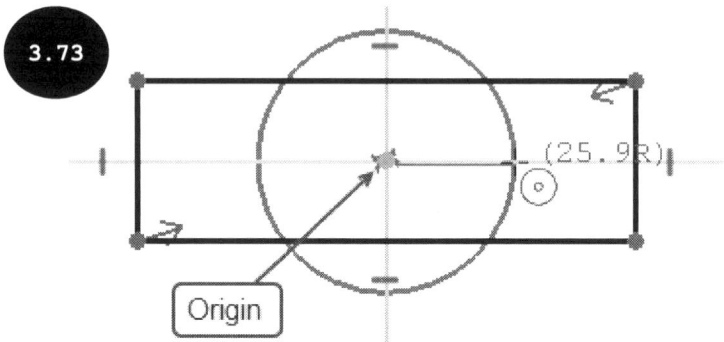

3.73

Now, you need to create another circle.

8.   Click to specify the center point of the circle at the origin and then click to specify a point when the radius of the circle appears close to 15 mm near the cursor, see Figure 3.74. A circle gets drawn. Next, right-click to exit the **Center and rim point** tool.

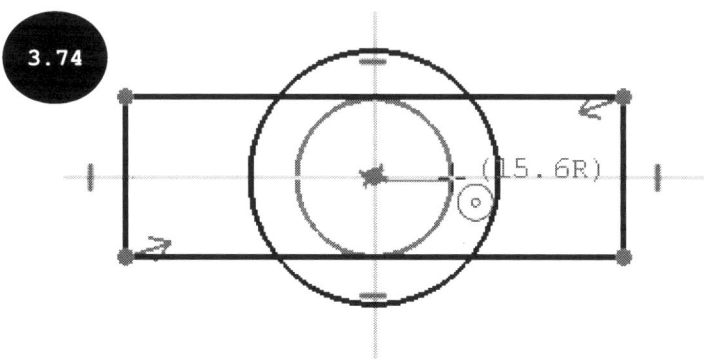

3.74

Now, you need to trim the unwanted sketch entities to their nearest intersection.

9. Click on the **Trim edge** tool in the **Sketcher geometries** toolbar, see Figure 3.75. The **Trim edge** tool gets activated and the appearance of the cursor changes to cross mark with the display of a red trim icon.

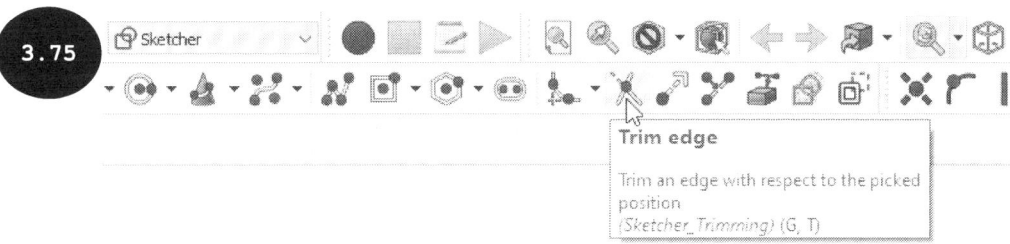

3.75

Trim edge

Trim an edge with respect to the picked position
(Sketcher_Trimming) (G, T)

10. Click to trim the unwanted entities of the sketch to their nearest intersection one by one. Figure 3.76 shows the final sketch after trimming all the unwanted entities of the sketch. Next, right-click in the 3D View area to exit the **Trim edge** tool.

Now, you need to apply the required geometric constraints and dimensions to make the sketch fully defined.

11. Apply the horizontal and vertical constraints to all the horizontal and vertical lines of the sketch, if not applied by default.

12. Apply the horizontal constraint between the endpoints of the upper arc of the sketch to make them aligned horizontally, see Figure 3.77.

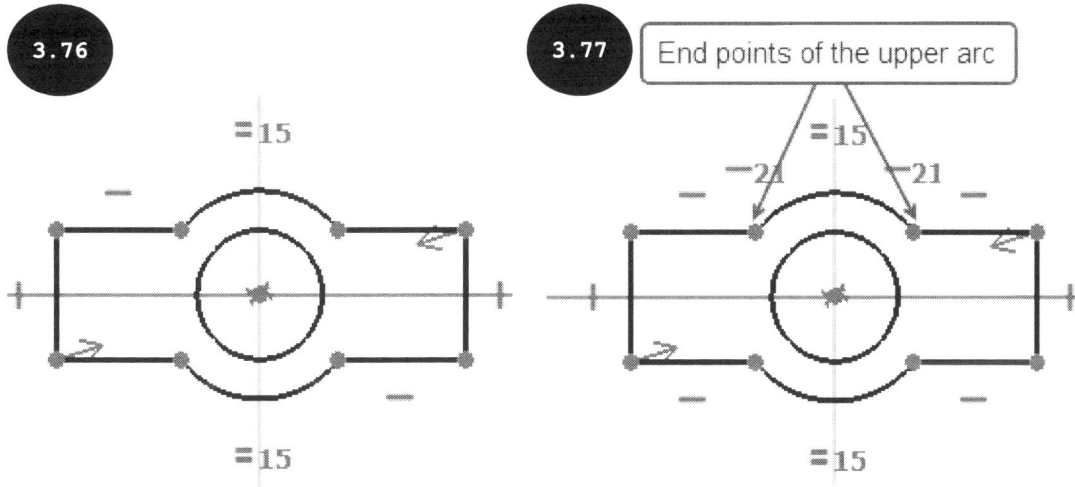

3.76

3.77   End points of the upper arc

13. Similarly, apply the horizontal constraint between the endpoints of the lower arc of the sketch to make them aligned horizontally.

Now, you need to apply the required dimensions.

14. Apply all the required dimensions to the sketch by using the respective dimension tools. Figure 3.78 shows a fully defined sketch after applying all the required dimensions.

After creating the sketch, you need to exit the Sketch editing mode of the **Sketcher** workbench.

15. Click on the **Close** button in the **Task Plane** of the **Combo View** to exit the **Sketcher** workbench (see Figure 3.79) and switch back to the **Part Design** workbench.

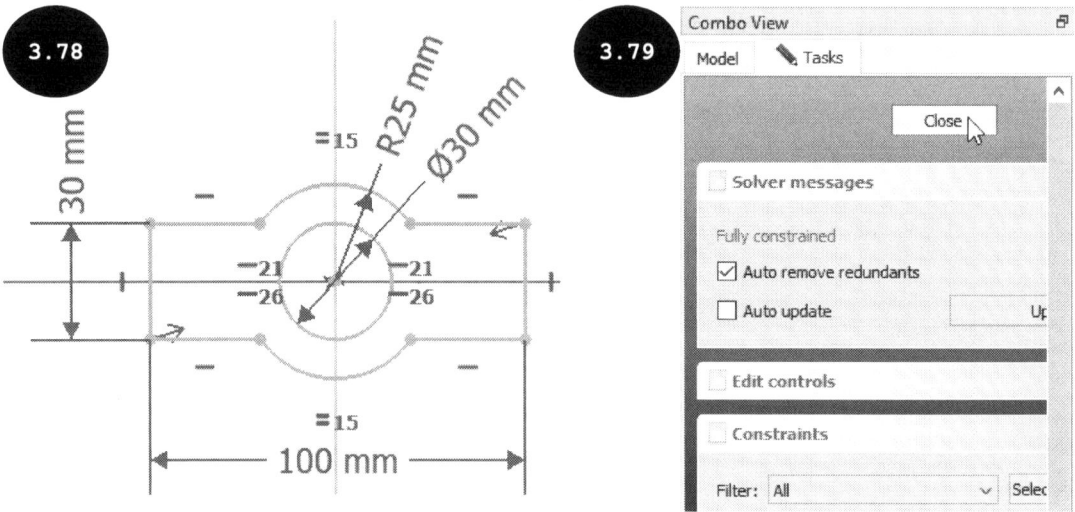

Section 6: Creating a Pad Feature

Now, you need to create a pad feature by extruding the sketch to a depth of 16 mm symmetrically on both sides of the sketching plane.

1. Click on the **Pad** tool in the **Part Design Modeling** toolbar, see Figure 3.80. The preview of a pad feature appears in the 3D View area with default parameters since the sketch gets selected automatically. Also, the **Pad parameters** sub-window appears in the **Task Panel** of the **Combo View**, see Figure 3.81.

2. Ensure that the **Dimension** option is selected in the **Type** drop-down list of the **Pad parameters** sub-window in the **Task Panel**.

3. Enter **16** mm in the **Length** field of the **Pad parameters** sub-window as the extrusion length of the pad feature.

4. Select the **Symmetric to plane** check box in the **Pad parameters** sub-window for extruding the sketch symmetrically on both sides of the sketching plane, see Figure 3.82.

5. Click on the **OK** button in the **Task Panel**. The pad feature of specified parameters gets created in the 3D View area, see Figure 3.83.

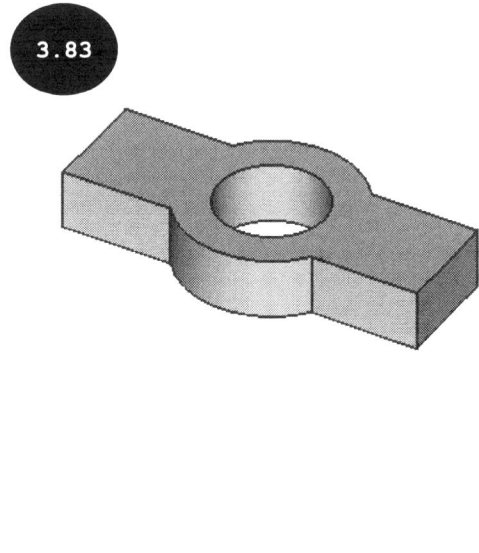

Section 7: Saving the Model

Now, you can save the model.

1. Click on the **Save** tool in the **File** toolbar (see Figure 3.84) or press the CTRL + S keys. The **Save FreeCAD Document** dialog box appears.

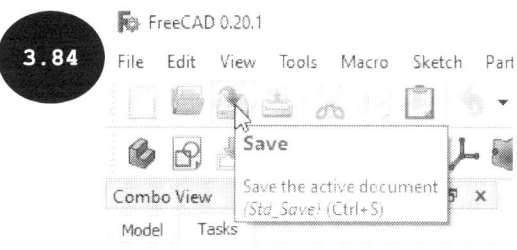

2. Browse the **FreeCAD** folder in the local drive of your system. Next, create a new folder with the name **Chapter 03** inside this folder.

3. Enter **Ch03-Tutorial 1** in the **File name** field of the dialog box. Next, click on the **Save** button in the dialog box. The model gets saved with the name **Ch03-Tutorial 1** at the specified location (> *FreeCAD* > *Chapter 03*).

4. Click on **File** > **Close** in the **Standard Menu** to close the current document.

Tutorial 2

Create a sketch of the model shown in Figure 3.85 and then revolve it around the vertical axis at an angle of 270 degrees. All dimensions are in inches (in).

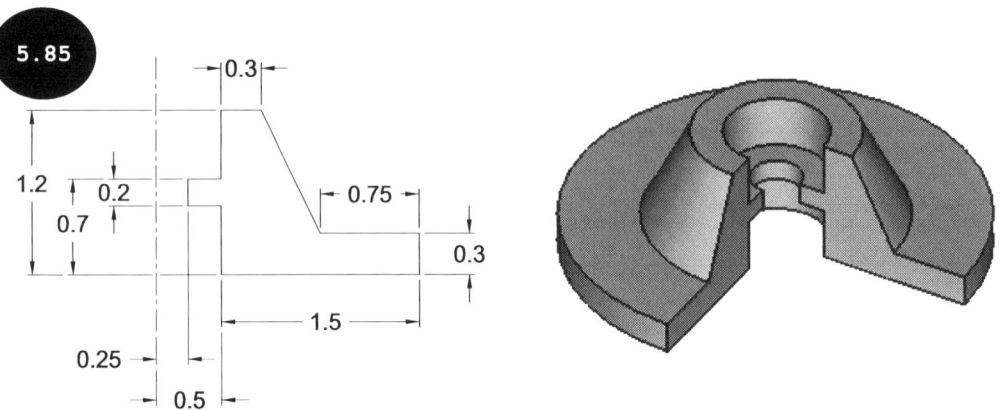

Section 1: Invoking a New Empty Document

1. Start FreeCAD by double-clicking on the **FreeCAD 0.20** icon on your desktop. The startup user interface of FreeCAD appears.

2. Click on the **New** tool in the **File** toolbar (see Figure 3.86) or press the **CTRL + N** keys. A new empty document gets invoked with the default name "**unnamed: 1**" and it becomes active by default.

Section 2: Invoking the Part Design Workbench

Now, you can invoke the **Part Design** workbench for creating a 3D solid model.

1. Invoke the **Workbench Selector** in the **Workbench** toolbar and then select the **Part Design** workbench, see Figure 3.87. The **Part Design** workbench gets invoked.

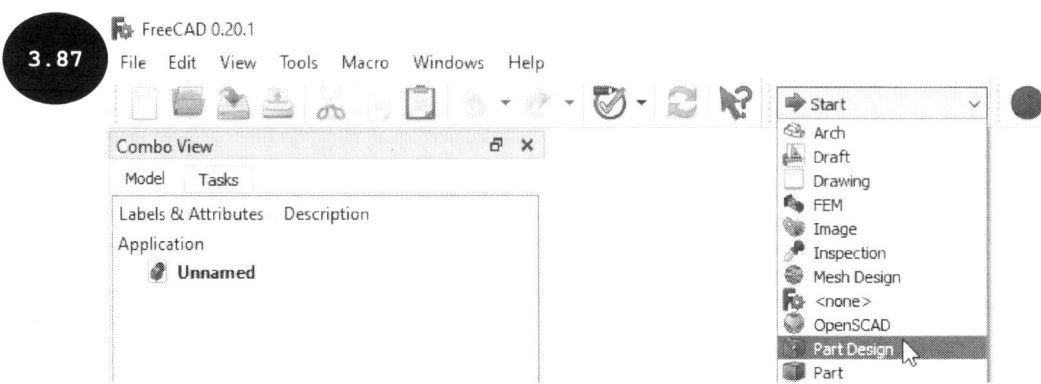

Section 3: Invoking the Sketcher Workbench

Now, you need to invoke the **Sketcher** workbench for creating a sketch of the base feature.

1. Click on the **Create sketch** tool 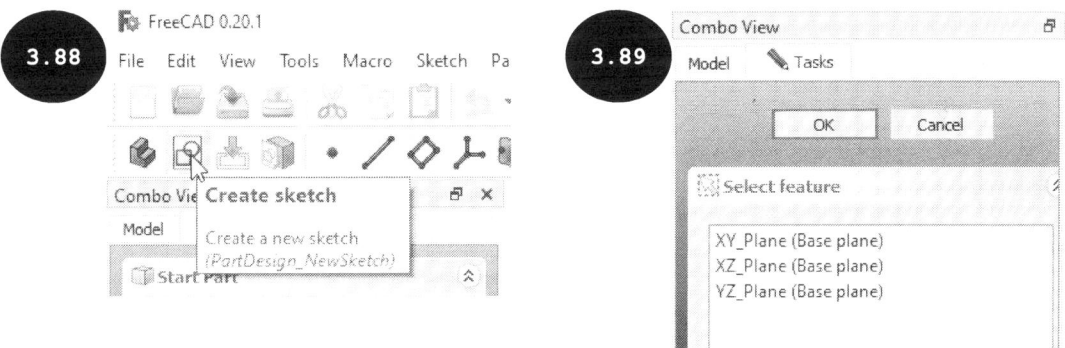 in the **Part Design Helper** toolbar, see Figure 3.88. The three default planes appear in the 3D View area. Also, the **Task Panel** appears in the **Tasks** tab of **Combo View** and displays the name of the three default planes, see Figure 3.89.

2. Select the **XZ_Plane** as the sketching plane in the **Task Panel** and then click on the OK button. You can also select the sketching plane in the 3D View area. The **Sketcher** workbench gets invoked and the selected plane gets oriented normal to the viewing direction.

Section 4: Specifying the Units

1. Click on **Edit > Preferences** in the **Standard Menu**, see Figure 3.90. The **Preferences** dialog box appears.

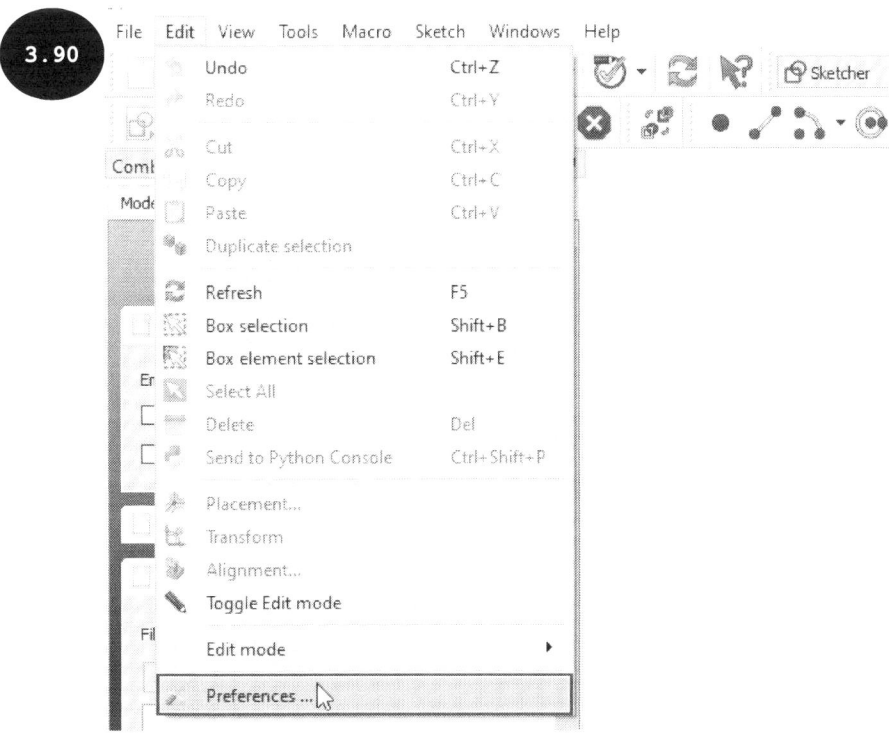

2. Ensure that the **General** section is selected in the left panel of the **Preferences** dialog box and then click on the **Units** tab. The options to define units appear in the dialog box, see Figure 3.91.

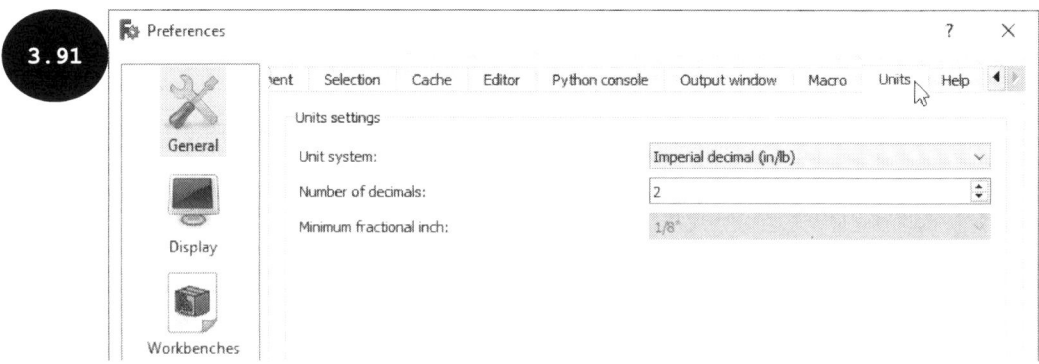

3. Select the **Imperial decimal (in/lb)** option in the **Unit system** drop-down list of the dialog box as the unit system. In this unit system, the length is measured in inches and the mass is calculated in pounds (lb).

4. Ensure that the **2** is specified in the **Number of decimals** field of the dialog box as the number of digits after the decimal point of measurements.

5. Click on the **Apply** button and then the **OK** button in the dialog box to accept the changes made and exit the **Preferences** dialog box.

Section 5: Creating the Sketch
Now, you can create a sketch of the revolution feature.

1. Click on the **Create polyline** tool in the **Sketcher geometries** toolbar for drawing a continuous chain of line entities, see Figure 3.92. The **Create polyline** tool gets activated.

2. Move the cursor over the horizontal axis, at a small distance from the origin and then click to specify the start point of the first line segment, refer to Figure 3.93.

3. Move the cursor vertically upward and then click anywhere to specify the endpoint of the vertical line, refer to Figure 3.93. A vertical line of any length gets created and the **Create polyline** tool remains activated.

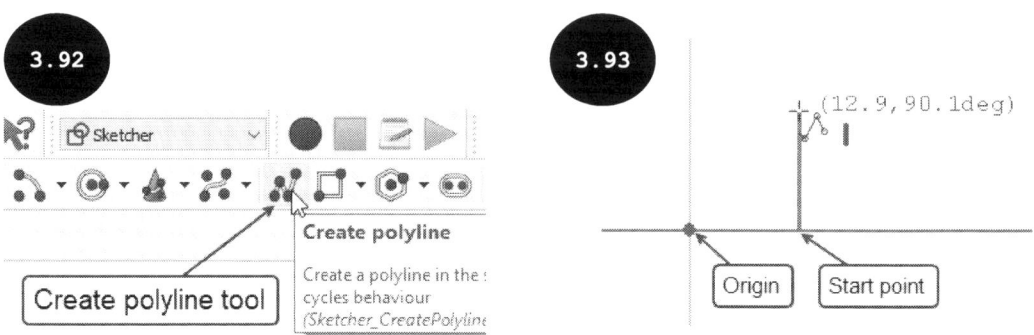

4. Continue creating a chain of line entities of the sketch by specifying points arbitrarily in the 3D View area like the one shown in Figure 3.94. It is a closed sketch where the start point of the first line segment and the endpoint of the last line segment coincide with each other.

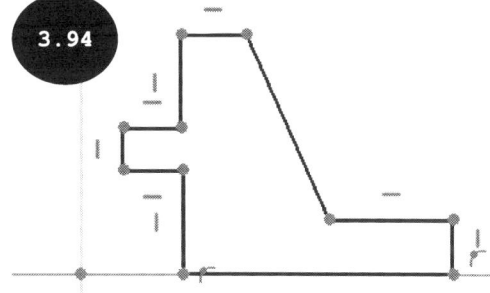

5. Right-click twice to exit the **Create polyline** tool.

Now, you need to apply the required geometric constraints and dimensions to make the sketch fully defined.

6. Apply horizontal and vertical constraints to the horizontal and vertical lines of the sketch, if not applied by default.

7. Apply the equal constraint between the lines of equal length, see Figure 3.95.

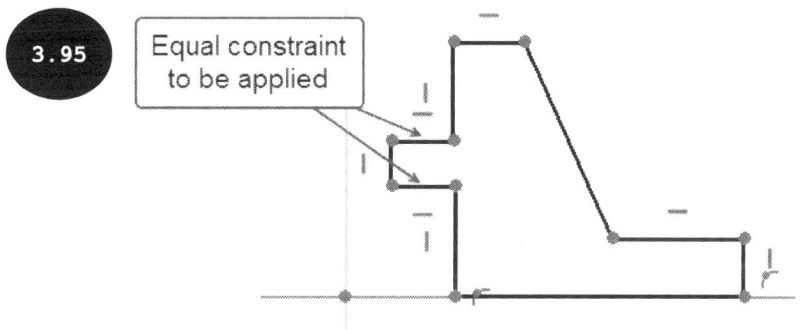

8. After applying the required geometric constraints, apply dimensions to the sketch by using the dimension tools. Figure 3.96 shows a fully defined sketch after applying the required dimensions.

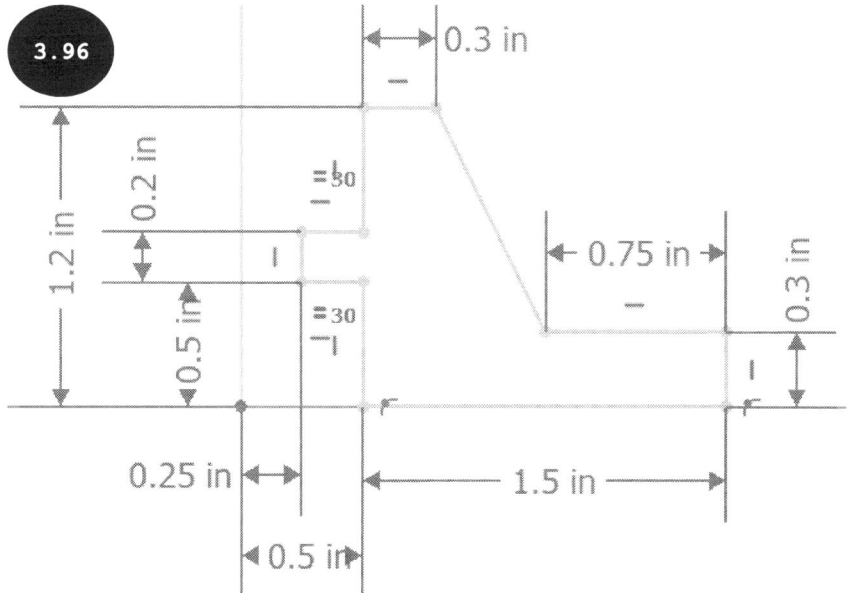

Now, you can exit the **Sketcher** workbench.

9. Click on the **Close** button in the **Task Plane** of the **Combo View** to exit the **Sketcher** workbench and switch back to the **Part Design** workbench.

Section 6: Creating a Revolution Feature

Now, you need to create a revolution feature by revolving the sketch at an angle of 270 degrees around the vertical axis.

1. Click on the **Revolution** tool in the **Part Design Modeling** toolbar, see Figure 3.97. The preview of a revolution feature appears in the 3D View area with the default angle of revolution, see Figure 3.98. Also, the **Revolution parameters** sub-window appears in the **Task Panel** of the **Combo View**, see Figure 3.99.

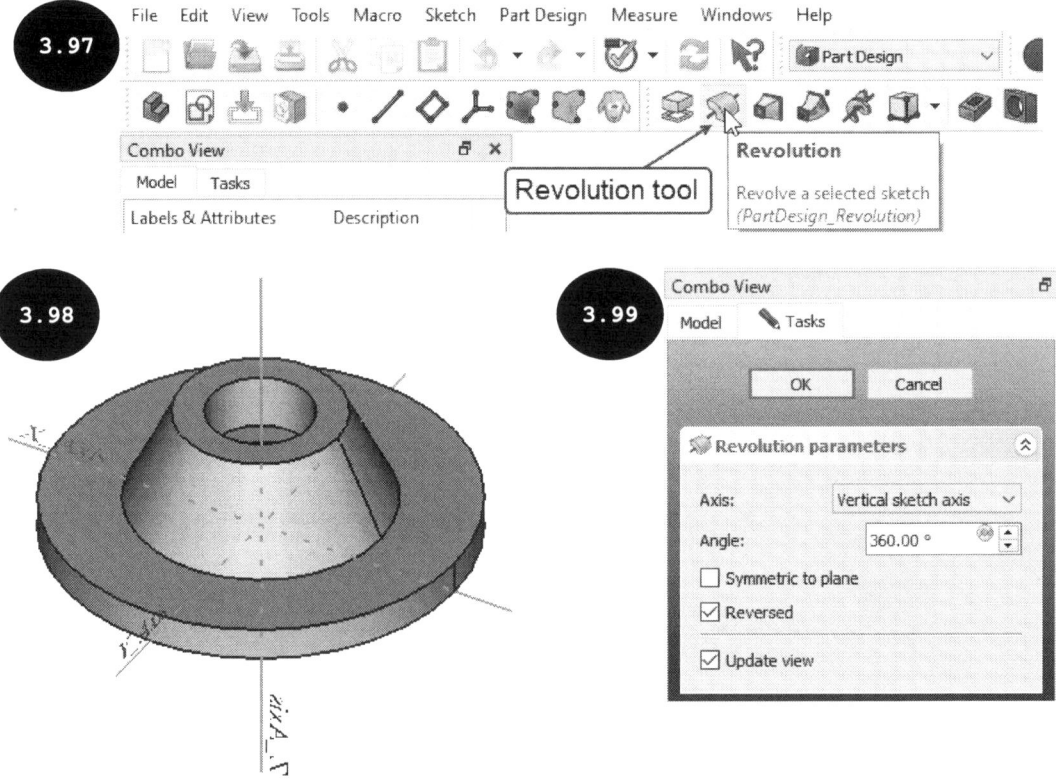

2. Ensure that the **Vertical sketch axis** option is selected in the **Axis** drop-down list of the **Task Panel** to define the vertical axis of the sketch as the axis of revolution.

3. Enter 270 degrees as the angle of revolution in the **Angle** field of the **Task Panel**. A preview of the revolution feature appears by revolving the sketch 270 degrees around the axis of the revolution.

4. If needed, clear the **Reversed** check box in the **Task Panel** to define the direction of revolution of the feature like the one shown in Figure 3.100.

5. Click on the **OK** button in the **Task Panel**. The revolution feature of the specified angle of revolution gets created in the 3D View area, see Figure 3.101.

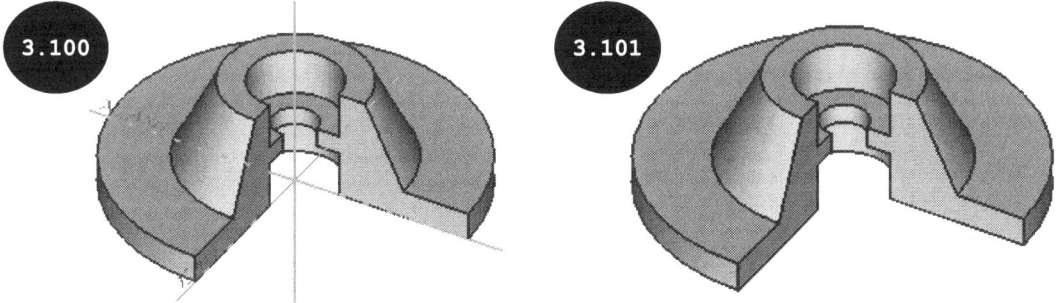

Section 7: Saving the Model

1. Click on the **Save** tool in the **File** toolbar (see Figure 3.102) or press the CTRL + S keys. The **Save FreeCAD Document** dialog box appears.

2. Browse to the *FreeCAD > Chapter 03* folder in the local drive of your system. You need to create these folders, if not created earlier.

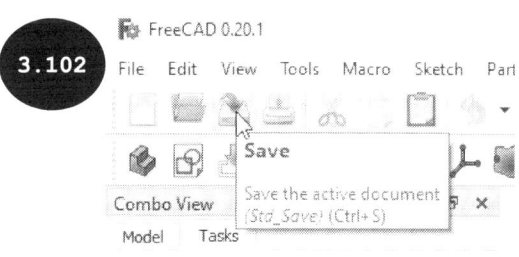

3. Enter **Ch03-Tutorial 2** in the **File name** field of the dialog box. Next, click on the **Save** button in the dialog box. The model gets saved at the specified location. Next, close the document by clicking on **File > Close** in the **Standard Menu**.

Hands-on Test Drive 1

Create the revolution model shown in Figure 3.103. The angle of revolution is 360 degrees around the vertical axis. All dimensions are in mm.

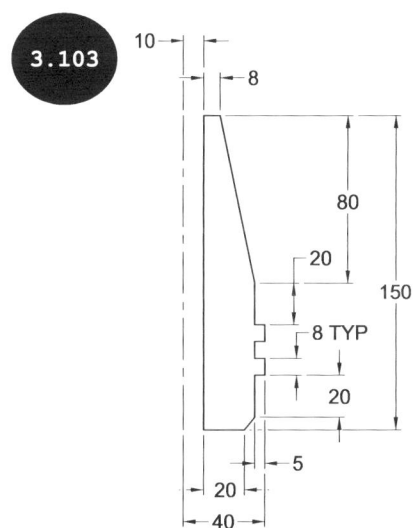

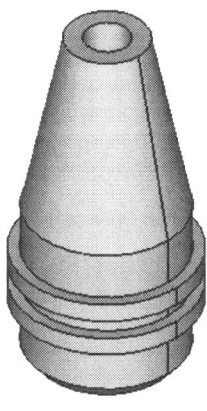

Hands-on Test Drive 2

Create the pad model shown in Figure 3.104. The depth of extrusion is 1.5 inches, symmetrically about the sketching plane. All dimensions are in inches (in).

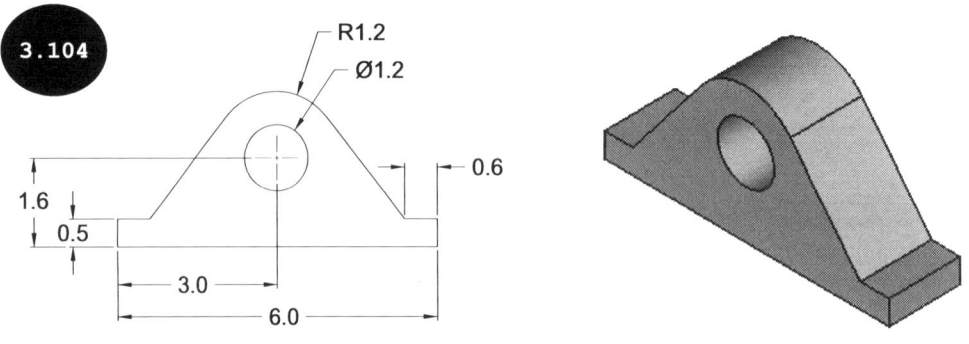

Summary

In this chapter, you have learned about creating the pad and revolution features. The chapter also described various methods for navigating a model, displaying standard views, and changing the display style of a model, in addition to the application of the Navigation Cube.

Questions

Complete and verify the following sentences:

- A _____ feature is created by extruding a sketch normal to the sketching plane.

- The _____ tool is used for creating a feature by revolving a sketch around an axis.

- The _____ tool is used for fitting a model completely inside the graphics area.

- The _____ is used to switch between various standard views of a model.

- In _____ display style, the edges and vertices of a model are displayed in a solid color, while the faces of the model are illuminated depending upon their orientation in the 3D View area.

- The _____ option is used for extruding a sketch on both sides of the sketching plane with different extrusion lengths.

- The _____ option is used for extruding a sketch up to its nearest intersection.

- By default, the direction of extrusion of a pad feature is normal to the sketching plane. (True/False)

- The position of the Navigation Cube is fixed at the upper right corner of the 3D View area. (True/False)

Creating Datum Geometries

This chapter discusses the following topics:

*   Creating Datum Planes
*   Creating Datum Lines/Axes
*   Creating Datum Points
*   Creating a Local Coordinate System

Datum geometries such as datum planes, datum lines, and datum points are used as references to create sketches, features, or other datum geometries. In FreeCAD, the three default datum planes (**XY_Plane**, **XZ_Plane**, and **YZ_Plane**) and three datum axes (**X_Axis**, **Y_Axis**, and **Z_Axis**) are available, by default. You can use these datum geometries for creating sketches and 3D solid features of a model, as discussed in earlier chapters. However, to create a real-world model having multiple features, you may need additional datum geometries, since the default datum geometries may not be enough for creating all features of a 3D model. FreeCAD allows you to create datum planes, datum axes, datum lines, and a local coordinate system by using the respective tools available in the **Part Design Helper** toolbar, see Figure 4.1.

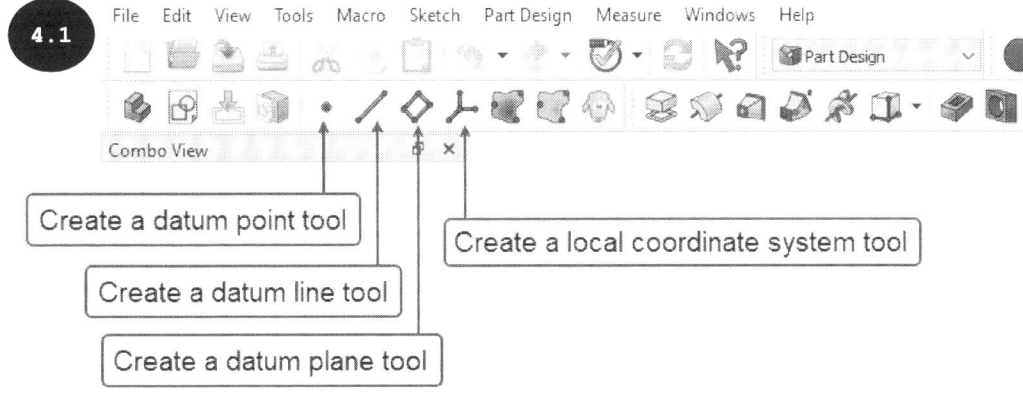

Consider the case of a 3D model shown in Figure 4.2, which consists of four features. Its first feature is a pad feature created on the **YZ_Plane**. The second feature of the model is a pocket feature created on the right planar face of the model by removing material. The third feature is a datum plane created at an angle by using the **Create a datum plane** tool. The fourth feature is a pad feature created on the datum plane. Figure 4.3 illustrates the model creation process.

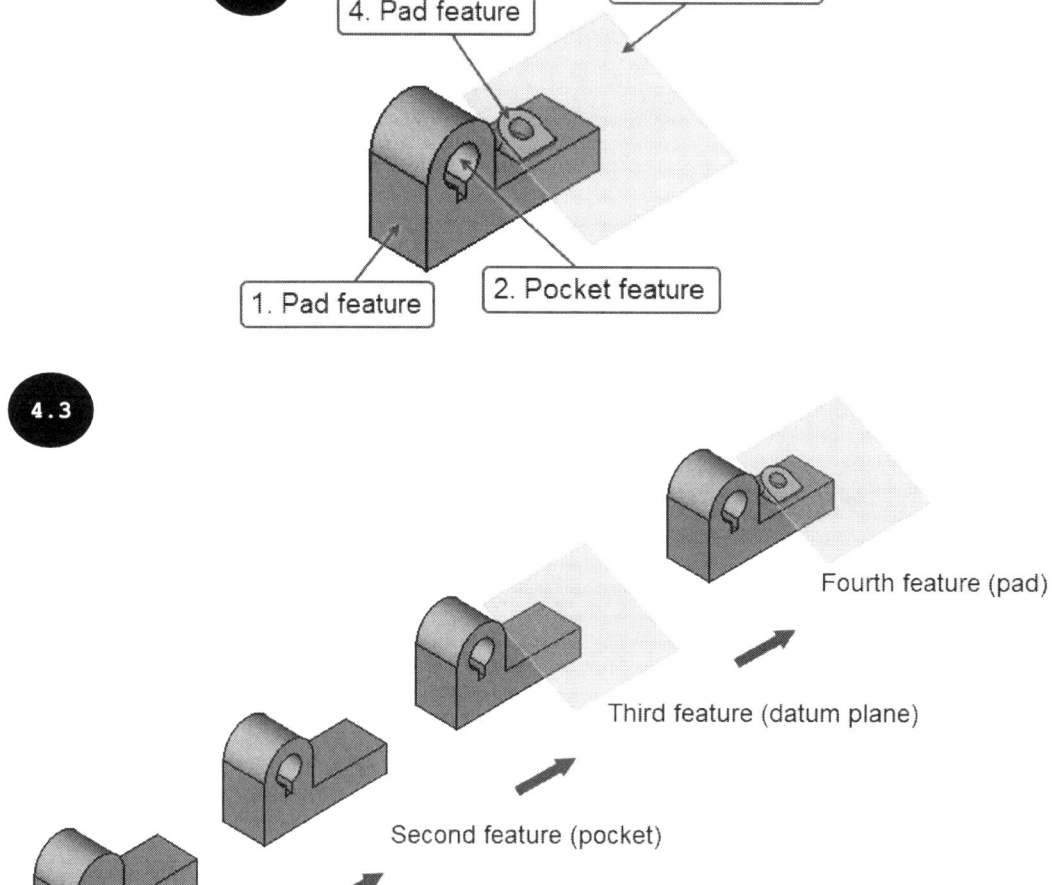

4.2

3. Datum plane

4. Pad feature

1. Pad feature

2. Pocket feature

4.3

Fourth feature (pad)

Third feature (datum plane)

Second feature (pocket)

First feature (pad)

Note: It is evident from the above model that additional datum planes may be needed to create certain features of a model.

Tip: In addition to selecting a datum plane, you can also select a planar face of a model as the sketching plane for creating the sketch of a feature.

Creating Datum Planes

In FreeCAD, you can create datum planes normal to an edge, passing through three vertices, passing through the first two vertices and normal to the third vertex, tangent to a face at a vertex, aligned to a planar face, aligned to the default XY plane, and so on by using the **Create a datum plane** tool.

To create a datum plane, click on the **Create a datum plane** tool in the **Part Design Helper** toolbar, see Figure 4.4. The **Datum Plane parameters** sub-window appears in the **Task Panel** of the **Combo View**, see Figure 4.5. Also, you are prompted to select the first reference for creating a datum plane. The options in the **Task Panel** are used for creating various types of datum planes.

By default, the **Reference1** button is activated and labeled as **Selecting** in the **Task Panel**, indicating that you can select the first reference in the 3D View area for creating a datum plane. You can select an edge, a vertex, a plane, a face, a curve, a circle, or a conic sketch entity as the first reference for creating a datum plane.

After selecting the first reference, the **Reference2** button gets activated automatically in the **Task Panel** and labeled as **Selecting**, indicating that you can select the second reference for creating the datum plane.

Tip: The selection of references depends upon the type of datum plane to be created. For example, to create a datum plane normal to an edge and passing through a vertex, then you need to select a linear edge as the first reference and a vertex as the second reference for creating the datum plane.

Depending upon the type of first reference selected, the list of attachment modes gets filtered in the **Attachment mode** area of the **Task Panel** for creating a datum plane. Also, among them, the most suitable attachment mode is applied to the selected first reference and is highlighted in the **Attachment mode** area of the **Task Panel**. Moreover, the name of the applied attachment mode appears as "**Attached with mode** <*name of the mode*>" at the top of the **Datum Plane parameters** sub-window in the **Task Panel** in green color, see Figure 4.6. The green color indicates that the application of the applied attachment mode is passed. However, if it appears in red, it indicates the application of the applied attachment mode failed to the selected reference geometries of the model. Figure 4.6 shows a list of attachment modes displayed in the **Attachment mode** area when a linear edge is selected as the first reference for creating a datum plane. The methods for creating some of the different types of datum planes are discussed next.

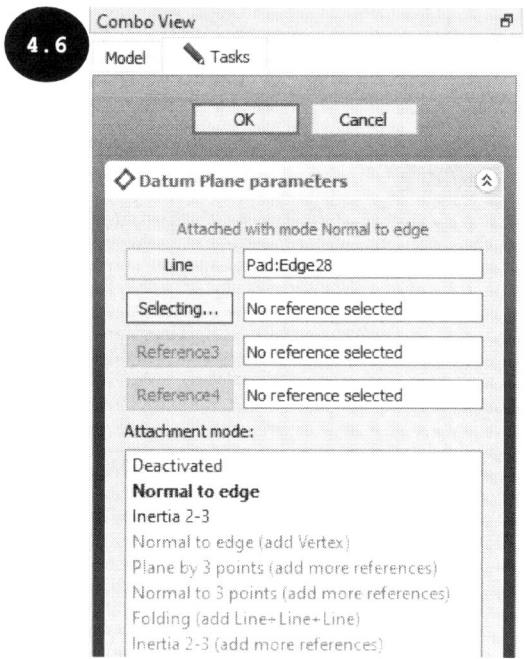

4.6

> **Note:**   An attachment mode is used to attach a plane being created to the selected reference geometries of the model. It creates an association with each other such that if any modification is made to the reference geometries of the model, then the associated datum plane will also be modified accordingly. Various attachment modes are discussed next.

Creating a Datum Plane Coplanar to the Default XY Plane

You can create a datum plane coplanar to the default XY Plane by using the **Deactivated** attachment mode and the method for creating the same is discussed below:

1. Click on the **Create a datum plane** tool in the **Part Design Helper** toolbar, see Figure 4.7. The **Datum Plane parameters** sub-window appears in the **Task Panel**, see Figure 4.8. Also, the preview of a datum plane appears coplanar to the default XY Plane in the 3D View area since, the **Deactivated** mode is activated in the **Attachment mode** area of the **Task Panel**, by default.

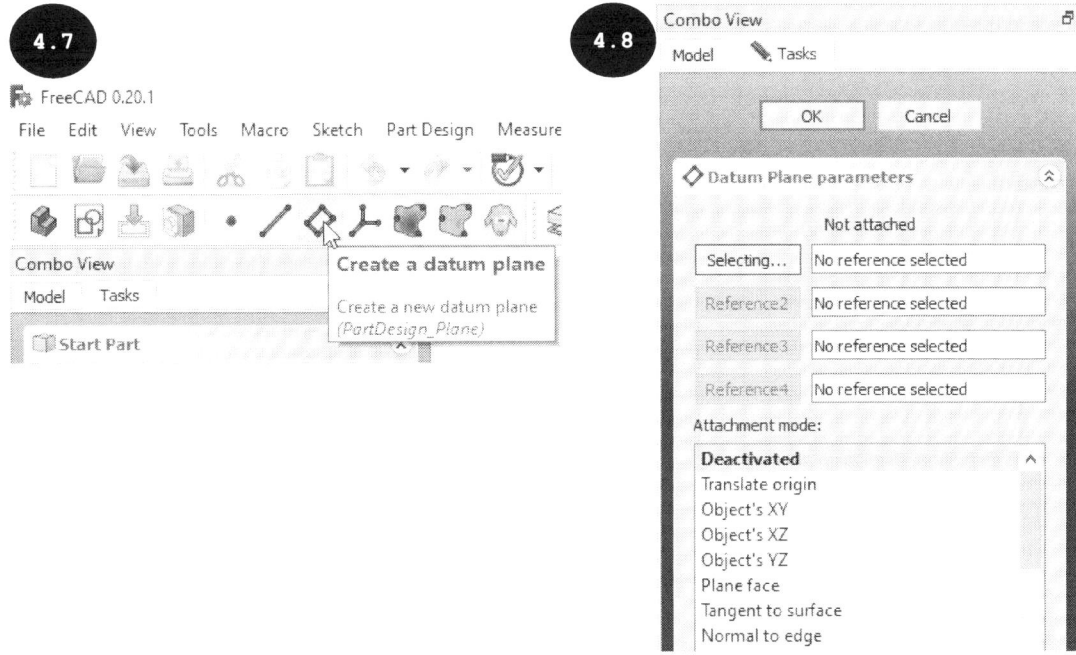

Note: The **Deactivated** mode is used for creating a datum plane coplanar to the default XY Plane. It is the default mode, and the selection of a reference geometry is not required for creating a datum plane by using this attachment mode.

2. Click on the **OK** button in the **Task Panel**. The **Incompatible reference set** window appears, informing that no attachment mode fits the current set of references. Click on the **Yes** button in this window to confirm the creation of the datum plane.

Creating a Datum Plane Normal to an Edge

You can create a datum plane normal to a linear edge of a model by using the **Normal to edge** attachment mode and the method for creating the same is discussed below:

1. Click on the **Create a datum plane** tool in the **Part Design Helper** toolbar, refer to Figure 4.7. The **Datum Plane parameters** sub-window appears in the **Task Panel**. Also, you are prompted to select a first reference for creating a datum plane.

2. Select a linear edge of a model as the first reference. The preview of a datum plane appears normal to the selected edge of the model, see Figure 4.9. Also, the **Normal to edge** mode gets activated in the **Attachment mode** area of the **Task Panel**.

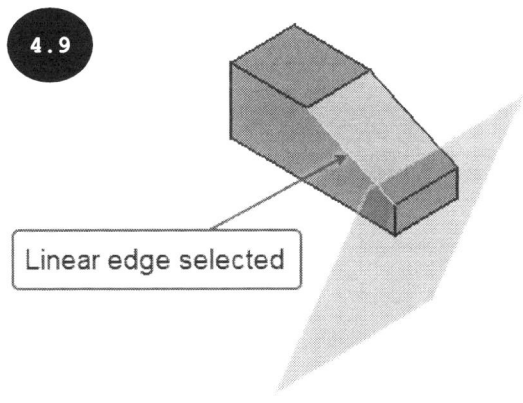

Linear edge selected

Note: You can also create a datum plane normal to a linear edge of a model and passing through a vertex. For doing so, after selecting a linear edge of a model as the first reference, select a vertex of the model as the second reference, see Figure 4.10. Ignore, if an error appears. Next, select the **Normal to edge** mode in the **Attachment mode** area of the **Task Panel**. The preview of a datum plane appears normal to the selected edge and passing through the selected vertex in the 3D View area, see Figure 4.10.

Tip: You can further control the placement and orientation of the datum plane in the 3D View area by specifying translational and rotational values in the respective fields of the **Attachment Offset** area of the **Task Panel**, see Figure 4.11.

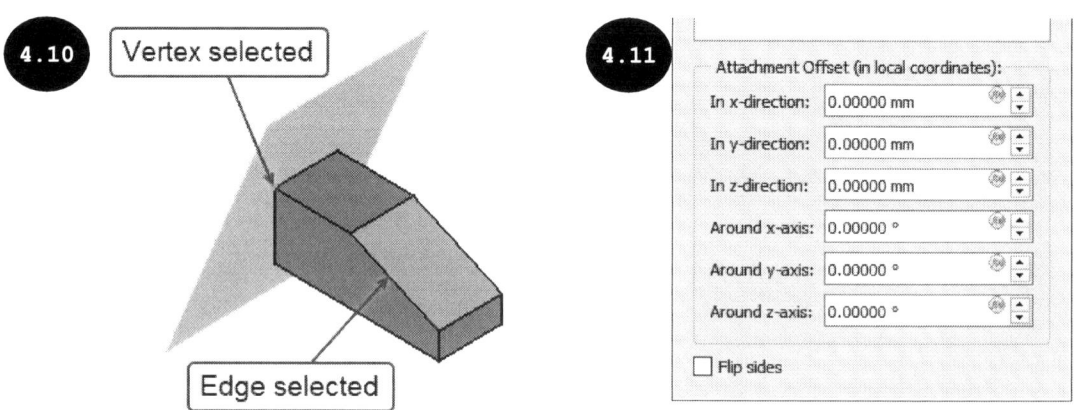

3.   Click on the **OK** button in the **Task Panel** to confirm the creation of the datum plane and exit the **Task Panel**.

Creating a Datum Plane Passing through a Vertex

The method for creating a datum plane passing through a vertex of a model and parallel to the default XY Plane is discussed below:

1.   Click on the **Create a datum plane** tool in the **Part Design Helper** toolbar, see Figure 4.12. The **Datum Plane parameters** sub-window appears in the **Task Panel**. Also, you are prompted to select a first reference for creating a datum plane.

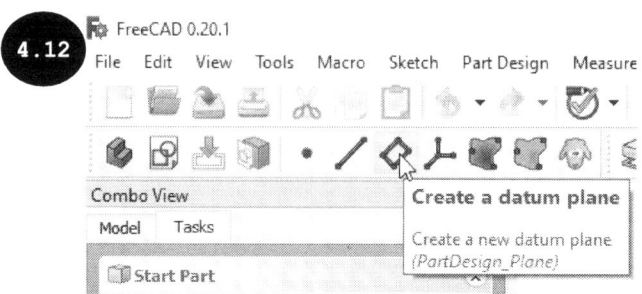

2. Select a vertex of a model as the first reference in the 3D View area. The preview of a datum plane appears passing through the selected vertex and parallel to the default XY Plane in the 3D View area, see Figure 4.13. Also, the **Translate origin** mode gets activated automatically in the **Attachment mode** area of the **Task Panel**.

> **Tip:** You can further control the placement of the datum plane in the 3D View area by specifying translational or offset distance values in the respective fields of the **Attachment Offset** area of the **Task Panel**, see Figure 4.14.

3. Click on the **OK** button in the **Task Panel** to confirm the creation of the datum plane and exit the **Task Panel**.

Creating a Datum Plane Coincide to a Planar Face

The method for creating a datum plane coincides with a plane or a planar face of a model is discussed below:

1. Click on the **Create a datum plane** tool ◇ in the **Part Design Helper** toolbar. The **Datum Plane parameters** sub-window appears in the **Task Panel**. Also, you are prompted to select a first reference for creating a datum plane.

2. Select a plane or a planar face of a model as the first reference in the 3D View area. The preview of a datum plane appears to coincide with the selected plane or planar face in the 3D View area, see Figure 4.15. Also, the **Plane face** mode gets activated automatically in the **Attachment mode** area of the **Task Panel**.

3. Click on the **OK** button in the **Task Panel** to confirm the creation of the datum plane and exit the **Task Panel**.

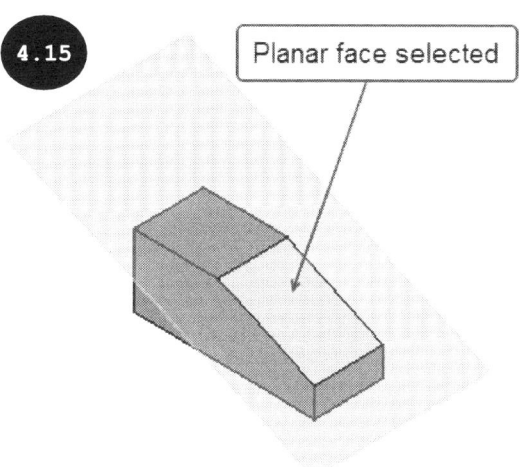

Creating a Datum Plane Tangent to a Face

The method for creating a datum plane tangent to a face of a model at a vertex is discussed below:

1.   Click on the **Create a datum plane** tool ◇ in the **Part Design Helper** toolbar. The **Datum Plane parameters** sub-window appears in the **Task Panel**. Also, you are prompted to select a first reference for creating a datum plane.

2.   Select a face of a model as the first reference and then a vertex as the second reference in the 3D View area. The preview of a datum plane appears such that it is tangent to the selected face of the model and normal to the selected vertex of the model, see Figure 4.16. Also, the **Tangent to surface** mode gets activated automatically in the **Attachment mode** area of the **Task Panel**.

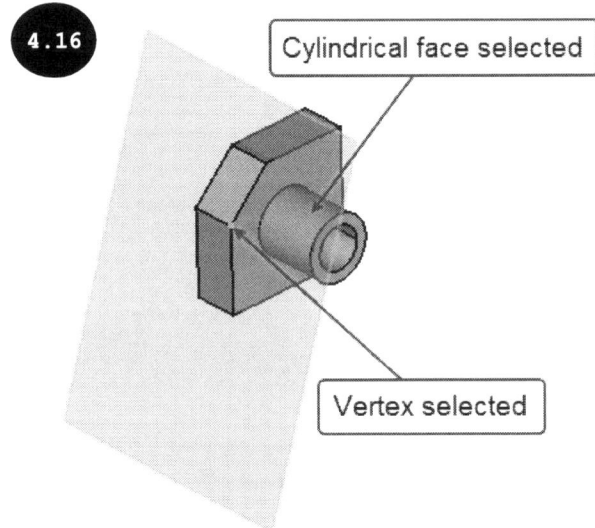

4.16

Cylindrical face selected

Vertex selected

3.   Click on the **OK** button in the **Task Panel** to confirm the creation of the datum plane and exit the Task Panel.

Creating a Datum Plane Aligned to the Plane of an Entity

The method for creating a datum plane aligned to the plane of a circular sketch entity (circle), a curve, or a circular edge of a model is discussed below:

1.   Click on the **Create a datum plane** tool ◇ in the **Part Design Helper** toolbar. The **Datum Plane parameters** sub-window appears in the **Task Panel**. Also, you are prompted to select a first reference for creating a datum plane.

2.   Select a circular sketch entity (circle), a curve, or a circular edge of a model as the first reference. The preview of a datum plane appears aligned to the plane of the selected reference, see Figure 4.17. Also, the **Concentric** mode gets activated automatically in the **Attachment mode** area of the **Task Panel**.

3.   If needed, you can also select a vertex or a point as the second reference to define the orientation of the datum plane.

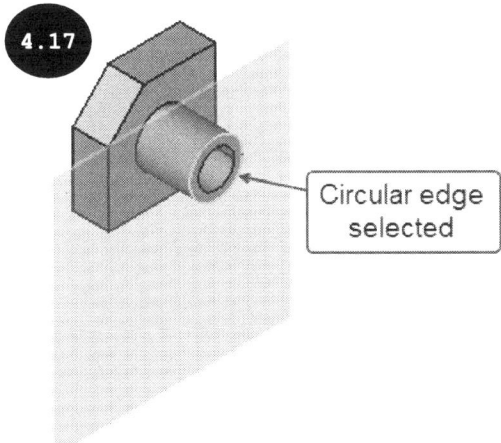

Circular edge
selected

4. Click on the **OK** button in the **Task Panel** to confirm the creation of the datum plane and exit the Task Panel.

Creating a Datum Plane Normal to the Plane of an Entity

The method for creating a datum plane normal to the plane of a circular sketch entity (circle), a curve, or a circular edge of a model is discussed below:

1. Click on the **Create a datum plane** tool ◇ in the **Part Design Helper** toolbar. The **Datum Plane parameters** sub-window appears in the **Task Panel**. Also, you are prompted to select a first reference for creating a datum plane.

2. Select a circular sketch entity (circle), a curve, or a circular edge of a model as the first reference in the 3D View area.

3. Select the **Revolution Section** mode in the **Attachment mode** area of the **Task Panel**. The preview of a datum plane appears normal to the plane of the selected reference, see Figure 4.18.

4. If needed, you can select a vertex or an endpoint of a curve as the second reference for creating a datum plane normal to the plane of the first reference and passing through the vertex selected as the second reference, see Figure 4.19.

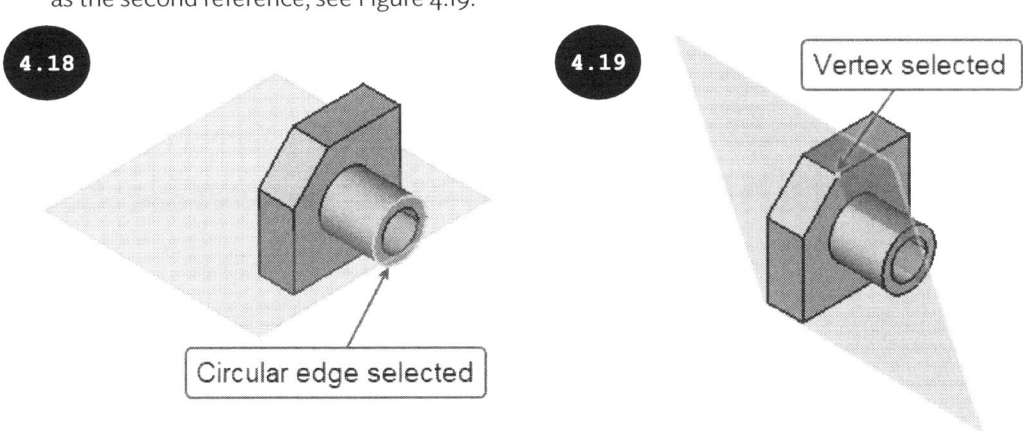

Circular edge selected

Vertex selected

5.   Click on the OK button in the **Task Panel** to confirm the creation of the datum plane and exit the **Task Panel**.

Creating a Datum Plane Passing Through Three Points/Vertices

The method for creating a datum plane passing through three points or vertices of a model is discussed below:

1.   Click on the **Create a datum plane** tool ◇ in the **Part Design Helper** toolbar. The **Datum Plane parameters** sub-window appears in the **Task Panel**. Also, you are prompted to select a first reference for creating a datum plane.

2.   Select three vertices of a model as the first, second, and third references one by one in the 3D View area, see Figure 4.20. The preview of a datum plane appears passing through the selected vertices. Also, the **Plane by 3 points** mode gets selected in the **Attachment mode** area of the **Task Panel**.

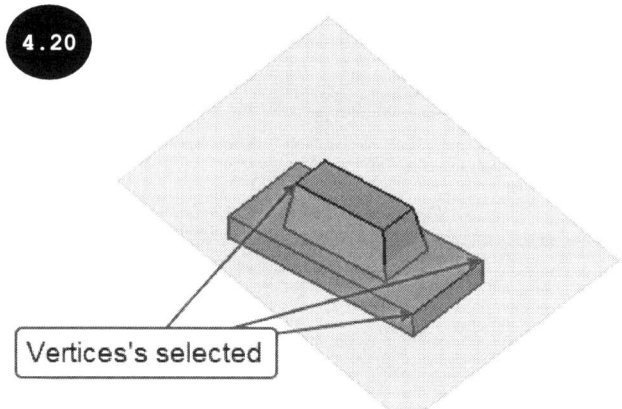

4.20

Vertices's selected

Note: Alternatively, you can also select a linear edge and a vertex or two linear edges as the first and second references for creating a datum plane passing through the selections using the **Plane by 3 points** attachment mode.

3.   Click on the OK button in the **Task Panel** to confirm the creation of the datum plane and exit the **Task Panel**.

Creating a Datum Plane Normal to Three Points/Vertices

The method for creating a datum plane normal to three points or vertices of a model is discussed below:

1.   Click on the **Create a datum plane** tool ◇ in the **Part Design Helper** toolbar. The **Datum Plane parameters** sub-window appears in the **Task Panel**. Also, you are prompted to select a first reference for creating a datum plane.

2.   Select three vertices of a model as the first, second, and third references one by one in the 3D View area.

3.   Select the **Normal to 3 points** mode in the **Attachment mode** area of the **Task Panel**. The preview of a datum plane appears normal to selected references in the **3D View** area.

Note: Alternatively, you can also select a linear edge and a vertex or two linear edges as the first and second references for creating a datum plane normal to the selections using the **Normal to 3 points** attachment mode.

---

4.   Click on the **OK** button in the **Task Panel** to confirm the creation of the datum plane and exit the Task Panel.

Creating a Datum Plane Normal to a Curve

The method for creating a datum plane normal to a curve is discussed below:

1.   Click on the **Create a datum plane** tool ◈ in the **Part Design Helper** toolbar. The **Datum Plane parameters** sub-window appears in the **Task Panel**. Also, you are prompted to select a first reference for creating a datum plane.

2.   Select a curve or a circular edge as the first reference in the 3D View area. The **Frenet NB** mode gets activated in the **Attachment mode** area of the **Task Panel**, automatically. Also, the preview of a datum plane appears normal to the selected curve such that the normal-binormal (NB) axes of the frenet-serret coordinate get aligned at an endpoint of the curve or the center of the circular edge, see Figures 4.21 and 4.22. Figure 4.21 shows the preview of a datum plane normal to a curve and Figure 4.22 shows the axes (N, B, and T) of the frenet-serret coordinate for your reference.

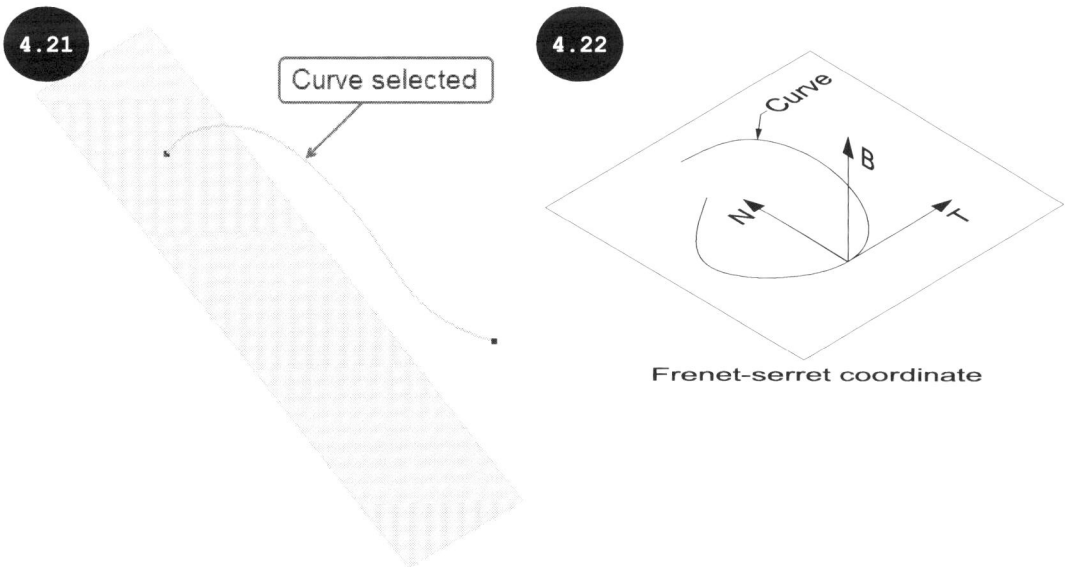

Frenet-serret coordinate

Tip: After selecting a curve as the first reference, you can also select a point as the second reference to define the location of the datum plane along the curve, if needed.

3.   Click on the **OK** button in the **Task Panel** to confirm the creation of the datum plane and exit the **Task Panel**.

Creating a Datum Plane Coincide to the Plane of a Curve

The method for creating a datum plane that coincides with the plane of a curve is discussed below:

1.   Click on the **Create a datum plane** tool ◈ in the **Part Design Helper** toolbar. The **Datum Plane parameters** sub-window appears in the **Task Panel**. Also, you are prompted to select a first reference for creating a datum plane.

2.   Select a curve or a circular edge as the first reference in the 3D View area. Next, select the **Frenet TN** mode in the **Attachment mode** area of the **Task Panel.** The preview of a datum plane appears coincident with the plane of the curve such that the tangent-normal (TN) axes of the frenet-serret coordinate get aligned to the plane of the curve. Refer to Figure 4.22 for the axes (N, B, and T) of the frenet-serret coordinate.

3.   Click on the **OK** button in the **Task Panel** to confirm the creation of the datum plane and exit the **Task Panel**.

Creating a Datum Plane Tangent to an Endpoint of a Curve

The method for creating a datum plane tangent to an endpoint of a curve is discussed below:

1.   Click on the **Create a datum plane** tool ◈ in the **Part Design Helper** toolbar. The **Datum Plane parameters** sub-window appears in the **Task Panel**. Also, you are prompted to select a first reference for creating a datum plane.

2.   Select a curve or a circular edge as the first reference in the 3D View area. Next, select the **Frenet TB** mode in the **Attachment mode** area of the **Task Panel.** The preview of a datum plane appears tangent to an endpoint of the selected curve such that the tangent-binormal (TB) axes of the frenet-serret coordinate get aligned at an endpoint of the curve, see Figure 4.23. Refer to Figure 4.22 for the axes (N, B, and T) of the frenet-serret coordinate.

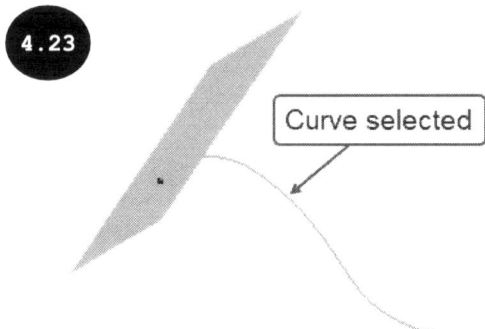

4.23

Curve selected

Tip: You can also select a point or a vertex as the second reference to define an endpoint of the curve for creating a datum plane tangent to it.

3.	Click on the OK button in the **Task Panel** to confirm the creation of the datum plane and exit the Task Panel.

Creating a Datum Plane Aligned to the XY Plane of a Conic Curve

The method for creating a datum plane aligned to the local XY plane of a conic curve or edge is discussed below:

1.	Click on the **Create a datum plane** tool ◇ in the **Part Design Helper** toolbar. The **Datum Plane parameters** sub-window appears in the **Task Panel**. Also, you are prompted to select a first reference for creating a datum plane.

2.	Select a conical edge or a conic curve (sketch) such as an ellipse, a hyperbolic arc, or a parabolic arc as the first reference in the 3D View area. The preview of a datum plane appears aligned to the local XY plane of the selected entity, see Figure 4.24. Also, the **Object's XY** mode gets selected in the **Attachment mode** area of the **Task Panel**.

3.	Click on the OK button in the **Task Panel** to confirm the creation of the datum plane and exit the Task Panel.

Creating a Datum Plane Aligned to the XZ Plane of a Conic Curve

The method for creating a datum plane aligned to the local XZ plane of a conic curve or edge is discussed below:

1.	Click on the **Create a datum plane** tool ◇ in the **Part Design Helper** toolbar. The **Datum Plane parameters** sub-window appears in the **Task Panel**. Also, you are prompted to select a first reference for creating a datum plane.

2.	Select a conical edge or a conic curve (sketch) such as an ellipse, a hyperbolic arc, or a parabolic arc as the first reference in the 3D View area. Next, select the **Object's XZ** mode in the **Attachment mode** area of the **Task Panel**. The preview of a datum plane appears aligned to the local XZ plane of the selected entity, see Figure 4.25.

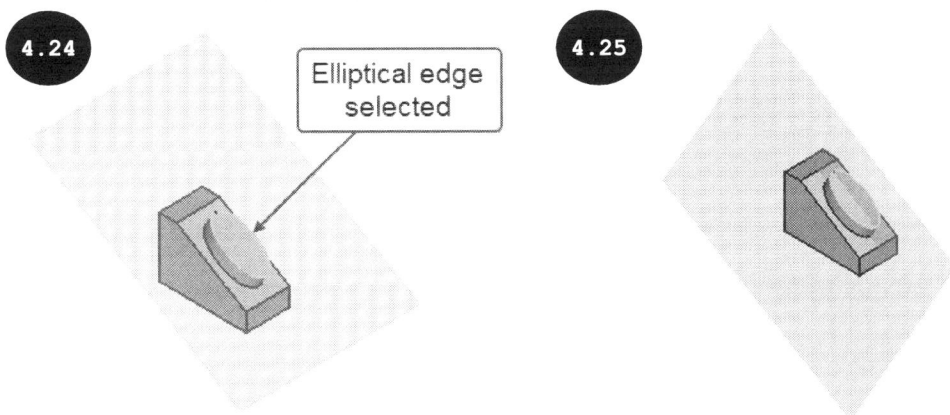

4.24   Elliptical edge selected

4.25

3.	Click on the OK button in the **Task Panel** to confirm the creation of the datum plane and exit the Task Panel.

Creating a Datum Plane Aligned to the YZ Plane of a Conic Curve

The method for creating a datum plane aligned to the local YZ plane of a conic curve or edge is discussed below:

1.   Click on the **Create a datum plane** tool ◇ in the **Part Design Helper** toolbar. The **Datum Plane parameters** sub-window appears in the **Task Panel**. Also, you are prompted to select a first reference for creating a datum plane.

2.   Select a conical edge or a conic curve (sketch) such as an ellipse, a hyperbolic arc, or a parabolic arc as the first reference in the 3D View area. Next, select the **Object's YZ** mode in the **Attachment mode** area of the **Task Panel**. The preview of a datum plane appears aligned to the local YZ plane of the selected entity, see Figure 4.26.

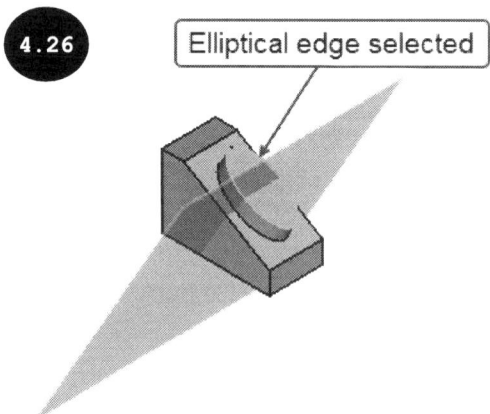

Figure 4.26 — Elliptical edge selected

3.   Click on the **OK** button in the **Task Panel** to confirm the creation of the datum plane and exit the Task Panel.

Creating a Datum Plane Passing Through 2 and 3 Axes of Inertia

The method for creating a datum plane passing through the second and third principal axes of inertia is discussed below:

1.   Click on the **Create a datum plane** tool ◇ in the **Part Design Helper** toolbar. The **Datum Plane parameters** sub-window appears in the **Task Panel**. Also, you are prompted to select a first reference for creating a datum plane.

2.   Select an object such as a plane, a face, an edge, a vertex, or a sketch as the first reference. The preview of a datum plane appears depending on the type of entity selected.

3.   Select the **Inertia 2-3** mode in the **Attachment mode** area of the **Task Panel**. The preview of a datum plane appears passing through the second and third principal axes of inertia of the selected entity.

4. Similarly, you can select an object as the second reference or second and third references one by one in the 3D View area, if needed. The preview of a datum plane appears passing through the second and third principal axes of inertia (center of mass) of the selected entities, accordingly.

5. Click on the OK button in the Task Panel to confirm the creation of the datum plane and exit the Task Panel.

Creating Datum Lines/Axes

You can also create datum lines that can be used as axes of revolution for creating features such as revolution, groove, and polar patterns similar to creating datum planes. To create a datum line/axis, click on the Create a datum line tool in the Part Design Helper toolbar, see Figure 4.27. The Datum Line parameters sub-window appears in the Task Panel of the Combo View, see Figure 4.28. Also, you are prompted to select the first reference for creating a datum line/axis. The options in the Task Panel are used for creating various types of datum lines. The methods for creating some of the different types of datum lines/axes are discussed next.

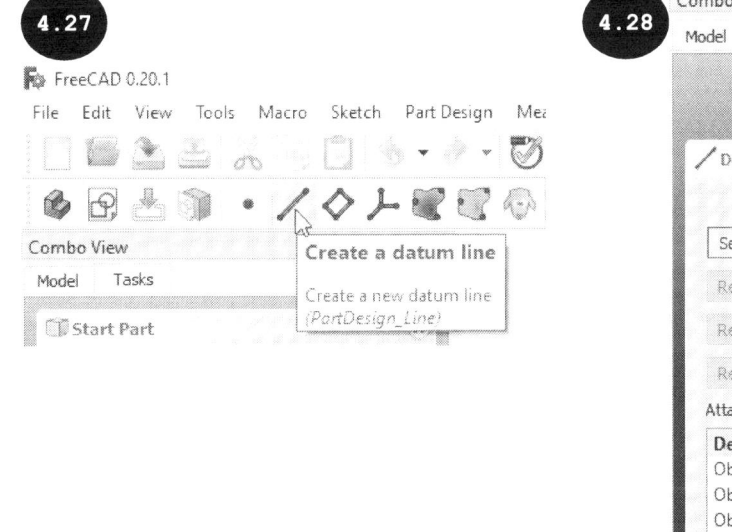

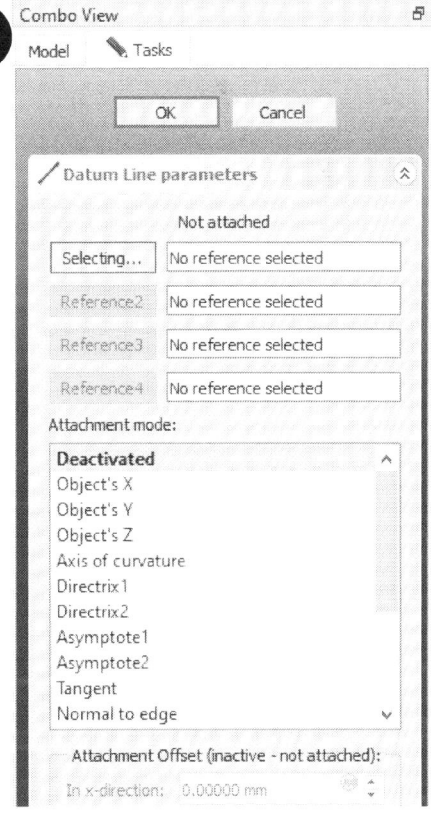

Creating a Datum Line Along the Default Z Axis

The method for creating a datum plane along the default Z axis is discussed below:

1. Click on the **Create a datum line** tool ✎ in the **Part Design Helper** toolbar, refer to Figure 4.27. The **Datum Line parameters** sub-window appears in the **Task Panel**. Also, the preview of a datum line appears along to the default Z axis in the 3D View area since, the **Deactivated** mode is activated in the **Attachment mode** area of the **Task Panel**, by default.

2. Click on the **OK** button in the **Task Panel**. The **Incompatible reference set** window appears, informing that no attachment mode fits the current set of references. Click on the **Yes** button in this window to continue with the creation of the datum axis along the default Z axis.

Creating a Datum Line Passing Through Two Points

The method for creating a datum line passing through two points or along an edge is discussed below:

1. Click on the **Create a datum line** tool ✎ in the **Part Design Helper** toolbar. The **Datum Line parameters** sub-window appears in the **Task Panel**, and you are prompted to select the first reference.

2. Select two vertices of a model as the first and second references one by one in the 3D View area. The preview of a datum axis/line appears passing through the selected vertices, see Figure 4.29. Also, the **Through two points** mode gets activated in the **Attachment mode** area of the **Task Panel**.

Note: Instead of selecting two vertices, you can also select a linear edge of a model as the first reference for creating a datum axis along it by using the **Through two points** attachment mode, see Figure 4.30.

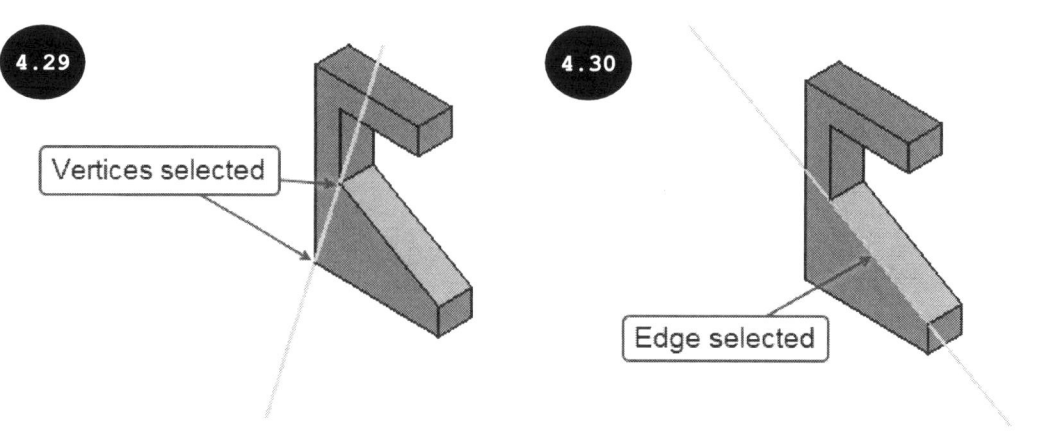

Tip: You can further control the placement and orientation of the datum line in the 3D View area by specifying translational and rotational values in the respective fields of the **Attachment Offset** area in the **Task Panel**, see Figure 4.31.

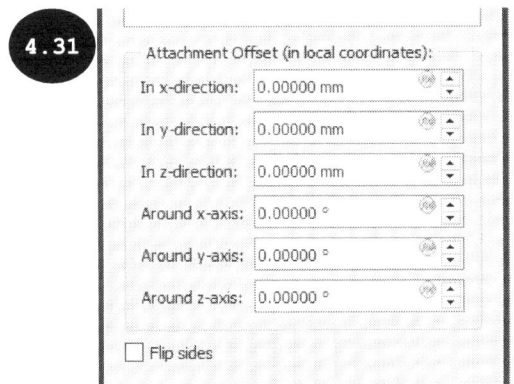

3. Click on the OK button in the **Task Panel** to confirm the creation of the datum axis and exit the Task Panel.

Creating a Datum Line Along the Axis of Curvature

The method for creating a datum line along the axis of curvature of a curved edge is discussed below:

1. Click on the **Create a datum line** tool ✏ in the **Part Design Helper** toolbar. The **Datum Line parameters** sub-window appears in the **Task Panel**, and you are prompted to select the first reference.

2. Select a curved edge of a model as the first reference in the 3D View area. The preview of a datum axis/line appears along the axis of curvature of the selected entity, see Figure 4.32. Also, the **Axis of Curvature** mode gets activated in the **Attachment mode** area of the **Task Panel**.

Tip: You can further control the placement and orientation of the datum line/axis in the 3D View area by specifying translational and rotational values in the respective fields of the **Attachment Offset** area in the **Task Panel**, see Figure 4.33.

3. Click on the OK button in the **Task Panel** to confirm the creation of the datum axis and exit the Task Panel.

Creating a Datum Line Tangent to an Edge

The method for creating a datum line tangent to an edge at a vertex is discussed below:

1. Click on the **Create a datum line** tool ✎ in the **Part Design Helper** toolbar. The **Datum Line parameters** sub-window appears in the **Task Panel**, and you are prompted to select the first reference.

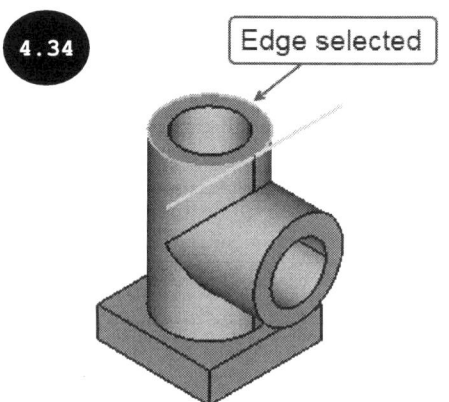

2. Select a curved edge of a model as the first reference in the 3D View area. Next, select the **Tangent** mode in the **Attachment mode** area of the **Task Panel**. The preview of a datum line appears tangent to the selected circular edge of the model, see Figure 4.34.

Tip: If needed, you can also select a vertex as the second reference to define the location of the datum line tangent to the selected edge of the model.

3. Click on the **OK** button in the **Task Panel** to confirm the creation of the datum axis and exit the **Task Panel**.

Creating a Datum Line Normal to a Curved Edge

The method for creating a datum line normal to a curved edge is discussed below:

1. Click on the **Create a datum line** tool ✎ in the **Part Design Helper** toolbar. The **Datum Line parameters** sub-window appears in the **Task Panel**.

2. Select a curved edge of a model as the first reference in the 3D View area. Next, select the **Normal to edge** mode in the **Attachment mode** area of the **Task Panel**. The preview of a datum plane appears normal to the selected edge such that it gets aligned to the N axis of its frenet-serret coordinate in the 3D View area, see Figures 4.35 and 4.36.

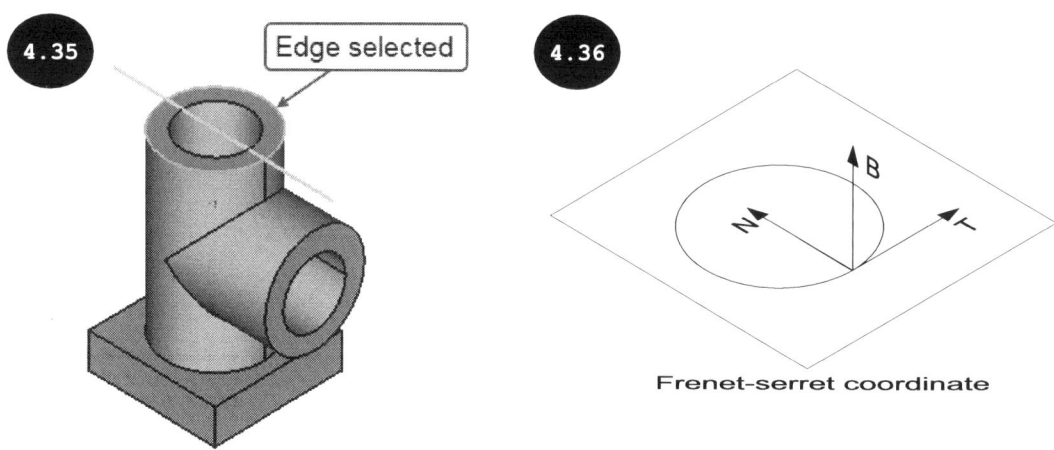

Frenet-serret coordinate

Tip: If needed, you can also select a vertex as the second reference to define the location of the datum line normal to the selected edge of the model.

3. Click on the **OK** button in the **Task Panel** to confirm the creation of the datum axis and exit the Task Panel.

Creating a Datum Line Binormal to a Curved Edge

The method for creating a datum line normal to a curved edge is discussed below:

1. Click on the **Create a datum line** tool ✏ in the **Part Design Helper** toolbar. The **Datum Line parameters** sub-window appears in the **Task Panel**, and you are prompted to select the first reference.

2. Select a curved edge of a model as the first reference in the 3D View area. Next, select the **Binormal** mode in the **Attachment mode** area of the **Task Panel**. The preview of a datum plane appears normal to the selected edge such that it gets aligned to the B axis of its frenet-serret coordinate in the 3D View area, see Figure 4.37. Refer to Figure 4.36 for the frenet-serret coordinate.

Tip: If needed, you can also select a vertex as the second reference to define the location of the datum line normal to the selected edge of the model.

3. Click on the **OK** button in the **Task Panel** to confirm the creation of the datum axis and exit the Task Panel.

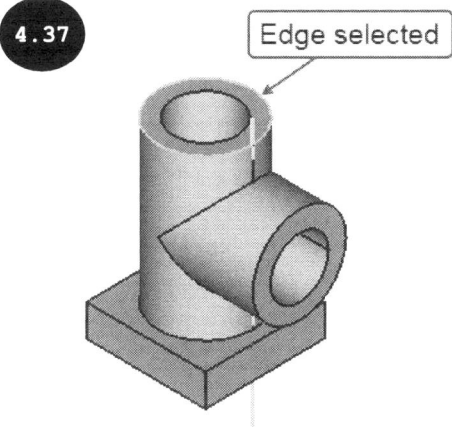

4.37

Edge selected

Creating a Datum Line along the First Principal Axis of Inertia

The method for creating a datum line along the first principal axis of inertia is discussed below:

1. Click on the **Create a datum line** tool ✏ in the **Part Design Helper** toolbar. The **Datum Line parameters** sub-window appears in the **Task Panel**, and you are prompted to select the first reference.

2.   Select a planar or curved face of a model as the first reference in the 3D View area. The preview of a datum plane appears such that it follows the first principal axis of inertia, see Figure 4.38. Also, the **1st principal axis** mode gets activated in the **Attachment mode** area of the **Task Panel**.

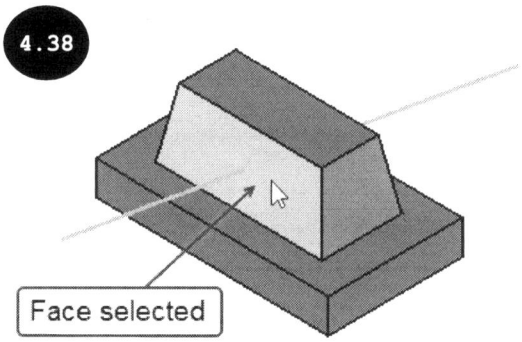

Face selected

Note: You can also select second, third, and/or fourth references (faces) one by one in the 3D View area for creating a datum line following the first principal axis of inertia of the selected references (faces).

3.   Click on the **OK** button in the **Task Panel** to confirm the creation of the datum axis and exit the Task Panel.

Creating a Datum Line along the Second Principal Axis of Inertia

The method for creating a datum line along the second principal axis of inertia is discussed below:

1.   Click on the **Create a datum line** tool ✎ in the **Part Design Helper** toolbar. The **Datum Line parameters** sub-window appears in the **Task Panel**, and you are prompted to select the first reference.

2.   Select a planar or curved face of a model as the first reference in the 3D View area. Next, select the **2nd principal axis** mode in the **Attachment mode** area of the **Task Panel**. The preview of a datum plane appears such that it follows the second principal axis of inertia, see Figure 4.39.

Note: You can also select the faces as the second, third, and/or fourth references one by one in the 3D View area for creating a datum line following the second principal axis of inertia of the selected references. After selecting the references, you need to activate the **2nd principal axis** mode in the **Attachment mode** area of the **Task Panel**.

3.   Click on the **OK** button in the **Task Panel** to confirm the creation of the datum axis and exit the Task Panel.

Creating a Datum Line along the Third Principal Axis of Inertia

The method for creating a datum line along the third principal axis of inertia is discussed below:

1. Click on the **Create a datum line** tool ✏ in the **Part Design Helper** toolbar. You are prompted to select the first reference.

2. Select a planar or curved face of a model as the first reference in the 3D View area. Next, select the **3rd principal axis** mode in the **Attachment mode** area of the **Task Panel**. The preview of a datum plane appears such that it follows the third principal axis of inertia, see Figure 4.40.

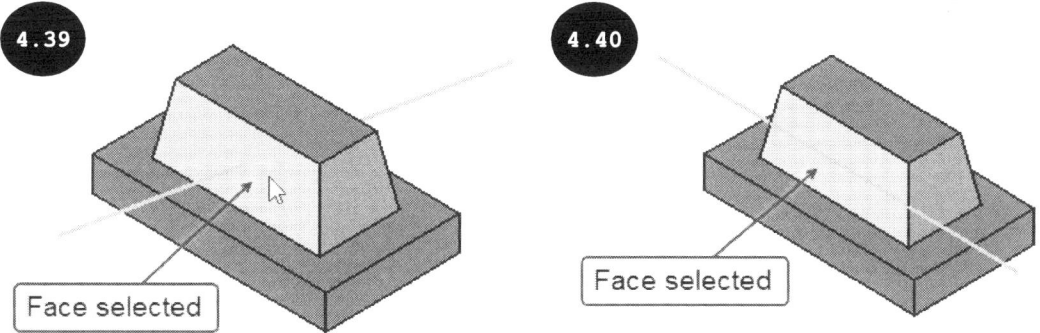

Note: You can also select the faces as the second, third, and/or fourth references one by one in the 3D View area for creating a datum line following the third principal axis of inertia of the selected references. After selecting the references, you need to activate the **3rd principal axis** mode in the **Attachment mode** area of the **Task Panel**.

3. Click on the OK button in the **Task Panel** to confirm the creation of the datum axis and exit the Task Panel.

Creating a Datum Line Along the Local X-Axis of a Conic Curve

The method for creating a datum line along the local X-axis of a conic curve/edge is discussed below:

1. Click on the **Create a datum line** tool ✏ in the **Part Design Helper** toolbar. The **Datum Line parameters** sub-window appears in the **Task Panel**.

2. Select a conical edge or a conic curve (sketch) such as an ellipse, a hyperbolic arc, or a parabolic arc as the first reference in the 3D View area. Next, select the **Object's X** mode in the **Attachment** mode area of the **Task Panel**. The preview of a datum line appears aligned to the local X-axis of the selected reference, see Figure 4.41.

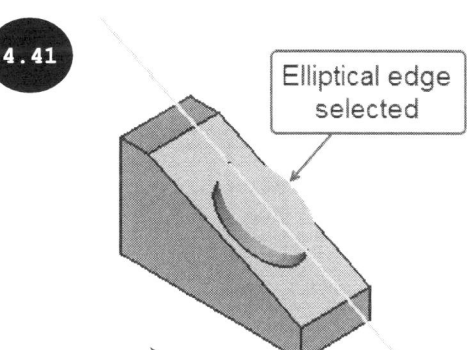

3.   Click on the **OK** button in the **Task Panel** to confirm the creation of the datum axis and exit the **Task Panel**.

Tip: As discussed earlier, you can further control the placement and orientation of the datum line in the 3D View area by specifying translational and rotational values in the respective fields of the **Attachment Offset** area in the **Task Panel**.

Creating a Datum Line Along the Local Y-Axis of a Conic Curve

The method for creating a datum line aligned along the local Y-axis of a conic curve or edge is discussed below:

1.   Click on the **Create a datum line** tool in the **Part Design Helper** toolbar. The **Datum Line parameters** sub-window appears in the **Task Panel**, and you are prompted to select the first reference.

2.   Select a conical edge or a conic curve (sketch) such as an ellipse, a hyperbolic arc, or a parabolic arc as the first reference in the 3D View area. Next, select the **Object's Y** mode in the **Attachment mode** area of the **Task Panel**. The preview of a datum line appears aligned to the local Y-axis of the selected reference, see Figure 4.42.

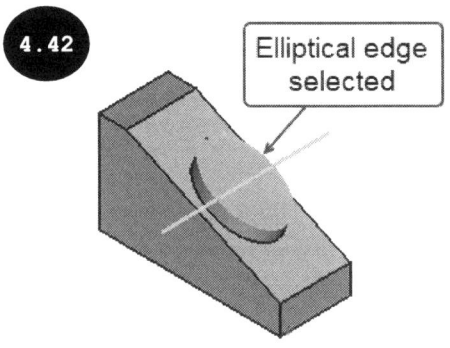

3.   Click on the **OK** button in the **Task Panel** to confirm the creation of the datum axis and exit the **Task Panel**.

Creating a Datum Line Along the Local Z-Axis of a Conic Curve

The method for creating a datum line aligned along the local Z-axis of a conic curve or edge is discussed below:

1.   Click on the **Create a datum line** tool in the **Part Design Helper** toolbar. The **Datum Line parameters** sub-window appears in the **Task Panel**, and you are prompted to select the first reference.

2.   Select a conical edge or a conic curve (sketch) such as an ellipse, a hyperbolic arc, or a parabolic arc as the first reference in the 3D View area. Next, select the **Object's Z** mode in the **Attachment mode** area of the **Task Panel**. The preview of a datum line appears aligned to the local Z-axis of the selected reference, see Figure 4.43.

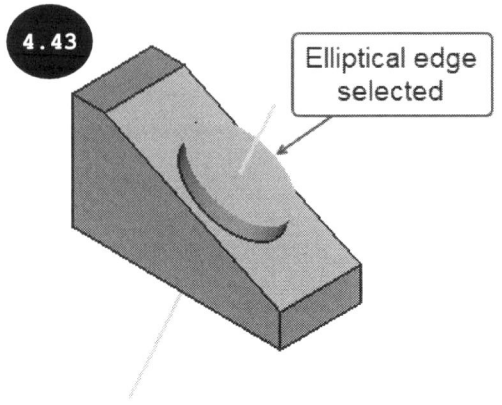

3.   Click on the **OK** button in the **Task Panel** to confirm the creation of the datum axis and exit the **Task Panel**.

Creating Datum Points

A datum point can be created anywhere on a 3D model or space. It can be used as a reference point for measuring distances, creating sketches and datum geometries, and so on. To create a datum point, click on the **Create a datum point** tool in the **Part Design Helper** toolbar, see Figure 4.44. The **Datum Point parameters** sub-window appears in the **Task Panel** of the **Combo View**, see Figure 4.45. Also, you are prompted to select the first reference for creating a datum point. The options in the **Task Panel** are used for creating various types of datum points. The methods for creating some of the different types of datum points are discussed next.

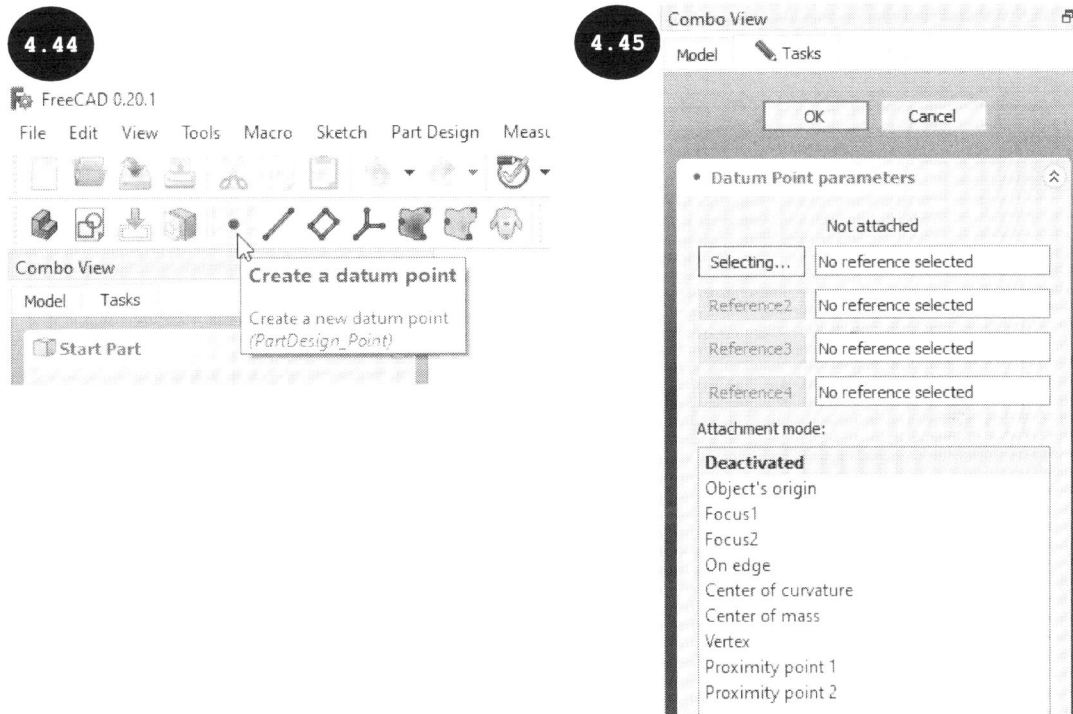

Creating a Datum Point at the Origin

The method for creating a datum point at the origin is discussed below:

1. Click on the **Create a datum point** tool ● in the **Part Design Helper** toolbar, refer to Figure 4.44. The **Datum Point parameters** sub-window appears in the **Task Panel**. Also, the preview of a datum point appears at the origin in the 3D View area since, the **Deactivated** mode is activated in the **Attachment mode** area of the **Task Panel**, by default.

2. Click on the **OK** button in the **Task Panel**. The **Incompatible reference set** window appears, informing that no attachment mode fits the current set of references. Click on the **Yes** button in this window to continue with the creation of the datum point at the origin.

Creating a Datum Point at the Center of Mass

The method for creating a datum point at the center of mass of the selected references (faces, edges, or vertices) is discussed below:

1. Click on the **Create a datum point tool** • in the **Part Design Helper** toolbar. The **Datum Point parameters** sub-window appears in the **Task Panel**.

2. Select a face, an edge, or a vertex of a model as the first reference. The preview of a datum point appears at the center of mass of the selected reference, see Figures 4.46 and 4.47. Ensure that the **Center of mass** mode gets activated in the **Attachment mode** area of the **Task Panel** for creating a datum point at the center of mass of the selected reference.

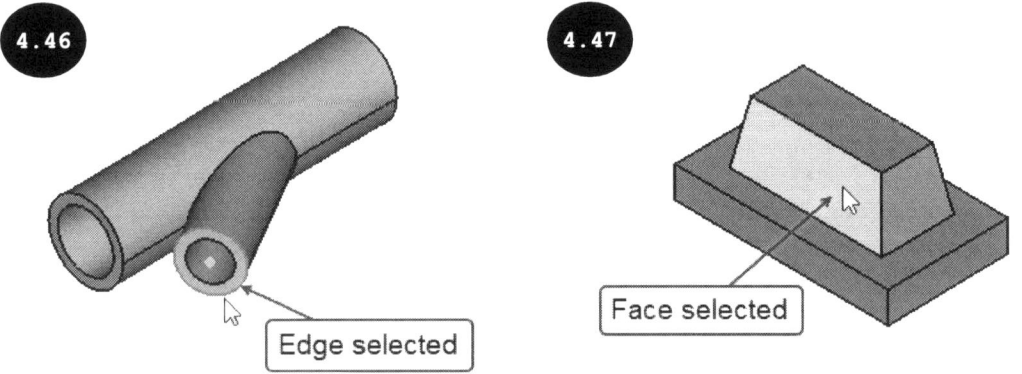

4.46 Edge selected

4.47 Face selected

> **Note:** When you select a vertex or an edge of a model as the first reference, you need to select the **Center of mass** mode manually in the **Attachment mode** area of the **Task Panel** for creating a datum point at the center of mass of the selected reference.

3. If needed, you can also select the second, third, and/or fourth references for creating a datum point at the center of mass of the selected references. You can select faces, edges, or vertices of a model as references in the 3D View area. After selecting the required references, ensure that the **Center of mass** mode is activated in the **Attachment mode** area of the **Task Panel**.

> **Tip:** You can further control the placement and orientation of the datum point in the 3D View area by specifying translational and rotational values in the respective fields of the **Attachment Offset** area in the **Task Panel**, see Figure 4.48.

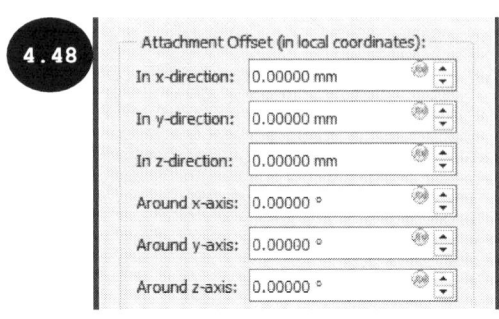

4.48

Attachment Offset (in local coordinates):	
In x-direction:	0.00000 mm
In y-direction:	0.00000 mm
In z-direction:	0.00000 mm
Around x-axis:	0.00000 °
Around y-axis:	0.00000 °
Around z-axis:	0.00000 °

4. Click on the **OK** button in the **Task Panel** to confirm the creation of the datum point and exit the **Task Panel**.

Creating a Datum Point at the Center of Curvature

The method for creating a datum point at the center of curvature of a circular edge, a circle, or a curve is discussed below:

1. Click on the **Create a datum point** tool ✷ in the **Part Design Helper** toolbar. The **Datum Point parameters** sub-window appears in the **Task Panel**, and you are prompted to select the first reference.

2. Select a circular edge of a model, a circle, or a curve as the first reference in the 3D View area. The preview of a datum point appears at the center of curvature of the selected reference, see Figure 4.49. Also, the **Center of curvature** mode gets activated in the **Attachment mode** area of the **Task Panel**.

Tip: You can further control the placement of the datum point in the 3D View area by specifying translational and rotational values in the respective fields of the **Attachment Offset** area in the **Task Panel**.

---

3. Click on the **OK** button in the **Task Panel** to confirm the creation of the datum point and exit the **Task Panel**.

Creating a Datum Point onto a Vertex

The method for creating a datum point onto a vertex of a model is discussed below:

1. Click on the **Create a datum point** tool ✷ in the **Part Design Helper** toolbar. The **Datum Point parameters** sub-window appears in the **Task Panel**, and you are prompted to select the first reference.

2. Select a vertex of a model as the first reference in the 3D View area. The preview of a datum point appears on the selected vertex of the model, see Figure 4.50. Next, select the **Vertex** mode in the **Attachment mode** area of the **Task Panel**.

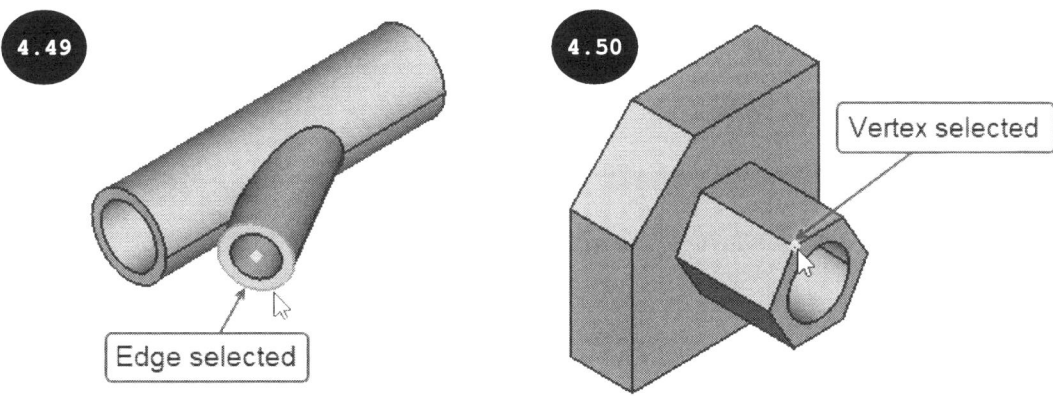

Note: Instead of selecting a vertex, you can select an edge or a line as the first reference for creating a datum point onto a vertex of the selected edge/line by using the **Vertex** attachment mode.

3. Click on the **OK** button in the **Task Panel** to confirm the creation of the datum point and exit the **Task Panel**.

Creating a Datum Point onto an Edge

The method for creating a datum point on an edge of a model is discussed below:

1. Click on the **Create a datum point** tool ● in the **Part Design Helper** toolbar. The **Datum Point parameters** sub-window appears in the **Task Panel**, and you are prompted to select the first reference.

2. Select an edge of a model as the first reference in the 3D View area. The preview of a datum point appears on an endpoint of the selected edge of the model.

3. Select a vertex of the model as the second reference in the 3D View area. The preview of a datum point appears by projecting the selected vertex onto the edge of the model, see Figure 4.51.

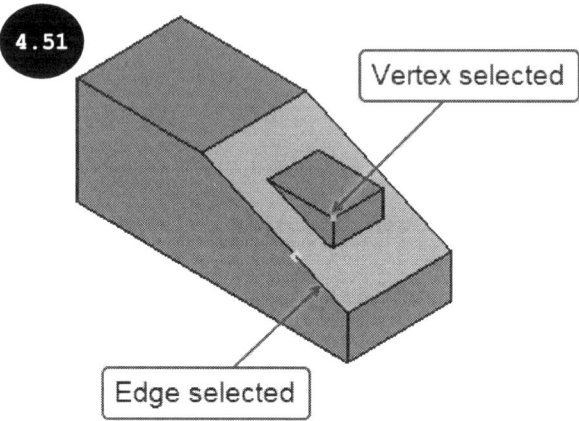

4. Click on the **OK** button in the **Task Panel** to confirm the creation of the datum point and exit the **Task Panel**.

Creating a Datum Point at the Origin of a Conical Edge

The method for creating a datum point at the origin of a conical edge such as an ellipse, a parabola, or a hyperbola is discussed below:

1. Click on the **Create a datum point** tool ● in the **Part Design Helper** toolbar. The **Datum Point parameters** sub-window appears in the **Task Panel**, and you are prompted to select the first reference.

2. Select a conical edge of a model such as an ellipse, a parabola, or a hyperbola as the first reference in the 3D View area, see Figure 4.52. Next, select the Object's origin mode in the **Attachment mode** area of the **Task Panel**. The preview of a datum point appears at the origin of the selected conical edge.

3. Click on the **OK** button in the **Task Panel** to confirm the creation of the datum point and exit the **Task Panel**.

Creating a Datum Point on a Focus of a Conical Edge

The method for creating a datum point on a focus of an ellipse, a parabola, or a hyperbola edge of a model is discussed below:

1. Click on the **Create a datum point tool** ✳ in the **Part Design Helper** toolbar. The **Datum Point parameters** sub-window appears in the **Task Panel**.

2. Select an ellipse, a parabola, or a hyperbola edge of a model as the first reference in the 3D View area. The preview of a datum point appears on a focus of the selected conical edge, see Figure 4.53.

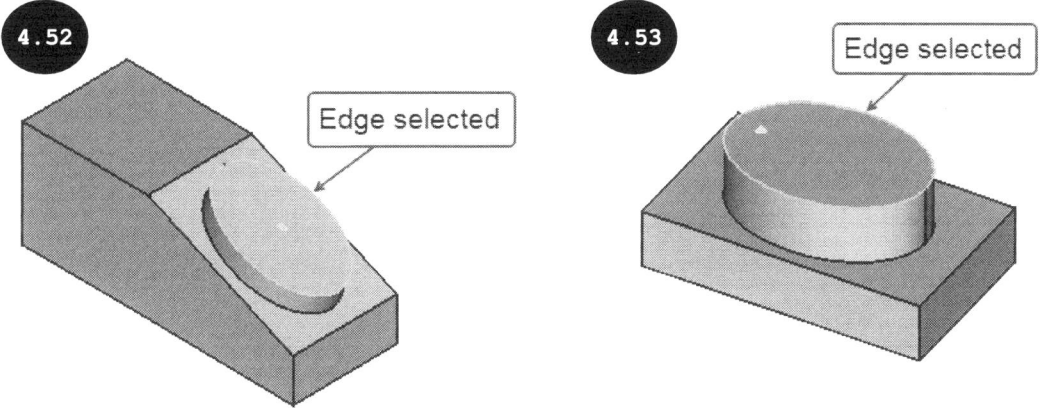

Note: After selecting an edge, if the **Focus2** mode gets activated in the **Attachment mode** area of the **Task Panel** by default, then you can select the **Focus1** mode for creating a datum point on the other focus of the selected edge or vice-versa.

3. Click on the **OK** button in the **Task Panel** to confirm the creation of the datum point and exit the **Task Panel**.

Creating a Local Coordinate System

In addition to creating a datum plane, a datum line, and a datum point, you can also create a local coordinate system by using the **Create a local coordinate system** tool of the **Part Design Helper** toolbar, see Figure 4.54. A local coordinate system can be used as a reference for creating other datum geometries. It can also be used for machining or analyzing a model by positioning the origin of the model relative to its features, identifying the orientation of the attached datum geometry, and so on. The method for creating a local coordinate system is discussed below:

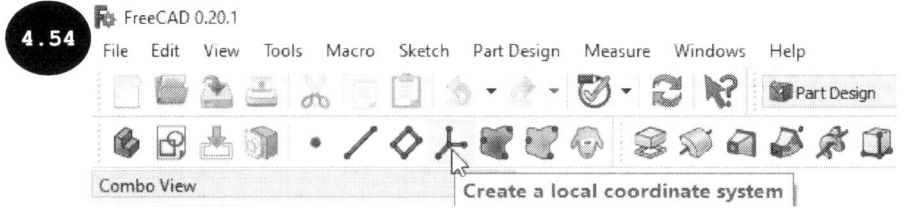

1.   Click on the **Create a local coordinate system** tool in the **Part Design Helper** toolbar. The **Local Coordinate System parameters** sub-window appears in the **Task Panel**.

2.   Select a plane, a planar face, a linear edge, a vertex, a conical edge (ellipse, parabola, or hyperbola), a circular edge, a curve, or a circle as the first reference geometry in the 3D View area. The preview of a local coordinate system appears depending upon the selected reference geometry, refer to Figure 4.55. Also, the respective mode gets activated automatically in the **Attachment mode** area of the **Task Panel**.

Planar face selected

Edge selected

a.

b.

Vertex selected

Conical Edge selected

c.

d.

Circular edge selected

Curve selected

e.

f.

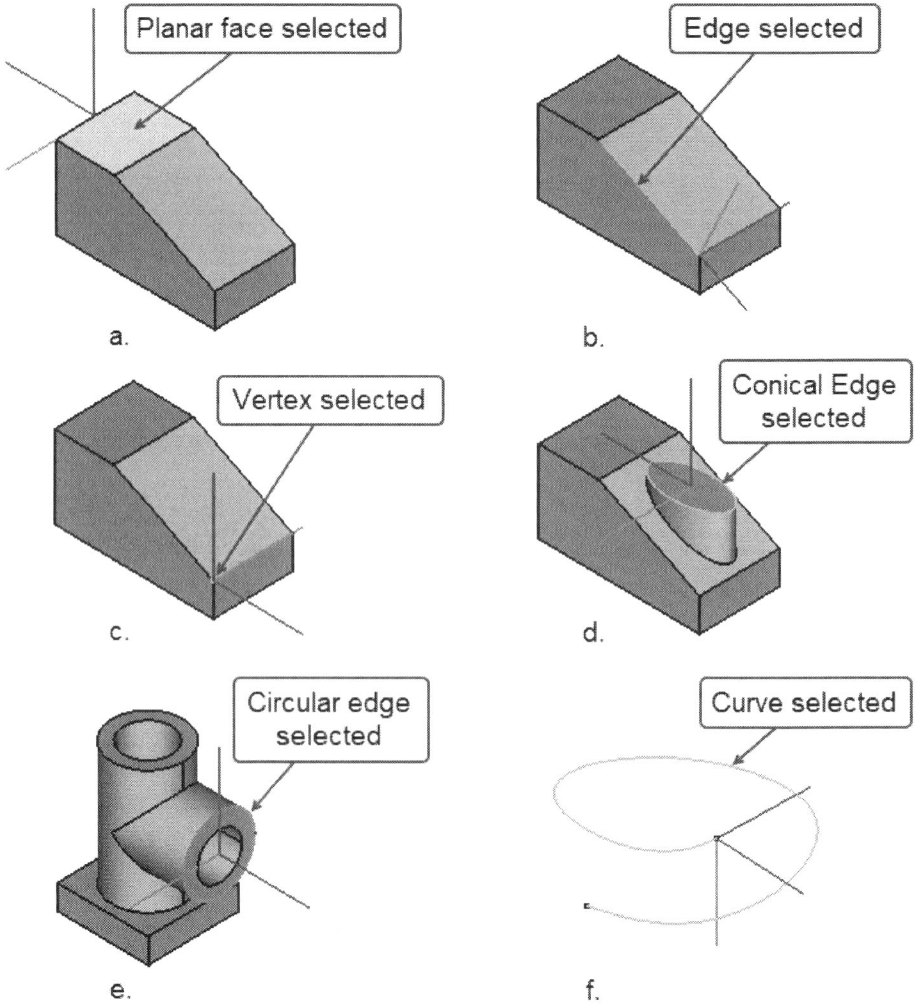

3. Ensure that the required attachment mode is activated in the **Attachment mode** area of the **Task Panel**.

> **Tip:** You can further control the placement and orientation of the local coordinate system in the 3D View area by specifying translational and rotational values in the respective fields of the **Attachment Offset** area in the **Task Panel**, see Figure 4.56.

4. If needed, you can also select second, third, and/or fourth references for creating a local coordinate system. For example, to create a local coordinate system by aligning its XY plane passing through three vertices, you need to select three vertices as the first, second, and third references.

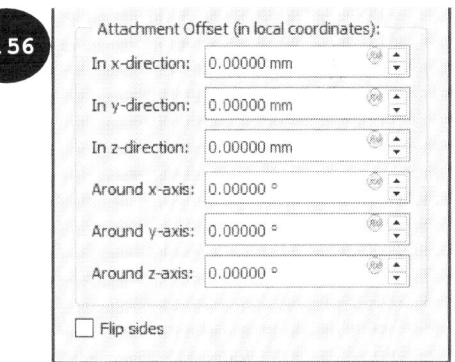

4.56

5. Click on the **OK** button in the **Task Panel** to confirm the creation of the local coordinate system and exit the **Task Panel**.

Tutorial 1

Create a multi-feature model, as shown in Figure 4.57. You need to create the model by creating all its features one by one. All dimensions are in mm.

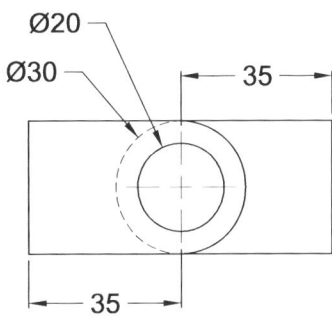

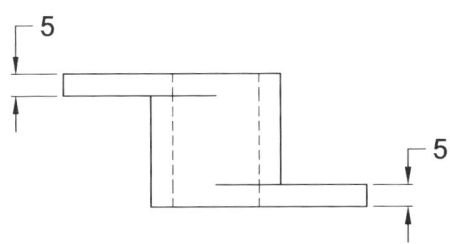

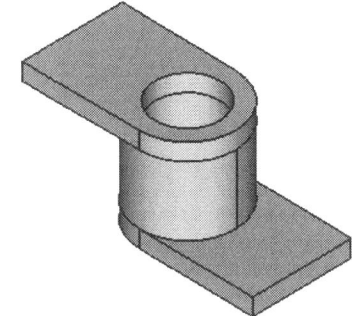

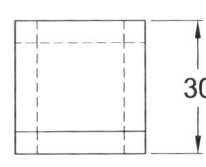

Section 1: Starting FreeCAD and a New Empty Document

1.   Start FreeCAD by double-clicking on the **FreeCAD 0.20** icon on your desktop. The startup user interface of FreeCAD appears, see Figure 4.58.

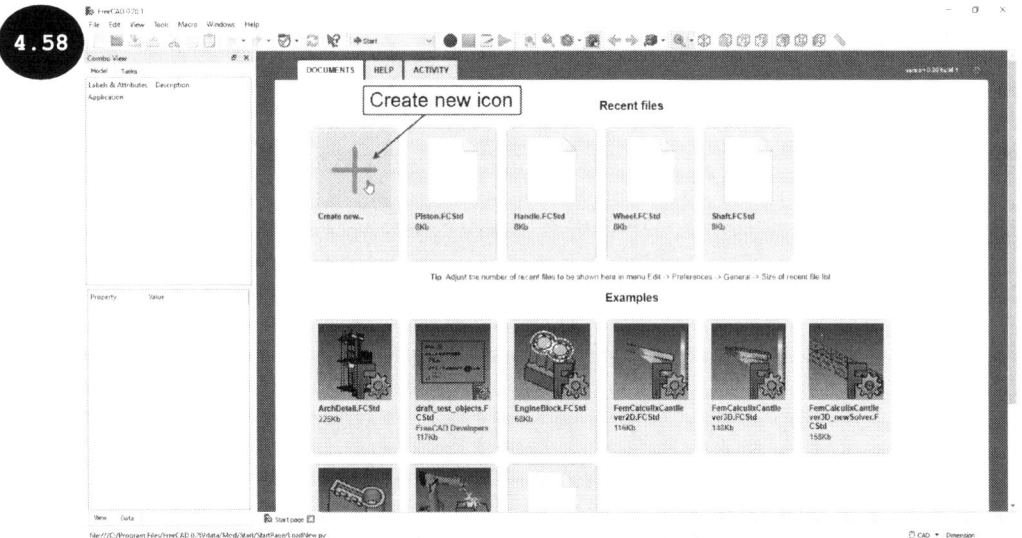

2.   Click on the **Create new** icon on the **Start** page (see Figure 4.58) or press the **CTRL + N** keys. A new empty document gets invoked with the default name "**unnamed: 1**" and it becomes active by default.

Section 2: Invoking the Part Design Workbench

Now, you can invoke the **Part Design** workbench for creating a 3D solid model.

1.   Invoke the **Workbench Selector** in the **Workbench** toolbar and then select the **Part Design** workbench, see Figure 4.59. The **Part Design** workbench gets invoked.

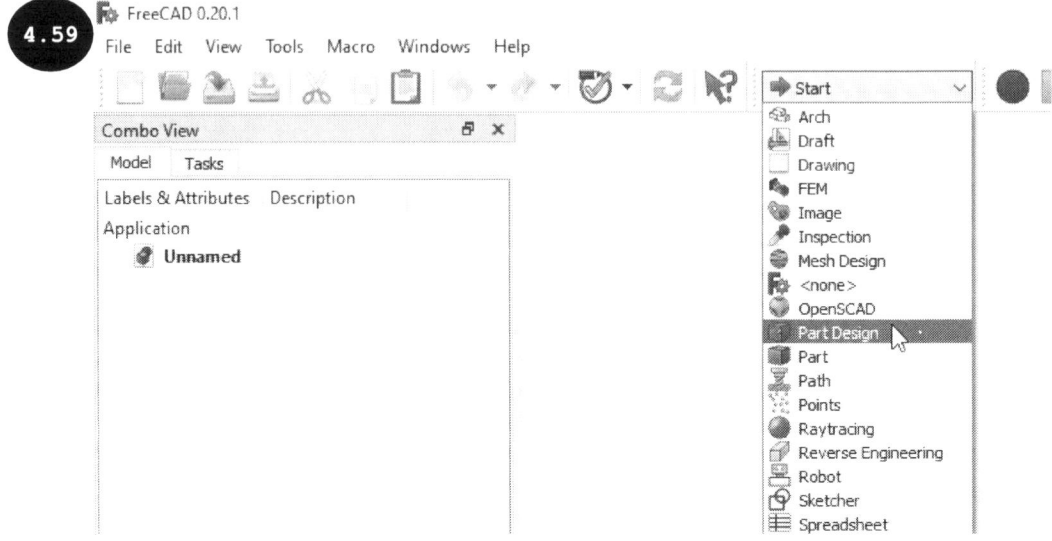

Section 3: Specifying the Unit

Now, you need to specify millimeters (mm) as the measurement unit for the document.

1. Click on **Edit > Preferences** in the **Standard Menu**, see Figure 4.60. The **Preferences** dialog box appears.

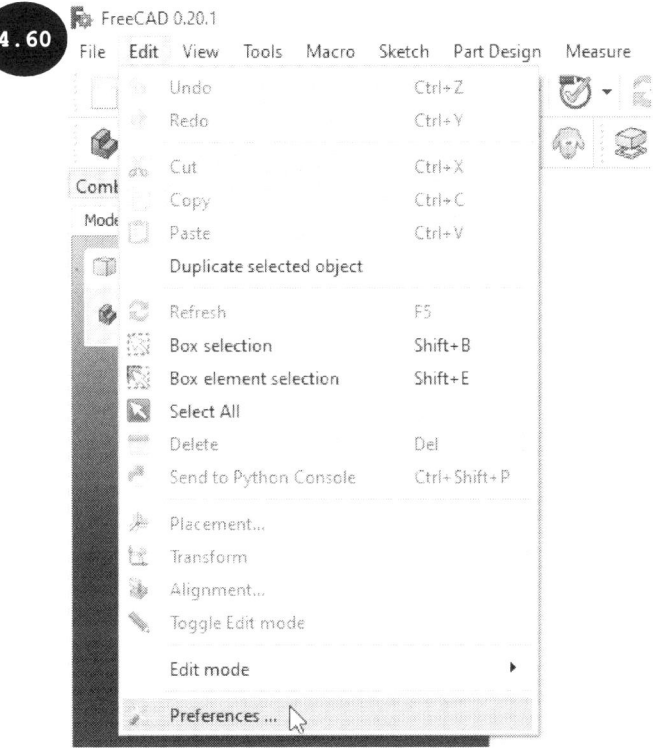

2. Ensure that the **General** section is selected in the left panel of the **Preferences** dialog box and then click on the **Units** tab, see Figure 4.61.

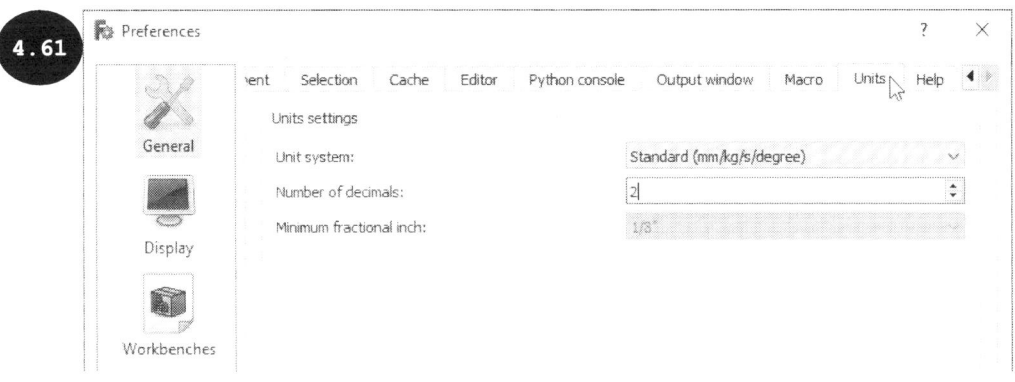

Tip: You may need to click on the arrow ▸ at the upper right corner of the **Preferences** dialog box for displaying the **Units** tab.

3. Ensure that the **Standard (mm/kg/s/degree)** option is selected in the **Unit system** drop-down list of the dialog box. In this unit system, the length is measured in millimeters, the mass is calculated in kilograms, the time is represented in seconds, and the angle is measured in degrees.

4. Ensure that the **2** is specified in the **Number of decimals** field of the dialog box as the number of digits after the decimal point of measurements.

5. Click on the **Apply** button and then the **OK** button in the **Preferences** dialog box. The selected unit system is defined, and the dialog box is closed.

Section 4: Creating the Base Feature
Now, you can create the base feature of the model, which is a pad feature.

1. Click on the **Create sketch** tool ◙ in the **Part Design Helper** toolbar, see Figure 4.62. The three default planes appear in the 3D View area. Also, the **Task Panel** appears in the **Tasks** tab of **Combo View** with a list of three default planes.

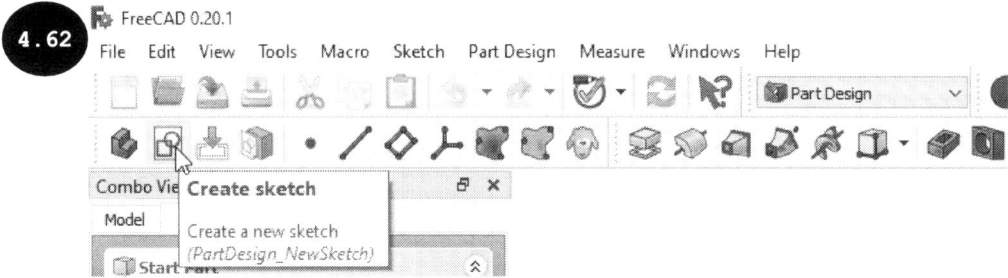

2. Select the **XY_Plane** as the sketching plane in the 3D View area for creating the sketch of the base feature. The **Sketcher** workbench gets invoked. Note that the selected plane becomes the sketching plane for drawing the sketch and is oriented normal to the viewing direction.

    Now, you can create a sketch of the base feature.

3. Create the sketch of the base feature and then apply the required constraints and dimensions to the sketch, see Figure 4.63.

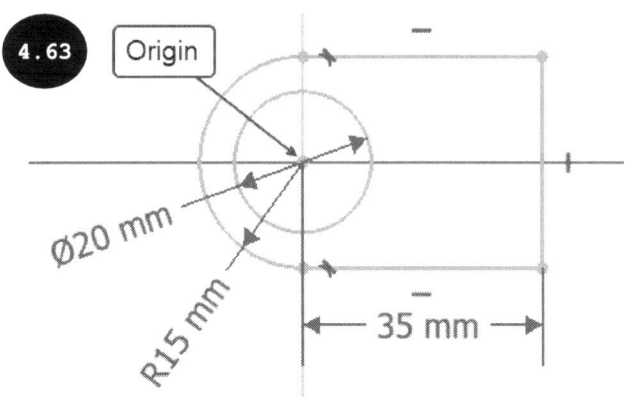

Note: In Figure 4.63, a tangent constraint is applied between each set of connected arc and line entities to make the sketch fully constrained.

After creating the sketch, you need to exit the **Sketcher** workbench.

4. Click on the **Close** button in the **Task Plane** of the **Combo View** to exit the **Sketcher** workbench (see Figure 4.64) and switch back to the **Part Design** workbench.

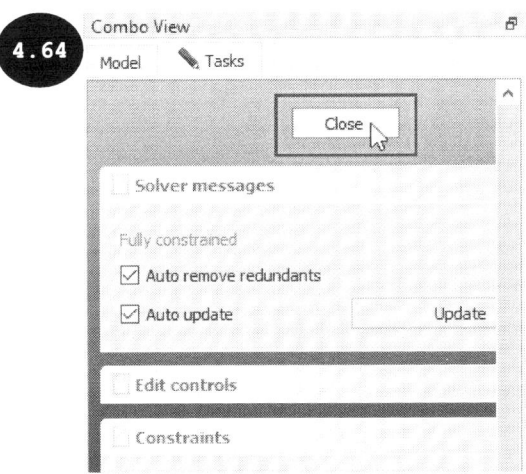

Now, you need to create a pad feature.

5. Click on the **Pad** tool in the **Part Design Modeling** toolbar, see Figure 4.65. The preview of a pad feature appears in the 3D View area with default parameters. Also, the **Pad parameters** sub-window appears in the **Task Panel** of **Combo View**, see Figure 4.66.

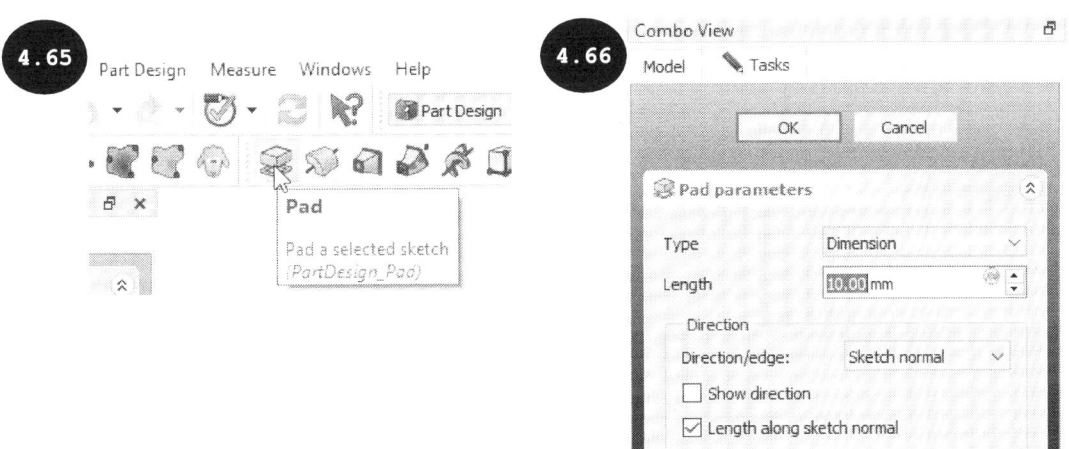

6.   Ensure that the **Dimension** option is selected in the **Type** drop-down list for creating a pad feature by specifying its length.

7.   Enter **5** mm as the length of the pad feature in the **Length** field of the **Task Panel**. Next, press the TAB key or click anywhere in the 3D View area to update the preview of the pad feature.

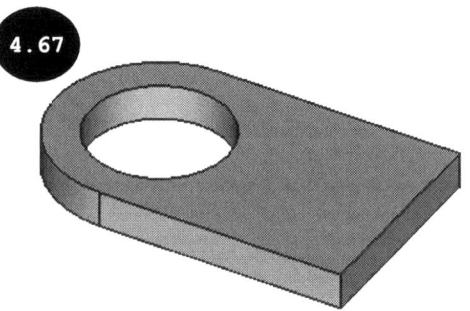

8.   Click on the **OK** button in the **Task Panel** to confirm the creation of the pad feature and exit the **Task Panel**. The pad feature gets created, see Figure 4.67.

Section 5: Creating the Second Feature

Now, you can create the second feature of the model.

1.   Click to select the top planar face of the base feature as the sketching plane for creating the sketch of the second feature of the model, see Figure 4.68.

2.   Click on the **Create sketch** tool in the **Part Design Helper** toolbar, see Figure 4.69. The **Sketcher** workbench gets invoked and the top planar face of the base feature gets oriented normal to the viewing direction.

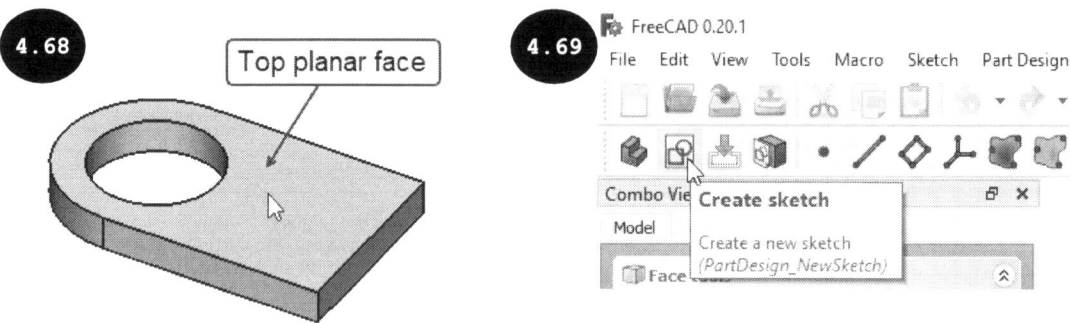

3.   Create two circles as the sketch of the second feature and then apply the required dimensions, see Figure 4.70.

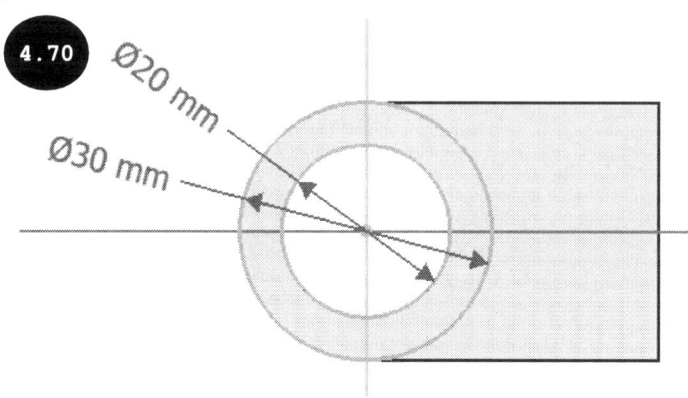

4. After creating the sketch, click on the **Close** button in the **Task Plane** of the **Combo View** to exit the **Sketcher** workbench (see Figure 4.71) and switch back to the **Part Design** workbench.

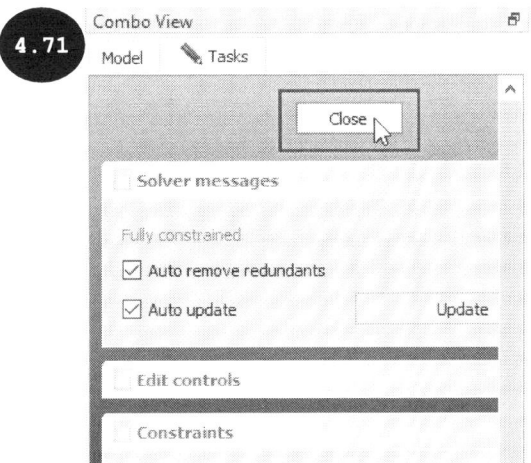

Now, you can convert the sketch into a pad feature.

5. Click on the **Pad** tool in the **Part Design Modeling** toolbar, see Figure 4.72. The preview of a pad feature appears in the 3D View area with default parameters. Also, the **Pad parameters** sub-window appears in the **Task Panel** of **Combo View**.

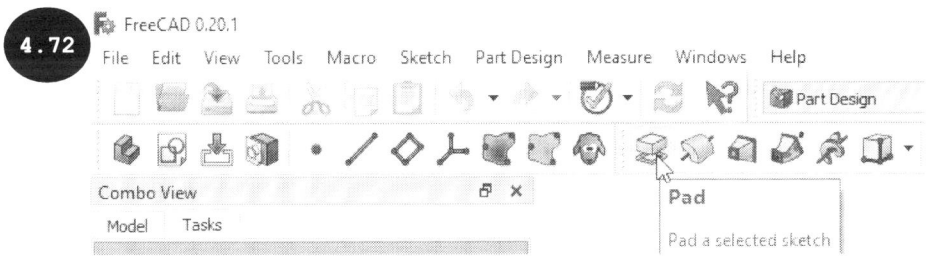

6. Enter **20** mm as the length of the pad feature in the **Length** field of the **Task Panel**. Next, press the TAB key or click anywhere in the 3D View area to update the preview of the pad feature.

7. Click on the **OK** button in the **Task Panel** to confirm the creation of the pad feature and exit the **Task Panel**. The second feature gets created, see Figure 4.73.

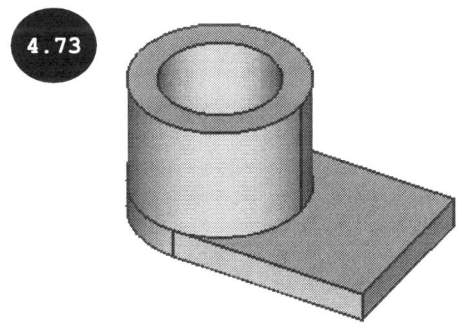

Section 6: Creating the Third Feature

Now, you need to create the third feature of the model.

1. Click to select the top planar face of the second feature as the sketching plane for creating the sketch of the third feature, see Figure 4.74.

2. Click on the **Create sketch** tool 🗺 in the **Part Design Helper** toolbar, see Figure 4.75. The **Sketcher** workbench gets invoked and the top planar face of the model gets oriented normal to the viewing direction.

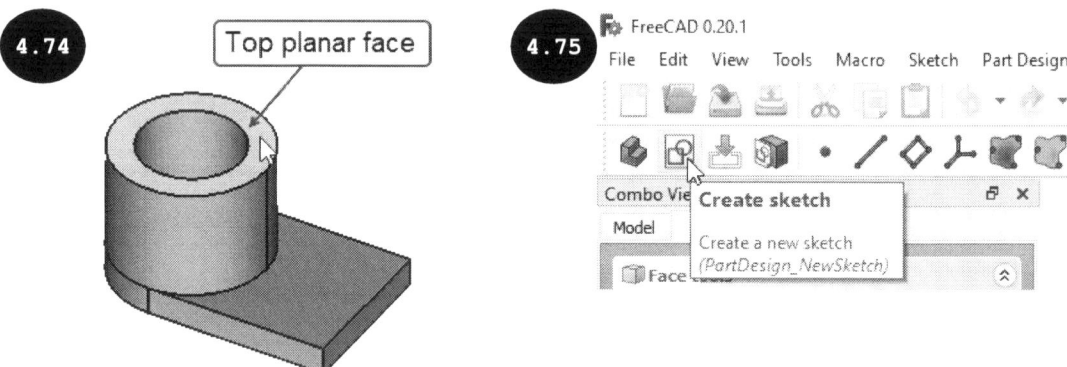

3. Create the sketch of the third feature and then apply the required constraints and dimensions, see Figure 4.76.

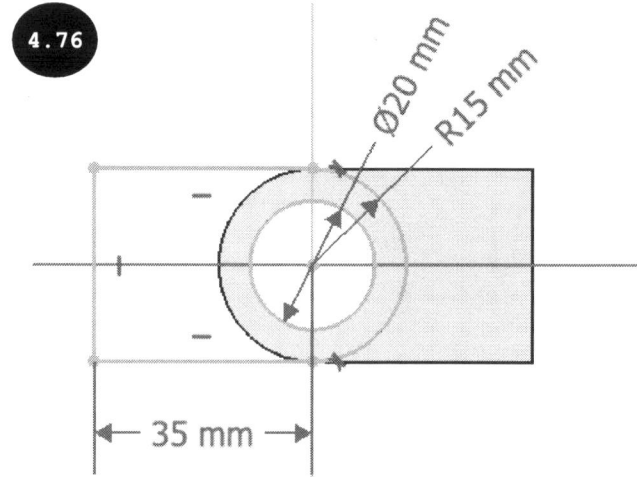

4. After creating the sketch, click on the **Close** button in the **Task Plane** of the **Combo View** to exit the **Sketcher** workbench and switch back to the **Part Design** workbench.

5. Click on the **Pad** tool in the **Part Design Modeling** toolbar, see Figure 4.77. The preview of a pad feature appears in the 3D View area with default parameters. Also, the **Pad parameters** sub-window appears in the **Task Panel** of the **Combo View**.

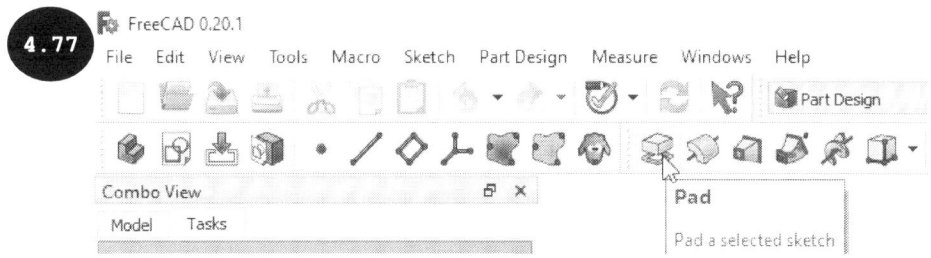

6. Enter **5** mm as the length of the pad feature in the **Length** field of the **Task Panel**. Next, press the TAB key or click anywhere in the 3D View area to update the preview of the pad feature.

7. Click on the **OK** button in the **Task Panel** to confirm the creation of the feature and exit the **Task Panel**. Figure 4.78 shows the final model after creating all its features.

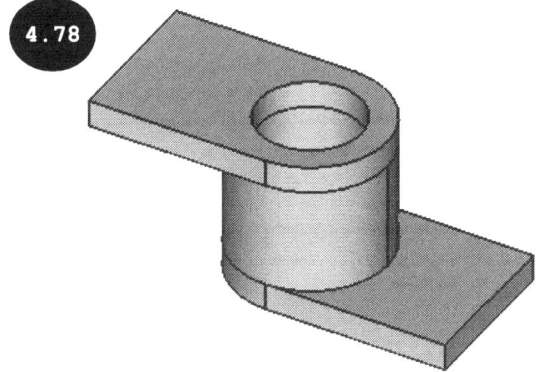

Section 7: Saving the Model

1. Click on the **Save** tool in the **File** toolbar (see Figure 4.79) or press the CTRL + S keys. The **Save FreeCAD Document** dialog box appears.

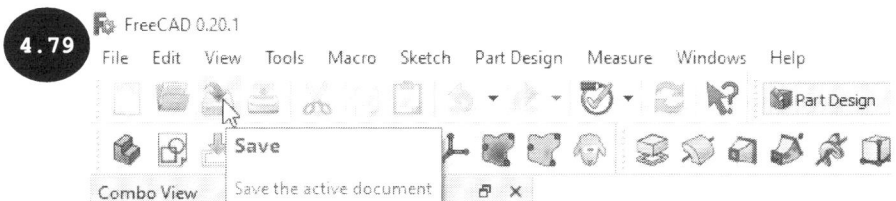

2. Browse to the **FreeCAD** folder in the local drive of your system. Next, create a new folder with the name **Chapter 04** inside it.

3. Enter **Ch04-Tutorial 1** in the **File name** field of the dialog box. Next, click on the **Save** button in the dialog box. The mode gets saved with the name **Ch04-Tutorial 1** at the specified location (> *FreeCAD* > *Chapter 04*).

4. Click on **File** > **Close** in the **Standard Menu** to close the current document.

Tutorial 2

Create a multi-feature model, as shown in Figure 4.80. You need to create the model by creating all its features one by one. All dimensions are in inches (in).

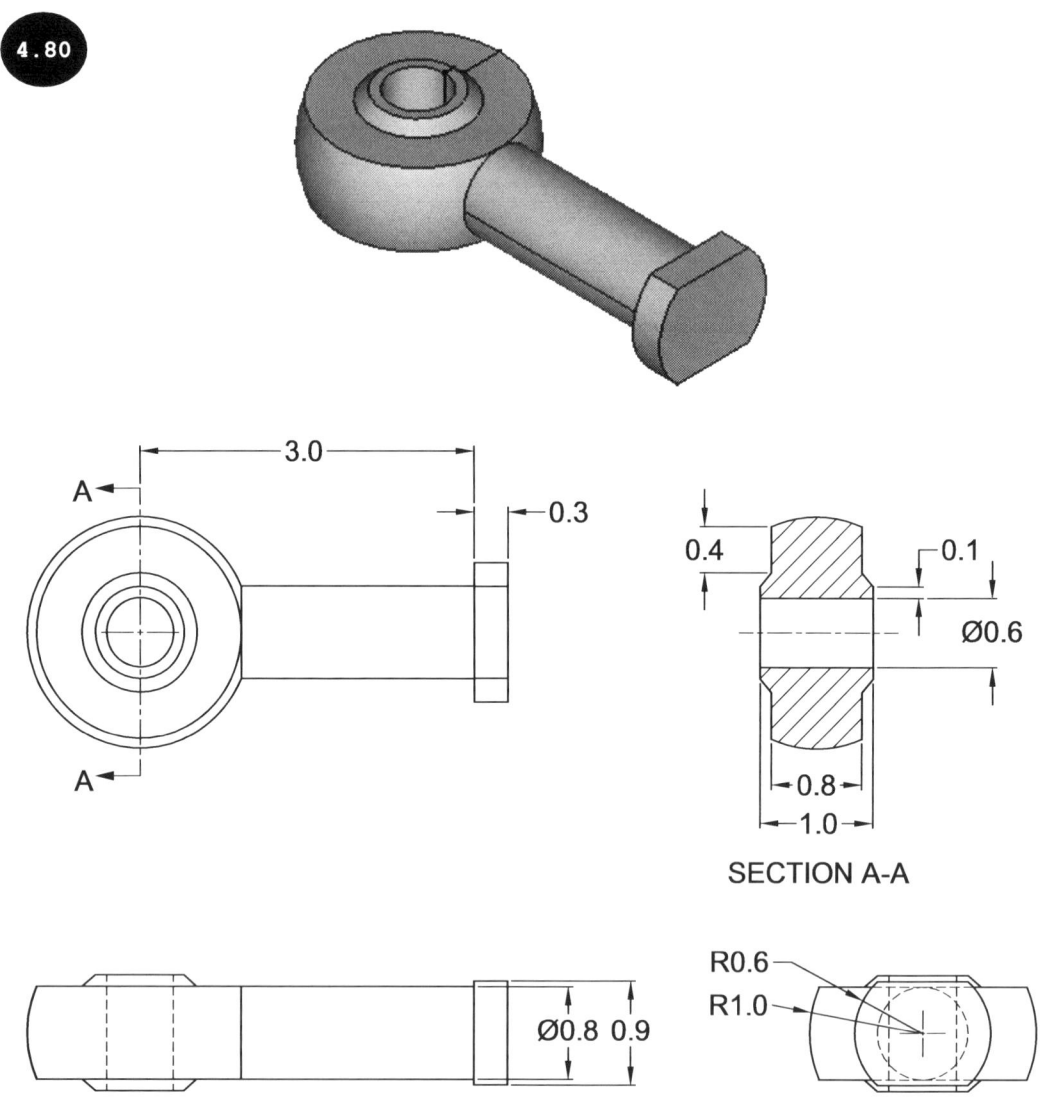

4.80

SECTION A-A

Section 1: Starting FreeCAD and a New Empty Document

1. Start FreeCAD by double-clicking on the **FreeCAD 0.20** icon on your desktop, if not started already. The startup user interface of FreeCAD appears.

2. Click on the **New** tool in the **File** toolbar (see Figure 4.81) or press the **CTRL + N** keys. A new empty document gets invoked with the default name and gets activated, by default.

Section 2: Invoking the Part Design Workbench

Now, you can invoke the **Part Design** workbench.

1. Invoke the **Workbench Selector** in the **Workbench** toolbar and then select the **Part Design** workbench, see Figure 4.82. The **Part Design** workbench gets invoked.

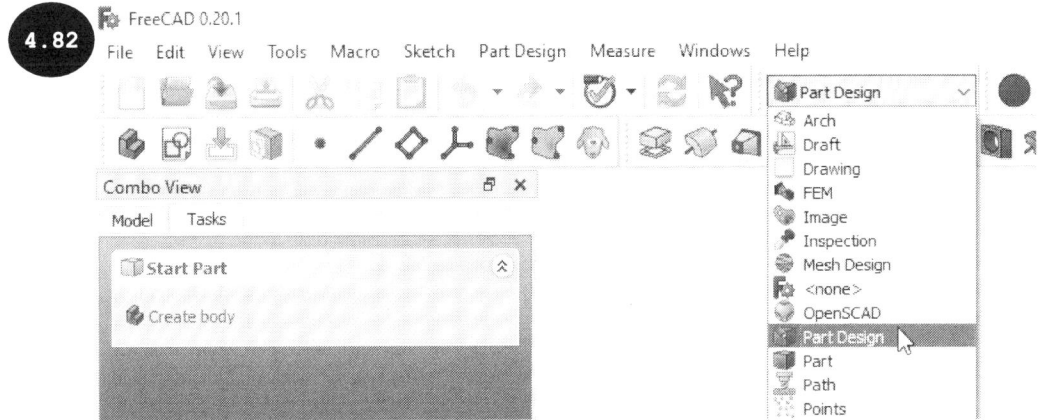

Section 3: Specifying the Unit

Now, you need to specify inches (in) as the measurement unit for the document.

1. Click on **Edit > Preferences** in the **Standard Menu**. The **Preferences** dialog box appears.

2. Ensure that the **General** section is selected in the left panel of the **Preferences** dialog box and then click on the **Units** tab, refer to Figure 4.83.

> **Tip:** You may need to click on the arrow ▶ at the upper right corner of the **Preferences** dialog box for displaying the **Units** tab.

3. Select the **Imperial decimal (in/lb)** option in the **Unit system** drop-down list of the dialog box as the unit system, see Figure 4.83. In this unit system, the length is measured in inches and the mass is calculated in pounds (lb).

4. Ensure that the **2** is specified in the **Number of decimals** field of the dialog box as the number of digits after the decimal point of measurements, see Figure 4.83.

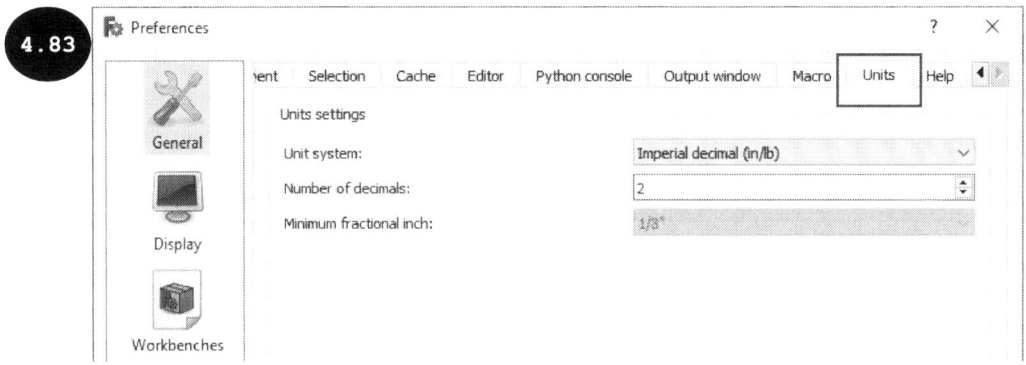

5. Click on the **Apply** button and then the **OK** button in the **Preferences** dialog box. The selected unit system is defined, and the dialog box is closed.

Section 4: Creating the Base Feature

Now, you can create the base feature of the model, which is a revolution feature.

1. Click on the **Create sketch** tool in the **Part Design Helper** toolbar, see Figure 4.84. The three default planes appear in the 3D View area. Also, the **Task Panel** appears in the **Tasks** tab of the **Combo View**.

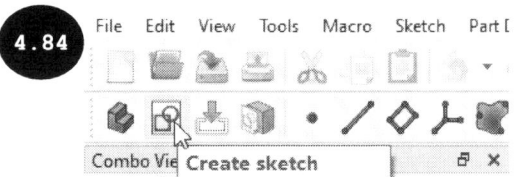

2. Select the **YZ_Plane** as the sketching plane in the 3D View area. The **Sketcher** workbench gets invoked and the selected plane gets oriented normal to the viewing direction.

3. Create the sketch of the base feature of the model and then apply the required constraints and dimensions, see Figure 4.85.

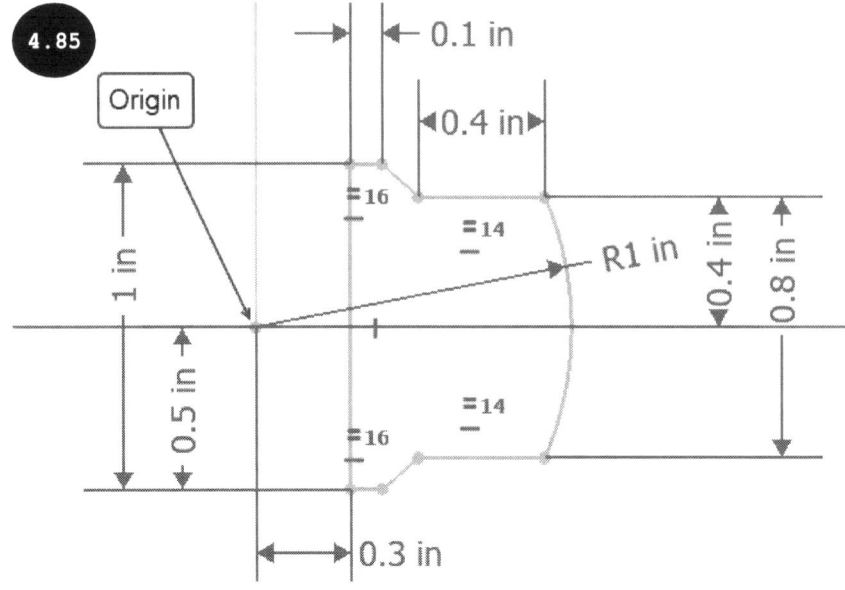

4. After creating the sketch, click on the **Close** button in the **Task Plane** of the **Combo View** to exit the **Sketcher** workbench and switch back to the **Part Design** workbench.

5. Click on the **Revolution** tool in the **Part Design Modeling** toolbar, see Figure 4.86. The preview of a revolution feature appears in the 3D View area with default parameters. Also, the **Revolution parameters** sub-window appears in the **Task Panel** of the **Combo View**.

6. Ensure that the **Vertical sketch axis** option is selected in the **Axis** drop-down list of the **Task Panel** to define the vertical axis of the sketch as the axis of revolution.

7. Ensure that the **360** degrees is specified as the angle of revolution in the **Angle** field of the **Task Panel**.

8. Click on the **OK** button in the **Task Panel**. The revolution feature gets created in the 3D View area, see Figure 4.87.

Section 5: Creating the Second Feature

Now, you can create the second feature of the model, which is a pad feature. To create the second feature of the model, you first need to create a datum plane at an offset distance of 3 inches from the YZ_Plane.

1. Click on the **Create a datum plane** tool ◇ in the **Part Design Helper** toolbar. The **Datum Plane parameters** sub-window appears in the **Task Panel**. Also, you are prompted to select a first reference for creating a datum plane.

2. Select the top circular edge of the base feature as the first reference, see Figure 4.88. The preview of a datum plane appears aligned to the plane of the selected reference, see Figure 4.89. Also, the **Concentric** mode gets activated automatically in the **Attachment mode** area of the **Task Panel**.

Edge to be selected

3. Select the **Revolution Section** mode in the **Attachment mode** area of the **Task Panel**. The preview of a datum plane appears normal to the plane of the selected reference, see Figure 4.90.

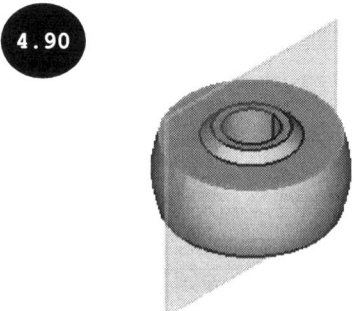

4. Enter 3 inches in the **In z-direction** field of the **Attachment Offset** area of the **Task Panel** as the offset distance along the z-axis, see Figure 4.91.

5. Select the **Flip sides** check box in the **Attachment Offset** area of the **Task Panel** to reverse the direction of the datum plane like the one shown in Figure 4.92.

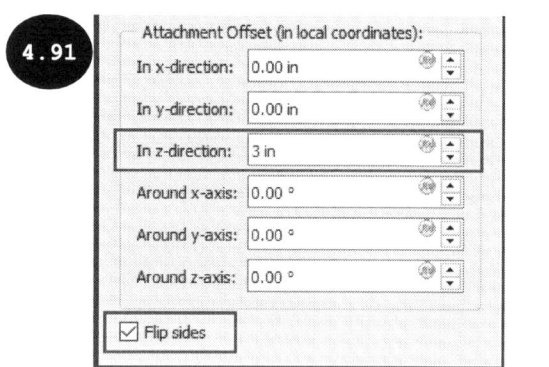

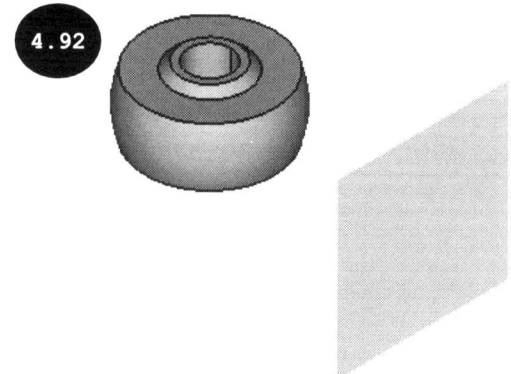

6. Click on the **OK** button in the **Task Panel** to confirm the creation of the datum plane and exit the **Task Panel**.

   Now, you can create the second feature of the model.

7. Click on the **Create sketch** tool in the **Part Design Helper** toolbar, see Figure 4.93. The three default planes appear in the 3D View area. Also, the **Task Panel** appears in the **Tasks** tab of **Combo View**.

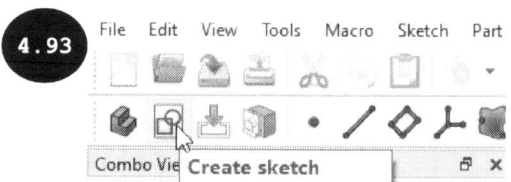

8. Select the newly created datum plane as the sketching plane in the 3D View area. The **Sketcher** workbench gets invoked and the selected plane gets oriented normal to the viewing direction.

9. Create a circle of diameter 0.8 inches as the sketch of the second feature and then apply the required dimensions, see Figure 4.94.

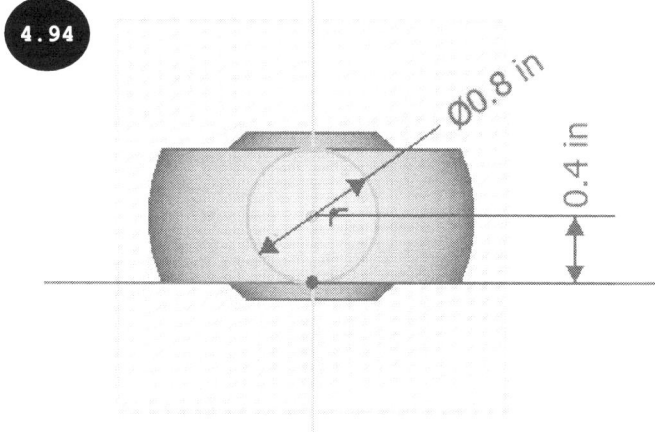

4.94

Ø0.8 in

0.4 in

10. After creating the sketch, click on the **Close** button in the **Task Plane** of the **Combo View** to exit the **Sketcher** workbench and switch back to the **Part Design** workbench.

11. Click on the **Pad** tool in the **Part Design Modeling** toolbar, see Figure 4.95. The **Pad parameters** sub-window appears in the **Task Panel** of the **Combo View**. Also, an error appears informing that the creation of a feature gets failed.

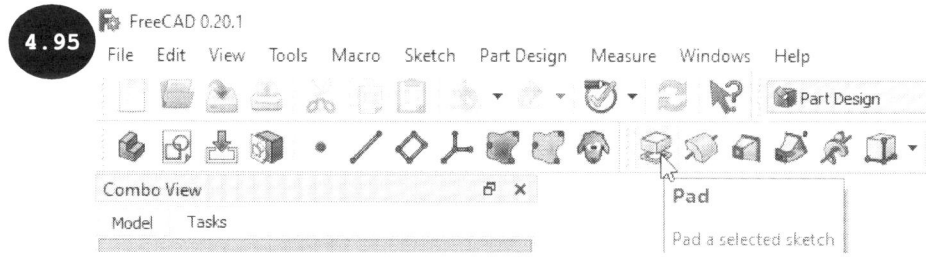

4.95

12. Select the **Reversed** check box in the **Task Panel** to reverse the direction of extrusion towards the base feature of the model.

13. Select the **To first** option in the **Type** drop-down list of the **Task Panel**. The preview of a pad feature appears up to its next intersection in the 3D View area, see Figure 4.96.

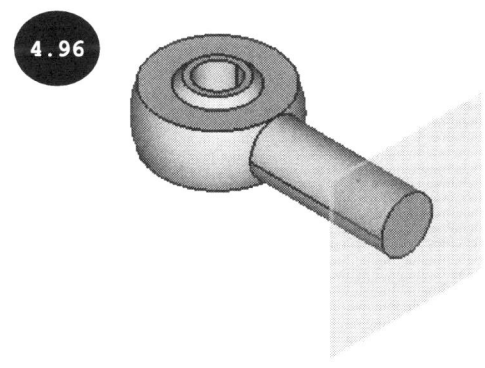

4.96

14. Click on the **OK** button in the **Task Panel** to confirm the creation of the pad feature and exit the **Task Panel**. The second feature gets created.

Section 6: Hiding the Datum Plane
Now, you can hide the datum plane in the 3D View area.

1. Click to select the datum plane in the 3D View area or the **Model** tab of the **Task Panel** and then press the SPACEBAR key. The datum plane gets hidden in the 3D View area, see Figure 4.97.

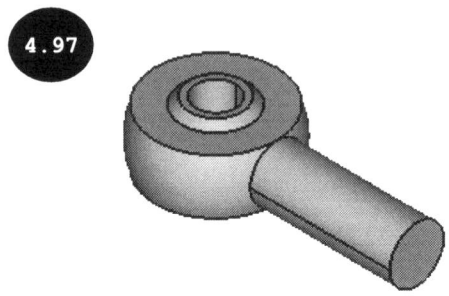

4.97

Tip: In FreeCAD, you can toggle the display of a datum plane or a feature in the 3D View area by selecting it in the **Model** tab of the **Task Panel** and then pressing the SPACEBAR key. You can select a datum plane or a feature in the 3D View area, if its current display status is turned on.

Section 7: Creating the Third Feature
Now, you need to create the third feature of the model.

1. Select the right planar face of the model as the sketching plane for creating the sketch of the third feature, see Figure 4.98.

2. Click on the **Create sketch** tool 🖉 in the **Part Design Helper** toolbar, see Figure 4.99. The **Sketcher** workbench gets invoked and the right planar face of the model gets oriented normal to the viewing direction.

4.98

Right planar face

4.99

3. Create the sketch of the third feature and then apply the required constraints and dimensions, see Figure 4.100.

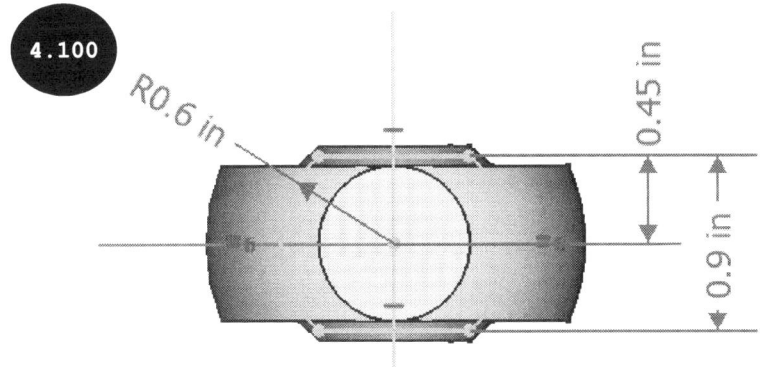

4. After creating the sketch, click on the **Close** button in the **Task Plane** of **Combo View** to exit the **Sketcher** workbench and switch back to the **Part Design** workbench.

5. Click on the **Pad** tool in the **Part Design Modeling** toolbar, see Figure 4.101. The preview of a pad feature appears in the 3D View area with default parameters. Also, the **Pad parameters** sub-window appears in the **Task Panel** of the **Combo View**.

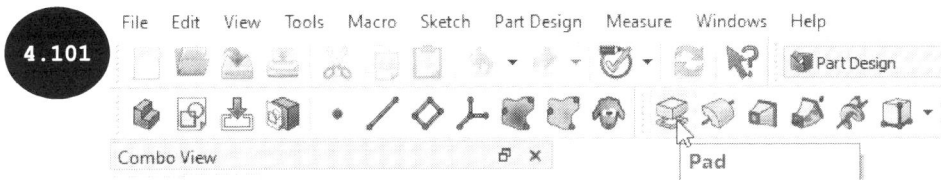

6. Enter **0.3** inches as the length of the pad feature in the **Length** field of the **Task Panel**. Next, press the TAB key or click anywhere in the 3D View area to update the preview of the pad feature.

7. Click on the **OK** button in the **Task Panel** to confirm the creation of the feature and exit the **Task Panel**. Figure 4.102 shows the final model after creating all its features.

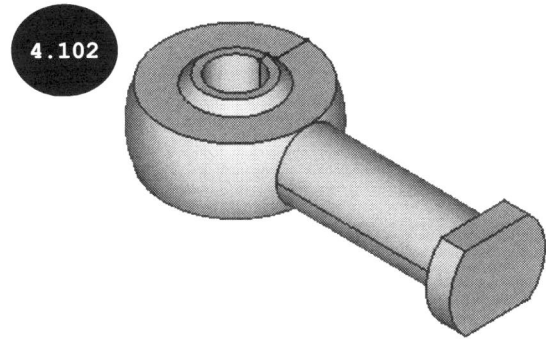

Section 8: Saving the Model

Now, you can save the model.

1. Click on the **Save** tool in the **File** toolbar (see Figure 4.103) or press the CTRL + S keys. The **Save FreeCAD Document** dialog box appears.

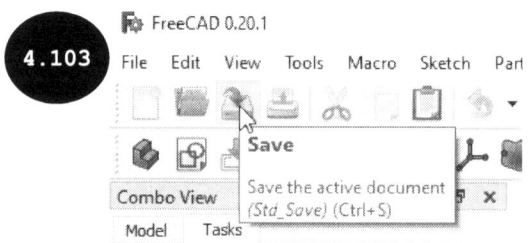

2. Browse to the *FreeCAD > Chapter 04* folder in the local drive of your system. You need to create these folders, if not created earlier.

3. Enter **Ch04-Tutorial 2** in the **File name** field of the dialog box. Next, click on the **Save** button in the dialog box. The mode gets saved with the name **Tutorial 2** at the specified location. Next, close the document by clicking on **File > Close** in the **Standard Menu**.

Hands-on Test Drive 1

Create the model shown in Figure 4.104. You need to create the model by creating all its features one by one. All dimensions are in inches (in).

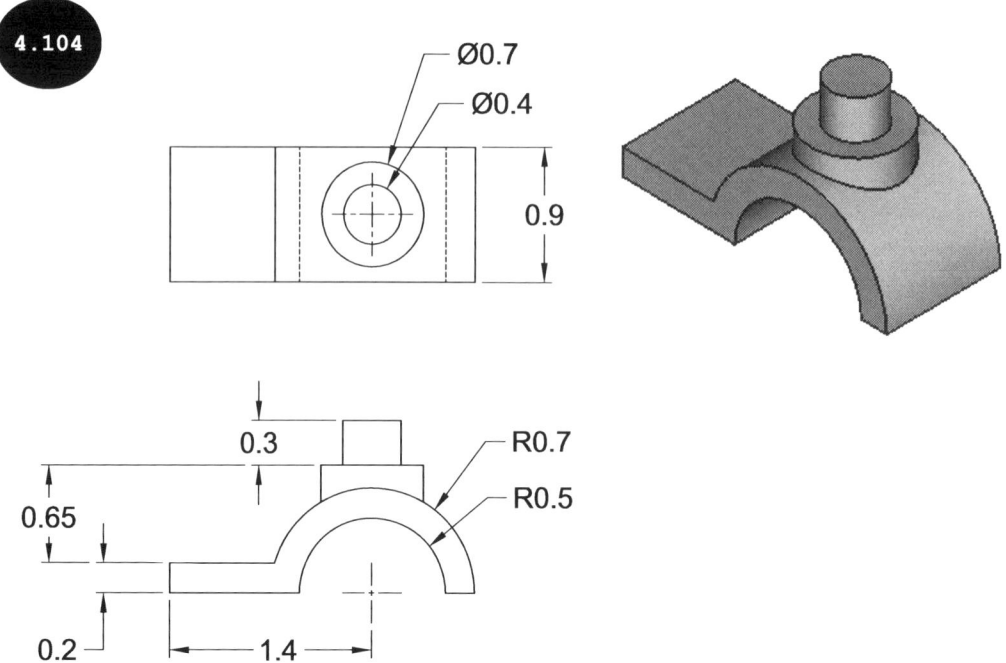

Hands-on Test Drive 2

Create the model shown in Figure 4.105. You need to create the model by creating all its features one by one. All dimensions are in mm.

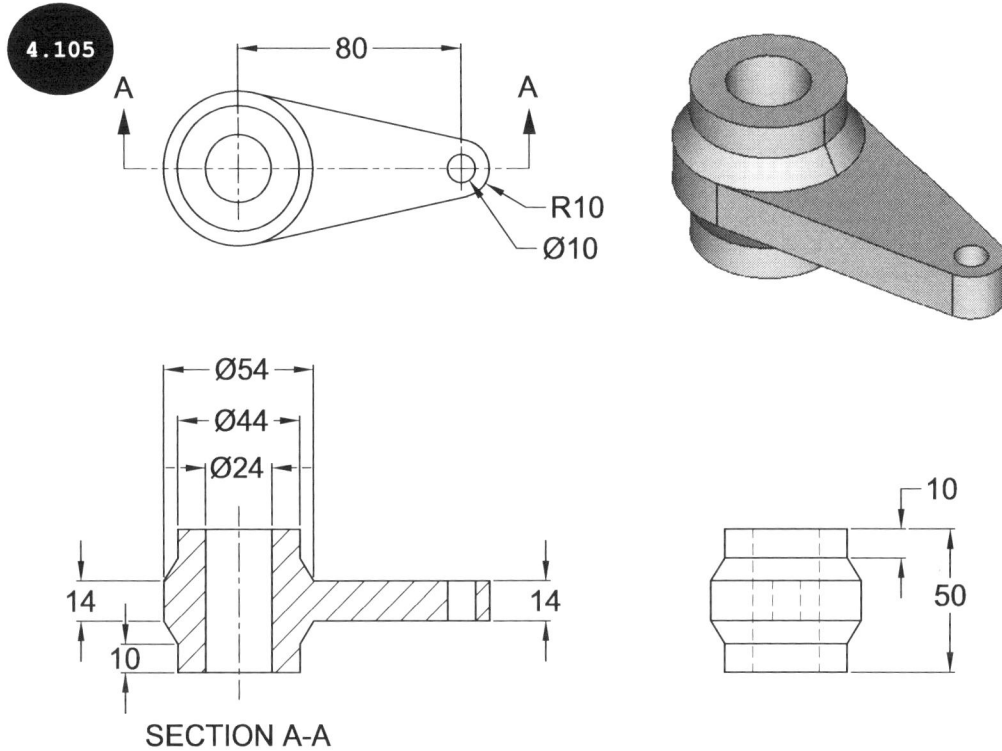

SECTION A-A

*Hint: While creating a sketch of a feature, you may need to take references from the edges of an existing feature of the model for applying constraints and dimensions. In FreeCAD, you can project the edges of an existing feature onto the current sketching plane to take references by using the **External geometry** tool. You will learn about projecting the edges of a model onto the current sketching plane as reference entities in Chapter 7.*

Summary

In this chapter, you have learned various methods for creating additional datum planes, axes, and points by using the respective tools.

Questions

Complete and verify the following sentences:

- In FreeCAD, you can create various types of datum planes by using the _____ tool.

- The _____, _____, and _____ are the three default datum planes of a document.

- To create a datum plane normal to a linear edge of a model, you need to select a _____ of a model as the first reference.

- To create a datum plane passing through three vertices, you need to select _____ vertices of a model as the _____, _____, and _____ references.

- The _____ attachment mode is used for creating a datum plane aligned to the local XZ plane of a conical edge or curve (ellipse, hyperbola, or parabola).

- You can create various types of datum lines by using the _____ tool.

- The _____ tool is used for creating a datum point.

- The _____ attachment mode is used for creating a datum plane passing through the second and third principal axes of inertia of the selected entity.

- The _____ tool is used for creating a local coordinate system.

- In FreeCAD, you can control the placement and orientation of a datum plane by specifying the required translational and rotational values in the respective fields of the _____ area in the **Task Panel**.

- An attachment mode is used to attach a plane being created to the selected reference geometries of the model such that if any modification is made to the reference geometries, then the associated datum plane will also be modified accordingly. (True/False)

- The **Deactivated** attachment mode is used for creating a datum plane, coplanar with the default XY Plane without selecting any reference geometry. (True/False)

CHAPTER

5

Creating Pocket and Groove Features

This chapter discusses the following topics:

- Creating a Pocket Feature
- Creating a Groove Feature
- Projecting External Geometries into the Sketch
- Displaying Section View in the Sketch Model
- Displaying an Earlier State of a Model
- Reordering Features of a Model
- Deleting a Feature of a Model
- Editing Features and Sketches
- Defining Display Properties or Appearance
- Measuring Distance Between Two Geometries

In the previous chapters, you have learned about creating pad features and revolution features by adding material. In this chapter, you will learn about creating pocket and groove features by subtracting material from an existing body. Besides, you will also learn about displaying an earlier state of a model, editing features and sketches, measuring distance, and assigning appearance to a body.

Creating a Pocket Feature

A pocket feature is created by subtracting material from an existing body, see Figure 5.1. You can create a pocket feature by using the **Pocket** tool in the **Part Design Modeling** toolbar. Note that the sketch of a pocket feature should be closed. The method for creating a pocket feature is discussed below:

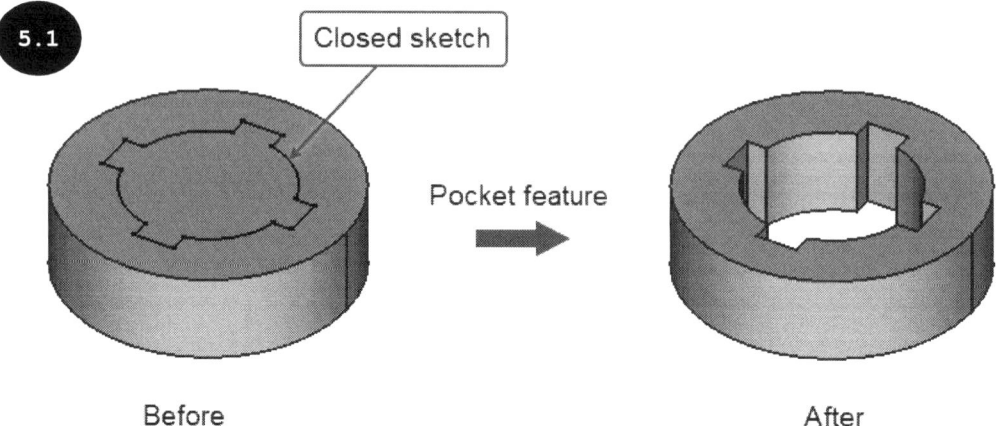

1. Invoke the **Sketcher** workbench by selecting a plane or a planar face as the sketching plane and then create a closed sketch of a pocket feature. After creating a sketch, exit the **Sketcher** workbench to switch back to the **Part Design** workbench.

2. In the **Part Design** workbench, click on the **Pocket** tool in the **Part Design Modeling** toolbar, see Figure 5.2. The preview of a pocket feature appears in the 3D View area, since the sketch of the pocket feature gets selected automatically, refer to Figure 5.3. Also, the **Pocket parameters** sub-window appears in the **Task Panel** of the **Tasks** tab in **Combo View**, see Figure 5.4.

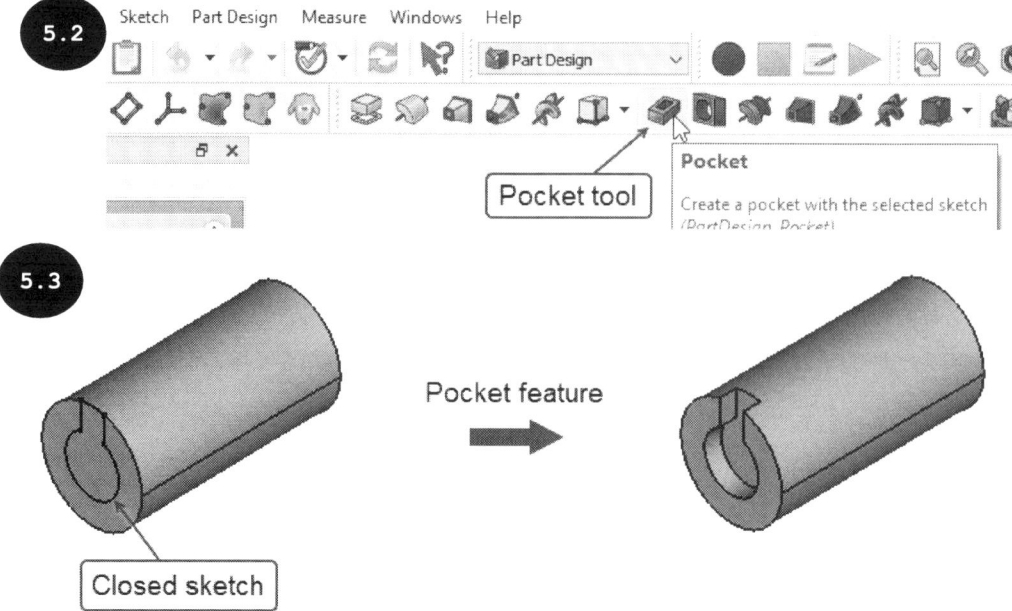

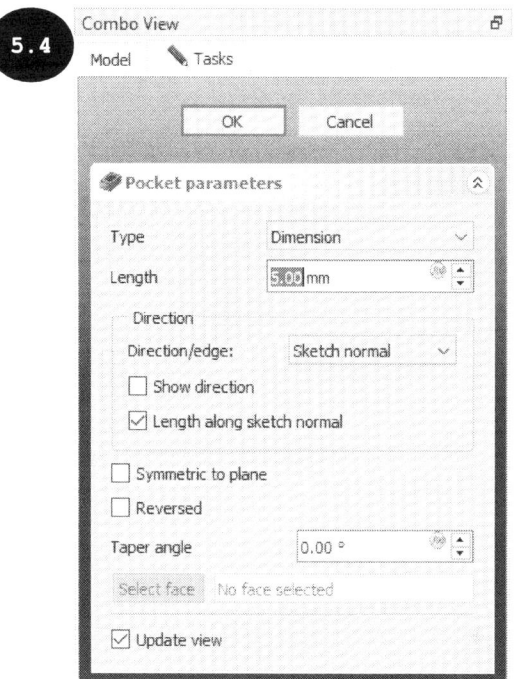

5.4

Note: If only one closed sketch is available in the 3D View area, then on invoking the **Pocket** tool, it will be selected automatically, and the preview of a pocket feature appears. However, if two or more closed sketches are available in the 3D View area, then on invoking the **Pocket** tool, you need to select a sketch of the pocket feature, manually. You can select a sketch in the 3D View area or in the **Select feature** sub-window that will be appeared in the **Task Panel**.

3. Select the required option in the **Type** drop-down list of the **Task Panel** for specifying the depth of the pocket feature. The options in this drop-down list are the same as discussed earlier while creating a pad feature by adding material except the **Through all** option (see Figure 5.5), which is discussed next.

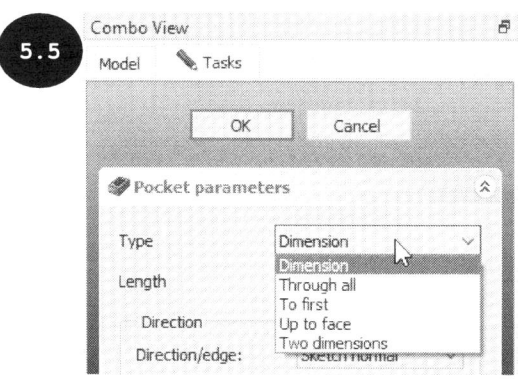

5.5

Through all: The **Through all** option is used for creating a pocket feature by removing the material through the entire model, see Figure 5.6.

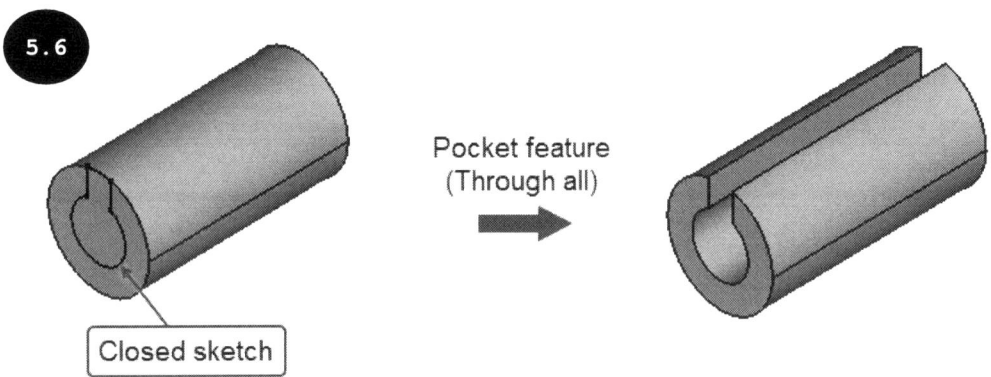

Pocket feature
(Through all)

Closed sketch

4.   Specify all the required parameters in the **Pocket parameters** sub-window of the **Task Panel** for creating the pocket feature.

Note: The options in the **Pocket parameters** sub-window are the same as those discussed earlier while creating a pad feature with the only difference being that the options in the **Pocket parameters** sub-window are used for creating a pocket feature by removing material from the model.

5.   After specifying all the required parameters for creating a pocket feature, click on the **OK** button in the **Task Panel**, see Figure 5.7. The pocket feature of specified parameters gets created. Also, its default name gets added under the **Body** node of the **Tree View** in the **Model** tab, see Figure 5.8. You can click on the **Model** tab of the **Combo View** to display the **Tree View**.

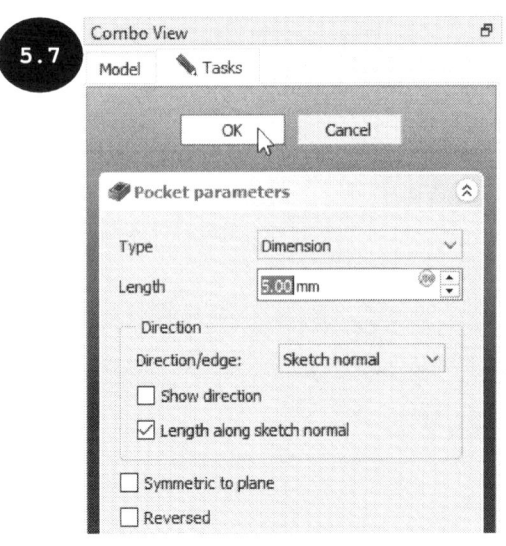

Creating a Groove Feature

A groove feature is created such that the material is subtracted from an existing body by revolving a sketch around an axis, see Figure 5.9. In FreeCAD, you can create a groove feature by using the **Groove** tool in the **Part Design Modeling** toolbar. The method for creating a groove feature is discussed below:

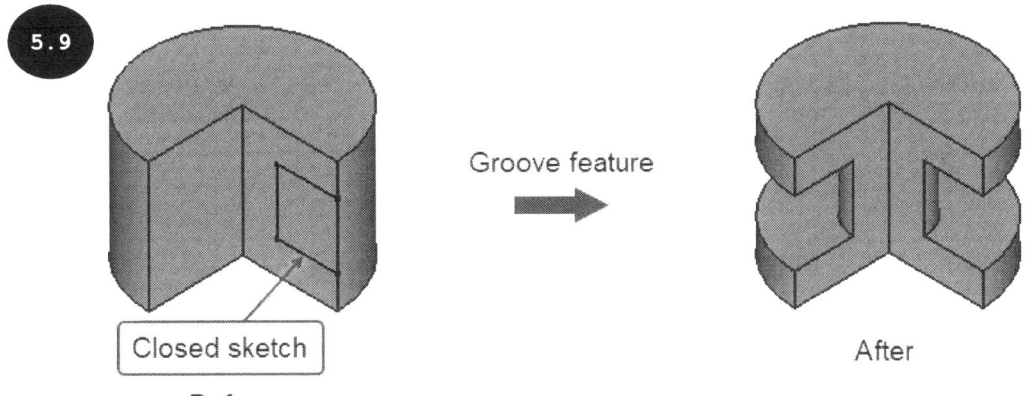

Closed sketch

Before

Groove feature

After

1. Invoke the **Sketcher** workbench by selecting a plane or a planar face as the sketching plane and then create a closed sketch of a groove feature. After creating a sketch, exit the **Sketcher** workbench to switch back to the **Part Design** workbench. Note that the sketch of a groove feature should be closed. Also, it should be on either side of its axis of revolution.

2. Click on the **Groove** tool in the **Part Design Modeling** toolbar, see Figure 5.10. Ignore if an error message is displayed since the vertical axis is chosen by default as the axis of revolution.

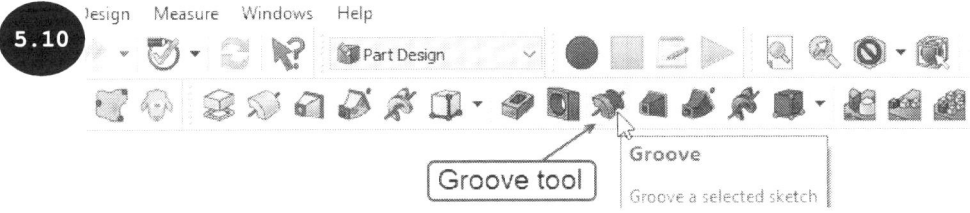

Groove tool

Groove
Groove a selected sketch

3. Select the required axis of rotation in the **Axis** drop-down list of the **Revolution parameters** sub-window that appears in the **Task Panel**, see Figure 5.11. The preview of a groove feature appears such that the material is removed from the existing body by revolving the sketch around the selected axis of revolution in the 3D View area, see Figure 5.12. In this figure, the **Horizontal sketch axis** option is selected as the axis of revolution for creating the groove feature. Note that the options in the **Axis** drop-down list are the same as discussed earlier while creating a revolution feature.

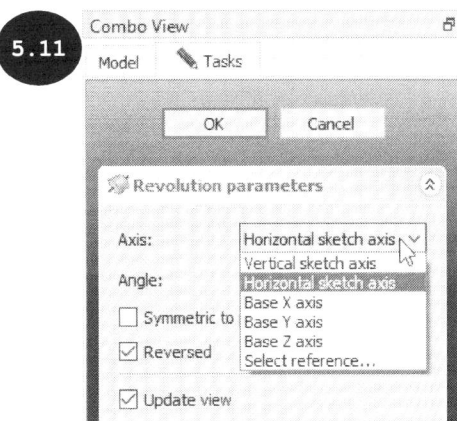

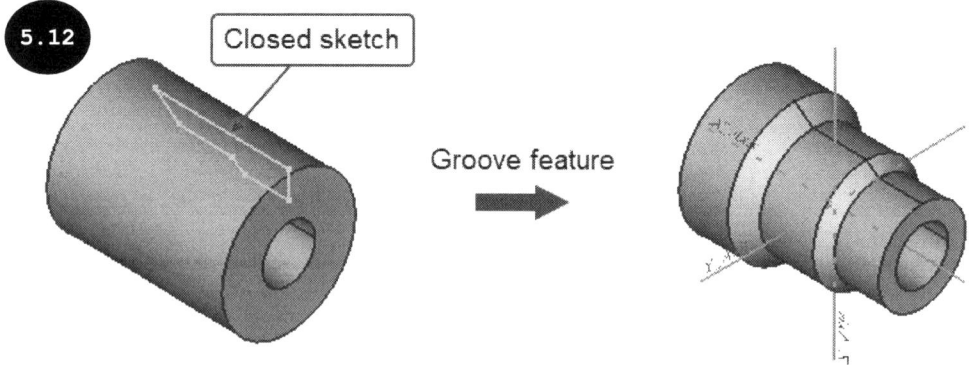

4.   Enter the required angle of revolution in the **Angle** field of the **Revolution parameters** sub-window.

5.   Specify other parameters for creating a groove feature in the **Revolution parameters** sub-window and then click on the **OK** button, see Figure 5.13. A groove feature of specified parameters gets created in the 3D View area by removing material from the model. Also, its default name gets added under the **Body** node of the **Tree View**, see Figure 5.14. You can click on the **Model** tab of the **Combo View** to display the **Tree View**.

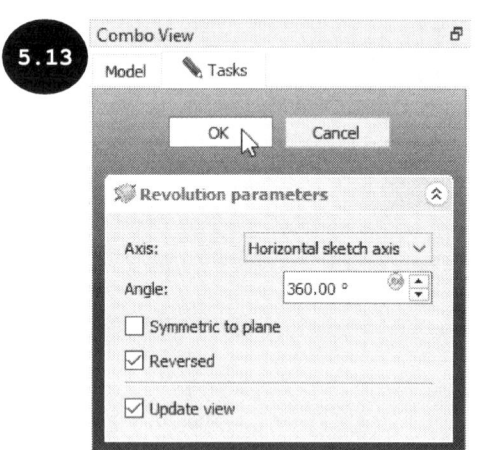

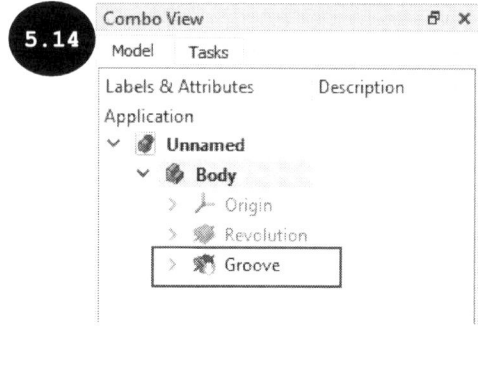

Projecting External Geometries into the Sketch

In FreeCAD, while creating a sketch in the **Sketcher** workbench, you can project external geometries such as edges and vertices of the model as linked construction entities into the sketch by using the **External geometry** tool, see Figure 5.15. In this figure, the external edges of the model are projected as linked construction entities into the sketch. You can use these construction entities as reference entities for applying geometrical and dimensional constraints to the sketch entities. By default, the linked construction entities are displayed in magenta color. The method for projecting external geometries as linked construction entities into the sketch is discussed below:

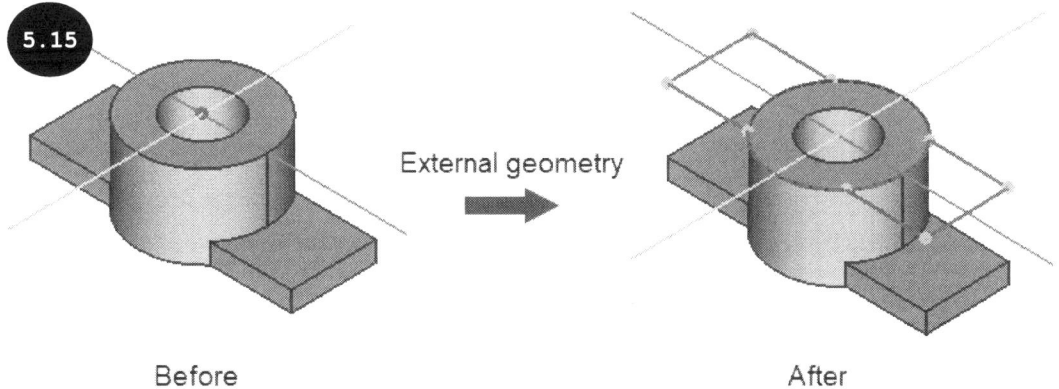

External geometry

Before   After

1. Invoke the **Sketcher** workbench by selecting a plane or a planar face as the sketching plane using the **Create sketch** tool, see Figure 5.16.

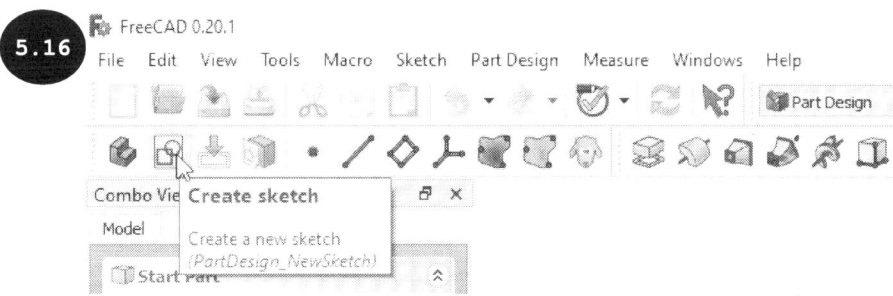

2. In the **Sketcher** workbench, click on the **External geometry** tool in the **Sketcher geometries** toolbar, see Figure 5.17. The **External geometry** tool gets activated.

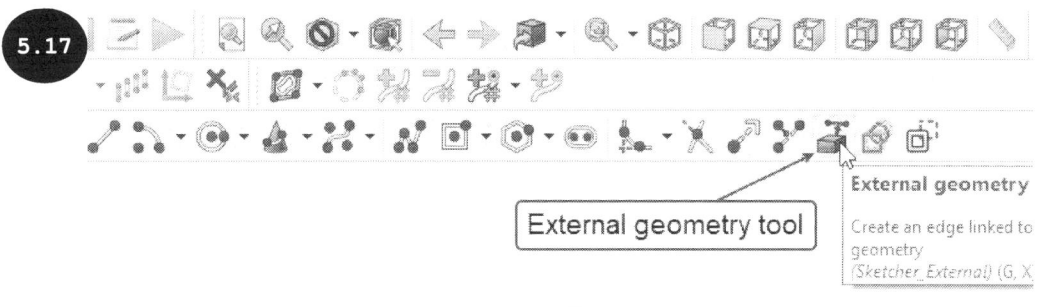

3. Select one or more edges or vertices of the existing features of the body to be projected as the linked construction entities into the sketch. The selected external geometries (edges or vertices) get projected as linked construction entities into the sketch, see Figure 5.18. You can also select sketch entities and points of an existing sketch to be projected as the linked construction entities

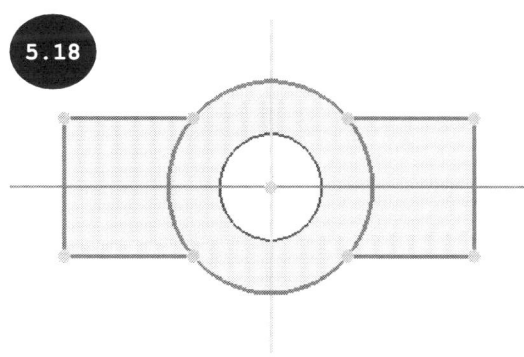

into the current sketch. Note that the linked construction entities are displayed in magenta color, by default. In Figure 5.18, the outer edges of the body are projected as linked construction entities into the sketch.

4.   Press the ESC key to exit the **External geometry** tool.

Note: After projecting external geometries as linked construction entities into the sketch, you can use them as reference entities for applying geometrical and dimensional constraints to the sketch entities, see Figure 5.19. In this figure, two horizontal dimensions of 12 mm are applied to the sketch by using the linked construction entities.

The linked construction entities are only visible in the **Sketcher** workbench when you are creating or editing a sketch.

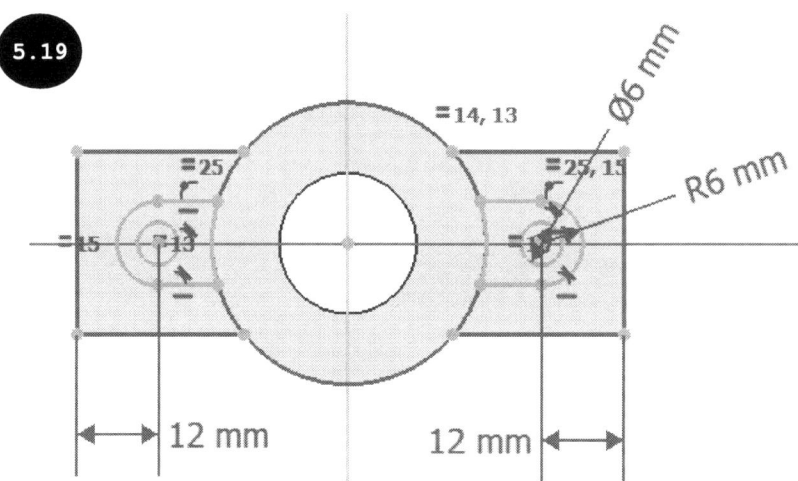

Displaying Section View in the Sketch Mode

In FreeCAD, you can switch between the section view and the full view in the Sketch editing mode of the **Sketcher** workbench, see Figure 5.20. A section view is created by temporarily hiding the material in front of the current sketching plane so that the sketch appears in front.

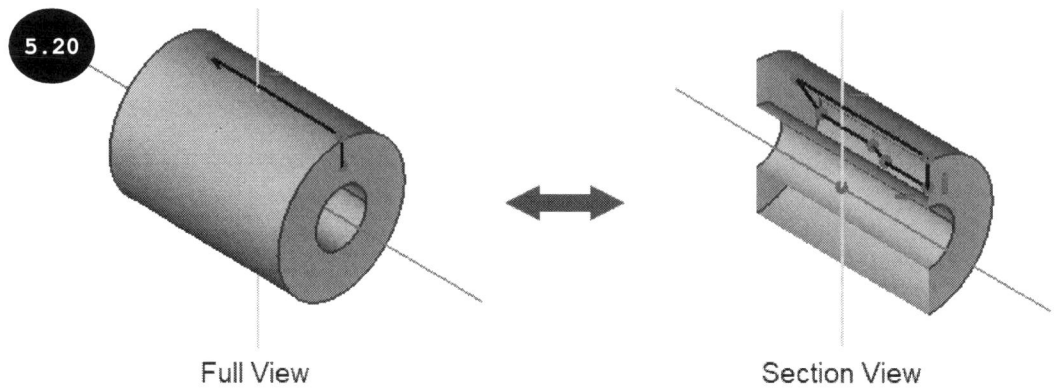

Full View   Section View

To display a section view of a model in the Sketch editing mode of the **Sketcher** workbench, click on the **View Section** tool in the **Sketcher** toolbar, see Figure 5.21. The section view of the model appears in the 3D View area by temporarily hiding the material that is in front of the sketching plane. Note that it is a toggle tool. As a result, to display the model back to its original full-view state, you need to click on this tool again.

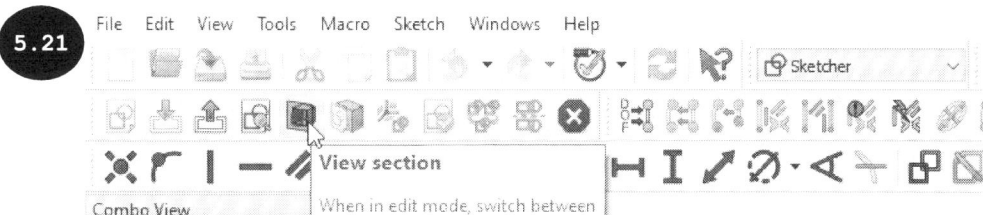

Displaying an Earlier State of a Model

In FreeCAD, when you create a new feature of a model, it gets added at the end of the feature list in **Tree View** and is activated as the last feature of the model, see Figure 5.22. Also, the model is displayed in the 3D View area with all its features.

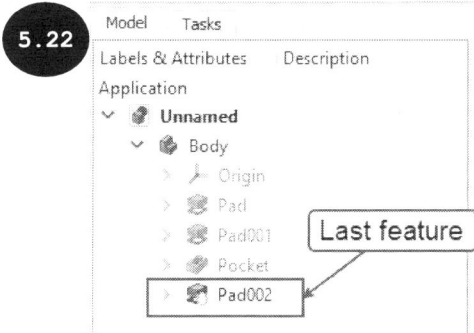

To display the earlier state of a model, click on the feature to be activated as the last feature of the model in **Tree View** (see Figure 5.23) and then press SPACEBAR. The selected feature gets activated as the last feature of the model, see Figure 5.24. Also, the earlier state of the model appears in the 3D View area such that all the features that are below the activated feature are not displayed in the model.

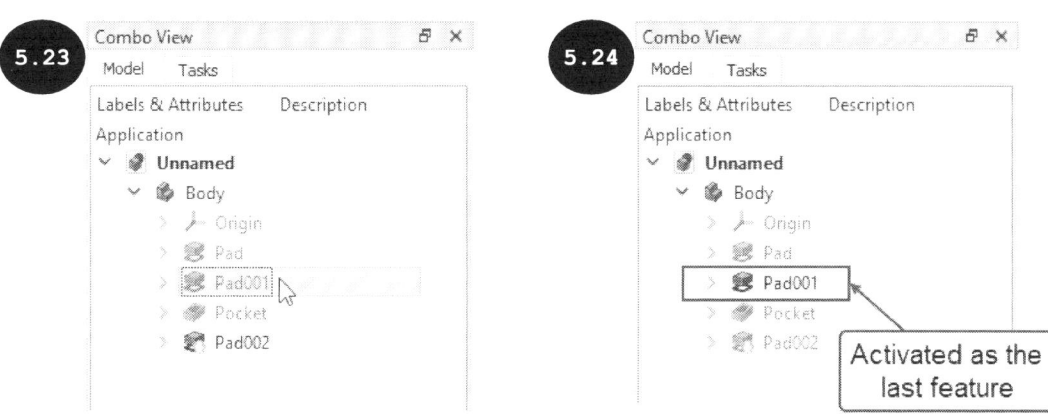

To display the complete model in its original state, select the last feature of the model in **Tree View** and then press SPACEBAR to activate it. The model is displayed in the 3D View area including all its features.

Reordering Features of a Model

By default, the features of a model are organized one after the other in the order of their creation in the **Tree View**. However, you may change the order of a feature by moving it after the other feature of the model, if desired. For doing so, right-click on the feature whose order is to be changed and then click on the **Move object after other object** option in the shortcut menu that appears, see Figure 5.25. The **Select feature** dialog box appears, see Figure 5.26.

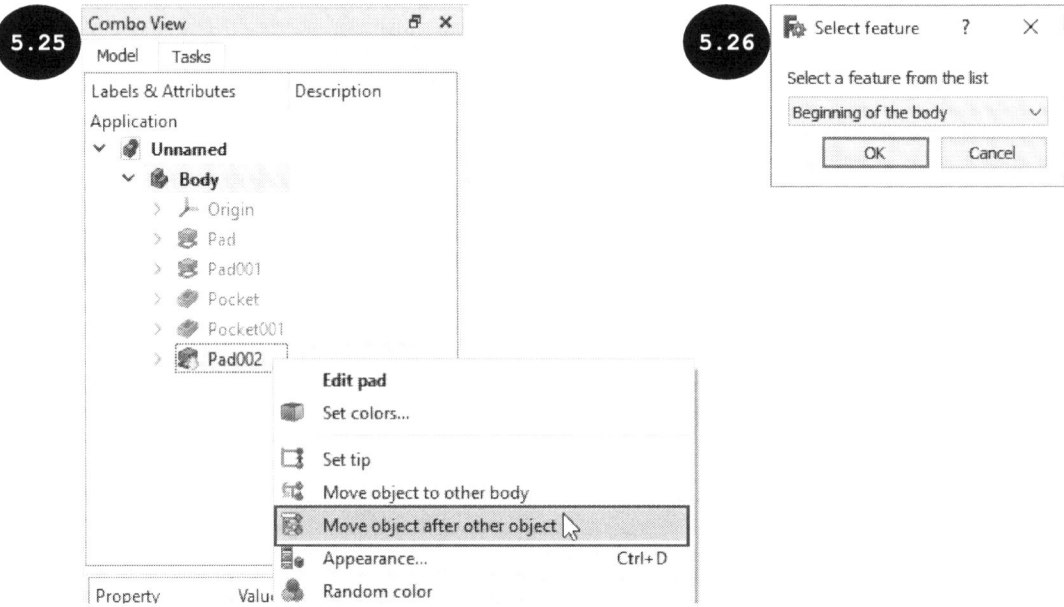

In the drop-down list of the **Select feature** dialog box, select a desired feature of the model after which the selected feature is to be moved, see Figure 5.27. Next, click on the OK button. The feature gets moved after the selected feature of the model in **Tree View**. Also, it gets activated as the last feature of the model. Note that you cannot move a child feature above its parent feature in the **Tree View**.

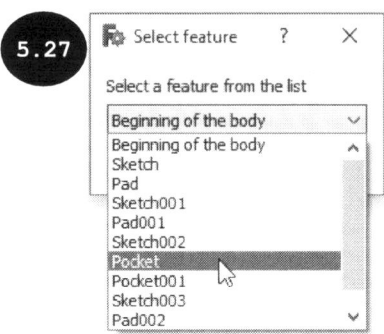

Note: Features that display below the active feature of the model in the **Tree View** are greyed out and are not included in the model in the 3D View area. To display the entire model, you need to activate its last feature by selecting it in the **Tree View** and then pressing the SPACEBAR key.

Deleting a Feature of a Model

To delete an existing feature of a model, select the feature to be deleted in **Tree View** and then right-click to display a shortcut menu, see Figure 5.28. In this shortcut menu, select the **Delete** option. The selected feature gets deleted from the model.

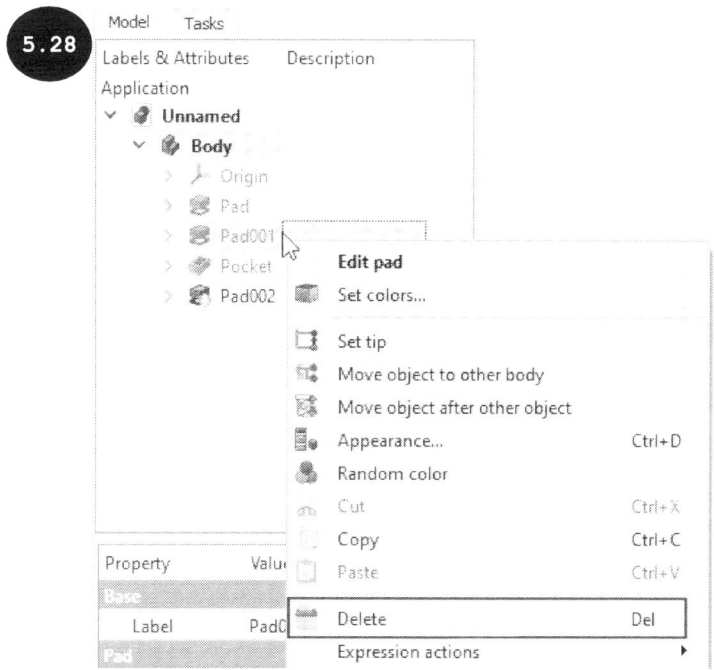

Note: If the selected feature has some dependent features, then while deleting it, the **Object dependencies** dialog box appears, see Figure 5.29. This dialog box displays a list of all dependent/child features of the feature being deleted. You can confirm or decline to delete the selected feature by clicking on the **Yes** or **No** button in the dialog box, respectively.

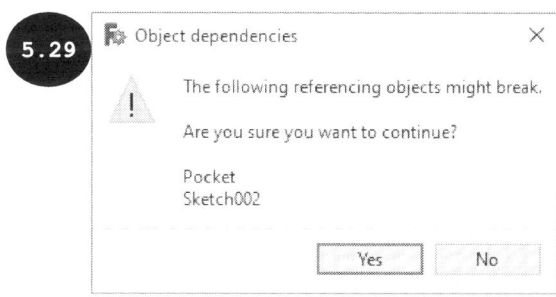

Editing Features and Sketches

FreeCAD lets you edit the individual features of a model and their sketches at any point in the design. The methods for editing a feature and its sketch are discussed next.

Editing a Feature

The method for editing a feature of a model is discussed below:

1. Select a feature to be edited in the **Tree View** of the **Model** tab and then right-click to display a shortcut menu, see Figure 5.30.

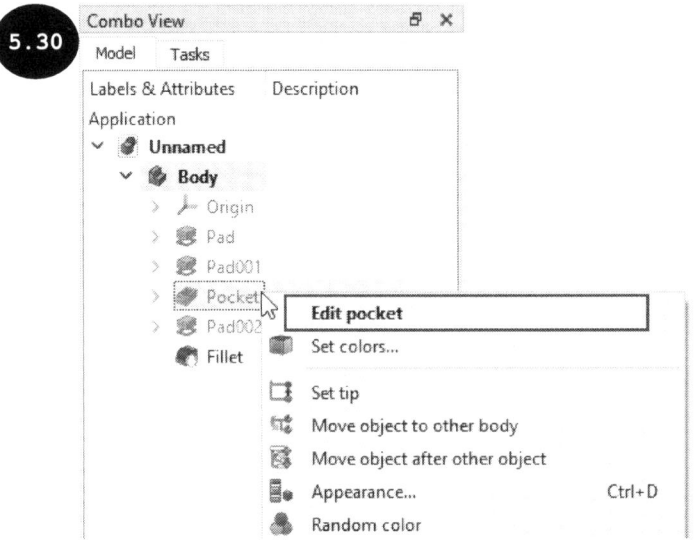

2. Click on the **Edit <feature type>** option in the shortcut menu, refer to Figure 5.30. The options to edit the parameters of the selected features appear in the **Task Panel**, see Figure 5.31.

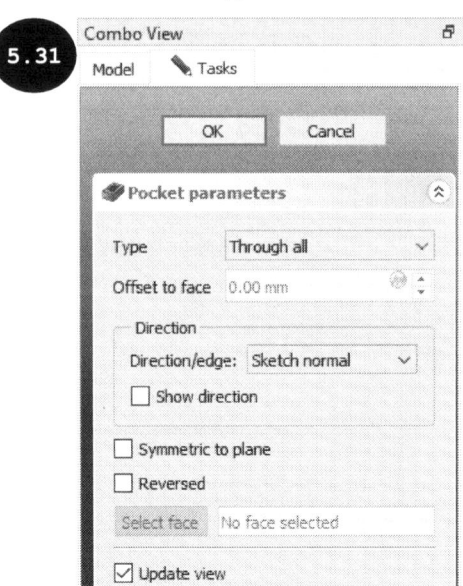

3. Edit the required parameters of the selected feature by using the respective options in the **Task Panel**.

4. After editing the required parameters, click on the **OK** button in the **Task Panel**. The selected feature of the model gets modified, accordingly.

5. Similarly, you can edit the other features of the model one by one.

Editing a Sketch

The method for editing a sketch of a feature or an individual sketch is discussed below:

1. Select the sketch of a feature or an individual sketch to be edited in the **Tree View** of the **Model** tab and then right-click to display a shortcut menu, see Figure 5.32. Note that to select the sketch of a feature, you need to expand its feature node in **Tree View**.

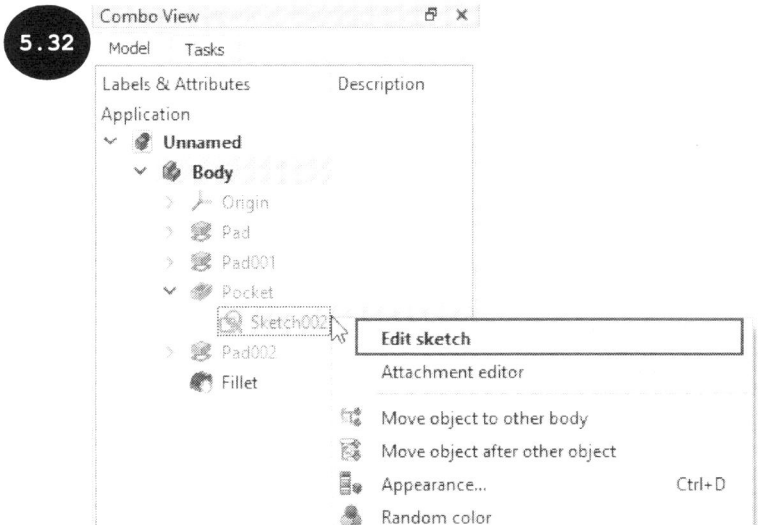

2. Click on the **Edit sketch** option in the shortcut menu. The Sketch editing mode gets invoked with the display of the selected sketch normal to the viewing direction.

3. Edit the sketch by using the sketching tools, as required.

4. After editing the sketch, exit the Sketch editing mode by clicking on the **Close** button in the **Task Panel**. The sketch gets modified.

5. Similarly, you can edit the other sketches of the model one by one.

Defining Display Properties or Appearance

In FreeCAD, you can define the required display properties or appearance of a model. The method for defining the display properties of a model is discussed below:

1. Right-click on the **Body** node in the **Tree View** and then click on the **Appearance** option in the shortcut menu that appears, see Figure 5.33. The **Display properties** sub-window appears in the **Task Panel**, see Figure 5.34. Alternatively, select the **Body** node in the **Tree View** or a face of the model in the 3D View area and then click on **View > Appearance** in the **Standard Menu** or press the CTRL + D keys for invoking the **Display properties** sub-window in the **Task Panel**.

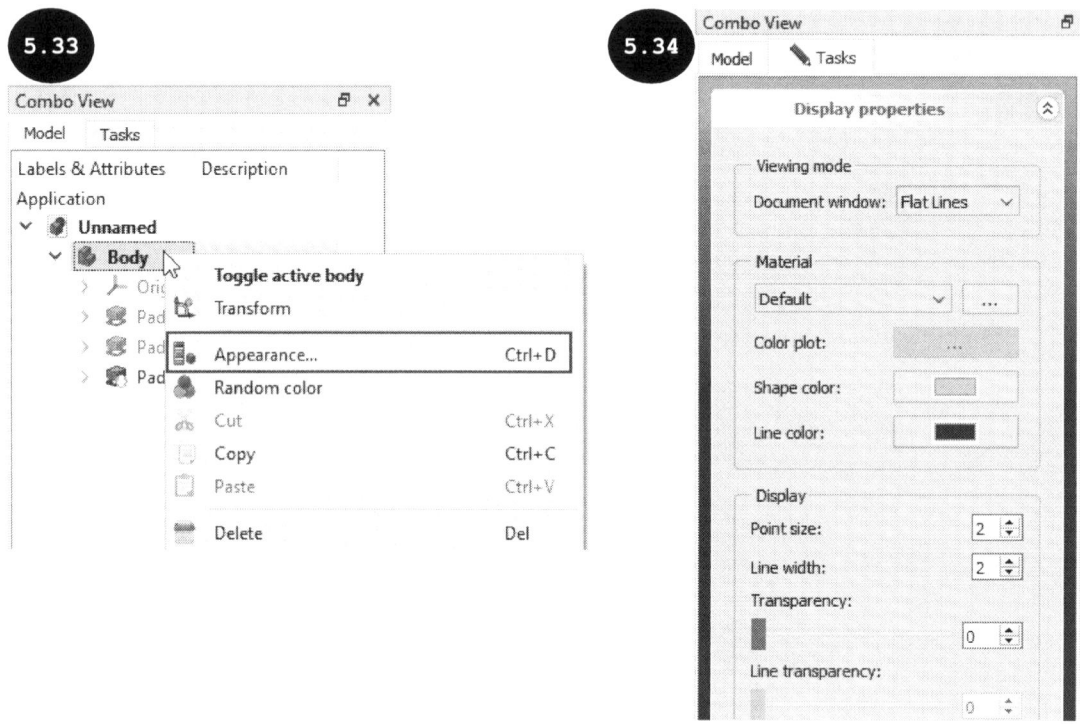

2. Select the required option (**Flat Lines**, **Shaded**, **Wireframe**, or **Points**) as the display style of the model in the **Document window** drop-down list in the **Task Panel**, see Figure 5.35.

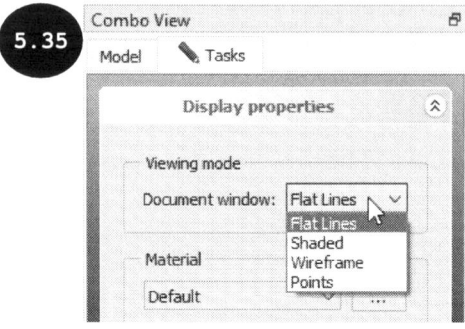

3. Select a predefined material such as Aluminum, Brass, Bronze, Copper, or Chrome in the **Material** drop-down list of the **Task Panel**, see Figure 5.36. The predefined shape and line colors of the selected material appear in the respective color swatches of the **Material** area (see Figure 5.37), and are assigned to the model, respectively.

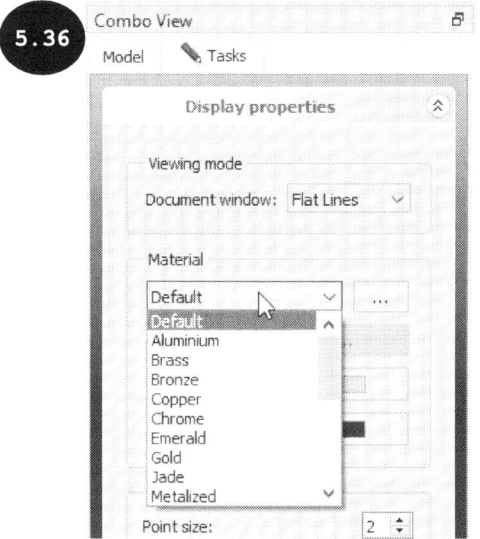

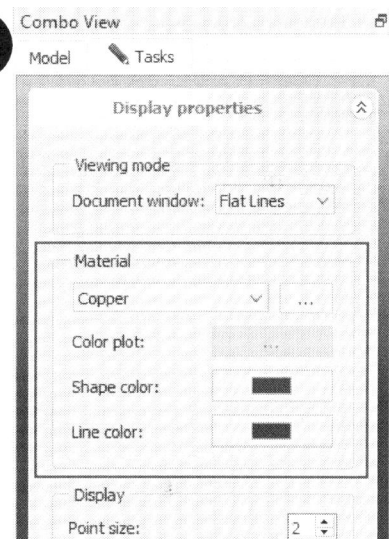

4. Edit the predefined shape and line colors of the selected material by clicking the respective color swatches (**Shape color** and **Line color**) in the **Material** area of the **Task Panel**, if needed. Note that when you click on a color Swatch (**Shape color** or **Line color**), the **Select Color** dialog box appears. In this dialog box, you can select the required color to be assigned and then click on the **OK** button to exit the dialog box.

Note: You can also customize the properties such as ambient, diffuse, emissive, specular, and shininess of the material by clicking on the [...] button next to the **Material** drop-down list of the **Task Panel**. On doing so, the **Material properties** dialog box appears, see Figure 5.38. In this dialog box, edit the material properties as required and then click on the **Close** button to exit the dialog box. The custom material properties get assigned to the selected model.

5. Accept or edit the default point size, line width, and transparency display settings of the model in the respective fields of the **Display** area in the **Task Panel**, see Figure 5.39. You can also edit the transparency of the model by dragging the **Transparency** slider available in the **Display** area of the **Task Panel**. In Figure 5.40, the transparency of the model is changed to 75%.

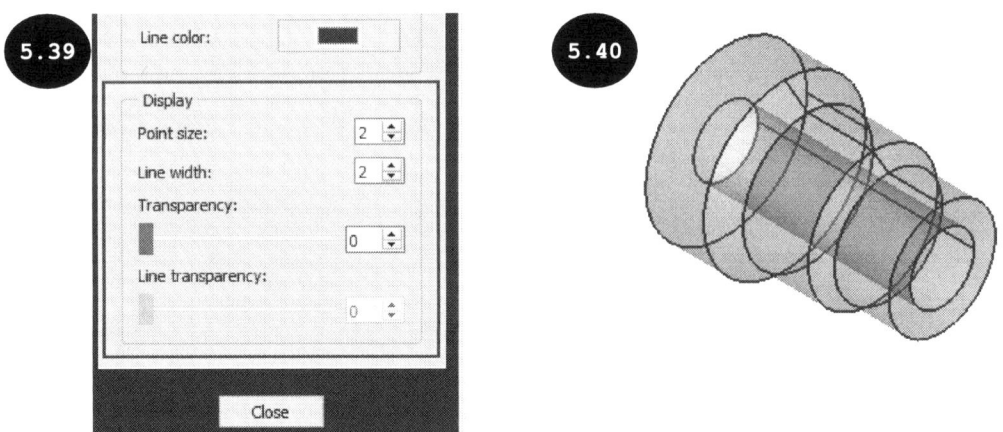

6. After defining the required display properties, click on the **Close** button in the **Task Panel**. The defined display properties or appearance get assigned to the model. Click anywhere in the 3D View area to exit the current selection set.

Measuring Distance Between Two Geometries

You can measure the linear and angular distances between two geometries such as vertices, edges, or faces of a model. The methods for measuring linear and angular distances are discussed next.

Measuring a Linear Distance

You can measure a linear distance between two geometries (vertices, edges, or faces) of a model and display the measurement results in the 3D View area, see Figure 5.41. The method for measuring a linear distance between two geometries of a model is discussed below:

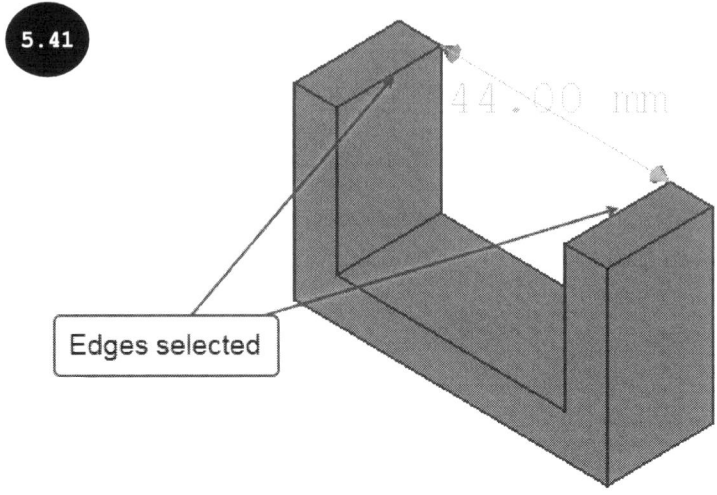

1. Click on the **Measure Linear** tool in the **Measure** toolbar, see Figure 5.42. The **Selections** and **Control** sub-windows appear in the **Task Panel**, see Figure 5.43. Also, you are prompted to select the first geometry of a model, since the **Selection 01** button is activated in the **Selections** sub-window of the **Task Panel**, by default.

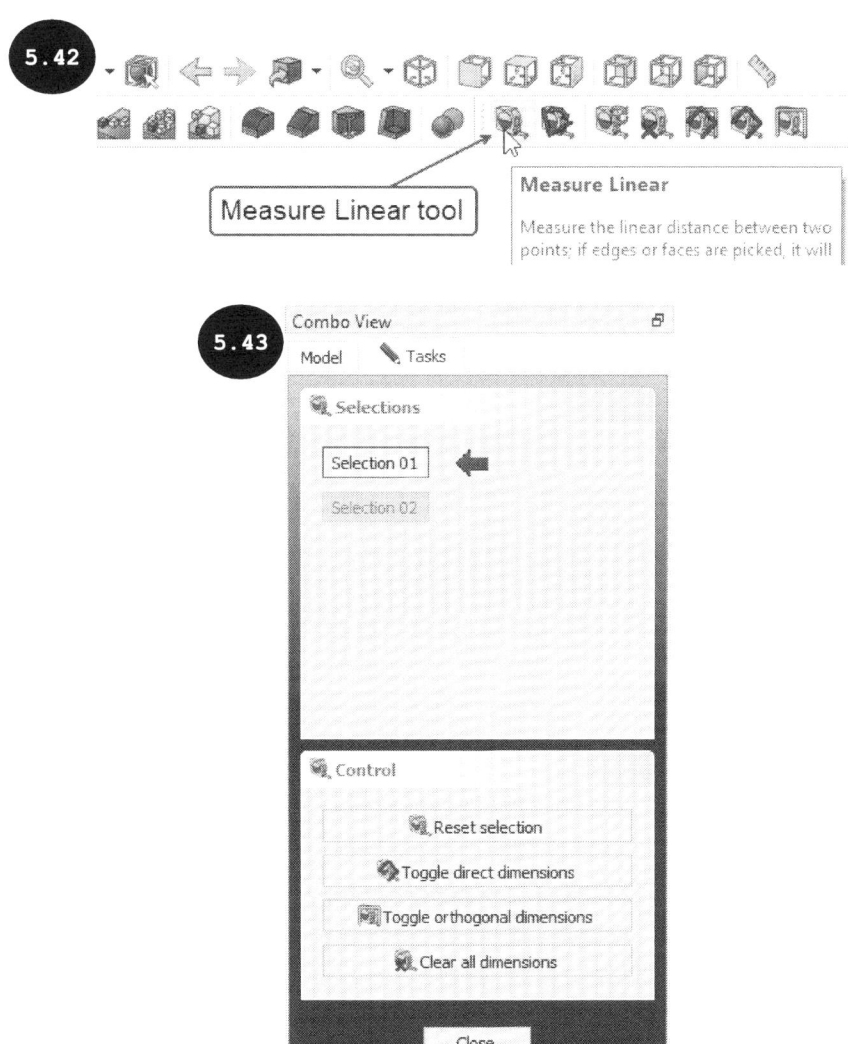

Measure Linear tool

Measure Linear

Measure the linear distance between two points; if edges or faces are picked, it will

---

Tip: The options in the **Selections** sub-window are used for selecting the geometries of the model to be measured and the options in the **Control** sub-window are used for controlling the display of the measurement results in the 3D View area.

---

2. Select the first geometry of the model in the 3D View area, see Figure 5.44. You can select a vertex, an edge, or a face of a model as the geometry. Note that after selecting the first geometry of the model, the **Selection 02** button gets activated automatically in the **Selections** sub-window and you are prompted to select the second geometry of the model.

3. Select the second geometry (vertex, edge, or face) of the model in the 3D View area. The measurement results between the selected geometries appear in the 3D View area, see Figure 5.44. Also, the **Selection 01** button gets activated again in the **Selections** sub-window of the **Task Panel**. It indicates that you continue to measure the distance between other sets of geometries.

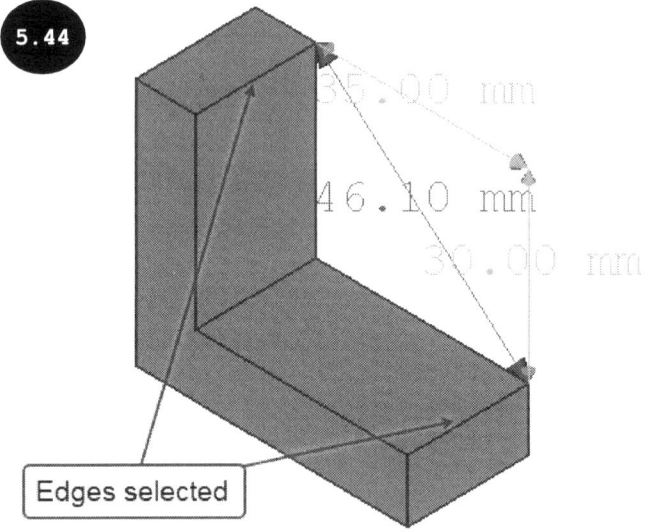

Edges selected

Note: The shortest (direct) distance between the two selected geometries and the delta measurement (orthogonal dimensions) parallel to the global X, Y, and Z axes are displayed in the 3D View area, refer to Figure 5.44. In this figure, two linear edges of the model are selected as the geometries to measure the distance between them.

---

4. Similarly, you can measure the distance between other sets of geometries one by one.

    After measuring the distance between one or more sets of geometries, you can control the display of measurement results in the 3D View area by using the options available in the **Control** sub-window of the **Task Panel**, see Figure 5.45. These options are discussed next.

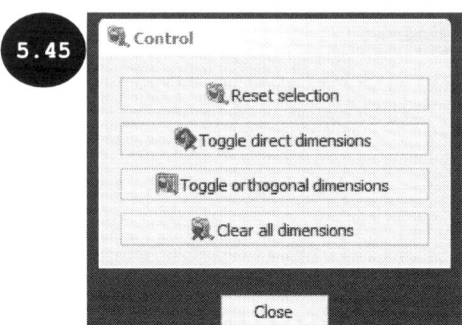

Reset selection: The Reset selection button in the **Control** sub-window is used to reset the current selection of the first geometry.

Toggle direct dimensions: The Toggle direct dimensions button is used to toggle the display of the shortest (direct) dimension between the selected geometries, see Figure 5.46.

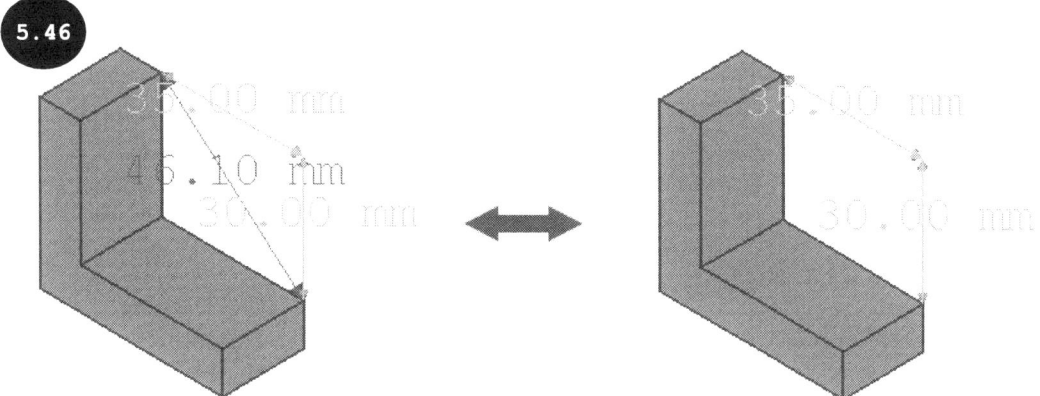

Toggle orthogonal dimensions: The Toggle orthogonal dimensions button is used to toggle the delta measurements (orthogonal dimensions) between the selected geometries, see Figure 5.47.

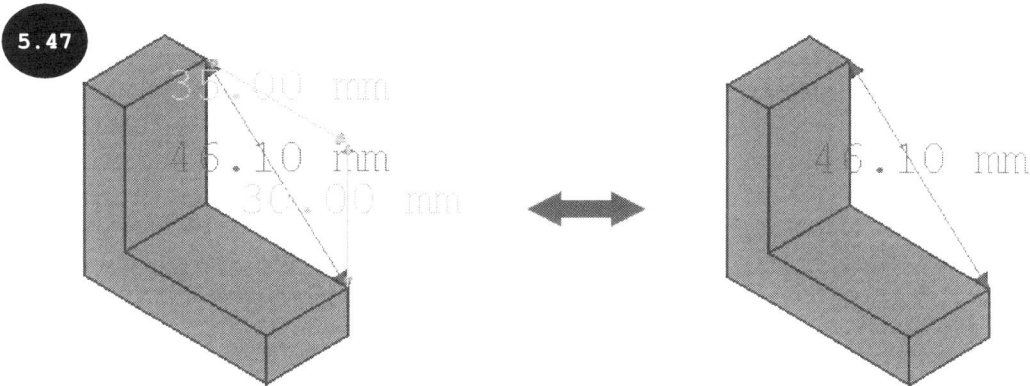

Clear all dimensions: The Clear all dimensions button is used to clear or remove the display of all the measurement results or dimensions in the 3D View area.

5. After measuring the distance between the geometries and controlling the display of the measurement results in the 3D View area if required, click on the **Close** button to exit the **Task Panel**.

Note: You can also control the display of dimensions in the 3D View area by using the tools (**Clear All**, **Toggle All**, **Toggle 3D**, and **Toggle Delta**) available in the **Measure** toolbar, see Figure 5.48.

The **Clear All** tool is used to clear or remove the display of all the measurement results or dimensions in the 3D View area. The **Toggle All** tool is used to turn on or off the display of measurement results or dimensions in the 3D View area. The **Toggle 3D** tool is used to toggle the display of shortest or direct dimensions in the 3D View area. The **Toggle Delta** tool is used to toggle the delta/orthogonal dimensions in the 3D View area.

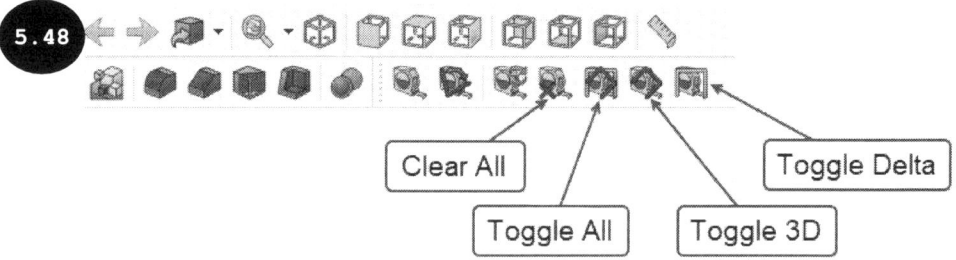

Measuring an Angular Distance

You can measure an angular distance between two linear edges, two planar faces, or a linear edge and a planar face of a model and display the measurement results in the 3D View area, see Figure 5.49. In this figure, the angular distance between two linear edges is measured. The method for measuring an angular distance between two geometries is discussed below:

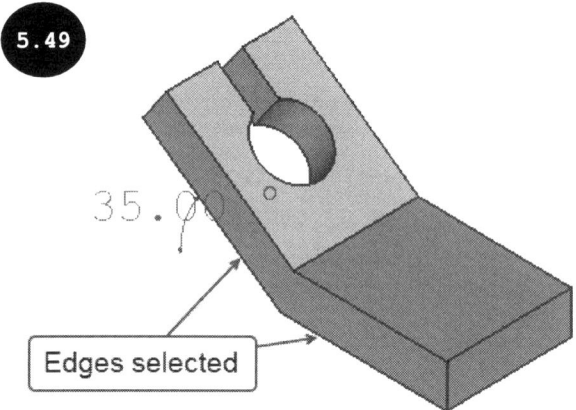

1. Click on the **Measure Angular** tool in the **Measure** toolbar, see Figure 5.50. The **Selections** and **Control** sub-windows appear in the **Task Panel**. Also, you are prompted to select the first geometry of a model, since the **Selection 01** button is activated in the **Selections** sub-window of the **Task Panel**, by default.

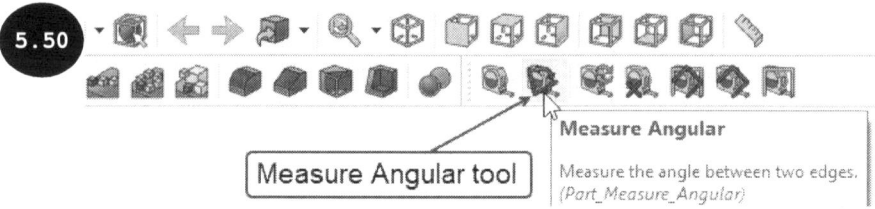

2. Select the first geometry of the model in the 3D View area. You can select a linear edge or a planar face as the first geometry. Note that after selecting the first geometry, the **Selection 02** button gets activated in the **Selections** sub-window for selecting the second geometry of the model.

3. Select a linear edge or a planar face of a model as the second geometry. The angular distance between the selected geometries of the model appears in the 3D View area.

4. Similarly, you can measure the angular distance between other sets of model geometries one by one.

> **Note:** The options in the **Control** sub-window of the **Task Panel** are used to control the display of the measurement results in the 3D View area and are the same as discussed earlier.

5. Click on the **Close** button to exit the **Task Panel**.

> **Tip:** If the position of measured geometries of a model are moved or updated, then you need to refresh or recalculate their measurement dimensions in the 3D View area by clicking on the **Refresh** tool in the **Measure** tool, see Figure 5.51.

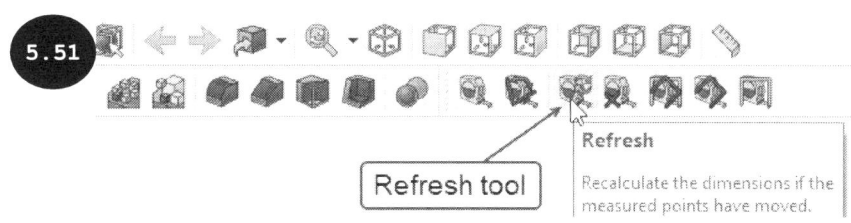

5.51

Refresh tool

Refresh

Recalculate the dimensions if the measured points have moved.

Tutorial 1

Create a model, as shown in Figure 5.52. Different views and dimensions of the model are given in the same figure. All dimensions are in mm.

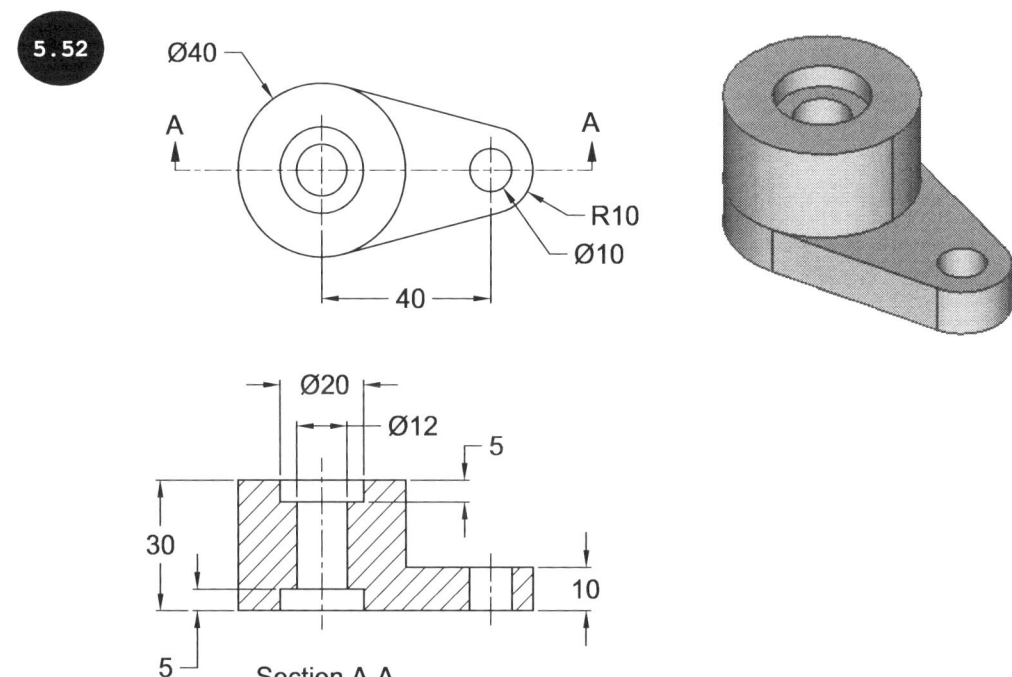

5.52

Section A-A

Section 1: Starting FreeCAD and a New Empty Document

1. Start FreeCAD by double-clicking on the **FreeCAD 0.20** icon on your desktop. The startup user interface of FreeCAD appears, see Figure 5.53.

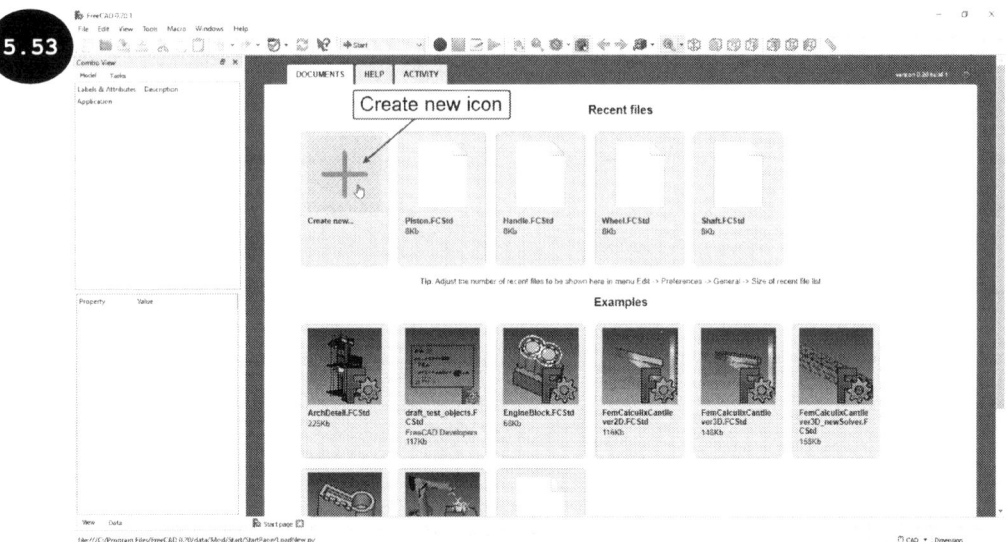

2. Click on the **Create new** icon on the **Start** page (refer to Figure 5.53) or press the **CTRL + N** keys. A new empty document gets invoked with the default name "**unnamed: 1**" and it becomes active by default.

Section 2: Invoking the Part Design Workbench

Now, you can invoke the **Part Design** workbench for creating a 3D solid part.

1. Invoke the **Workbench Selector** in the **Workbench** toolbar and then select the **Part Design** workbench, see Figure 5.54. The **Part Design** workbench gets invoked.

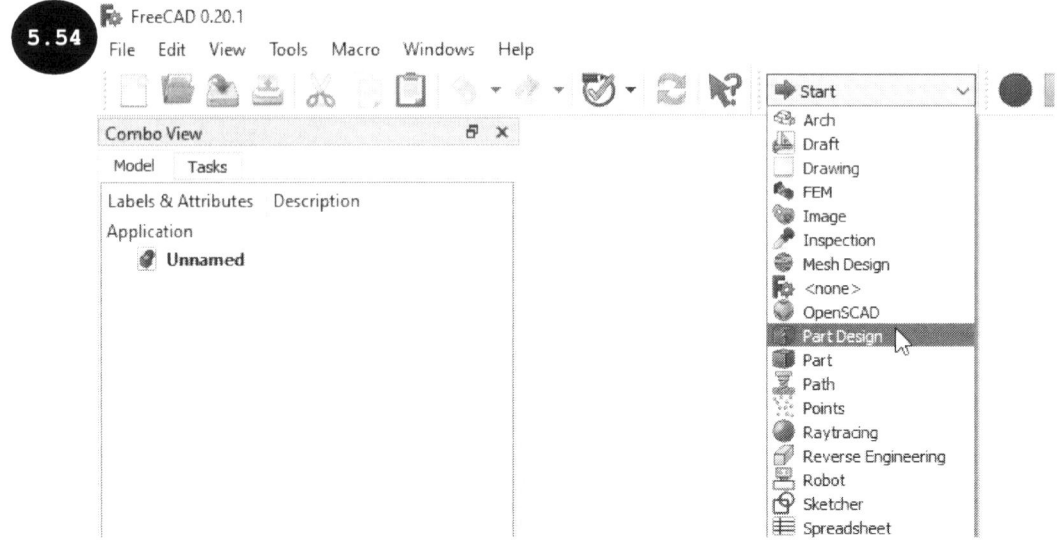

Section 3: Specifying the Unit

Now, you need to specify millimeters (mm) as the measurement unit for the document.

1. Click on **Edit > Preferences** in the **Standard Menu**, see Figure 5.55. The **Preferences** dialog box appears.

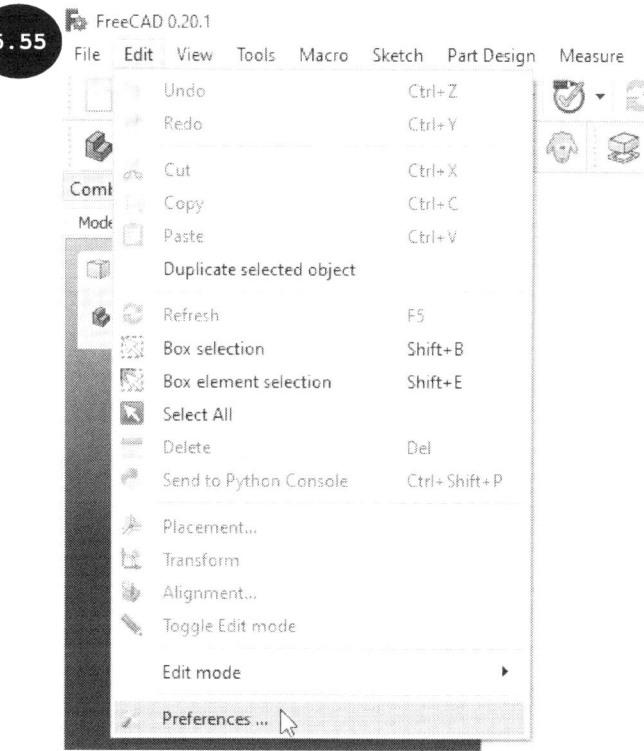

2. Ensure that the **General** section is selected in the left panel of the **Preferences** dialog box and then click on the **Units** tab, see Figure 5.56.

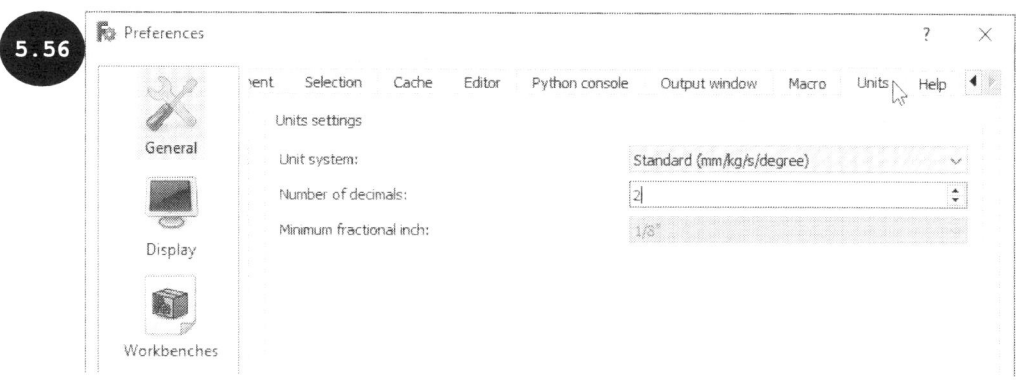

Tip: You may need to click on the arrow ▶ at the upper right corner of the **Preferences** dialog box for displaying the **Units** tab.

3. Ensure that the **Standard (mm/kg/s/degree)** option is selected in the **Unit system** drop-down list of the dialog box. In this unit system, the length is measured in millimeters, the mass is calculated in kilograms, the time is represented in seconds, and the angle is measured in degrees.

4. Ensure that the **2** is specified in the **Number of decimals** field of the dialog box as the number of digits after the decimal point of measurements.

5. Click on the **Apply** button and then the **OK** button in the **Preferences** dialog box. The selected unit system is defined, and the dialog box is closed.

Section 4: Creating the Base Feature

Now, you can create the base feature of the model, which is a pad feature.

1. Click on the **Create sketch** tool in the **Part Design Helper** toolbar, see Figure 5.57. The three default planes appear in the 3D View area. Also, the **Task Panel** appears in the **Tasks** tab of **Combo View** with a list of three default planes.

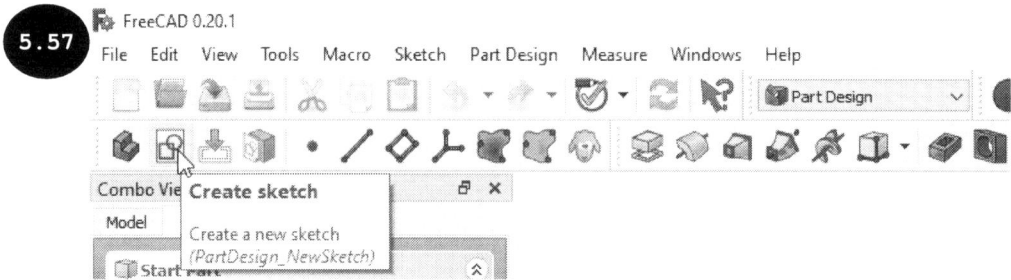

2. Select the **XY_Plane** as the sketching plane in the 3D View area for creating the sketch of the base feature. The **Sketcher** workbench gets invoked. Also, the selected plane becomes the sketching plane for drawing the sketch and is oriented normal to the viewing direction.

    Now, you can create a sketch of the base feature.

3. Create the sketch of the base feature and then apply the required constraints and dimensions to the sketch, see Figure 5.58.

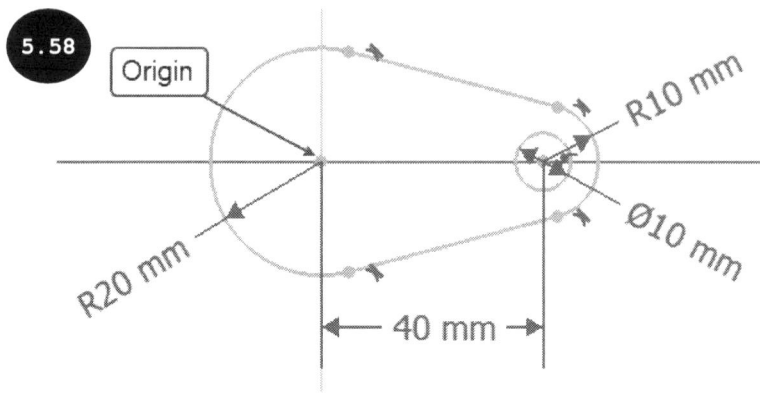

Note: In Figure 5.58, a tangent constant is applied between each set of connected arc and line entities of the sketch to make it fully constrained.

After creating the sketch, you need to exit the **Sketcher** workbench.

4. Click on the **Close** button in the **Task Plane** of the **Combo View** to exit the **Sketcher** workbench (see Figure 5.59) and switch back to the **Part Design** workbench.

Now, you need to create a pad feature.

5. Click on the **Pad** tool in the **Part Design Modeling** toolbar, see Figure 5.60. The preview of a pad feature appears in the 3D View area with default parameters. Also, the **Pad parameters** sub-window appears in the **Task Panel**, see Figure 5.61.

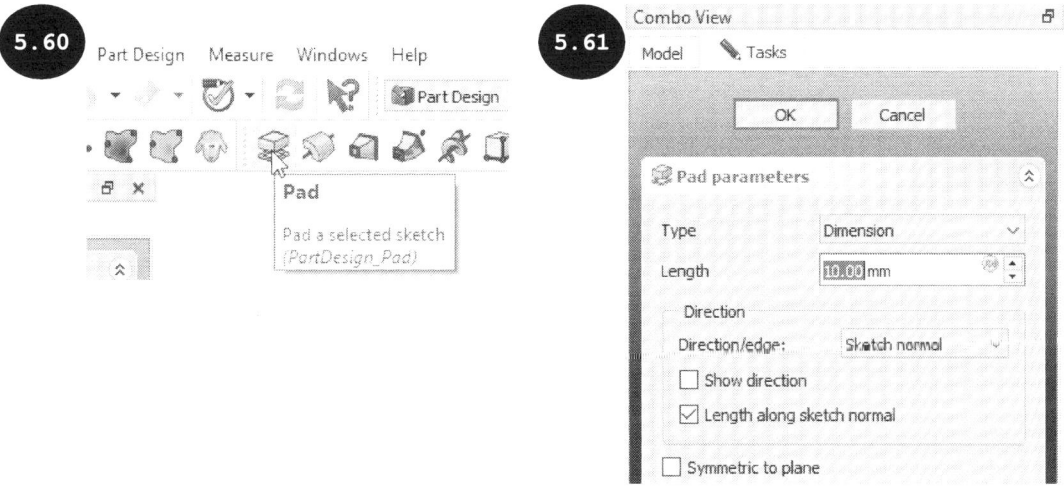

6. Ensure that the **Dimension** option is selected in the **Type** drop-down list for creating a pad feature by specifying its length.

7.   Enter 10 mm as the length of the pad feature in the **Length** field of the **Task Panel**. Next, press the TAB key or click anywhere in the 3D View area to update the preview of the pad feature.

8.   Click on the **OK** button in the **Task Panel** to confirm the creation of the pad feature and exit the **Task Panel**. The pad feature gets created, see Figure 5.62.

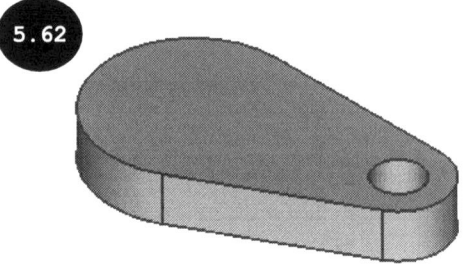

Section 5: Creating the Second Feature
Now, you can create the second feature of the model.

1.   Click to select the top planar face of the base feature as the sketching plane for creating the sketch of the second feature of the model, see Figure 5.63.

2.   Click on the **Create sketch** tool in the **Part Design Helper** toolbar, see Figure 5.64. The **Sketcher** workbench gets invoked and the top planar face of the base feature gets oriented normal to the viewing direction.

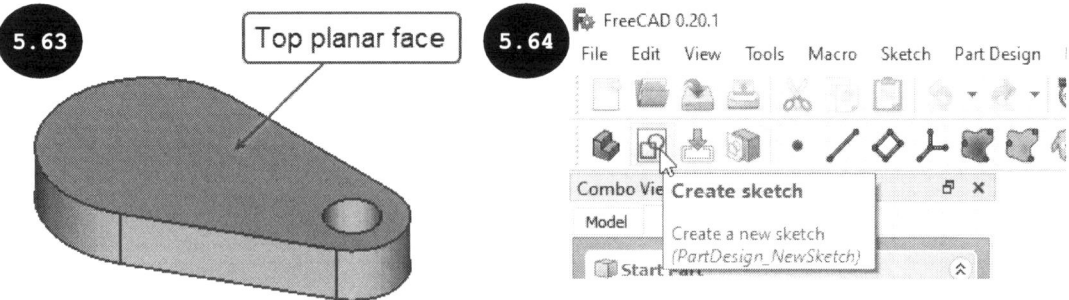

3.   Create a circle of diameter 40 mm as the sketch of the second feature, see Figure 5.65. Note that the center point of the circle is at the origin.

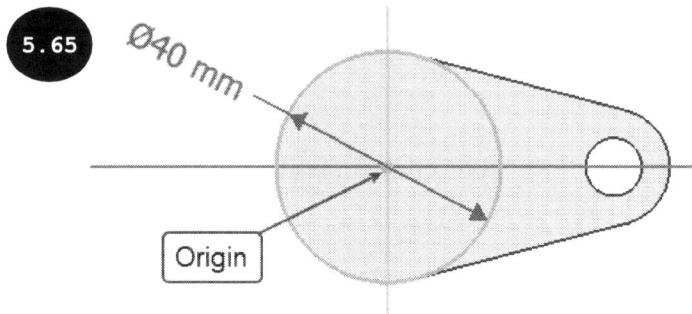

4. After creating the sketch, click on the **Close** button in the **Task Plane** of the **Combo View** to exit the **Sketcher** workbench (see Figure 5.66) and switch back to the **Part Design** workbench.

Now, you can extrude the sketch to create a pad feature.

5. Click on the **Pad** tool in the **Part Design Modeling** toolbar, see Figure 5.67. The preview of a pad feature appears in the 3D View area with default parameters. Also, the **Pad parameters** sub-window appears in the **Task Panel**.

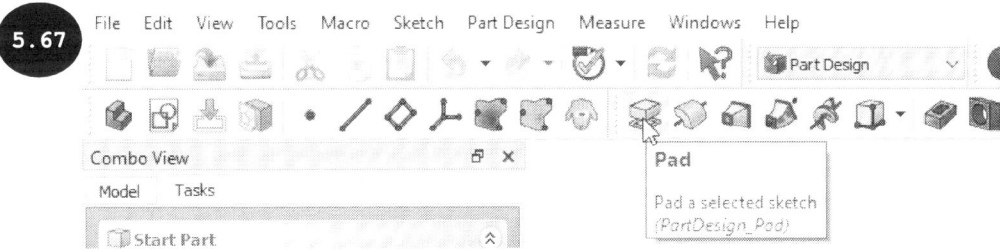

6. Enter **20** mm as the length of the pad feature in the **Length** field of the **Task Panel**. Next, press the TAB key or click anywhere in the 3D View area to update the preview of the pad feature.

7. Click on the **OK** button in the **Task Panel** to confirm the creation of the pad feature and exit the **Task Panel**. The second feature gets created, see Figure 5.68. Click anywhere in the 3D View area to exit the current selection set.

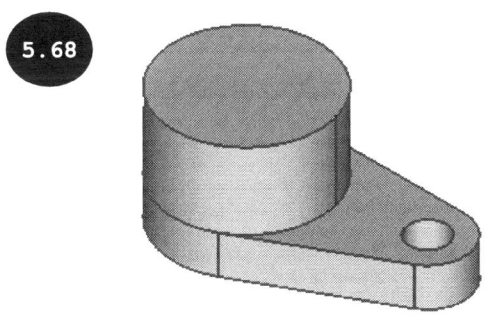

Section 6: Creating the Third Feature

Now, you need to create the third feature of the model, which is a groove feature.

1. Click on the **Create sketch** tool ![sketch icon] in the **Part Design Helper** toolbar, see Figure 5.69. The three default planes appear in the 3D View area, and you are prompted to select a sketching plane for creating the sketch of the third feature.

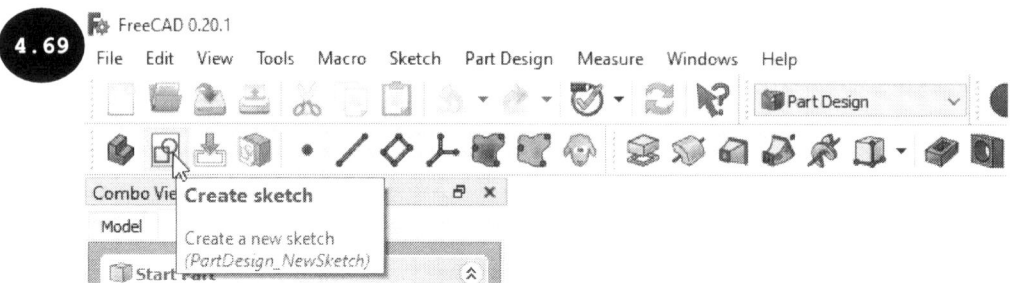

2. Select the **XZ_Plane** as the sketching plane in the 3D View area for creating the sketch of the third feature. The **Sketcher** workbench gets invoked. Also, the selected plane gets oriented normal to the viewing direction.

3. Select the **View section** tool in the **Sketcher** toolbar, see Figure 5.70. The section view of the model appears in the 3D View area by temporarily hiding the material that is in front of the sketching plane.

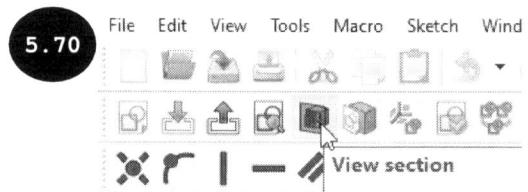

4. Create the sketch of the third feature and then apply the required constraints and dimensions, see Figure 5.71.

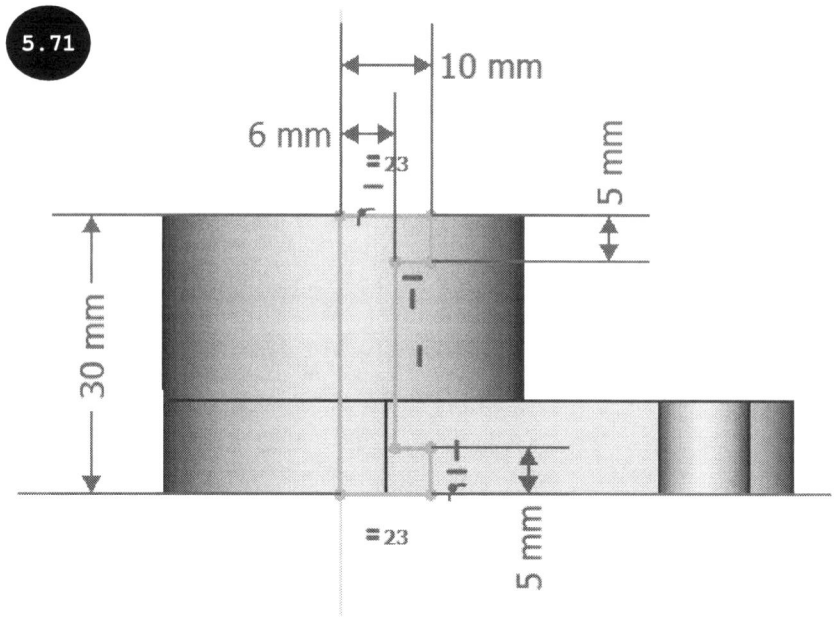

5. After creating the sketch, click on the **Close** button in the **Task Plane** to exit the **Sketcher** workbench and switch back to the **Part Design** workbench.

6. Click on the **Groove** tool in the **Part Design Modeling** toolbar, see Figure 5.72. The preview of a groove feature appears such that the material is removed from the model by revolving the sketch around its vertical axis in the 3D View area, see Figure 5.73. It is because the **Vertical sketch axis** option is selected by default in the **Axis** drop-down list of the **Revolution parameters** sub-window that appears in the **Task Panel**, see Figure 5.74.

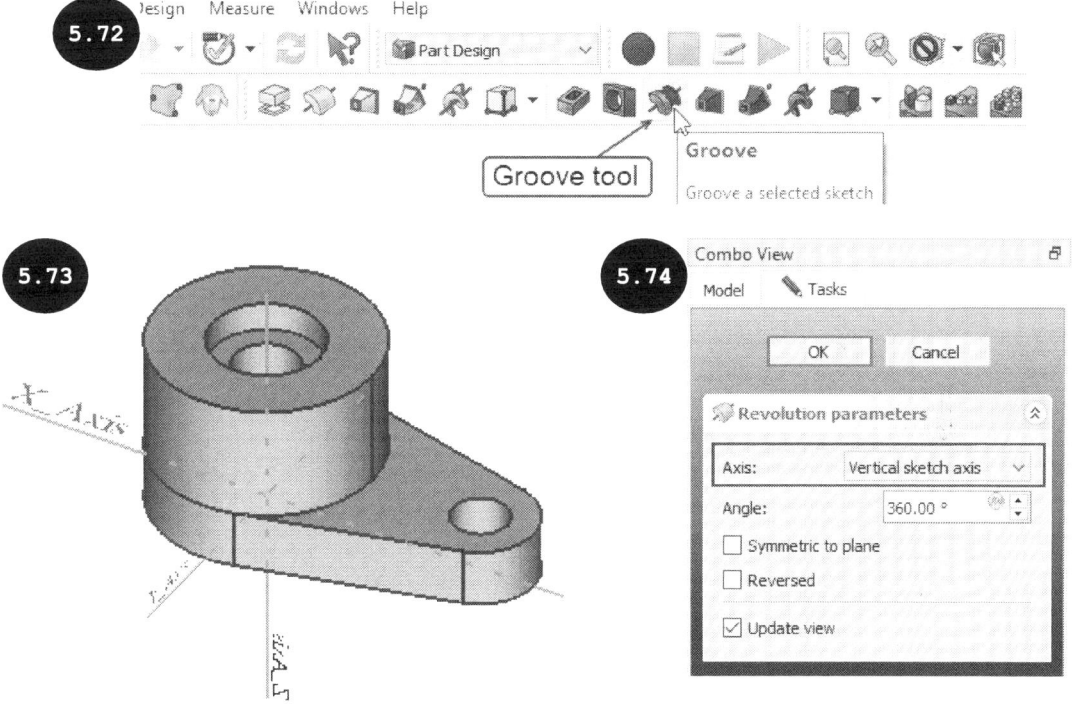

7. Ensure that the **360** degrees is specified as the angle of revolution in the **Angle** field of the **Task Panel**.

8. Click on the **OK** button in the **Task Panel** to confirm the creation of the feature and exit the **Task Panel**. Figure 5.75 shows the final model after creating all its features.

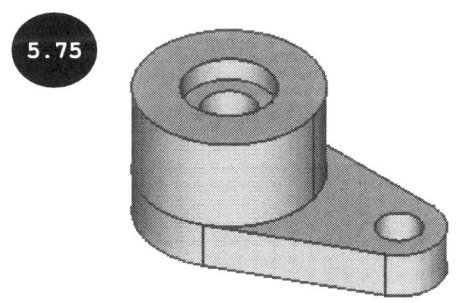

Section 7: Saving the Model

1. Click on the **Save** tool in the **File** toolbar (see Figure 5.76) or press the CTRL + S keys. The **Save FreeCAD Document** dialog box appears.

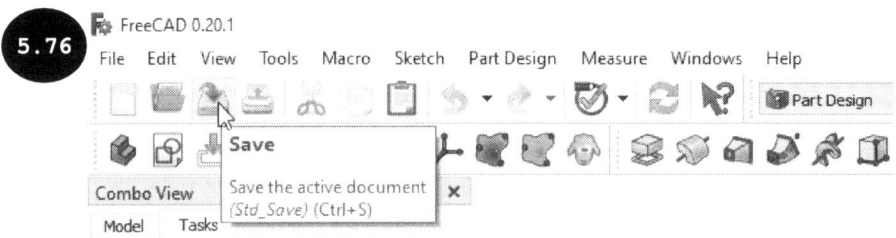

2. Browse to the required folder (:*FreeCAD* > *Chapter 05*) in the local drive of your system. Note that you need to create the Chapter 05 sub-folder inside the FreeCAD folder.

3. Enter **Ch05-Tutorial 1** in the **File name** field of the dialog box. Next, click on the **Save** button in the dialog box. The model gets saved with the name **Tutorial 1** at the specified location (:*FreeCAD* > *Chapter 05*).

4. Click on **File** > **Close** in the **Standard Menu** to close the current document.

Tutorial 2

Create a model, as shown in Figure 5.77. Different views and dimensions of the model are given in Figure 5.78. All dimensions are in inches (in).

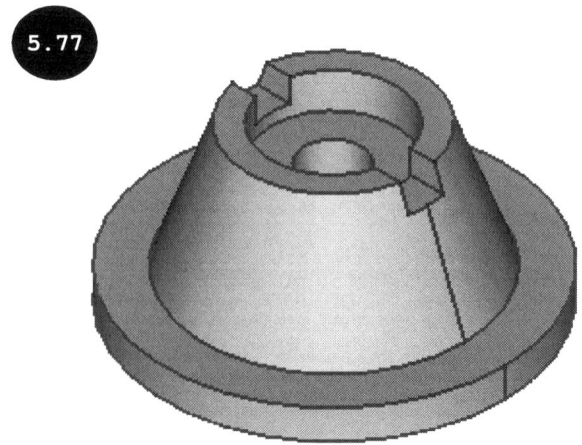

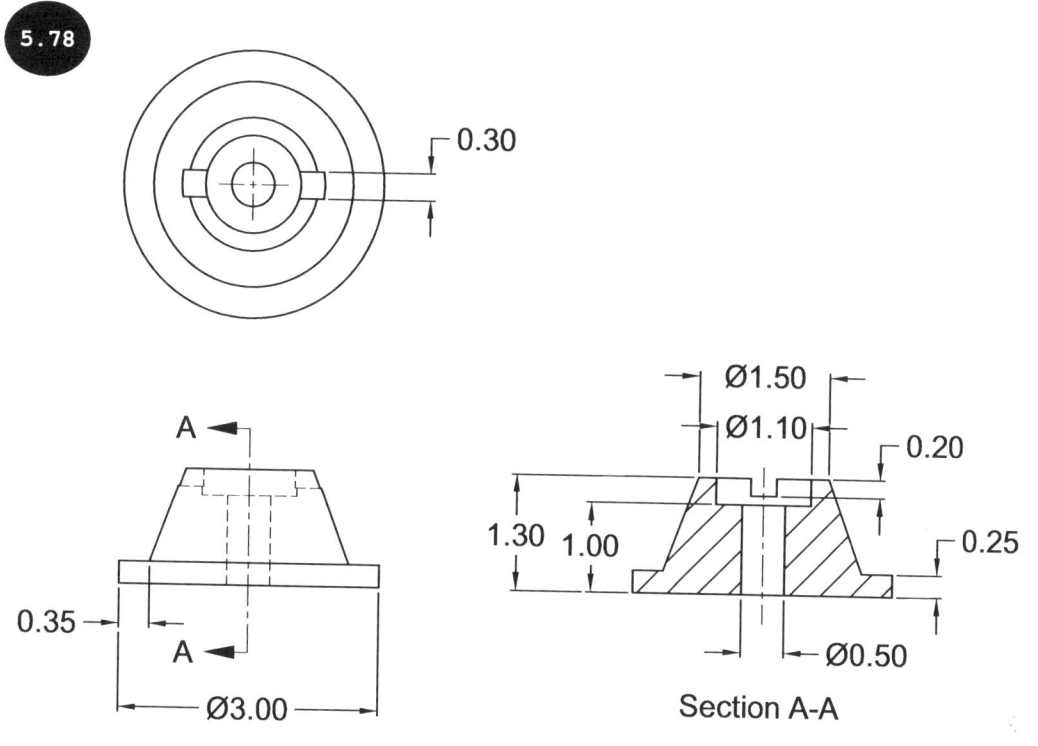

Section 1: Starting FreeCAD and a New Empty Document

1. Start FreeCAD by double-clicking on the **FreeCAD 0.20** icon on your desktop, if not started already. The startup user interface of FreeCAD appears.

2. Click on the **New** tool in the **File** toolbar (see Figure 5.79) or press the **CTRL + N** keys. A new empty document gets invoked with the default name and gets activated, by default.

Section 2: Invoking the Part Design Workbench

Now, you can invoke the **Part Design** workbench.

1. Invoke the **Workbench Selector** in the **Workbench** toolbar and then select the **Part Design** workbench, see Figure 5.80. The **Part Design** workbench gets invoked.

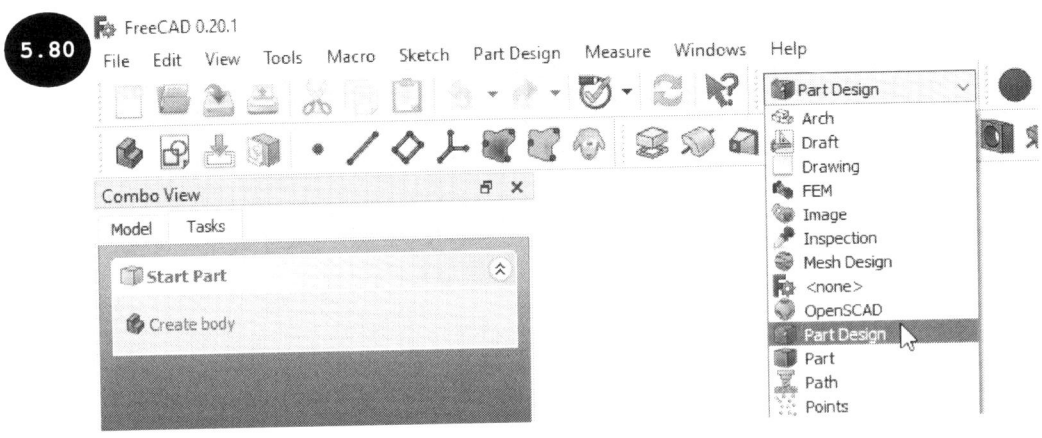

Section 3: Specifying the Unit

Now, you need to specify inches (in) as the measurement unit for the document.

1.   Click on **Edit > Preferences** in the **Standard Menu**. The **Preferences** dialog box appears.

2.   Ensure that the **General** section is selected in the left panel of the **Preferences** dialog box and then click on the **Units** tab, refer to Figure 5.81.

Tip: You may need to click on the arrow ▶ at the upper right corner of the **Preferences** dialog box for displaying the **Units** tab.

3.   Select the **Imperial decimal (in/lb)** option in the **Unit system** drop-down list of the dialog box as the unit system, see Figure 5.81. In this unit system, the length is measured in inches and the mass is calculated in pounds (lb).

4.   Ensure that the **2** is specified in the **Number of decimals** field of the dialog box as the number of digits after the decimal point of measurements, see Figure 5.81.

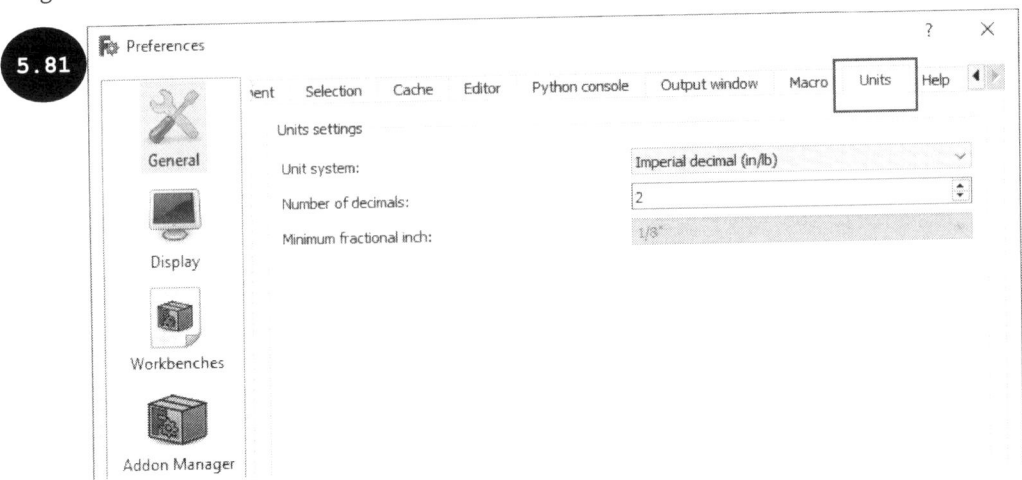

5. Click on the **Apply** button and then the **OK** button in the **Preferences** dialog box. The selected unit system is defined, and the dialog box is closed.

Section 4: Creating the Base Feature

Now, you can create the base feature of the model, which is a revolution feature.

1. Click on the **Create sketch** tool in the **Part Design Helper** toolbar, see Figure 5.82. The three default planes appear in the 3D View area. Also, the **Task Panel** appears in the **Tasks** tab of **Combo View**.

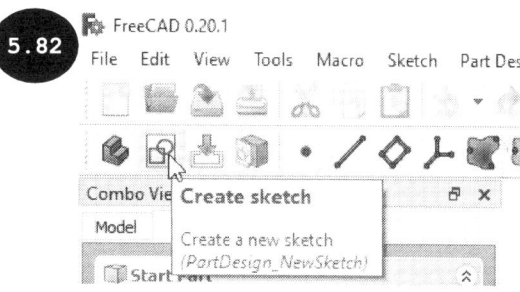

2. Select the **XZ_Plane** as the sketching plane in the 3D View area. The **Sketcher** workbench gets invoked and the selected plane gets oriented normal to the viewing direction.

3. Create the sketch of the base feature of the model and then apply the required constraints and dimensions, see Figure 5.83.

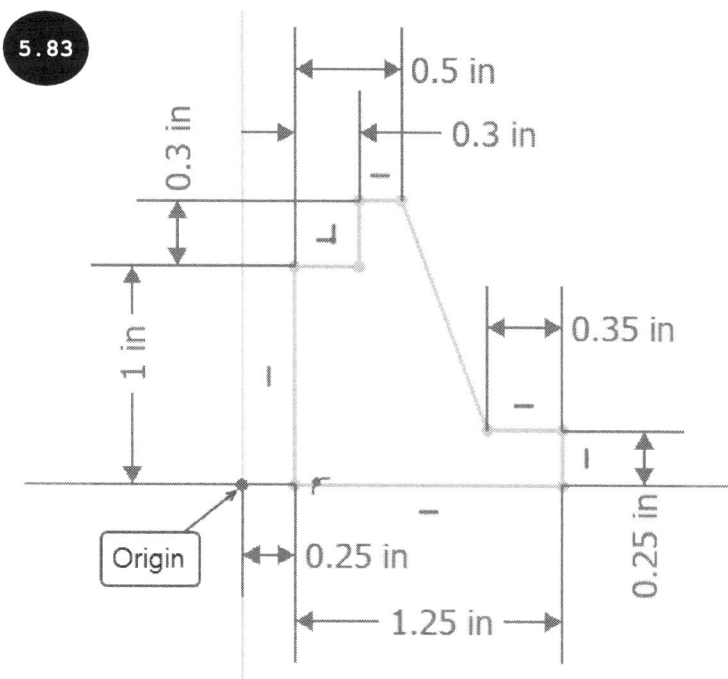

4. After creating the sketch, click on the **Close** button in the **Task Plane** to exit the **Sketcher** workbench and switch back to the **Part Design** workbench.

5. Click on the **Revolution** tool in the **Part Design Modeling** toolbar, see Figure 5.84. The preview of a revolution feature appears in the 3D View area with default parameters. Also, the **Revolution parameters** sub-window appears in the **Task Panel** of the **Combo View**.

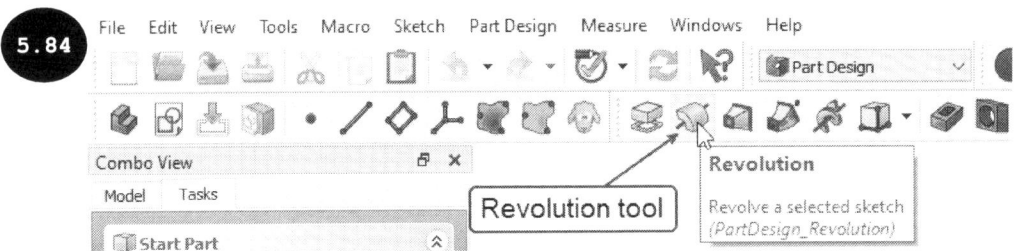

6. Ensure that the **Vertical sketch axis** option is selected in the **Axis** drop-down list of the **Task Panel** as the axis of revolution.

7. Ensure that the **360** degrees is specified as the angle of revolution in the **Angle** field of the **Task Panel**.

8. Click on the **OK** button in the **Task Panel**. The revolution feature gets created in the 3D View area, see Figure 5.85.

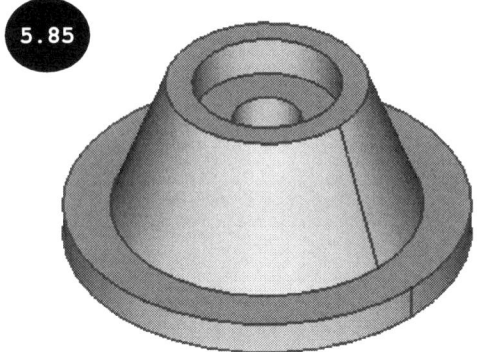

Section 5: Creating the Second Feature
Now, you can create the second feature of the model, which is a pocket feature.

1. Select the top planar face of the base feature as the sketching plane for creating the sketch of the second feature, see Figure 5.86.

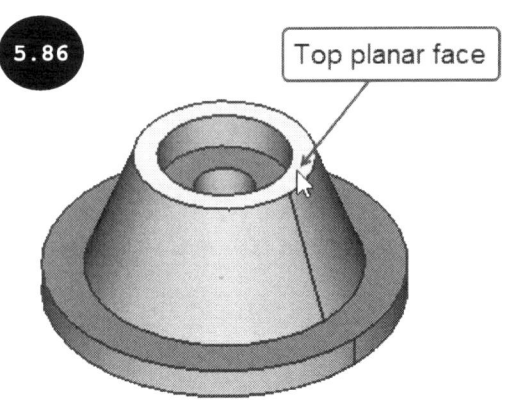

2. Click on the **Create sketch** tool in the **Part Design Helper** toolbar, see Figure 5.87. The **Sketcher** workbench gets invoked and the top planar face of the base feature gets oriented normal to the viewing direction.

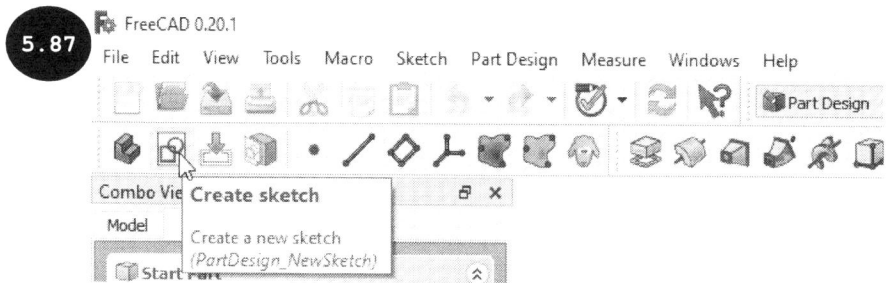

3. Create a rectangle as the sketch of the second feature, see Figure 5.88. Note that the center point of the rectangle is at the origin.

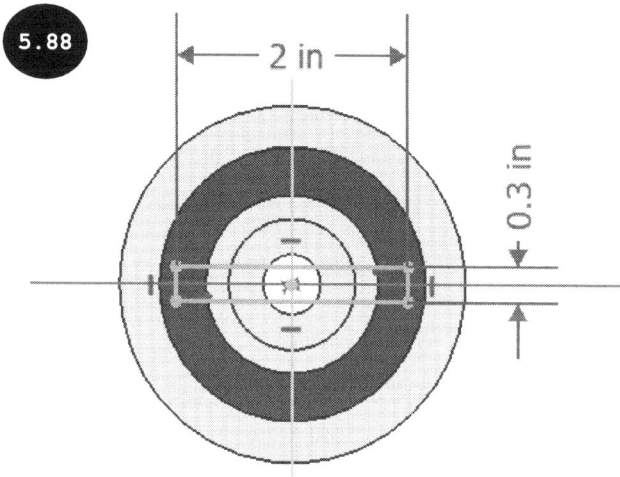

4. After creating the sketch, click on the **Close** button in the **Task Plane** to exit the **Sketcher** workbench and switch back to the **Part Design** workbench.

Now, you can create a pocket feature by removing the material from the model.

5. Click on the **Pocket** tool in the **Part Design Modeling** toolbar, see Figure 5.89. The preview of a pocket feature appears in the 3D View area by removing material from the model up to a default length. Also, the **Pocket parameters** sub-window appears in the **Task Panel**.

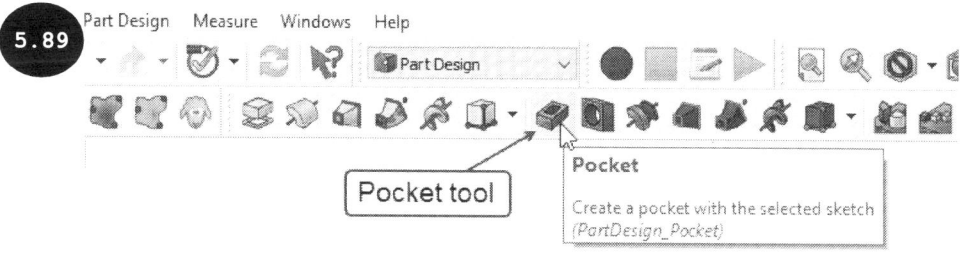

6. Ensure that the **Dimension** option is selected in the **Type** drop-down list of the **Task Panel** for extruding the sketch up to a specified length.

7. Enter **0.2** inches in the **Length** field of the Task Panel as the length of extrusion and then press the TAB key to update the preview of the pocket feature in the 3D View area.

8. Accept the remaining default options and then click on the **OK** button in the **Task Panel** to confirm the creation of the pocket feature by removing the material from the model. Figure 5.90 shows the final model after creating all its features.

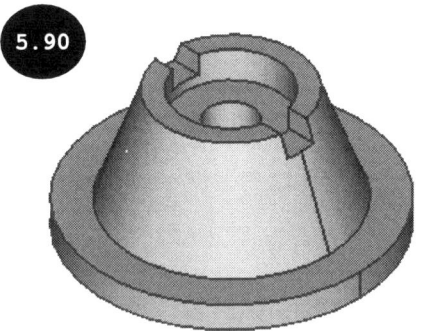

Section 6: Assigning the Material/Appearance
Now, you can assign the chrome material/appearance to the model.

1. Right-click on the **Body** node in the **Model** tab of the **Combo View** and then click on the **Appearance** option in the shortcut menu that appears, see Figure 5.91. The **Display properties** sub-window appears in the **Task Panel**, see Figure 5.92.

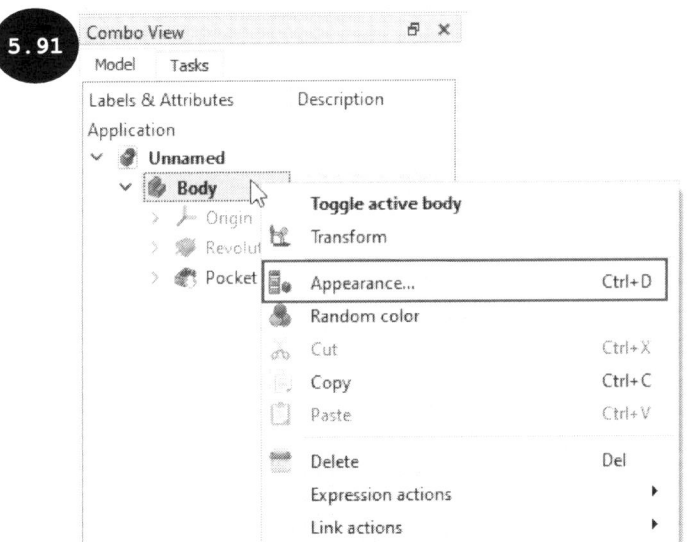

2. Select the **Chrome** option in the Material drop-down list of the dialog box as the material or appearance to be applied to the selected model.

3. Accept the remaining default display properties and then click on the **Close** button to exit the **Task Panel**. The Chrome material or appearance gets applied to the model, see Figure 5.93.

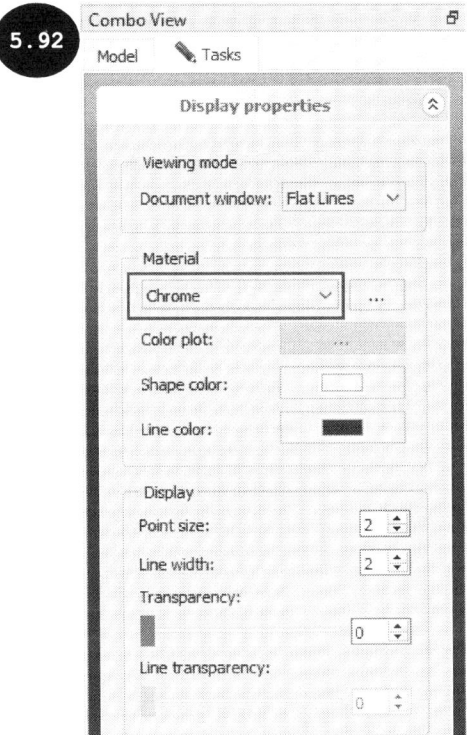

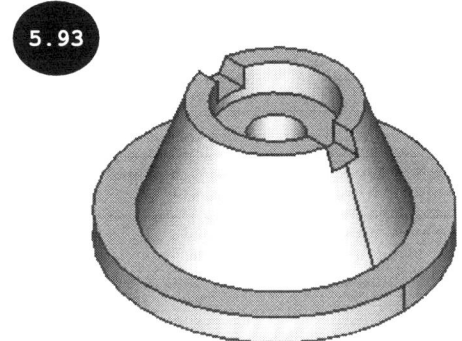

Section 7: Saving the Model
Now, you can save the model.

1. Click on the **Save** tool in the **File** toolbar (see Figure 5.94) or press the CTRL + S keys. The **Save FreeCAD Document** dialog box appears.

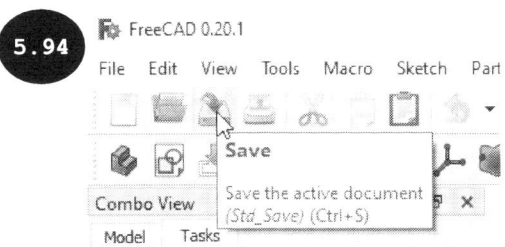

2. Browse to the *FreeCAD > Chapter 05* folder in the local drive of your system. You need to create these folders, if not created earlier.

3. Enter **Ch05-Tutorial 2** in the **File name** field of the dialog box. Next, click on the **Save** button in the dialog box. The mode gets saved at the specified location.

4. Close the document by clicking on **File** > **Close** in the **Standard Menu**.

Hands-on Test Drive 1

Create the model shown in Figure 5.95. You need to create the model by creating all its features one by one. All dimensions are in mm.

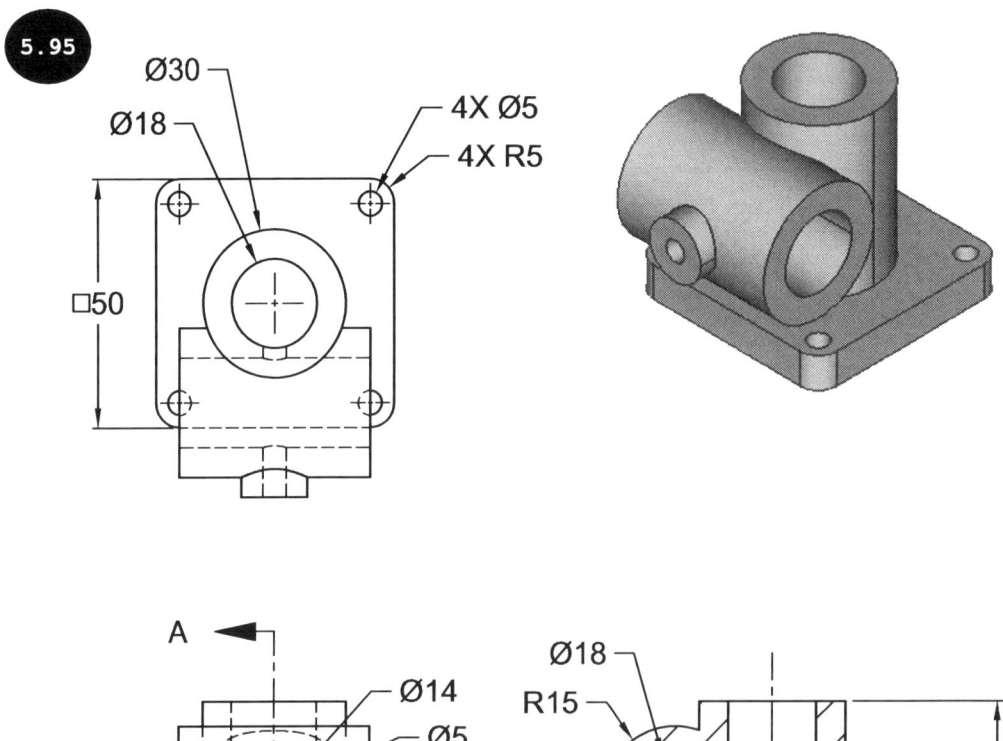

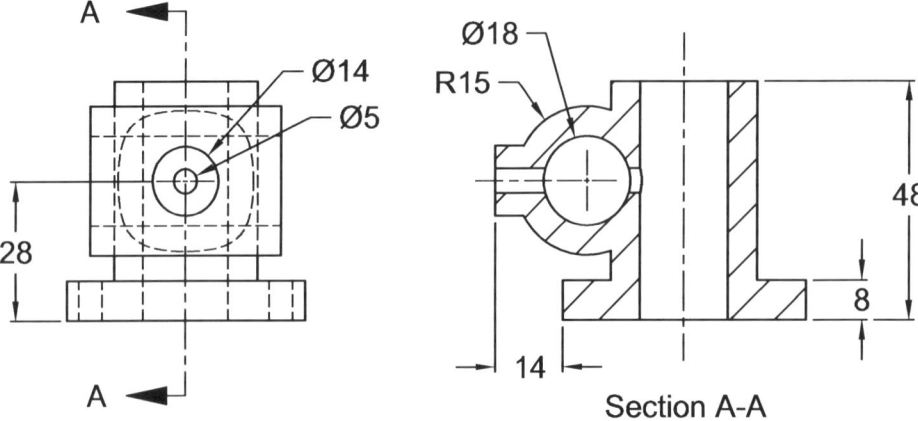

Hands-on Test Drive 2

Create the model shown in Figure 5.96. You need to create the model by creating all its features one by one. All dimensions are in inches.

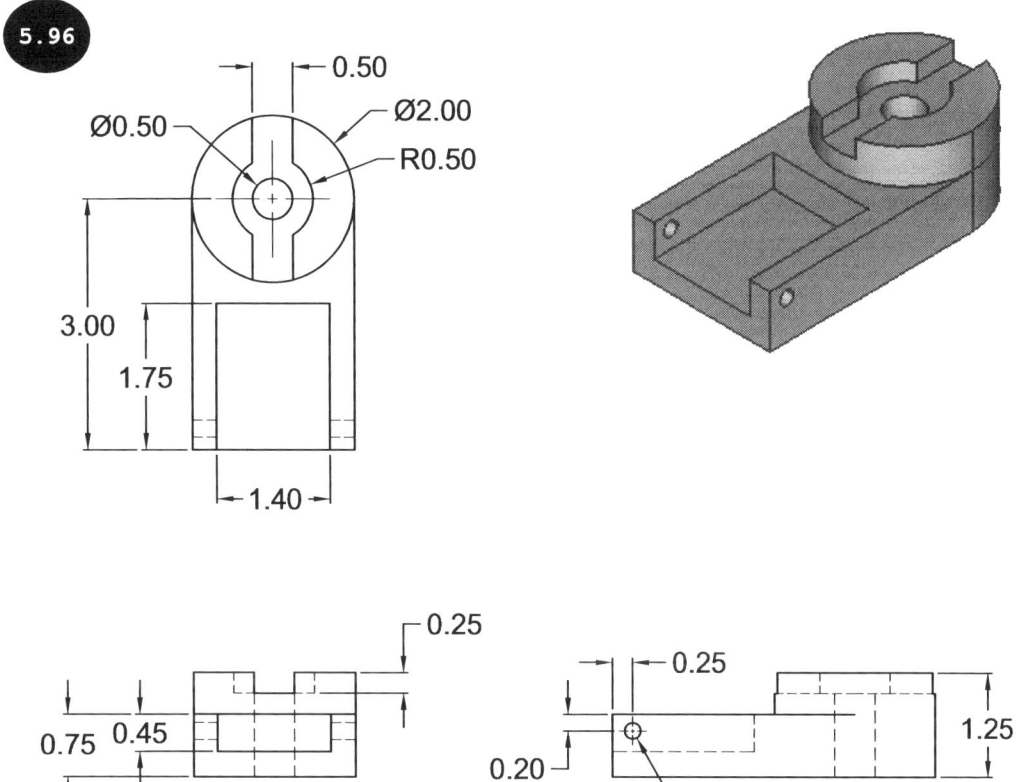

Summary

In this chapter, you have learned how to create pocket and groove features by removing the material from the model. The chapter also described methods for projecting external geometries into the sketch, displaying section view and an earlier state of a model, reordering features, deleting, and editing features, and defining display properties to the model. It also discussed how to measure the distance between two geometries of a model.

Questions

Complete and verify the following sentences:

- A _____ feature is created by subtracting material, normal to the sketching plane from an existing body.

- The _____ option is used for creating a pocket feature by removing the material throughout the entire model.

- A _____ feature is created such that the material is subtracted from an existing body by revolving a sketch around an axis.

- The _____ tool is used for projecting external geometries such as edges and vertices of the model as linked construction entities into the sketch.

- The _____ entities are only visible in the **Sketcher** workbench while creating or editing a sketch.

- In the **Sketcher** workbench, you can create a _____ view by temporarily hiding the material in front of the current sketching plane.

- You can measure the _____ and _____ distances between two geometries such as vertices, edges, or faces of a model.

- The _____ tool is used for creating a section view of a model in the Sketch editing mode of the **Sketcher** workbench.

- FreeCAD lets you edit the individual features of a model and their sketches at any point in the design. (True/False)

- The linked construction entities of a sketch can be only used as reference entities for applying geometrical and dimensional constraints to the sketch entities. (True/False)

- In the **Tree View**, you can change the order of a feature by moving it above its parent feature. (True/False)

Creating Pipe, Loft, and Helix Features

This chapter discusses the following topics:

- Creating an Additive Pipe Feature
- Creating a Multi-section Additive Pipe Feature
- Creating a Subtractive Pipe Feature
- Creating an Additive Loft Feature
- Creating a Subtractive Loft Feature
- Creating an Additive Helix Feature
- Creating a Subtractive Helix Feature
- Creating a Helical Curve

In the previous chapters, you have learned about the primary modeling tools that are used for creating features like pad, revolution, pocket, and groove. You have also learned about the basic workflow of creating models, which is to first create the base feature of a model and then create the remaining features of the model one after the other.

In this chapter, you will explore some of the advanced modeling features such as additive pipe, additive loft, additive helix, subtractive pipe, subtractive loft, and subtractive helix.

Creating an Additive Pipe Feature

An additive pipe feature is created by adding material by sweeping a profile (closed sketch) along a path (open or closed sketch). Figure 6.1 shows a profile and a path as well as the resultant additive pipe feature.

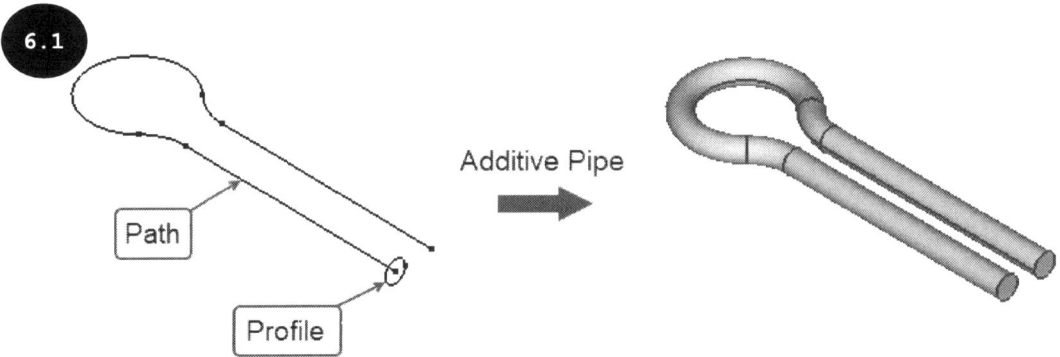

It is evident from the above figures that for creating an additive pipe, you first need to create a path and a profile where the profile follows the path and creates an additive pipe feature. The profile defines the cross-section of the feature, and the path defines the route taken by the profile for creating the pipe feature. In FreeCAD, you can create an additive pipe feature by using the **Additive Pipe** tool. Note that for creating an additive pipe feature, you need to be sure of the following:

- The profile must be a closed sketch.
- The path can be an open or a closed sketch, which is made up of a set of end-to-end connected sketched entities, a curve, or a set of model edges.
- The path should start or pass through the plane of the profile to get better results.
- The profile and path as well as the resultant pipe feature must not be self-intersected.

The method for creating an additive pipe feature is discussed below:

1. Create a path and a profile as separate sketches in the **Sketcher** workbench, refer to Figure 6.2.

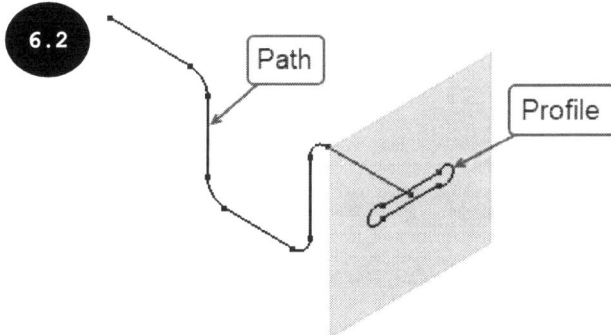

Note: In Figure 6.2, the path is created on the XZ Plane (front plane), and the profile is created on a datum plane that is normal to the right horizontal entity of the path as separate sketches one by one. The methods for creating datum planes are discussed in Chapter 4.

2. After creating a path and a profile, click on the **Additive pipe** tool in the **Part Design Modeling** toolbar, see Figure 6.3. The **Select feature** sub-window appears in the **Task Panel** and displays a list of sketches available in the 3D View area, see Figure 6.4. Also, you are prompted to select a sketch as the profile of the feature.

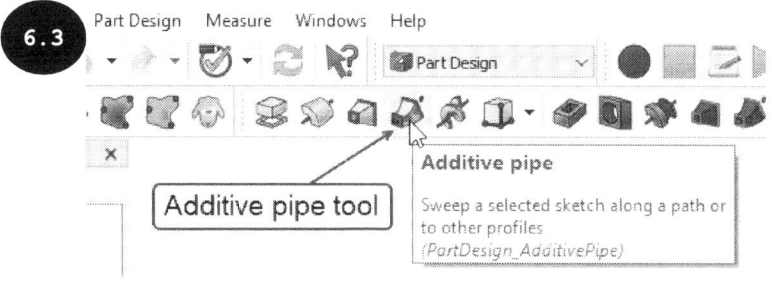

Note: You can also first select the profile and then the path by pressing the CTRL key in the **Task Panel** before invoking the **Additive pipe** tool. On doing so, the preview of the resultant additive pipe feature appears in the 3D View area, directly. Also, the names of the selected profile and the path get displayed in the respective fields of the **Task Panel** that appears.

3. Select a closed sketch as the profile of the feature in the 3D View area or the **Select feature** sub-window of the **Task Panel** and then click on the **OK** button. The options for creating an additive pipe feature appear in the **Task Panel**, see Figure 6.5. Also, the name of the selected sketch appears in the **Profile** field of the **Pipe parameters** sub-window in the **Task Panel**. Ignore the error message that may appear in the **Report view** window at the bottom of the screen after selecting the profile of the additive pipe feature. You can close the **Report view** window by clicking on the cross mark ✕ that appears in its top right corner.

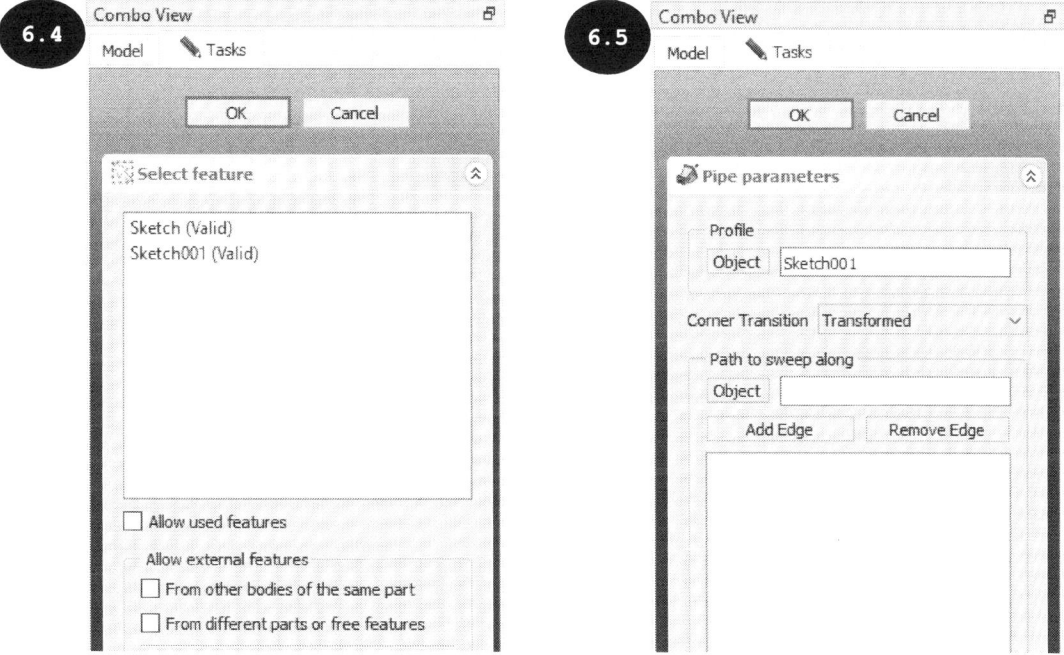

Tip: You can also select a closed sketch or a face of a 3D model as the profile of an additive feature prior to invoking the **Additive pipe** tool.

4. Click on the **Object** button in the **Path to sweep along** area of the **Pipe parameters** sub-window in the **Task Panel** (see Figure 6.6) for selecting a path of the additive pipe feature.

5. Select an open or closed sketch as the path of the feature. A preview of the additive pipe feature appears in the 3D View area, see Figure 6.7. Note that on selecting an entity of a sketch, the whole sketch gets selected as the path of the feature.

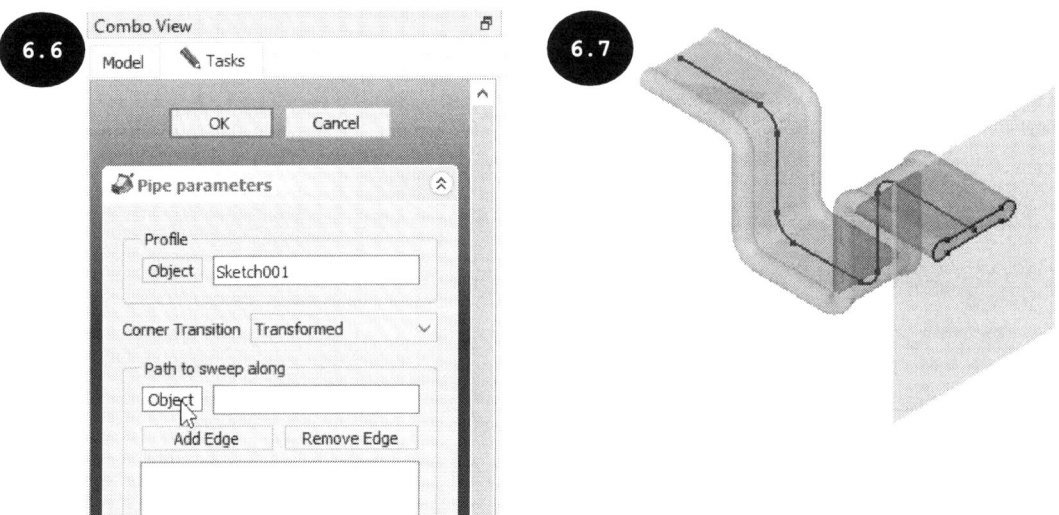

The options to control other settings such as corner transition and orientation of an additive pipe feature in the **Task Panel** are discussed next.

Corner Transition: The Corner Transition drop-down list is used for defining the transformed, right corner, or round corner transition of the profile at the corners of the path by selecting the respective options, see Figures 6.8 through 6.10.

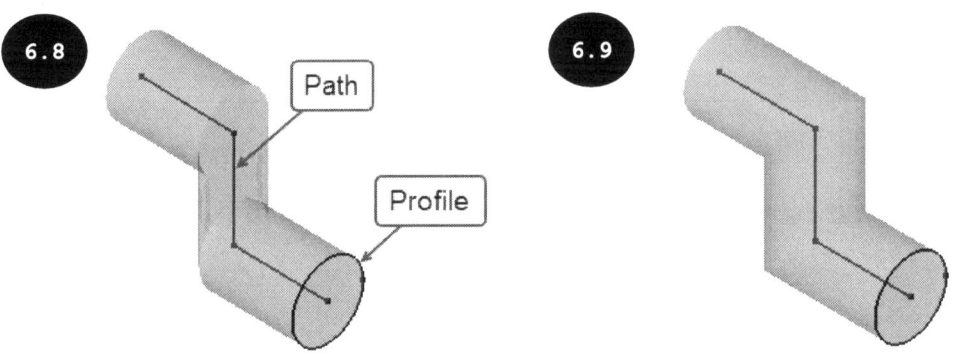

Transformed option selected   Right Corner option selected

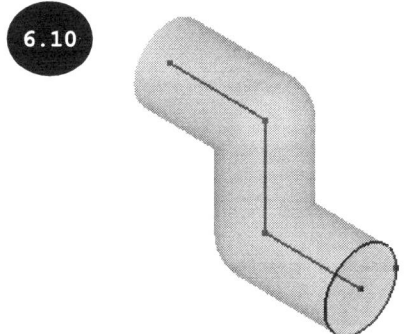

Round Corner option selected

Add Edge: The Add Edge button is used for selecting a single sketch entity or an edge of a 3D model as the path of an additive pipe feature. For doing so, click on the **Add Edge** button in the **Task Panel** and then select a sketch entity or an edge of a 3D model as the path of the additive pipe feature in the 3D View area, see Figures 6.11 and 6.12. The preview of an additive pipe feature appears such that the profile follows only the selected sketch entity or the edge, see Figures 6.11 and 6.12. Also, the name of the selected sketch entity or edge appears in the selection field that appears below the **Add Edge** button in the **Task Panel**.

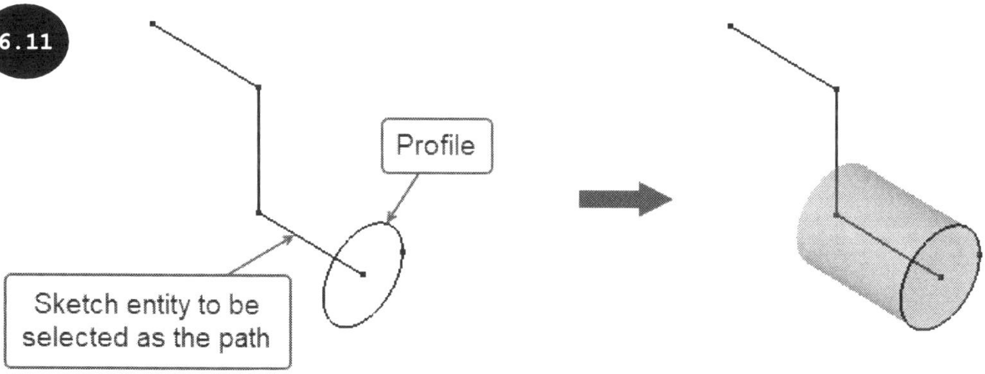

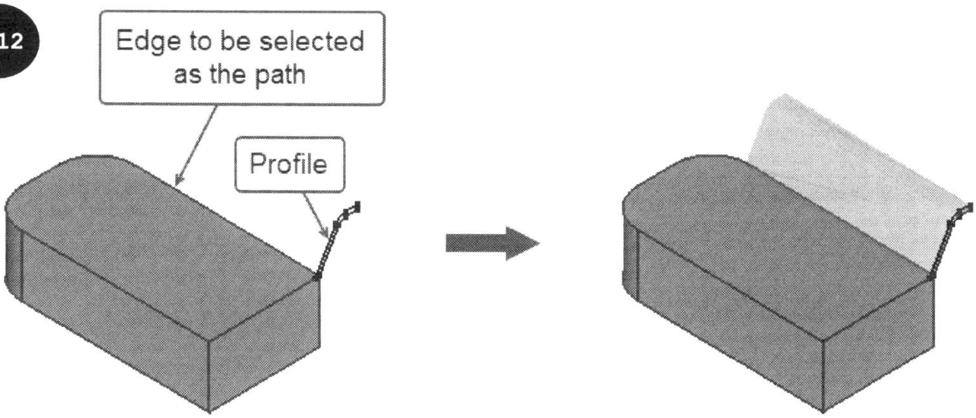

You can also select multiple sketch entities or edges as the path of an additive pipe feature by clicking on the **Add Edge** button every time before making a selection, see Figures 6.13 and 6.14. Note that you must select continuous sketch entities or edges with no branches.

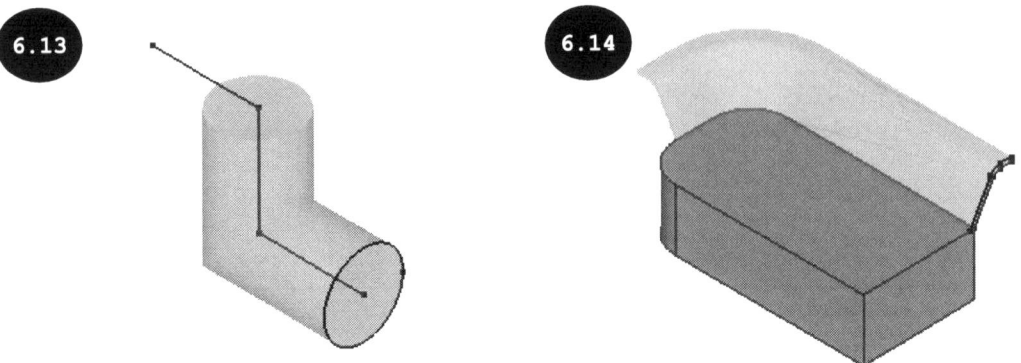

Remove Edge: The **Remove Edge** button is used for removing a sketch entity or an edge from the list of entities/edges selected as the path of the additive pipe feature. For doing so, click on the **Remove Edge** button in the **Task Panel** and then click on a sketch entity or edge in the 3D View area to be removed from the path selection set. Note that you need to click on the **Remove Edge** button every time before removing a sketch entity or edge from the path selection set.

Orientation mode: The options in the Orientation mode drop-down list of the **Section orientation** sub-window are used for controlling the orientation of the profile along the path, see Figure 6.15. The options are discussed next.

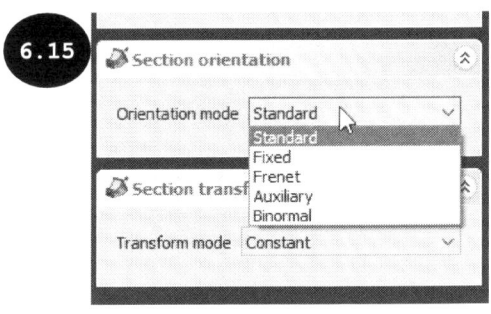

Standard: By default, the **Standard** option is selected in the **Orientation mode** drop-down list. As a result, the profile follows the path such that the cross-section shape of the resultant feature is kept perpendicular throughout the path, see Figure 6.16.

Fixed: On selecting the **Fixed** option, the profile follows the path such that it remains parallel throughout the path, see Figure 6.17. It means the cross-section shape of the resultant feature will not be rotated with the path and kept constant throughout.

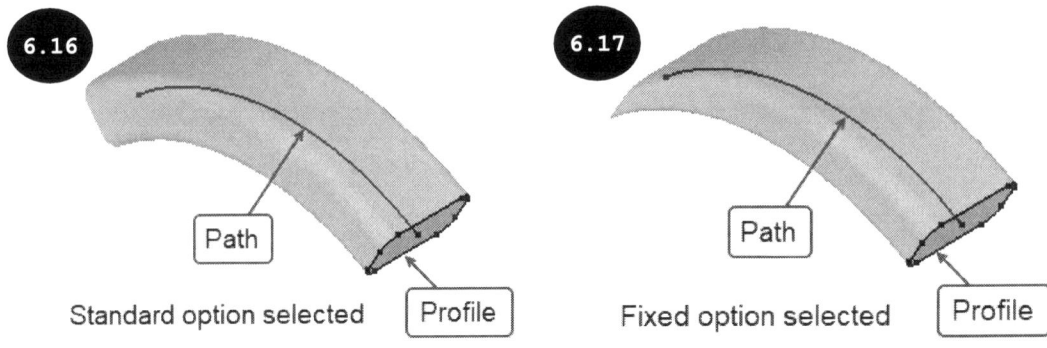

Standard option selected   Profile   Fixed option selected   Profile

Frenet: On selecting the **Frenet** option, a minimum possible twisting is applied to the profile while following the path, see Figure 6.18. This figure shows a path, a profile, and the preview of the resultant additive pipe feature when the **Frenet** option is selected. Figure 6.19 shows the preview of an additive pipe feature when the **Standard** option is selected to better understand the difference between the **Frenet** and **Standard** options.

6.18

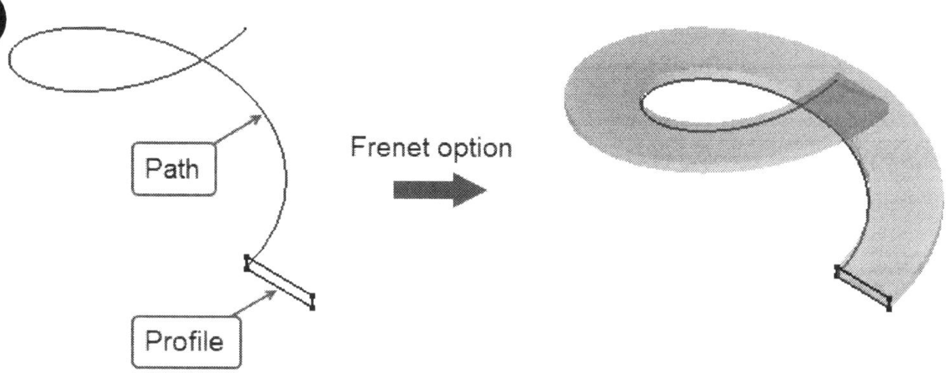

Path

Frenet option

Profile

6.19

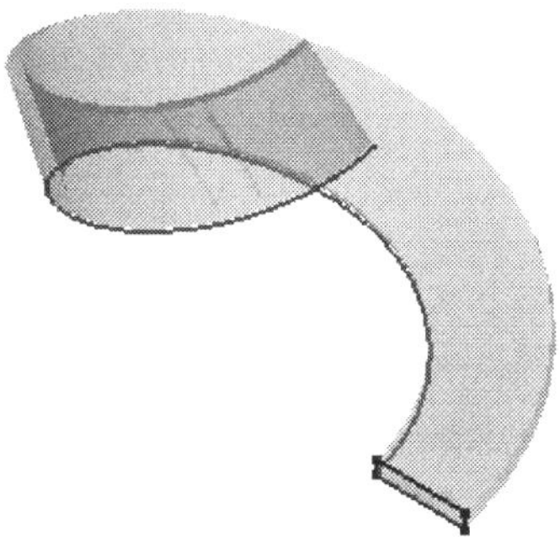

Note: In Figures 6.18 and 6.19, a helical curve is selected as the path of the additive pipe feature. You will learn about creating a helical curve later in this chapter.

Auxiliary: On selecting the **Auxiliary** option, the **Profile** area appears in the **Section orientation** sub-window of the **Task Panel** for selecting a secondary path to guide the profile of the additive pipe feature, see Figure 6.20.

6.20

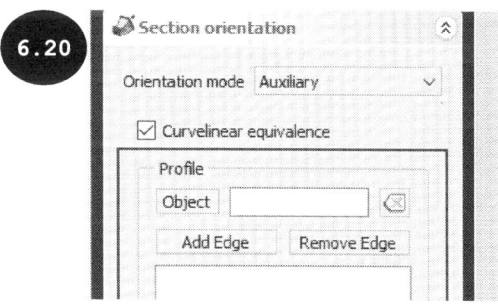

After selecting the **Auxiliary** option in the **Orientation mode** drop-down list, click on the **Object** button in the **Profile** area that appears and then select a secondary path (guide curve) to guide the orientation of the profile while following the path, see Figure 6.21.

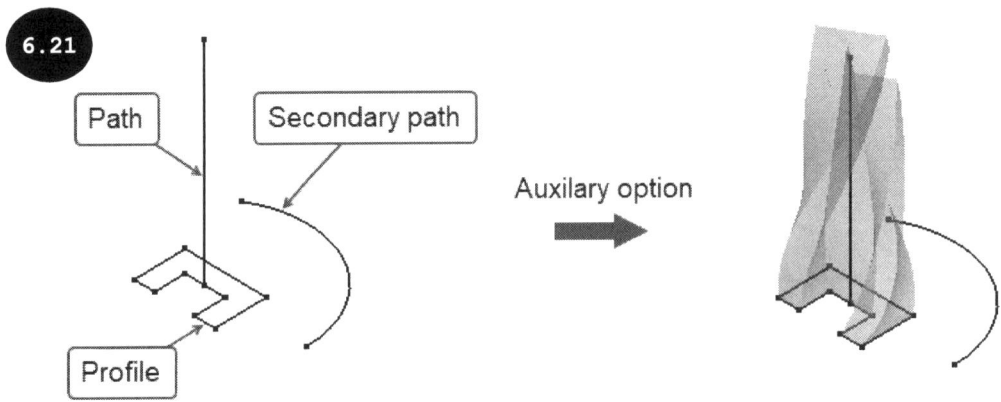

Tip: In Figure 6.21, an arc is created on the XY Plane (top plane) as the secondary path to guide the orientation of the profile. Also, the profile is created on the XY Plane (top plane), and the path is created on the XZ Plane (front plane) as separate sketches.

Binormal: On selecting the **Binormal** option, the **X**, **Y**, and **Z** fields appear in the **Selection orientation** sub-window of the **Task Panel** (see Figure 6.22) for specifying the respective binormal vector to define the orientation of the profile.

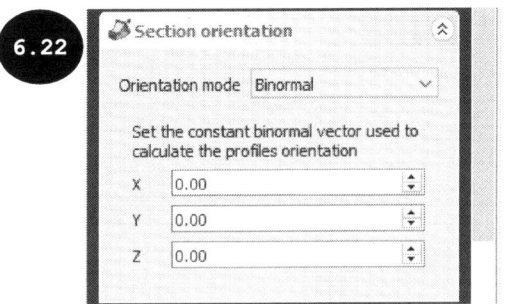

Transform mode: By default, the **Constant** option is selected in the **Transform mode** drop-down list of the **Section transformation** sub-window in the **Task Panel**, see Figure 6.23. As a result, you can create an additive pipe feature by using a single profile, see Figure 6.24. This figure shows an additive pipe feature created by using a single profile. Note that it has a constant cross-section.

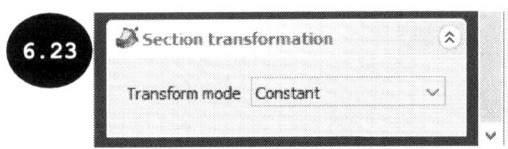

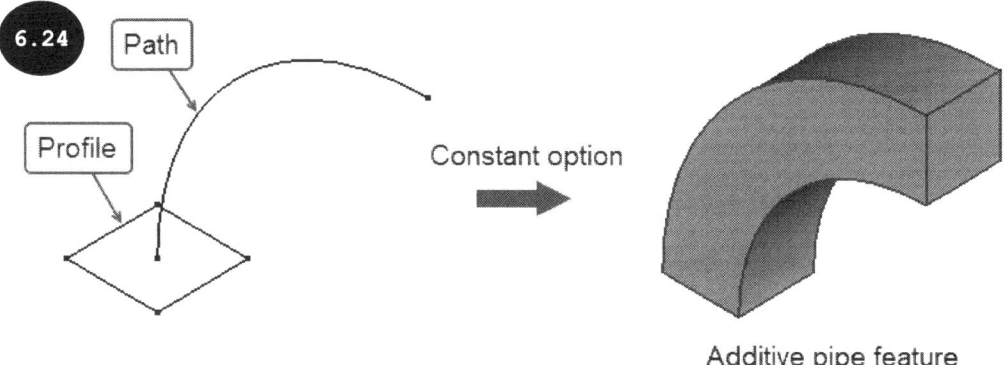

Additive pipe feature

On selecting the **Multisection** option in the **Transform mode** drop-down list of the **Section transformation** sub-window (see Figure 6.25), you can create an additive pipe feature by using multiple profiles, see Figure 6.26. In this figure, an additive pipe feature is created by using two different profiles. You will learn about creating a multi-section additive pipe feature later in this chapter.

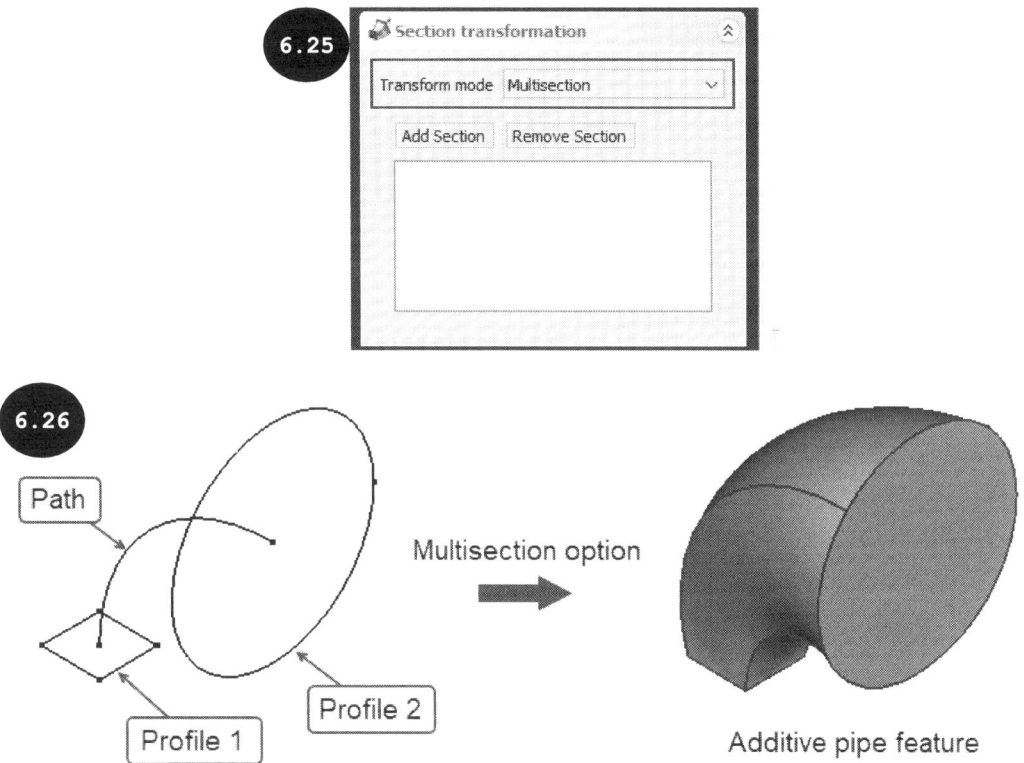

Multisection option

Additive pipe feature

6. After selecting the required options for creating an additive pipe feature, click on the **OK** button in the **Task Panel**. An additive feature of specified settings gets created.

Creating a Multi-section Additive Pipe Feature

As discussed earlier, you can also create a multi-section additive pipe feature by using two or more profiles, see Figure 6.27. The method for creating a multi-section additive pipe feature is discussed below:

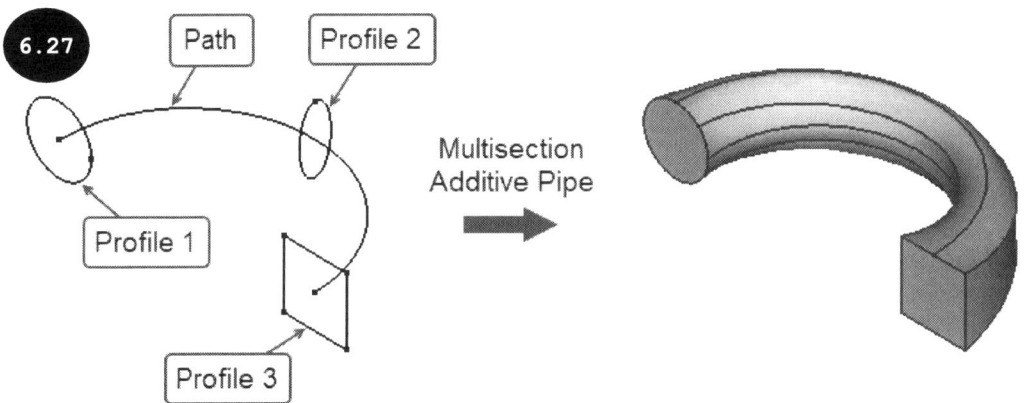

1. Create a path and the required number of profiles as separate sketches for creating a multi-section additive pipe feature, refer to Figure 6.27.

2. After creating a path and the required profiles, click on the **Additive pipe** tool in the **Part Design Modeling** toolbar, see Figure 6.28. The **Select feature** sub-window appears in the **Task Panel** and displays a list of sketches available in the 3D View area. Also, you are prompted to select a sketch as the profile of the feature.

3. Select a closed sketch as the first profile of the feature in the 3D View area or the **Select feature** sub-window of the **Task Panel** and then click on the **OK** button. The options for creating an additive pipe feature appear in the **Task Panel**, see Figure 6.29. Ignore the error message that may appear in the **Report view** window at the bottom of the screen after selecting a profile. You can close the **Report view** window by clicking on the cross mark ✕ that appears in its top right corner.

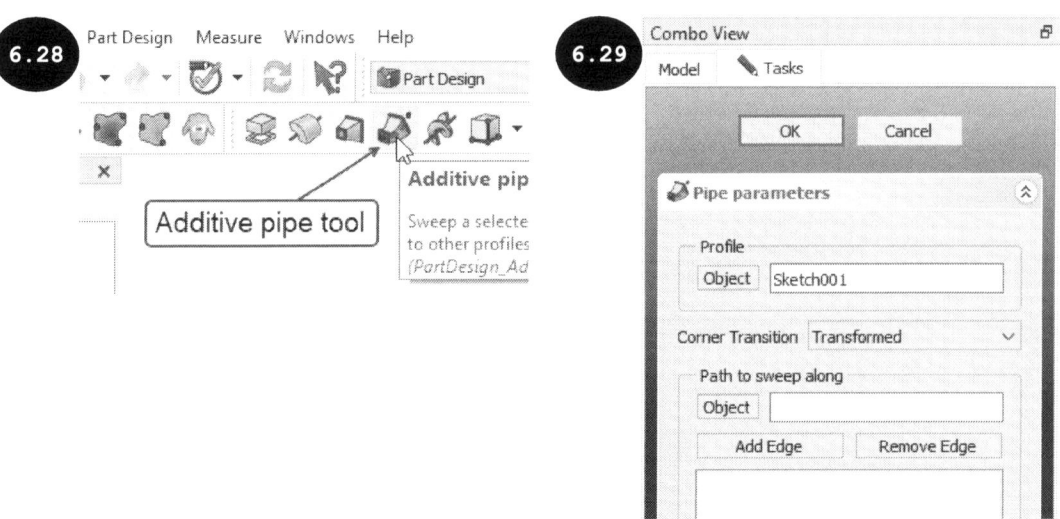

4. Click on the **Object** button in the **Path to sweep along** area of the **Pipe parameters** sub-window in the **Task Panel** (see Figure 6.30) and then select an open or a closed sketch as the path of the feature in the 3D View area. A preview of the additive pipe feature appears such that the profile follows the path, see Figure 6.31.

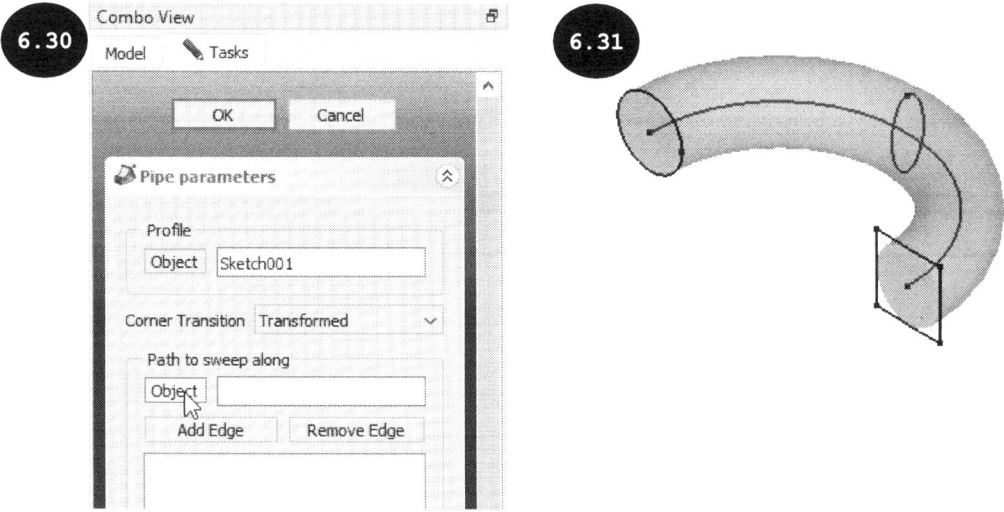

5. Select the **Multisection** option in the **Transform mode** drop-down list of the **Section transformation** sub-window for selecting multiple profiles to create a multi-section additive pipe feature, see Figure 6.32.

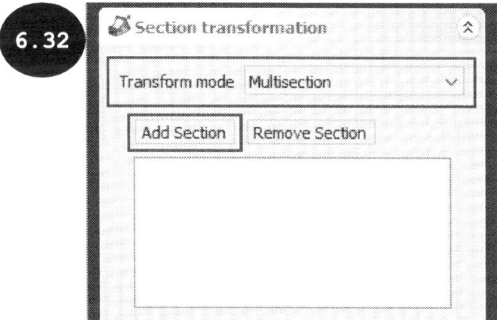

Now, you can select multiple profiles for creating a multi-section additive pipe feature.

6. Click on the **Add Section** button that appears below the **Transform mode** drop-down list, refer to Figure 6.32.

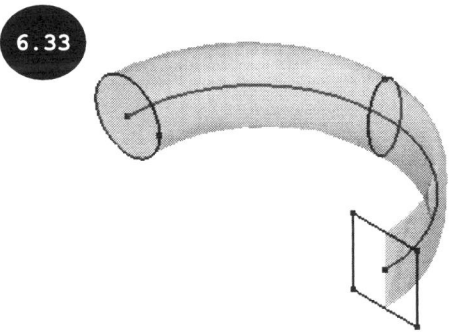

7. Select a closed sketch as the second profile of the additive pipe feature in the 3D View area. The preview of the additive pipe feature gets updated in the 3D View area such that its cross-sectional shape gets transformed from one profile to another while following the path, see Figure 6.33.

8. Click on the **Add Section** button again and then select the third profile of the additive pipe feature in the 3D View area, if needed. The preview of the additive pipe feature gets updated in the 3D View area, see Figure 6.34.

9. Similarly, you can select other profiles of the additive pipe feature, if needed.

10. After selecting all the required profiles of the additive pipe feature, click on the **OK** button in the **Task Panel**. A multi-section additive pipe feature of specified settings gets created in the 3D View area, see Figure 6.35.

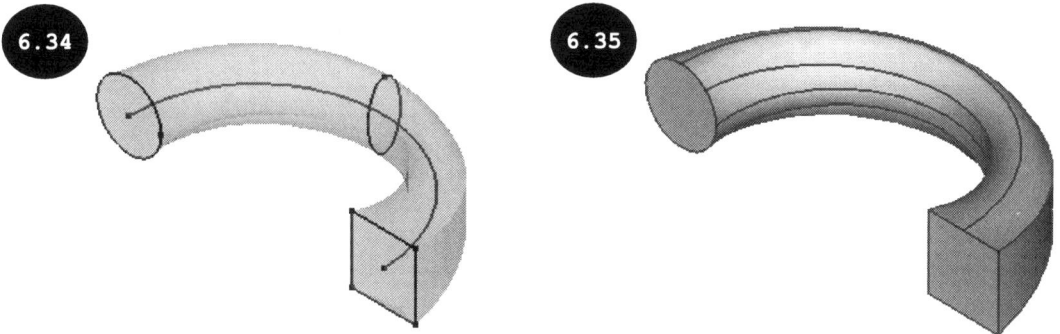

Creating a Subtractive Pipe Feature

In FreeCAD, you can create a subtractive pipe feature like that of creating an additive pipe feature with the only difference being that the subtractive pipe feature is created by subtracting or removing material from an existing body, see Figure 6.36. The method for creating a subtractive pipe feature is discussed below:

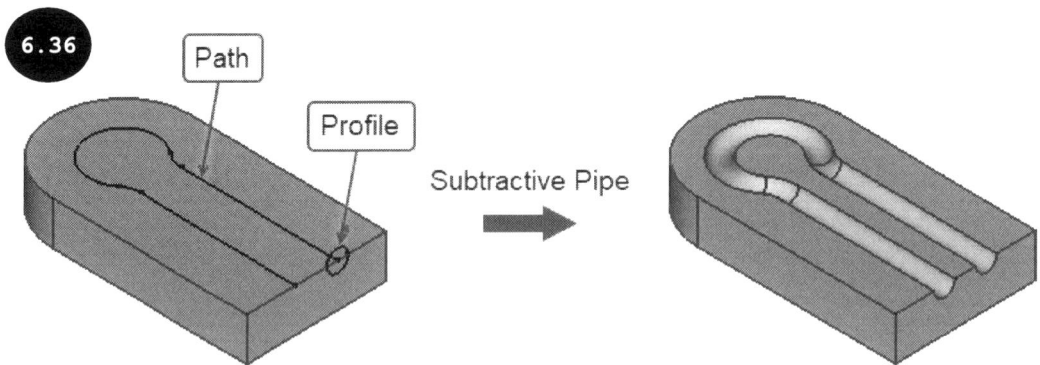

1. Create a path and a profile of a subtractive pipe feature as separate sketches one by one in the **Sketcher** workbench, refer to Figure 6.37.

Note: In Figure 6.37, the path is created on the top planar face of the model and the profile is created on the right planar face of the model as separate sketches.

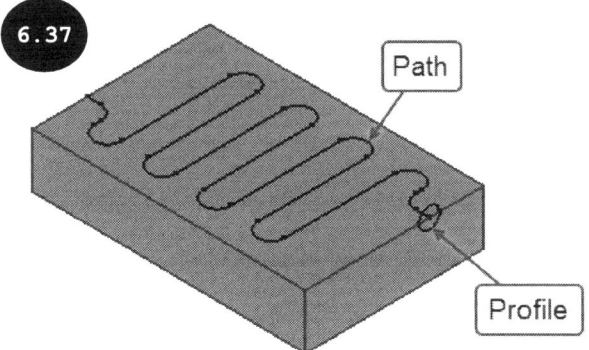

2. After creating a path and a profile, click on the **Subtractive pipe** tool in the **Part Design Modeling** toolbar, see Figure 6.38. The **Select feature** sub-window appears in the **Task Panel** and displays a list of sketches available in the 3D View area. Also, you are prompted to select a sketch as the profile of the feature.

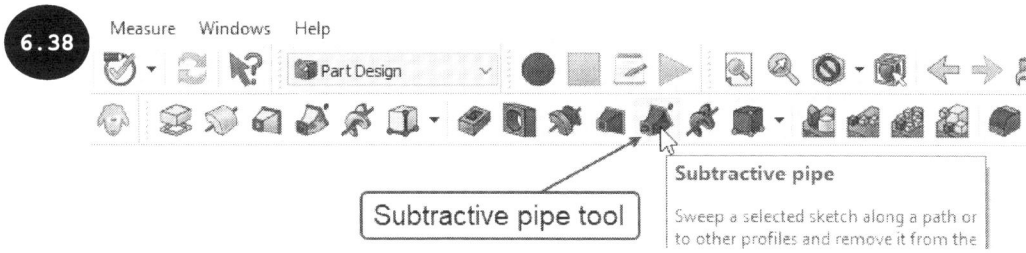

Note: You can also first select the profile and then the path by pressing the CTRL key in the **Task Panel** before invoking the **Subtractive pipe** tool. On doing so, the preview of the resultant subtractive pipe feature appears in the 3D View area, directly. Also, the names of the selected profile and the path get displayed in the respective fields of the **Task Panel** that appears.

3. Select a closed sketch as the profile of the feature in the 3D View area or the **Select feature** sub-window of the **Task Panel** and then click on the **OK** button. The options for creating a subtractive pipe feature appear in the **Task Panel**, see Figure 6.39. Also, the name of the selected sketch appears in the **Profile** field of the **Pipe parameters** sub-window in the **Task Panel**. Ignore the error message that may appear in the **Report view** window at the bottom of the screen after selecting the profile of the subtractive pipe feature. You can close the **Report view** window by clicking on the cross mark ✕ that appears in its top right corner.

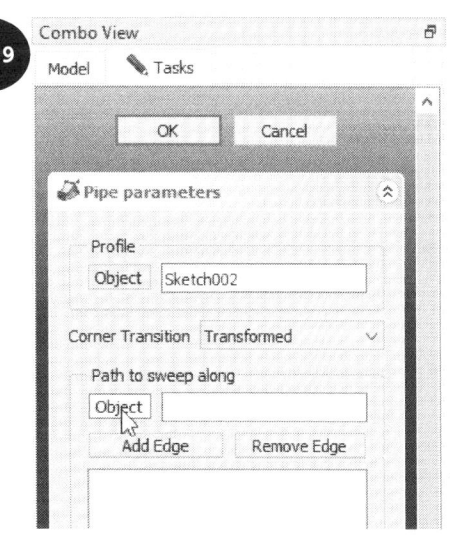

4. Click on the **Object** button in the **Path to sweep along** area of the **Pipe parameters** sub-window in the **Task Panel** (refer to Figure 6.39) for selecting a path of the subtractive pipe feature.

5. Select an open or closed sketch as the path of the feature. A preview of the subtractive pipe feature appears in the 3D View area, see Figure 6.40. Note that on selecting an entity of a sketch, the whole sketch gets selected as the path of the feature.

6. Click on the **OK** button in the **Task Panel**. A subtractive pipe feature gets created by removing the material from the model, see Figure 6.41.

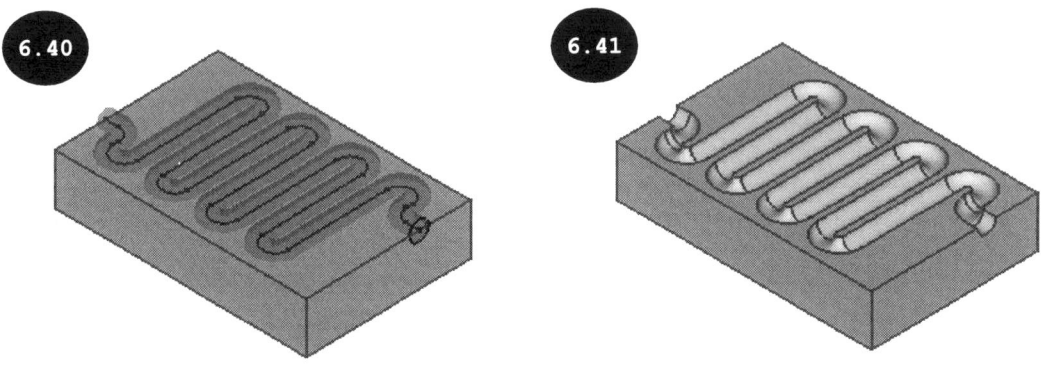

Note: In the **Task Panel**, the options to control the corner transition and orientation settings of a subtractive pipe feature are the same as discussed earlier.

Creating an Additive Loft Feature

An additive loft feature is created by making a transition between two or more profiles. Figure 6.42 shows three different profiles and the resultant additive loft feature.

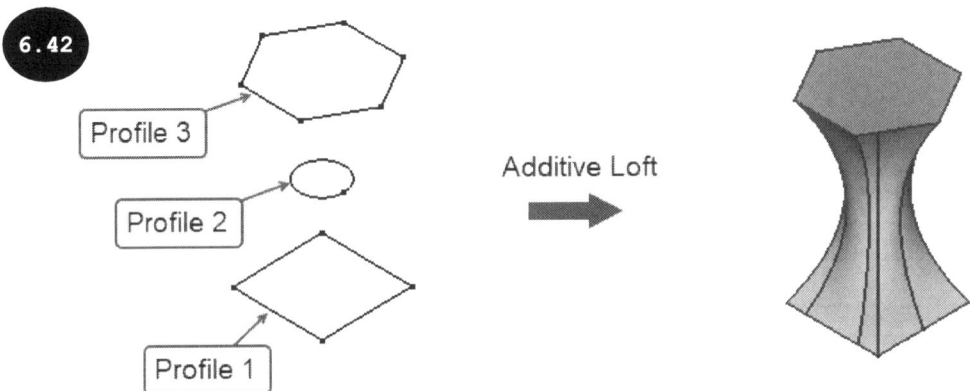

To create an additive loft feature, you first need to create all its profiles that define its cross-sectional shape. In FreeCAD, you can create an additive loft feature by using the **Additive Loft** tool. Note that for creating an additive loft feature, you need to be sure of the following:

- Two or more similar or dissimilar sketch profiles must be available in the 3D View area before invoking the **Additive Loft** tool.
- Profiles must be closed sketches. You can also select faces or edges as profiles.
- All sketch profiles must be created as separate sketches.
- The profiles and the resultant loft feature must not be self-intersected.

The method for creating an additive loft feature is discussed below:

1. Create all profiles of the loft feature as separate sketches one by one in the 3D View Area, refer to Figure 6.43. In this figure, three closed sketches are created as profiles on different planes.

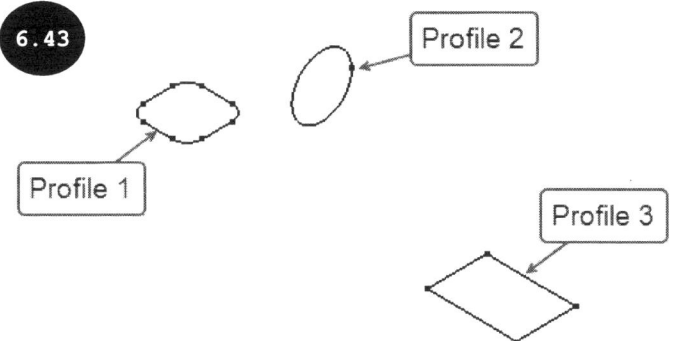

2. After creating the profiles, click on the **Additive loft** tool in the **Part Design Modeling** toolbar, see Figure 6.44. The **Select feature** sub-window appears in the **Task Panel** and displays a list of sketches available in the 3D View area.

3. Select a closed sketch as the profile of the feature in the 3D View area or the **Select feature** sub-window of the **Task Panel** and then click on the **OK** button. The options for creating an additive loft feature appear in the **Task Panel**, see Figure 6.45. Also, the name of the selected sketch appears in the **Profile** field of the **Loft parameters** sub-window in the **Task Panel**. Ignore the error message that may appear in the **Report view** window at the bottom of the screen after selecting a profile. You can close the **Report view** window by clicking on the cross mark ✕ that appears in its top right corner.

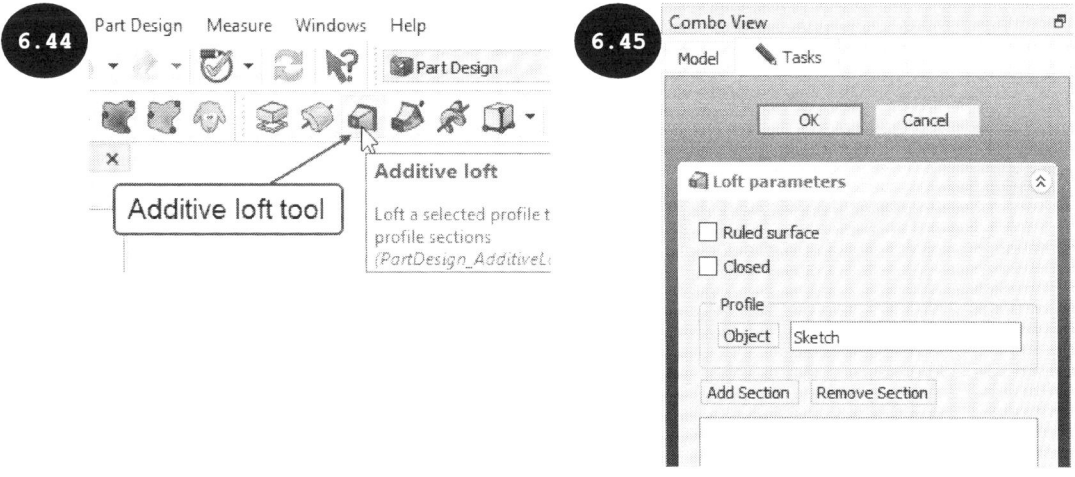

Tip: You can also select two or more sketches as the profiles of an additive loft feature prior to invoking the **Additive loft** tool.

Moreover, you can also select a face as the profile of a loft feature.

4. Click on the **Add Section** button in the **Loft parameters** sub-window (see Figure 6.46) and then select the second profile of the loft feature. The preview of an additive loft feature appears in the 3D View area, see Figure 6.47. Note that you can select a closed sketch or a face of an existing feature as the profile of a loft feature.

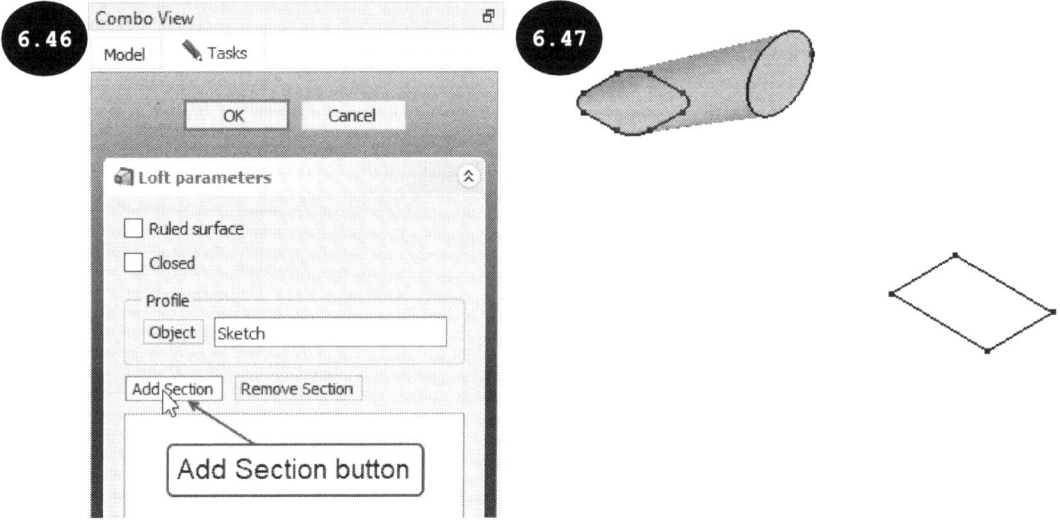

5. Click on the **Add Section** button again in the **Loft parameters** sub-window and then select the third profile of the loft feature in the 3D View area, if needed. The preview of the loft feature gets updated in the 3D View area, see Figure 3.48.

6. Similarly, you can select other profiles of the additive loft feature by using the **Add Section** button, if needed.

7. Ensure that the **Ruled surface** check box is cleared in the **Task Panel** for creating an additive loft feature with smooth transitions between its profiles, see Figure 6.49. On selecting this **Ruled surface** check box, the additive loft feature will be created with straight transitions between its profiles or cross-sections, see Figure 6.50.

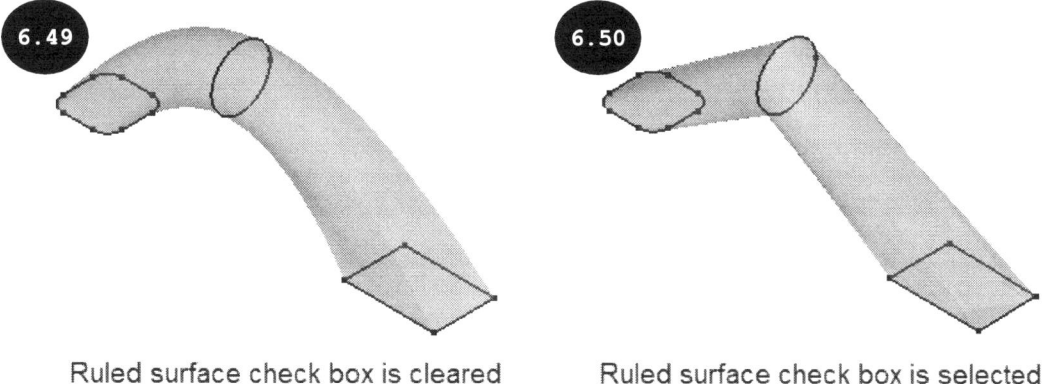

Ruled surface check box is cleared   Ruled surface check box is selected

8.   After selecting all the profiles (sections) of the additive loft feature, click on the **OK** button in the **Task Panel**. The additive loft feature gets created, see Figure 6.51.

Creating a Subtractive Loft Feature

In FreeCAD, you can create a subtractive loft feature like that of creating an additive loft feature with the only difference being that the subtractive loft feature is created by subtracting or removing material from an existing body, see Figure 6.52. The method for creating a subtractive loft feature is discussed below:

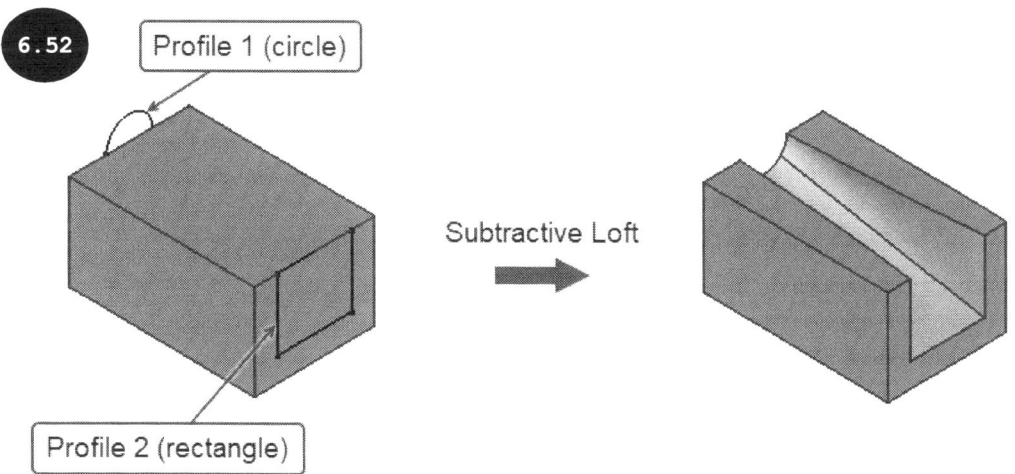

1. Create all profiles of a subtractive loft feature as separate sketches one by one in the 3D View Area, refer to Figure 6.53. In this figure, three closed sketches (an ellipse, a circle, and a rectangle) are created as profiles on different planes.

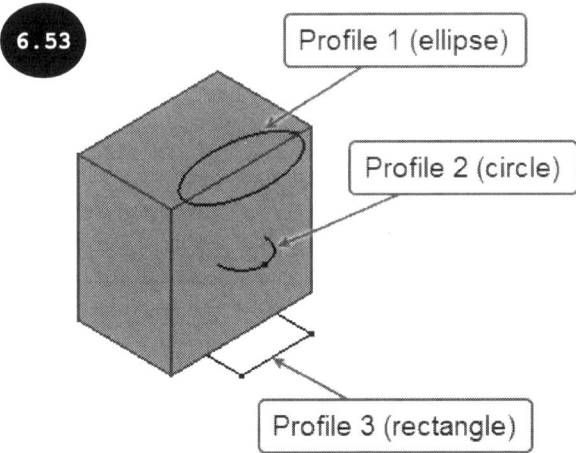

Note: In Figure 6.53, half a portion of Profile 2 (circle) and Profile 3 (rectangle) overlap or pass into the existing object, so are not visible.

Now, you can create the subtractive loft feature.

2. Select all the profiles in the **Task Panel** by pressing the CTRL key and then click on the **Subtractive loft** tool in the **Part Design Modeling** toolbar, see Figure 6.54. The preview of a subtractive loft feature appears in the 3D View area, see Figure 6.55. Also, the **Loft parameters** sub-window appears in the **Task Panel**. The options in this sub-window are the same as discussed earlier.

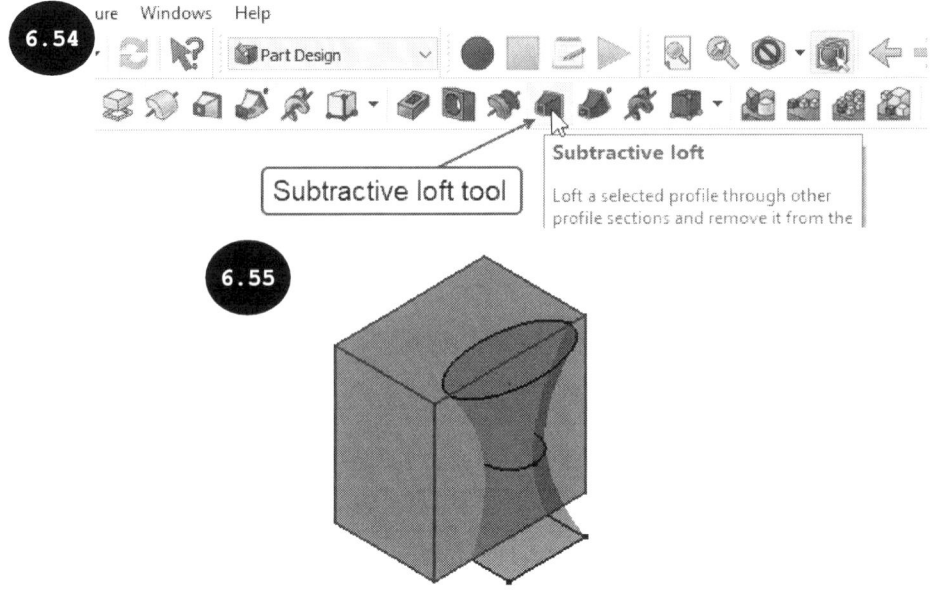

Tip: You can select the profiles of a subtractive loft feature before or after invoking the **Subtractive loft** tool.

3. Click on the **OK** button in the **Task Panel**. The subtractive loft feature gets created by removing the material from the model, see Figure 6.56.

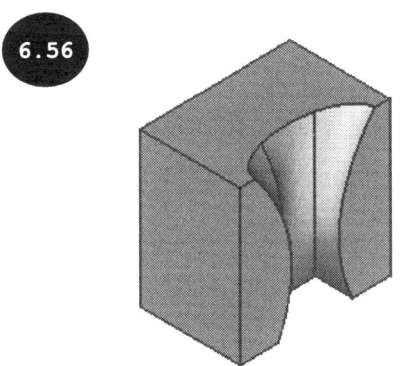

6.56

Creating an Additive Helix Feature

In FreeCAD, you can create an additive helix feature by sweeping a closed sketch (profile) along a helix path around an axis, see Figure 6.57. In this figure, an additive helix feature (helical coil) is created by sweeping a rectangular sketch around the vertical axis. The method for creating an additive helix feature is discussed below:

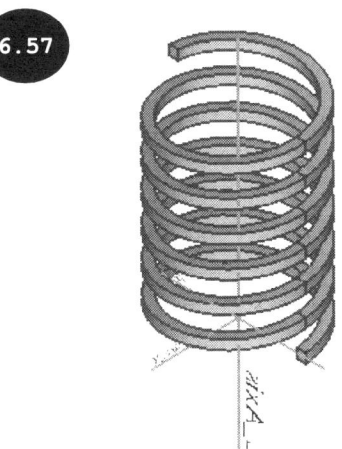

6.57

1. Create a closed sketch as the profile of an additive helix feature in the **Sketcher** workbench, see Figure 6.58. In this figure, a circle is created as the profile of the helix feature. After creating a sketch, exit the **Sketcher** workbench to switch back to the **Part Design** workbench.

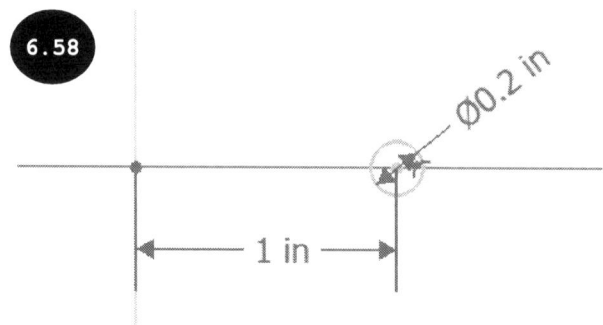

Note: The sketch of an additive helix feature should be a closed sketch and on either side of its axis of revolution.

2. Click on the **Additive helix** tool in the **Part Design Modeling** toolbar, see Figure 6.59. The preview of an additive helix feature appears in the 3D View area by revolving the sketch along a helix path around the vertical axis of the sketch, see Figure 6.60. It is because the **Vertical sketch axis** option is selected, by default in the **Axis** drop-down list of the **Helix parameters** sub-window that appears in the **Task Panel**, see Figure 6.61.

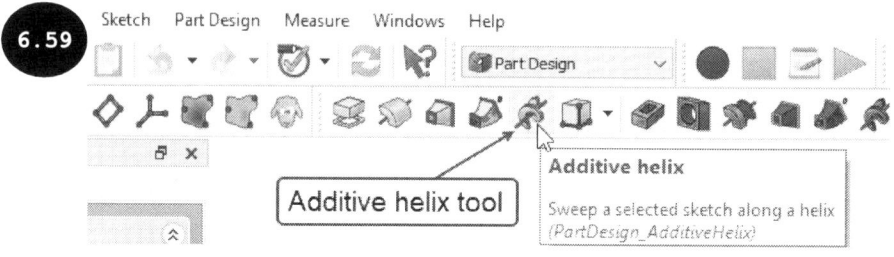

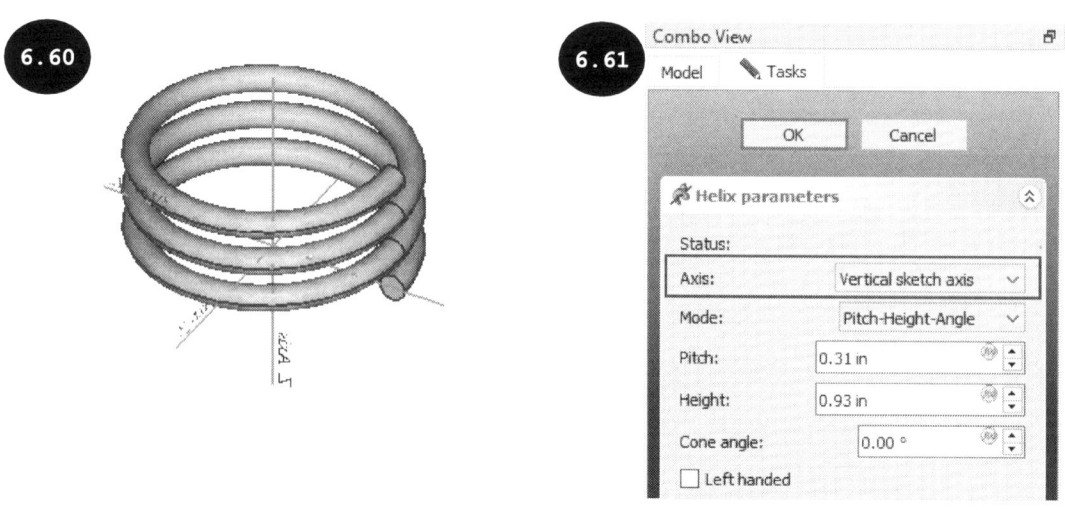

Note: If the sketch of an additive helix feature is not on either side of its vertical axis, then on invoking the **Additive helix** tool, an error will occur, and a preview of the feature does not appear in the 3D View area. It is because the sketch cannot be revolved about its vertical axis that intersect with it. In this case you need to define an axis of revolution for the sketch other than its vertical axis by selecting the required option in the **Axis** drop-down list of the **Helix parameters** sub-window.

3. Specify the required option in the **Axis** drop-down list of the **Helix parameters** sub-window for defining the axis of revolution of the feature, see Figure 6.62. The options in this drop-down list are the same as discussed in earlier chapters while creating a revolution feature.

4. Specify the required option in the **Mode** drop-down list of the **Helix parameters** sub-window for creating a helix by specifying the respective set of parameters, see Figure 6.63. The options are discussed next.

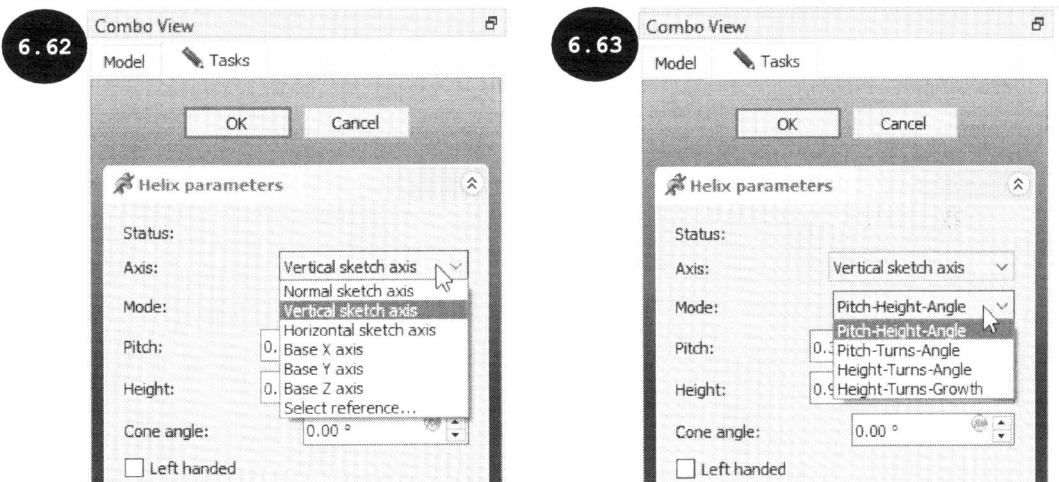

Pitch-Height-Angle: The **Pitch-Height-Angle** option is used for creating a helix by defining its pitch and total height, see Figure 6.64. When this option is selected, the **Pitch**, **Height**, and **Cone angle** fields get displayed in the **Task Panel** for defining the pitch, the total height, and the taper angle of the helix, respectively.

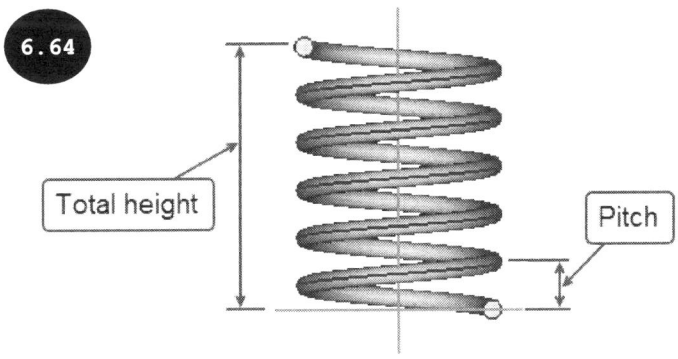

Note: On specifying a taper angle value in the **Cone angle** field of the **Task Panel**, you can create a tapered helix of a defined angle, see Figure 6.65.

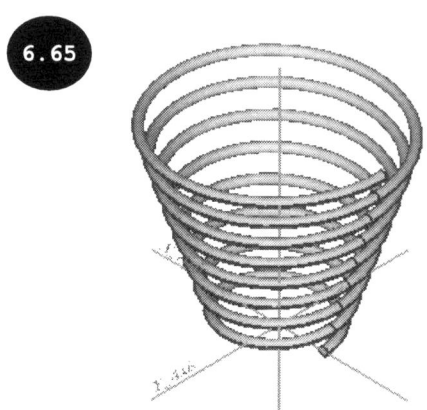

Pitch-Turns-Angle: The Pitch-Turns-Angle option is used for creating a helix by defining its pitch and number of revolutions (turns). When this option is selected, the **Pitch, Turns, Cone angle** fields get enabled in the dialog box for defining the pitch, the number of revolutions, and the taper angle of the helix, respectively.

Height-Turns-Angle: The Height-Turns-Angle option is used for creating a helix by defining its total height and number of revolutions (turns). When this option is selected, the **Height, Turns,** and **Cone angle** fields get enabled in the dialog box for defining the total height, the number of revolutions (turns), and the taper angle of the helix, respectively.

Height-Turns-Growth: The Height-Turns-Growth option is used for creating a helix by defining its total height, number of revolutions (turns), and incremental growth of the helical radius, see Figure 6.66. When this option is selected, the **Height, Turns,** and **Radial growth** fields get enabled in the **Task Panel** for defining the total height, the number of revolutions (turns), and the incremental growth value of the helical radius of the helix, respectively.

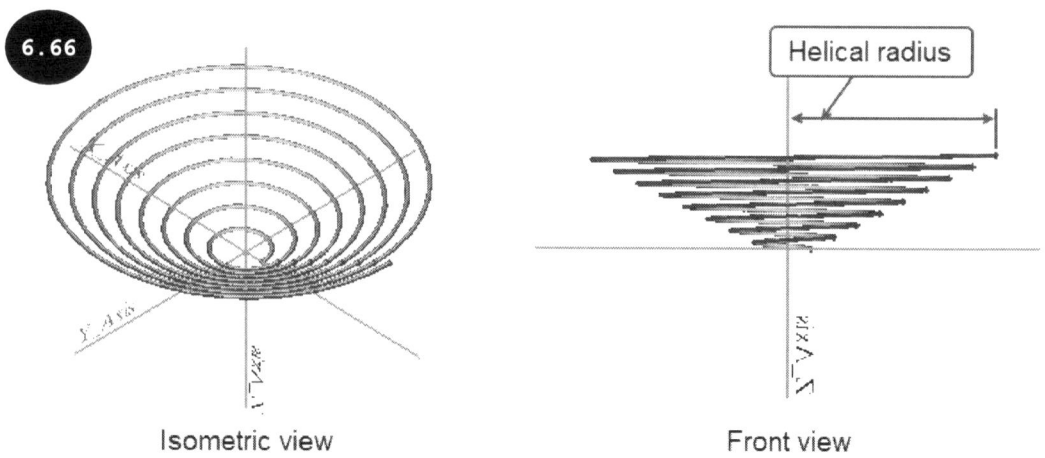

Isometric view   Front view

Note: You can also create a spiral coil by using the **Height-Turns-Growth** option, see Figure 6.67. For doing so, after selecting the **Height-Turns-Growth** option in the **Mode** drop-down list, enter **0** in the **Height** field and then enter the required number of revolutions (turns) and the incremental growth of the helical radius in the respective **Turns** and **Radial growth** fields of the **Task Panel**. The preview of a spiral coil of specified parameters gets appeared in the 3D View area, see Figure 6.67.

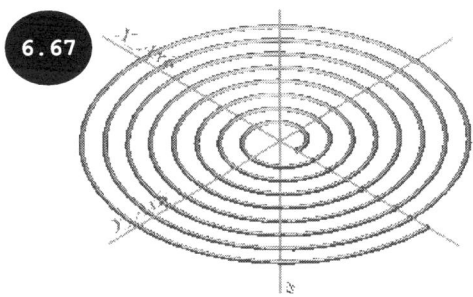

5. Specify the required parameters for creating an additive helix feature depending upon the option selected in the **Mode** drop-down list of the **Task Panel**, as discussed above.

6. Select the **Left handed** check box to reverse the direction of the helix from default clockwise to counterclockwise if needed.

7. Select the **Reversed** check box to reverse the axis direction of the helix to its other side, if needed.

8. After specifying all the required parameters for creating an additive helix feature, click on the **OK** button in the **Task Panel**. The additive helix feature of specified parameters gets created.

Creating a Subtractive Helix Feature

In FreeCAD, you can create a subtractive helix like that of creating an additive helix feature with the only difference that the subtractive helix is created by subtracting or removing material from an existing body, see Figure 6.68. In this figure, a subtractive helix feature is created by sweeping a circular profile along a helix path around the vertical axis. The method for creating a subtractive helix feature is discussed below:

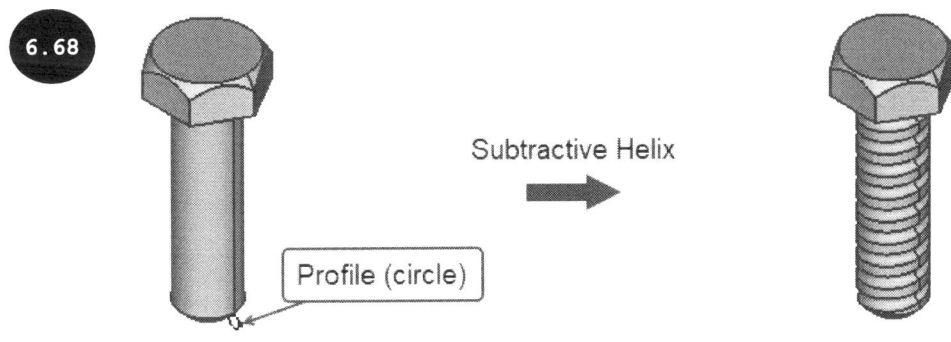

Subtractive Helix

Profile (circle)

1. Create a closed sketch as the profile of a subtractive helix feature, see Figure 6.69. In this figure, a rectangle is created as the profile of the helix feature.

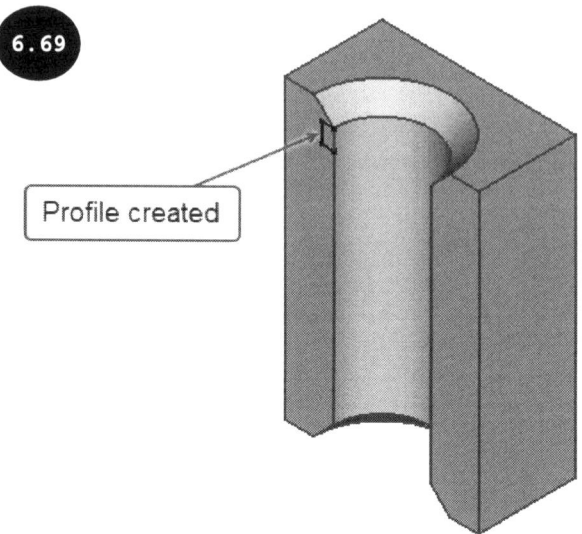

Profile created

2. Click on the **Subtractive helix** tool in the **Part Design Modeling** toolbar, see Figure 6.70. The preview of a subtractive helix feature appears with default parameters in the 3D View area, see Figure 6.71. Also, the **Helix parameters** sub-window appears in the **Task Panel** with the **Vertical sketch axis** option selected in its **Axis** drop-down list, by default. As a result, the preview of a subtractive helix feature appears by revolving the profile around the vertical axis.

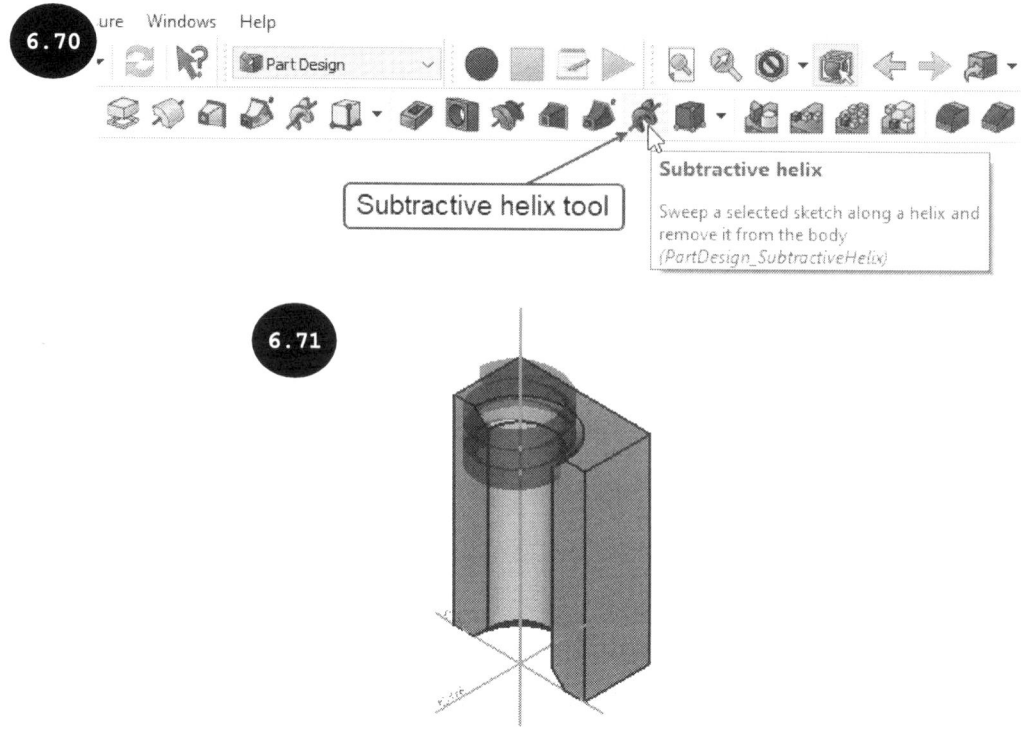

Subtractive helix tool

Subtractive helix
Sweep a selected sketch along a helix and remove it from the body
(PartDesign_SubtractiveHelix)

3. Specify the required option in the **Axis** drop-down list of the **Helix parameters** sub-window for defining the axis of revolution. The options in this drop-down list are the same as discussed earlier.

4. Specify the required option (**Pitch-Height-Angle, Pitch-Turns-Angle, Height-Turns-Angle,** or **Height-Turns-Growth**) in the **Mode** drop-down list of the **Helix parameters** sub-window for creating a helix, see Figure 6.72. The options in this drop-down list are the same as discussed earlier.

5. Specify the required parameters for creating a subtractive helix feature in the respective fields of the **Task Panel.** Note that the availability of fields for specifying the parameters depends upon the option selected in the **Mode** drop-down list of the **Task Panel.**

6. Select the **Left handed** check box to reverse the direction of the helix, if needed.

7. Select the **Reversed** check box to reverse the axis direction of the helix to its other side, if needed. The preview of the feature gets updated in the 3D View area, see Figure 6.73.

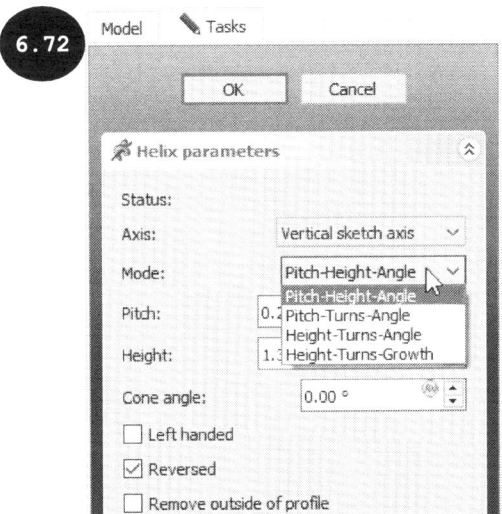

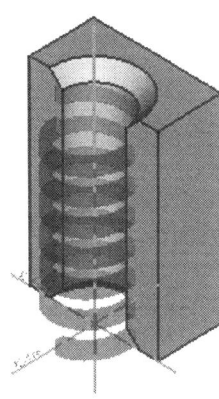

Note that all the options in the **Task Panel** are the same as discussed earlier except the **Remove outside of profile** option, which is discussed next.

Remove outside of profile: On selecting the Remove outside of profile check box, only the intersection of the helix and the existing body will be retained in the resultant feature.

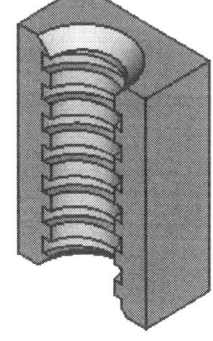

8. After specifying all the required parameters, click on the **OK** button in the **Task Panel.** The subtractive helix feature of specified parameters gets created, see Figure 7.74.

Creating a Helical Curve

In FreeCAD, you can create a helical curve as a primitive in the **Part** workbench. The method for creating a helical curve in the **Part** workbench is discussed below:

1. Invoke the **Part** workbench by selecting the **Part** option in the **Workbench Selector**.

2. In the **Part** workbench, click on the **Create primitives** tool of the **Solid** toolbar, see Figure 6.75. The **Geometric Primitives** and **Location** sub-windows appear in the **Task Panel** with options to create various types of primitives such as box, cylinder, cone, sphere, prism, helix, and spiral, refer to Figure 6.76.

3. Select the **Helix** option in the **Primitives** drop-down list of the **Geometric Primitives** sub-window, see Figure 6.76. The options to create a helical curve appear.

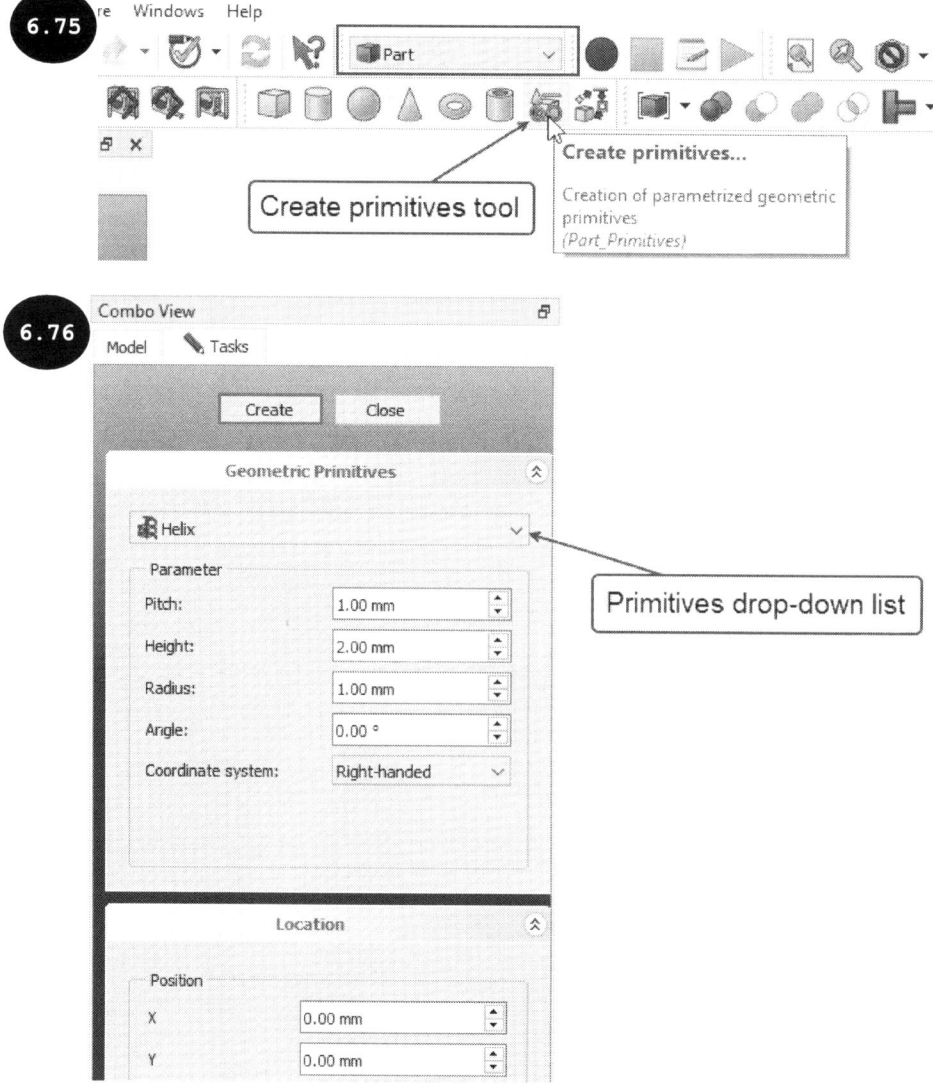

4. Specify the required parameters such as pitch, height, radius, and angle of the helical curve in the respective fields of the **Task Panel**. You can also define the position of the helical curve in the 3D View area by specifying the required X, Y, and Z coordinates in the **Location** sub-window of the **Task Panel**.

5. After specifying the required parameters, click on the **Create** button in the Task Panel. A helical curve of specified parameters gets created in the 3D View area, see Figure 6.77.

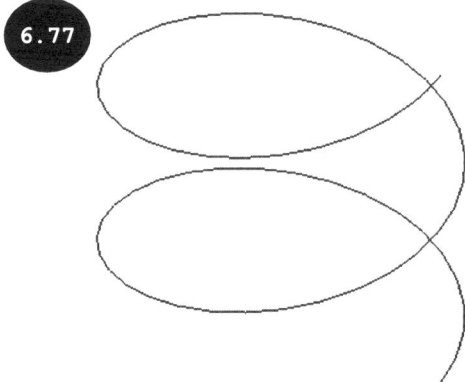

6. Exit the **Task Panel** by clicking on the **Close** button.

7. After creating a helical curve, switch back to the **Part Design** workbench by selecting it in the **Workbench Selector**.

Tip: You can use a helical curve as a path to create a feature like pipe, refer to Figure 6.78.

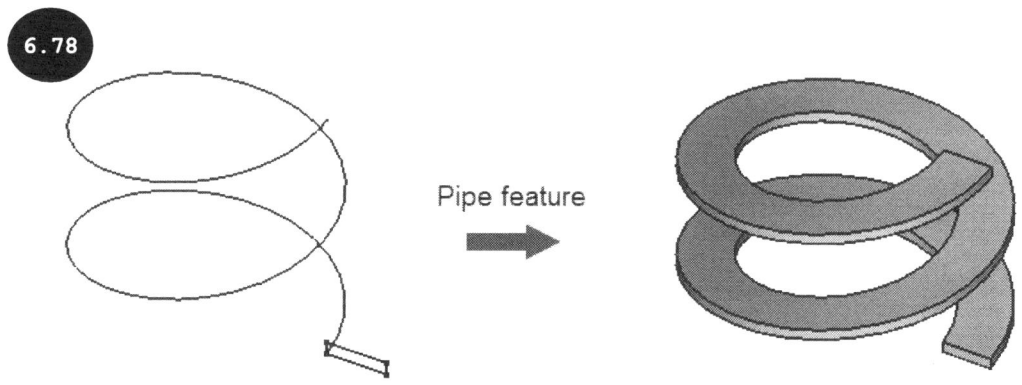

Pipe feature

Note: This textbook covers the **Part Design** workbench for creating 3D solid parametric models. The **Part** workbench is also used for creating solid models of relatively simple shapes.

Tutorial 1

Create a model, as shown in Figure 6.79. The different views and dimensions are given in the same figure. All dimensions are in mm.

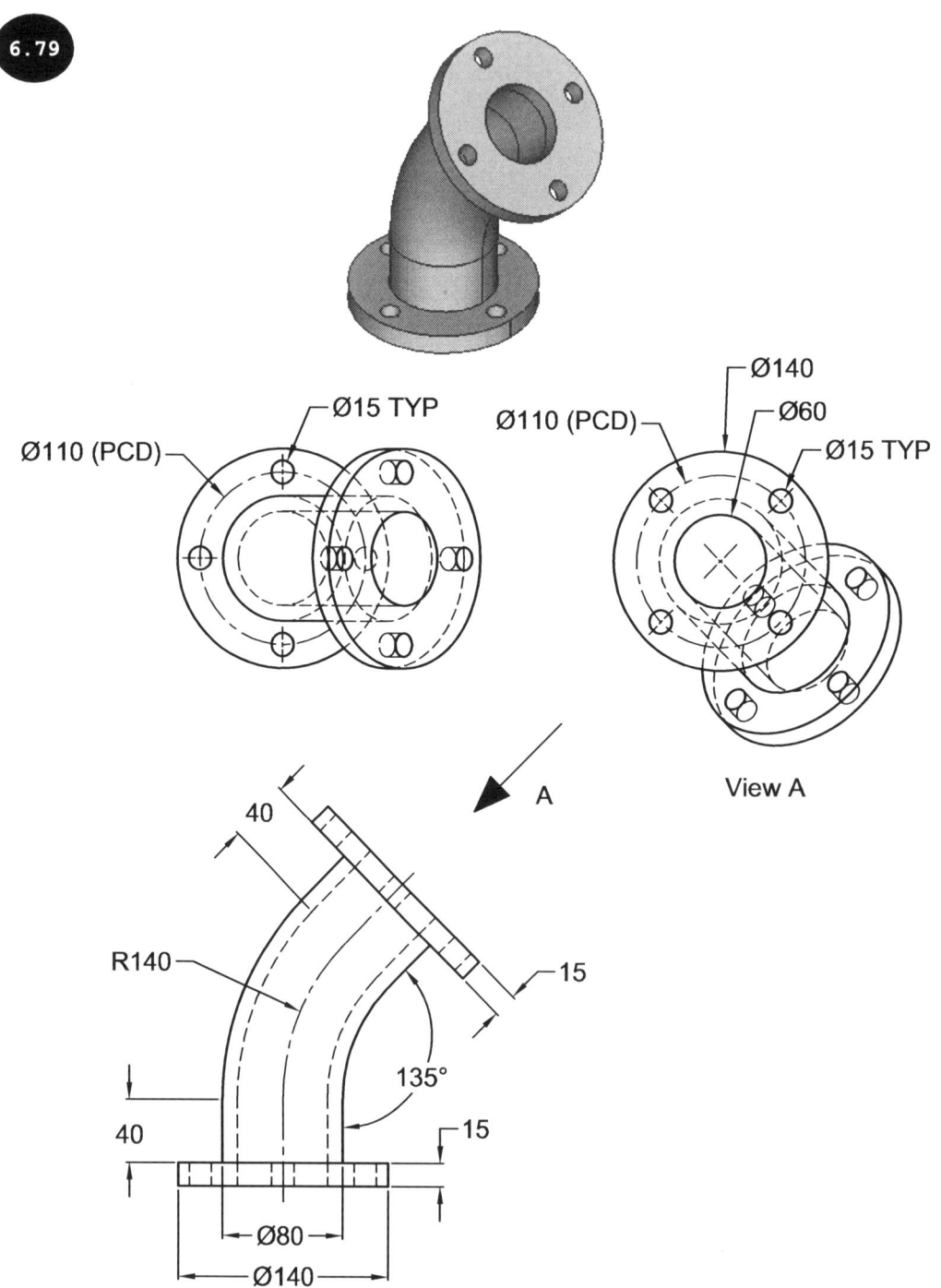

6.79

Ø110 (PCD)

Ø15 TYP

Ø110 (PCD)

Ø140

Ø60

Ø15 TYP

A

View A

40

R140

15

40

135°

15

Ø80

Ø140

Section 1: Starting FreeCAD and a New Empty Document

1. Start FreeCAD by double-clicking on the **FreeCAD 0.20** icon on your desktop. The startup user interface of FreeCAD appears, see Figure 6.80.

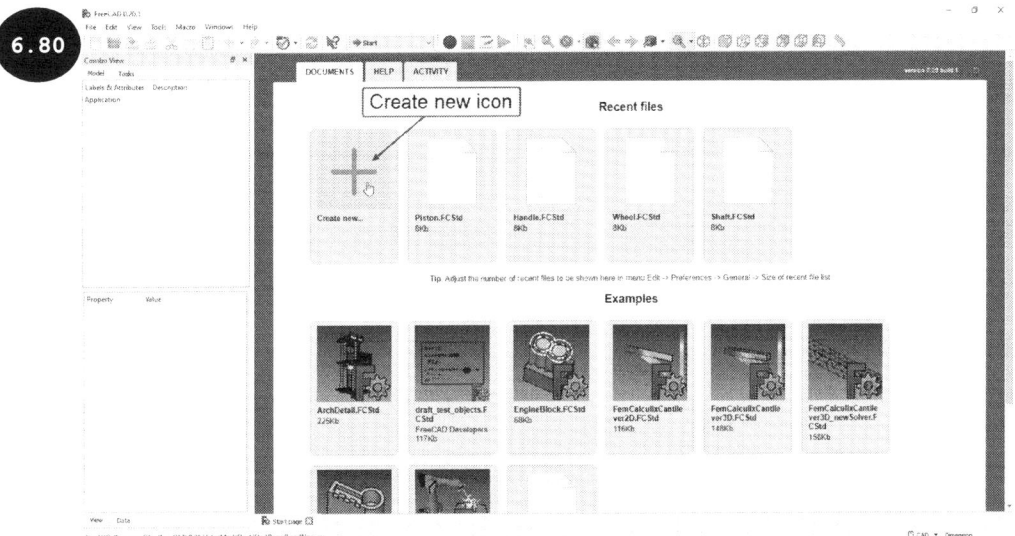

2. Click on the **Create new** icon on the **Start** page (refer to Figure 6.80) or press the **CTRL + N** keys. A new empty document gets invoked with the default name "**unnamed: 1**" and it becomes active by default.

Section 2: Invoking the Part Design Workbench

Now, you can invoke the **Part Design** workbench for creating a 3D solid part.

1. Invoke the **Workbench Selector** in the **Workbench** toolbar and then select the **Part Design** workbench, see Figure 6.81. The **Part Design** workbench gets invoked.

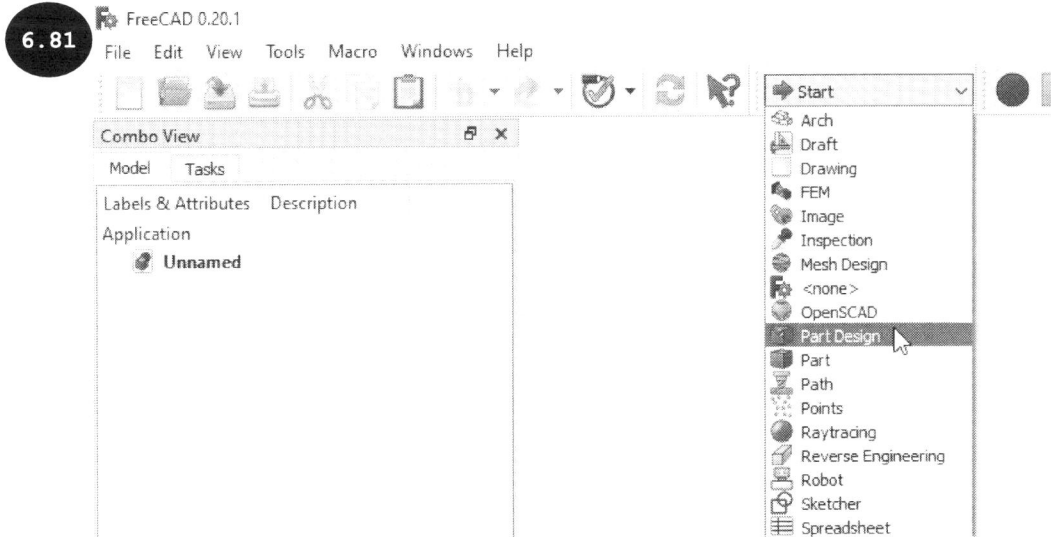

Section 3: Specifying the Unit

Now, you need to specify millimeters (mm) as the measurement unit for the document.

1. Click on **Edit** > **Preferences** in the **Standard Menu**, see Figure 6.82. The **Preferences** dialog box appears.

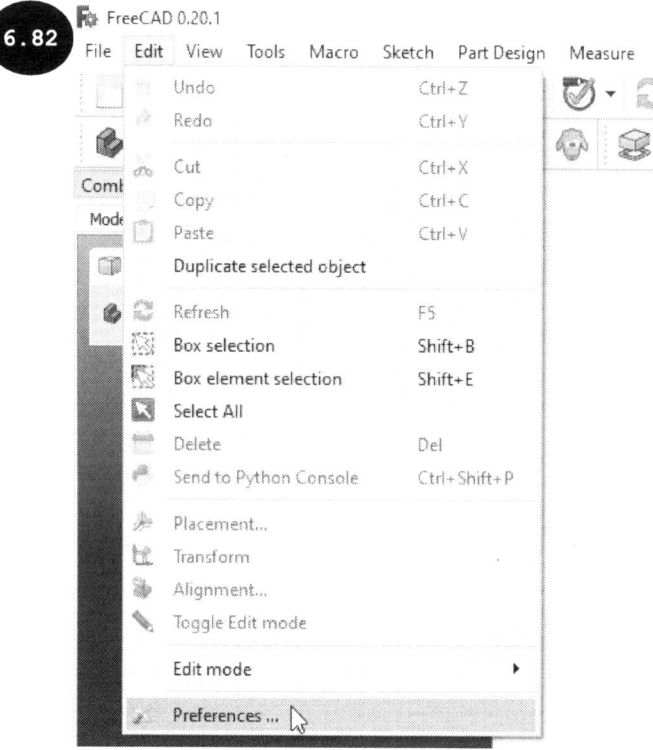

2. Ensure that the **General** section is selected in the left panel of the **Preferences** dialog box and then click on the **Units** tab, see Figure 6.83.

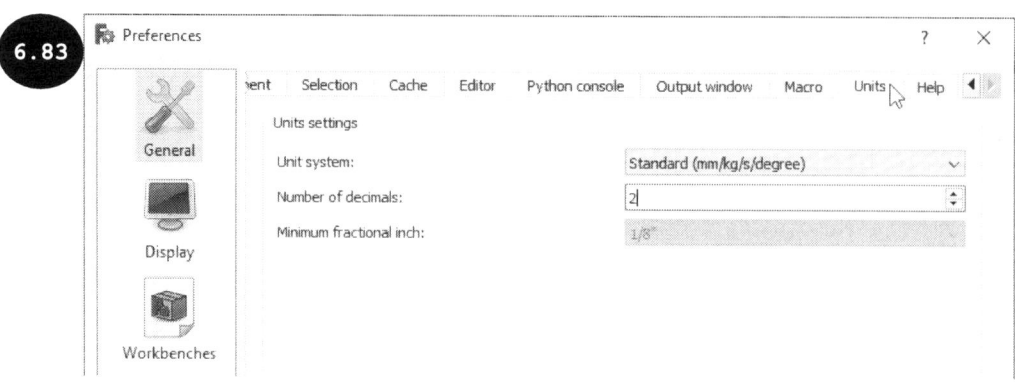

Tip: You may need to click on arrow ▶ at the upper right corner of the **Preferences** dialog box for displaying the **Units** tab.

3. Select the **Standard (mm/kg/s/degree)** option in the **Unit system** drop-down list of the dialog box as the unit system of the current document.

4. Ensure that the 2 is specified in the **Number of decimals** field of the dialog box as the number of digits after the decimal point of measurements.

5. Click on the **Apply** button and then the **OK** button in the **Preferences** dialog box. The selected unit system is defined, and the dialog box is closed.

Section 4: Creating the Base Feature
Now, you can create the base or first feature of the model, which is an additive pipe feature.

1. Invoke the **Sketcher** workbench by selecting the **XZ_Plane** as the sketching plane and then create a sketch, which consists of an arc and two-line entities as the path of the additive pipe feature, see Figure 6.84. Note that the connected line and arc entities of the sketch are tangent to each other. After creating the sketch, exit the **Sketcher** workbench to switch back to the **Part Design** workbench.

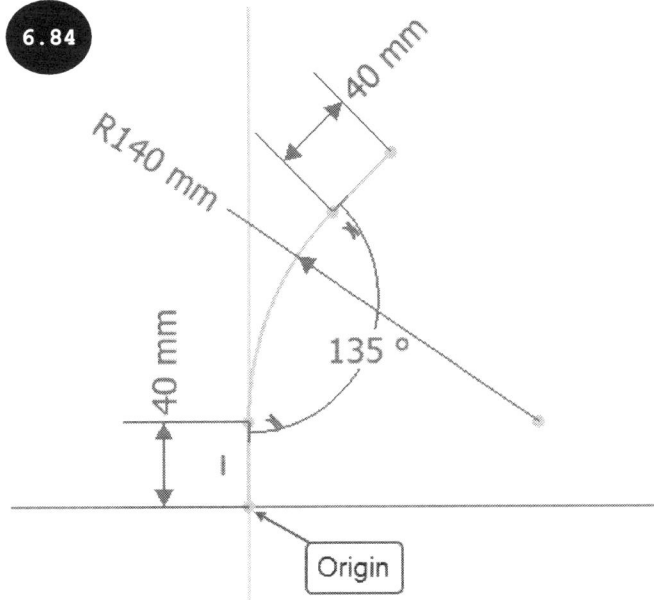

Note: You need to apply the required dimensions and constraints to make the sketch (path) fully constrained.

Now, you need to create the profile of the additive pipe feature.

2. Invoke the **Sketcher** workbench by selecting the **XY_Plane** as the sketching plane and then create a sketch (two concentric circles) as the profile of the additive pipe feature, see Figure 6.85. Note that the center point of both circles is at the origin.

3. After creating the profile, exit the **Sketcher** workbench and then change the view orientation to isometric, see Figure 6.86. Click anywhere in the 3D View area to exit the current selection set.

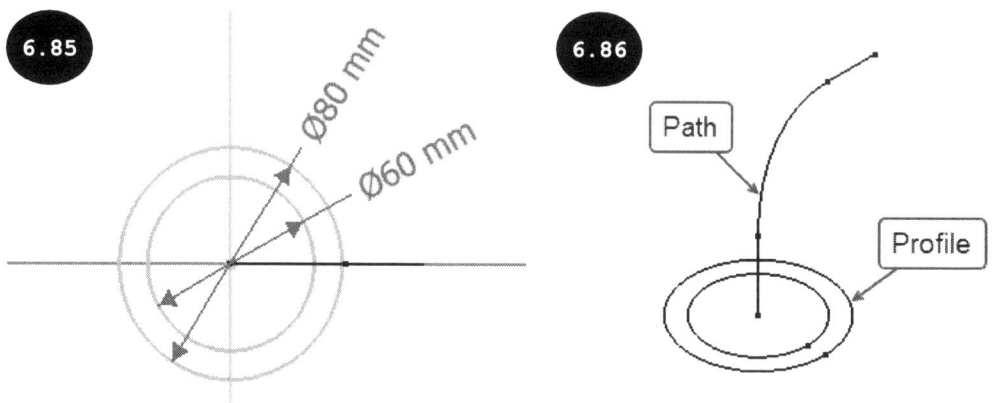

Now, you can create the additive pipe feature.

4. Select the sketch of the profile and then the sketch of the path in the **Tree View** of the **Model** tab in the **Task Panel** by pressing the CTRL key. Next, release the CTRL key.

5. After selecting the profile and the path in the **Tree View**, click on the **Additive pipe** tool in the **Part Design Modeling** toolbar, see Figure 6.87. The preview of the additive pipe feature appears in the 3D View area such that the profile follows the path, see Figure 6.88. Also, the **Pipe parameters** sub-window appears in the **Task Panel** with the options to create an additive pipe feature.

Note: You can also select the profile and the path of the feature after invoking the **Additive pipe** tool.

6. Accept the default settings in the **Pipe parameters** sub-window of the **Task Panel** and then click on the **OK** button. The additive pipe feature gets created, see Figure 6.89.

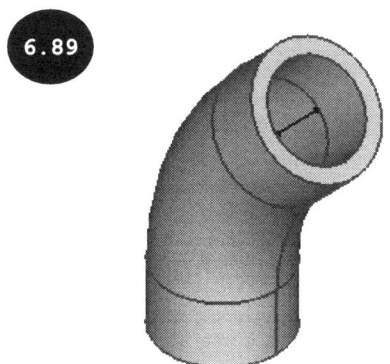

Section 5: Creating the Second Feature

Now, you can create the second feature of the model, which is a pad feature.

1. Click on the **Create sketch** tool ⬚ in the **Part Design Helper** toolbar (see Figure 6.90) and then select the **XY_Plane** as the sketching plane. The **Sketcher** workbench gets invoked and the selected plane gets oriented normal to the viewing direction.

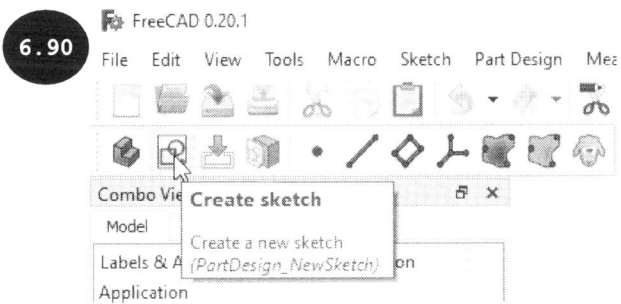

2. Select the **View section** tool in the **Sketcher** toolbar, see Figure 6.91. The section view of the model appears in the 3D View area by temporarily hiding the material that is in front of the sketching plane.

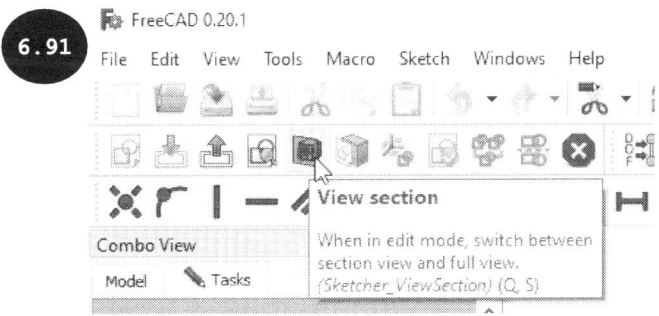

3. Create the sketch of the pad feature by using the sketching tools, see Figure 6.92.

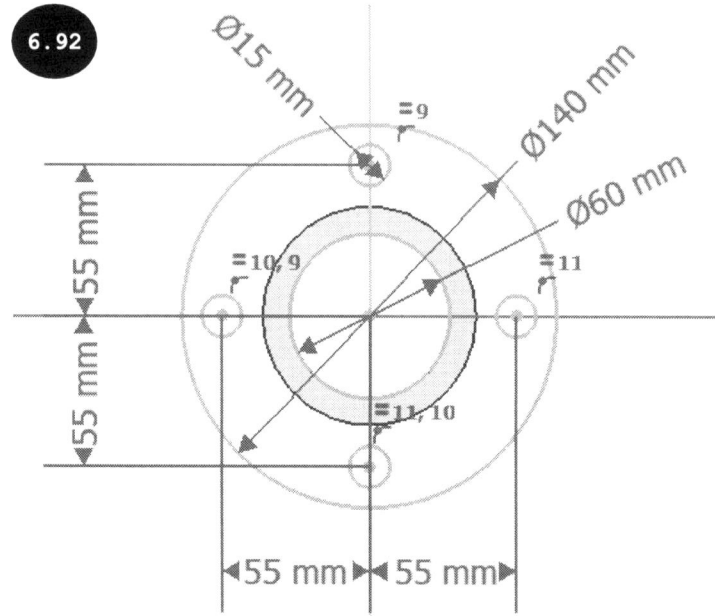

4. After creating the sketch, exit the **Sketcher** workbench to switch back to the **Part Design** workbench.

   Now, you can extrude the sketch to create a pad feature.

5. Click on the **Pad** tool in the **Part Design Modeling** toolbar, see Figure 6.93. The preview of a pad feature appears in the 3D View area with default parameters, see Figure 6.94. Also, the **Pad parameters** sub-window appears in the **Task Panel**.

6. Enter **15** mm in the **Length** field of the **Task Panel** and then press the TAB key to update the preview of the pad feature.

7. Select the **Reversed** check box in the **Pad parameters** sub-windows of the **Task Panel** to reverse the direction of extrusion downward.

8. Click on the **OK** button in the **Task Panel** to confirm the creation of the pad feature and exit the **Task Panel**. The second feature gets created, see Figure 6.95.

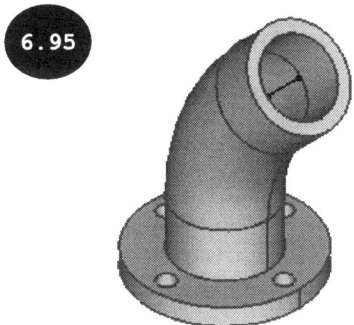

6.95

Section 6: Creating the Third Feature
Now, you can create the third feature of the model, which is also a pad feature.

1. Select the top planar face of the base feature (additive pipe) as the sketching plane (see Figure 6.96) and then click on the **Create sketch** tool in the **Part Design Helper** toolbar, see Figure 6.97. The **Sketcher** workbench gets invoked and the selected planar face gets oriented normal to the viewing direction.

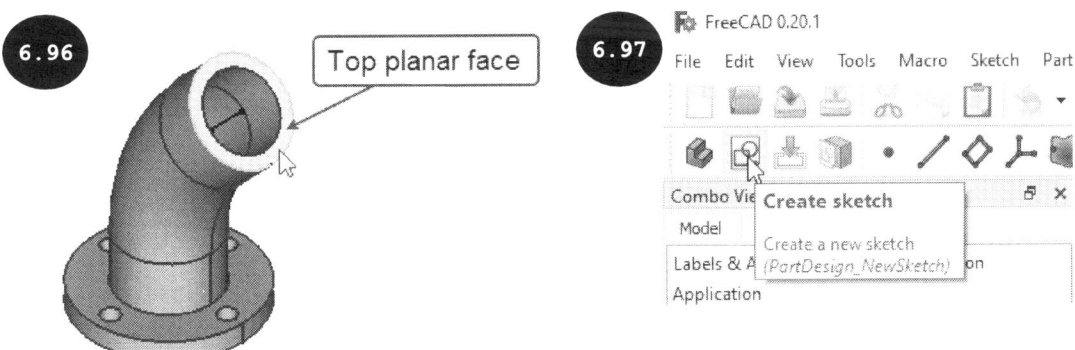

6.96   Top planar face

6.97   FreeCAD 0.20.1

Create sketch
Create a new sketch
(PartDesign_NewSketch)

2. Click on the **External geometry** tool in the **Sketcher geometries** toolbar (see Figure 6.98) to project the edges of existing features as the linked construction entities into the sketch.

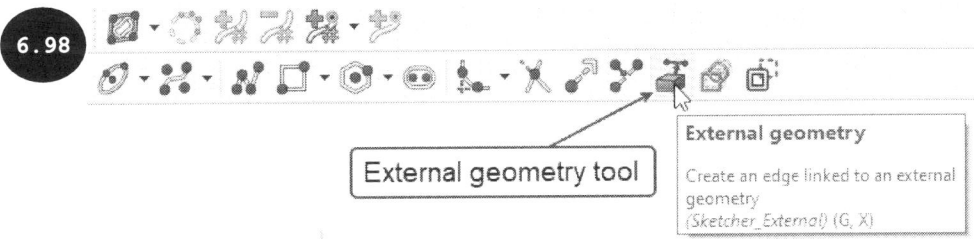

6.98

External geometry tool

External geometry
Create an edge linked to an external geometry
(Sketcher_External) (G, X)

3. Select the inner circular edge of the top planar face of the base feature to be projected as the linked construction entity into the sketch, see Figure 6.99. Next, press the ESC key to exit the tool.

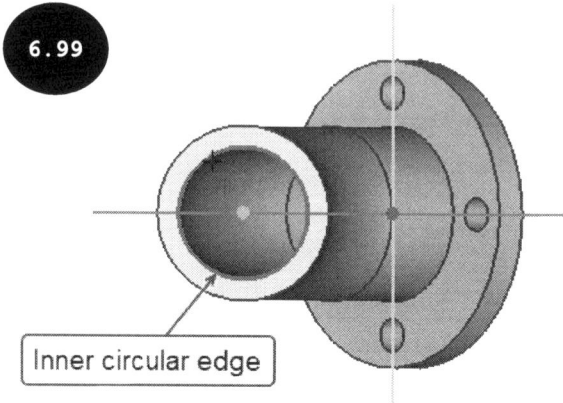

Inner circular edge

Now, you can take reference of the linked construction entity for creating the sketch of the pad feature.

4. Create the sketch of the pad feature by using the sketching tools, see Figure 6.100.

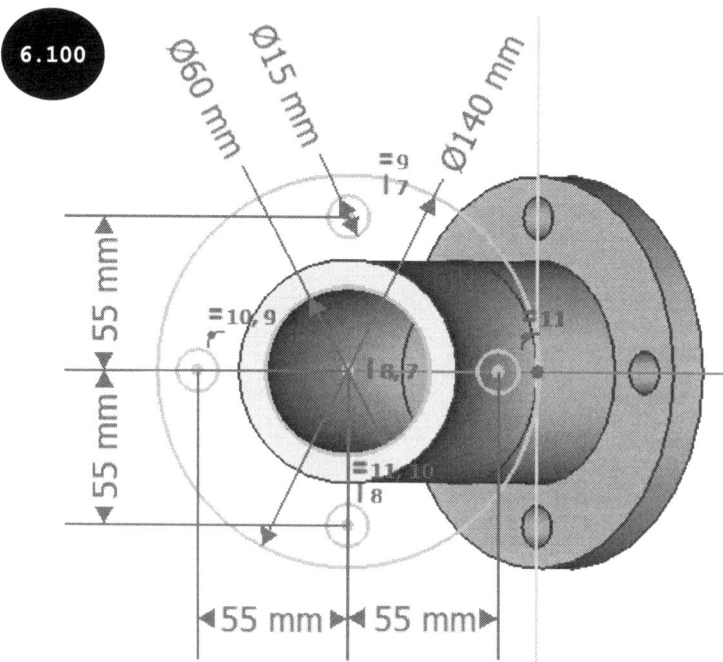

5. After creating the sketch, exit the **Sketcher** workbench to switch back to the **Part Design** workbench.

Now, you can extrude the sketch to create a pad feature.

6. Click on the **Pad** tool in the **Part Design Modeling** toolbar, see Figure 6.101. The preview of a pad feature appears in the 3D View area with default parameters. Also, the **Pad parameters** sub-window appears in the **Task Panel**.

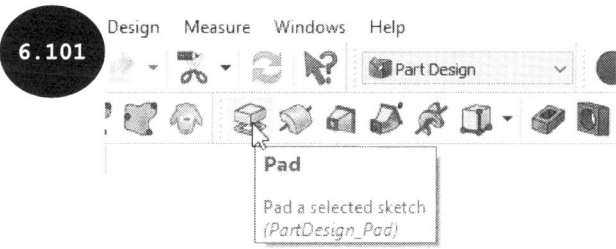

7. Enter **15** mm in the **Length** field of the **Task Panel** and then press the TAB key to update the preview of the pad feature.

8. Click on the **OK** button in the **Task Panel** to confirm the creation of the pad feature and exit the **Task Panel**. The pad feature of specified length gets created, see Figure 6.102.

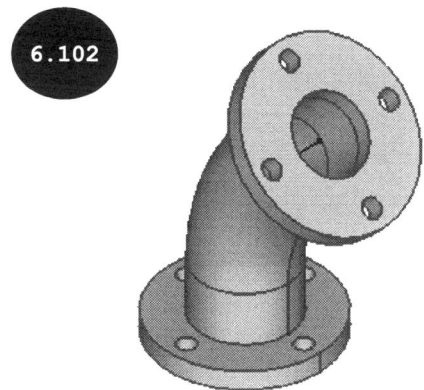

Section 7: Saving the Model

1. Click on the **Save** tool in the **File** toolbar or press the CTRL + S keys. The **Save FreeCAD Document** dialog box appears.

2. Browse to the required folder (*:\FreeCAD > Chapter 06*) in the local drive of your system. Note that you need to create the Chapter 06 sub-folder inside the FreeCAD folder.

3. Enter **Ch06-Tutorial 1** in the **File name** field of the dialog box. Next, click on the **Save** button in the dialog box. The model gets saved at the specified location (*:\FreeCAD > Chapter 06*).

4. Click on **File > Close** in the **Standard Menu** to close the current document.

Tutorial 2

Create the model shown in Figure 6.103. All dimensions are in inches (in).

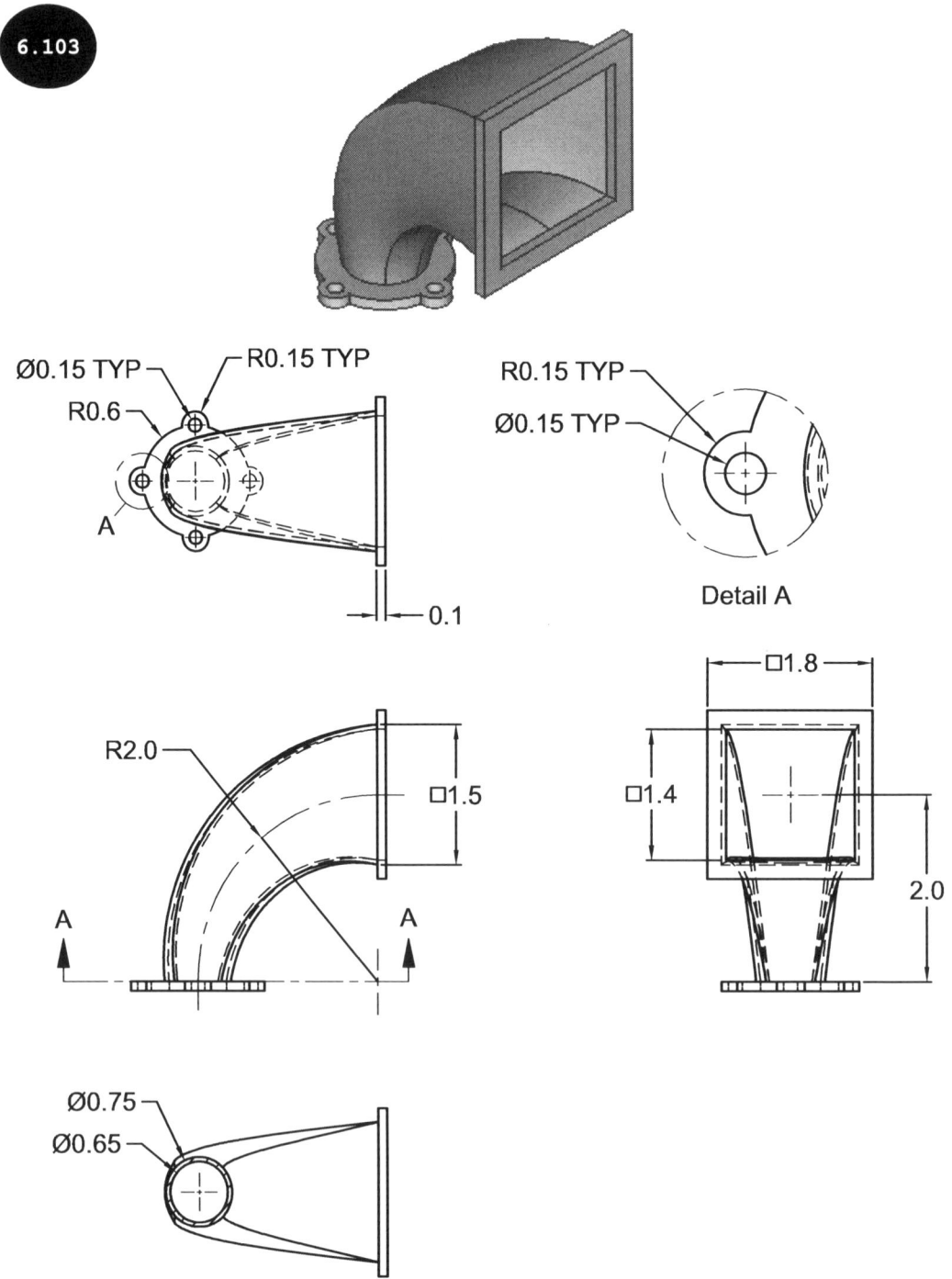

6.103

Ø0.15 TYP — ┌─ R0.15 TYP

R0.6

A

0.1

R0.15 TYP —

Ø0.15 TYP —

Detail A

R2.0

□1.5

A

A

□1.8

□1.4

2.0

Ø0.75

Ø0.65

Section A-A

Section 1: Starting FreeCAD and a New Empty Document

1. Start FreeCAD by double-clicking on the **FreeCAD 0.20** icon on your desktop. The startup user interface of FreeCAD appears, see Figure 6.104.

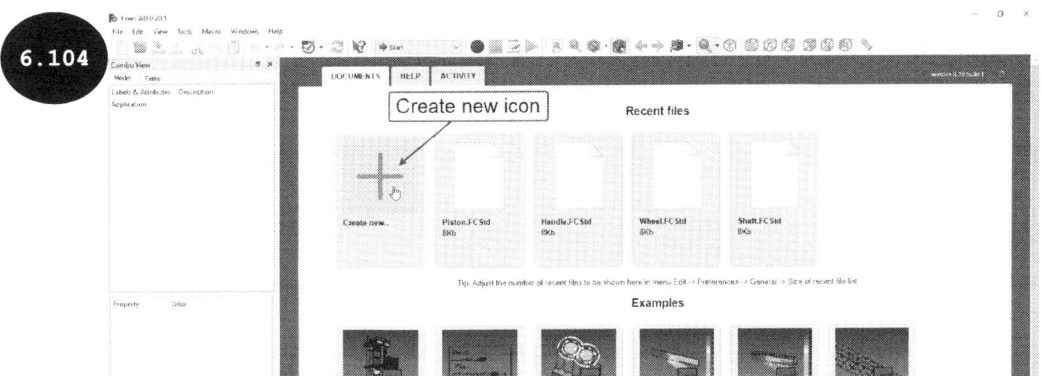

2. Click on the **Create new** icon on the **Start** page (refer to Figure 6.104) or press the **CTRL + N** keys. A new empty document gets invoked with the default name "**unnamed: 1**" and it becomes active by default.

Section 2: Invoking the Part Design Workbench and Specifying the Unit

Now, you can invoke the **Part Design** workbench for creating a 3D solid part and then specify the required unit system.

1. Invoke the **Workbench Selector** in the **Workbench** toolbar and then select the **Part Design** workbench, see Figure 6.105. The **Part Design** workbench gets invoked.

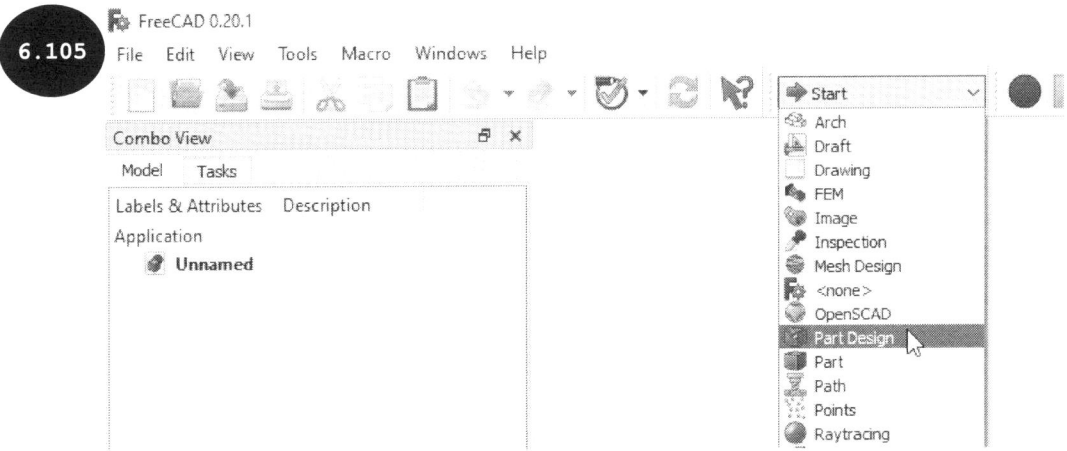

Now, you need to specify inches (in) as the measurement unit for the document.

2. Specify the **Imperial decimal (in/lb)** as the unit system for the current document by using the **Preferences** dialog box.

Section 3: Creating the Base Feature
Now, you can create the base or first feature of the model, which is an additive pipe feature.

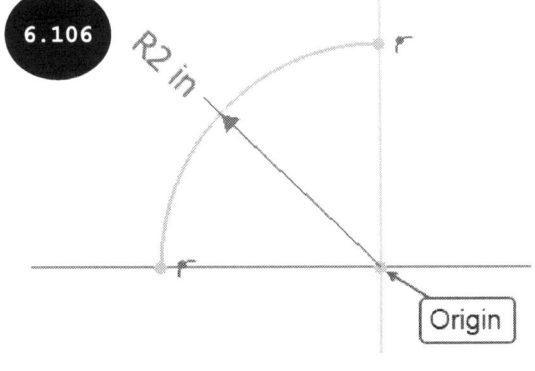

1. Invoke the **Sketcher** workbench by selecting the **XZ_Plane** as the sketching plane and then create an arc as the path of the additive pipe feature, see Figure 6.106. After creating the sketch, exit the **Sketcher** workbench to switch back to the **Part Design** workbench.

   Now, you need to create two different profiles of the additive pipe feature.

2. Invoke the **Sketcher** workbench by selecting the **XY_Plane** as the sketching plane for creating the first profile of the additive pipe feature.

3. Click on the **External geometry** tool in the **Sketcher geometries** toolbar (see Figure 6.107) to project the existing sketch (path) as the linked construction entities into the sketch.

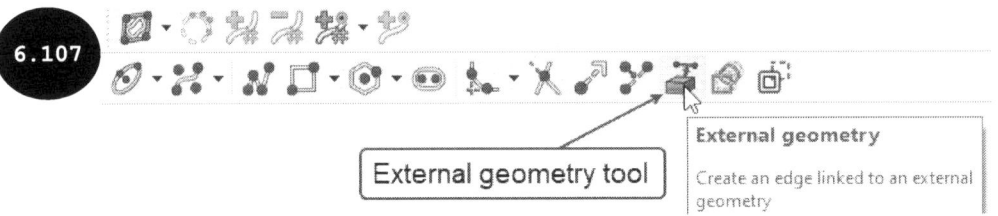

4. Select the existing sketch to be projected as the linked construction entity into the sketch and then press the ESC key to exit the **External geometry** tool. The existing sketch gets projected as the linked construction entity into the sketch.

   Now, you can take reference of the linked construction entity for creating the first profile of the additive pipe feature.

5. Create a sketch (two concentric circles) as the first profile, see Figure 6.108. Note that the center point of both circles is at the left endpoint of the linked construction entity.

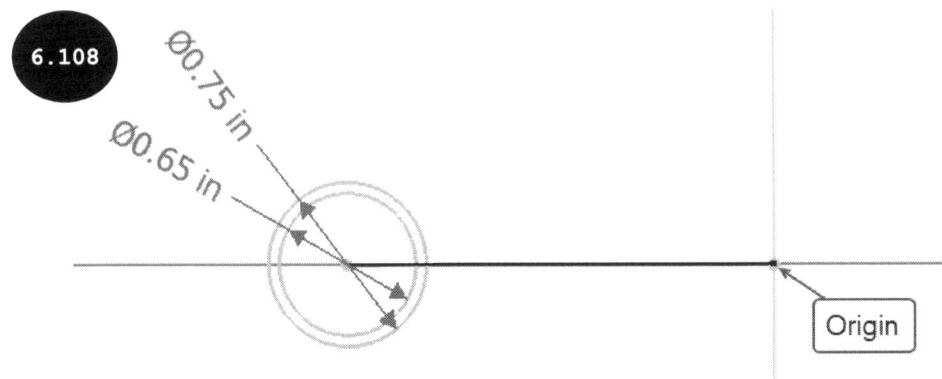

6. After creating the profile, exit the **Sketcher** workbench and then change the view orientation to isometric, see Figure 6.109. Click anywhere in the 3D View area to exit the current selection set.

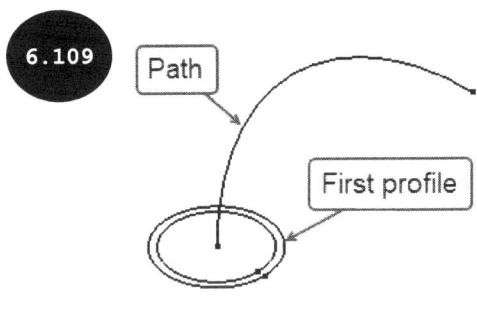

Now, you need to create two profiles of the additive pipe feature.

7. Invoke the **Sketcher** workbench by selecting the **YZ_Plane** as the sketching plane and then create the sketch (two concentric rectangles) of the second profile of the additive pipe feature, see Figure 6.110.

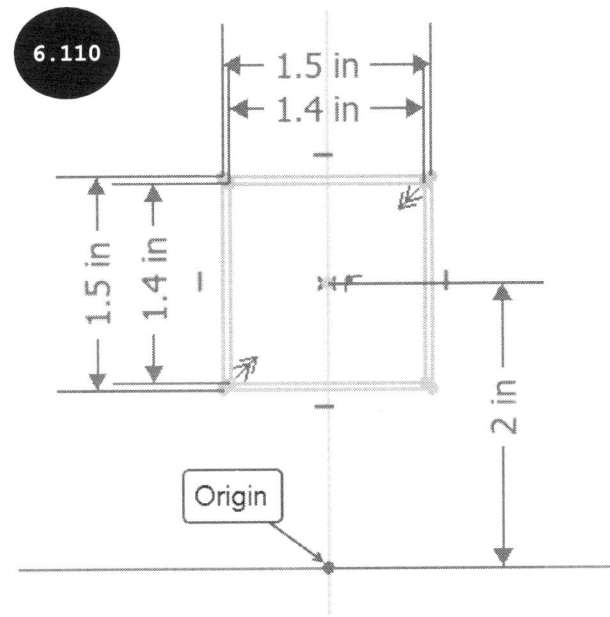

8. After creating the second profile, exit the **Sketcher** workbench and then change the view orientation to isometric, see Figure 6.111. Click anywhere in the 3D View area to exit the current selection set.

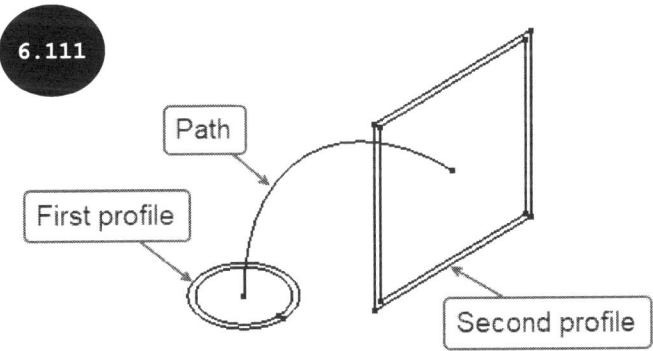

Now, you can create the additive pipe feature.

9.   Click on the **Additive pipe** tool in the **Part Design Modeling** toolbar, see Figure 6.112. The **Select feature** sub-window appears in the **Task Panel**.

10. Select the sketch of the first profile in the 3D View area. The options to create an additive pipe feature appear in the **Pipe parameters** sub-window of the **Task Panel**. Also, the name of the selected sketch appears in its **Profile** field. Ignore the error message that may appear in the **Report view** window at the bottom of the screen. You can close the **Report view** window by clicking on the cross mark ✕ that appears in its top right corner.

11. Click on the **Object** button in the **Path to sweep along** area of the **Pipe parameters** sub-window in the **Task Panel** (see Figure 6.112) and then select the path of the additive feature in the 3D View area. The preview of an additive pipe feature appears such that the first selected profile follows the path, see Figure 6.113.

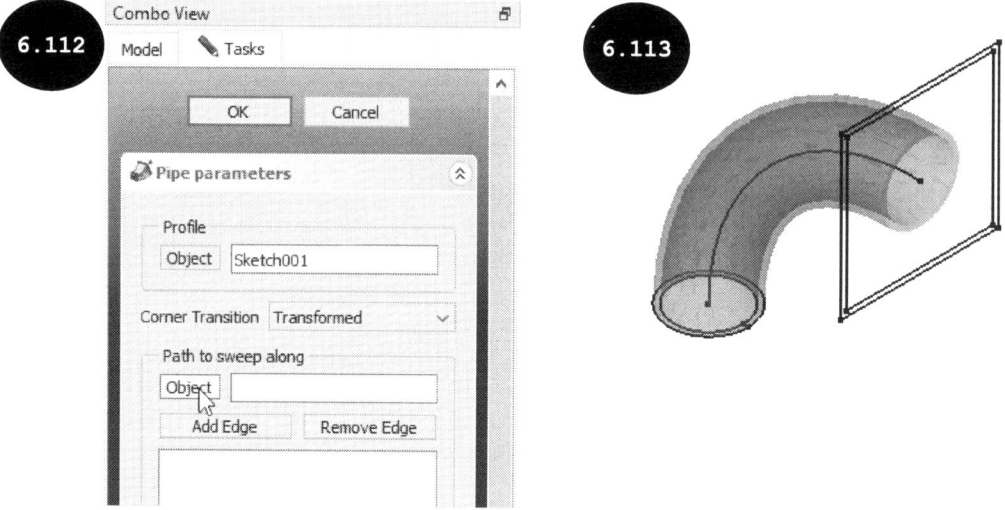

Now, you can select the section profile of the additive pipe feature.

12. Select the **Multisection** option in the **Transform mode** drop-down list of the **Section transformation** sub-window to create a multi-section additive pipe feature, see Figure 6.114.

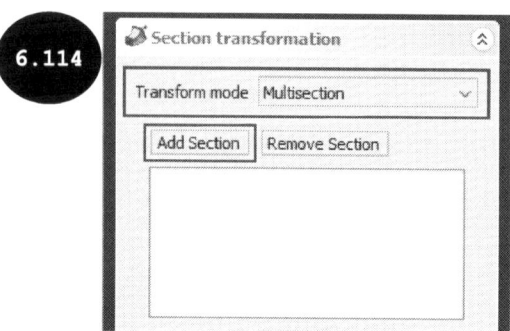

Now, you can select the second profile of the additive pipe feature.

13. Click on the **Add Section** button that appears below the **Transform mode** drop-down list, refer to Figure 6.114.

14. Select the second profile of the additive pipe feature in the 3D View area. The preview of the additive pipe feature gets modified in the 3D View area such that its cross-sectional shape gets transformed from one profile to another while following the path, see Figure 6.115.

15. Click on the **OK** button in the **Task Panel**. The additive pipe feature gets created, see Figure 6.116.

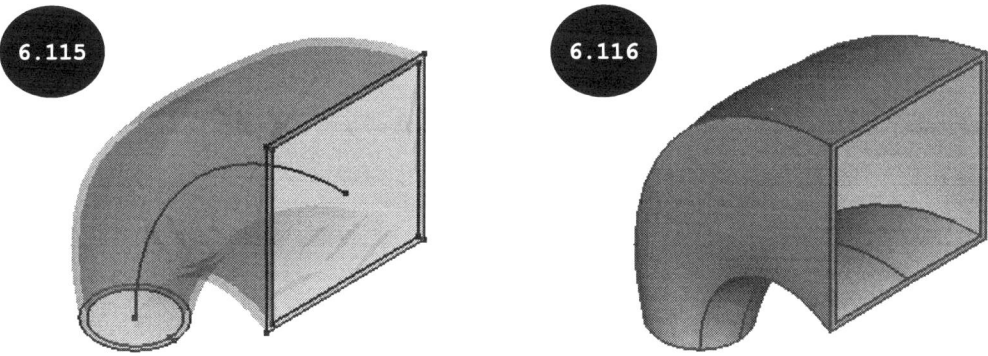

Section 4: Creating the Second Feature

Now, you can create the second feature of the model, which is a pad feature.

1. Invoke the **Sketcher** workbench by selecting the **XY_Plane** or the bottom planar face of the base feature as the sketching plane.

2. Select the **View section** tool in the **Sketcher** toolbar, see Figure 6.117. The section view of the model appears in the 3D View area by temporarily hiding the material that is in front of the sketching plane.

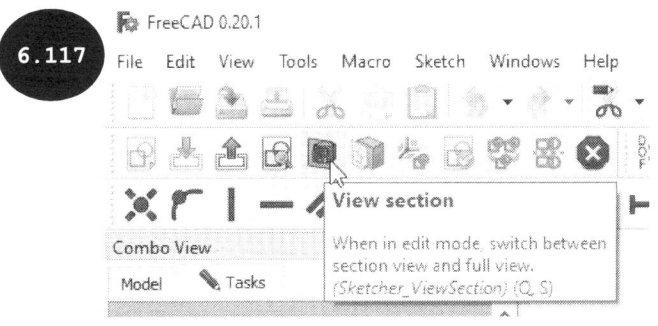

3. Create the sketch of the pad feature by using the sketching tools, see Figure 6.118. In this figure, the display of geometric constraints is turned off for a better understanding of the sketch.

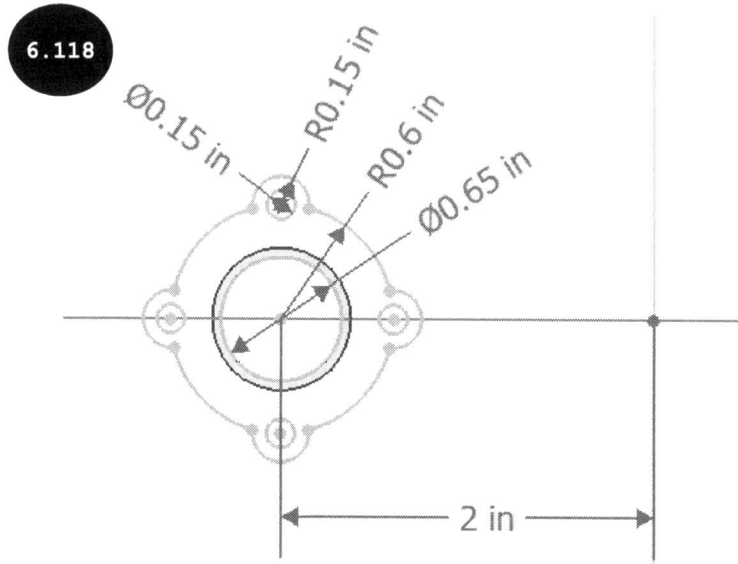

Note: In Figure 6.118, the display of the geometric constraints is turned off for a better understanding of the sketch. For doing so, select the **Geometric** option in the **Filter** drop-down list of the **Constraints** sub-window in the **Task Panel**. A list of applied geometric constraints of the sketch gets filtered and displayed in the **Constraints** sub-window in the **Task Panel**. Next, click on the **Hide Listed** button in the **Constraints** sub-window in the **Task Panel**. The display of geometric constraints gets turned off in the 3D View area. To turn on the display of geometric constraints, click on the **Show Listed** button in the **Constraints** sub-window of the **Task Panel**.

4. After creating the sketch, exit the **Sketcher** workbench to switch back to the **Part Design** workbench.

Now, you can extrude the sketch to create a pad feature.

5. Click on the **Pad** tool in the **Part Design Modeling** toolbar, see Figure 6.119. The preview of a pad feature appears in the 3D View area with default parameters. Also, the **Pad parameters** sub-window appears in the **Task Panel**.

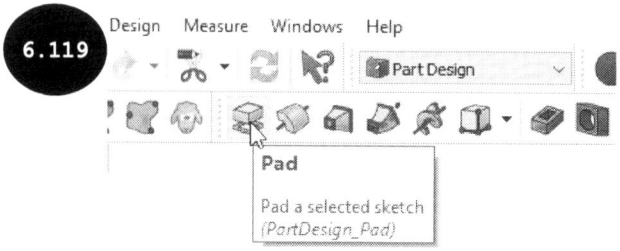

6. Enter **0.1** inches in the **Length** field of the **Task Panel** and then press the TAB key to update the preview of the pad feature.

7. Select the **Reversed** check box in the **Pad parameters** sub-windows of the **Task Panel** to reverse the direction of extrusion downward.

8. Click on the **OK** button in the **Task Panel** to confirm the creation of the pad feature and exit the **Task Panel**. The second feature gets created, see Figure 6.120.

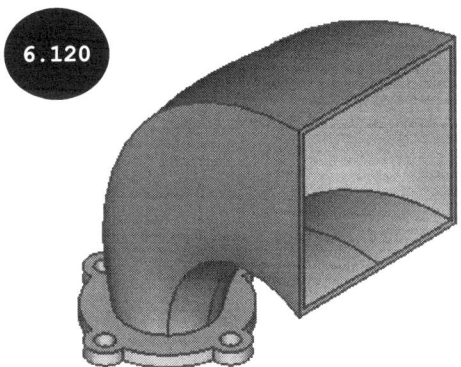

6.120

Section 5: Creating the Third Feature

Now, you can create the third feature of the model, which is also a pad feature.

1. Select the right planar face of the base feature (additive pipe) as the sketching plane (see Figure 6.121) and then click on the **Create sketch** tool in the **Part Design Helper** toolbar, see Figure 6.122. The **Sketcher** workbench gets invoked and the selected planar face gets oriented normal to the viewing direction.

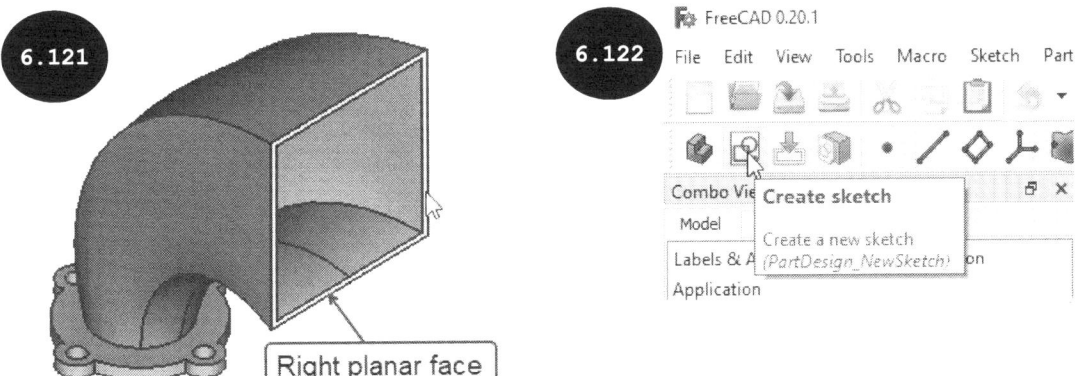

6.121

Right planar face

6.122

FreeCAD 0.20.1

File   Edit   View   Tools   Macro   Sketch   Part

Combo Vie **Create sketch**

Model

Labels & A   Create a new sketch
            (PartDesign_NewSketch)   on
Application

2.   Create the sketch of the pad feature by using the sketching tools, see Figure 6.123.

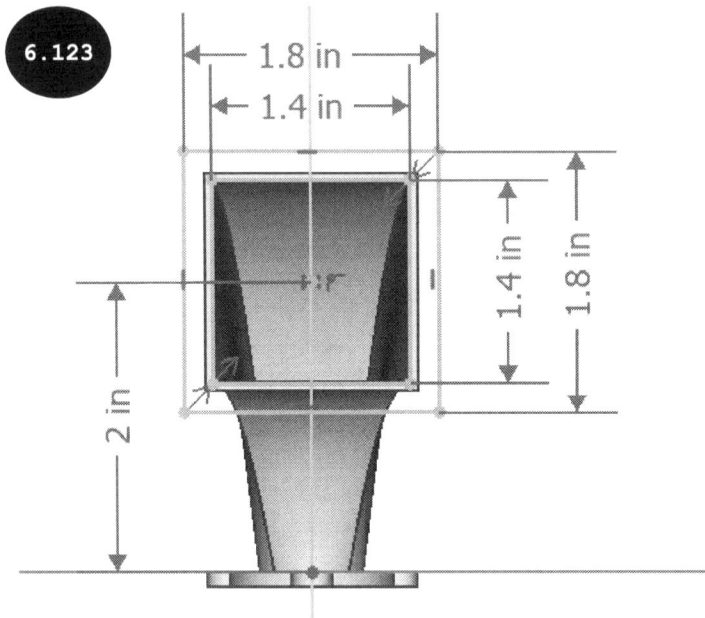

3.   After creating the sketch, exit the **Sketcher** workbench to switch back to the **Part Design** workbench.

Now, you can extrude the sketch to create a pad feature.

4.   Click on the **Pad** tool in the **Part Design Modeling** toolbar and then enter **0.1** inches in the **Length** field of the **Task Panel** that appears. Next, press the TAB key to update the preview of the pad feature.

5.   Click on the **OK** button in the **Task Panel** to confirm the creation of the pad feature and exit the **Task Panel**. The pad feature of specified length gets created, see Figure 6.124.

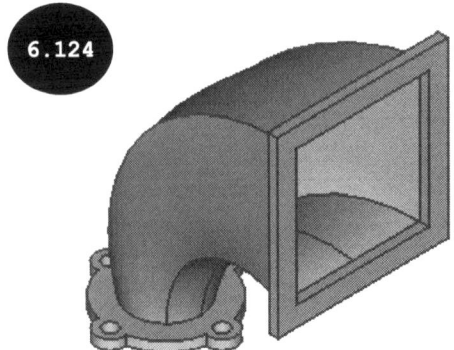

Section 6: Saving the Model

1. Click on the **Save** tool 🔖 in the **File** toolbar (see Figure 6.125) or press the CTRL + S keys. The **Save FreeCAD Document** dialog box appears.

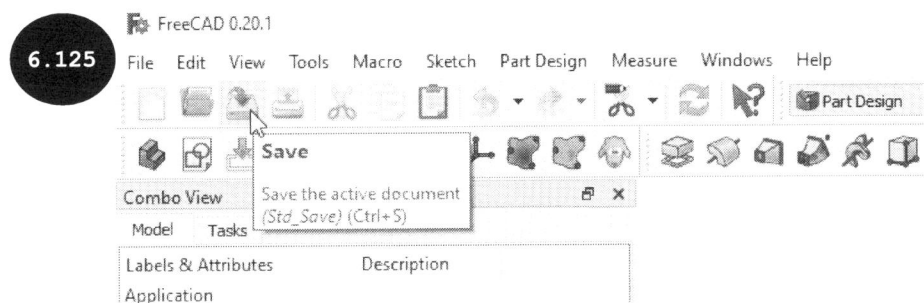

2. Browse to the required folder (:\FreeCAD > Chapter 06) in the local drive of your system. Note that you need to create the Chapter 06 sub-folder inside the FreeCAD folder, if not created earlier.

3. Enter **Ch06-Tutorial 2** in the **File name** field of the dialog box. Next, click on the **Save** button in the dialog box. The model gets saved at the specified location (:\FreeCAD > Chapter 06).

4. Click on the **File > Close** in the **Standard Menu** to close the current document, see Figure 6.126.

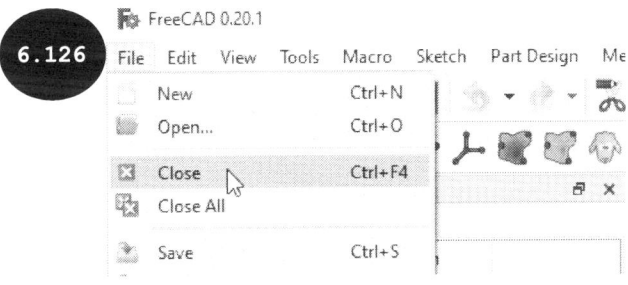

Hands-on Test Drive 1

Create the model shown in Figure 6.127. Different drawing views and dimensions of the model are given in Figure 6.128. All dimensions are in inches (in).

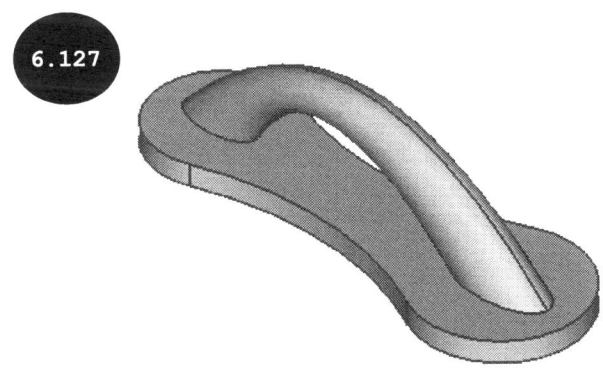

6.128

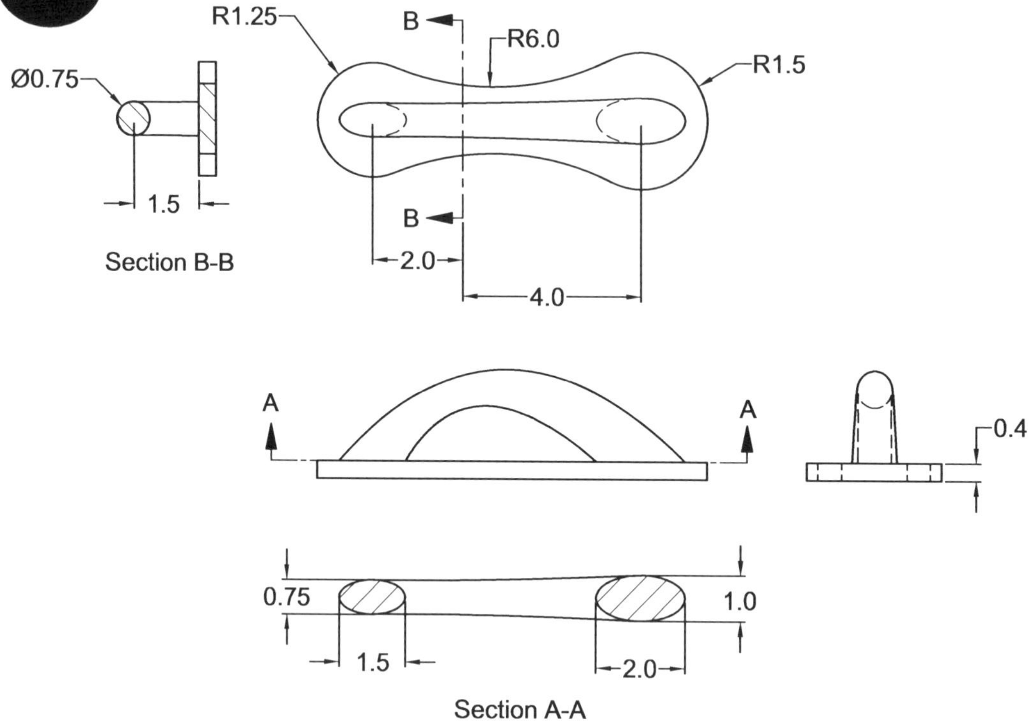

R1.25

B

R6.0

Ø0.75

R1.5

1.5

Section B-B

B

2.0

4.0

A

A

0.4

0.75

1.0

1.5

2.0

Section A-A

Hands-on Test Drive 2

Create the model shown in Figure 6.129. Different drawing views and dimensions of the model are given in Figure 6.130. All dimensions are in mm.

6.129

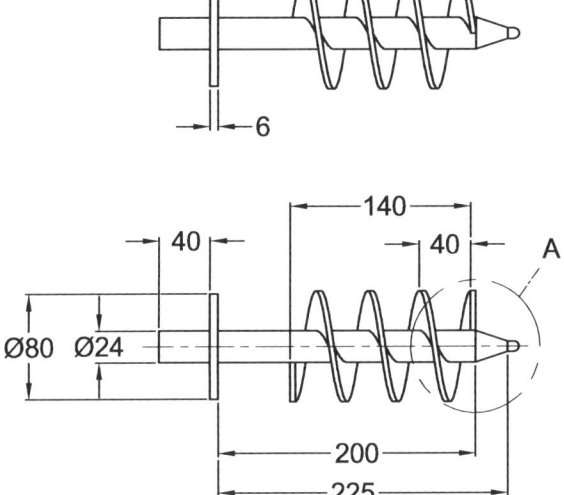

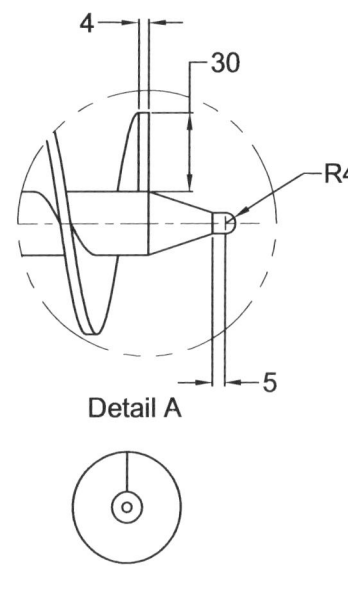

Detail A

Summary

This chapter discussed how to create additive pipe features, multi-section additive pipe features, subtractive pipe features, additive loft features, and subtractive loft features, in addition to additive and subtractive helix features. The method for creating a helical curve in the **Part** workbench has also been discussed in this chapter.

Questions

Complete and verify the following sentences:

- The _____ tool is used for creating a pipe feature by adding material.

- While creating an additive pipe feature, the _____ option is selected in the **Orientation mode** drop-down list, by default. As a result, the profile follows the path such that the cross-section shape of the resultant feature is kept perpendicular throughout the path.

- The _____ option is used for creating an additive pipe feature with a single profile.
.
- The _____ option is used for creating an additive pipe feature with multiple profiles.

- An _____ feature is created by making a transition between two or more profiles.

- The _____ tool is used for creating a loft feature by removing the material from an existing body.

- The _____ tool is used for creating a helix feature by adding material.

- The _____ option is used for creating a helix by defining its total height, number of revolutions (turns), and incremental growth of the helical radius.

- The _____ option allows you to create a spiral coil.

- The profiles of an additive loft feature can either be opened or closed sketches. (True/False)

- In FreeCAD, you cannot create a tapered helix feature. (True/False)

- To create an additive loft feature, you first need to create all its profiles that define its cross-sectional shape. (True/False)

Mirroring and Patterning Features

This chapter discusses the following topics:

- Mirroring Features of a Model
- Patterning Features of a Model
- Create a Multi-transform Pattern

Mirroring and Patterning tools are used for transforming existing features of a model. The methods for mirroring and patterning one or more features of a model are discussed next.

Mirroring Features of a Model

In FreeCAD, you can mirror one or more features of a model about a mirroring plane by using the **Mirrored** tool. Figure 7.1 shows a feature to be mirrored, a mirroring plane, and the resultant mirrored feature. The method for mirroring features of a model is discussed next.

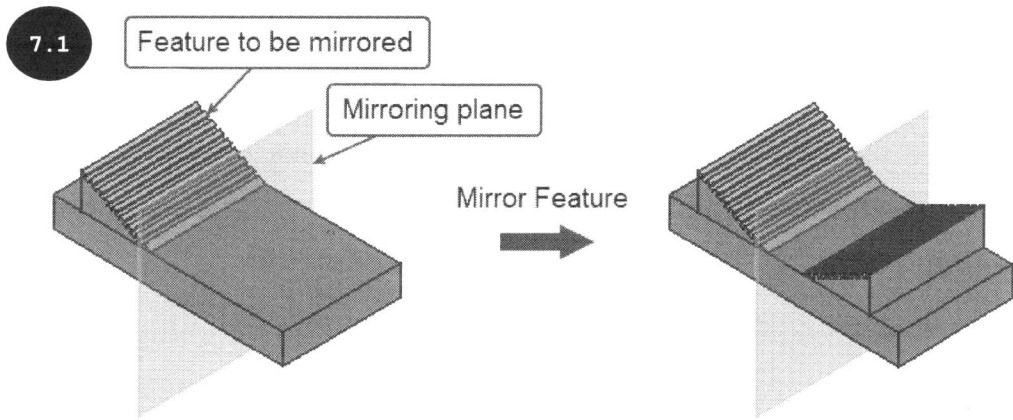

7.1

Feature to be mirrored

Mirroring plane

Mirror Feature

1. Click on the **Mirrored** tool in the **Part Design Modeling** toolbar, see Figure 7.2. The **Select feature** sub-window appears in the **Task Panel** and displays a list of existing features of the model, see Figure 7.3. Also, you are prompted to select one or more features to be mirrored.

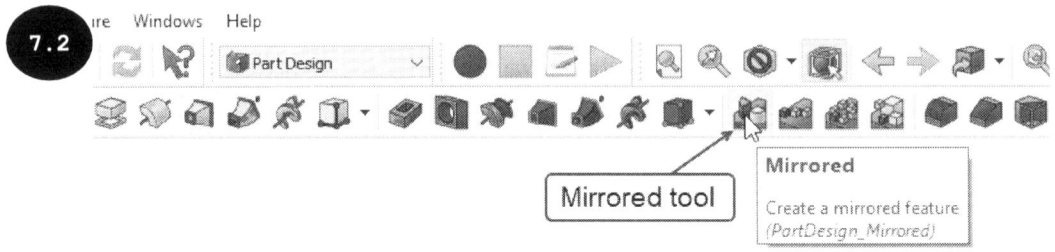

Note: You can select features to be mirrored before or after invoking the **Mirrored** tool.

If a feature is selected prior to invoking the **Mirrored** tool, then a preview of its mirrored feature appears about the vertical axis of its sketch directly in the 3D View area.

2. Select one or more features of a model to be mirrored in the **Select feature** sub-window of the **Task Panel** and then click on the OK button. The **Mirrored parameters** sub-window appears in the **Task Panel** and the names of the selected features appear in its field, see Figure 7.4. Also, the preview of a mirrored feature appears about the vertical axis of its sketch, since the **Vertical sketch axis** option is selected in the **Plane** drop-down list of the **Task Panel**, by default.

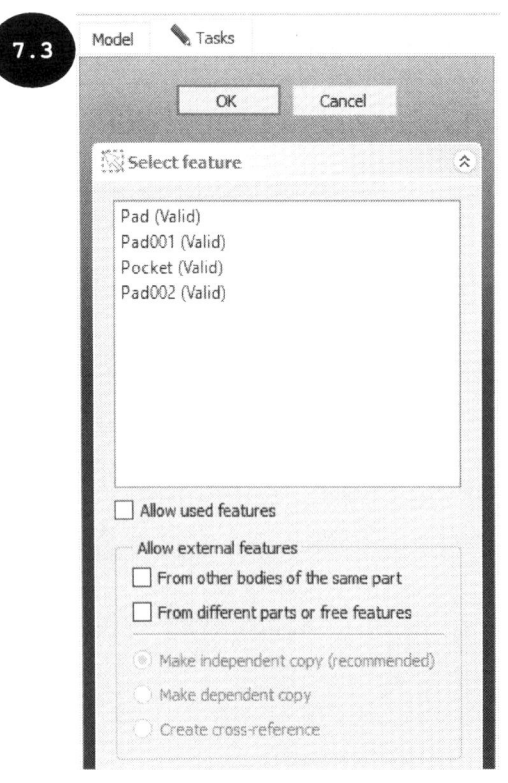

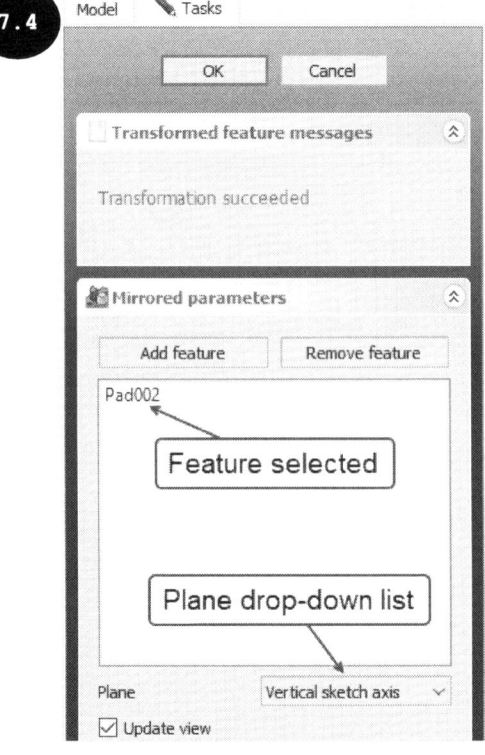

Note: If the sketch of the selected feature is not on either side of its vertical axis, then the preview of the mirrored feature does not appear in the 3D View area. It is because the feature cannot be mirrored about the vertical axis of its sketch that intersects with it. In this case, you need to define a mirroring plane other than its vertical axis by selecting the required option in the **Plane** drop-down list of the **Mirrored parameters** sub-window in the **Task Panel**.

Tip: You can add additional features to be mirrored or remove already selected features by using the **Add feature** and **Remove feature** buttons of the **Mirrored parameters** sub-window, respectively.

3. Specify the required option in the **Plane** drop-down list of the **Mirrored parameters** sub-window for defining the mirroring plane, refer to Figure 7.4. The preview of the mirrored feature appears about the selected mirroring plane in the 3D View area, see Figure 7.5. In this figure, the feature is mirrored about the YZ Plane by selecting the **Base YZ plane** option in the **Plane** drop-down list. The options in the **Plane** drop-down list are discussed next.

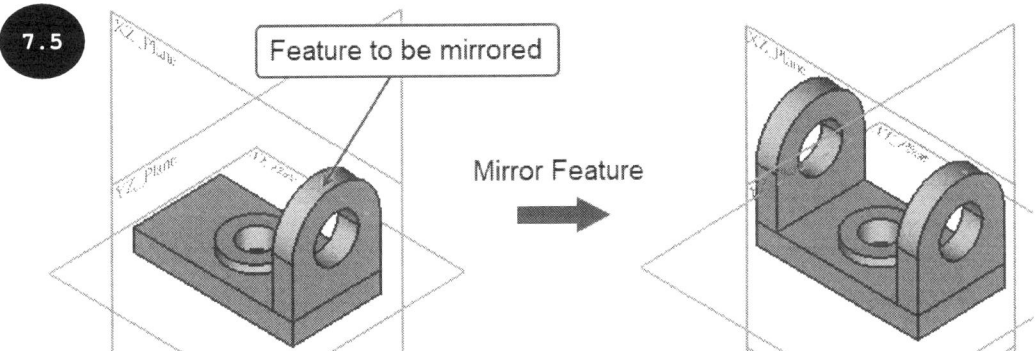

Vertical sketch axis: The Vertical sketch axis option is used for mirroring the selected feature of the model about the vertical axis of its sketch.

Horizontal sketch axis: The Horizontal sketch axis option is used for mirroring the selected feature of the model about the horizontal axis of its sketch.

Base XY plane: The Base XY plane option is used for mirroring the selected feature of the model about the XY plane.

Base YZ plane: The Base YZ plane option is used for mirroring the selected feature of the model about the YZ plane.

Base XZ plane: The Base XZ plane option is used for mirroring the selected feature of the model about the XZ plane.

Select reference: The Select reference option is used for selecting a plane or a planar face of an existing feature as the mirroring plane for creating the mirrored feature.

4.   Click on the **OK** button in the **Task Panel**. The selected feature of the model gets mirrored about the mirroring plane, see Figure 7.6.

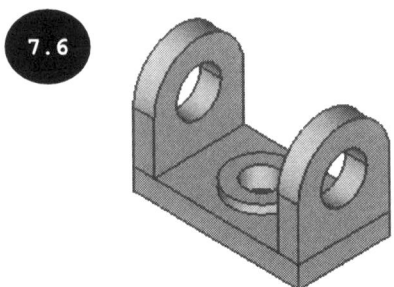

Patterning Features of a Model

In FreeCAD, you can create a linear pattern and a polar pattern of one or more features by using the **Linear Pattern** and **Polar Pattern** tools, respectively. The methods for creating both these types of patterns are discussed next.

Creating a Linear Pattern

A linear pattern creates multiple instances of one or more features of a model in a linear direction, see Figure 7.7. The method for creating a linear pattern is discussed below:

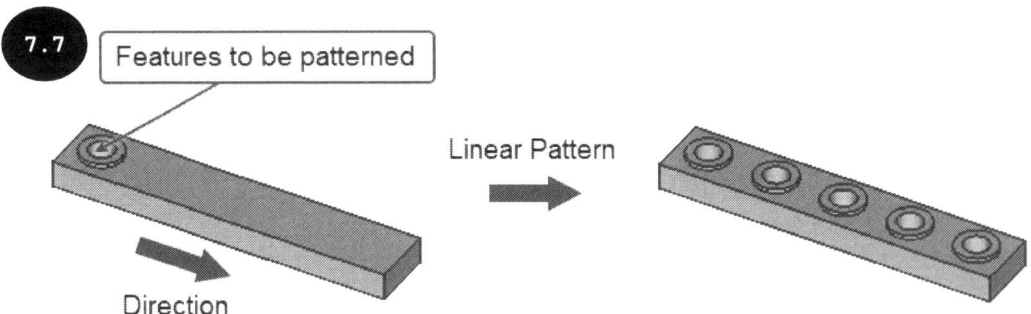

1.   Select a feature to be patterned in the **Tree View** or the 3D View area. You can also select multiple features to be patterned by pressing the CTRL key in sequential order for better results.

2.   After selecting a feature, click on the **LinearPattern** tool in the **Part Design Modeling** toolbar, see Figure 7.8. The **LinearPattern parameters** sub-window appears in the **Task Panel** and the name of the selected feature appears in its field, see Figure 7.9. Also, the preview of a linear pattern of the selected feature appears along the horizontal axis of its sketch with default parameters, since the **Horizontal sketch axis** option is selected in the **Direction** drop-down list of the **Task Panel**, by default.

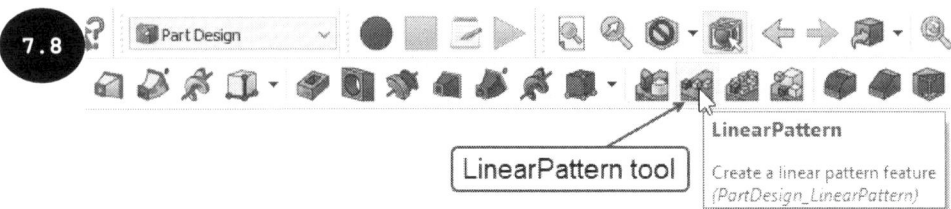

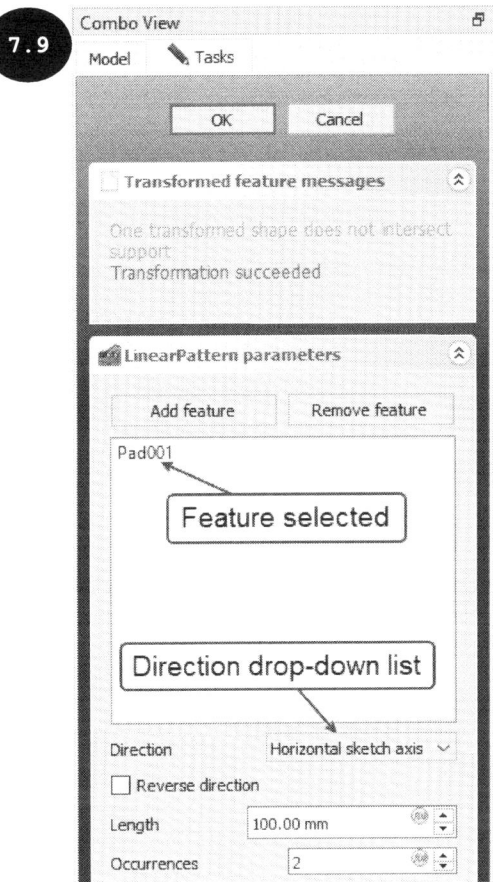

Note: You can select features to be patterned before or after invoking the **LinearPattern** tool.

If a feature to be patterned is not selected prior to invoking the **LinearPattern** tool, then the **Select feature** sub-window appears in the **Task Panel**, which displays a list of existing features of the model. You can select one or more features to be patterned in this **Select feature** sub-window. You need to press the CTRL key for selecting multiple features to be patterned, simultaneously.

Tip: You can add additional features to be patterned or remove already selected features by using the **Add feature** and **Remove feature** buttons of the **LinearPattern parameters** sub-window, respectively. You can also remove an already selected feature from the pattern list by right-clicking on its name in the **LinearPattern parameters** sub-window and then selecting the **Remove** option in the shortcut menu that appears.

3. Specify the required option in the **Direction** drop-down list of the **LinearPattern parameters** sub-window for defining the direction of a linear pattern, see Figure 7.10. The preview of a linear pattern of the selected feature appears along the defined direction in the 3D View area.

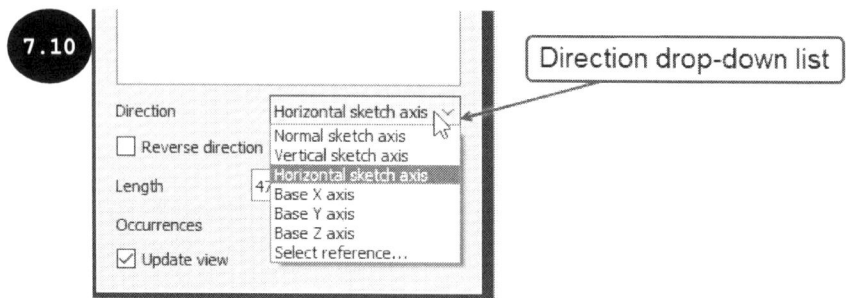

7.10

Direction drop-down list

> **Note:** The options to define the direction of a linear pattern work the same way as described earlier.

4. Enter the required total length of the linear pattern in the **Length** field of the **Task Panel** between which the specified number of pattern occurrences is to be created.

5. Enter the required number of pattern occurrences to be created in the **Occurrences** field of the Task Panel, see Figure 7.11. This figure shows the preview of a linear pattern after specifying **5** as the number of pattern occurrences to be created along the pattern direction.

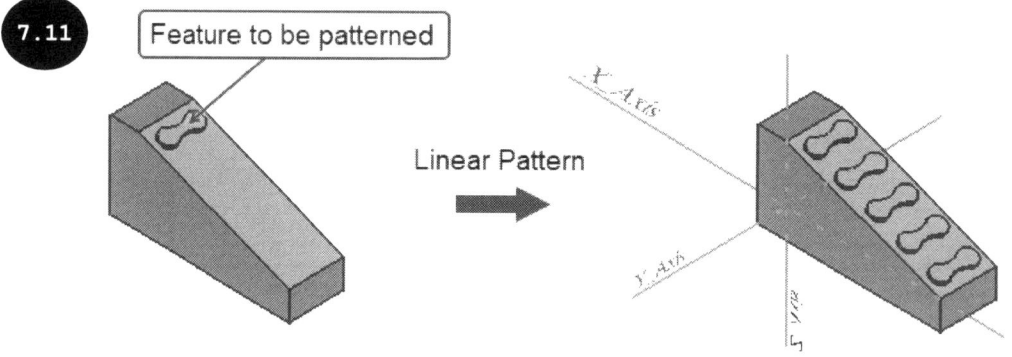

7.11

Feature to be patterned

Linear Pattern

> **Note:** The specified number of pattern occurrences is arranged equally between the total length specified in the **Length** field of the **Task Panel**.
>
> Also, the number of pattern occurrences specified in the **Occurrences** field includes the source or parent feature.

6. Select the **Reverse direction** check box in the **LinearPattern parameters** sub-window to reverse the pattern direction if needed.

7. After specifying all the required parameters, click on the **OK** button in the **Task Panel**. The linear pattern of a specified number of pattern occurrences of the selected feature gets created, see Figure 7.12.

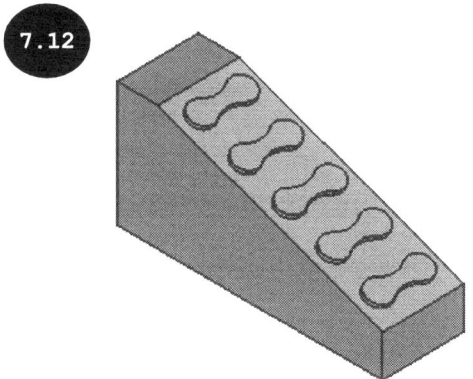

Creating a Polar Pattern

A polar pattern creates multiple instances of one or more features of a model around an axis of revolution, see Figure 7.13. The method for creating a polar pattern is discussed below:

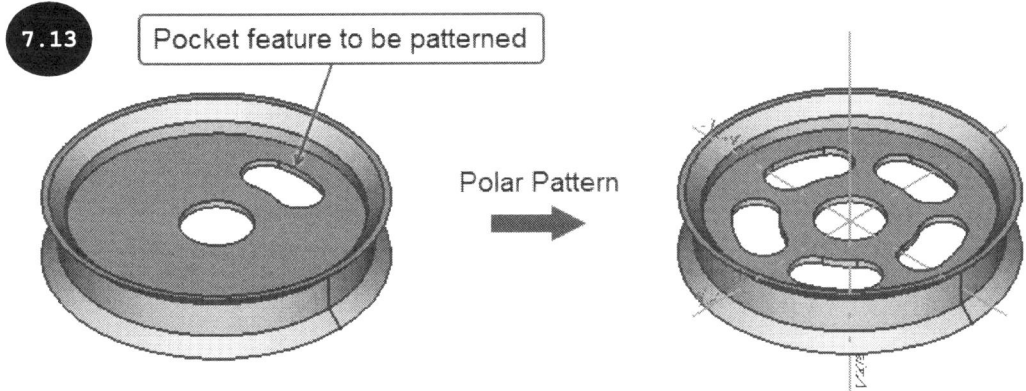

Pocket feature to be patterned

Polar Pattern

1. Select a feature to be patterned in the **Tree View** or the 3D View area. You can also select multiple features to be patterned by pressing the CTRL key.

2. After selecting a feature, click on the **PolarPattern** tool in the **Part Design Modeling** toolbar, see Figure 7.14. The preview of a polar pattern of the selected feature appears around the normal axis of its sketch in the 3D View area, since the **Normal sketch axis** option is selected in the **Axis** drop-down list of the **PolarPattern parameters** sub-window that appears in the **Task Panel**, see Figure 7.15.

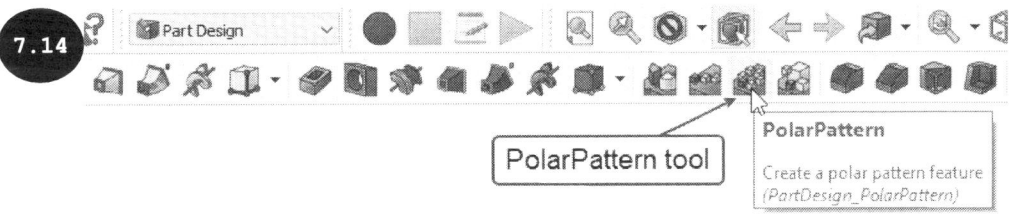

PolarPattern tool

PolarPattern

Create a polar pattern feature
(PartDesign_PolarPattern)

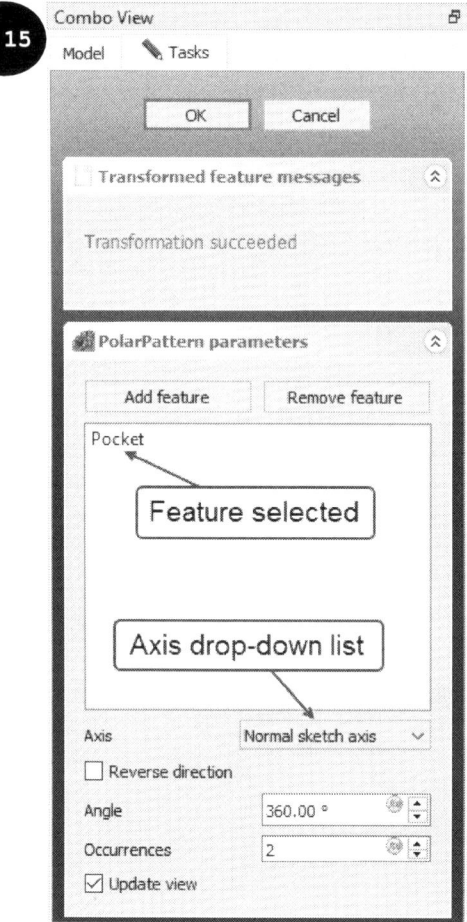

Note: You can select features to be patterned before or after invoking the **PolarPattern** tool.

If a feature to be patterned is not selected before invoking the **PolarPattern** tool, then the **Select feature** sub-window appears in the **Task Panel**, which displays a list of existing features of the model. You can select one or more features to be patterned in this **Select feature** sub-window of the **Task Panel**. You need to press the CTRL key for selecting multiple features to be patterned, simultaneously.

Tip: You can add additional features to be patterned or remove already selected features by using the **Add feature** and **Remove feature** buttons of the **PolarPattern parameters** sub-window of the **Task Panel**, respectively.

3. Specify the required option in the **Axis** drop-down list of the **PolarPattern parameters** sub-window for defining the axis of revolution of the polar pattern, see Figure 7.16. A preview of the polar pattern of the selected feature appears around the defined axis of revolution in the 3D View area.

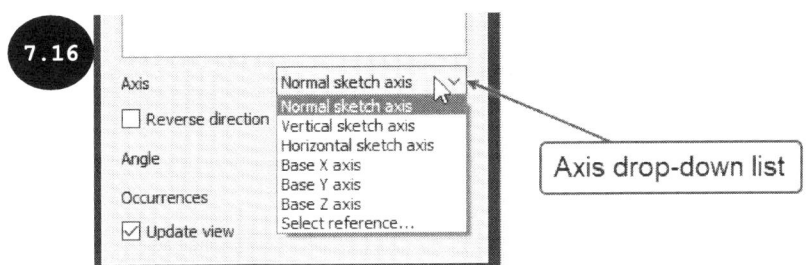

Tip: On selecting the **Select reference** option in the **Axis** drop-down list, you can select a circular edge, a cylindrical face, a linear edge, or an axis to define the axis of revolution.

4. Enter the required total angle value of the polar pattern in the **Angle** field of the **Task Panel** between which the specified number of pattern occurrences is to be arranged with equal angular spacing among all occurrences. By default, the 360 degrees angle value is defined in this field.

5. Enter the required number of pattern occurrences to be created in the **Occurrences** field of the **Task Panel**, see Figure 7.17. This figure shows the preview of a polar pattern after specifying 3 as the number of pattern occurrences to be created between the specified angle value. Note that the number of pattern occurrences specified in the **Occurrences** field includes the parent feature.

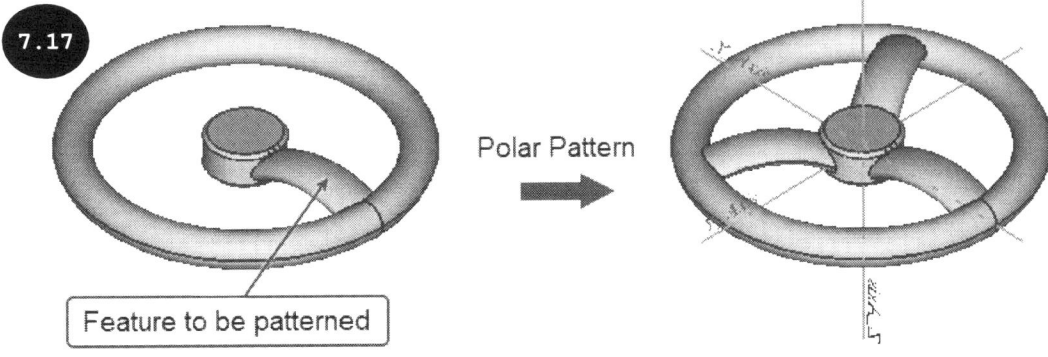

6. Select the **Reverse direction** check box in the **PolarPattern parameters** sub-window to reverse the pattern direction if needed. It works better if the angle value is specified less than 360 degrees.

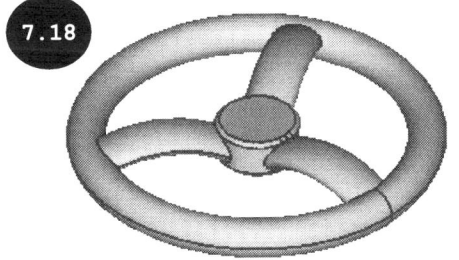

7. After specifying all the required parameters, click on the **OK** button in the **Task Panel**. The polar pattern of a specified number of pattern occurrences gets created, see Figure 7.18.

Create a Multi-transform Pattern

In FreeCAD, you can create a multi-transform pattern by combining multiple transformations: Mirrored, Linear Pattern, Polar pattern, and/or Scaled by using the **MultiTransform** tool. The method for creating a multi-transform pattern is discussed below:

1. Select a feature to be patterned in the **Tree View** or the 3D View area. You can also select multiple features to be patterned by pressing the CTRL key.

2. After selecting a feature, click on the **Create MultiTransform** tool in the **Part Design Modeling** toolbar, see Figure 7.19. The **MultiTransform parameters** sub-window appears in the **Task Panel** and the name of the selected feature appears in its field, see Figure 7.20.

Now, you can define the first transformation (Mirrored, Linear Pattern, Polar pattern, or Scaled) to be applied to the selected feature.

3. Right-click on the **Transformations** field of the **Task Panel** and then select the required transformation (**Add mirrored transformation, Add linear pattern, Add polar pattern,** or **Add scaled transformation**) to be created in the shortcut menu that appears, see Figure 7.21. The transformation gets selected, and its name appeared in the **Transformations** field of the **Task Panel**, see Figure 7.22. Also, the options to create the selected transformation appear at the bottom of the **Task Panel**. In Figure 7.22, the linear pattern transformation is selected. As a result, the options to create a linear pattern appear at the bottom of the **Task Panel**. These options are the same as discussed earlier.

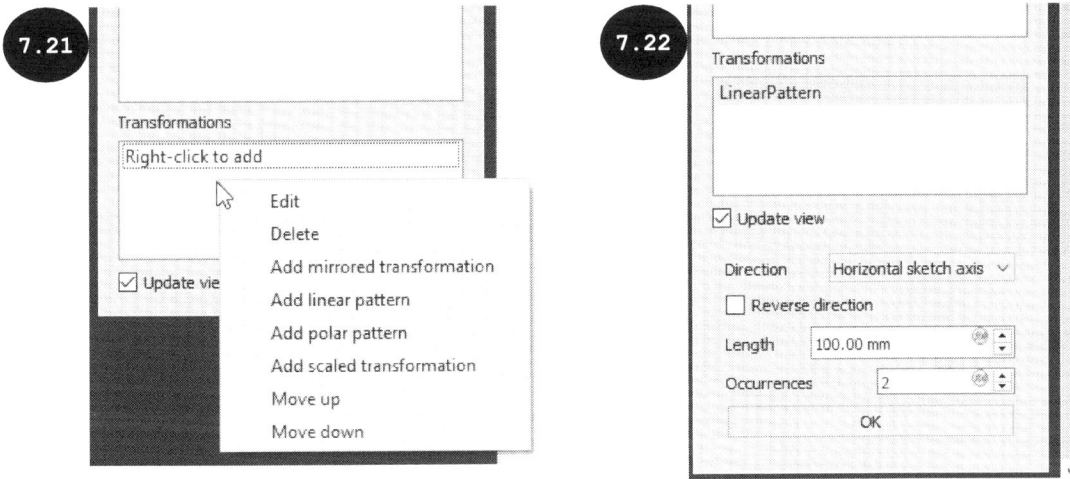

Transformation Options: The **Add mirrored transformation** option is used to add a mirrored transformation to the selected feature. The **Add linear pattern** option is used to add a linear pattern transformation to the selected feature. The **Add polar pattern** option is used to add a polar pattern transformation to the selected feature. The **Add scaled transformation** option is used to add a scaled transformation to the selected feature. All these transformations are discussed earlier and can be performed separately, except the scaled transformation.

4. Specify the required parameters for creating the selected transformation by using the respective options in the **Task Panel**. The preview of the transformation appears in the 3D View area, see Figure 7.23. This figure shows the preview of a linear pattern transformation of the hole feature.

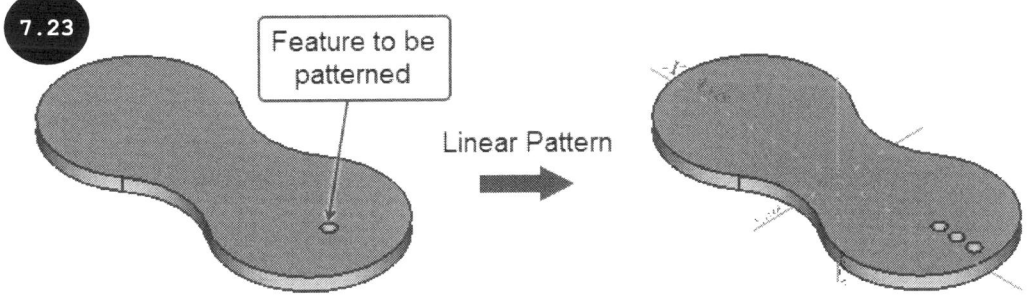

5. After specifying the required transformation parameters, click on the **OK** button at the bottom of the **Task Panel**. The selected transformation gets created, see Figure 7.24. In this figure, the linear pattern transformation of the hole feature gets created by specifying 3 number of pattern occurrences.

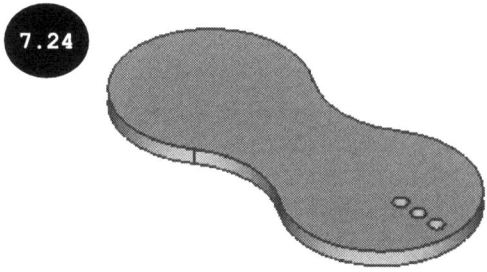

Now, you can create the second transformation (Mirrored, Linear Pattern, Polar pattern, or Scaled) to the selected feature.

6. Right-click on the **Transformations** field of the **Task Panel** and then select the required transformation (**Add mirrored transformation, Add linear pattern, Add polar pattern,** or **Add scaled transformation**) to be created in the shortcut menu that appears, see Figure 7.25. The transformation gets selected, and its name appears below the first created transformation in the **Transformations** field of the **Task Panel**, see Figure 7.26. Also, the options to create the selected transformation appear at the bottom of the **Task Panel**. In Figure 7.26, the polar pattern transformation is selected as the second transformation.

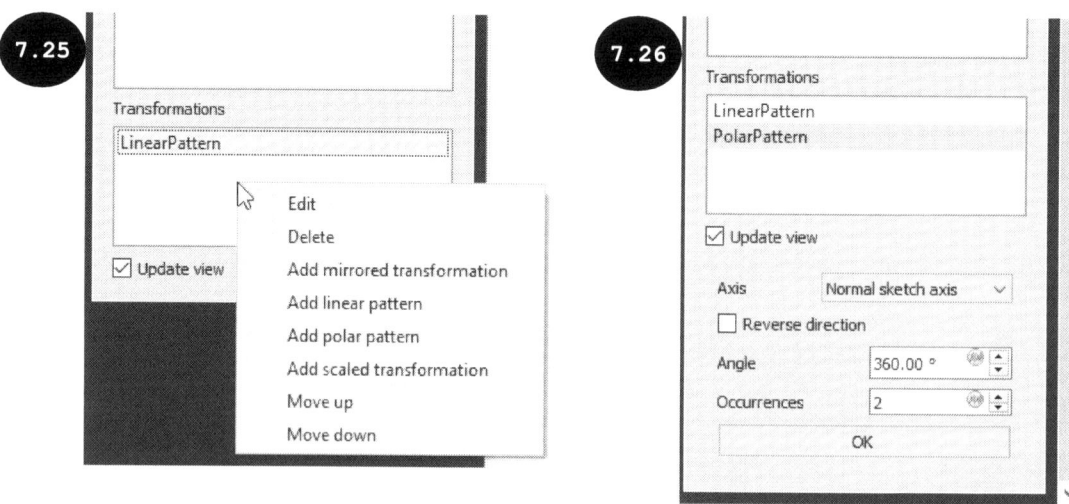

7. Specify the required parameters for creating the selected transformation by using the respective options in the **Task Panel**. The preview of the transformation appears in the 3D View area, see Figure 7.27. This figure shows the preview of a polar pattern transformation of the result of the previous transformation.

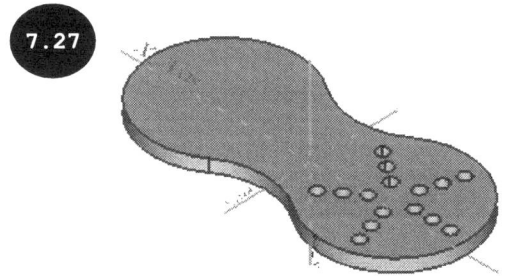

Note: Each subsequent transformation is applied to the result of the previous transformation.

8. Similarly, you can create the remaining transformations one after another. In Figure 7.28, the mirror transformation is created as the result of the previous transformation shown in Figure 7.27.

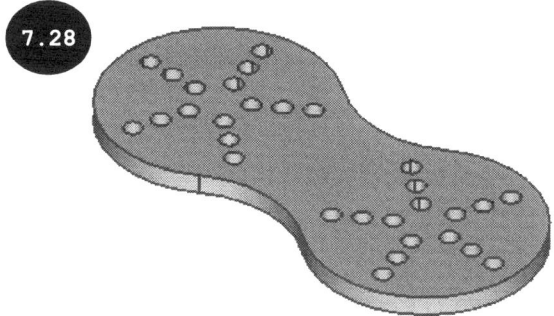

Note: As mentioned earlier, you can also perform a scaled transformation by using the **Add scaled transformation** option, see Figure 7.29. In this figure, first, a linear pattern transformation is performed for creating 5 occurrences of the pad feature, and then a scaled transformation is performed with a scale factor of 2 for 5 occurrences.

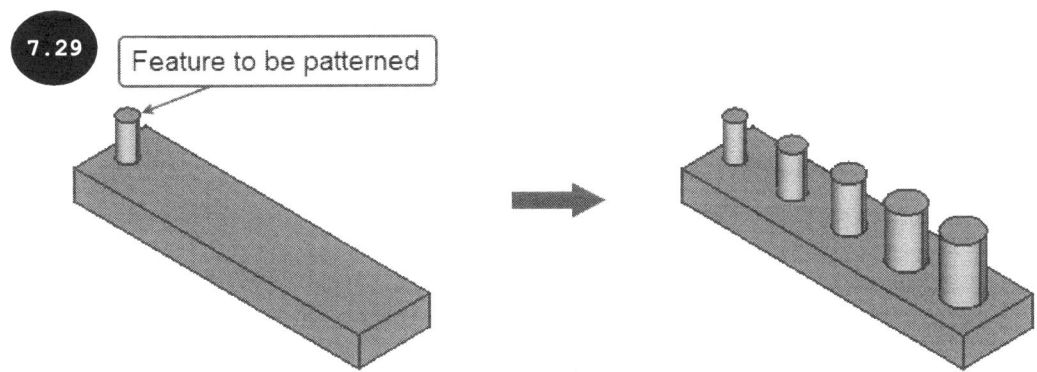

Feature to be patterned

9.   Click on the **OK** button to confirm the creation of a multi-transformation pattern and exit the Task Panel.

Tutorial 1

Create the model shown in Figure 7.30. All dimensions are in mm.

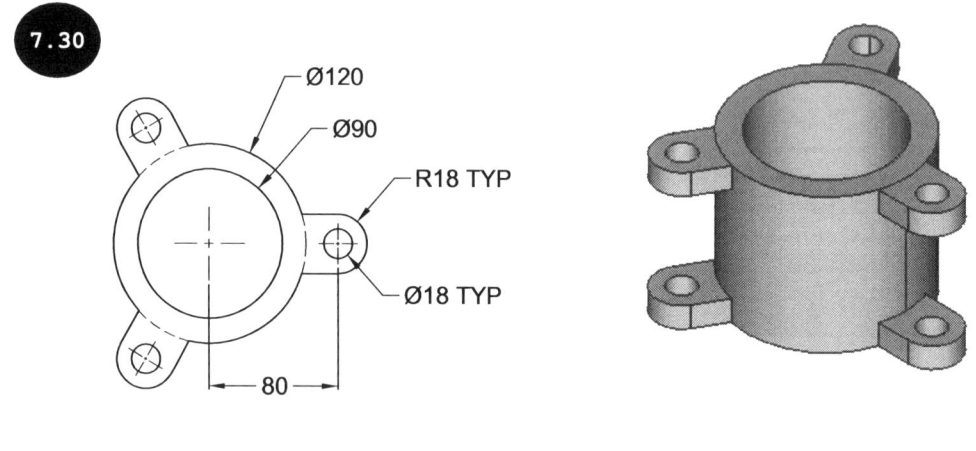

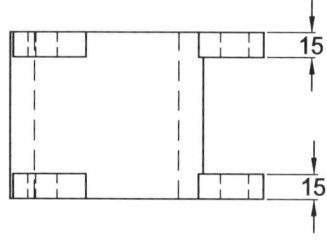

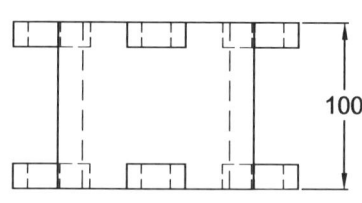

Section 1: Starting FreeCAD and a New Empty Document

1.   Start FreeCAD by double-clicking on the **FreeCAD 0.20** icon on your desktop. The startup user interface of FreeCAD appears, see Figure 7.31.

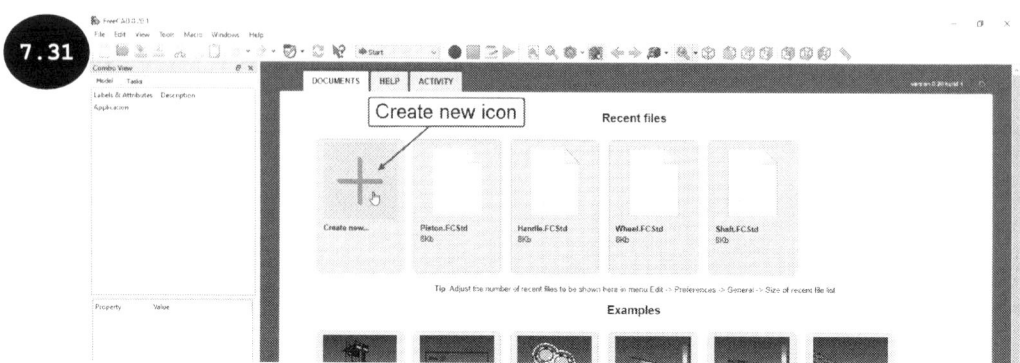

2. Click on the **Create new** icon on the **Start** page (refer to Figure 7.31) or press the **CTRL + N** keys. A new empty document gets invoked with the default name "**unnamed: 1**".

Section 2: Invoking the Part Design Workbench

Now, you can invoke the **Part Design** workbench for creating a 3D solid part.

1. Invoke the **Workbench Selector** in the **Workbench** toolbar and then select the **Part Design** workbench, see Figure 7.32. The **Part Design** workbench gets invoked.

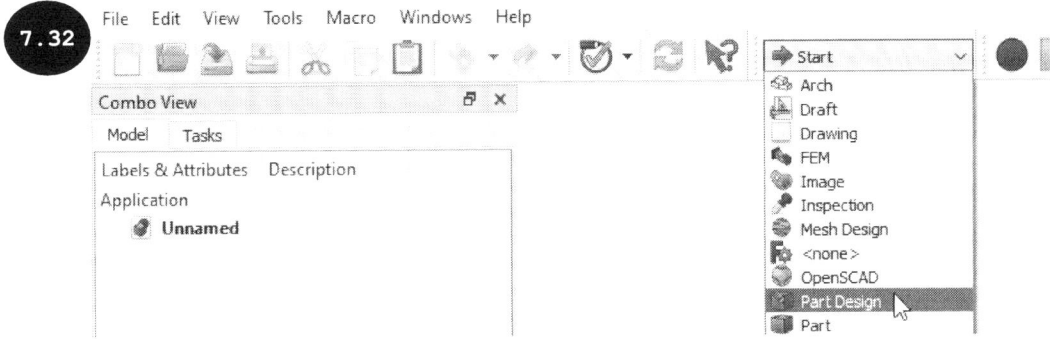

Section 3: Specifying the Unit

Now, you need to specify millimeters (mm) as the measurement unit for the document.

1. Click on **Edit > Preferences** in the **Standard Menu**, see Figure 7.33. The **Preferences** dialog box appears.

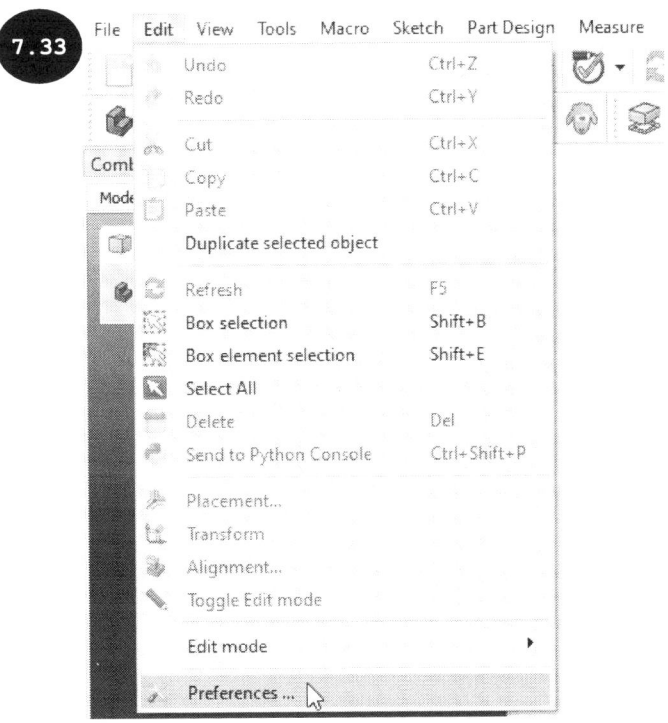

2. Ensure that the **General** section is selected in the left panel of the **Preferences** dialog box and then click on the **Units** tab, see Figure 7.34.

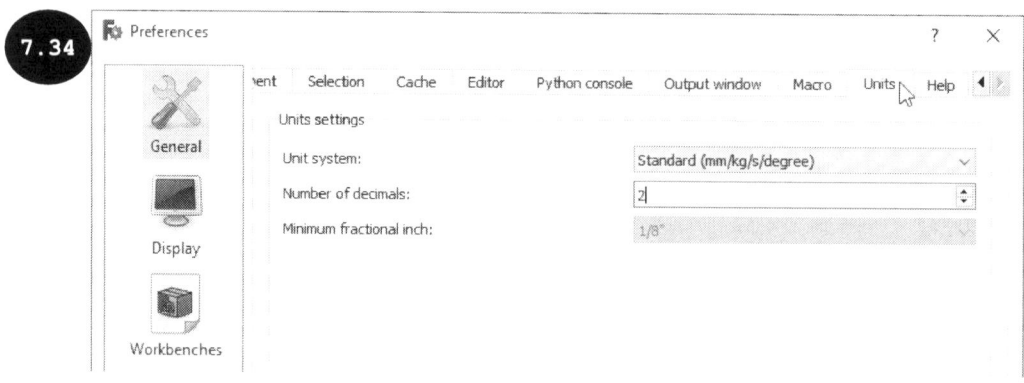

Tip: You may need to click on the arrow ▶ at the upper right corner of the **Preferences** dialog box for displaying the **Units** tab.

3. Select the **Standard (mm/kg/s/degree)** option in the **Unit system** drop-down list of the dialog box as the unit system of the current document.

4. Ensure that the **2** is specified in the **Number of decimals** field of the dialog box as the number of digits after the decimal point of measurements.

5. Click on the **Apply** button and then the **OK** button in the **Preferences** dialog box. The selected unit system is defined, and the dialog box is closed.

Section 4: Creating the Base Feature

Now, you can create the base or first feature of the model, which is a pad feature.

1. Invoke the **Sketcher** workbench by selecting the **XY_Plane** as the sketching plane using the **Create sketch** tool and then create the sketch (two concentric circles) of the pad feature, see Figure 7.35. The center point of the circles is at the origin.

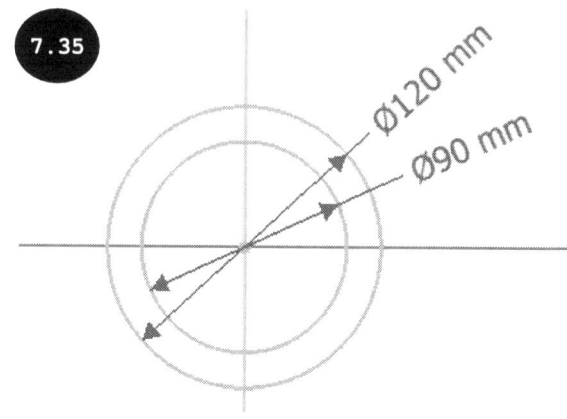

2. After creating the sketch, exit the **Sketcher** workbench to switch back to the **Part Design** workbench.

Now, you can extrude the sketch to create a pad feature.

3. Click on the **Pad** tool in the **Part Design Modeling** toolbar, see Figure 7.36. The preview of a pad feature appears in the 3D View area with default parameters. Also, the **Pad parameters** sub-window appears in the **Task Panel**.

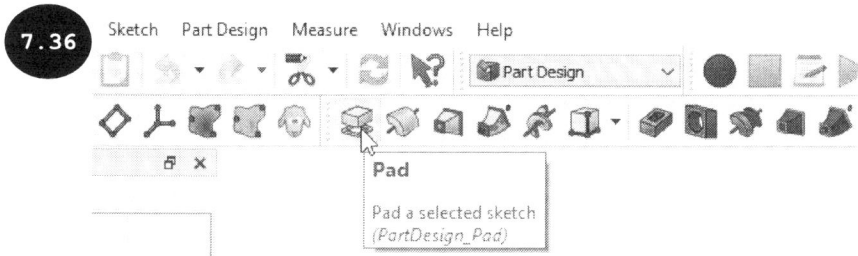

4. Enter **100** mm in the **Length** field of the **Task Panel** and then press the TAB key to update the preview of the pad feature.

5. Select the **Symmetric to plane** check box in the **Pad parameters** sub-windows of the **Task Panel** to add material symmetrically on both sides of the sketching plane.

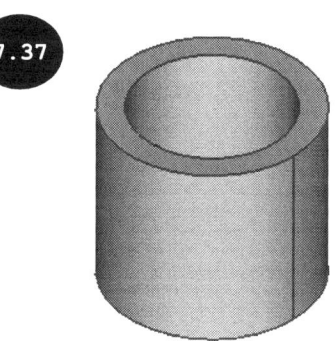

6. Click on the **OK** button in the **Task Panel** to confirm the creation of the pad feature and exit the **Task Panel**. The pad (base) feature of specified length gets created, see Figure 7.37.

Section 5: Creating the Second Feature
Now, you can create the second feature of the model, which is also a pad feature.

1. Select the top planar face of the base feature (see Figure 7.38) and then click on the **Create sketch** tool in the **Part Design Helper** toolbar, see Figure 7.39. The **Sketcher** workbench gets invoked and the selected planar face gets oriented normal to the viewing direction.

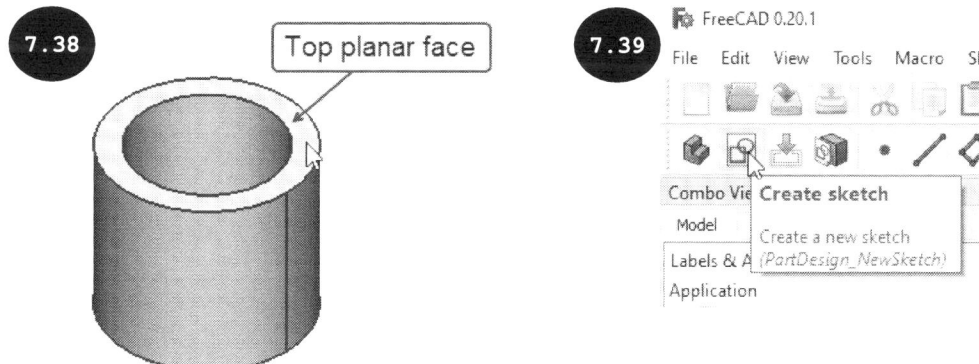

2. Create the sketch of the feature by using the sketching tools, see Figure 7.40.

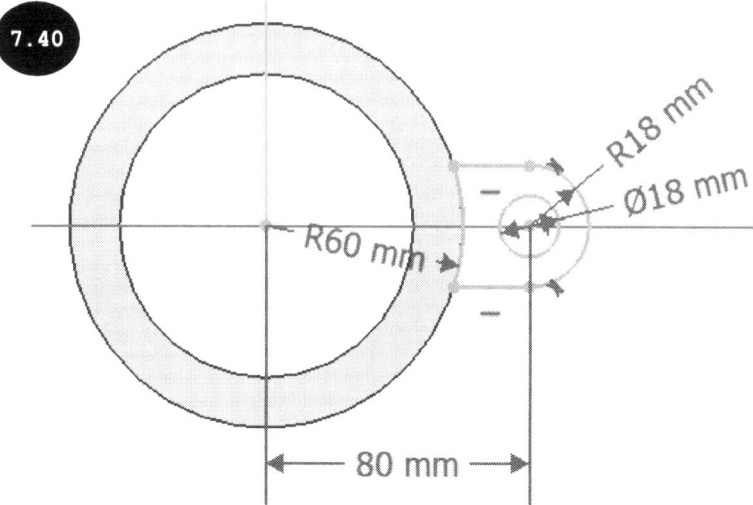

3. After creating the sketch, exit the **Sketcher** workbench to switch back to the **Part Design** workbench.

    Now, you can extrude the sketch to create a pad feature.

4. Click on the **Pad** tool in the **Part Design Modeling** toolbar, see Figure 7.41. The **Pad parameters** sub-window appears in the **Task Panel**. Ignore the error message that may appear in the **Report view** window at the bottom of the screen. You can close the **Report view** window by clicking on the cross mark ⊠ that appears in its top right corner.

5. Select the **Reversed** check box in the **Pad parameters** sub-windows of the **Task Panel** to reverse the direction of extrusion downward. The preview of the pad feature appears in the 3D View area.

6. Enter **15 mm** in the **Length** field of the **Task Panel** and then press the TAB key to update the preview of the pad feature.

7. Click on the **OK** button in the **Task Panel** to confirm the creation of the pad feature and exit the **Task Panel**. The pad feature of specified length gets created, see Figure 7.42.

Section 6: Creating the Multi-transform Pattern Feature

Now, you can create the third feature of the model, which is a multi-transform pattern feature.

1. Select the previously created pad feature (second) in the **Tree View** or the 3D View area.

2. After selecting a feature, click on the **Create MultiTransform** tool in the **Part Design Modeling** toolbar, see Figure 7.43. The **MultiTransform parameters** sub-window appears in the **Task Panel** and the name of the selected feature appears in its field.

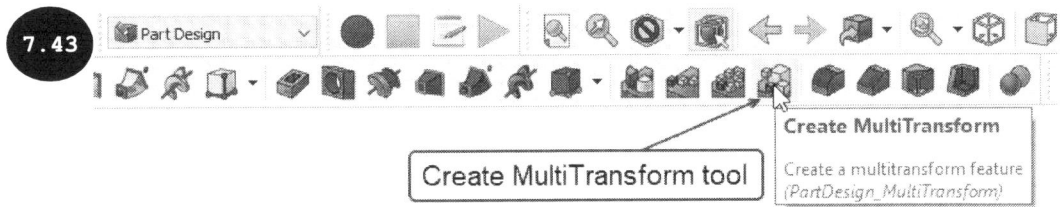

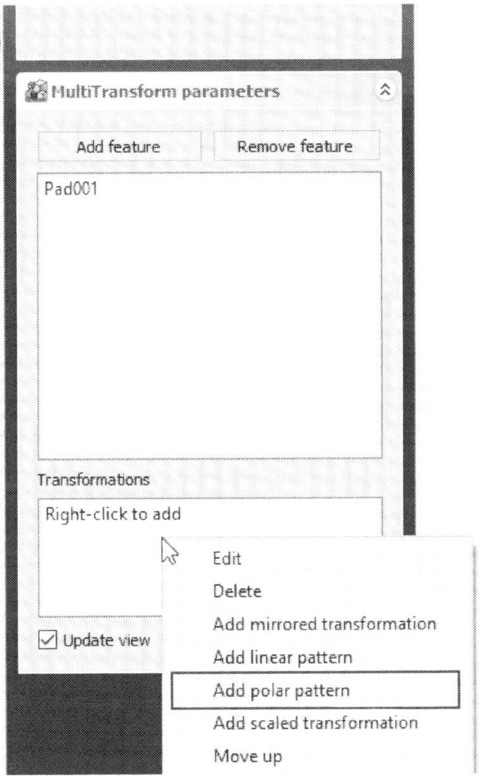

Now, you can define the first transformation to be applied to the selected feature.

3. Right-click on the **Transformations** field of the **Task Panel** and then select the **Add polar pattern** option in the shortcut menu that appears, see Figure 7.44. The polar pattern transformation gets selected and appeared in the **Transformations** field of the **Task Panel**, see Figure 7.45. Also, the options to create a polar pattern appear at the bottom of the **Task Panel**.

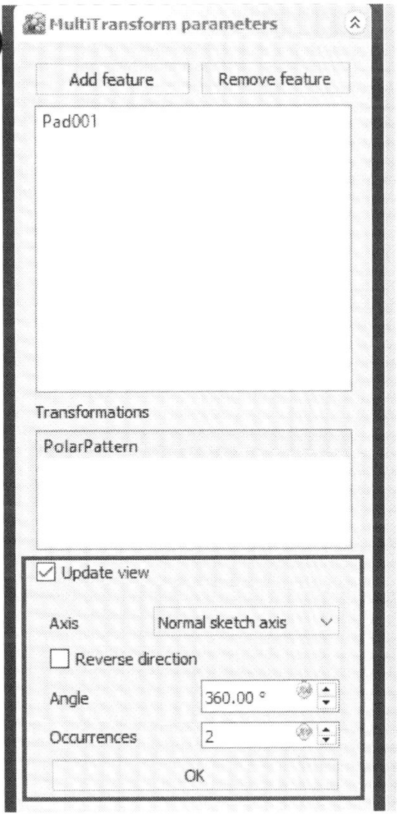

4. Ensure that the **Normal sketch axis** option is selected in the **Axis** drop-down list of the **Task Panel** to define the axis of revolution of the polar pattern, normal to the sketch of the selected feature.

5. Ensure that the **360** degrees angle value is defined in the **Angle** field of the **Task Panel**.

6. Enter **3** as the number of pattern occurrences to be created in the **Occurrences** field of the **Task Panel**.

7. Click on the **OK** button available at the bottom of the **Task Panel**. A polar pattern of specified parameters gets created, see Figure 7.46.

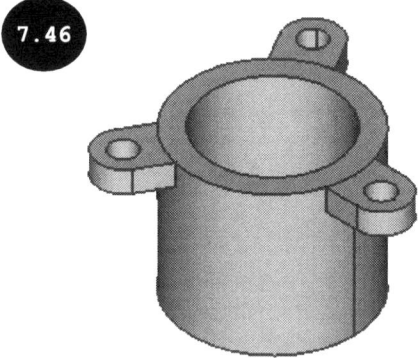

Now, you can create a mirrored transformation to mirror the result of the previously created polar pattern transformation.

8. Right-click on the **Transformations** field of the **Task Panel** and then select the **Add mirrored transformation** option in the shortcut menu that appears, see Figure 7.47. The options to mirror the result of the previously created polar pattern appear at the bottom of the **Task Panel**, see Figure 7.48.

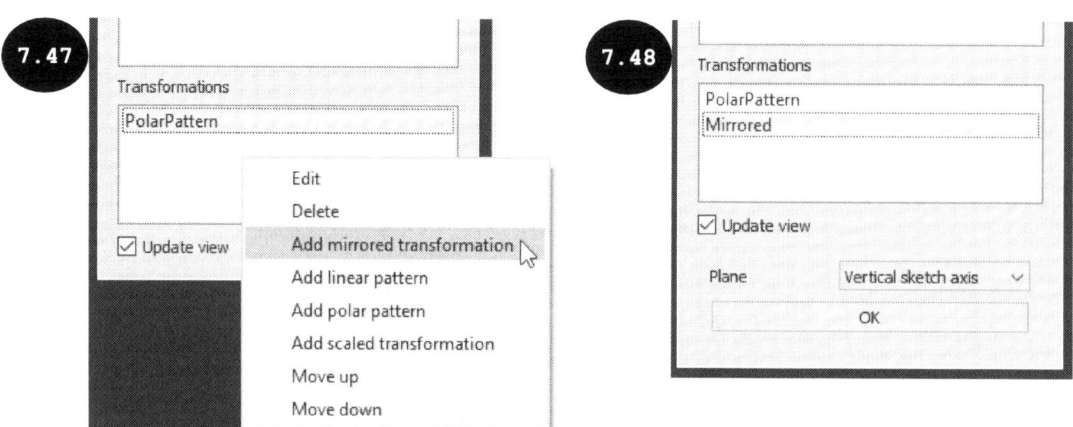

9. Select the **Base XY plane** option as the mirroring plane in the **Plane** drop-down list of the **Task Panel**. The preview of the mirrored transformation appears in the 3D View area, see Figure 7.49.

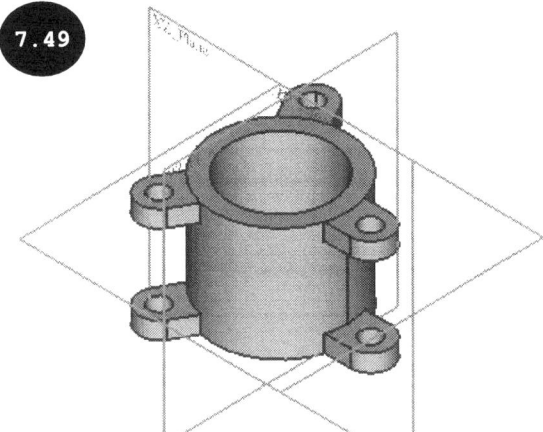

7.49

10. Click on the **OK** button available at the bottom of the **Task Panel**. The mirrored transformation gets created.

11. Select the **OK** button to exit the **Task Panel**. Figure 7.50 shows the final model.

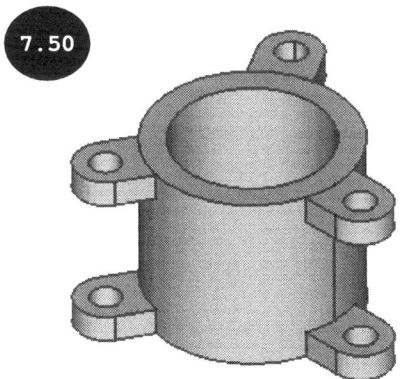

7.50

Section 7: Saving the Model

1. Click on the **Save** tool ![save icon] in the **File** toolbar or press the CTRL + S keys. The **Save FreeCAD Document** dialog box appears.

2. Browse to the required folder (:*FreeCAD* > *Chapter 07*) in the local drive of your system. Note that you need to create the Chapter 07 sub-folder inside the FreeCAD folder.

3. Enter **Ch07-Tutorial 1** in the **File name** field of the dialog box. Next, click on the **Save** button in the dialog box. The model gets saved at the specified location (:*FreeCAD* > *Chapter 07*).

4. Click on **File > Close** in the **Standard Menu** to close the current document.

Tutorial 2

Create a model, as shown in Figure 7.51. Different views and dimensions of the model are given in the same figure. All dimensions are in inches (in).

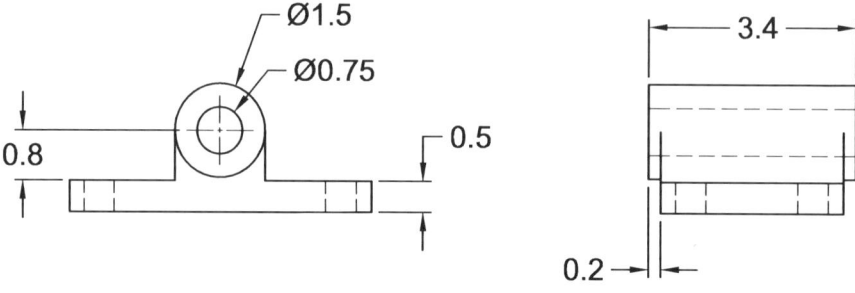

7.51

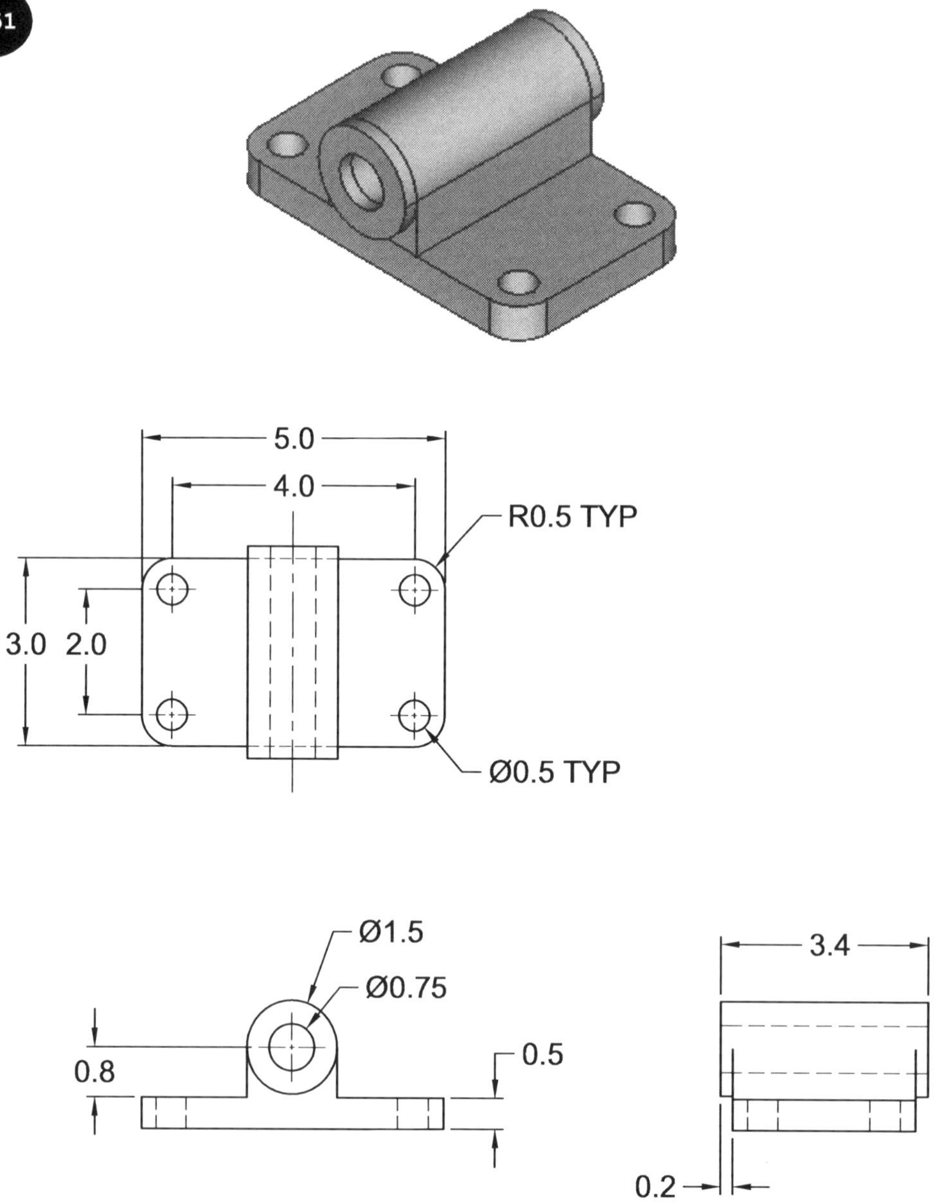

Section 1: Starting FreeCAD and a New Empty Document

1. Start FreeCAD by double-clicking on the **FreeCAD 0.20** icon on your desktop. The startup user interface of FreeCAD appears, see Figure 7.52.

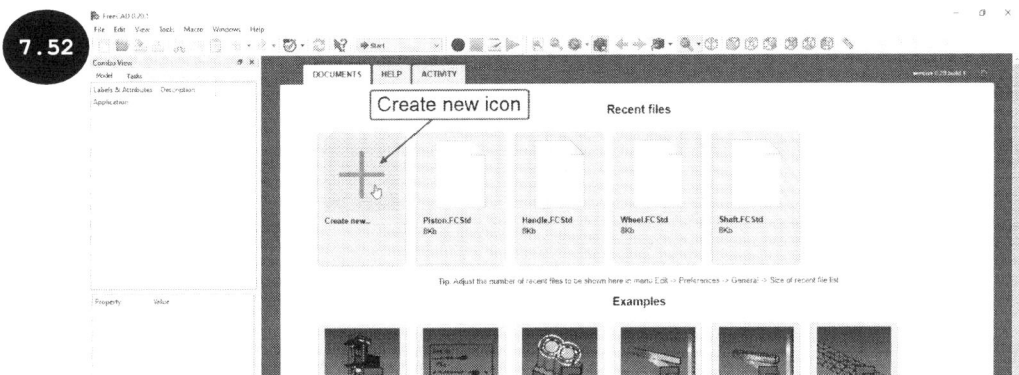

2. Click on the **Create new** icon on the **Start** page (refer to Figure 7.52) or press the **CTRL + N** keys. A new empty document gets invoked with the default name "**unnamed: 1**".

Section 2: Invoking the Part Design Workbench and Specifying the Unit

Now, you can invoke the **Part Design** workbench for creating a 3D solid part and then specify the required unit system.

1. Invoke the **Workbench Selector** in the **Workbench** toolbar and then select the **Part Design** workbench, see Figure 7.53. The **Part Design** workbench gets invoked.

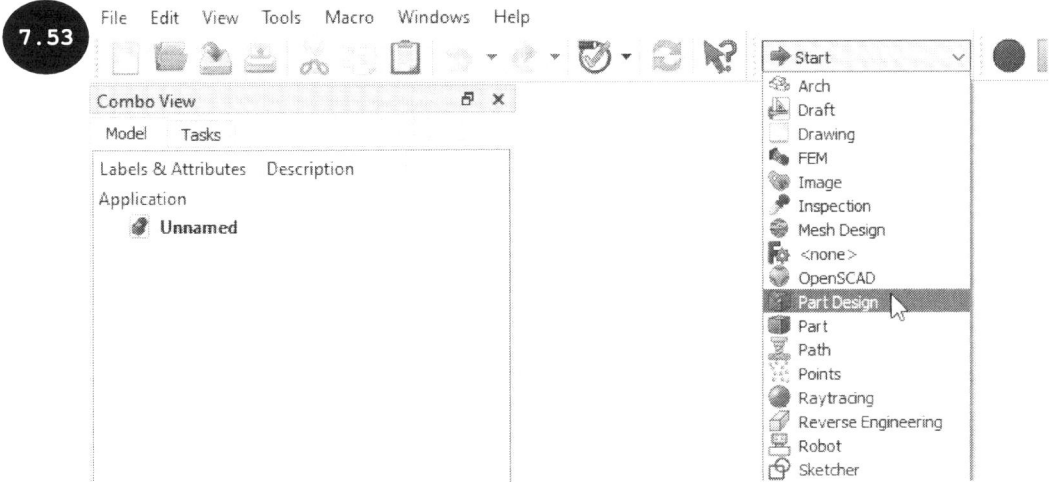

Now, you need to specify inches (in) as the measurement unit for the document.

2. Specify the **Imperial decimal (in/lb)** as the unit system for the current document by using the **Preferences** dialog box.

Section 3: Creating the Base Feature

Now, you can create the base or first feature of the model, which is a pad feature.

1.   Invoke the **Sketcher** workbench by selecting the **XY_Plane** as the sketching plane using the **Create sketch** tool and then create the sketch of the pad feature, see Figure 7.54.

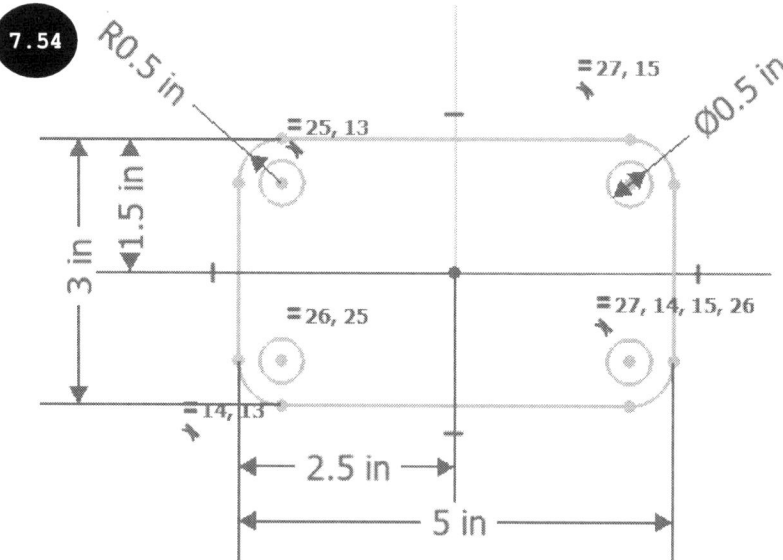

2.   After creating the sketch, exit the **Sketcher** workbench to switch back to the **Part Design** workbench.

Now, you can extrude the sketch to create a pad feature.

3.   Click on the **Pad** tool in the **Part Design Modeling** toolbar, see Figure 7.55. The preview of a pad feature appears in the 3D View area with default parameters. Also, the **Pad parameters** sub-window appears in the **Task Panel**.

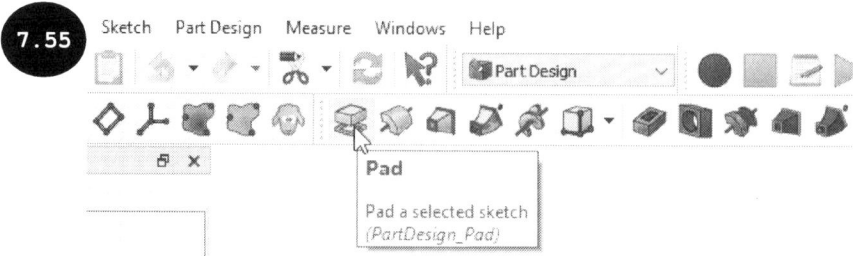

4.   Enter **0.5** inches in the **Length** field of the **Task Panel** and then press the TAB key to update the preview of the pad feature.

5.   Click on the **OK** button in the **Task Panel** to confirm the creation of the pad feature and exit the **Task Panel**. The pad (base) feature of specified length gets created, see Figure 7.56.

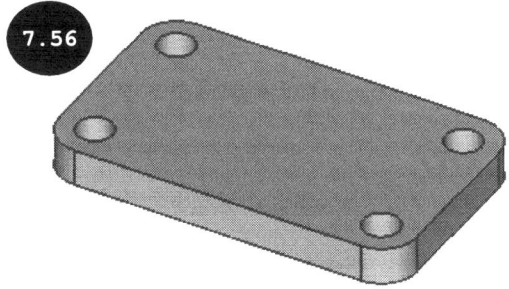

7.56

Section 4: Creating the Second Feature

Now, you can create the second feature of the model, which is also a pad feature.

1. Select the front planar face of the base feature (see Figure 7.57) and then click on the **Create sketch** tool in the **Part Design Helper** toolbar, see Figure 7.58. The **Sketcher** workbench gets invoked and the selected planar face gets oriented normal to the viewing direction.

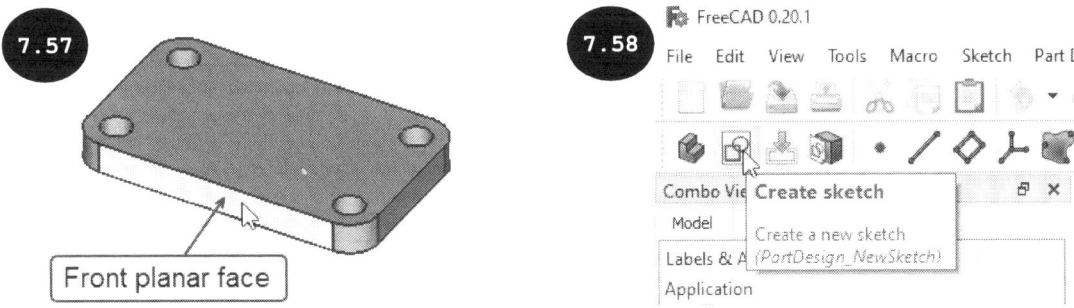

7.57

Front planar face

7.58

2. Click on the **External geometry** tool in the **Sketcher geometries** toolbar (see Figure 7.59) for projecting the top edge of the model as the linked construction entity into the sketch.

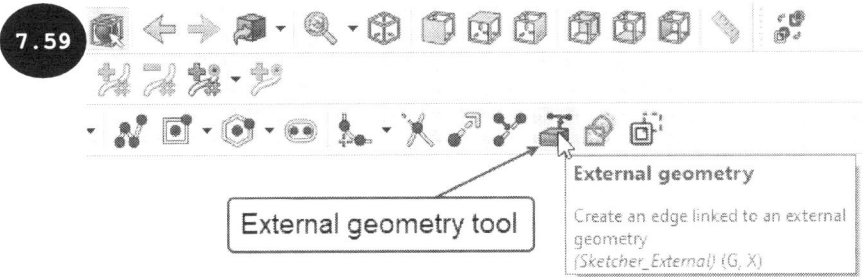

7.59

External geometry tool

External geometry

Create an edge linked to an external geometry
(Sketcher_External) (G, X)

3. Select the top edge of the model in the 3D View area. The edge gets projected as the linked construction entity in the sketch, see Figure 7.60. Next, press the ESC key to exit the tool.

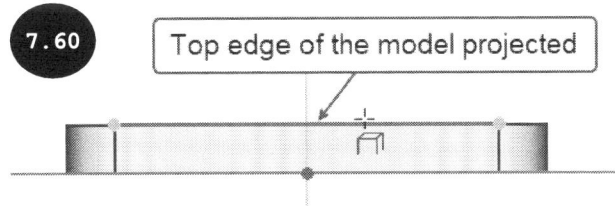

7.60

Top edge of the model projected

Now, you can create the sketch by taking reference toappear the linked construction entity.

4.   Create the closed sketch of the feature by using the sketching tools, see Figure 7.61.

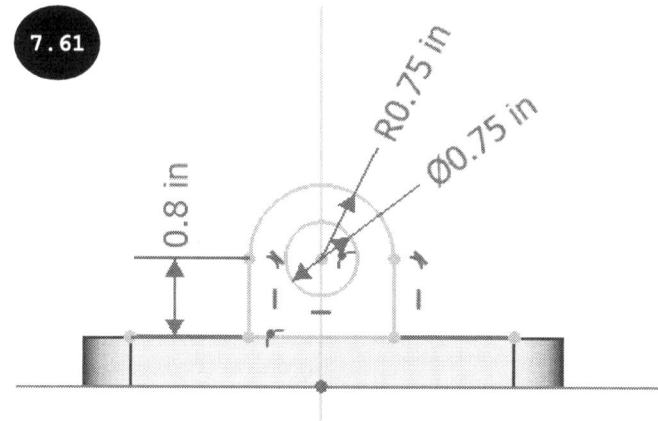

5.   After creating the sketch, exit the **Sketcher** workbench to switch back to the **Part Design** workbench.

Now, you can extrude the sketch to create a pad feature.

6.   Click on the **Pad** tool in the **Part Design Modeling** toolbar, see Figure 7.62. The **Pad parameters** sub-window appears in the **Task Panel**. Ignore the error message that may appear in the **Report view** window at the bottom of the screen. You can close the **Report view** window by clicking on the cross mark ☒ that appears in its top right corner.

7.   Select the **Reversed** check box in the **Pad parameters** sub-windows of the **Task Panel** to reverse the direction of extrusion towards the back. The preview of a pad feature appears in the 3D View area.

8.   Enter **3** inches in the **Length** field of the **Task Panel** and then press the TAB key to update the preview of the pad feature.

9.   Click on the **OK** button in the **Task Panel** to confirm the creation of the pad feature and exit the **Task Panel**. The pad feature of specified length gets created, see Figure 7.63.

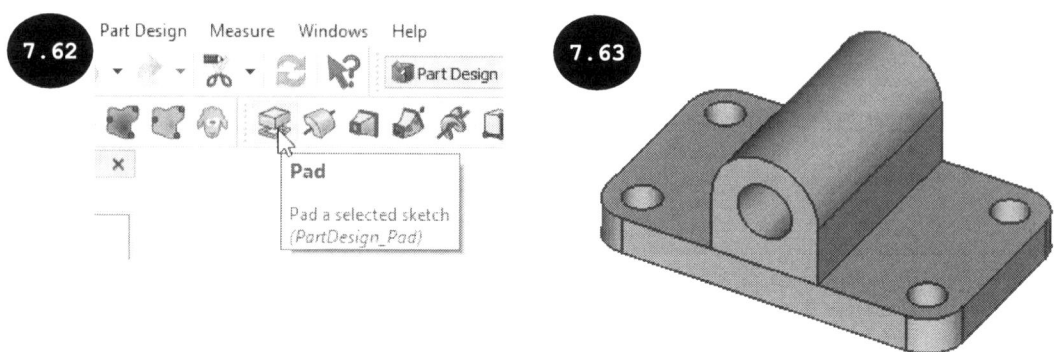

Section 5: Creating the Third Feature

Now, you can create the third feature of the model, which is also a pad feature.

1. Select the front planar face of the second feature (see Figure 7.64) and then click on the **Create sketch** tool in the **Part Design Helper** toolbar, see Figure 7.65. The **Sketcher** workbench gets invoked and the selected planar face gets oriented normal to the viewing direction.

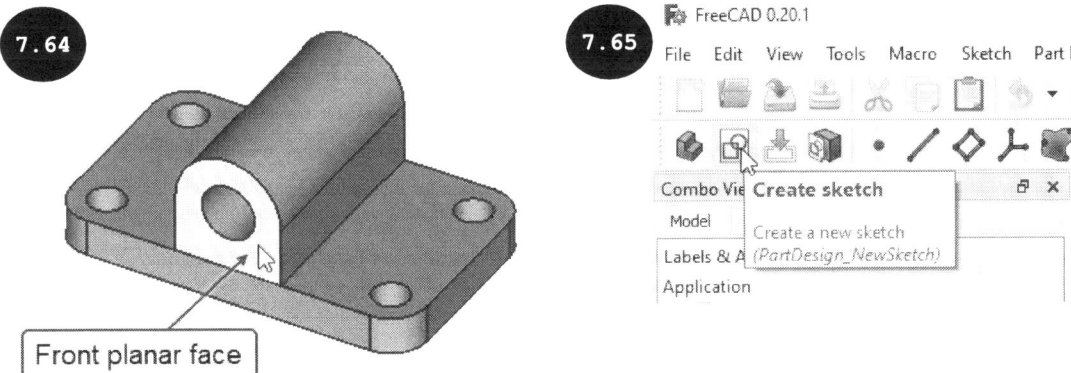

Front planar face

2. Create the sketch (two concentric circles) of the feature by using the sketching tools, see Figure 7.66.

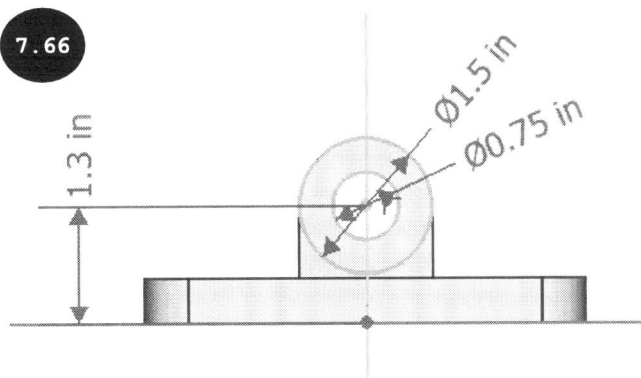

3. After creating the sketch, exit the **Sketcher** workbench to switch back to the **Part Design** workbench.

Now, you can extrude the sketch to create a pad feature.

4. Click on the **Pad** tool in the **Part Design Modeling** toolbar, see Figure 7.67. The **Pad parameters** sub-window appears in the **Task Panel**. Also, the preview of the pad feature appears in the 3D View area.

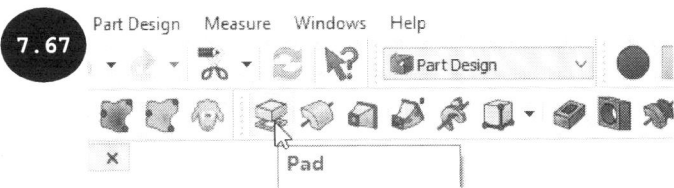

5. Enter **0.2** inches in the **Length** field of the **Task Panel** and then press the TAB key to update the preview of the pad feature.

6. Click on the **OK** button in the **Task Panel** to confirm the creation of the pad feature and exit the **Task Panel**. The pad feature of specified length gets created, see Figure 7.68.

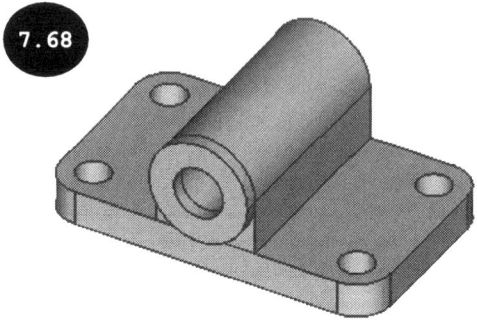

Section 6: Mirroring the Feature
Now, you need to mirror the previously created pad feature.

1. Select the previously created pad feature in the **Tree View** or the 3D View area and then click on the **Mirrored** tool in the **Part Design Helper** toolbar, see Figure 7.69. The **Mirrored parameters** sub-window appears in the **Task Panel**.

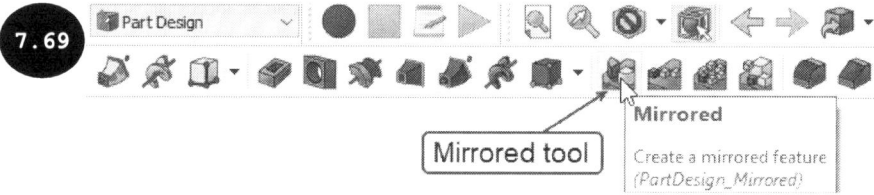

2. Select the **Base XZ plane** option as the mirroring plane in the Plane drop-down list of the Task Panel, see Figure 7.70. The preview of a mirror feature appears about the XZ plane of the model, see Figure 7.71.

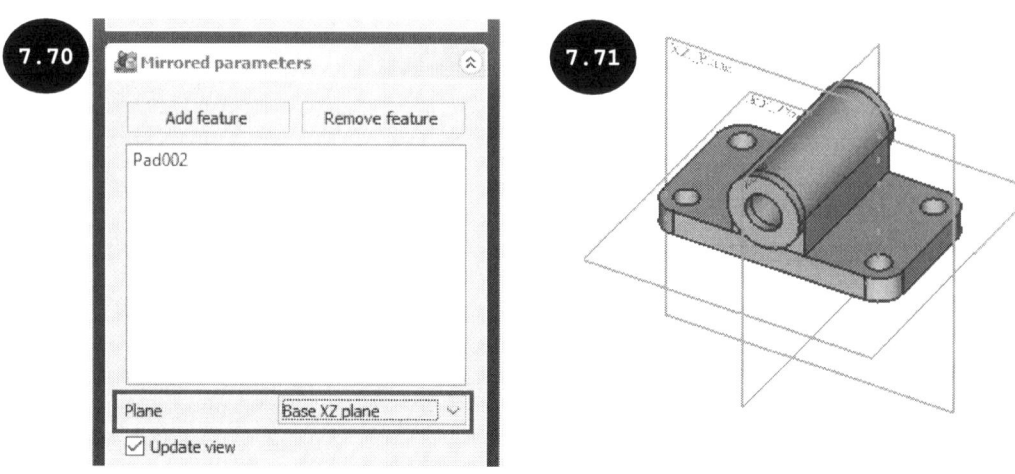

3. Click on the **OK** button in the **Task Panel** to confirm the creation of the mirrored feature and exit the **Task Panel**. The mirrored feature gets created. Figure 7.72 shows the final model.

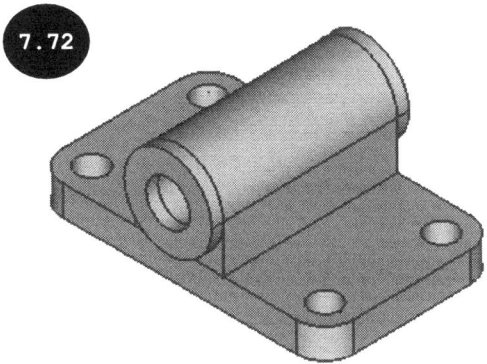

7.72

Section 7: Saving the Model

1. Click on the **Save** tool in the **File** toolbar or press the CTRL + S keys. The **Save FreeCAD Document** dialog box appears.

2. Browse to the required folder (:\FreeCAD > Chapter 07) in the local drive of your system. Note that you need to create the Chapter 07 sub-folder inside the FreeCAD folder, if not created earlier.

3. Enter **Ch07-Tutorial 2** in the **File name** field of the dialog box. Next, click on the **Save** button in the dialog box. The model gets saved at the specified location (:\FreeCAD > Chapter 07).

4. Click on **File > Close** in the **Standard Menu** to close the current document.

Hands-on Test Drive 1

Create a model shown in Figure 7.73. Different views and dimensions of the model are given in Figure 7.74. All dimensions are in inches (in).

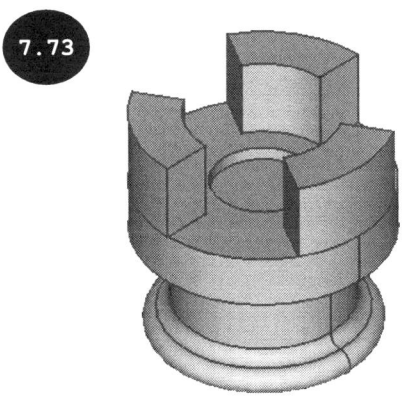

7.73

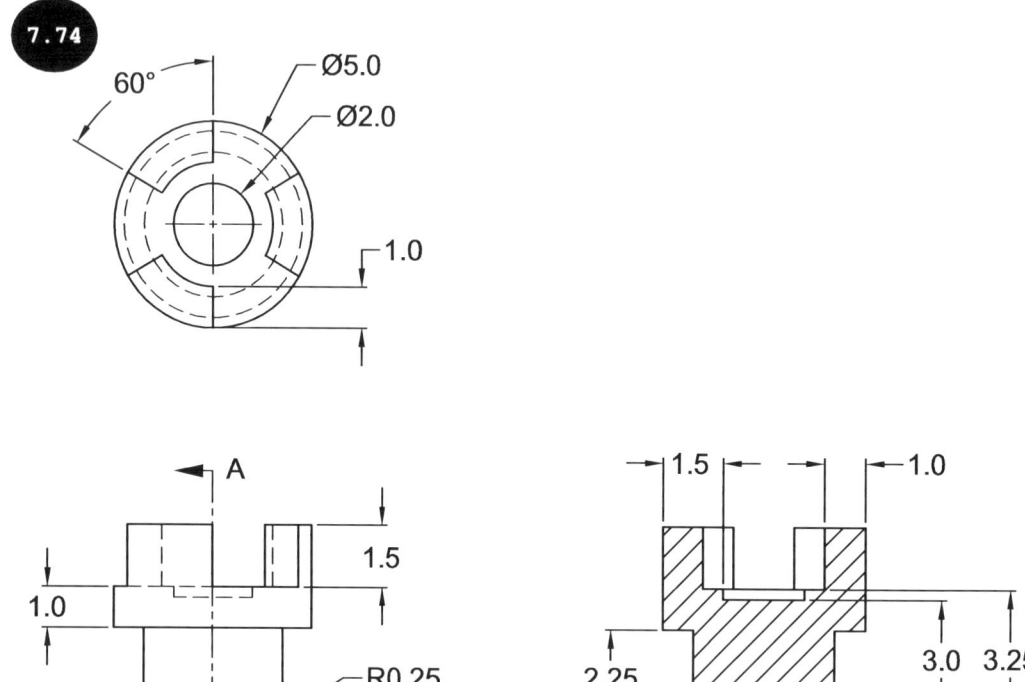

Hands-on Test Drive 2

Create a model shown in Figure 7.75. Different views and dimensions of the model are given in Figure 7.76. All dimensions are in mm.

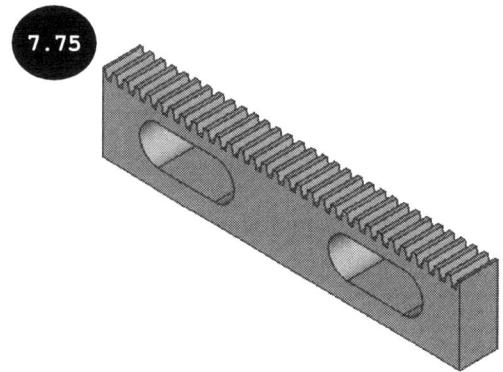

7.76

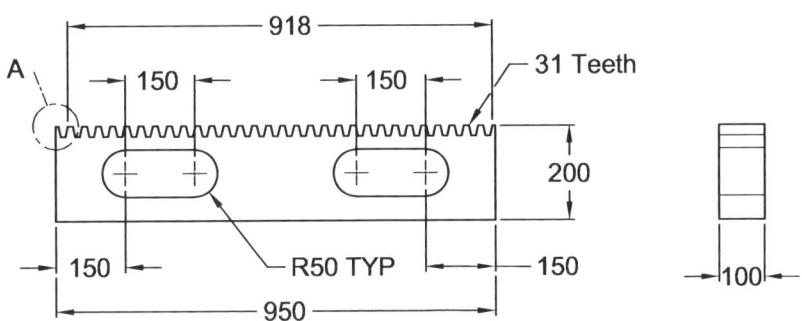

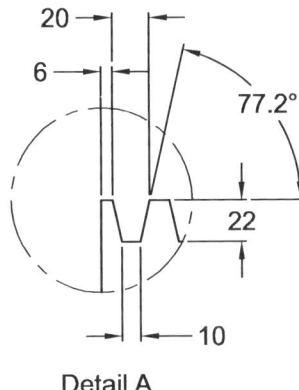

Detail A

Summary

This chapter discussed how to mirror features of a model about a mirroring plane. It also discussed creating a linear pattern, a polar pattern, and a multi-transform pattern.

Questions

Complete and verify the following sentences:

• The _____ tool is used for creating multiple occurrences of one or more features along a linear direction.

• A _____ pattern creates multiple occurrences of one or more features of a model around an axis of revolution.

• The _____ tool is used for mirroring one or more features of a model about a mirroring plane.

- The _____ option allows you to select a plane or a planar face of an existing feature as the mirroring plane while creating a mirrored feature.

- The _____ tool is used for creating a multi-transform pattern by combining _____, linear pattern, _____, and/or _____ transformations.

- While creating a linear pattern, the number of occurrences specified in the **Occurrences** field also includes the parent or source feature. (True/False)

- In FreeCAD, you cannot select features to be patterned after invoking the tool. (True/False)

- In FreeCAD, the scaled transformation cannot be performed separately. (True/False)

Creating Holes and Dress-up Features

This chapter discusses the following topics:

* Creating Holes
* Creating Fillets
* Creating Chamfers
* Creating a Thick Shell Model
* Adding an Angular Draft

In this chapter, you will learn about creating standard or customized holes as per the standard specifications by using the **Hole** tool. You will also learn how to create dress-up features such as fillet, chamfer, and thickness (shell) for applying treatment to the existing edges and faces of a model.

Creating Holes

In FreeCAD, you can create standard or customized holes such as counterbore, countersink, and straight from a sketch containing one or more circles, see Figures 8.1 and 8.2. Figure 8.1 shows a counterbore hole created from a sketch containing one circle and Figure 8.2 shows two countersink holes created from a sketch containing two circles.

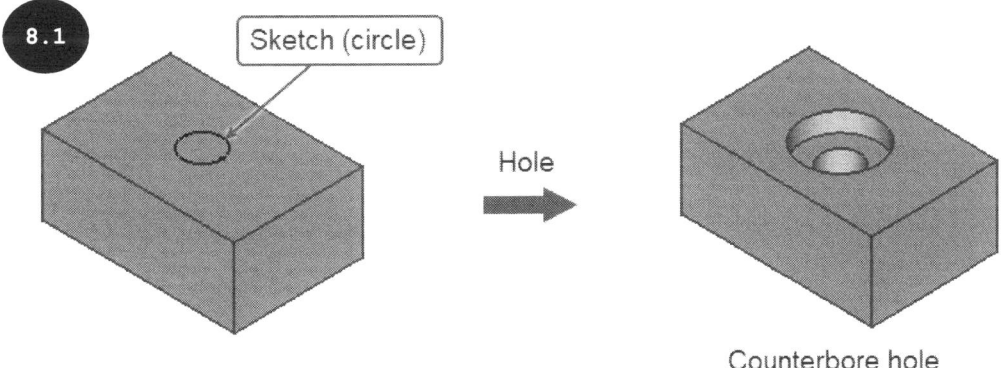

Sketch (circle)

Hole

Counterbore hole

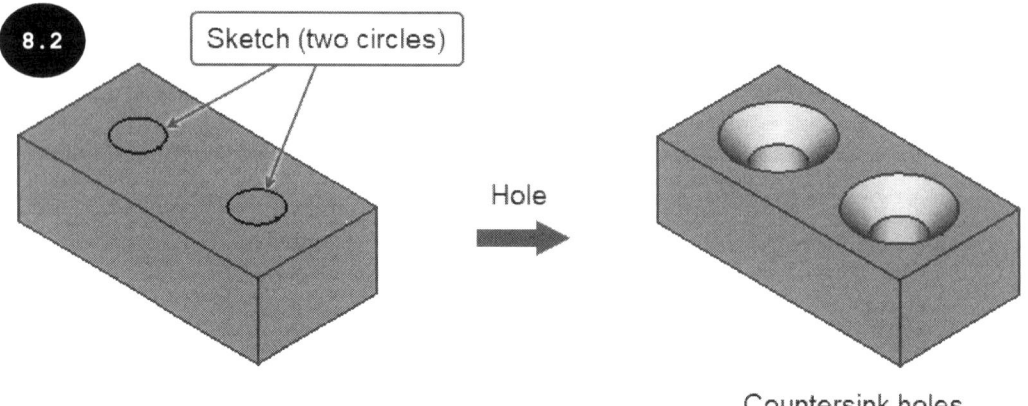

Countersink holes

You can create different types of holes by using the **Hole** tool. The method for creating holes is discussed below:

1. Create a sketch containing one or more circles on a planar face of an existing model, see Figure 8.3. In this figure, a circle is created on the top planar face of the model for creating a hole feature.

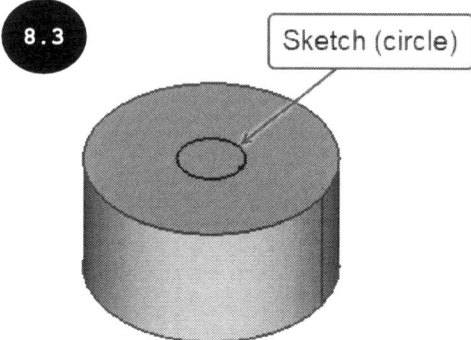

Note: A sketch of a hole feature may also contain arc entities. However, they must be a part of a closed contour/profile of the sketch.

The non-arc or non-circle entities of the sketch will be ignored, but they still must be a part of a closed contour/profile of the sketch.

2. After creating a sketch, click on the **Hole** tool in the **Part Design Modeling** toolbar, see Figure 8.4. The preview of a hole feature appears with default parameters, see Figure 8.5. Also, the **Hole parameters** sub-window appears in the **Task Panel** for defining hole parameters, see Figure 8.6.

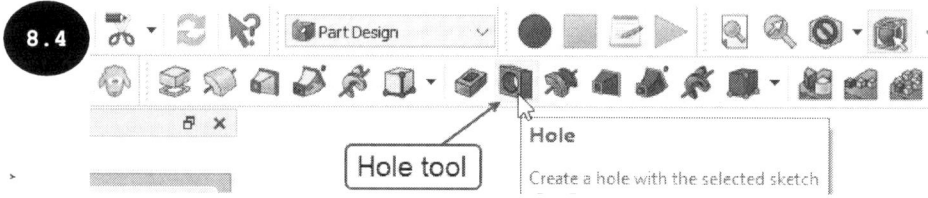

8.5

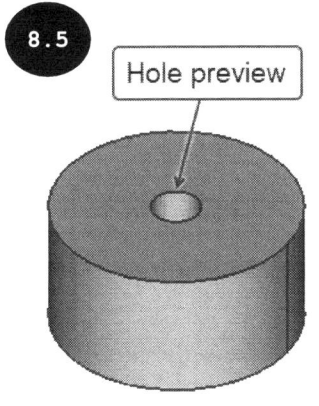

Hole preview

8.6

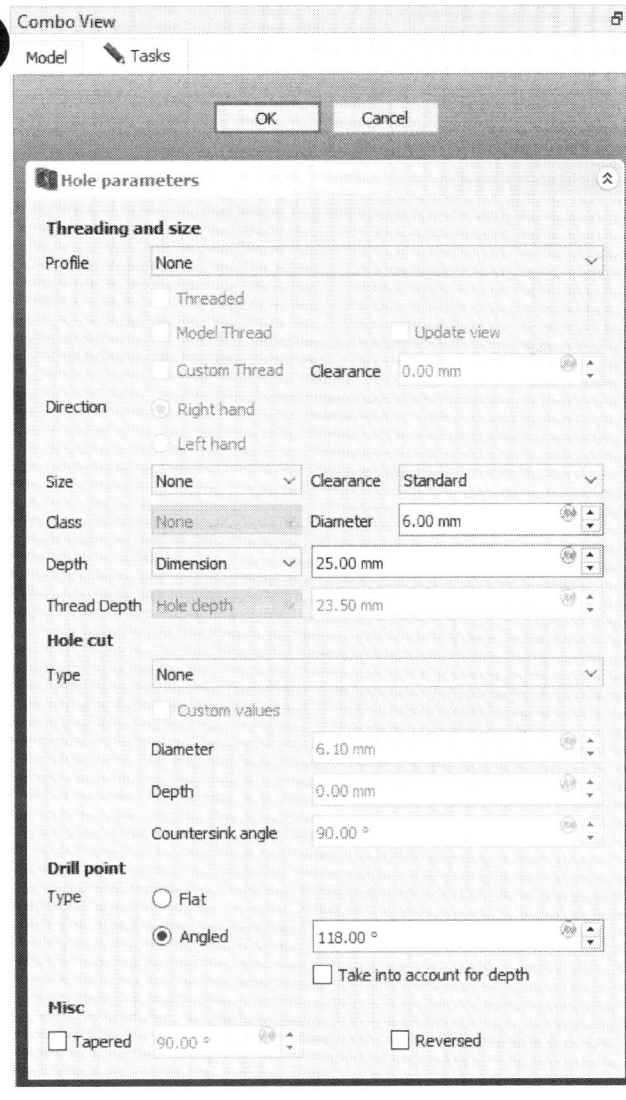

Note: The center of a circle or an arc entity of the sketch is used to define the center of the hole on the planar face of the model. However, its radius is not considered, and the diameter of the resultant hole is based on the defined parameters.

Tip: If only one sketch is available in the 3D View area, then on invoking the **Hole** tool, it will automatically be selected, and the preview of the hole appears in the 3D View area. However, if more than one sketch is available in the 3D View area, then the **Select feature** sub-window appears in the **Task Panel** for selecting a sketch of the hole feature.

The options in the **Hole parameters** sub-window are used for defining the required hole parameters and are discussed below:

Profile: The **Profile** drop-down list is used for selecting the type of standard profile such as ISO or UTS for creating a hole, see Figure 8.7. By default, the **None** option is selected in this drop-down list. As a result, the options to define the thread parameters and the standard size of the hole are not enabled in the **Task Panel**. The **None** option is used for creating a simple hole with a user-defined hole diameter.

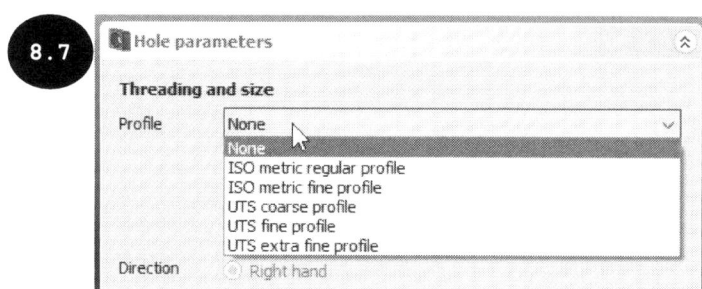

Threaded: The **Threaded** check box is used for creating a threaded hole. On selecting this **Threaded** check box, the options to define threaded data such as thread class and thread depth to the hole feature are enabled in the **Task Panel**.

Model Thread: On selecting the **Model Thread** check box, a real thread is modeled on a threaded hole by removing material from the model, see Figures 8.8 and 8.9. Note that you need to select the **Update view** check box in the **Task Panel** to update the preview of the threaded hole in the 3D View area. The **Model Thread** check box is enabled only when the **Threaded** check box is selected in the **Task Panel**.

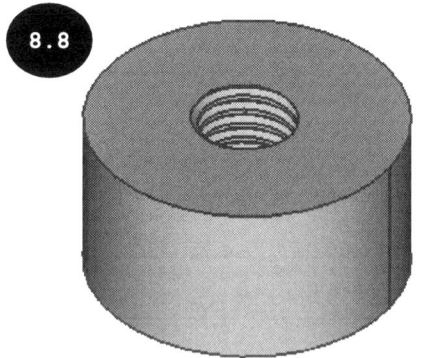

Threaded hole with Model Thread
check box is selected

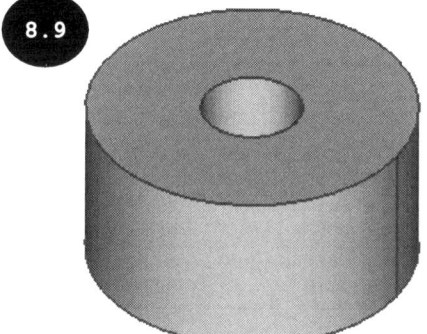

Threaded hole with Model Thread
check box is cleared

Note: Creating a real thread by removing material from a model consumes more computing power. Therefore, it is recommended to create a threaded hole without removing the material to increase the overall system performance.

Custom Thread: On selecting the **Custom Thread** check box, a real thread is modeled on the threaded hole as per the custom clearance value specified in the **Clearance** field that is enabled in front of this check box in the **Task Panel**. Note that this check box is enabled only when the **Model Thread** check box is selected in the **Task Panel**.

Direction: The **Right hand** and the **Left hand** radio buttons in the **Direction** area of the **Task Panel** are used for defining the thread direction to the right hand or left hand, respectively. These radio buttons are enabled only when the **Threaded** check box is selected in the **Task Panel**.

Size: The Size drop-down list is used for selecting a standard size of the hole to insert a fastener, see Figure 8.10. Note that the availability of options in this drop-down list depends upon the option selected in the **Profile** drop-down list of the **Task Panel**.

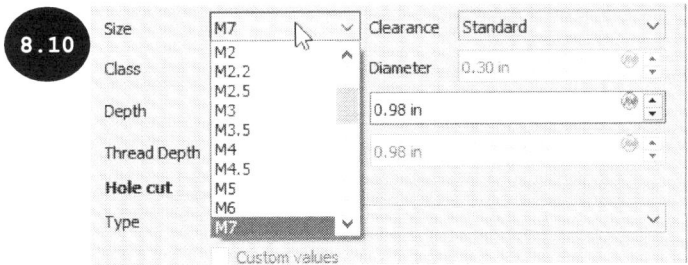

Clearance: The Clearance drop-down list is used for selecting the required option (**Standard**, **Close**, or **Wide**) to define the type of clearance/fit between the fastener and the hole. This drop-down list is enabled only while creating a non-threaded hole.

Class: The Class drop-down list is used for selecting the required tolerance class for the threaded hole.

Diameter: The Diameter field is used for specifying a user-defined hole diameter. Note that this field is enabled only when the **None** option is selected in the **Profile** drop-down list of the **Task Panel**.

Depth: The options in the **Depth** drop-down list are used for defining the depth of the hole from its placement plane. The **Dimension** option is used for specifying a depth value of the hole in the field that is enabled in front of the drop-down list, see Figure 8.11. The **Through all** option is used for creating a hole through the depth of the whole body, see Figure 8.12.

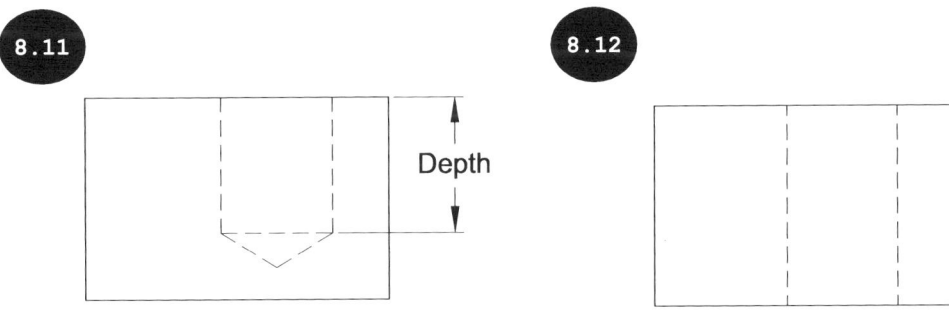

Thread Depth: The options in the **Thread Depth** drop-down list are used for defining the depth of the thread that is modeled on a threaded hole by removing the material. This drop-down list is enabled only when the **Model Thread** check box is selected in the **Task Panel** for creating a real thread by removing material from the model.

Hole Cut: The options in the **Hole Cut** area of the **Task Panel** are shown in Figure 8.13 and are discussed below:

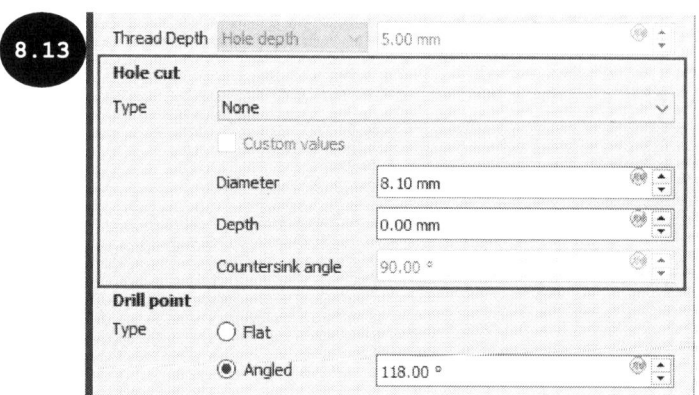

Type: The options in the **Type** drop-down list are used for defining the type of hole such as counterbore, countersink, or cap screw to be created, see Figure 8.14.

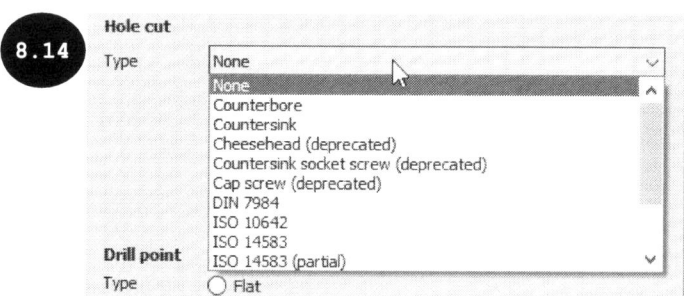

Diameter: The **Diameter** field is used for defining the upper diameter such as counterbore diameter or countersink diameter of the hole depending upon the type of hole selected in the **Type** drop-down list of the **Task Panel**, refer to Figure 8.15.

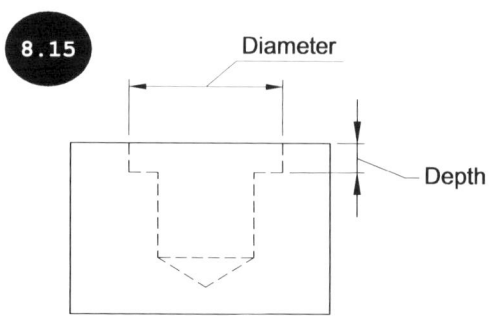

Depth: The **Depth** field is used for defining the depth of the upper hole such as counterbore depth or countersink depth depending upon the type of hole selected in the **Type** drop-down list, refer to Figure 8.15.

Countersink angle: The **Countersink angle** field is used for defining an angle value of the upper conical cut of the countersink hole, see Figure 8.16.

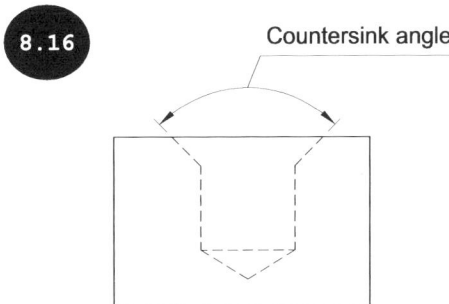

Countersink angle

Drill point: The **Flat** radio button in the **Drill point** area of the **Task Panel** is used for creating a hole with a flat end, see Figure 8.17. The **Angled** radio button is used for creating a hole with a drilled/angled end, see Figure 8.18. You can also specify an angle value in the field that is enabled when the **Angled** radio button is selected in the **Task Panel**.

Hole with flat end   Hole with angled end

Misc: On selecting the **Tapered** check box in the **Misc** area of the **Task Panel**, you can create a hole with a taper angle specified in the field that appears in front of this check box. Note that the taper angle value specified in this field is calculated from the placement face of the hole. By default, 90 degrees is defined as the taper angle. As a result, a straight hole is created. A taper angle value less than 90 degrees creates a smaller hole radius at the bottom of the hole, whereas a taper angle value greater than 90 degrees creates an enlarged hole radius at the bottom of the hole. You can also reverse the hole extrusion direction by selecting the **Reversed** check box in the **Misc** area of the **Task Panel**.

3. Specify all the required hole parameters in the **Hole parameters** sub-window of the **Task Panel**, as discussed above.

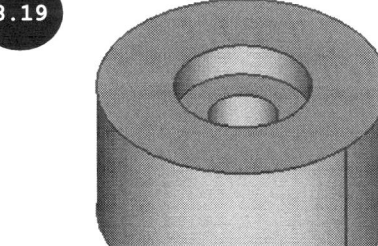

4. After specifying all the hole parameters, click on the **OK** button in the **Task Panel**. A hole of specified parameters gets created, see Figure 8.19.

Creating Fillets

A fillet is a rounded face of a constant radius. It is used to remove the sharp edges of a model. Figure 8.20 shows a model before and after creating fillets on the edges of a model. In FreeCAD, you can create fillets by using the **Fillet** tool. The method for creating fillets is discussed below:

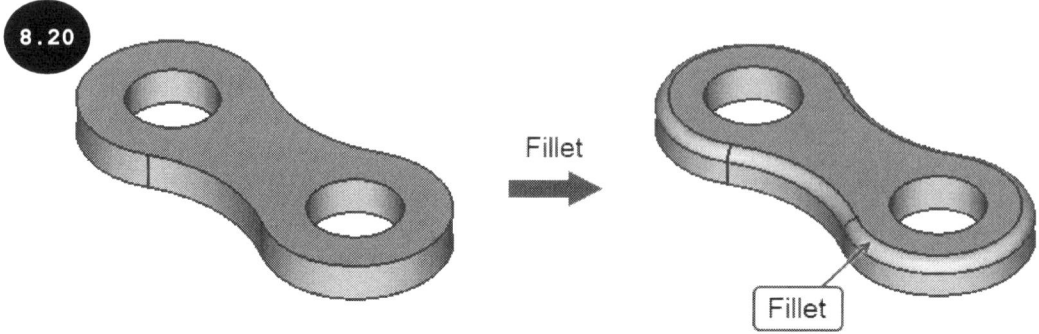

1. Select one or more edges, faces, or a feature of a model for creating a fillet in the 3D View area, see Figure 8.21. In this figure, an edge of a model is selected. To select multiple edges or faces of a model, you need to press the CTRL key.

2. After selecting edges, faces, or a feature of a model, click on the **Fillet** tool in the **Part Design Modeling** toolbar, see Figure 8.22. The preview of a fillet appears on the selected edges of the model with the default radius, see Figure 8.23. Also, the **Fillet parameters** sub-window appears in the **Task Panel**, see Figure 8.24.

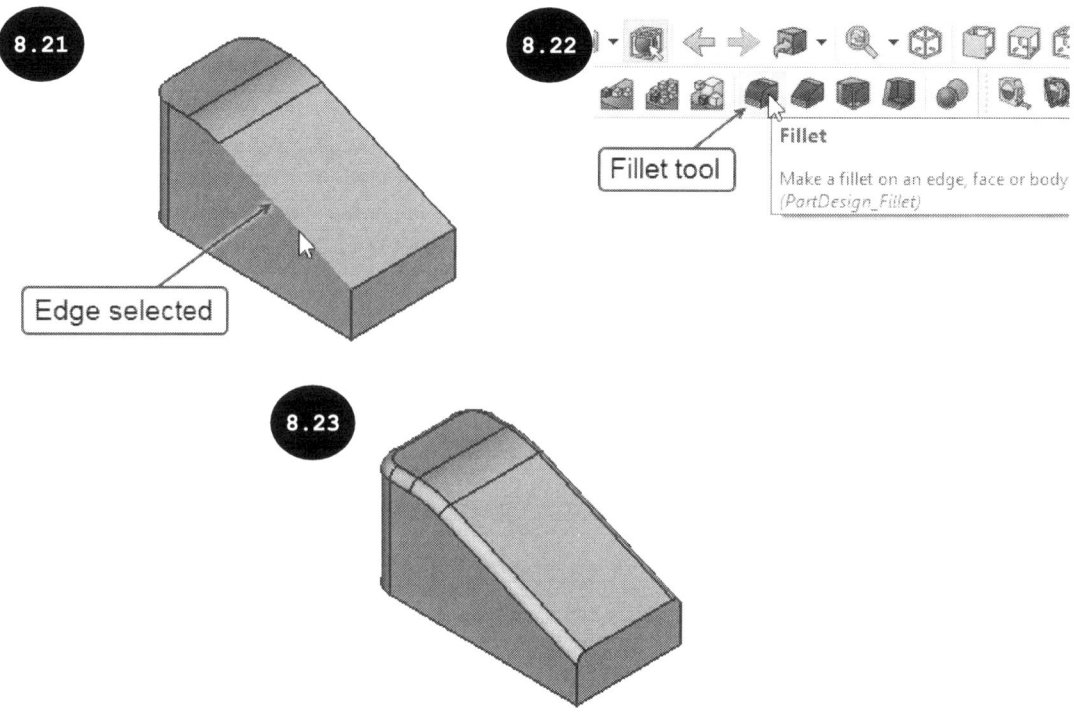

8.24

Note: On selecting an edge of a model, all the edges that are connected tangentially to the selected edge of the model will also be filleted, refer to Figure 8.23.

If you select a face, all the edges of the selected face get filleted (see Figure 8.25) and if you select a feature, all the edges of the selected feature get filleted, see Figure 8.26. You can select a feature in the **Tree View** of the **Model** tab in the **Task Panel**.

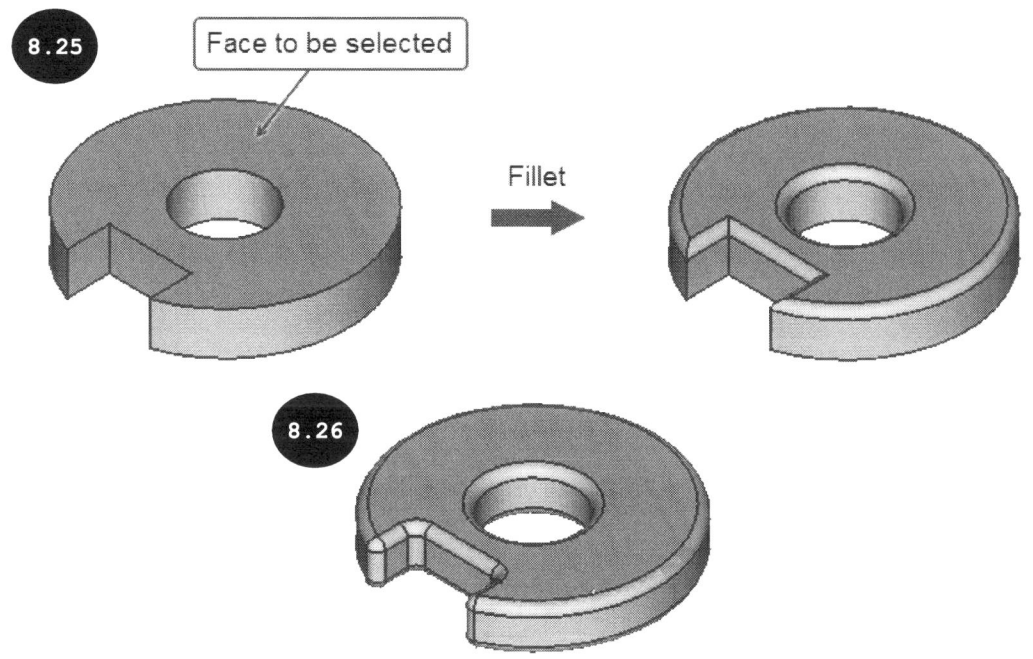

8.25   Face to be selected   Fillet

8.26

Tip: After invoking the **Fillet** tool, you can add additional edges to be filleted or remove already selected edges by using the **Add** or **Remove** button of the **Fillet parameters** sub-window, respectively. You can also remove an already selected edge, face, or feature from the list by right-clicking on the name of the item (edge, face, or feature) to be removed in the **Tree View** and then selecting the **Remove** option in the shortcut menu that appears.

3.   Enter the required radius value in the **Radius** field of the **Task Panel** and then press the TAB key. The preview of the fillet gets updated in the 3D View area.

Use All Edges: On selecting the **Use All Edges** check box, all the edges of the model get filleted in the 3D View area.

4.   After defining all the fillet parameters, click on the **OK** button in the **Task Panel**. A fillet feature of a specified radius gets created on the selected edges of the model.

Creating Chamfers

A chamfer is a beveled face that is not perpendicular to its adjacent faces. Figure 8.27 shows a model before and after creating a chamfer on its edge. In FreeCAD, you can create a chamfer by using the **Chamfer** tool. The method for creating a chamfer is discussed below:

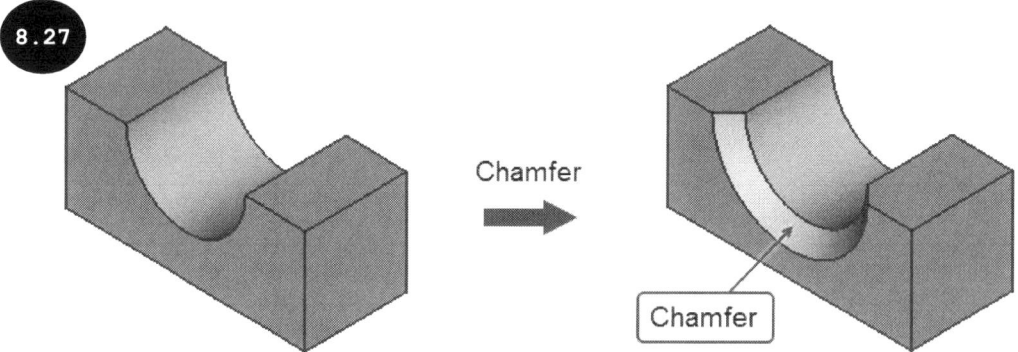

Chamfer

Chamfer

1.   Select one or more edges, faces, or a feature of a model for creating a chamfer in the 3D View area, see Figure 8.28. In this figure, an edge of a model is selected. To select multiple edges or faces of a model, you need to press the CTRL key.

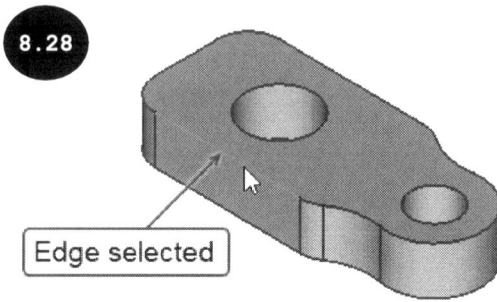

Edge selected

2. After selecting edges, faces, or a feature of a model, click on the **Chamfer** tool in the **Part Design Modeling** toolbar, see Figure 8.29. The preview of a chamfer appears on the selected edge or edges of the model with default parameters, see Figure 8.30. Also, the **Chamfer parameters** sub-window appears in the **Task Panel**, see Figure 8.31.

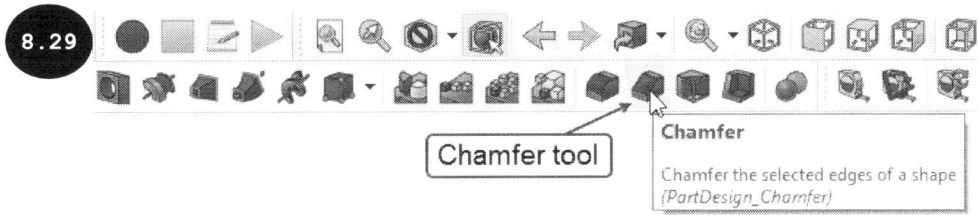

Chamfer tool

Chamfer

Chamfer the selected edges of a shape
(PartDesign_Chamfer)

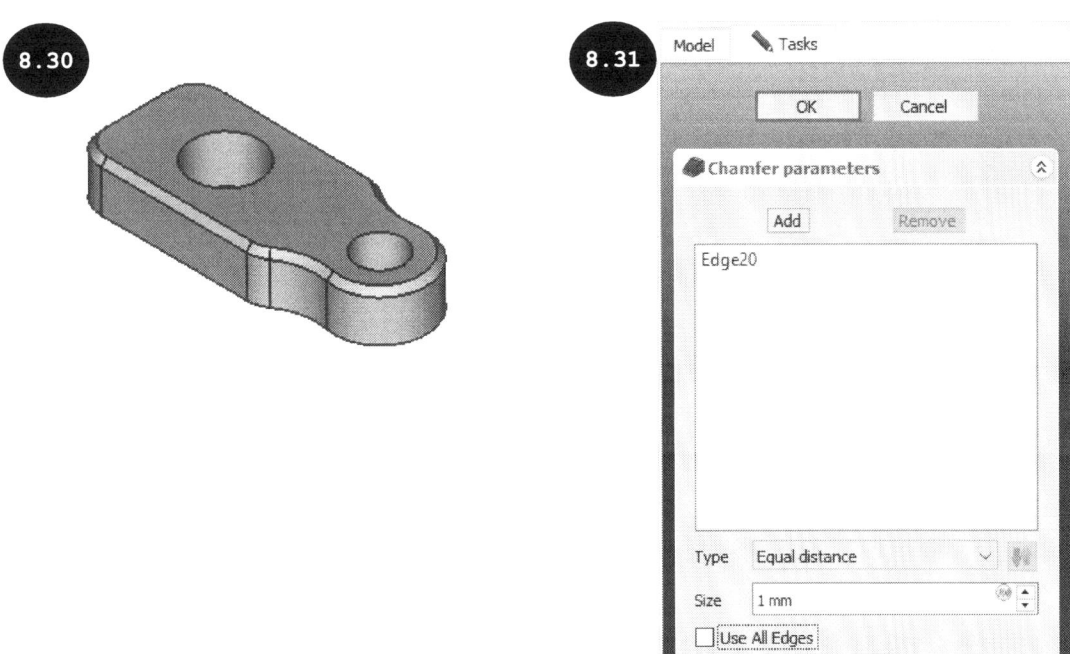

Note: It is evident from Figure 8.30 that on selecting an edge of a model, all the edges that are connected tangentially to the selected edge of the model will also be chamfered.

Also, if you select a face, all the edges of the selected face will be chamfered and if you select a feature, all the edges of the selected feature will be chamfered.

Tip: The **Add** and **Remove** buttons of the **Chamfer parameters** sub-window are used for adding additional edges or removing already selected edges of the model for creating a chamfer feature.

Type: The options in the **Type** drop-down list of the **Task Panel** are used to define a method for creating the respective type of chamfer, see Figure 8.32. These options are discussed next.

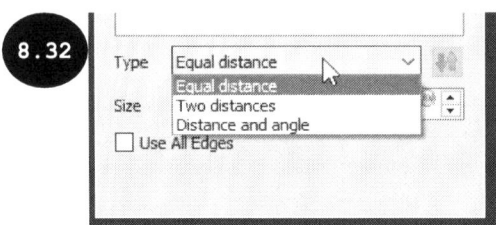

Equal distance: The **Equal distance** option creates a chamfer by specifying one distance value that is equally applied on both sides of the chamfered edge, see Figure 8.33.

On selecting the **Equal distance** option, the **Size** field appears in the **Task Panel**. Note that the distance value specified in this **Size** field is equally applied on both sides of the chamfer edge.

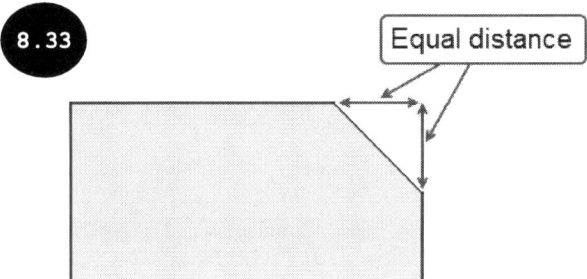

Two distances: The **Two distances** option creates a chamfer by specifying different distance values on both sides of the chamfered edge, see Figure 8.34.

On selecting the **Two distances** option, the **Size** and **Size 2** fields appear in the **Task Panel**. In the **Size** and **Size 2** fields, you can specify different distance values on both sides of the selected chamfered edge. You can also flip the sides of the chamfered edge by clicking on the **Flip direction** button available next to the **Type** drop-down list of the **Task Panel**.

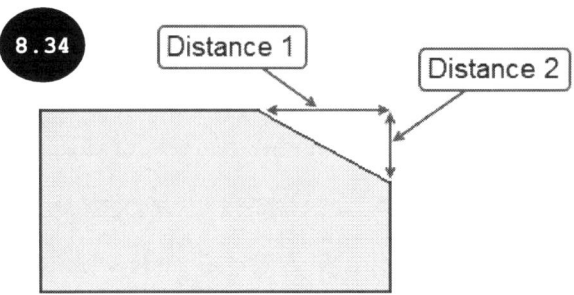

Distance and angle: The **Distance and angle** option creates a chamfer by specifying distance and angle values on the selected edge of the model, see Figure 8.35.

On selecting the **Distance and angle** option, the **Size** and **Angle** fields appear in the **Task Panel**. In these fields, you can specify the distance and angle values of the chamfer, respectively. You can also flip the sides of the chamfered edge by clicking on the **Flip direction** button available next to the **Type** drop-down list of the **Task Panel**.

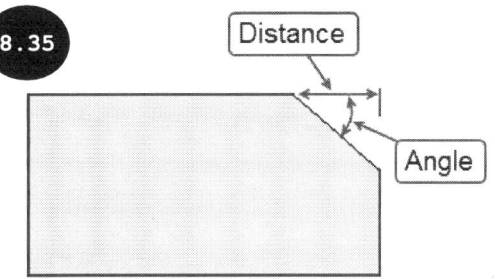

3. Select the required option (**Equal distance**, **Two distances**, or **Distance and angle**) in the **Type** drop-down list of the Task Panel for creating a chamfer, as discussed above.

4. Enter an equal distance, two distance values, or a distance and an angle value in the respective fields that appear depending upon the option selected in the **Type** drop-down list of the **Task Panel**.

Use All Edges: On selecting the Use All Edges check box, all the edges of the model get chamfered in the 3D View area.

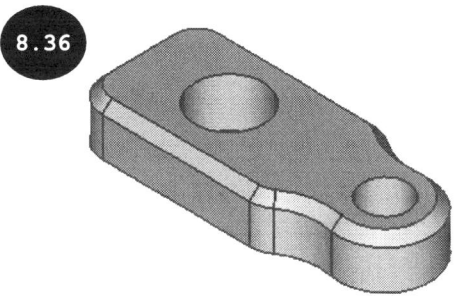

5. After defining all the required parameters, click on the **OK** button in the **Task Panel**. A chamfer feature of specified parameters gets created on the selected edge or edges of the model, see Figure 8.36.

Creating a Thick Shell Model

In FreeCAD, you can transform a 3D solid model into a thick shell model with a uniform wall thickness by removing at least one of its faces, see Figure 8.37. You can create a thick shell model by using the **Thickness** tool. The method for creating a thick shell model is discussed below:

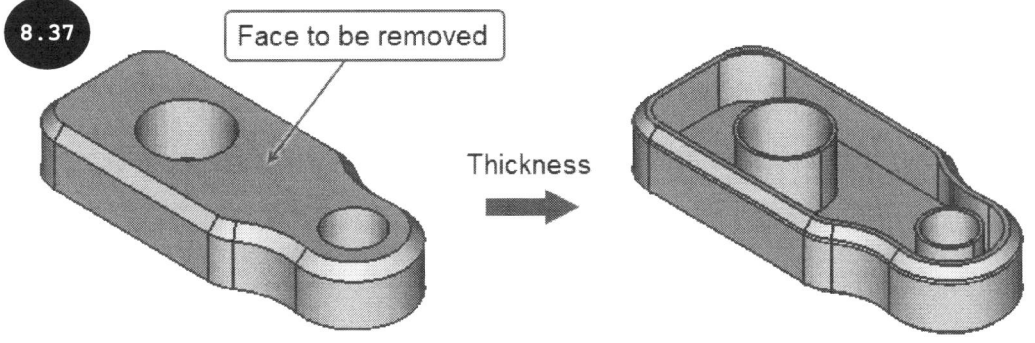

1. Select one or more faces of a model to be removed from the resultant shell model, see Figure 8.38. In this figure, the face of a model is selected to be removed. To select multiple faces of a model, you need to press the CTRL key.

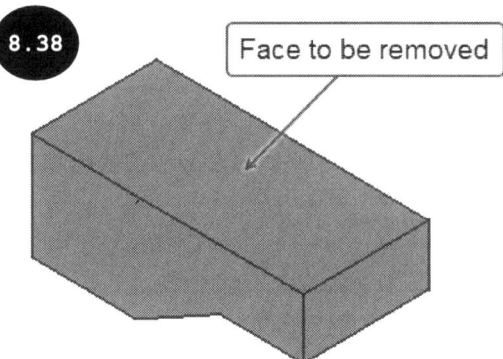

8.38   Face to be removed

2. After selecting a face to be removed, click on the **Thickness** tool in the **Part Design Modeling** toolbar, see Figure 8.39. The preview of a thick shell model with default thickness appears in the 3D View area by removing the selected face of the model, see Figure 8.40. Also, the **Thickness parameters** sub-window appears in the **Task Panel**, see Figure 8.41.

8.39

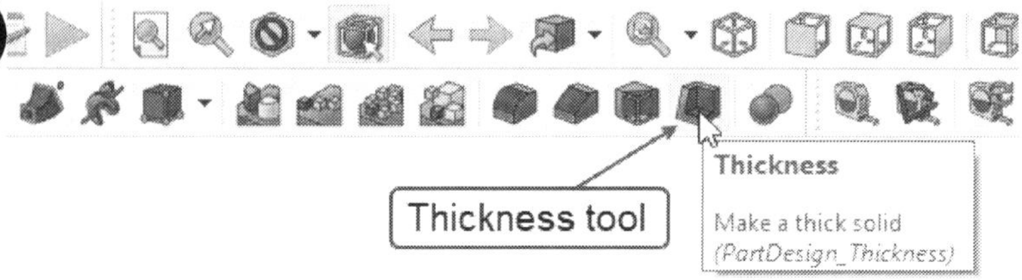

Thickness tool

Thickness

Make a thick solid
(PartDesign_Thickness)

8.40

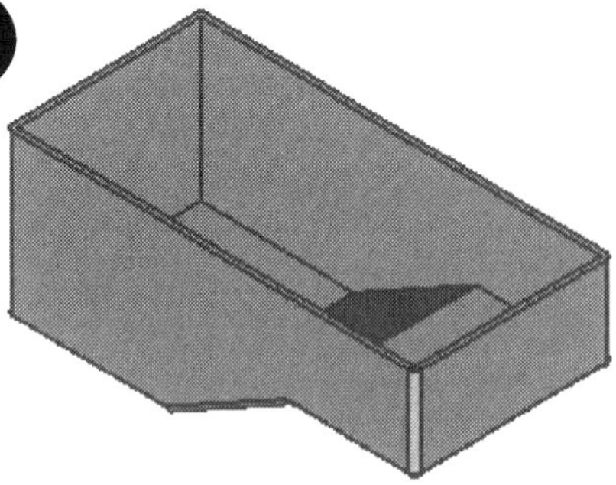

8.41

Model	Tasks

| OK | Cancel |

Thickness parameters

| Add face | Remove face |

Face5

Thickness	1.00 mm
Mode	Skin
Join Type	Arc

3. Enter the required wall thickness value in the **Thickness** field of the **Task Panel** and then press the TAB key. The thickness gets updated in the preview of the shell model, accordingly.

4. Select the required option (**Arc** or **Intersection**) in the **Join Type** drop-down list of the **Task Panel**, see Figures 8.42 and 8.43.

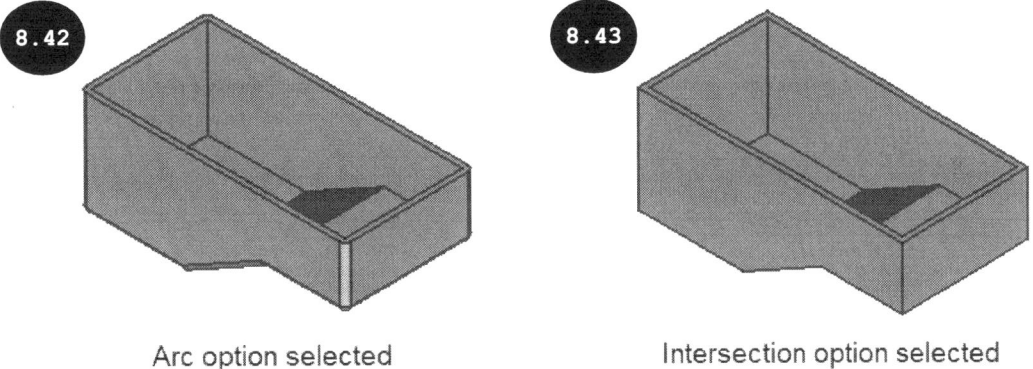

Arc option selected   Intersection option selected

Note: When the non-tangent faces of a model are offset to add thickness, a gap is created between them, refer to Figure 8.44. You can fill this gap by adding a fillet of the same radius as the defined thickness by using the **Arc** option, refer to Figure 8.45. You can also extend the offset faces at their virtual intersection to create a sharp corner by using the **Intersection** option, refer to Figure 8.46.

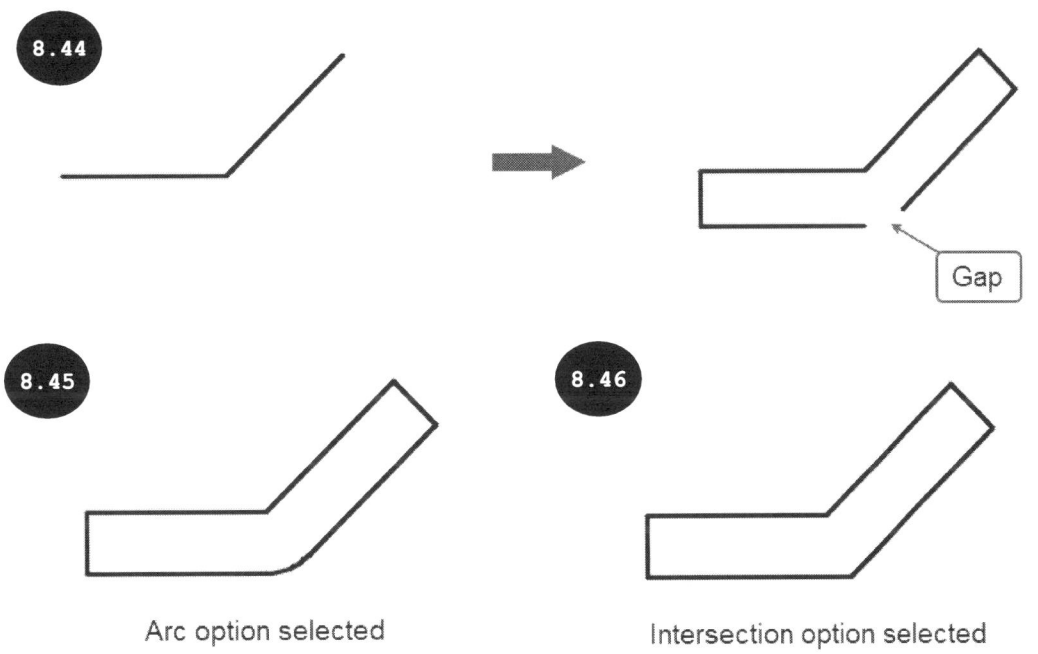

Arc option selected   Intersection option selected

5.   Select the **Make thickness inwards** check box if you want to add thickness inward to the model.

6.   Click on the **OK** button in the **Task Panel**. A thick shell model of specified thickness gets created, see Figure 8.47.

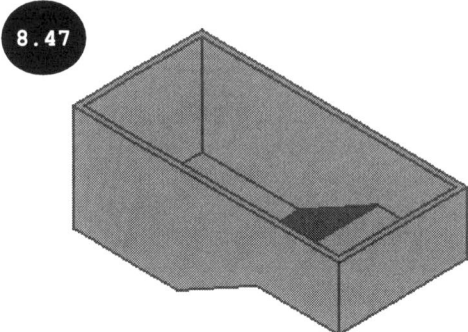

Adding an Angular Draft

Adding an angular draft is a process of tapering one or more faces of a component so that it can easily separate from its cast while manufacturing. In FreeCAD, you can add an angular draft to selected faces of a model by using the **Draft** tool. The method for adding an angular draft is discussed below:

1.   Select one or more faces of a model to add an angular draft to them in the 3D View area, see Figure 8.48. You can select multiple faces of a model by pressing the CTRL key.

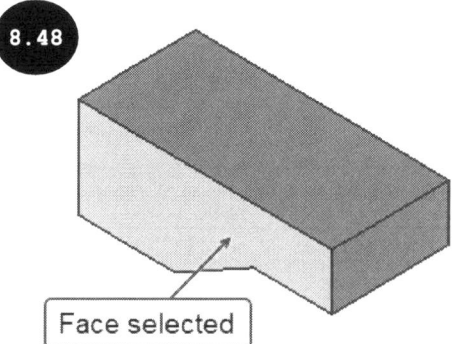

Face selected

2.   Click on the **Draft** tool in the **Part Design Modeling** toolbar, see Figure 8.49. The **Draft parameters** sub-window appears in the **Task Panel**, see Figure 8.50. Ignore the error message that may appear in the **Report view** window at the bottom of the screen. You can close the **Report view** window by clicking on the cross mark ✕ that appears in its top right corner.

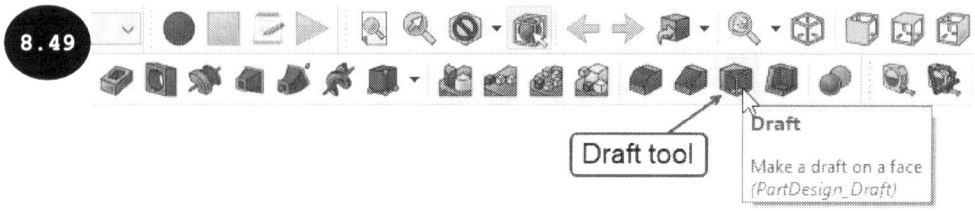

Draft tool

Draft
Make a draft on a face
(PartDesign_Draft)

Now, you need to select a neutral plane for adding a draft.

3. Click on the **Neutral Plane** button in the Task Panel and then select a plane or a planar face as the neutral plane, see Figure 8.51.

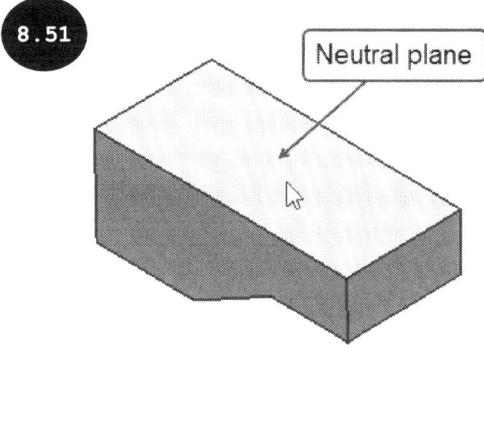

Note: The neutral plane is also known as a fixed plane which remains dimensionally unchanged while adding an angular draft angle to the selected face(s) of a model.

Now, you need to define the pulling direction for adding a draft.

4. Click on the **Pull direction** button in the **Task Panel** and then select a linear edge of the model to define the pulling direction of the angular draft to be applied, see Figure 8.52.

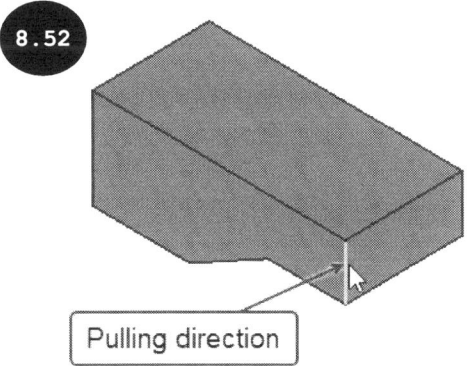

5. Enter the required draft angle value in the **Draft angle** field of the **Task Panel** and then press the TAB key. The preview appears such that the draft angle is applied to the selected face(s) of the model concerning the neutral plane and the pulling direction, see Figure 8.53.

6. Select the **Reverse pull direction** check box if you want to reverse the direction of the draft from outward to inward, see Figure 8.54.

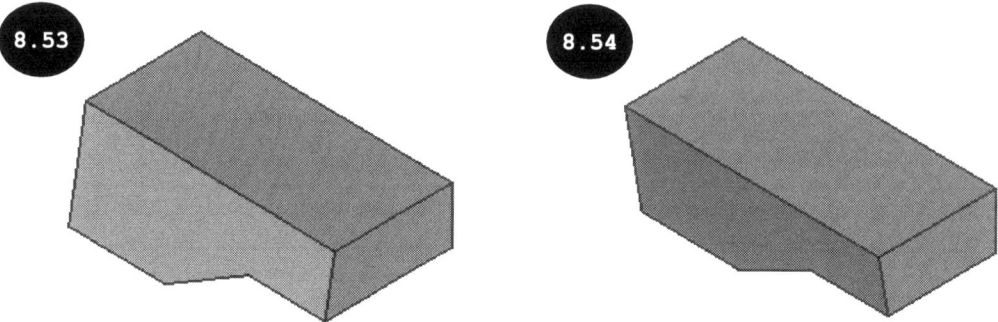

7. Click on the **OK** button in the **Task Panel**. The draft angle gets applied to the selected face(s) of the model concerning the neutral plane and the pulling direction.

Tutorial 1

Create the model shown in Figure 8.55. Different views and dimensions for creating the model are shown in Figure 8.56. All dimensions are in inches (in).

8.56

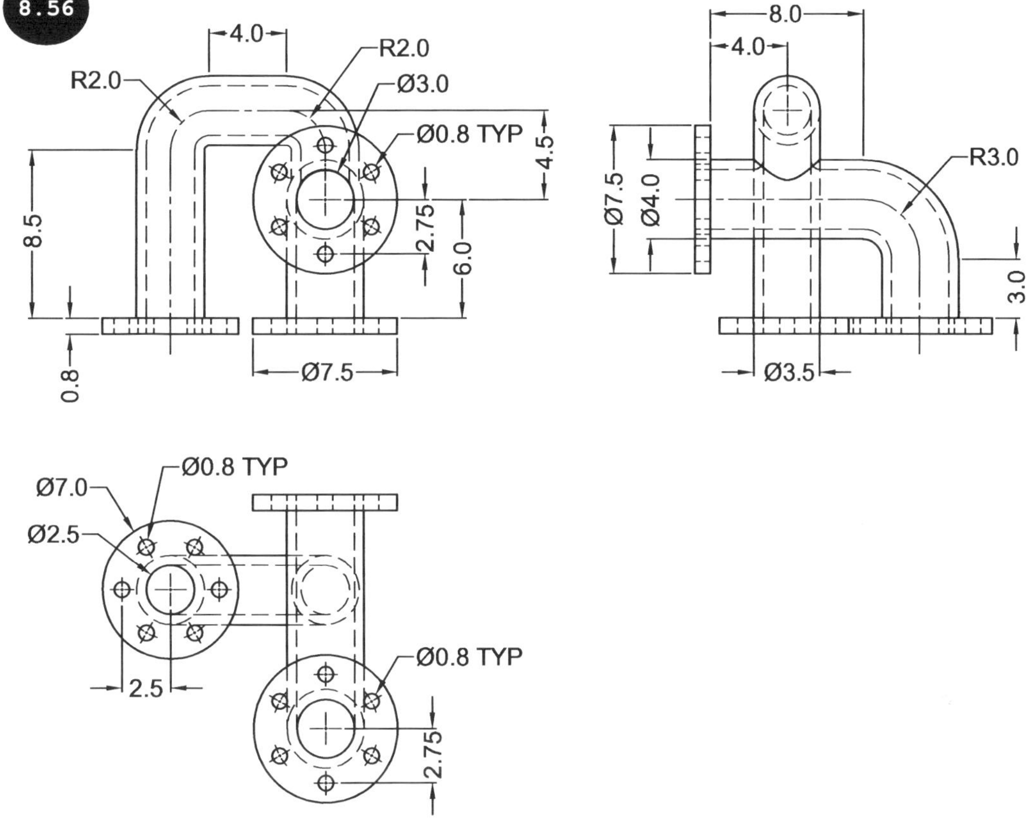

R2.0

R2.0

─4.0─

Ø3.0

Ø0.8 TYP

8.5

4.5

2.75

6.0

0.8

Ø7.5

─8.0─

─4.0─

Ø7.5

Ø4.0

R3.0

3.0

Ø3.5

Ø0.8 TYP

Ø7.0

Ø2.5

2.5

Ø0.8 TYP

2.75

Section 1: Starting FreeCAD and a New Empty Document

1. Start FreeCAD by double-clicking on the **FreeCAD 0.20** icon on your desktop. The startup user interface of FreeCAD appears, see Figure 8.57.

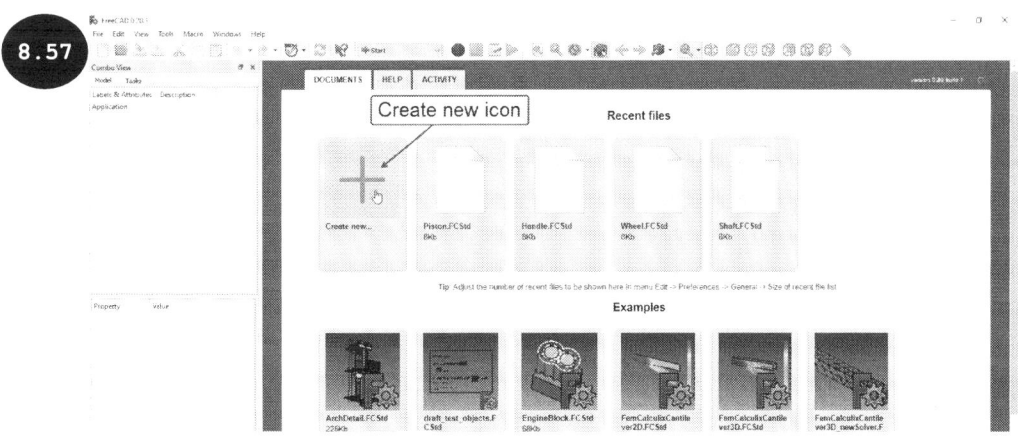

8.57

2. Click on the **Create new** icon on the **Start page** (refer to Figure 8.57) or press the **CTRL + N** keys. A new empty document gets invoked with the default name "**unnamed: 1**".

Section 2: Invoking the Part Design Workbench and Specifying Units

1. Invoke the **Workbench Selector** in the **Workbench** toolbar and then select the **Part Design** workbench, see Figure 8.58. The **Part Design** workbench gets invoked.

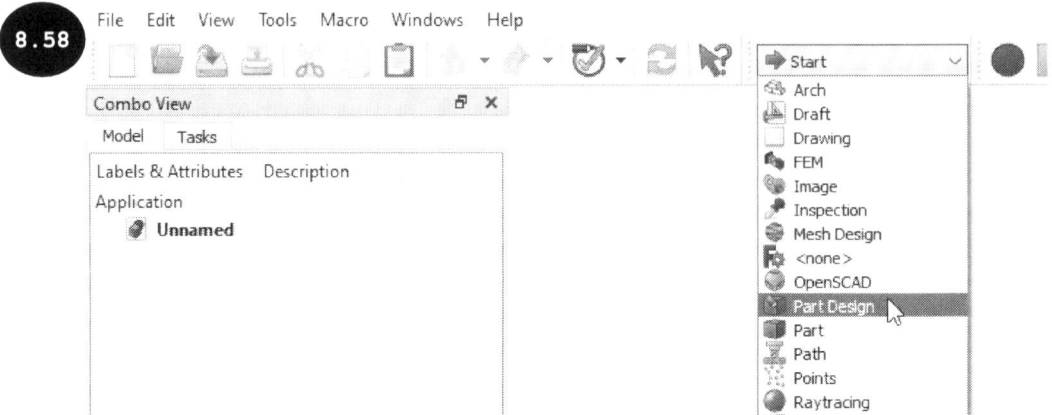

Now, you need to define the units of measurement for the current document.

2. Specify inches (in) as the measurement unit for the document by using the **Preferences** dialog box.

Section 3: Creating the Base Feature

Now, you can create the base or first feature of the model, which is an additive pipe feature.

1. Invoke the **Sketcher** workbench by selecting the **YZ_Plane** as the sketching plane using the **Create sketch** tool and then create the sketch (path) of the additive pipe feature, see Figure 8.59.

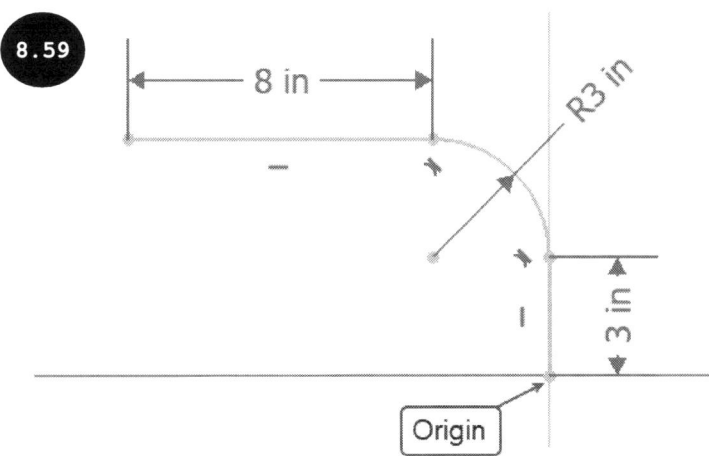

2. After creating the sketch, exit the **Sketcher** workbench to switch back to the **Part Design** workbench.

Now, you can create the profile of the additive pipe feature.

3. Invoke the **Sketcher** workbench by selecting the **XY_Plane** as the sketching plane and then create a circle as the profile of the additive pipe feature, see Figure 8.60. Note that the center point of the circle is at the origin.

4. After creating the profile, exit the **Sketcher** workbench and then change the view orientation to isometric, see Figure 8.61. Click anywhere in the 3D View area to exit the current selection set.

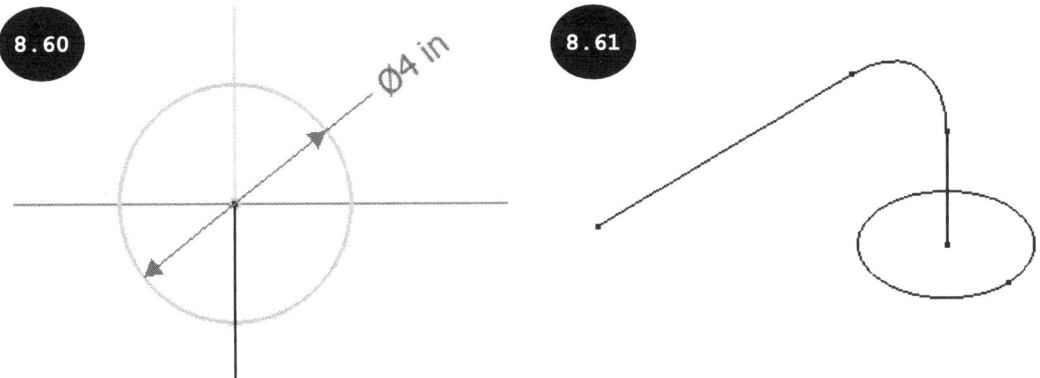

Now, you can create the additive pipe feature.

5. Select the profile (**Sketch001**) and then the path (**Sketch**) in the **Tree View** of the **Model** tab in the **Task Panel** by pressing the CTRL key. Next, release the CTRL key.

6. After selecting the profile and the path in the **Tree View**, click on the **Additive pipe** tool in the **Part Design Modeling** toolbar, see Figure 8.62. The preview of the additive pipe feature appears in the 3D View area such that the profile follows the path, see Figure 8.63. Also, the **Pipe parameters** sub-window appears in the **Task Panel** with the options to create an additive pipe feature.

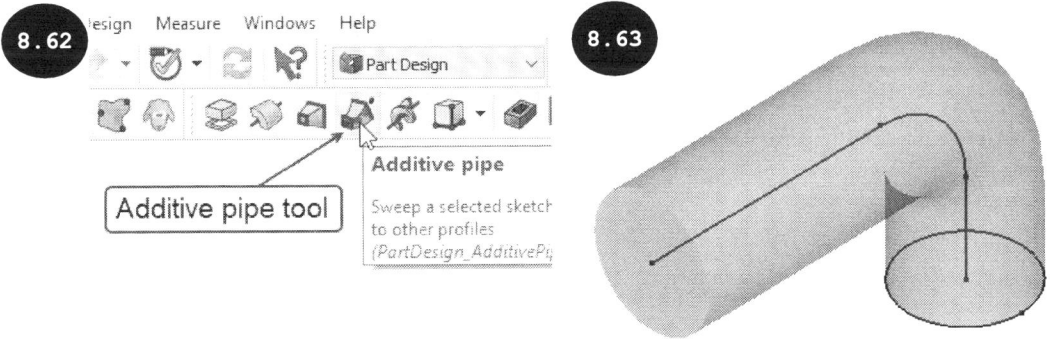

Tip: You can also select the profile and the path of the feature after invoking the **Additive pipe** tool.

7. Click on the OK button in the Task Panel and then click on the OK button. The additive pipe feature gets created, see Figure 8.64.

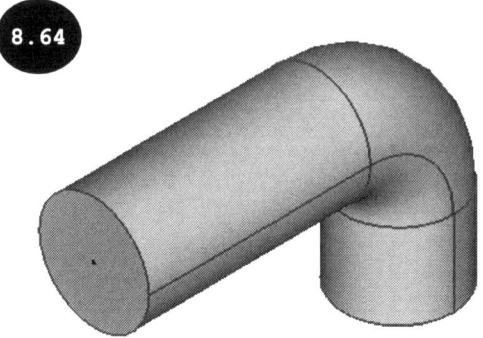

8.64

Section 4: Creating the Second Feature

Now, you can create the second feature of the model, which is also an additive pipe feature. To create this additive pipe feature, you need to first create a datum plane at an offset distance of 4 inches from the front planar face of the base feature.

1. Click on the Create a datum plane tool in the Part Design Helper toolbar, see Figure 8.65. The Datum Plane parameters sub-window appears in the Task Panel. Also, you are prompted to select a first reference for creating a datum plane.

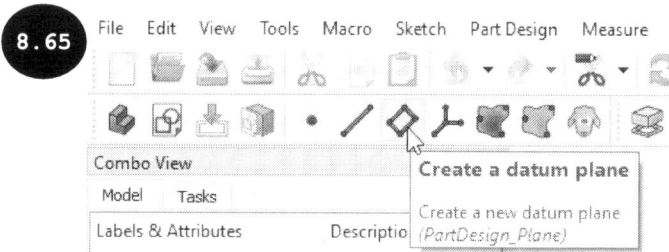

8.65

2. Select the front planar face of the base feature (additive pipe) as the first reference, see Figure 8.66. The preview of a datum plane appears in the 3D View area. Also, the Plane face mode gets activated automatically in the Attachment mode area of the Task Panel.

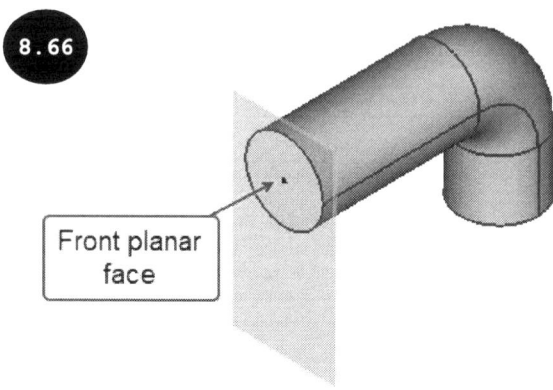

8.66

Front planar face

3. Enter **-4** inches in the **In z-direction** field of the **Attachment Offset** area in the **Task Panel** as the offset distance between the selected planar face and the datum plane being created, see Figure 8.67. Next, press the TAB key. The preview of the datum plane gets updated in the 3D View area and appears like the one shown in Figure 8.68.

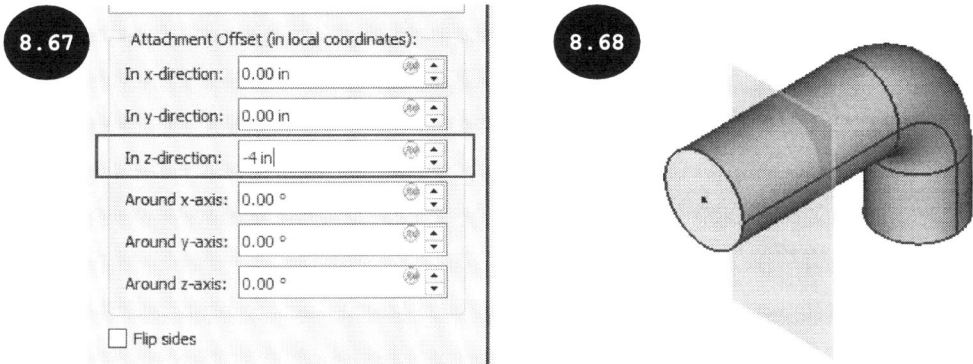

4. Click on the **OK** button in the **Task Panel** to confirm the creation of the datum plane and exit the **Task Panel**.

Now, you can create the path of the additive pipe feature on the newly created datum plane.

5. Invoke the **Sketcher** workbench by selecting the newly created datum plane as the sketching plane using the **Create sketch** tool 🗹 and then create the sketch (path) of the additive pipe feature, see Figure 8.69.

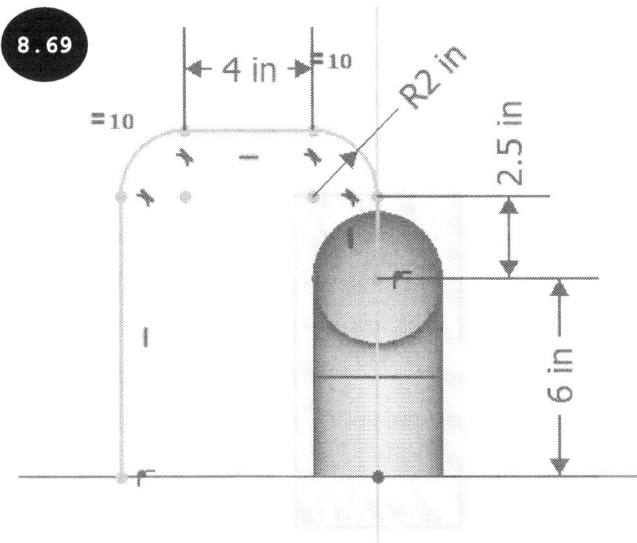

6. After creating the path, exit the **Sketcher** workbench to switch back to the **Part Design** workbench.

Now, you can create the profile of the additive pipe feature.

7. Invoke the **Sketcher** workbench by selecting the **XY_Plane** as the sketching plane for creating the profile of the additive pipe feature.

8. Click on the **External geometry** tool in the **Sketcher geometries** toolbar (see Figure 8.70) and then click on the endpoint of the previously created sketch (path) as the entity to be projected into the sketch, see Figure 6.71. Next, press the ESC key to exit the tool.

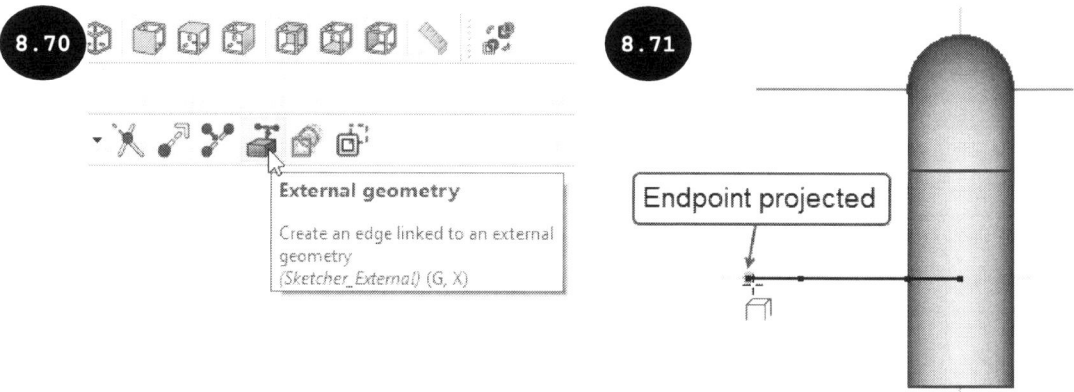

9. Create a circle as the profile of the additive pipe feature by taking reference of the projected construction endpoint, see Figure 6.72. Note that the center point of the circle is at the projected endpoint.

10. After creating the profile, exit the **Sketcher** workbench and then change the view orientation to isometric, see Figure 8.73. Click anywhere in the 3D View area to exit the current selection set.

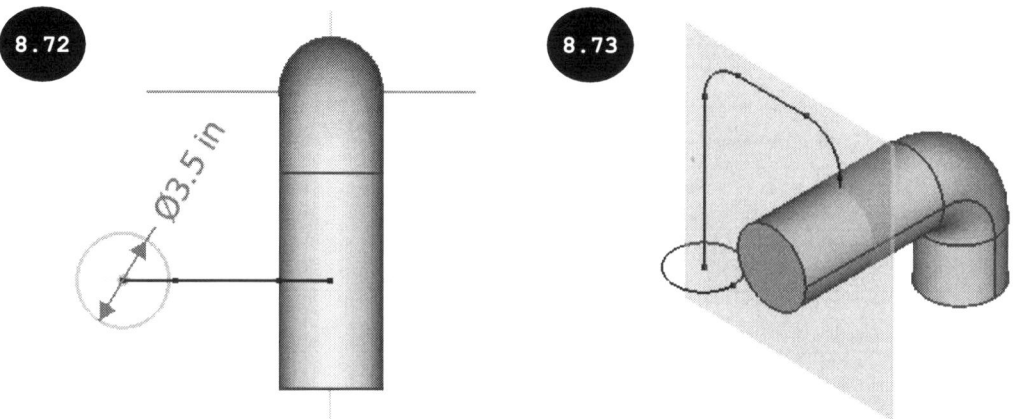

11. Select the datum plane in the 3D View area and then press SPACEBAR to hide the display of the datum plane in the 3D View area.

Now, you can create the additive pipe feature.

12. Select the profile (**Sketch003**) and then the path (**Sketch002**) in the **Tree View** of the **Model** tab in the **Task Panel** by pressing the CTRL key. Next, release the CTRL key.

13. After selecting the profile and the path in the **Tree View**, click on the **Additive pipe** tool in the **Part Design Modeling** toolbar, see Figure 8.74. The preview of the additive pipe feature appears in the 3D View area such that the profile follows the path, see Figure 8.75. Also, the **Pipe parameters** sub-window appears in the **Task Panel** with the options to create an additive pipe feature.

14. Click on the **OK** button in the **Task Panel** and then click on the **OK** button. The additive pipe feature gets created, see Figure 8.76.

Section 5: Creating the Third Feature

Now, you can create the third feature of the model, which is a thick shell feature.

1. Rotate the model and then select all the end planar faces (three) of the model in the 3D View area as the faces to be removed while creating the thick shell feature, see Figure 8.77.

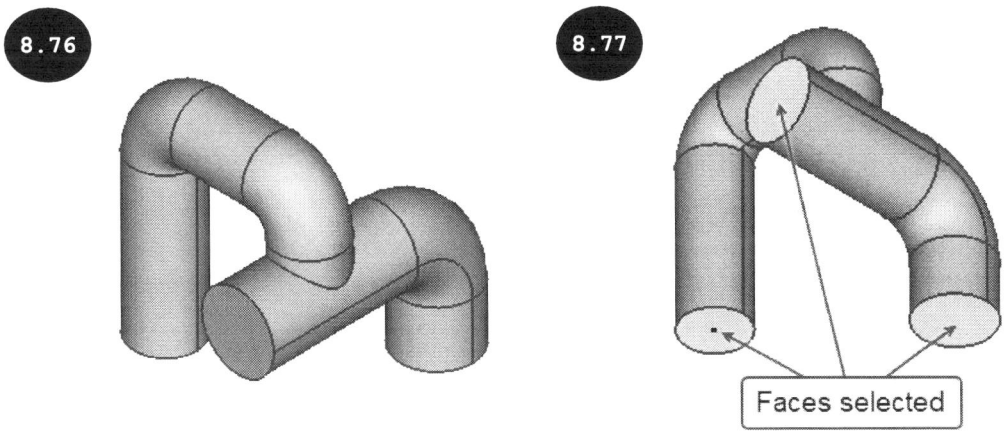

2. After selecting the faces, click on the **Thickness** tool in the **Part Design Modeling** toolbar, see Figure 8.78. The **Thickness parameters** sub-window appears in the **Task Panel**. Also, the preview of a thick shell model of default wall thickness appears in the 3D View area.

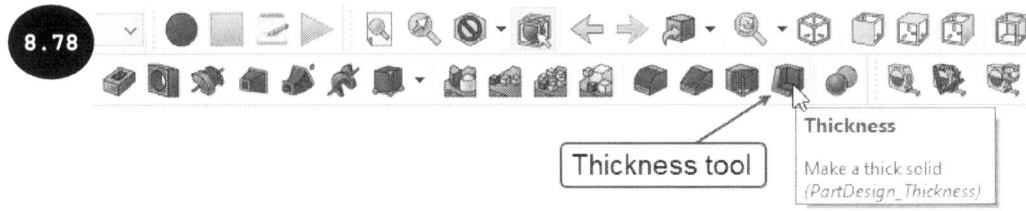

Thickness tool

Thickness

Make a thick solid
(PartDesign_Thickness)

3. Enter **0.5** inches in the **Thickness** field of the **Task Panel** and then press the TAB key to update the preview in the 3D View area as per the specified wall thickness.

4. Select the **Make thickness inwards** check box in the **Task Panel** to add thickness inward.

5. Click on the **OK** button in the **Task Panel**. A thick shell model of specified wall thickness gets created by removing the selected faces of the model, see Figure 8.79. Next, change the view orientation of the model to isometric, see Figure 8.80.

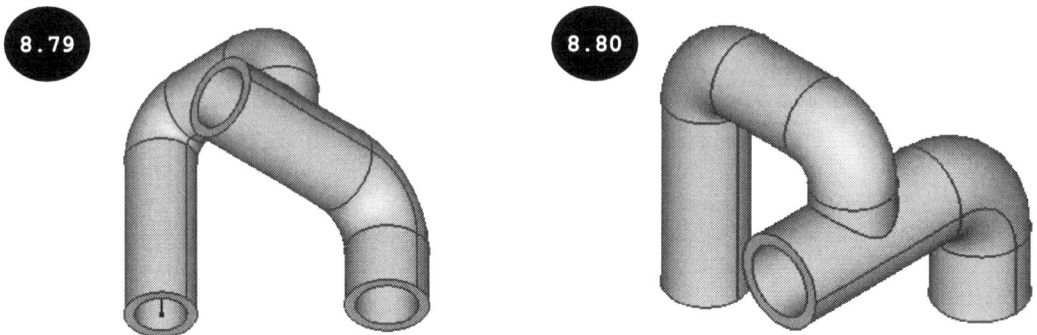

Section 6: Creating the Fourth Feature
Now, you can create the fourth feature of the model, which is a pad feature.

1. Select the front planar face of the model as the sketching plane (see Figure 8.81) and then click on the **Create sketch** tool for invoking the **Sketcher** workbench.

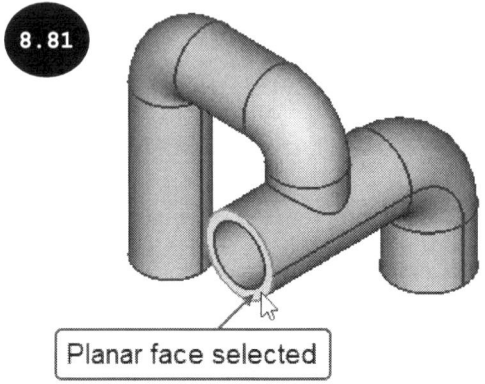

Planar face selected

2. Create two concentric circles as the sketch of the pad feature, see Figure 8.82.

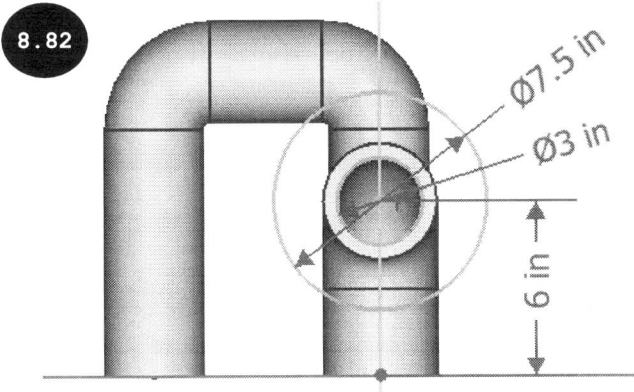

3. After creating the sketch, exit the **Sketcher** workbench and then extrude the sketch to **0.8** inches by using the **Pad** tool. Figure 8.83 shows the model after creating the pad feature.

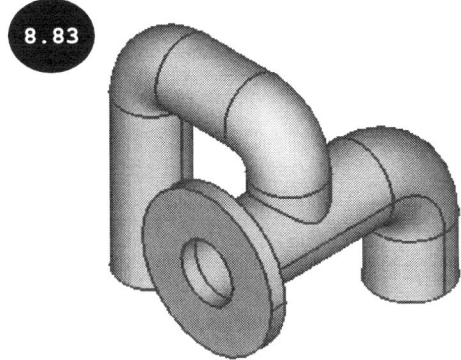

Section 7: Creating the Fifth Feature

Now, you can create the fifth feature of the model, which is a pocket feature.

1. Select the front planar face of the model as the sketching plane (see Figure 8.84) and then click on the **Create sketch** tool for invoking the **Sketcher** workbench.

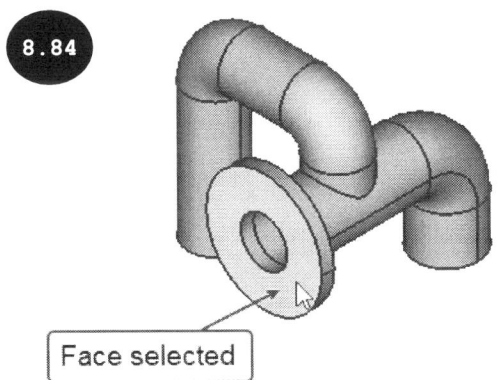

Face selected

2. Create a circle of diameter **0.8** inches as the sketch of the pocket feature, see Figure 8.85.

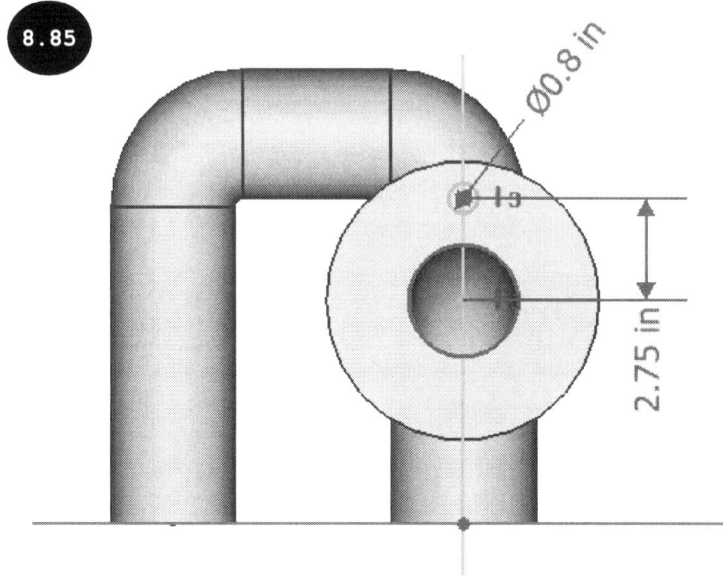

3. After creating the sketch, exit the **Sketcher** workbench and then click on the **Pocket** tool in the **Part Design Modeling** toolbar, see Figure 8.86. The **Pocket parameters** sub-window appears in the **Task Panel**. Also, the preview of the pocket feature appears in the 3D View area.

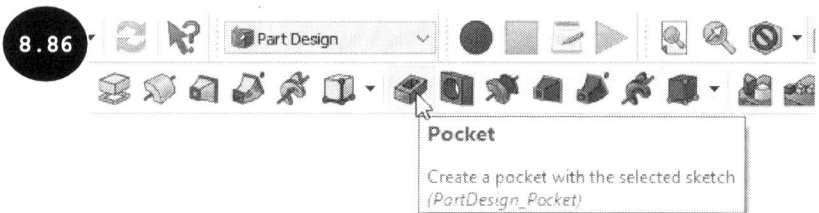

4. Select the **To first** option in the **Type** drop-down list of the **Pocket parameters** sub-window (see Figure 8.87) for creating a pocket feature by extruding the sketch up to its first or nearest intersecting face of the model.

5. Click on the **OK** button in the **Task Panel**. A pocket feature gets created, see Figure 8.88.

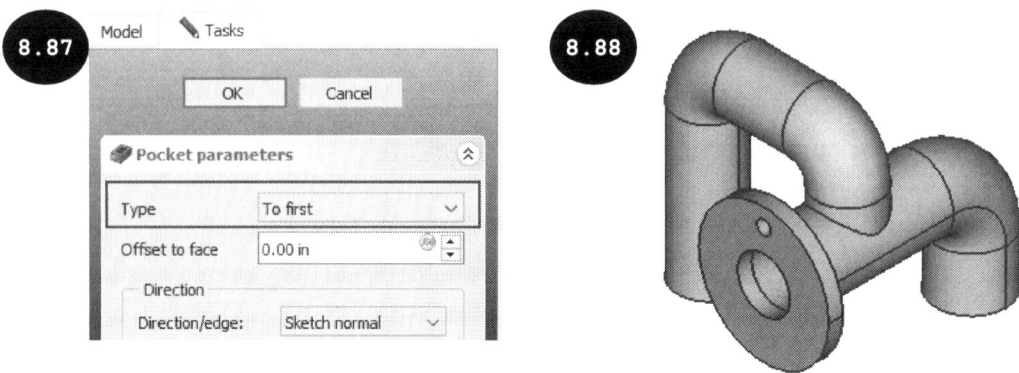

Section 8: Creating the Polar Pattern

Now, you can create the polar pattern of the previously created pocket feature for creating its remaining occurrences.

1. Select the previously created pocket feature in the **Tree View** of the **Model** tab in the **Task Panel** or the 3D View area.

2. After selecting the feature, click on the **PolarPattern** tool in the **Part Design Modeling** toolbar, see Figure 8.89. The **PolarPattern parameters** sub-window appears in the **Task Panel**.

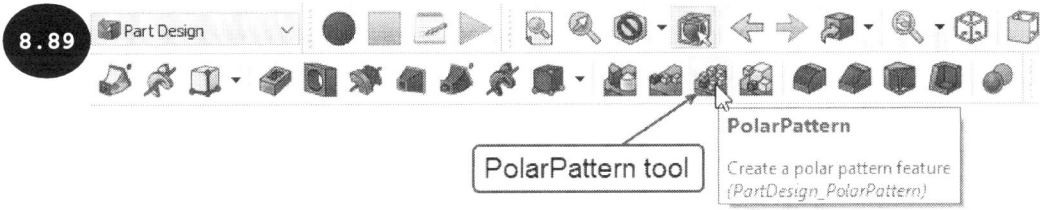

PolarPattern tool

PolarPattern

Create a polar pattern feature
(PartDesign_PolarPattern)

3. Select the **Select reference** option in the **Axis** drop-down list in the **Task Panel**, see Figure 8.90. You are prompted to select a reference entity to define the axis of revolution.

4. Select the front circular edge of the model to define the axis of revolution of the polar pattern, see Figure 8.91.

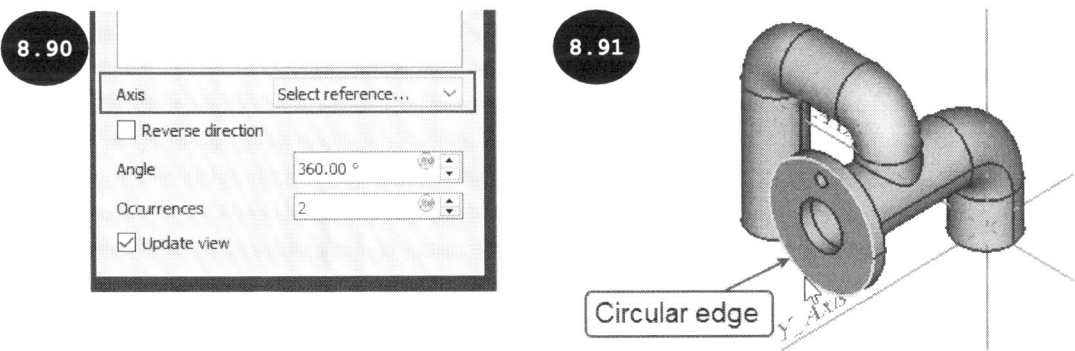

Circular edge

5. Enter **6** in the **Occurrences** field of the **Task Panel** as the number of occurrences to be created. The preview of the polar pattern of specified occurrences appears around the axis of revolution, see Figure 8.92.

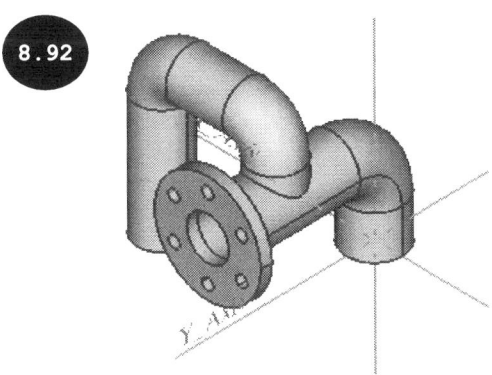

6. Ensure that the **360** degrees is specified in the **Angle** field of the **Task Panel** as the total angle between which the specified number of occurrences is to be arranged equally.

7. Click on the **OK** button in the **Task Panel**. A polar pattern of the specified number of occurrences of the selected pocket feature gets created, see Figure 8.93.

Section 9: Creating the Remaining Features

Now, you can create the remaining features of the model.

1. Create two more flanges on the other ends of the model one by one in a similar manner as described above. Note that each flange compresses a pad, a pocket, and a polar pattern feature. Figure 8.94 shows the final model after creating all its features. Refer to Figure 8.56 for the dimensions of each feature of the model.

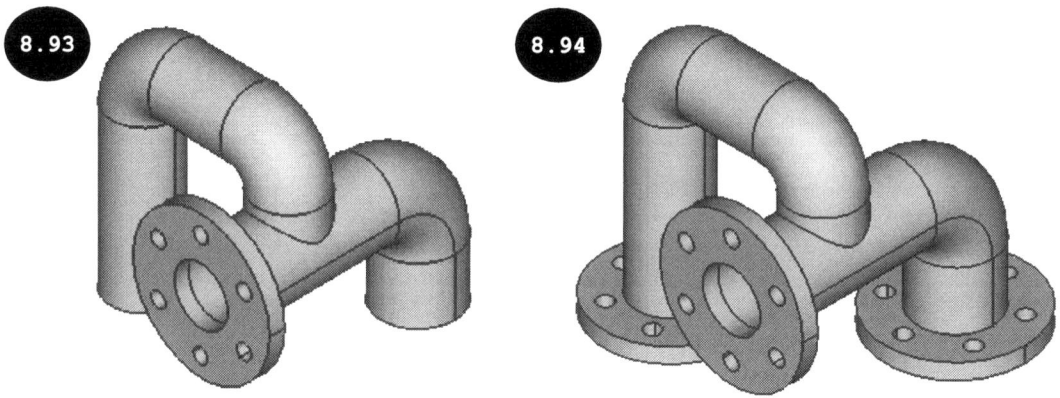

Section 10: Saving the Model

1. Click on the **Save** tool in the **File** toolbar (see Figure 8.95) or press the CTRL + S keys. The **Save FreeCAD Document** dialog box appears.

2. Browse to the required folder (:*FreeCAD* > *Chapter 08*) in the local drive of your system. Note that you need to create the Chapter 08 sub-folder inside the FreeCAD folder.

3. Enter **Ch08-Tutorial 1** in the **File name** field of the dialog box. Next, click on the **Save** button in the dialog box. The model gets saved at the specified location (:*FreeCAD* > *Chapter 08*).

4. Click on **File** > **Close** in the **Standard Menu** to close the current document.

Tutorial 2

Create the model shown in Figure 8.96. Different views and dimensions for creating the model are shown in the same figure. All dimensions are in mm.

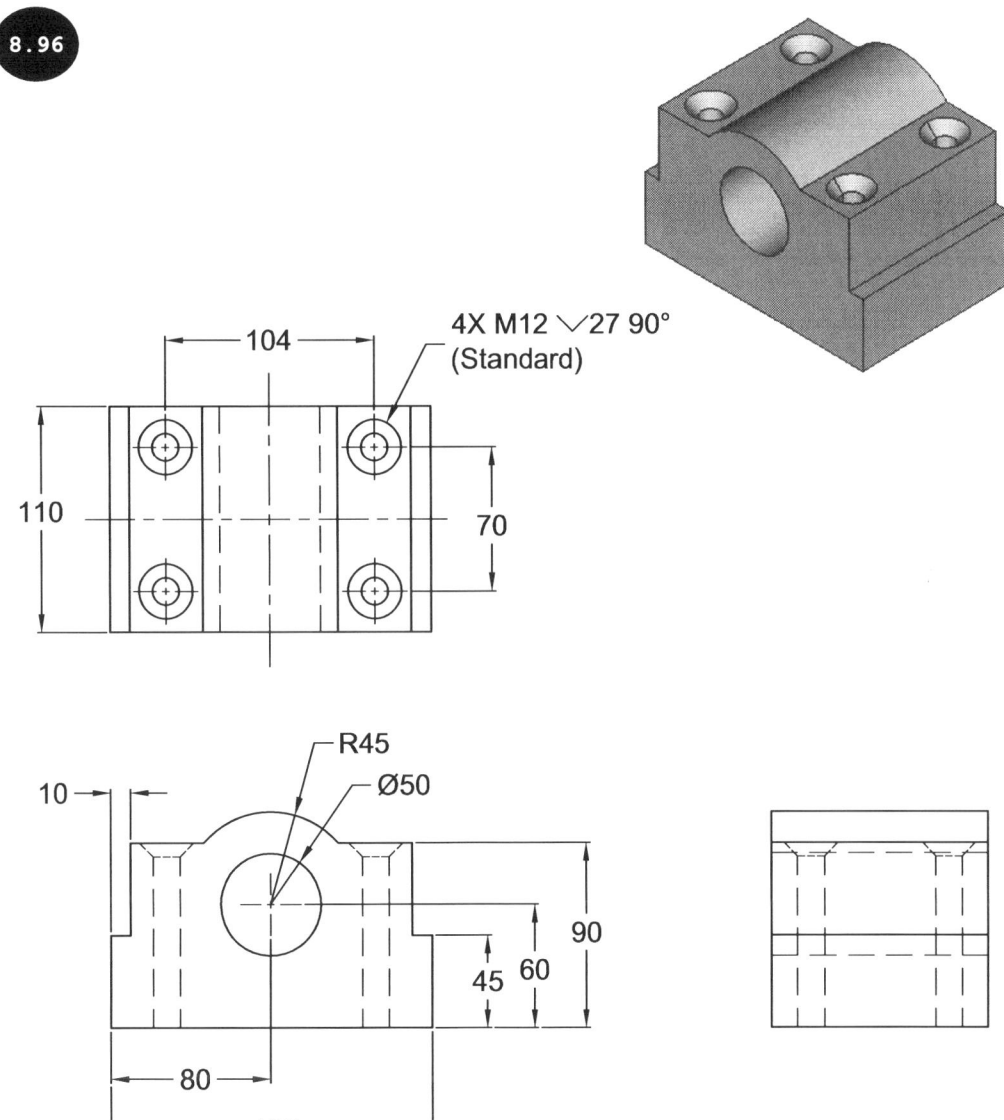

8.96

104

4X M12 ∨27 90°
(Standard)

110

70

R45
Ø50

10

90

45 60

80

160

Section 1: Invoking the Part Design Workbench and Specifying Units

1. Start FreeCAD by double-clicking on the **FreeCAD 0.20** icon on your desktop, if not launched already.

2. Click on the **New** tool in the **File** toolbar, see Figure 8.97. A new empty document gets invoked with a default name.

3. Invoke the **Workbench Selector** in the **Workbench** toolbar and then select the **Part Design** workbench, see Figure 8.98. The **Part Design** workbench gets invoked.

Now, you need to define the units of measurement for the current document.

4. Specify millimeter (mm) as the measurement unit for the document by using the **Preferences** dialog box.

Section 2: Creating the Base Feature
Now, you can create the base or first feature of the model, which is a pad feature.

1. Invoke the **Sketcher** workbench by selecting the **XZ_Plane** as the sketching plane using the **Create sketch** tool and then create the sketch of the pad feature, see Figure 8.99.

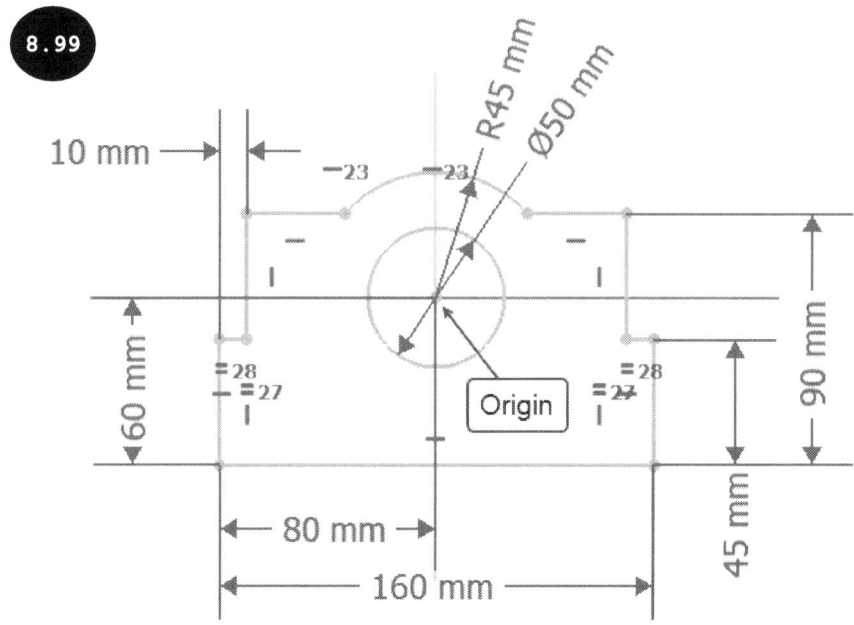

2. After creating the sketch, exit the **Sketcher** workbench to switch back to the **Part Design** workbench.

Now, you can extrude the sketch to create a pad feature.

3. Click on the **Pad** tool in the **Part Design Modeling** toolbar, see Figure 8.100. The preview of a pad feature appears in the 3D View area with default parameters. Also, the **Pad parameters** sub-window appears in the **Task Panel**.

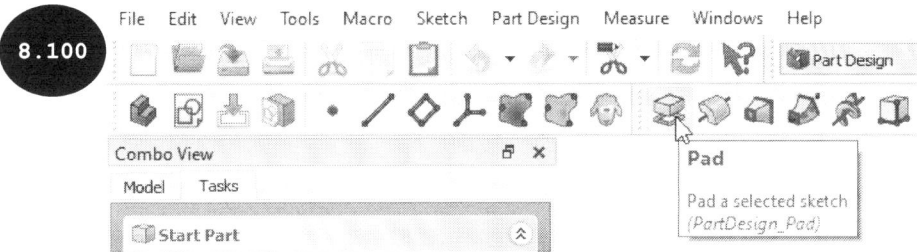

4. Enter **110** mm in the **Length** field of the **Task Panel** and then press the TAB key to update the preview of the pad feature in the 3D View area.

5. Select the **Symmetric to plane** check box in the **Task Panel** for adding material symmetrically on both sides of the sketching plane.

6. Click on the **OK** button in the **Task Panel** to confirm the creation of the pad feature and exit the **Task Panel**. The pad (base) feature of specified length gets created, see Figure 8.101.

Section 3: Creating the Holes

Now, you can create countersink holes in the model.

1. Select the top planar face of the model as the sketching plane (see Figure 8.102) and then click on the **Create sketch** tool. The **Sketcher** workbench gets invoked and the selected planar face gets oriented normal to the viewing direction.

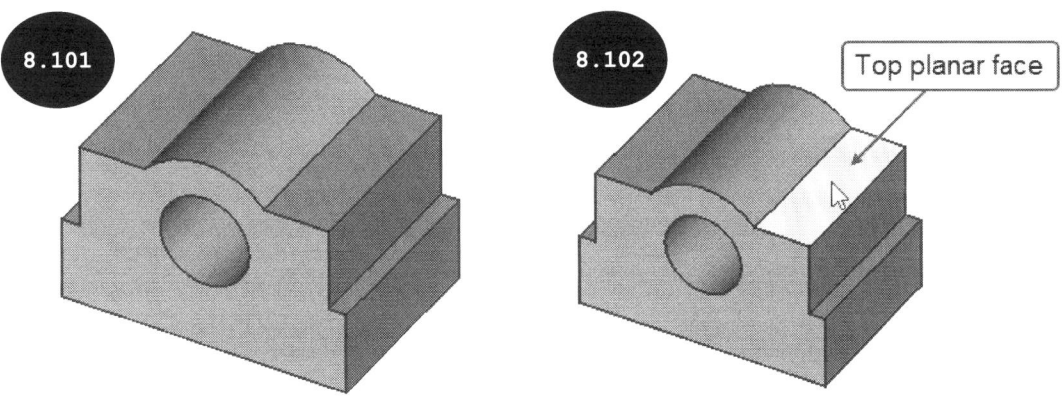

Top planar face

2. Select the **View section** tool in the **Sketcher** toolbar, see Figure 8.103. The section view of the model appears in the 3D View area by temporarily hiding the material that is in front of the sketching plane.

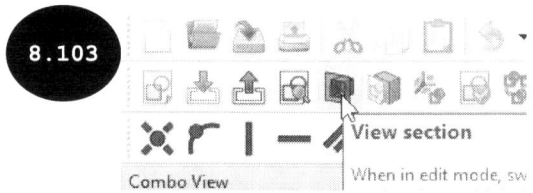

3. Create a circle to define the center of a hole concerning the origin, see Figure 8.104.

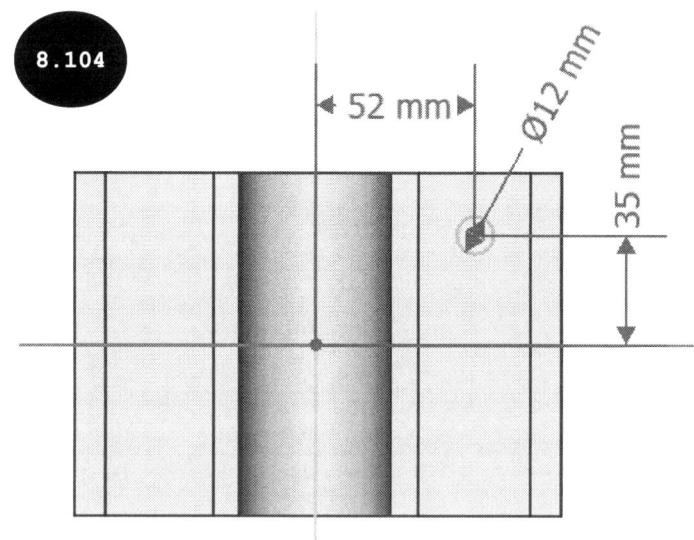

Note: The center of a circle defines the position of the hole center on the planar face of the model and its diameter will be ignored or not taken into account.

---

4. Exit the **Sketcher** workbench and then click on the **Hole** tool in the **Part Design Modeling** toolbar, see Figure 8.105. The preview of a hole appears in the 3D View area with default parameters. Also, the **Hole parameters** sub-window appears in the **Task Panel**.

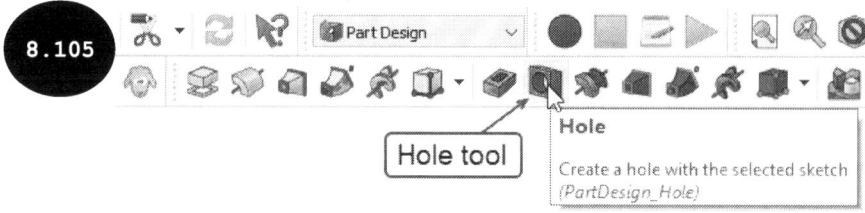

5. Select the **ISO metric regular profile** option in the **Profile** drop-down list of the **Task Panel**, see Figure 8.106.

6. Select the **M12** option in the **Size** drop-down list of the **Task Panel**, see Figure 8.106.

7. Select the **Through all** option in the **Depth** drop-down list of the **Task Panel**, see Figure 8.106.

8. Select the **Countersink** option in the **Type** drop-down list of the **Task Panel**, see Figure 8.106.

9. Enter **27** mm as the countersink diameter of the hole in the **Diameter** field of the **Hole cut** area in the **Task Panel**, see Figure 8.106.

10. Ensure that the **90** degrees is specified in the **Countersink angle** field of the **Task Panel**.

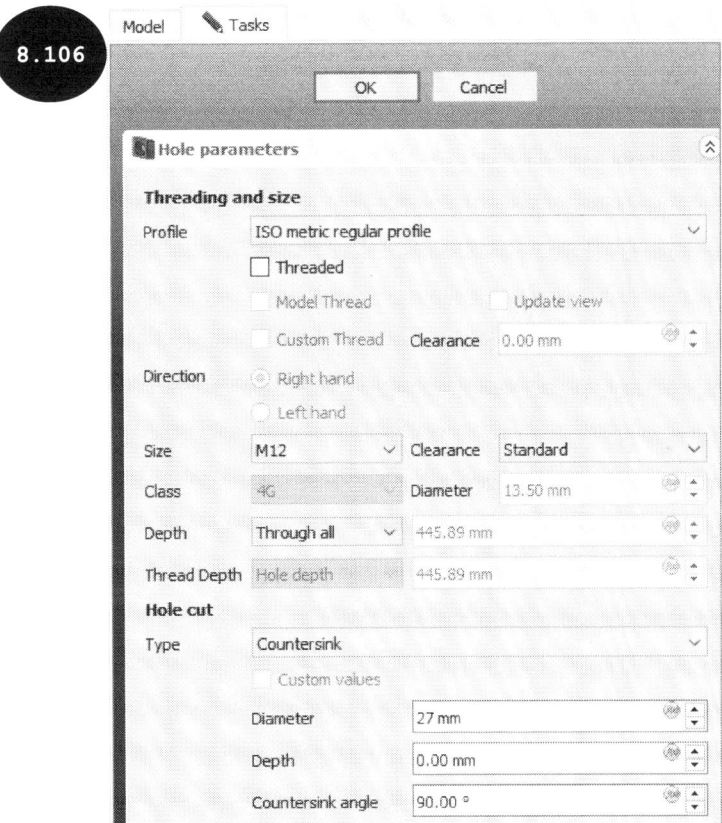

11. After specifying all the required parameters, click on the **OK** button in the **Task Panel**. The countersink hole of specified parameters gets created, see Figure 8.107.

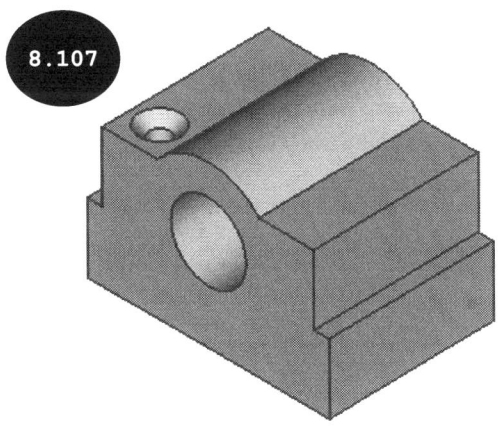

Section 4: Creating the Multi-transform Pattern Feature

Now, you can create a multi-transform pattern feature to create the remaining holes of the model.

1. Select the previously created countersink hole in the **Tree View** or the 3D View area.

2. Click on the **Create MultiTransform** tool in the **Part Design Modeling** toolbar, see Figure 8.108. The **MultiTransform parameters** sub-window appears in the **Task Panel** and the name of the selected feature appears in its field.

Create MultiTransform tool

Create MultiTransform

Create a multitransform feat[
(PartDesign_MultiTransform)

Now, you can define the first transformation (linear pattern) to be applied to the selected hole.

3. Right-click on the **Transformations** field of the **Task Panel** and then select the **Add linear pattern** option in the shortcut menu that appears, see Figure 8.109. The linear pattern transformation gets selected and appeared in the **Transformations** field of the **Task Panel**, see Figure 8.110. Also, the options to create a linear pattern appeared at the bottom of the **Task Panel**.

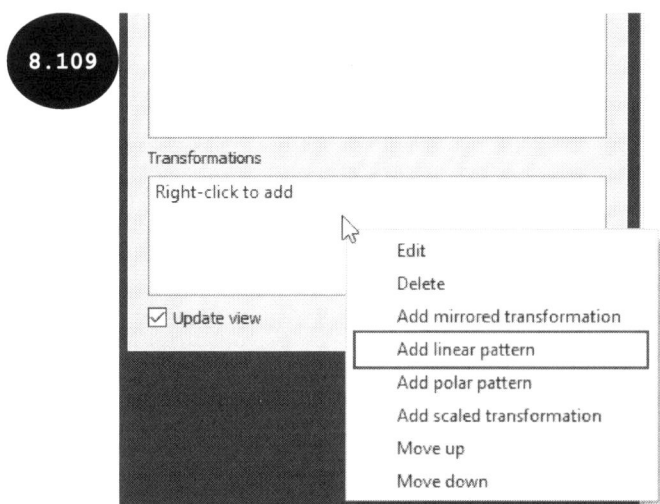

4. Enter **70** mm in the **Length** field of the **Task Panel** as the distance between two occurrences, see Figure 8.110.

5. Select the **Y axis** option in the **Direction** drop-down list of the **Task Panel** to define the pattern direction along the Y-axis of the model, see Figure 8.110. If the preview of the linear pattern does not appear like the one shown in Figure 8.111, then you can select any other option in this **Direction** drop-down list to define the correct pattern direction. If needed, you can also reverse the pattern direction by selecting the **Reverse direction** check box.

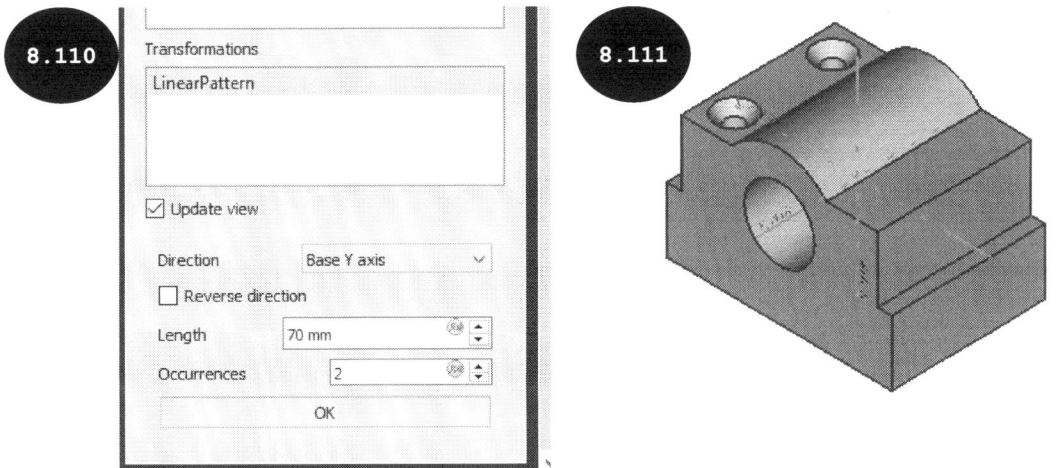

6. Ensure that **2** is specified in the **Occurrences** field of the **Task Panel** as the number of hole occurrences to be created along the defined pattern direction.

7. Click on the **OK** button available at the bottom of the **Task Panel**. A linear pattern of specified parameters gets created, see Figure 8.112.

Now, you can create a mirrored transformation to mirror the result of the previously created linear pattern transformation.

8. Right-click on the **Transformations** field of the **Task Panel** and then select the **Add mirrored transformation** option in the shortcut menu that appears, see Figure 8.113. The options to mirror the result of the previously created linear pattern appear at the bottom of the **Task Panel**.

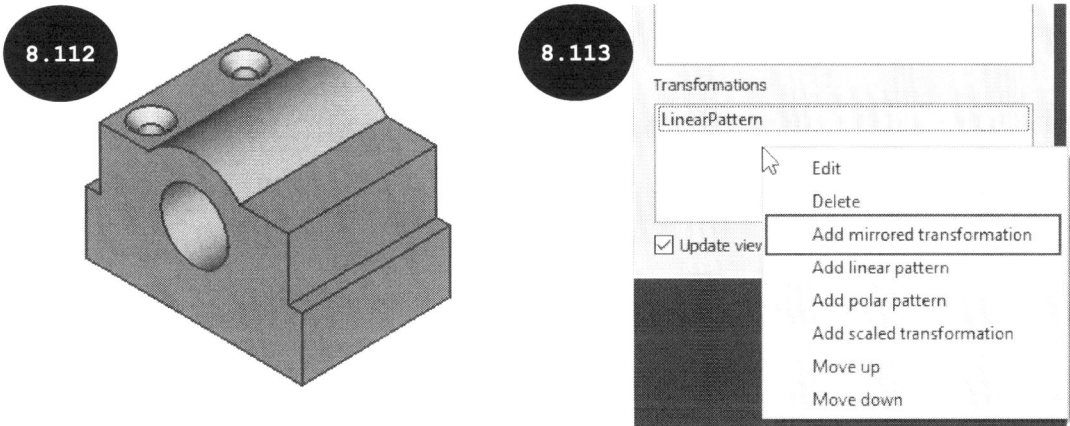

9. Ensure that the **Vertical sketch axis** is selected to define the mirroring plane in the **Plane** drop-down list of the **Task Panel**. If the preview of the resultant mirror feature does not appear like the one shown in Figure 8.114, then you need to select any other option in this **Plane** drop-down list to define the correct mirroring plane.

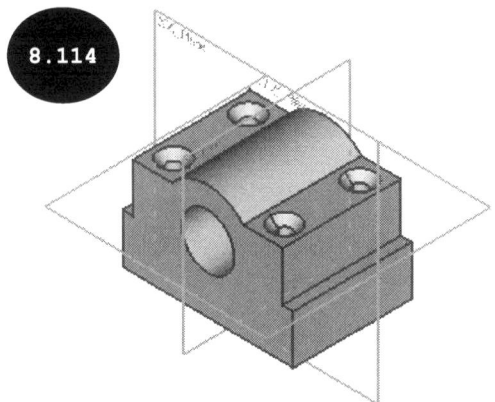

10. Click on the **OK** button available at the bottom of the **Task Panel**. The mirrored transformation gets created, see Figure 8.115.

11. Click on the **OK** button to exit the **Task Panel**. Figure 8.115 shows the final model.

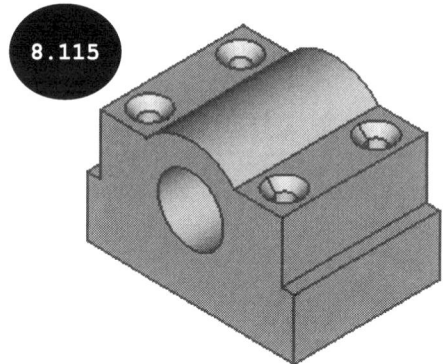

Section 5: Saving the Model

1. Click on the **Save** tool in the **File** toolbar or press the CTRL + S keys. The **Save FreeCAD Document** dialog box appears.

2. Browse to the required folder (*:\FreeCAD > Chapter 08*) in the local drive of your system. Note that you need to create the Chapter 08 sub-folder inside the FreeCAD folder, if not created earlier.

3. Enter **Ch08-Tutorial 2** in the **File name** field of the dialog box. Next, click on the **Save** button in the dialog box. The model gets saved at the specified location (*:\FreeCAD > Chapter 08*).

4. Click on **File** > **Close** in the **Standard Menu** to close the current document.

Hands-on Test Drive 1

Create the model shown in Figure 8.116. Different views and dimensions for creating the model are shown in the same figure. All dimensions are in mm.

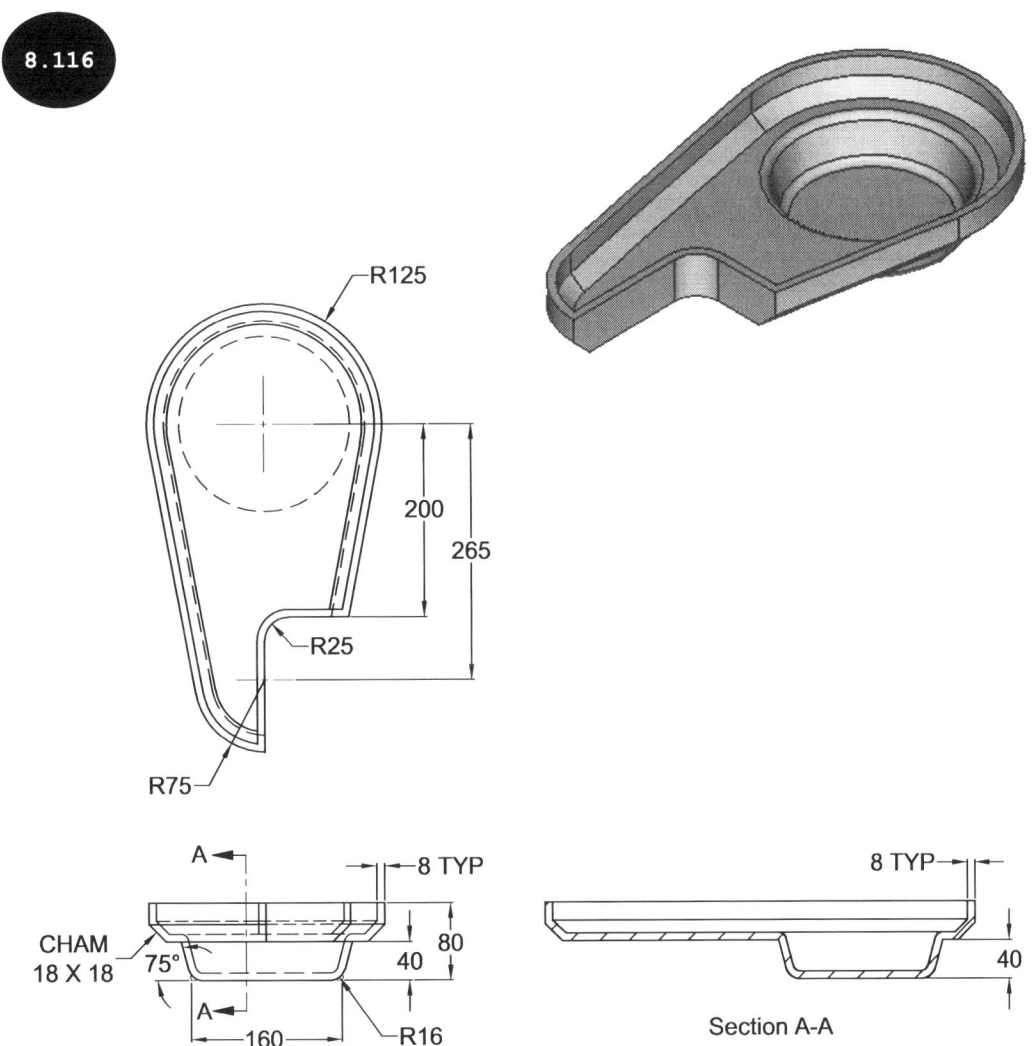

8.116

Summary

The chapter discussed how to create standard or customized holes such as counterbores and countersinks as per standard specifications. The chapter also described methods for creating different types of dress-up features: fillet, chamfer, thickness (shell), and angular draft for applying treatment to the existing edges and faces of a model.

Questions

Complete and verify the following sentences:

- The _____ tool is used for creating standard and customized holes such as counterbore and countersink.

- In FreeCAD, you can create dress-up features such as _____, _____, and _____ for applying treatment to the existing edges and faces of a model.

- On selecting the _____ check box in the **Hole parameters** sub-window, a real thread is modeled on a threaded hole by removing material from the model.

- A _____ is a rounded face of a constant radius.

- A _____ is a beveled face that is not perpendicular to its adjacent faces.

- The _____ tool is used for transforming a 3D solid model into a thick shell model of a uniform wall thickness by removing one or more faces.

- In FreeCAD, you add an angular draft to one or more selected faces of a model by using the _____ tool.

- The _____ plane is known as a fixed plane which remains dimensionally unchanged while adding an angular draft to the selected face(s) of a model.

- It is recommended to create a threaded hole without removing the material to increase the overall system performance. (True/False)

- You can create a thick shell model without removing any of its faces. (True/False)

- You can create a chamfer by specifying different distance values on both sides of the selected edge. (True/False)

- Adding an angular draft is a process of tapering one or more faces of a component so that it can easily separate from its cast while manufacturing. (True/False)

CHAPTER

9

Creating Assemblies

In this chapter, the following topics will be discussed:

- Creating an Assembly Using Top-down Approach
- Creating an Assembly Using Bottom-up Approach
- Checking or Tagging Degrees of Freedom
- Moving a Component along its Free DOFs
- Moving a Component along its Fixed DOFs

In the previous chapters, you have learned about various tools and techniques for creating real-world mechanical 3D solid parts. In this chapter, you will learn how to create mechanical assemblies. An assembly consists of two or more parts that are connected. Figure 9.1 shows an assembly in which multiple parts are connected.

9.1

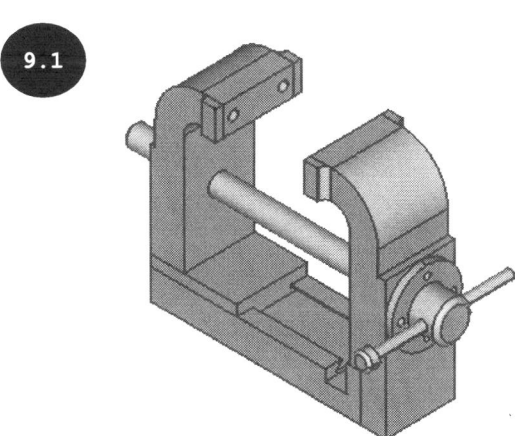

In FreeCAD, you can create an assembly by using two approaches: the Top-down assembly approach and the Bottom-up assembly approach. In the Top-down assembly approach, all the components of an assembly are created as individual bodies within a single part document of the **Part Design** workbench. Whereas, in the Bottom-up assembly approach, the existing components of an assembly are inserted one by one into an assembly workbench and then assembled by applying constraints to create an assembly. Note that the assembly workbench uses constraints and expressions to assemble components concerning each other.

Note: As of this release of FreeCAD, there is no official assembly workbench included by default. However, you can use the **A2plus** assembly workbench for creating assemblies by using the Bottom-up assembly approach. The method for creating assemblies in the **A2plus** assembly workbench is discussed later in this chapter.

Creating an Assembly Using Top-down Approach

Creating all the components of an assembly as individual bodies within a single part document of the **Part Design** workbench is known as the Top-down assembly approach. The method of creating an assembly by using this approach is discussed below:

1. Start FreeCAD and then click on the **Create new** icon in the **Start page**, refer to Figure 9.2. A new empty document gets invoked with the default name "**unnamed: 1**".

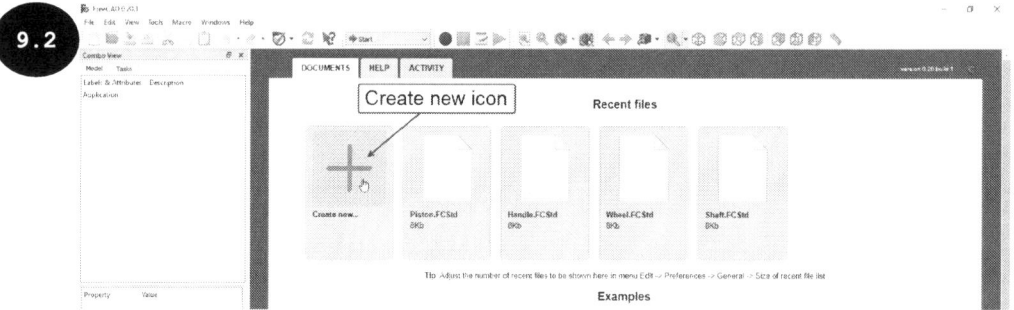

2. Invoke the **Part Design** workbench and then specify the required measurement unit for the document by using the **Preferences** dialog box.

    Now, you can create an assembly by creating its components as individual bodies.

3. Click on the **Create body** tool in the **Part Design Helper** toolbar, see Figure 9.3. A new empty body with the default name "**Body**" gets created and appears in the **Tree View** of the **Model** tab, see Figure 9.4. Also, it becomes the active body of the current document.

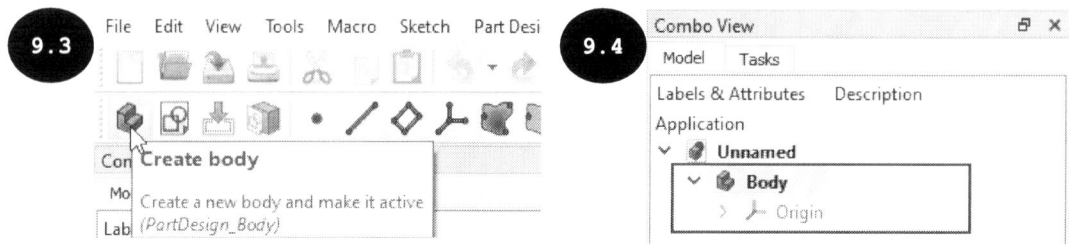

Now, you can rename the newly added body, as required.

4. Click on the **Model** tab of the **Combo View** for displaying the **Tree View** and then right-click on the newly created body to display a shortcut menu, see Figure 9.5.

5. Click on the **Rename** option in the shortcut menu and then enter the name for the body/part in the edit field that appears in **Tree View**. Next, click anywhere in the 3D View area.

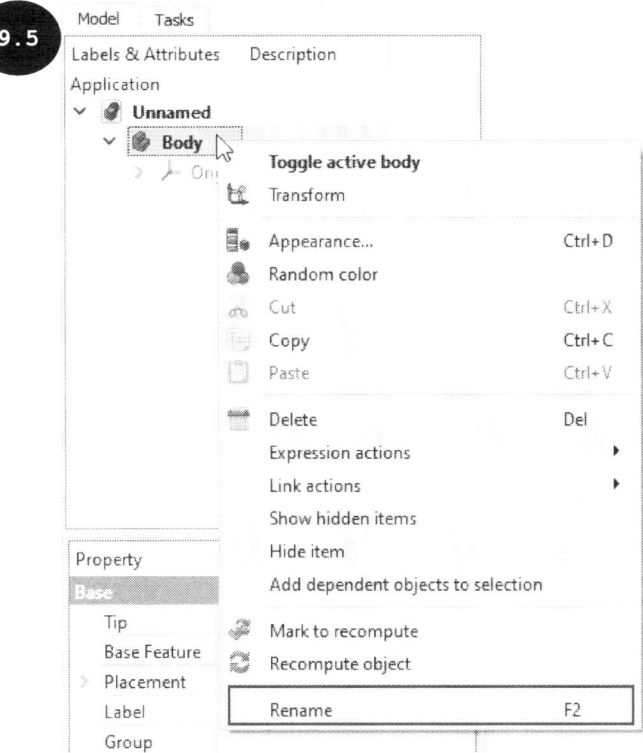

Now, you can create features of the active body/part similarly as discussed in earlier chapters.

6. Click on the **Create sketch** tool in the **Part Design Helper** toolbar (see Figure 9.6) and then select a plane for creating the sketch of the base feature. The **Sketcher** workbench gets invoked.

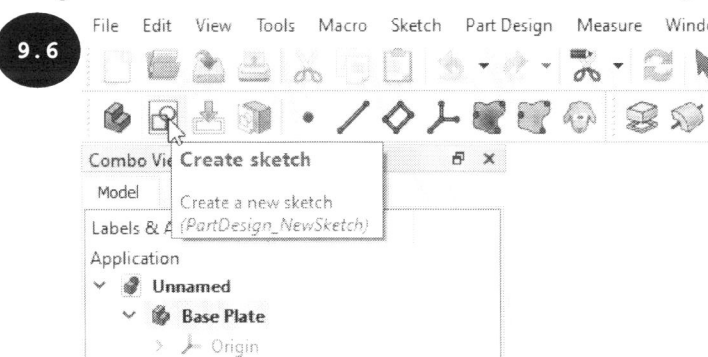

7. Create the sketch of the feature by using the sketching tool, refer to Figure 9.7.

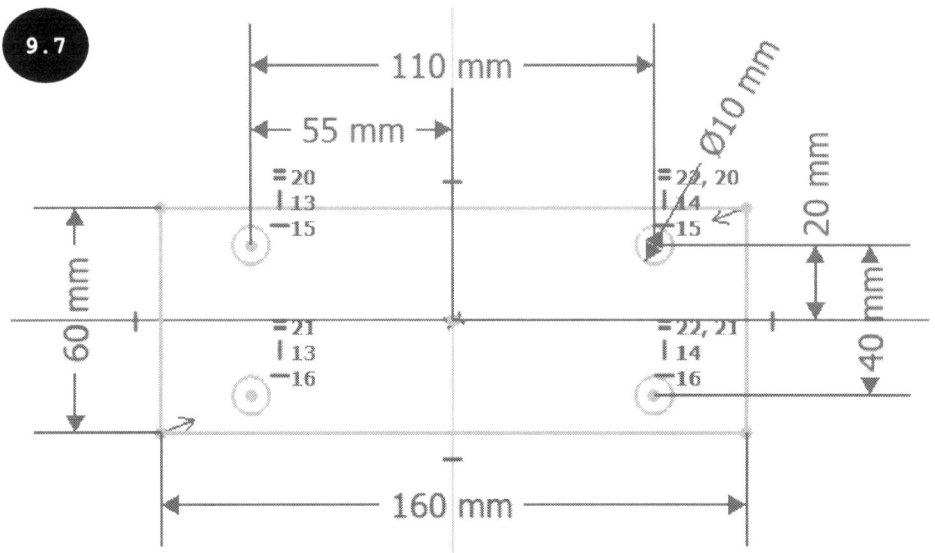

8. After creating the sketch, exit the **Sketcher** workbench and then convert the sketch into a 3D solid feature by using the solid modeling tool such as **Pad** and **Revolution**, refer to Figure 9.8. In this figure, a pad feature is created by extruding the sketch to a depth of 10 mm by using the **Pad** tool.

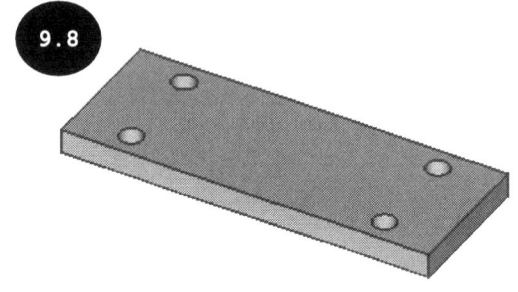

9. Similarly, you can create the remaining features of the body/part one by one.

    After creating all the features of the first body/part, you can create the second body/part of the assembly.

10. Click on the **Create body** tool in the **Part Design Helper** toolbar, see Figure 9.9. A new empty body with the default name "**Body001**" gets created and appears in the **Tree View** of the **Model** tab, see Figure 9.10. Also, it becomes the active body of the current document.

Now, you can rename the newly added body, as required.

11. Rename the newly added body/part in the **Tree View** of the **Model** tab, as discussed earlier.

Now, you can create features of the second body/part of the assembly.

12. Ensure that the second body/part is activated in the **Tree View**.

Note: You can activate a body at any point in time by double-clicking on its name in the **Tree View**.

13. Click on the **Create sketch** tool in the **Part Design Helper** toolbar (see Figure 9.11) and then select a plane for creating the sketch of the base feature of the second body. The **Sketcher** workbench gets invoked.

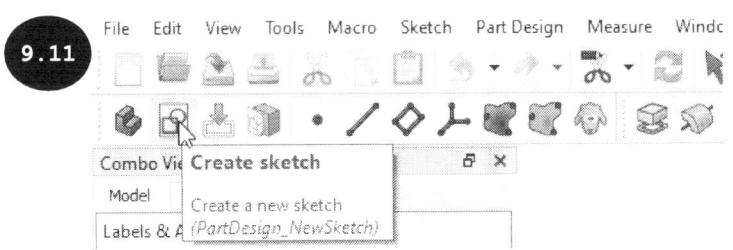

Note: You can also select a planar face of an existing body/part as the sketching plane for creating the base feature of the currently active body. For doing so, select a planar face of an existing body in the 3D View area and then click on the **Create sketch** tool in the **Part Design Helper** toolbar. The **Reference** dialog box appears, see Figure 9.12. In this dialog box, select the **Make dependent copy** radio button for making the currently active body a dependent body of the existing selected body. Next, click on the **OK** button in the dialog box. The **Sketcher** workbench gets invoked. Ignore the error message that may appear in the **Report view** window at the bottom of the screen and close the **Report view** window by clicking on the cross mark that appears in its top right corner.

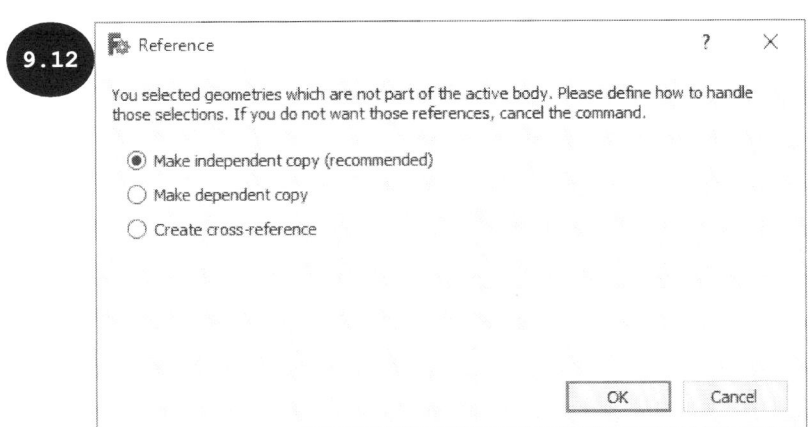

14. Create the sketch of the feature by using the sketching tool, refer to Figure 9.13.

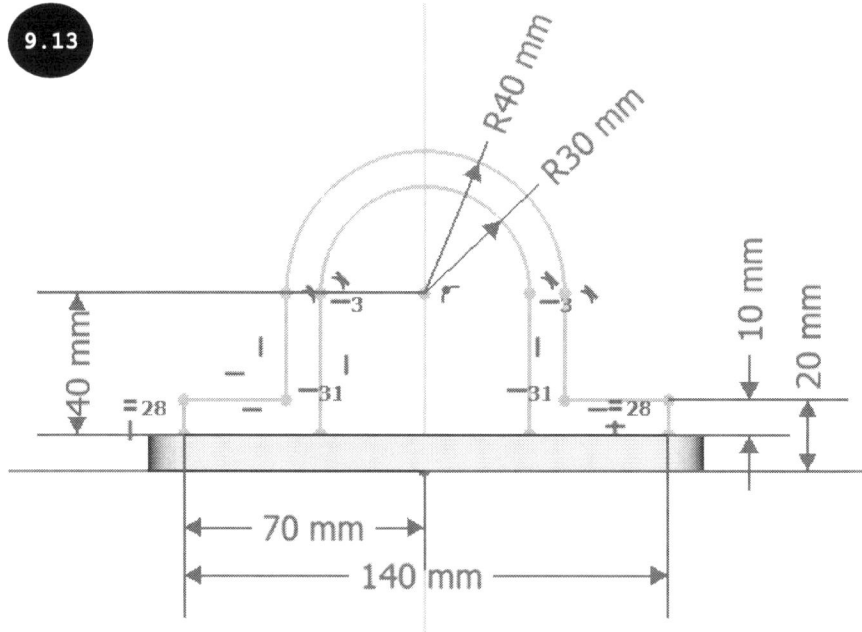

9.13

15. After creating the sketch, exit the **Sketcher** workbench and then convert the sketch into a 3D solid feature by using the solid modeling tool such as **Pad** and **Revolution**, refer to Figure 9.14. In this figure, a pad feature is created by extruding the sketch symmetrically to a depth of 60 mm by using the **Pad** tool.

16. Create the remaining features of the body/part one by one, refer to Figure 9.15.

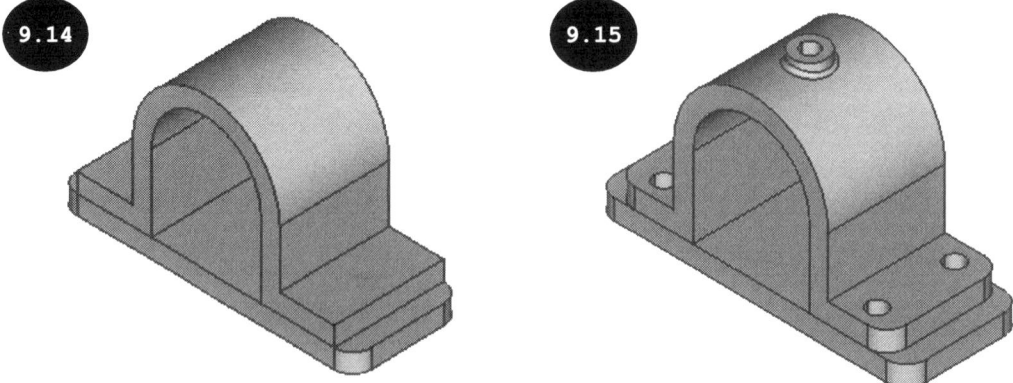

9.14   **9.15**

17. Similarly, you can create the other parts of the assembly one by one as separate bodies within the same part document.

18. After creating all the components of an assembly as individual bodies, you can save the document by using the **Save** tool of the **File** toolbar.

Creating an Assembly Using Bottom-up Approach

Inserting already created components of an assembly one by one into an assembly workbench and then assembling them by applying constraints is known as the Bottom-up assembly approach.

As mentioned earlier, as of this release of FreeCAD, there is no official assembly workbench included with the system, by default. However, you can use the **A2plus** assembly workbench for creating assemblies. The **A2plus** is an external workbench to assemble different parts of an assembly in FreeCAD. It is an add-on to FreeCAD and it can be installed easily in FreeCAD via **Addon Manager**.

Installing the A2plus Workbench

1. Click on the **Tools > Addon manager** in the **Standard Menu**, see Figure 9.16. After checking the connection to GitHub, the **Addon Manager** window appears with a list of external workbenches, see Figure 9.17.

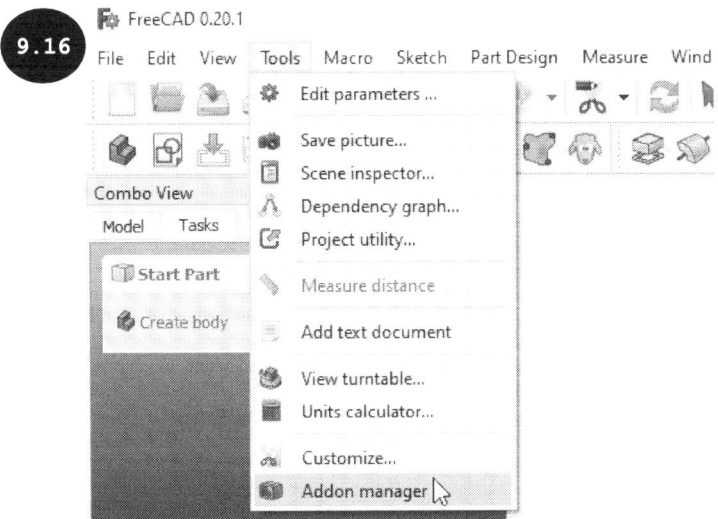

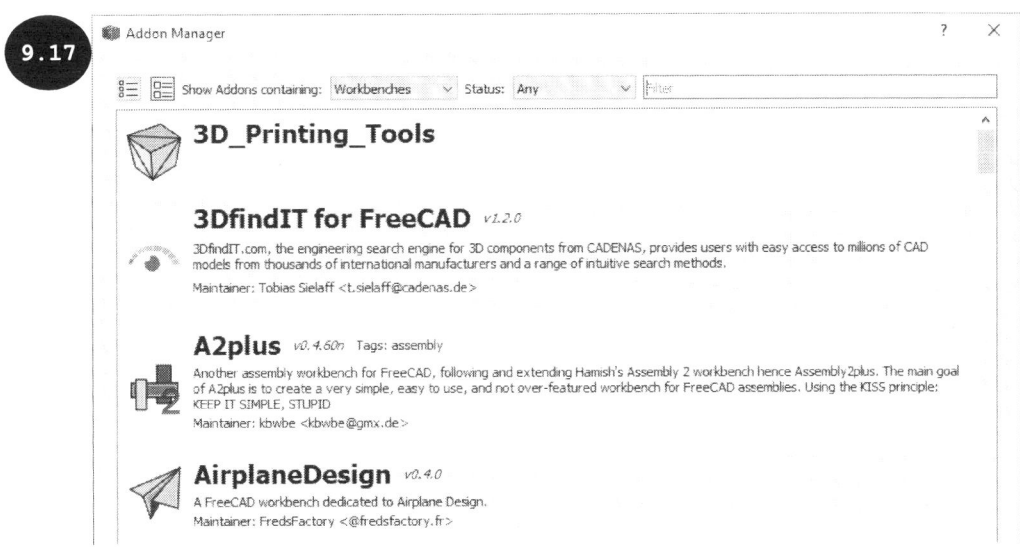

Tip: The **A2plus** code is developed and hosted on GitHub and can also be installed manually by copying it into FreeCAD's **Mod** directory.

2. Click on the **A2plus** workbench in the **Addon Manager** window. The **A2plus** documentation page appears in the **Addon Manager** window, see Figure 9.18.

3. Click on the **Install** button available in the upper right corner of the **Addon Manager** window, see Figure 9.18. The installation process gets started, and once it is completed, the **Installation succeeded** window appears informing that the **A2plus** gets installed successfully. Click on the **Close** button in this window.

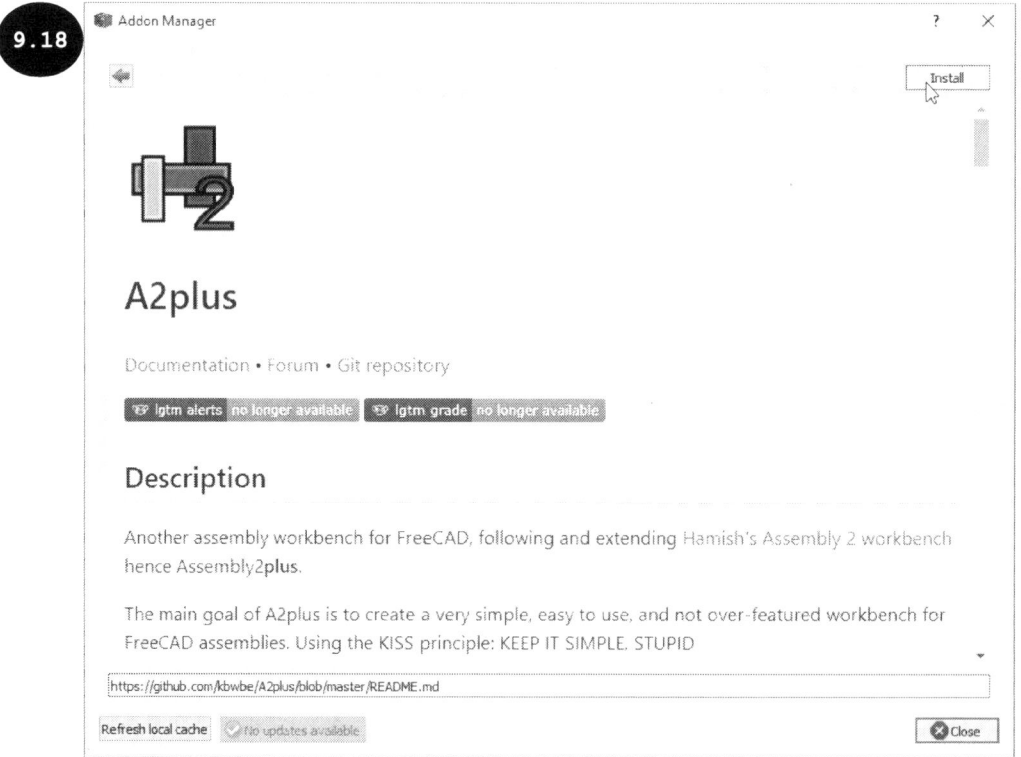

4. Exit the **Addon Manager** window by clicking on the **Close** button. You are prompted to restart FreeCAD for changes to take effect, see Figure 9.19.

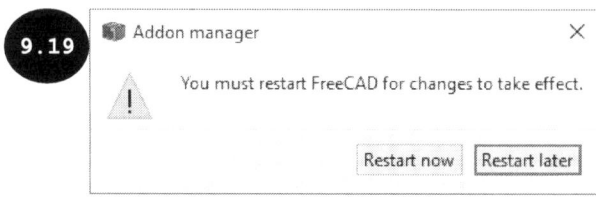

5. Click on the **Restart now** button to restart FreeCAD. Ensure that you have saved all your work before restarting FreeCAD.

Now, you can invoke the **A2plus** workbench.

6. Start a new empty document by clicking on the **Create new** icon on the **Start page** (see Figure 9.20) or pressing the CTRL + N keys.

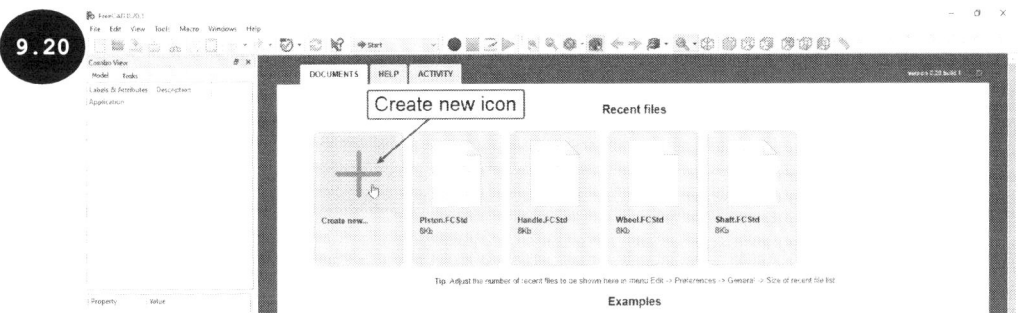

7. Invoke the **Workbench Selector** in the **Workbench** toolbar and then select the **A2plus** workbench, see Figure 9.21. The **A2plus** workbench gets invoked. Now, you can insert components of an assembly in this workbench and assemble them by applying constraints.

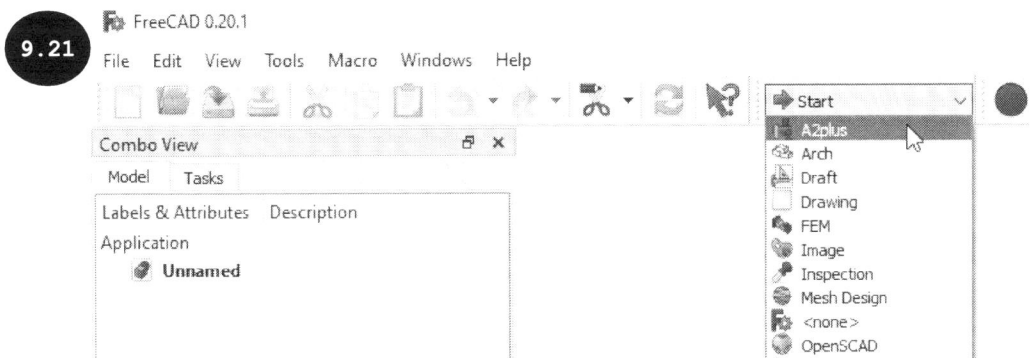

Inserting Components of an Assembly

Before you insert components of an assembly in the **A2plus** workbench, you need to save the document. After saving the document, you can insert components. The method for inserting components of an assembly in the **A2plus** workbench is discussed below:

1. Save the document by using the **Save** tool of the **File** toolbar, see Figure 9.22. It is recommended to save the document with a unique name for the assembly, in the same location where all the components of the assembly are saved.

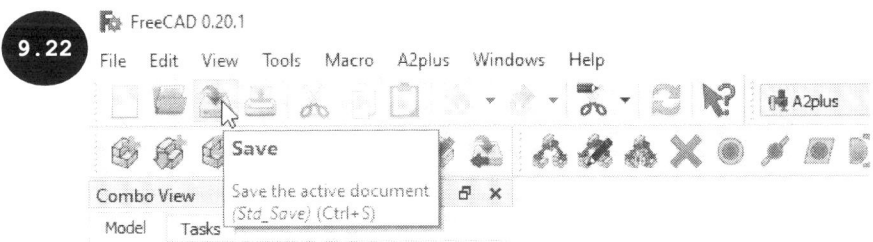

Now, you can insert a component of an assembly in the **A2plus** workbench.

2.   Click on the **Add a part from an external file** tool in the **A2p_Part** toolbar, see Figure 9.23. The **Select FreeCAD document to import part from** dialog box appears, see Figure 9.24.

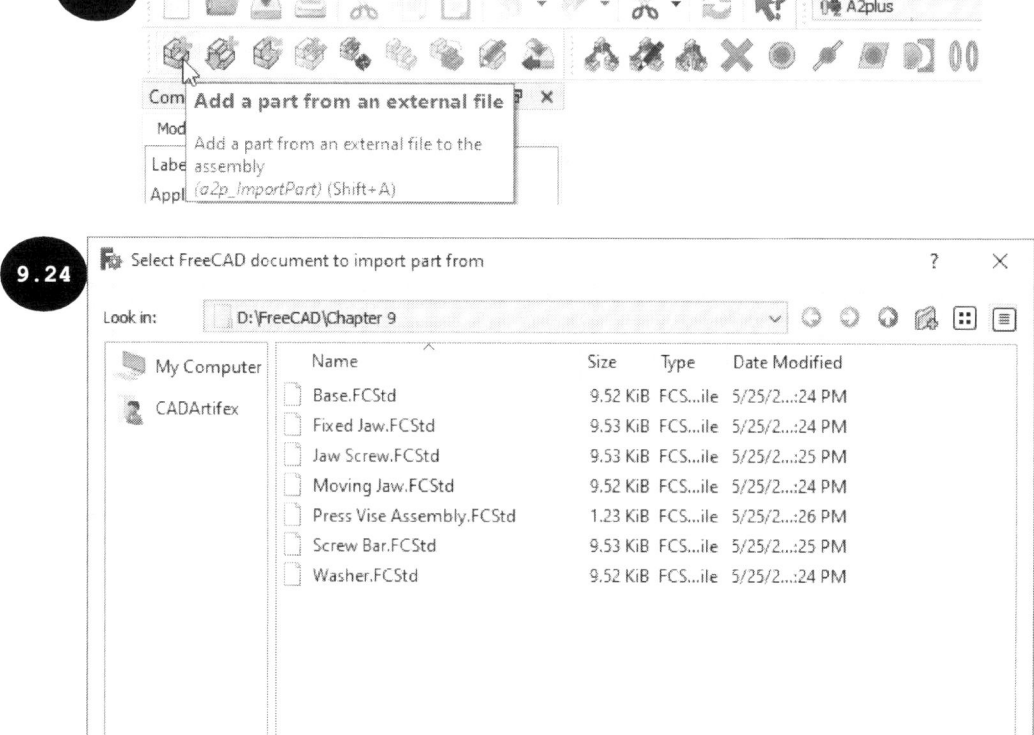

3.   Browse to the required location and then select the component to be inserted. Next, click on the **Open** button in the dialog box. The selected component gets inserted and placed at the default location (origin) in the 3D View area of the workbench. Also, it becomes a fixed component, by default. Notice that the name of the inserted component is listed in the **Tree View** of the **Model** tab under the name of the assembly document, see Figure 9.25.

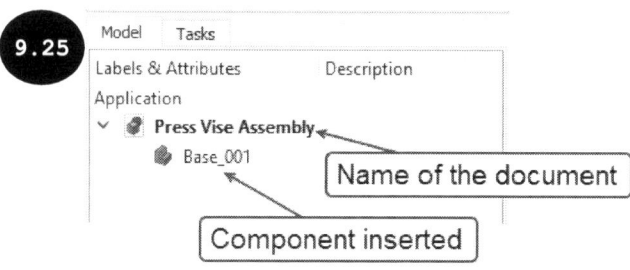

Tip: The number **001** is added as a suffix to the name of the inserted component indicating that it is the first occurrence of the component.

Now, you need to insert the second component of the assembly.

4. Click on the **Add a part from an external file** tool in the **A2p_Part** toolbar, see Figure 9.26. The **Select FreeCAD document to import part from** dialog box appears.

5. Select the component to be inserted and then click on the **Open** button in the dialog box. The selected component gets attached to the cursor.

6. Click the left mouse button anywhere in the 3D View area to define the position of the attached component. The component is placed in the defined location in the 3D View area, see Figure 9.27. Also, its name gets added in the **Tree View** of the **Model** tab.

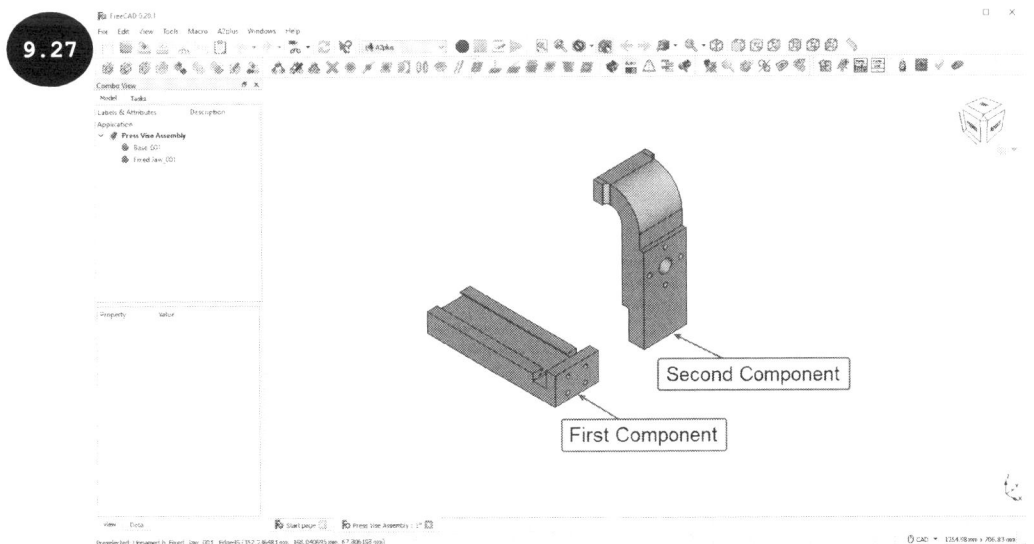

Note that the position of the second component is not fixed in the 3D View area, by default. You need to fix its position by applying constraints.

7. Similarly, you can insert other components of the assembly one by one. However, it is recommended to first fix the position of the second component concerning the first component by applying the required constraints.

Applying Constraints

Constraints are used for positioning components of an assembly by restricting or reducing their degrees of freedom. In FreeCAD, you can apply a constraint between two geometries (faces, edges, planes, or vertices) of different components. The method for applying a constraint is discussed below:

1. Select two geometries such as faces, edges, planes, vertices, or a combination of these, from two different components by pressing the CTRL key, see Figure 9.28. In this figure, two planar faces of different components are selected as geometries to apply a constraint. Notice that as soon as you select geometries for applying a constraint, the constraint tools that can be applied between the selected geometries get enabled in the **A2p_Constraint** toolbar, see Figure 9.29.

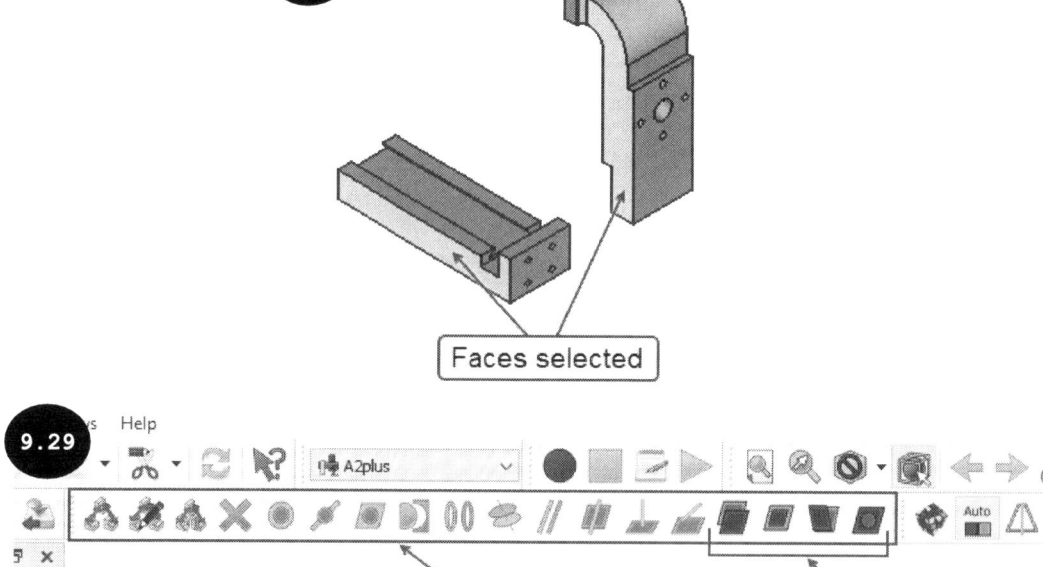

Note that the tools to apply constraints get enabled in the **A2p_Constraint** toolbar depending upon the type of geometries selected. Different types of constraints are discussed next.

Point on Point ● **:** The Point on Point constraint is used for making vertices or points of two components coincident with each other. You can also select circles or spheres for applying this constraint between their respective center points. You can apply this constraint by clicking on the **Add PointIdentity constraint** tool that is enabled in the **A2p_Constraint** toolbar after selecting two vertices or points of different components.

Point on Line ⬦ **:** The Point on Line constraint is used for placing a vertex or a point of one component on the edge of another component. You can apply this constraint by clicking on the **Add PointOnLine constraint** tool that is enabled in the **A2p_Constraint** toolbar after selecting a vertex or a point of one component and an edge of another component.

Point on Plane : The Point on Plane constraint is used for placing a vertex or a point of one component lying on a plane or a planar face of another component. You can apply this constraint by clicking the **Add PointOnPlane constraint** tool that is enabled in the **A2p_Constraint** toolbar after selecting a vertex or a point of one component and a plane or a planar face of another component.

Sphere on Sphere : The Sphere on Sphere constraint is used for making centers of two spherical faces or vertices of different components coincident with each other. You can apply this constraint by clicking on the **Add SphereCenterIdent constraint** tool that is enabled in the **A2p_Constraint** toolbar after selecting two spherical faces or vertices of different components.

Circular Edge on Circular Edge : The Circular Edge on Circular Edge constraint is used for making two circular edges of different components concentric to each other. You can apply this constraint by clicking the **Add CircularEdge constraint** tool that is enabled in the **A2p_Constraint** toolbar after selecting two circular edges of different components.

Axis Coincident : The Axis Coincident constraint is used for making the axes of two cylindrical faces or the linear edges of different components coincide with each other. You can apply this constraint by clicking on the **Add AxisCoincident constraint** tool that is enabled in the **A2p_Constraint** toolbar after selecting two cylindrical faces or linear edges of different components.

Axis Parallel : The Axis Parallel constraint is used for making axes of two cylindrical faces or the linear edges of different components parallel to each other. You can apply this constraint by clicking on the **Add AxisParallel constraint** tool that is enabled in the **A2p_Constraint toolbar** after selecting two cylindrical faces or linear edges of different components.

Axis on Plane parallel : The Axis on Plane parallel constraint is used for making an axis of a cylindrical face or a linear edge of one component parallel to a plane or a planar face of another component. You can apply this constraint by clicking on the **Add AxisPlaneParallel constraint** tool that is enabled in the **A2p_Constraint** toolbar after selecting a cylindrical face or a linear edge of one component and a plane or a planar face of another component.

Axis on Plane normal : The Axis on Plane normal constraint is used for making an axis of a cylindrical face or a linear edge of one component normal to a plane or a planar face of another component. You can apply this constraint by clicking on the **Add AxisPlaneNormal constraint** tool that is enabled in the **A2p_Constraint** toolbar after selecting a cylindrical face or a linear edge of one component and a plane or a planar face of another component.

Axis on Plane angle : The Axis on Plane angle constraint is used for making an axis of a cylindrical face or a linear edge of one component at an angle to a plane or a planar face of another component. Note that you can specify an angle value in the **Constraint properties** dialog box that appears on clicking the **Add AxisPlaneAngle constraint** tool in the **A2p_Constraint** toolbar after selecting a cylindrical face or a linear edge of one component and a plane or a planar face of another component.

Plane Parallel : The Plane Parallel constraint is used for making two planes or planar faces of different components parallel to each other. You can apply this constraint by clicking on the **Add**

PlanesParallel constraint tool that is enabled in the **A2p_Constraint** toolbar after selecting two planes or planar faces of different components.

Plane on Plane : The Plane on Plane constraint is used for making two planes or planar faces of different components coincident with each other. You can apply this constraint by clicking on the **Add PlaneCoincident constraint** tool that is enabled in the **A2p_Constraint** toolbar after selecting two planes or planar faces of different components.

Plane Angular : The Plane Angular constraint is used for making two planes or planar faces of different components at an angle to each other. Note that you can specify an angle value in the **Constraint properties** dialog box that appears on clicking the **Add AngledPlanes constraint** tool in the **A2p_Constraint** toolbar after selecting two planes or planar faces of different components.

Coincidence at Center of Mass : The Coincidence at Center of Mass constraint is used for making the center of mass of two planes or planar faces of different components coincide. You can apply this constraint by clicking on the **Add CenterOfMass constraint** tool that is enabled in the **A2p_Constraint** toolbar after selecting two planes or planar faces of different components.

2. After selecting two geometries of different components, click on the required constraint tool to be applied between them in the **A2p_Constraint** toolbar. The **Constraint properties** dialog box appears, see Figure 9.30. Also, the preview of the components appears in the 3D View area, after the selected constraint is applied between the geometries, see Figure 9.31. In this figure, two planar faces of components coincide each other.

Note: The options in the **Constraint properties** dialog box are used to define the alignment type, flip the alignment direction, specify an offset distance between the selected geometries, and so on. Note that the availability of options in this dialog box depends upon the type of constraint being applied.

3. Specify the required options in the **Constraint properties** dialog box, if needed, and then click on the **Accept** button. The constraint gets applied between the selected geometries of the components. Also, the name of the applied constraint with a numerical label gets added under its component node in the **Tree View** of the **Model** tab, see Figure 9.32.

4. Similarly, you can apply other constraints between the geometries of the components to fix all their required degrees of freedom, see Figure 9.33. In this figure, three Plane on Plane constraints are applied between three different sets of planar faces of the components to fix all their degrees of freedom.

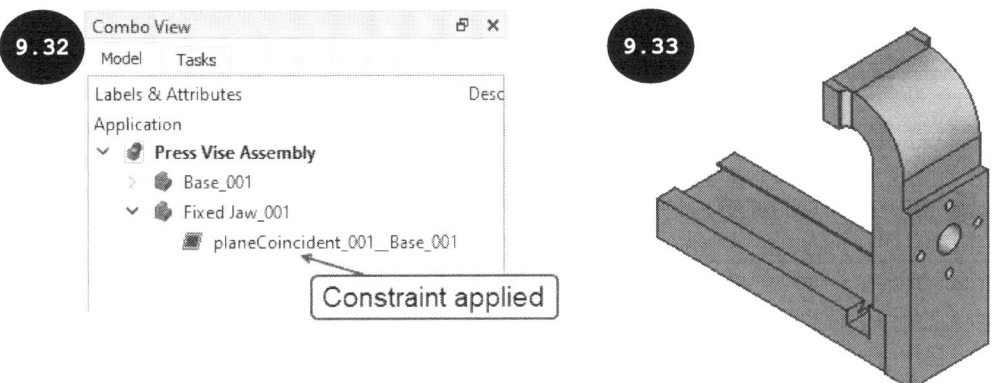

Constraint applied

Checking or Tagging Degrees of Freedom

In FreeCAD, you can tag the degrees of freedom information of each component of the assembly. For doing so, click on the **Print detailed DOF information** tool in the **A2p_View** toolbar, see Figure 9.34. The degrees of freedom information get tagged to each component of the assembly in the 3D View area, see Figure 9.35.

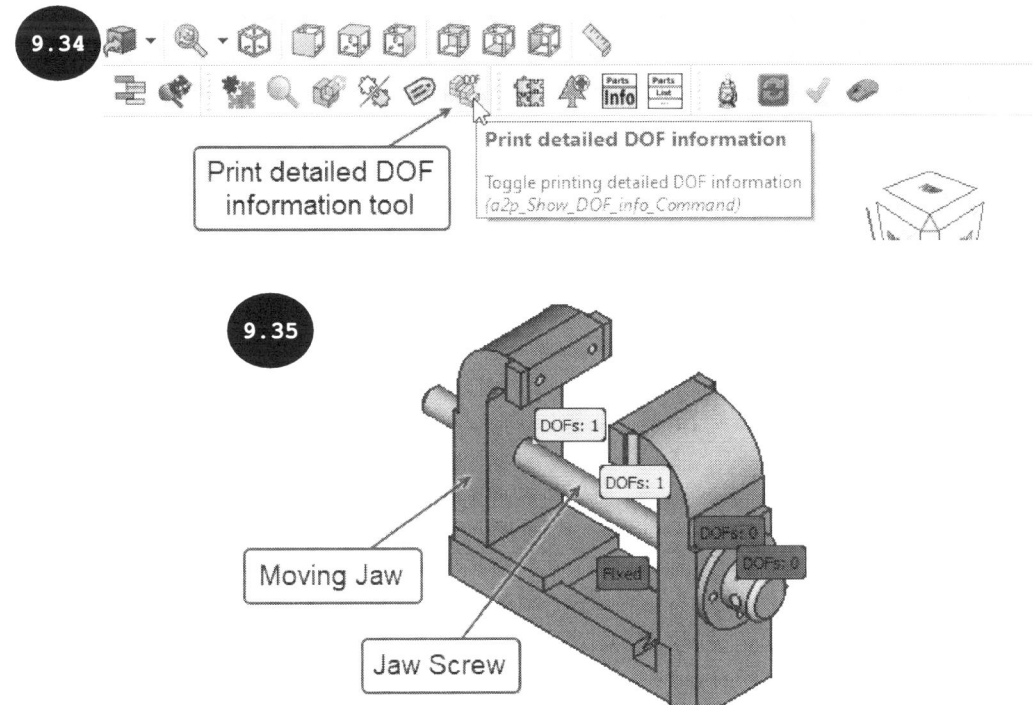

Print detailed DOF information tool

Print detailed DOF information

Toggle printing detailed DOF information (a2p_Show_DOF_info_Command)

DOFs: 1

DOFs: 1

DOFs: 0

DOFs: 0

Fixed

Moving Jaw

Jaw Screw

Note: In Figure 9.35, the degrees of freedom of all the components are fixed except the Moving Jaw and Jaw Screw components. Both these components have one free degree of freedom to enable a specific movement of the component. In the Moving Jaw component, one translational degree of freedom is kept free for its linear movement. In the Jaw Screw component, one rotational degree of freedom is kept free for its rotational movement.

To remove the display of degrees of freedom tags, click on the **Print detailed DOF information** tool 🥢 again in the **A2p_View** toolbar.

Moving a Component along its Free DOFs

In FreeCAD, you can move a component of an assembly along its free degrees of freedom for checking its movements. The method for moving a component along its free DOFs is discussed below:

1. Click on the **Move the selected part under constraints** tool in the **A2p_Part** toolbar, see Figure 9.36.

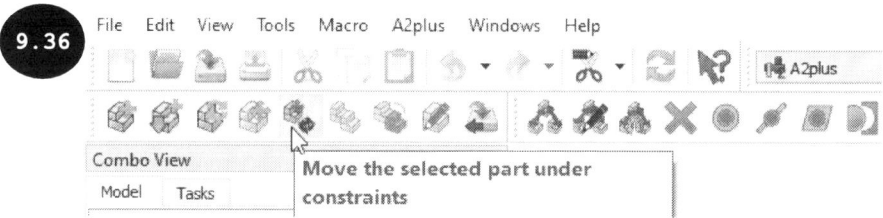

2. Click on the component to be moved into the 3D View area. The selected component gets attached to the cursor. Also, as you move the cursor, the component begins to move along its free degrees of freedom.

3. After moving the selected component along its free degree of freedom in the 3D View area, click to define its placement in a new location.

4. Similarly, you can move other components of an assembly one at a time along their free degrees of freedom by using the **Move the selected part under constraints** tool.

Moving a Component along its Fixed DOFs

In FreeCAD, you can also move a component of an assembly along its fixed or restricted degrees of freedom. The method for moving a component along its fixed DOFs is discussed below:

1. Select a component of an assembly to be moved in the 3D View area irrespective of its fixed degrees of freedom.

2. Click on the **Move the selected part** tool in the **A2p_Part** toolbar, see Figure 9.37. The three translational and rotational handles appear in the 3D View area, see Figure 9.38. Also, the **Increments** sub-window appears in the **Task Panel**, see Figure 9.39. Note that the **Move the selected part** tool is enabled only if one or more components of an assembly are inserted as external files in the **A2plus** workbench.

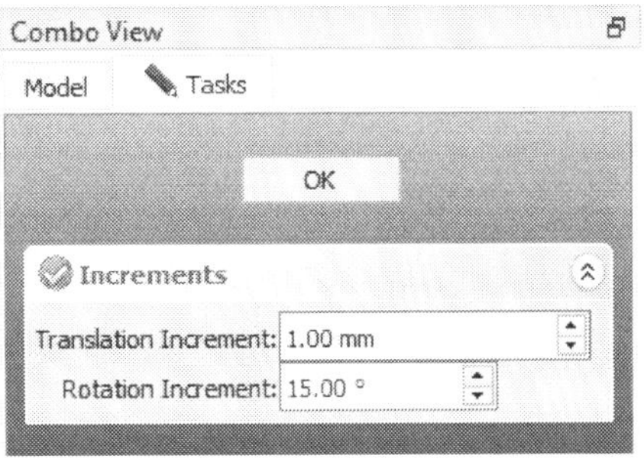

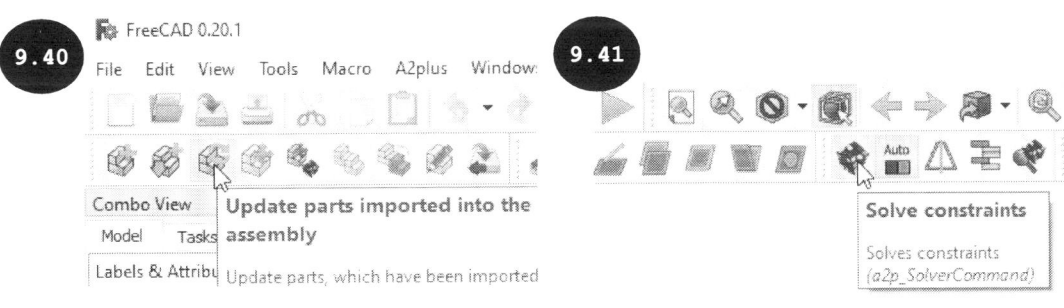

3. Drag the required translational or rotational handle of the selected component to move or rotate it along or about its respective direction irrespective of its fixed degrees of freedom. Alternatively, enter translational or rotational incremental values in the respective fields of the **Increments** sub-window for translating or rotating the selected component. Next, click on the **OK** button in the **Task Panel**.

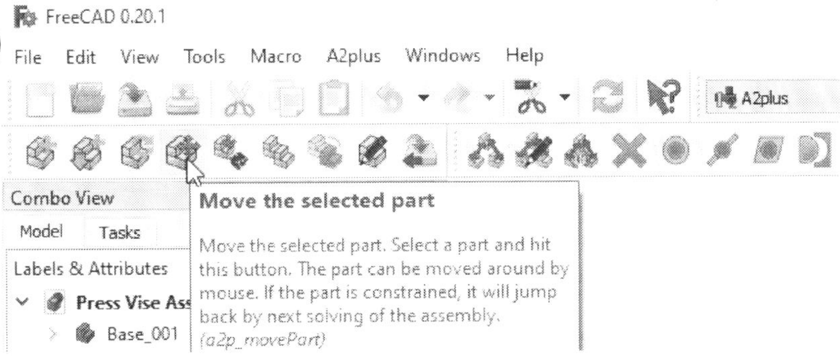

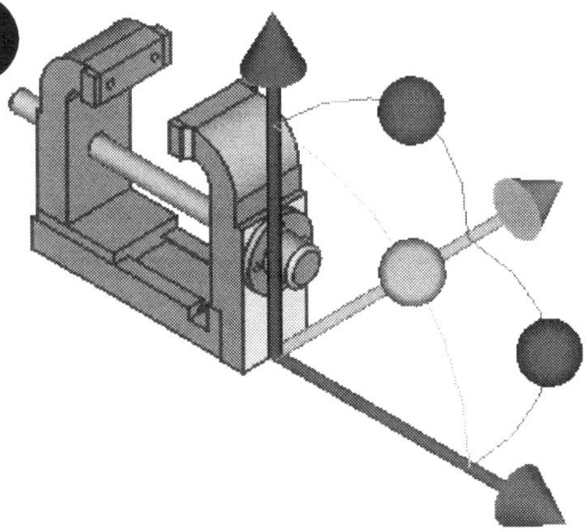

4. After moving or rotating a component along its fixed DOF, click on the **Update parts imported into the assembly** tool (see Figure 9.40) or the **Solve constraints** tool (see Figure 9.41) to solve the applied constraints and move the component back to its original position. Note that the component gets jumped to its original position only if it is moved or rotated in its fixed degree of freedom.

Tutorial 1

Create an assembly shown in Figure 9.42 by using the Top-down assembly approach in the **Part Design** workbench. Different views and dimensions of each component of the assembly are shown in Figures 9.43 through 9.46. All dimensions are in mm.

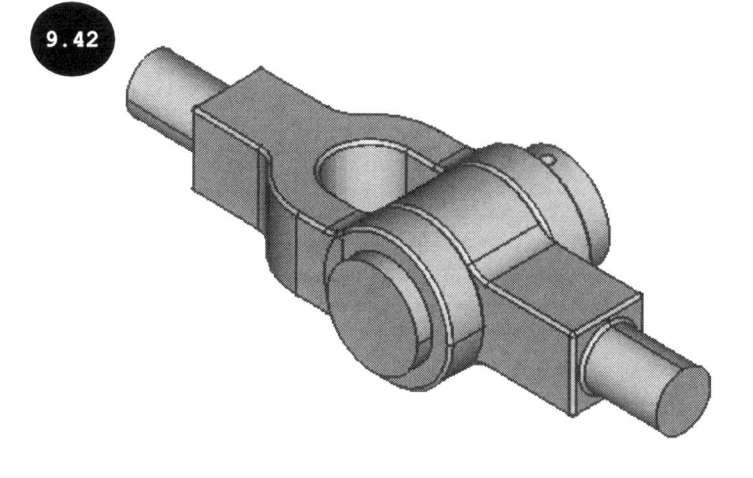

9.42

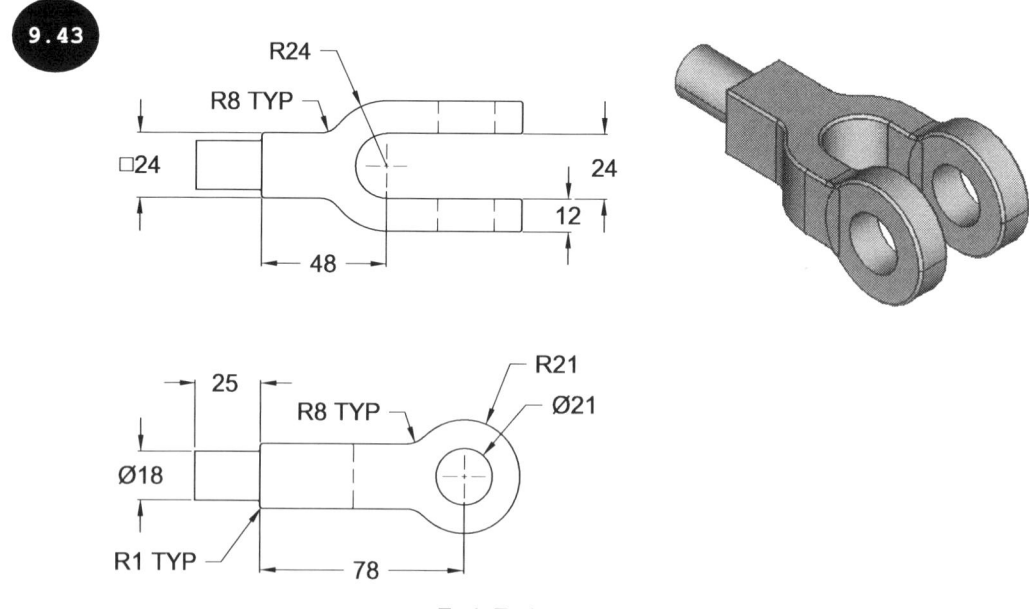

9.43

R24
R8 TYP
□24
24
12
48

25
R21
R8 TYP
Ø21
Ø18
R1 TYP
78

Fork End

9.44

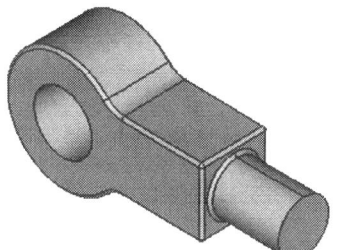

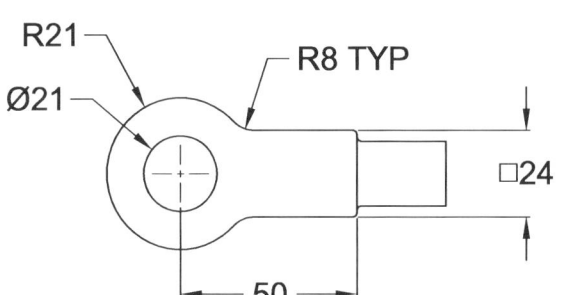

R21

Ø21

R8 TYP

□24

50

Eye End

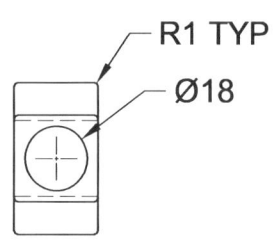

R1 TYP

Ø18

9.45

Ø4

53

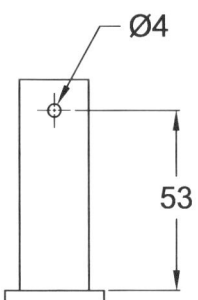

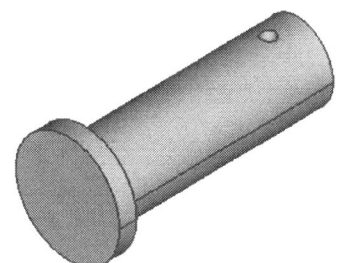

Ø30

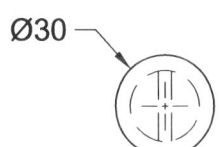

5

Ø21

62

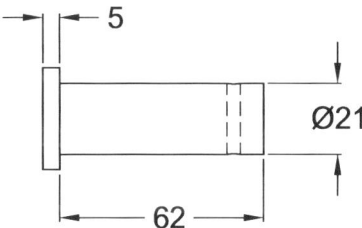

Pin

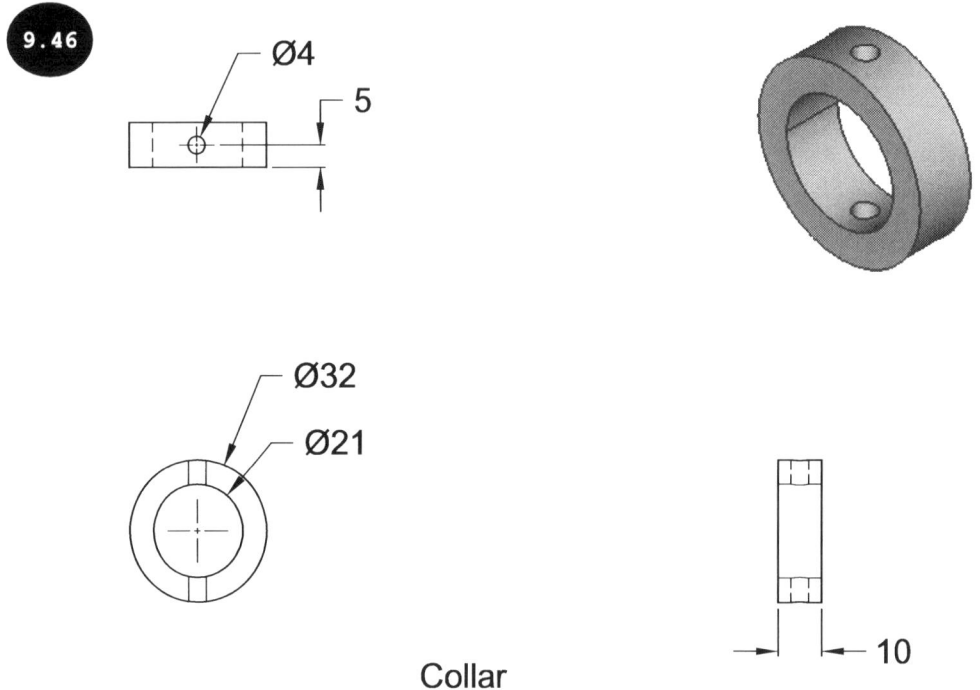

Collar

Section 1: Starting FreeCAD and a New Empty Document

1. Start FreeCAD by double-clicking on the **FreeCAD 0.20** icon on your desktop. The startup user interface of FreeCAD appears.

2. Click on the **New** tool in the **File** toolbar (see Figure 9.47) or press the **CTRL + N** keys. A new empty document gets invoked with the default name "**unnamed: 1**".

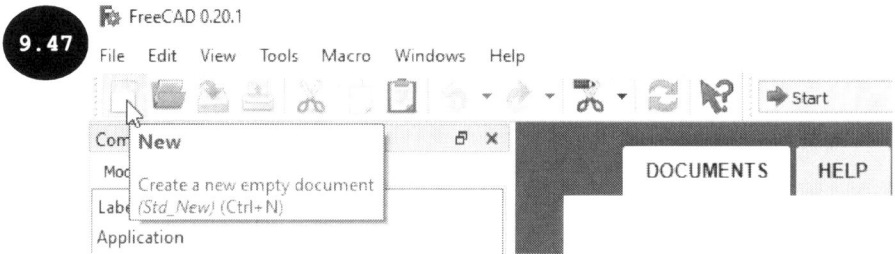

Section 2: Invoking the Part Design Workbench and Specifying Units

Now, you need to invoke the **Part Design** workbench for creating the assembly, as mentioned in the tutorial description.

1. Invoke the **Workbench Selector** in the **Workbench** toolbar and then select the **Part Design** workbench, see Figure 9.48. The **Part Design** workbench gets invoked.

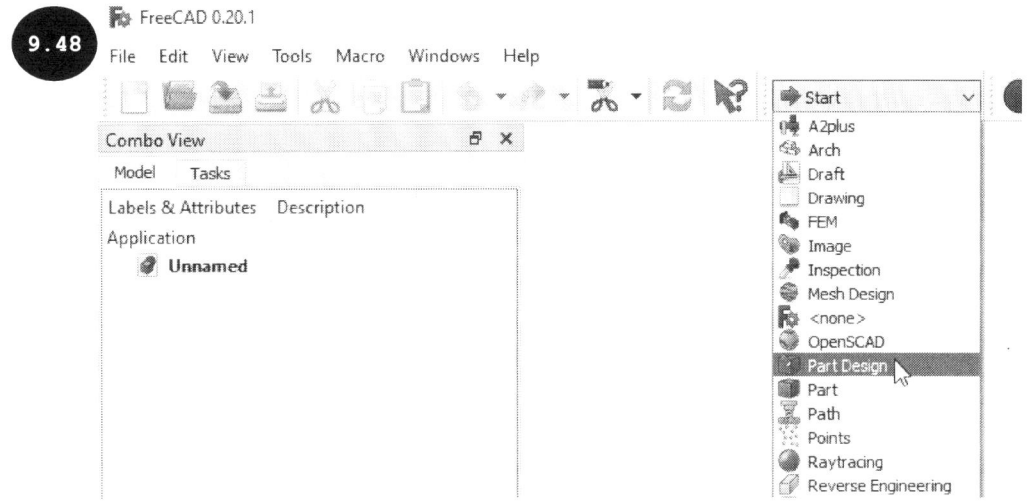

Now, you need to define the units of measurement for the current document.

2. Specify millimeter (mm) as the measurement unit for the document by using the **Preferences** dialog box.

Section 3: Creating the First Component of the Assembly

Now, you can create the first component (Fork End) of the assembly as a body within the **Part Design** workbench.

1. Click on the **Create body** tool in the **Part Design Helper** toolbar, see Figure 9.49. A new empty body with the default name "**Body**" gets created and appears in the **Tree View** of the **Model** tab, see Figure 9.50. Also, it becomes the active body of the current document.

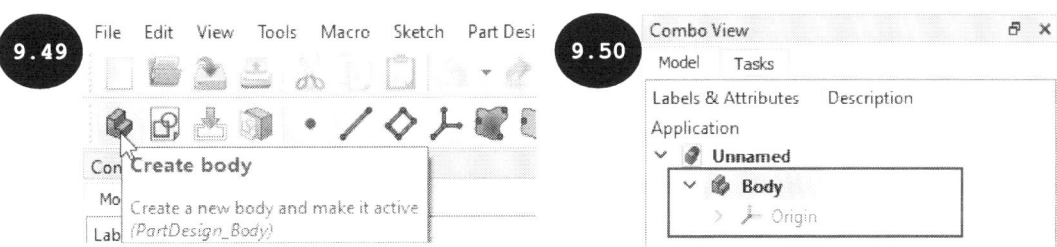

Now, you need to rename the newly added body.

2. Click on the **Model** tab of the **Combo View** for displaying the **Tree View** and then right-click on the newly created body to display a shortcut menu, see Figure 9.51.

3. Click on the **Rename** option in the shortcut menu.

4. Enter **Fork End** as the name of the body in the edit field that appears in the **Tree View**. Next, click anywhere in the 3D View area. The name of the body gets changed to Fork End, as specified.

Now, you can create features of the Fork End component of the assembly.

5. Click on the **Create sketch** tool in the **Part Design Helper** toolbar (see Figure 9.52) and then select the **XY_Plane** as the sketching plane. The **Sketcher** workbench gets invoked.

6. Create the sketch of the base feature by using the sketching tool, refer to Figure 9.53.

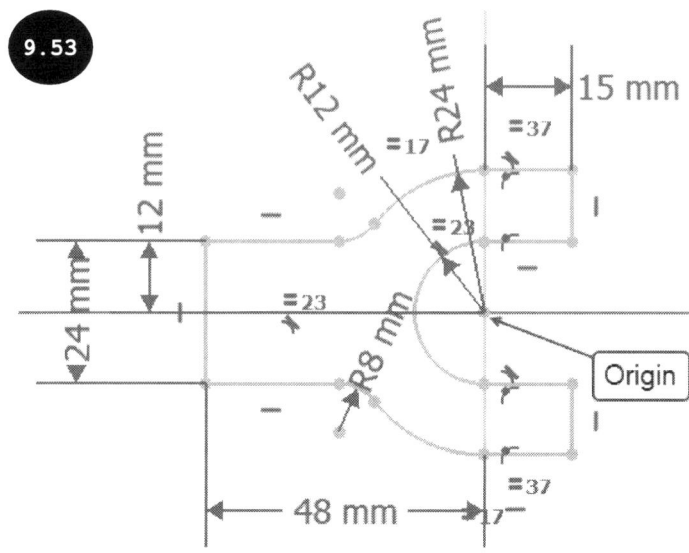

7. After creating the sketch, exit the **Sketcher** workbench and then extrude the sketch to a length of 24 mm, symmetrically on both sides of the sketching plane by using the **Pad** tool, see Figure 9.54.

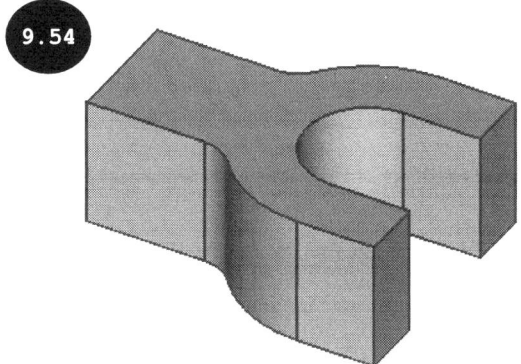

9.54

Now, you need to create the second feature of the Fork End component.

8. Select the front planar face of the base feature (see Figure 9.55) and then click on the **Create sketch** tool in the **Part Design Helper** toolbar, see Figure 9.56. The **Sketcher** workbench gets invoked and the selected planar face gets oriented normal to the viewing direction.

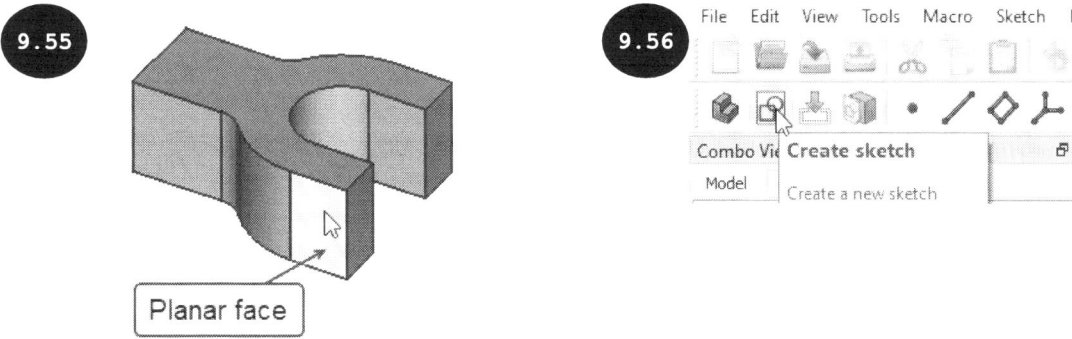

9.55

Planar face

9.56

9. Create the sketch (two concentric circles) of the second feature, see Figure 9.57.

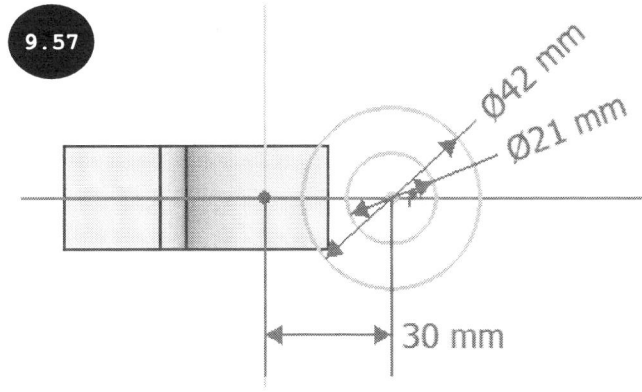

9.57

Ø42 mm

Ø21 mm

30 mm

10. Exit the **Sketcher** workbench and then extrude the sketch to a length of 12 mm toward the back side of the sketching plane by using the **Pad** tool. Figure 9.58 shows the model after creating the second feature.

9.58

Now, you need to create the third feature, which is a mirror feature.

11. Mirror the previously created feature by selecting the **XZ-Plane** as the mirroring plane using the **Mirrored** tool, see Figure 9.59.

9.59

Now, you need to create the fourth feature.

12. Invoke the **Sketcher** workbench by selecting the back planar face of the model as the sketching plane using the **Create sketch** tool, see Figure 9.60. Note that you need to rotate the model to select the back planar face of the model.

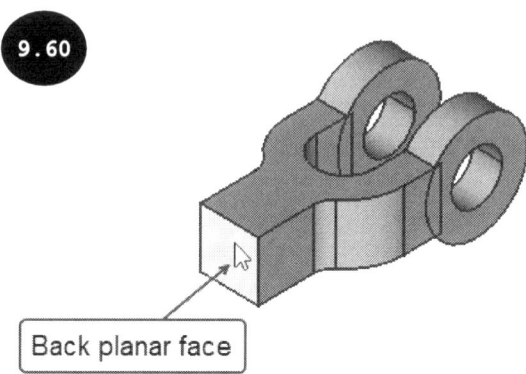

9.60

Back planar face

13. Create a circle of diameter 18 mm as the sketch of the fourth feature (see Figure 9.61). After creating the sketch, exit the **Sketcher** workbench.

14. Create a pad feature by extruding the sketch to a depth of 25 mm using the **Pad** tool, see Figure 9.62. Next, change the view orientation of the model to isometric.

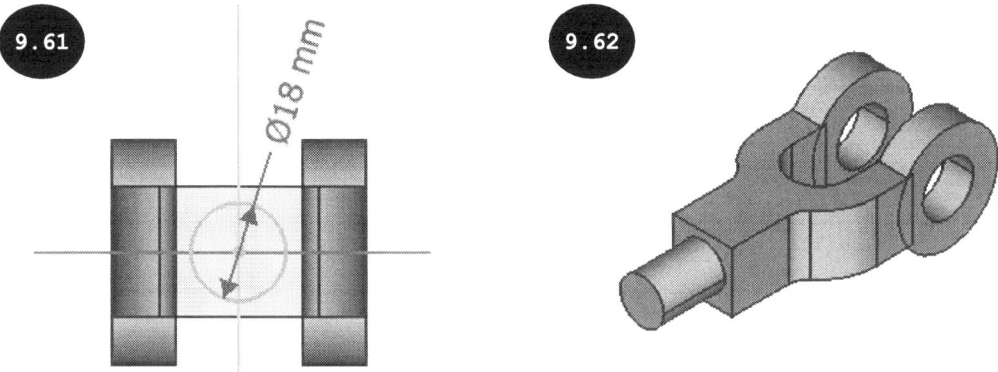

Now, you need to create fillets.

15. Select four edges of the model by pressing the CTRL key, see Figures 9.63 and 9.64. Note that you need to rotate the model for selecting these edges of the model.

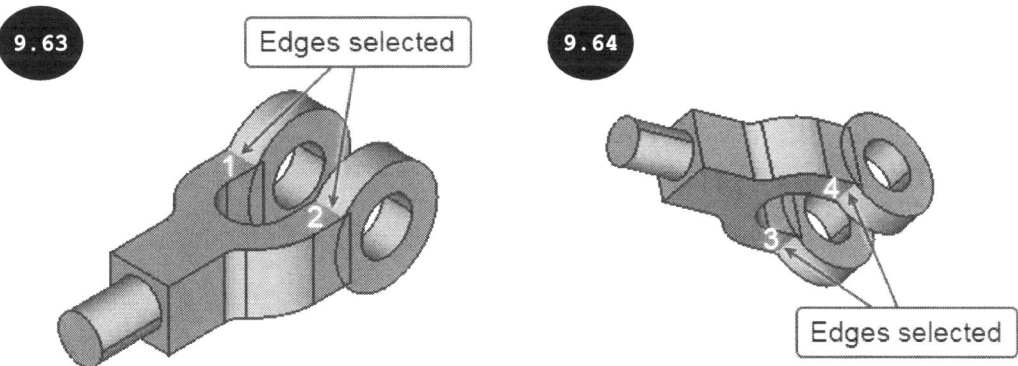

16. After selecting the edges, click on the **Fillet** tool, see Figure 9.65. The **Fillet parameters** sub-window appears in the **Task Panel**.

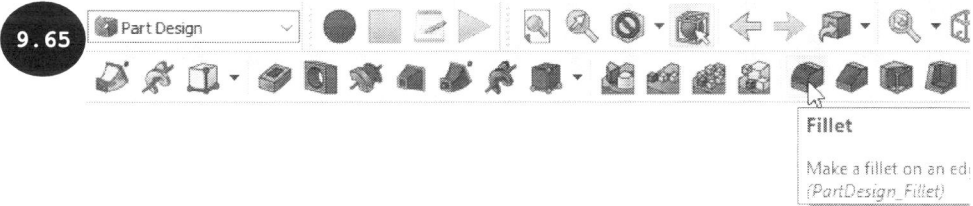

17. Enter **8** mm in the **Radius** field of the **Fillet parameters** sub-window and then click on the **OK** button in the **Task Panel**. A fillet of radius 8 mm gets created on the selected edges of the model, see Figure 9.66. Change the orientation of the model to isometric.

Now, you need to create fillets of radius 1 mm on the other edges of the model.

18. Rotate the model and then select the top and back planar faces of the model by pressing the CTRL key, see Figure 9.67.

19. Click on the **Fillet** tool and then enter **1** mm in the **Radius** field of the **Fillet parameters** sub-window that appears in the **Task Panel**. Next, click on the OK button. A fillet of radius 1 mm gets created on all the edges of the selected faces of the model, see Figure 9.68.

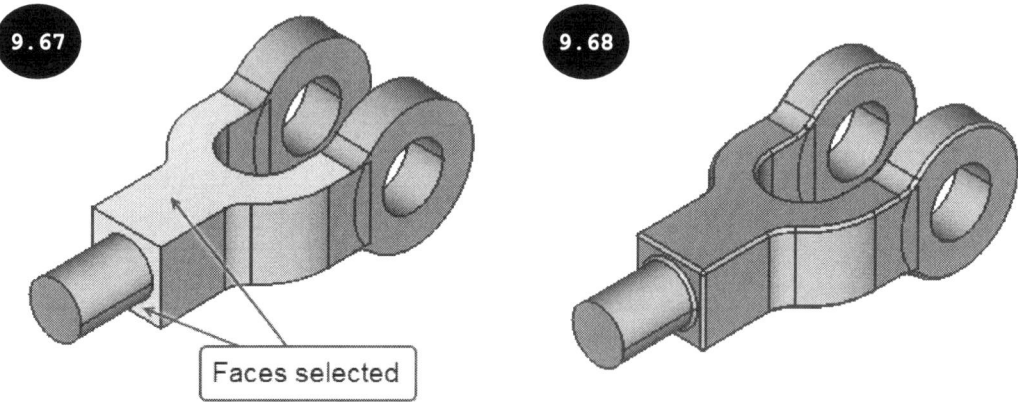

Faces selected

20. Change the orientation of the model to isometric, see Figure 9.69.

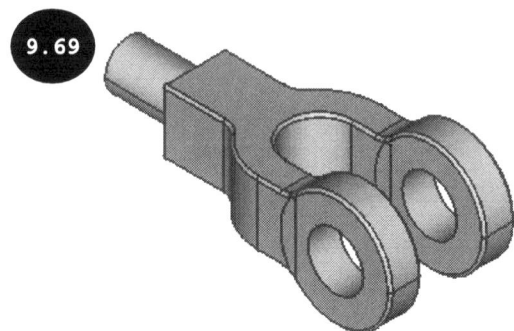

Section 4: Creating the Second Component

Now, you can create the second component (Eye End) of the assembly.

1. Click on the **Create body** tool in the **Part Design Helper** toolbar, see Figure 9.70. A new empty body with the default name "**Body001**" gets created and appears below the first component (Fork End) in the **Tree View** of the **Model** tab, see Figure 9.71. Also, it becomes the active body of the current document.

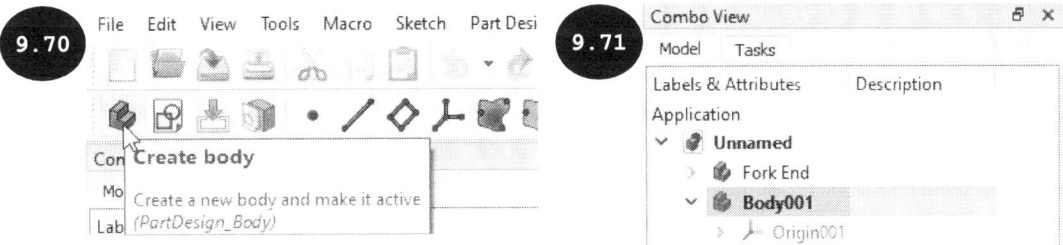

Now, you need to rename the newly added body.

2. Click on the **Model** tab of the **Combo View** for displaying the **Tree View** and then right-click on the newly created body "**Body001**" to display a shortcut menu, see Figure 9.72.

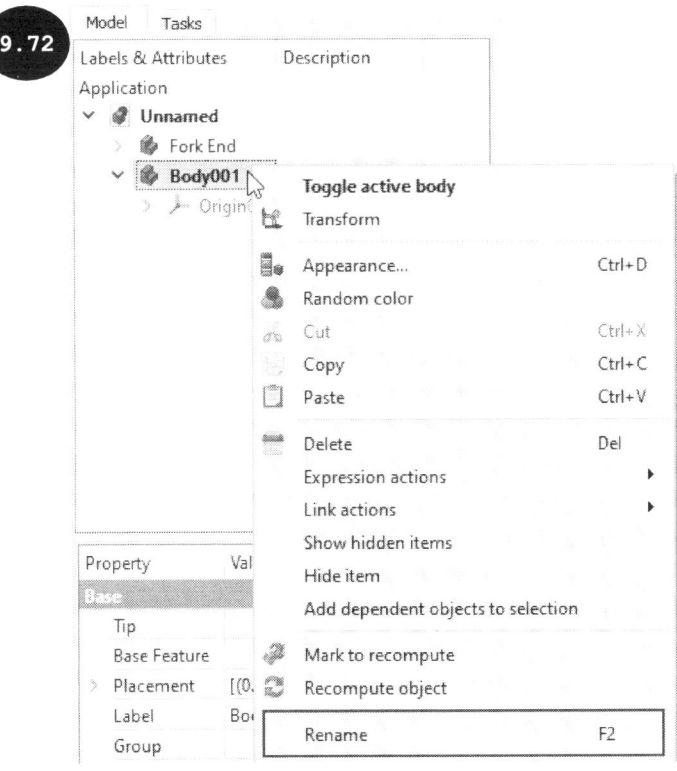

3. Click on the **Rename** option in the shortcut menu and then enter **Eye End** as the name of the body in the edit field that appears in **Tree View**. Next, click anywhere in the 3D View area. The name of the body gets changed to Eye End.

Now, you can create features of the **Eye End** component of the assembly.

4. Click on the **Create sketch** tool in the **Part Design Helper** toolbar (see Figure 9.73) and then select the **XZ_Plane** as the sketching plane in the 3D View area. The **Sketcher** workbench gets invoked.

5. Click on the **View section** tool in the **Part Design Helper** toolbar to temporarily hide the material that is in front of the sketching plane, see Figure 9.74.

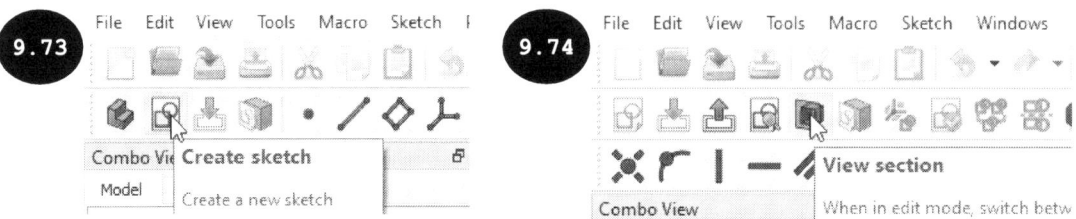

6. Create the sketch of the base feature of the component, refer to Figure 9.75.

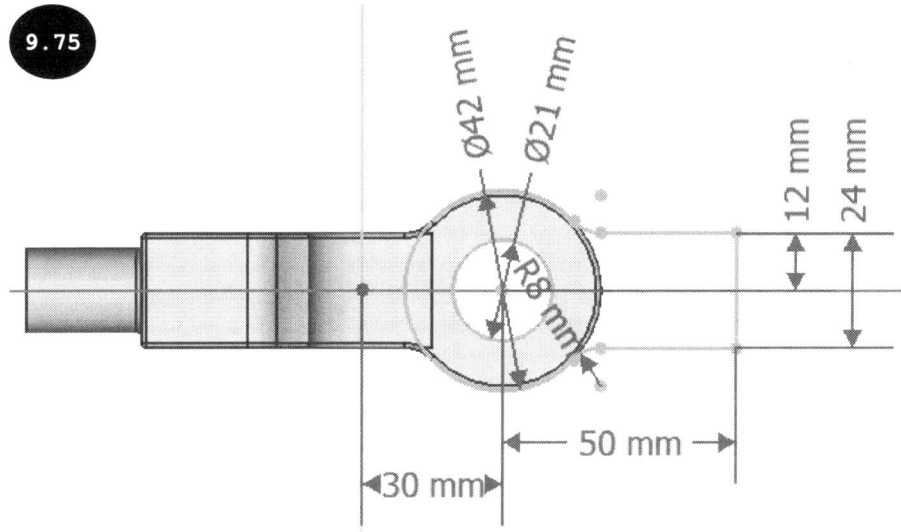

7. After creating the sketch, exit the **Sketcher** workbench and then extrude the sketch to a length of 24 mm, symmetrically on both sides of the sketching plane by using the **Pad** tool, see Figure 9.76.

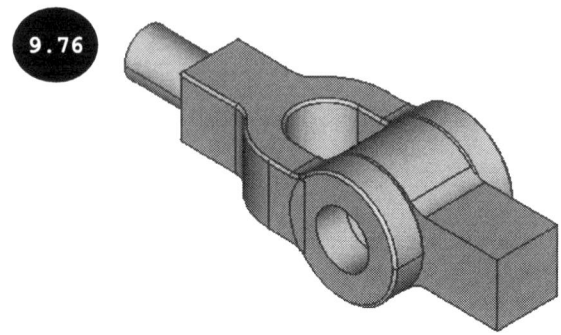

8. Invoke the Sketcher workbench by selecting the right planar face of the previously created base feature, see Figure 9.77.

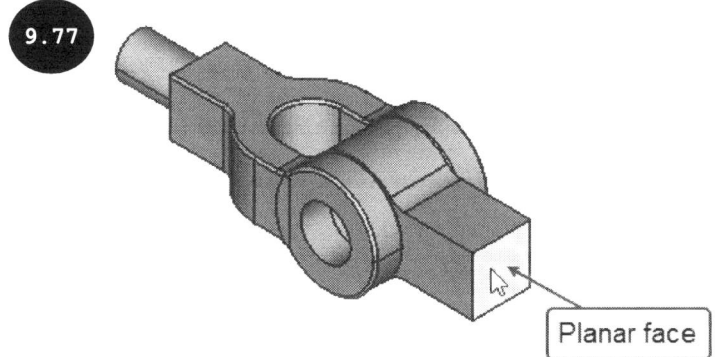

Planar face

9. Create a circle of diameter 18 mm as the sketch of the second feature, see Figure 9.78 and then create a pad feature by extruding it to a length of 25 mm using the **Pad** tool, see Figure 9.79.

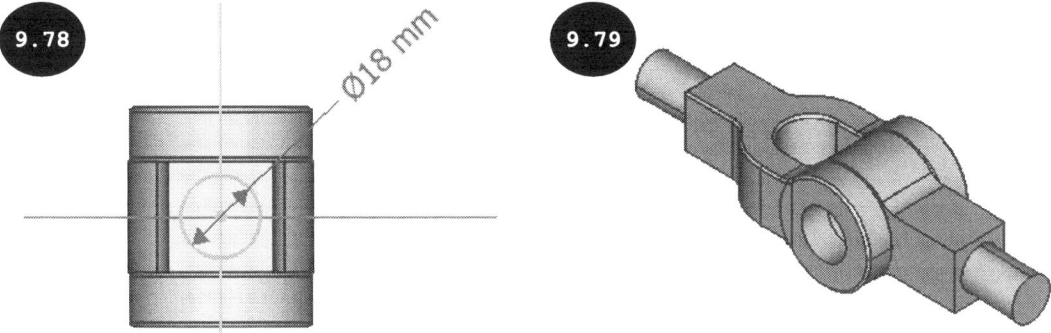

Ø18 mm

Now, you need to create the fillet on the edges of the Eye End component.

10. Select the top and right planar faces of the component by pressing the CTRL key, see Figure 9.80.

11. Click on the **Fillet** tool and then create a fillet of radius **1** mm on the edges of the selected faces, see Figure 9.81. The second component (Eye End) of the assembly gets created.

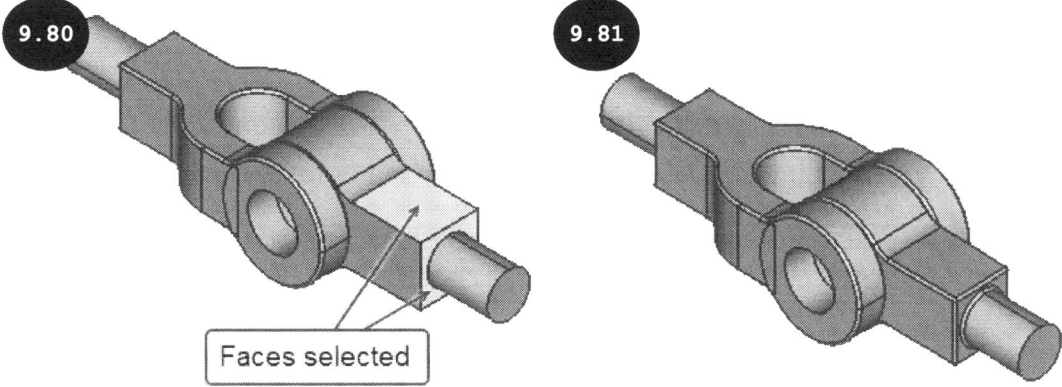

Faces selected

Section 5: Creating the Third Component

Now, you can create the third component (Pin) of the assembly.

1. Click on the **Create body** tool in the **Part Design Helper** toolbar, see Figure 9.82. A new empty body with the default name "**Body002**" gets created and appears below the second component (Eye End) in the **Tree View** of the **Model** tab, see Figure 9.83. Also, it becomes the active body of the current document.

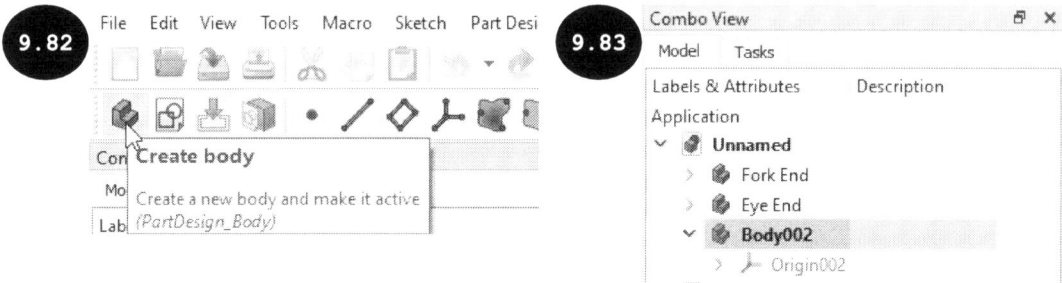

2. Rename the newly added body as **Pin** in the **Tree View**, as discussed earlier.

    Now, you can create features of the Pin component of the assembly.

3. Select the front planar face of the first component (see Figure 9.84) and then click on the **Create sketch** tool in the **Part Design Helper** toolbar, see Figure 9.85. The **Reference** dialog box appears.

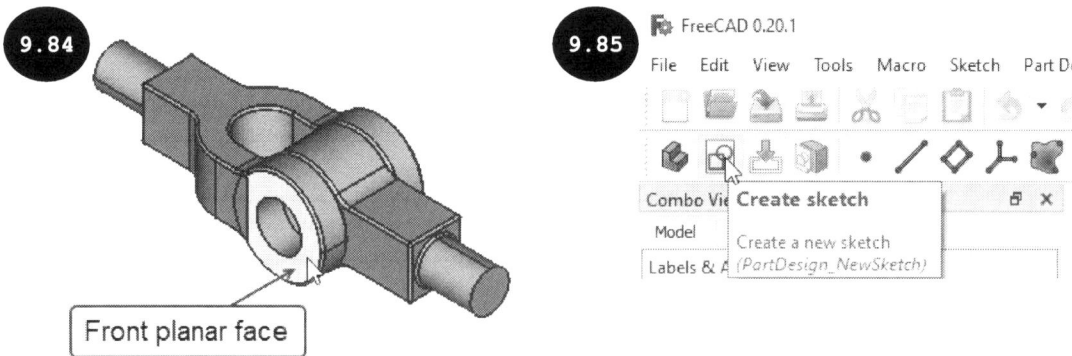

Front planar face

4. Select the **Make dependent copy** radio button in the **Reference** dialog box for creating a new body as the dependent copy of the first component. Next, click on the **OK** button in the dialog box. The **Sketcher** workbench gets invoked. Ignore the error message that may appear in the **Report view** window at the bottom of the screen. You can close the **Report view** window by clicking on the cross mark that appears in its top right corner.

5. Create a circle of diameter 21 mm as the sketch of the base feature of the Pin component, see Figure 9.86.

6. After creating the sketch, exit the **Sketcher** workbench and then extrude it to a length of 62 mm toward the back side of the sketching plane by using the **Pad** tool, see Figure 9.87.

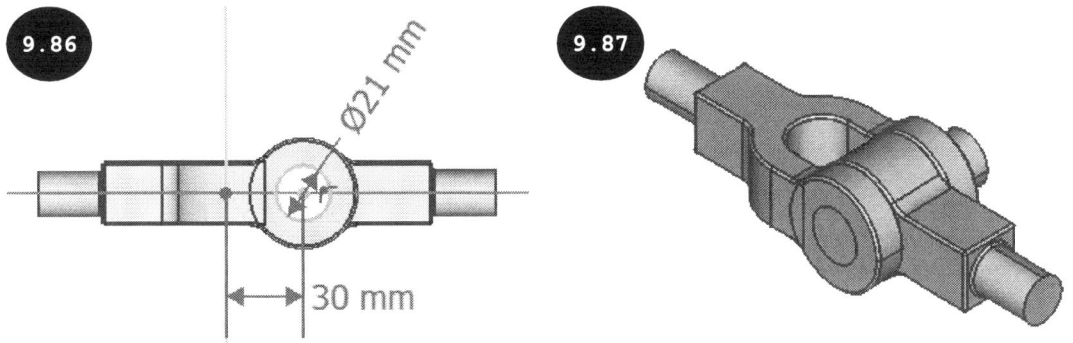

7. Similarly, create the remaining features (one pad and one pocket) of the Pin component one by one. Figure 9.88 shows the model after creating all its features. Refer to Figure 9.45 for dimensions to create these features of the Pin component.

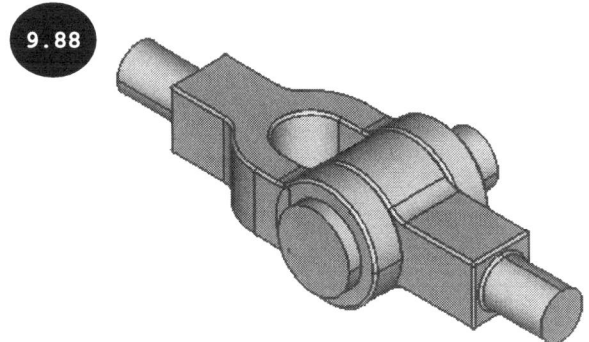

Section 6: Creating the Fourth Component

Now, you can create the fourth component (Collar) of the assembly.

1. Click on the **Create body** tool in the **Part Design Helper** toolbar, see Figure 9.89. A new empty body with the default name "**Body003**" gets created and appears below the third component (Pin) in the **Tree View** of the **Model** tab. Also, it becomes the active body of the current document.

2. Rename the newly added body as **Collar** in the **Tree View**, as discussed earlier.

   Now, you can create features of the Collar component of the assembly.

3. Rotate the assembly such that the back planar face of the first component can be visible, see Figure 9.90.

4.   Select the back planar face of the first component (see Figure 9.90) and then click on the **Create sketch** tool in the **Part Design Helper** toolbar, see Figure 9.91. The **Reference** dialog box appears.

Back planar face

5.   Select the **Make dependent copy** radio button in the **Reference** dialog box and then click on the **OK** button. The **Sketcher** workbench gets invoked. Ignore the error message that may appear in the **Report view** window at the bottom of the screen. You can close the **Report view** window by clicking on the cross mark that appears in its top right corner.

6.   Click on the **View section** tool in the **Part Design Helper** toolbar to temporarily hide the material that is in front of the sketching plane, see Figure 9.92.

7.   Create two concentric circles as the sketch of the base feature, see Figure 9.93.

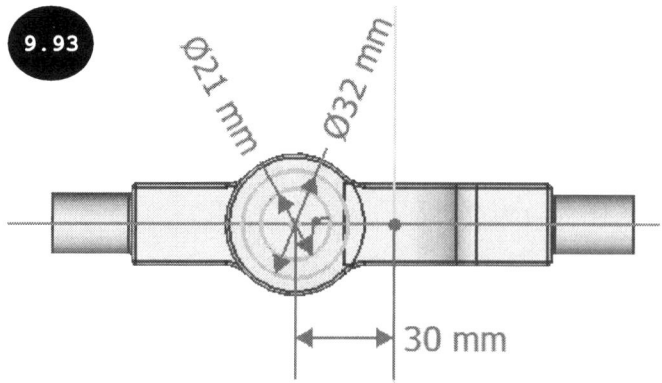

8.   After creating the sketch, exit the **Sketcher** workbench and then extrude it to a length of 10 mm toward the back side of the sketching plane by using the **Pad** tool, see Figure 9.94.

9.   Similarly, create a circular cut/hole of diameter 4 mm throughout the entire Collar component by using the **Pocket** tool, see Figure 9.95.

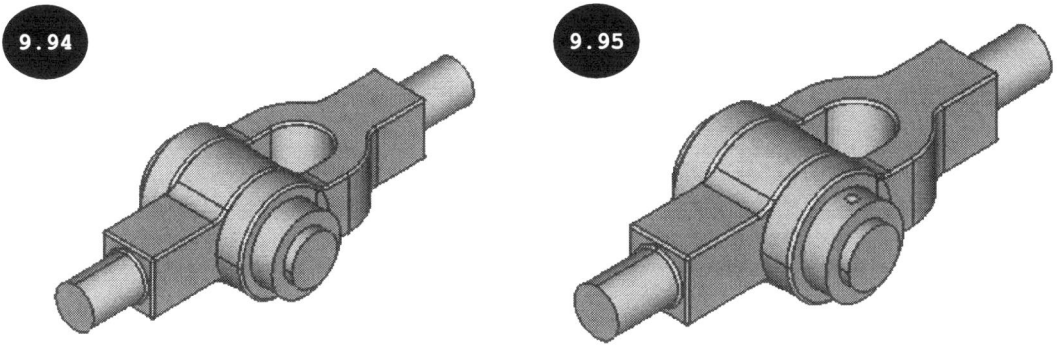

10. Change the view orientation of the model to isometric. Figure 9.96 shows the final assembly after creating all its components.

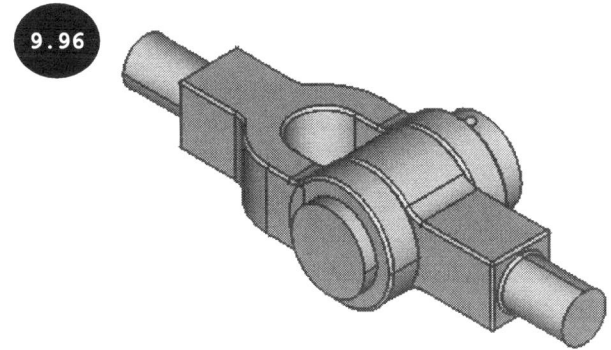

Section 7: Saving the Model

1. Click on the **Save** tool in the **File** toolbar (see Figure 9.97) or press the CTRL + S keys. The **Save FreeCAD Document** dialog box appears.

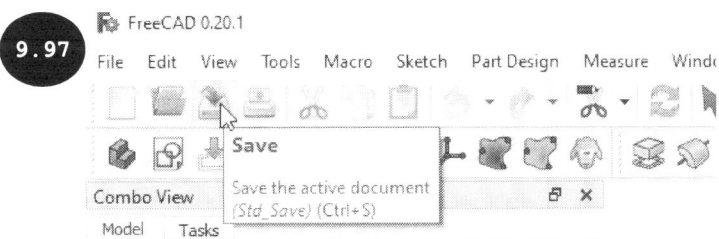

2. Browse to the required folder (:*FreeCAD* > *Chapter 09*) in the local drive of your system. Note that you need to create the Chapter 09 sub-folder inside the FreeCAD folder.

3. Enter **Ch09-Tutorial 1** in the **File name** field of the dialog box. Next, click on the **Save** button in the dialog box. The model gets saved at the specified location (:*FreeCAD* > *Chapter 09*).

4. Click on **File > Close** in the **Standard Menu** to close the current document.

Hands-on Test Drive 1

Create an assembly shown in Figure 9.98 by using the Top-down assembly approach in the **Part Design** workbench. Different views and dimensions of each component are shown in Figures 9.99 through 9.102. All dimensions are in inches.

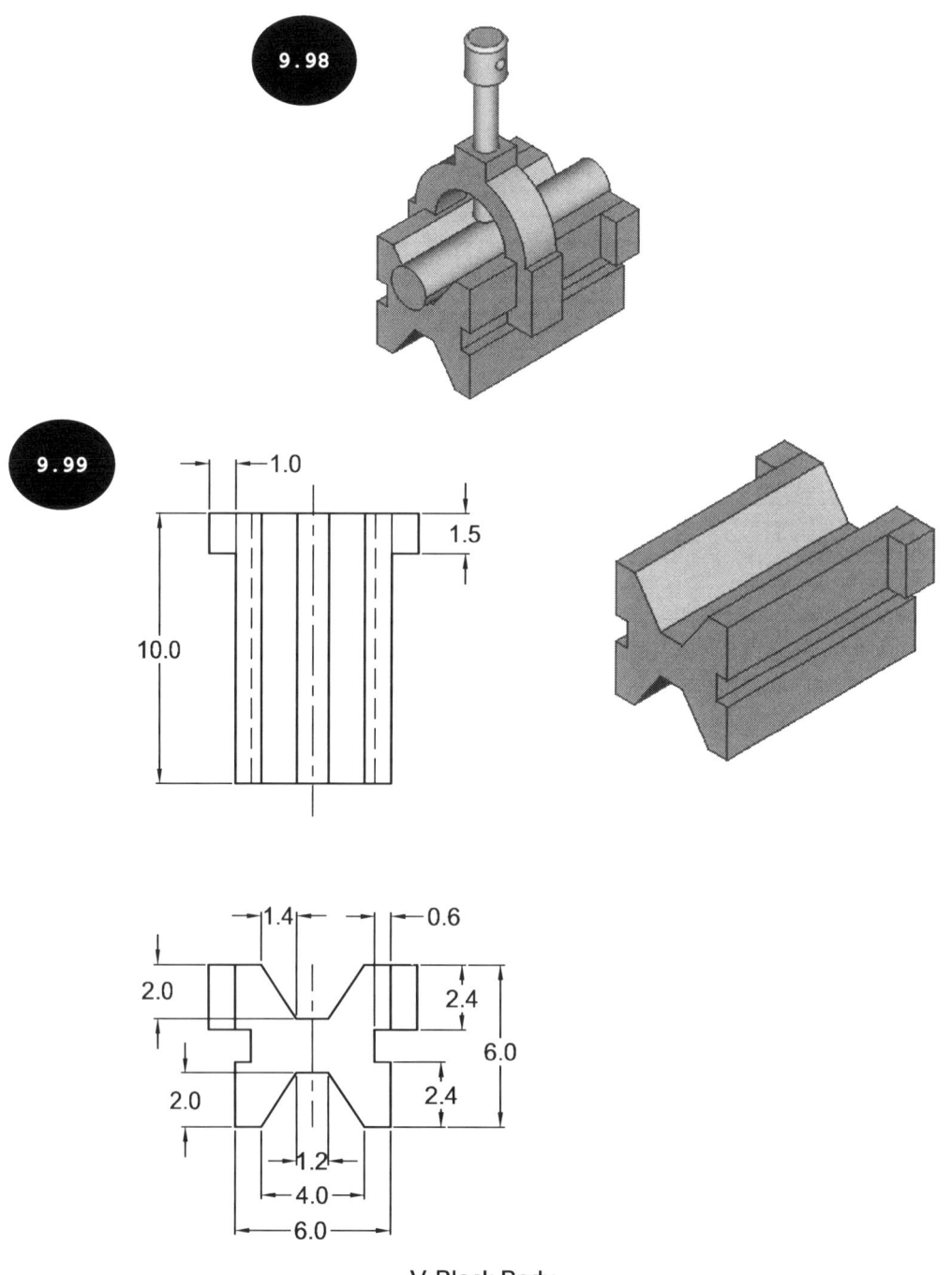

V-Block Body

9.100

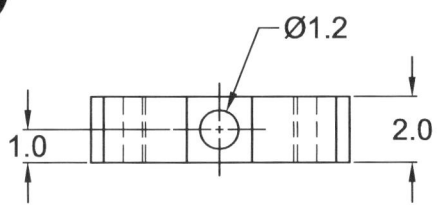

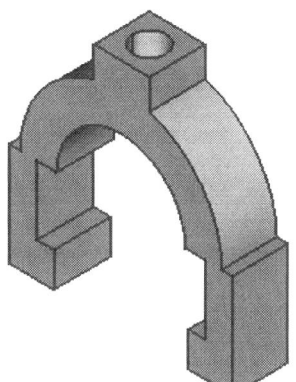

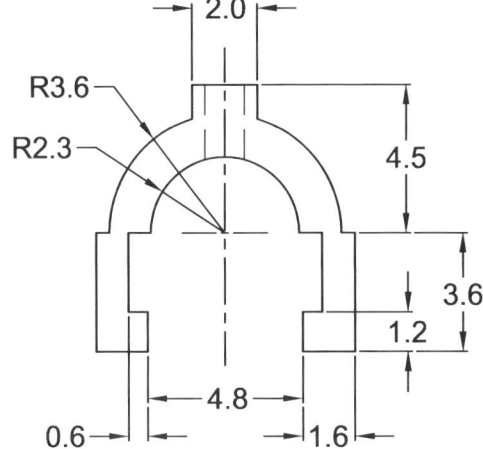

U-Clamp

9.101

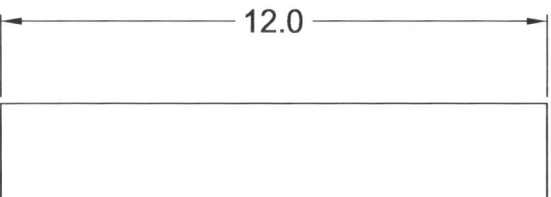

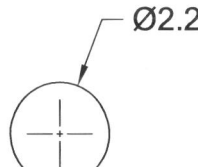

Pipe

9.102

R0.2   Ø2.0

8.0

CHAM 0.2 X 0.2

2.0   1.0   Ø0.6

Ø1.2

Fastener

Summary

The chapter discussed how to create assemblies by using the Top-down assembly approach and the Bottom-up assembly approach. The methods for installing the **A2plus** workbench, inserting components, and applying different types of constraints for assembling components were also discussed in this chapter. It also explained how to tag the degrees of freedom of assembly components and move a component along its free and fixed degrees of freedom.

Questions

Complete and verify the following sentences:

- In FreeCAD, you can create an assembly by using the _____ and _____ approaches.

- The _____ assembly approach, all the components of an assembly are created as individual bodies within a single part document.

- You can activate a body of a part document by _____ on its name in the **Tree View**.

- The _____ is an external workbench to assemble different components of an assembly.

- The _____ constraint is used for making vertices or points of two components coincident with each other.

- You can tag the degrees of freedom information of each component of the assembly. (True/False)

- In FreeCAD, you cannot create multiple bodies within a single part document. (True/False)

CHAPTER

10

Creating 2D Drawings

This chapter discusses the following topics:

- Invoking the TechDraw Workspace
- Inserting a Drawing Sheet
- Editing Title Block Text of a Sheet
- Creating an Independent 2D Projection View
- Modifying the Scale of a 2D Projection View
- Creating Multiple Linked 2D Projection Views
- Displaying Hidden Lines on the Views
- Creating a Section View
- Creating a Detail View
- Applying Dimensions
- Exporting Drawing as a DXF File
- Exporting Drawing as an SVG File

After creating a 3D model, you can create a 2D drawing. A 2D drawing is a traditional drafting document, which contains all the required information such as drawing views, dimensions, annotations, notes, etc. about the product to be manufactured. In FreeCAD, you can create basic technical drawings of 3D models created with another workbench such as **Part**, **Part Design**, or **A2plus** in the **TechDraw** workspace. You can also create technical drawings of 3D models that are imported from other CAD applications in the **TechDraw** workspace.

Invoking the TechDraw Workspace

The method for invoking the **TechDraw** workbench for creating a 2D drawing of a 3D model is discussed below:

1. Start FreeCAD by double-clicking on the **FreeCAD 0.20** icon on your desktop. The startup user interface of FreeCAD appears.

> **Note:** In FreeCAD, it is recommended to first open or create a 3D model before invoking the **TechDraw** workbench to create its 2D drawing views.

2. Start a new document and then create a 3D model in the **Part Design** workbench or open an existing 3D model for creating its 2D drawing, see Figure 10.1. In this figure, Tutorial 2 of Chapter 8 is opened for creating its drawing views.

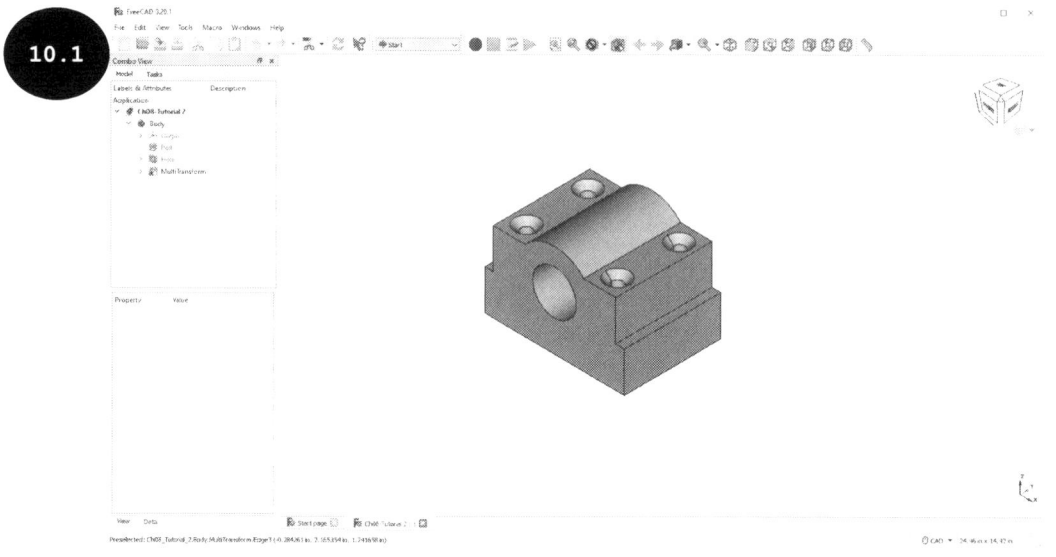

> **Tip:** In FreeCAD, you can open an existing 3D model by using the **Open** tool 📁 of the **File** toolbar. The method for opening a 3D model is discussed in Chapter 1.

> **Note:** You can also open an assembly for creating its 2D drawing. In addition, you can import a 3D model that is created in another CAD application for creating its 2D drawing. The method for importing a 3D model is discussed in Chapter 1.

Now, you can invoke the **TechDraw** workbench for creating a 2D drawing of the 3D model.

3. Invoke the **Workbench Selector** in the **Workbench** toolbar and then select the **TechDraw** workbench, see Figure 10.2. The **TechDraw** workbench gets invoked, see Figure 10.3.

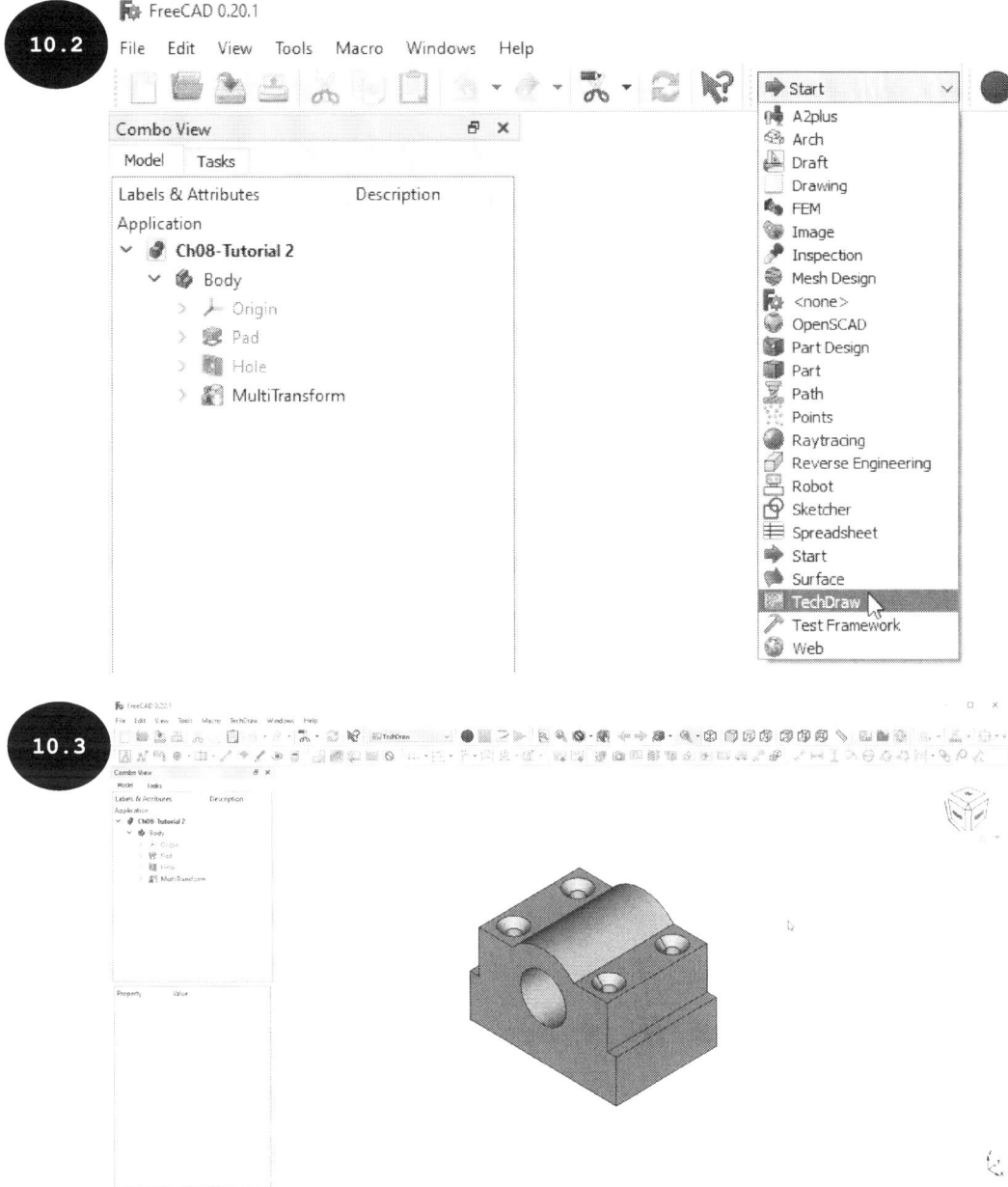

Note: Initially, most of the tools of the **TechDraw** workbench are not activated. Some of these tools get activated as soon as you insert a drawing sheet (page) of a specified template/size for creating different drawing views of the model and the remaining tools will be activated when you insert a drawing view on the sheet. The methods for inserting a sheet (page) and a drawing view of a 3D model are discussed next.

Inserting a Drawing Sheet

After invoking the **TechDraw** workbench, the first thing to do is to insert a drawing sheet (page) of a specific template to create different drawing views of a 3D model. In FreeCAD, you can insert a drawing sheet (page) using the default template or a selected template. Note that a template controls the sheet size, drafting standard, sheet border, etc. of a sheet. The methods for inserting a drawing sheet are discussed next.

Inserting a Drawing Sheet Using the Default Template

The method for inserting a drawing sheet using the default template is discussed below:

1. Click on the **Insert Default Page** tool in the **TechDraw Pages** toolbar, see Figure 10.4. A new drawing sheet (page) of the default template gets inserted with the default name "*Page*" in a separate tab and becomes active by default, see Figure 10.5.

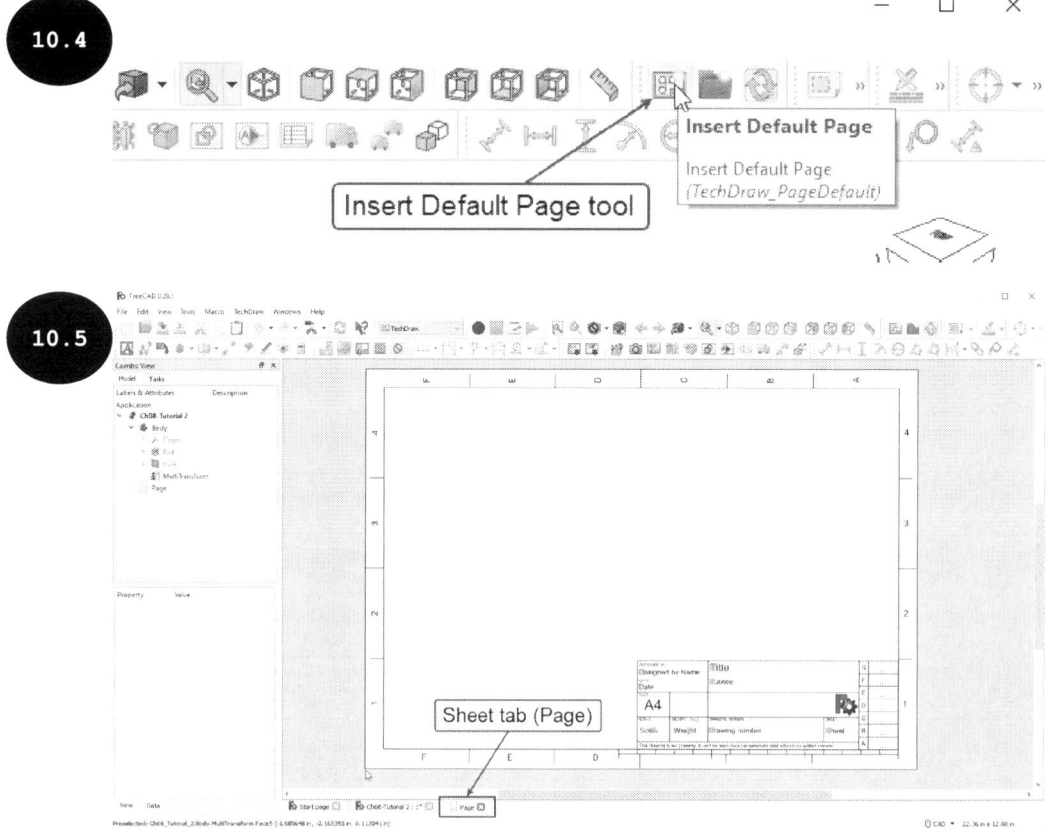

Tip: By default, the sheet gets inserted in a new separate tab. You may need to adjust or fit the sheet in the drawing display area by moving or zooming in or out it. You can move the sheet by pressing and holding the middle mouse button. You can zoom in or zoom out the sheet by scrolling the middle mouse button up or down on the sheet, respectively.

2. Similarly, you can insert multiple sheets (pages) using the default template for creating different drawing views of the 3D model, if needed.

Note: You can set the default template by using the **Preferences** dialog box, as required. For doing so, click on the **Edit > Preferences** in the **File** toolbar and then click on the **TechDraw** section in the left panel of the **Preferences** dialog box that appears, see Figure 10.6. The options to control the default template, drawing parameters, and other related settings appear on the right panel of the dialog box in the respective tabs. In the **General** tab of the dialog box, click on the **Browse** button next to the **Default Template** field in the **Files** area, see Figure 10.6. The **Select a file** window appears. In this window, browse to the **Templates** folder (*> \FreeCAD 0.20\data\Mod\TechDraw\Templates*) in the FreeCAD installation directory and then select the required template to be set as the default template for all new sheets/pages. Next, click on the **Open** button in the **Select a file** window and then click on the **Apply** button in the **Preferences** dialog box. The selected template gets set as the default template. Next, click on the **OK** button to exit the **Preferences** dialog box.

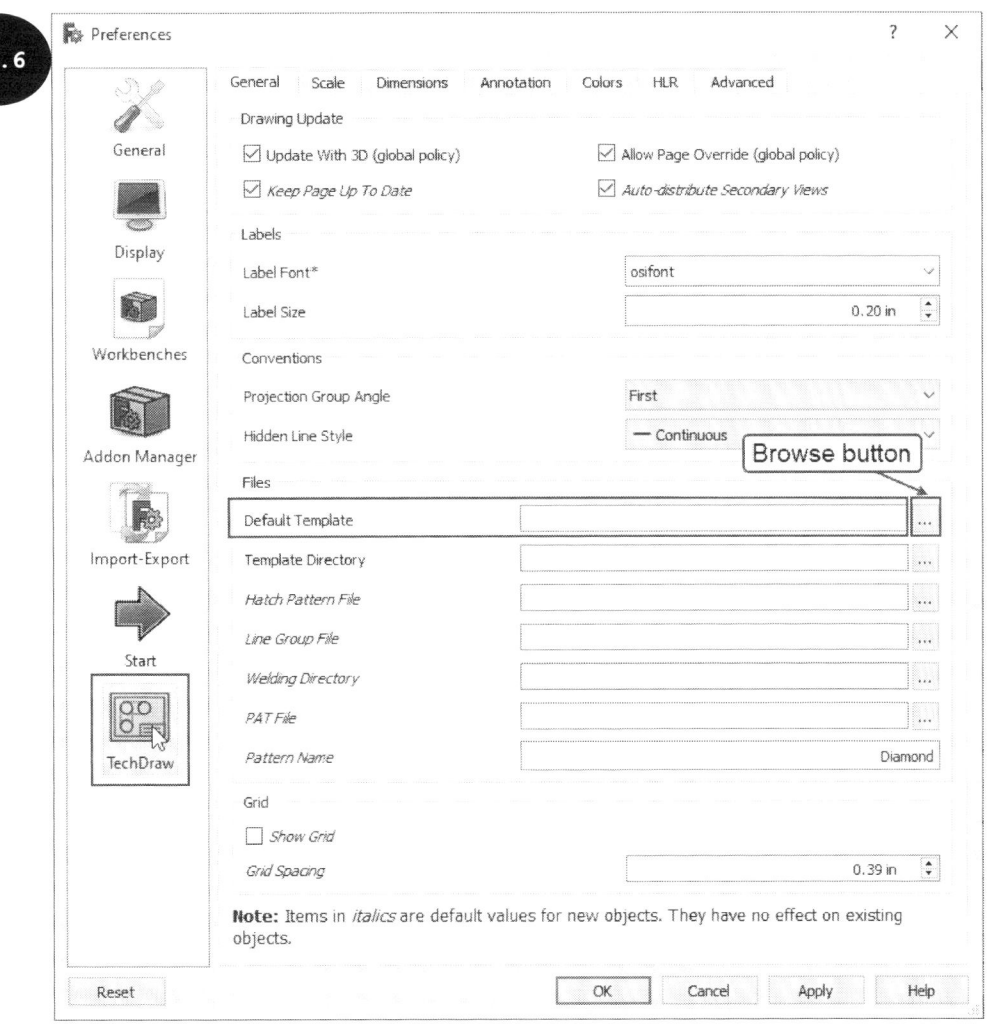

10.6

Inserting a Drawing Sheet Using a Selected Template

The method for inserting a drawing sheet using a selected template is discussed below:

1. Click on the **Insert Page using Template** tool in the **TechDraw Pages** toolbar, see Figure 10.7. The **Select a Template File** window appears with a list of available drawing templates, see Figure 10.8.

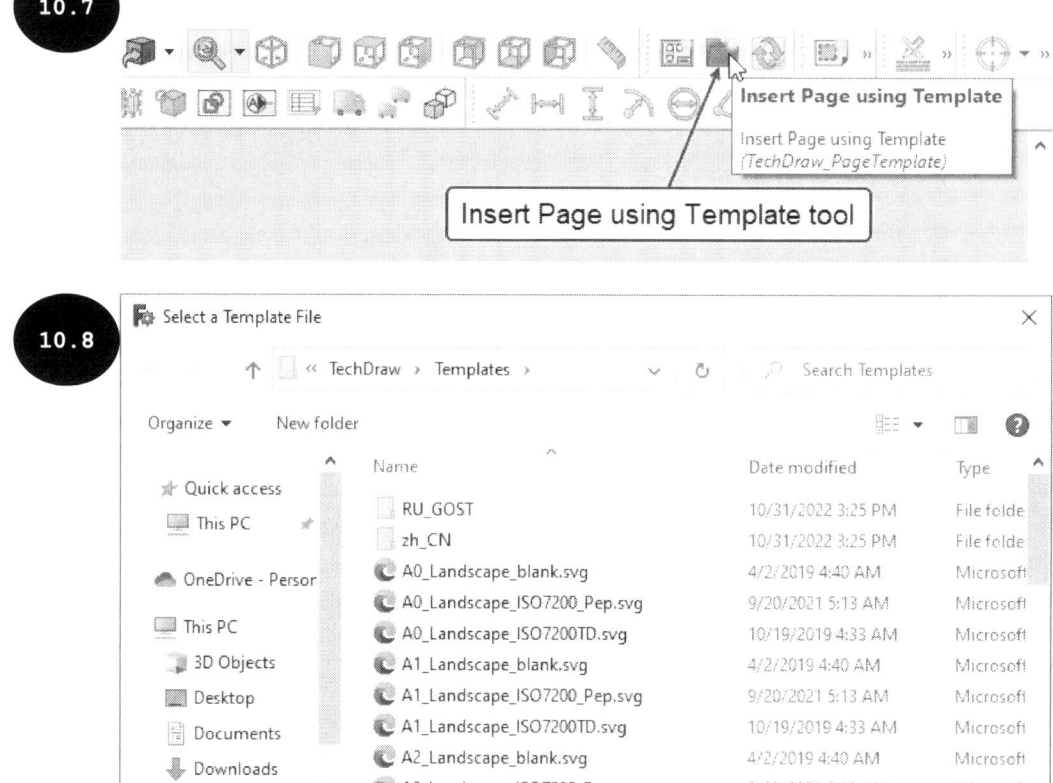

2. Select the required template in the **Select a Template File** window and then click on the **Open** button. A new drawing sheet (page) of the selected template gets inserted with a default name in a new separate tab and becomes active by default, see Figure 10.9.

Tip: FreeCAD has various drawing templates with pre-defined drafting standards to create drawing views of a model. A template controls size, drafting standard, border, etc. of a sheet.

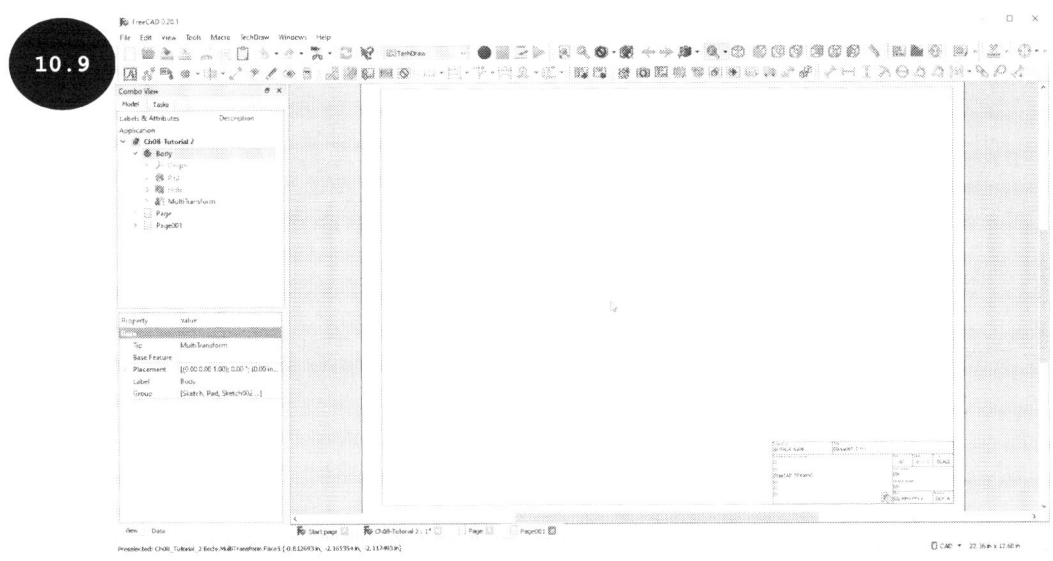

10.9

In Figure 10.9, a drawing sheet of **A2_Landscape_ISO7200TD** template is inserted for creating drawing views.

In FreeCAD, you can switch between different drawing sheets (pages) and the 3D model at any point in time by clicking on the respective tab available at the lower left corner of the drawing display area, see Figure 10.10.

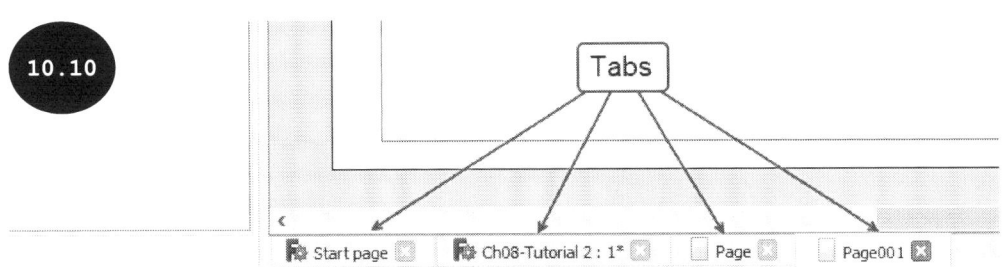

10.10

Editing Title Block Text of a Sheet

A drawing sheet/template contains the editable text for attributes such as Designed by Name, Date, Title, Subtitle, Scale, and Drawing number in its title block. These editable texts are highlighted in green color in the title block of the sheet. The method for editing an editable text of a sheet is discussed below:

1. Click on the highlighted portion of a text to be edited in the title block of the sheet, see Figure 10.11. The **Change Editable Field** dialog box appears, see Figure 10.12.

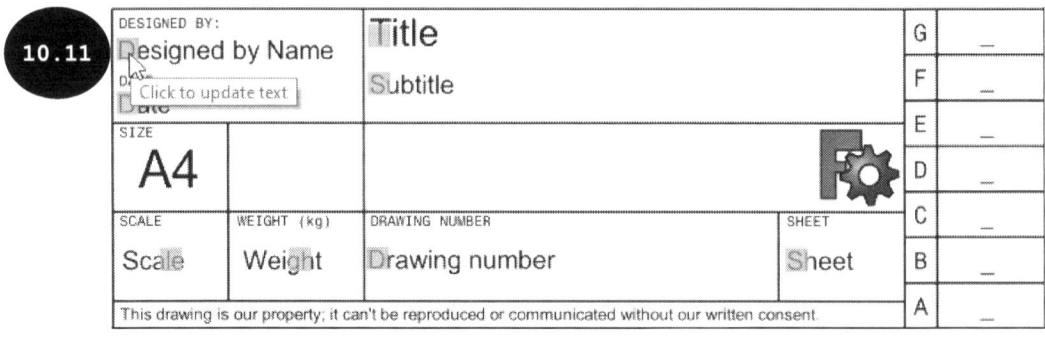

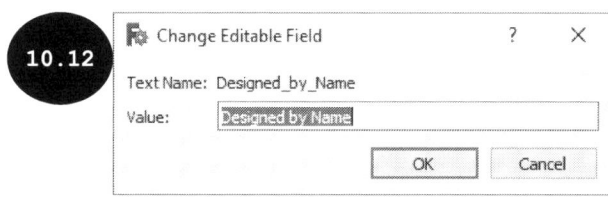

2.   Enter a new text in the **Value** field of the dialog box, as required, and then click on the **OK** button. The text gets modified in the title block, as specified.

3.   Similarly, you can edit the remaining editable texts of the sheet one by one by clicking on them.

Creating an Independent 2D Projection View

After creating or opening a 3D model and inserting a drawing sheet of a specified template, you can start creating 2D drawing views of the model. The method for creating an independent 2D projection view of the 3D model is discussed below:

1.   Switch to the 3D model by clicking on its tab at the lower left corner of the drawing display area whose drawing view is to be created, see Figure 10.13.

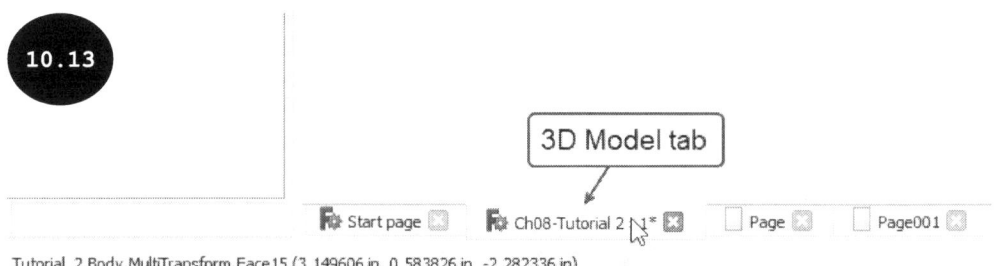

2.   Set the view orientation of the model to Front, Top, Right, Left, Back, Bottom, or Isometric by using the **Navigation Cube** as the view to be created on the sheet (page), see Figure 10.14. In this figure, the view orientation of the model is set to the Front view. You can also rotate the model to set its view orientation to an isometric or a custom view, as required.

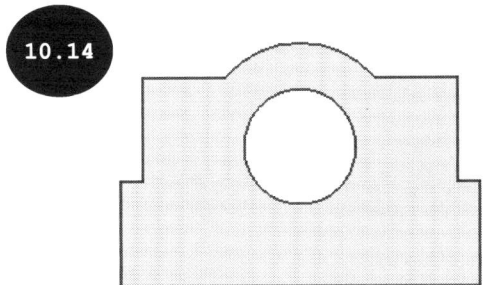

10.14

3. Click on the model "**Body**" in the **Tree View** for creating its view on the sheet as per its current orientation, see Figure 10.15.

10.15

Note: Instead of selecting the model "**Body**" in the **Tree View** for creating its view as per its current orientation in the 3D View area, you can select a face of the model in the 3D View area for creating its view normal to the selected face of the model.

4. After setting the desired view of the model in the 3D View area, switch to the drawing sheet (page) by clicking on its respective tab for creating the drawing view of the selected model, see Figure 10.16.

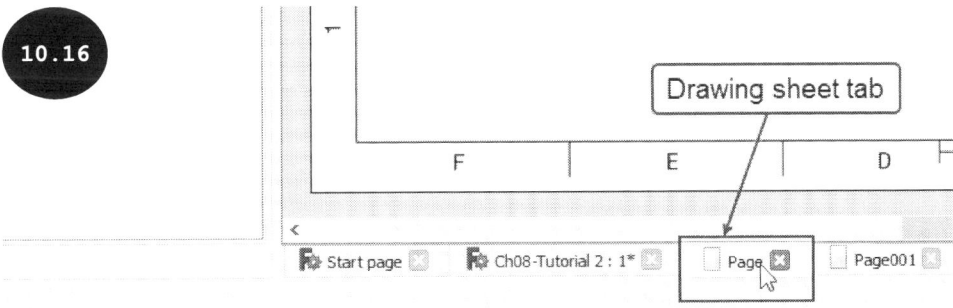

10.16

5. Click on the **Insert View** tool in the **TechDraw Views** toolbar, see Figure 10.17. A 2D projection view of the selected model gets created on the drawing sheet (page) as per its orientation in the 3D View area, see Figure 10.18.

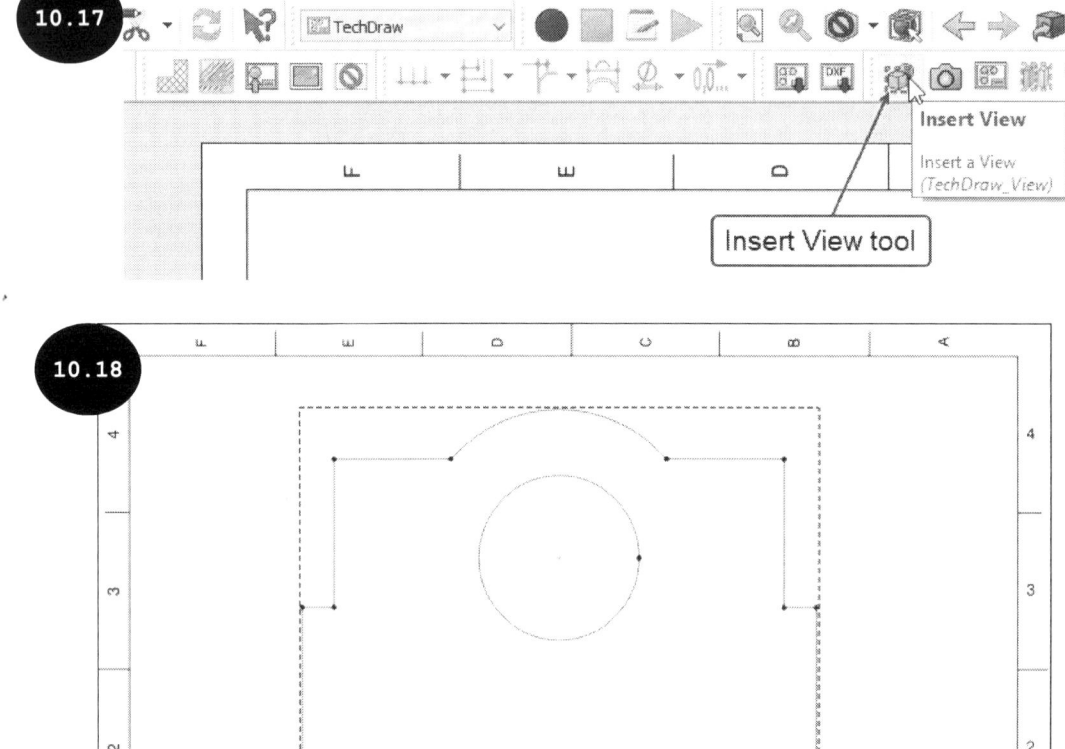

Insert View: The Insert View tool is used for creating an independent 2D projection view of the selected model on the drawing sheet (page).

6. Similarly, you can create multiple independent 2D projection views of the model on the sheet, if needed.

Modifying the Scale of a 2D Projection View

After creating a 2D projection view, you may need to modify its default scale value to adjust its display on the sheet (page), as required. The method for modifying the scale of a view is discussed below:

1. Select a drawing view in the sheet (page) whose scale value is to be modified. The **Property Editor** appears at the lower section of the **Model** tab in the **Combo View** with **View** and **Data** tabs at its bottom, see Figure 10.19.

2. Click on the **Data** tab at the bottom of the **Property Editor** for displaying the properties of the selected view, see Figure 10.19.

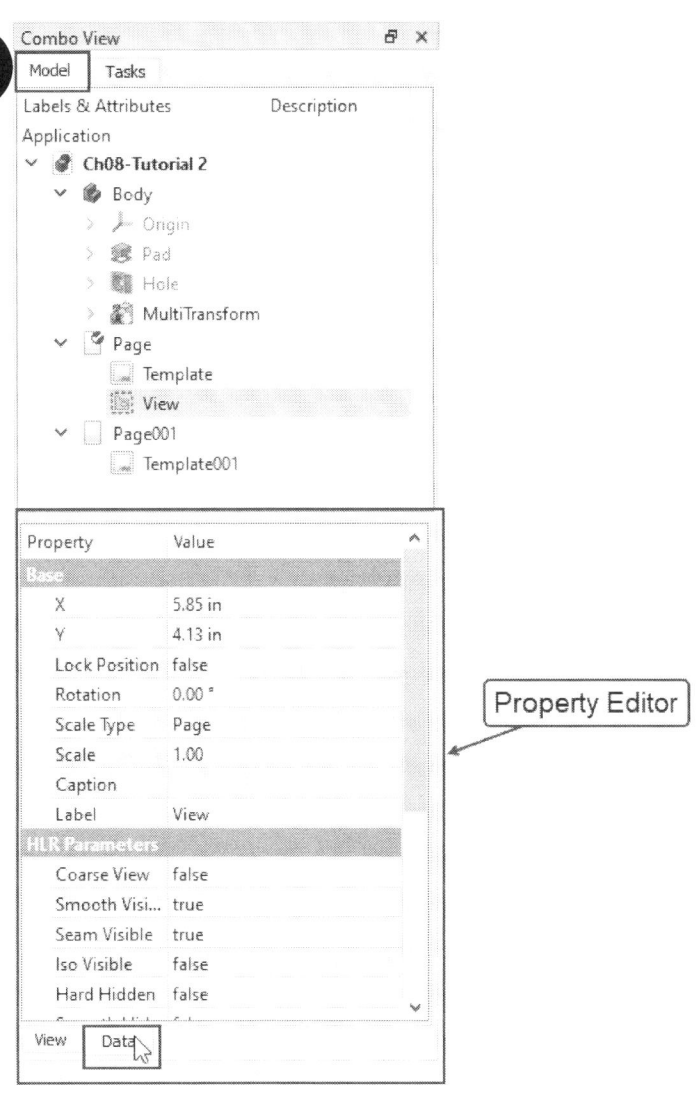

3. Click twice on the **Scale Type** field in the **Property Editor** and then select the **Custom** option in the drop-down list that appears, see Figure 10.20. The options in this drop-down list are discussed next.

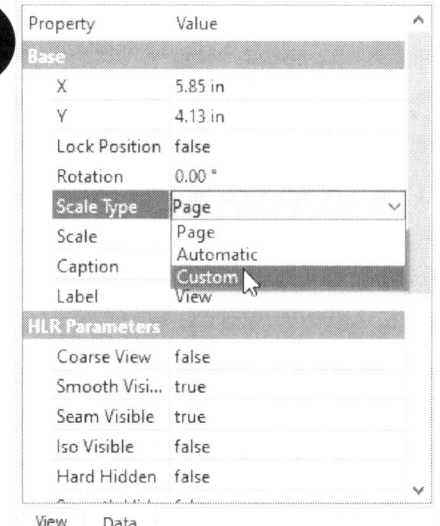

10.20

Property	Value
Base	
X	5.85 in
Y	4.13 in
Lock Position	false
Rotation	0.00 °
Scale Type	Page
Scale	
Caption	
Label	
HLR Parameters	
Coarse View	false
Smooth Visi...	true
Seam Visible	true
Iso Visible	false
Hard Hidden	false

Drop-down list options: Page / Automatic / Custom / View

View   Data

Page: The **Page** option is used to set the view scale as per the default specified scale of the sheet (page). This option is selected, by default. As a result, when you create a view, it displays on the sheet as per the default sheet (page) scale.

Note: You can set the default sheet (page) scale as required by using the **Preferences** dialog box. For doing so, invoke the **Preferences** dialog box by clicking on **Edit > Preferences** in the **File** toolbar and then click on the **TechDraw** section in its left panel. Next, click on the **Scale** tab on the right panel of the dialog box (see Figure 10.21) and then enter the required scale valve in the **Page Scale** field of the dialog box. Note that the modified values of the items/fields that appear in *italics* in the dialog box will be the default values of the new objects and will not affect the existing objects/views. Next, click on **Apply** and then **OK** button in the dialog box.

10.21

Preferences dialog box — Tabs: General | Scale | Dimensions | Annotation | Colors | HLR | Advanced

Left panel: General, Display, Workbenches

Scale
Page Scale	1.00
View Scale Type	Page
View Custom Scale	1.00

Size Adjustments
Vertex Scale	5.00
Center Mark Scale	0.50
Template Edit Mark	0.12 in

Automatic: The Automatic option is used to set the view scale automatically, to fit it on the sheet (page).

Custom: The Custom option is used to set a custom scale for the selected view. On selecting this option, the **Scale** field gets enabled below the **Scale Type** drop-down list in the **Property Editor**, see Figure 10.22. In this field, you can specify a custom scale value for the selected view, as required, and then press ENTER. Note that a scale factor like 1:2 can be written as 0.5 (1/2).

4. After selecting the **Custom** option in the **Scale Type** drop-down list of the **Property Editor**, enter the required scale value for the selected view in the **Scale** field, see Figure 10.22. Next, press ENTER.

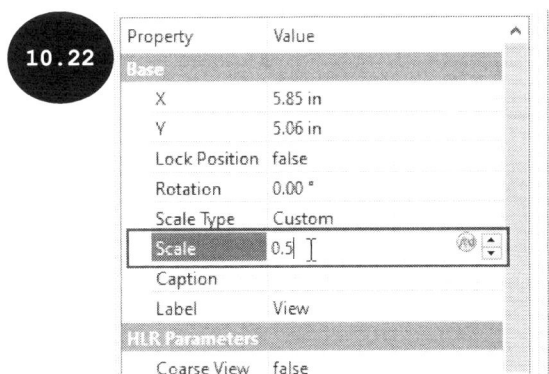

5. Click on the **Redraw Page** in the **TechDraw Pages** toolbar, see Figure 10.23. The drawing view gets updated on the sheet as per the newly defined scale value.

Note: To delete an existing drawing view of a model, select the view to be deleted on the sheet (page) and then press the DELETE key.

Creating Multiple Linked 2D Projection Views

The method for creating multiple linked 2D projection views such as the Front, Top, Left, and Right of a 3D model simultaneously on a sheet, is discussed below:

1.   Switch to the 3D model by clicking on its tab at the lower left corner of the drawing display area whose drawing views are to be created, see Figure 10.24.

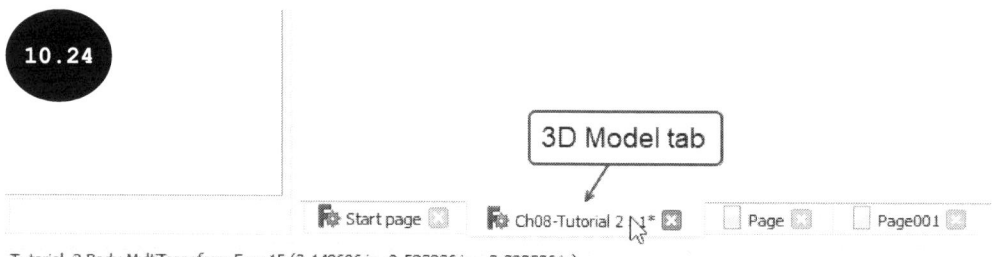

2.   Set the view orientation of the model to Front, Top, Right, Left, Back, Bottom, or Isometric by using the **Navigation Cube** as the primary view to be created on the sheet (page), see Figure 10.25. In this figure, the view orientation of the model is set to the Front. You can also rotate the model to set its view orientation to an isometric or a custom view, as required.

3.   Click on the model "**Body**" in the **Tree View** for creating its primary view (Front) as per its current orientation, see Figure 10.26.

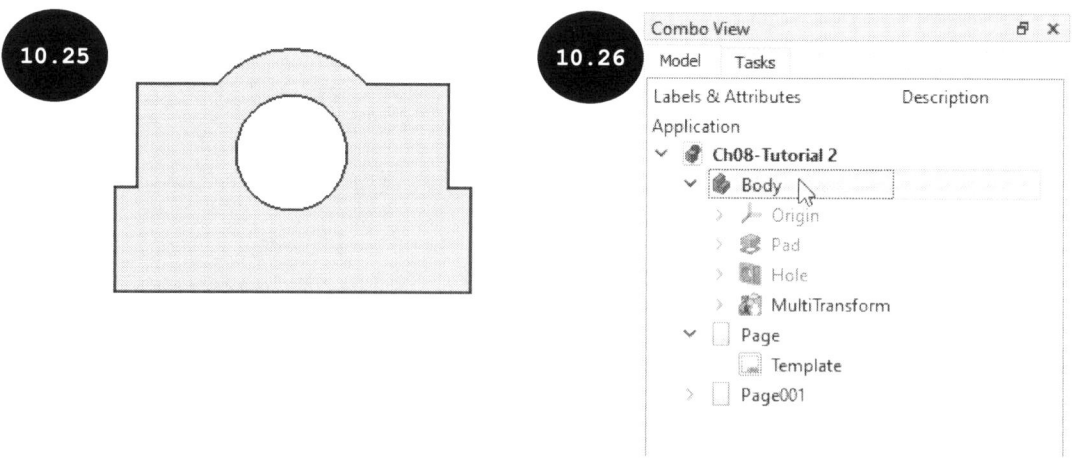

Note: Instead of selecting the model "**Body**" in the **Tree View** for creating its primary view as per its current orientation in the 3D View area, you can select a face of the model in the 3D View area for creating its primary view normal to the selected face.

4.   Switch to the drawing sheet (page) by clicking on its respective tab for creating the drawing views of the selected model, see Figure 10.27.

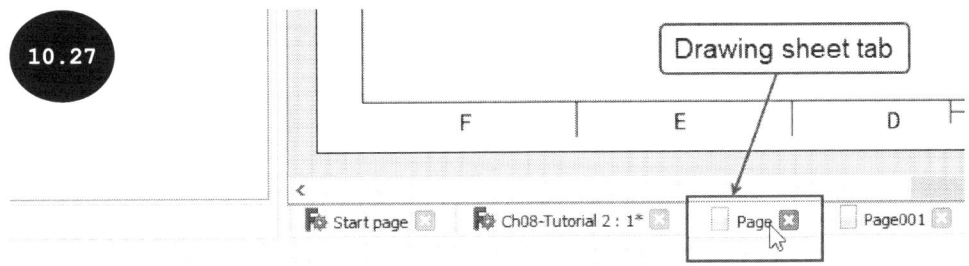

5. Click on the **Insert Projection Group** tool in the **TechDraw Views** toolbar, see Figure 10.28. A primary 2D projection view of the selected model gets created on the drawing sheet (page) as per its orientation set in the 3D View area. Also, the **Projection Group** sub-window appears in the **Task Panel**, see Figure 10.29.

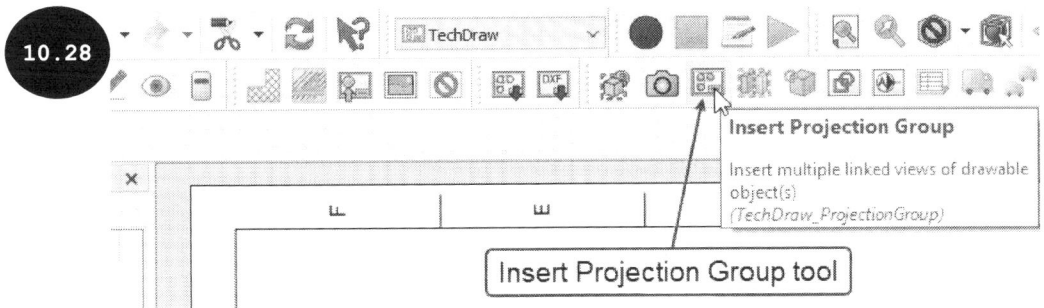

Projection: The options (**First Angle** and **Third Angle**) in the **Projection** drop-down list of the **Task Panel** are used for defining the angle of projection for creating the views.

Scale: The options (**Page**, **Automatic**, and **Custom**) in the **Scale** drop-down list are used for defining a scale factor for the views. All these options to define a scale are discussed earlier.

Adjust Primary Direction: The four arrows in the **Adjust Primary Direction** area of the **Task Panel** are used for adjusting the orientation of the primary view of the model. Note that each time you click on an arrow in this area, the primary view of the model rotates at an incremental angle of 90 degrees along the direction of the corresponding arrow.

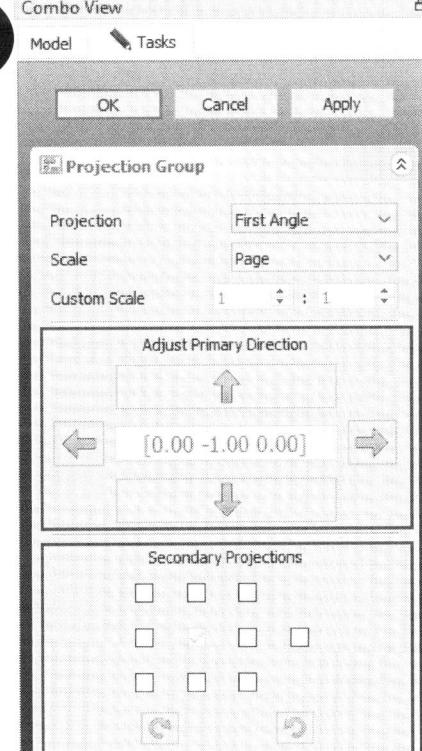

Secondary Projections: The check boxes in the **Secondary Projections** area of the **Task Panel** are used for creating the respective projection views such as the Top, Right, Left, and Isometric of the primary view. Note that the creation of projection views, by selecting the check boxes, depends on the angle of projection selected in the **Projection** drop-down list of the **Task Panel**.

6. Select the required angle of projection (**First Angle** or **Third Angle**) in the **Projection** drop-down list of the **Task Panel**.

7. Select the **Custom** option in the **Scale** drop-down list of the **Task Panel** and then enter a custom scale factor in the **Custom Scale** fields that are enabled in the **Task Panel**. Next, press the TAB key and then the F5 key to update the view on the sheet as per the specified scale factor.

8. Adjust the orientation of the primary view on the sheet by clicking on the arrows in the **Adjust Primary Direction** area of the **Task Panel**, if needed.

9. Select the required check boxes in the **Secondary Projections** area for creating the respective projection views of the model, see Figure 10.30. In this figure, the Top and Right projection views of the Front primary view are created as per the third angle of projection. Also, in Figure 10.30, the scale factor is set to 1:3 for the views.

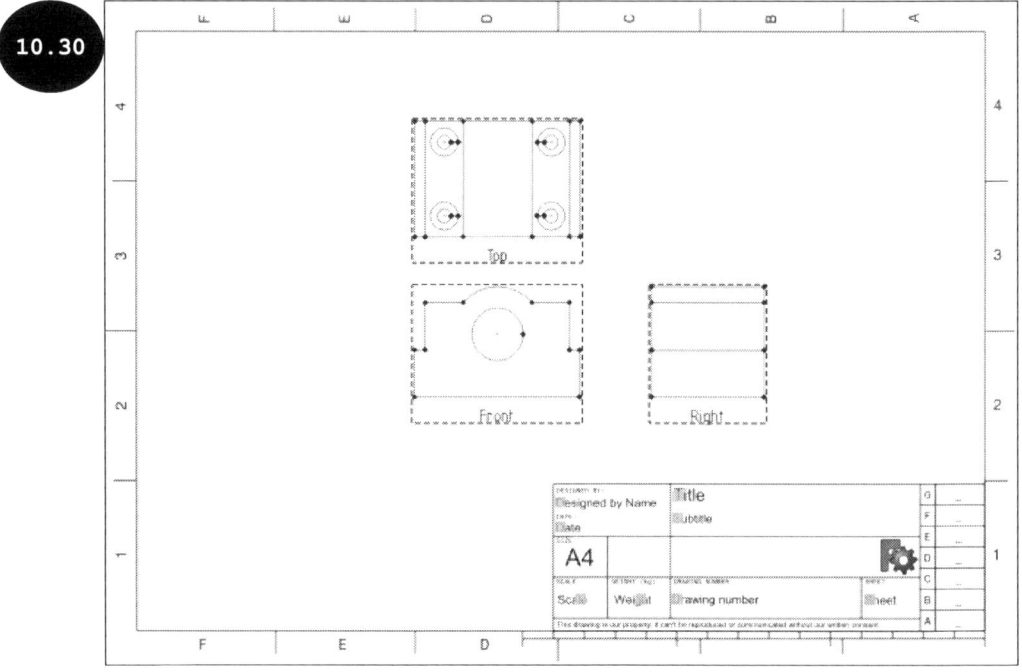

Tip: If needed, you can move the primary view of the model to a new location on the sheet, as required. For doing so, move the cursor over the outer frame of the primary view on the sheet and then drag it to a new location by pressing and holding the left mouse button. Notice that when you move the primary view, all its linked projection views will also be moved, accordingly. You can also move an individual projected view of a model by dragging its frame.

10. Enter the X and Y spacing values between the views in the **X Spacing** and **Y Spacing** fields of the **Task Panel**. You can also click on the up and down spinner arrows available next to these fields for specifying the spacing between the views. Note that these fields are enabled only when the **Auto Distribute** check box is selected in the **Task Panel**.

11. After selecting the required projection views to be created and other related settings, click on the OK button in the **Task Panel**. The multiple linked 2D projection views get created on the sheet.

Displaying Hidden Lines on the Views

In FreeCAD, you can toggle the display of hidden lines/edges of the model on the 2D projection views. The method for displaying the hidden lines/edges of the model on the views is discussed below.

1. Select one or more 2D projection views on the sheet (page) by clicking the left mouse button on the respective outer frame/boundary for displaying the hidden lines. Note that you need to press and hold the CTRL key to select multiple views in **Tree View**. The **Property Editor** appears at the lower section of the **Model** tab in the **Combo View** with **View** and **Data** tabs, refer to Figure 10.31.

2. Click on the **Data** tab at the bottom of the **Property Editor** for displaying the properties of the selected views, refer to Figure 10.31.

3. Click twice on the **Hard Hidden** field in the **Property Editor** and then select the **true** option in the drop-down list that appears, see Figure 10.31.

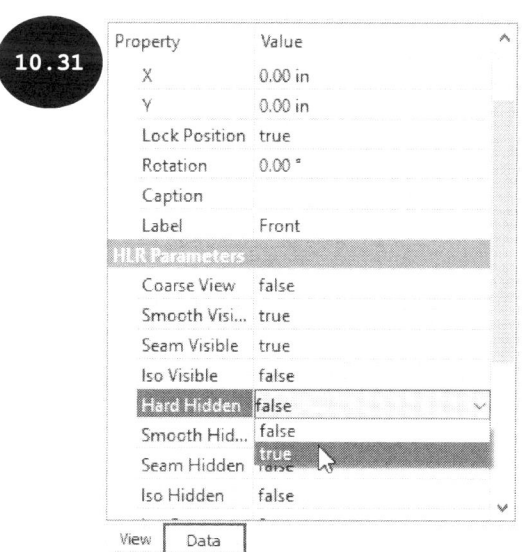

Note: The **true** option turns ON the display of hidden lines on the selected views, whereas the **false** option turns OFF the display of hidden lines on the selected views. You may need to update the views by clicking on the **Refresh** tool ↻ in the **File** toolbar to reflect the change made in the display of hidden lines.

4.   Click anywhere on the sheet. The display of hidden lines gets turned ON in the selected views with the default hidden line style, see Figure 10.32.

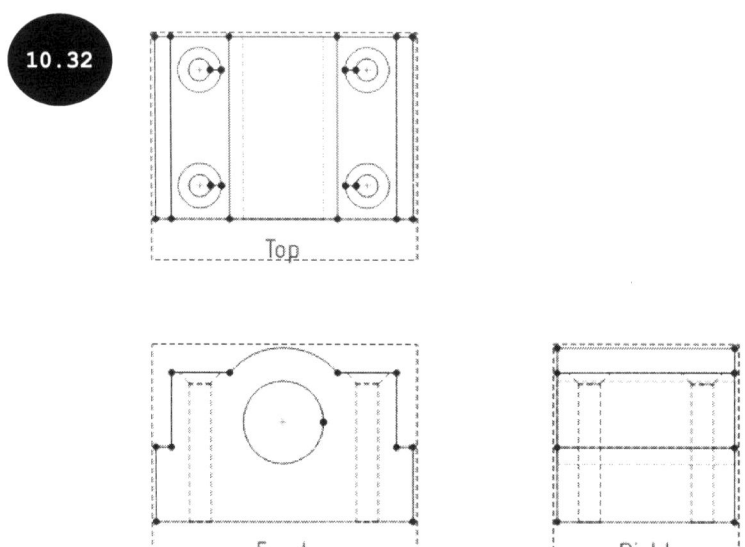

Note: In FreeCAD, you can set the default hidden line style to control the display of hidden lines of views using the **Preferences** dialog box. For doing so, invoke the **Preferences** dialog box by clicking on **Edit > Preferences** in the **File** toolbar and then click on the **TechDraw** section in its left panel. Next, select the required line type (**Continuous** or **Dashed**) in the **Hidden Line Style** drop-down list of the **Conventions** area in the **General** tab as the default hidden line style, see Figure 10.33. Next, click on the **Apply** button and then the **OK** button in the dialog box to confirm the change made and exit the dialog box.

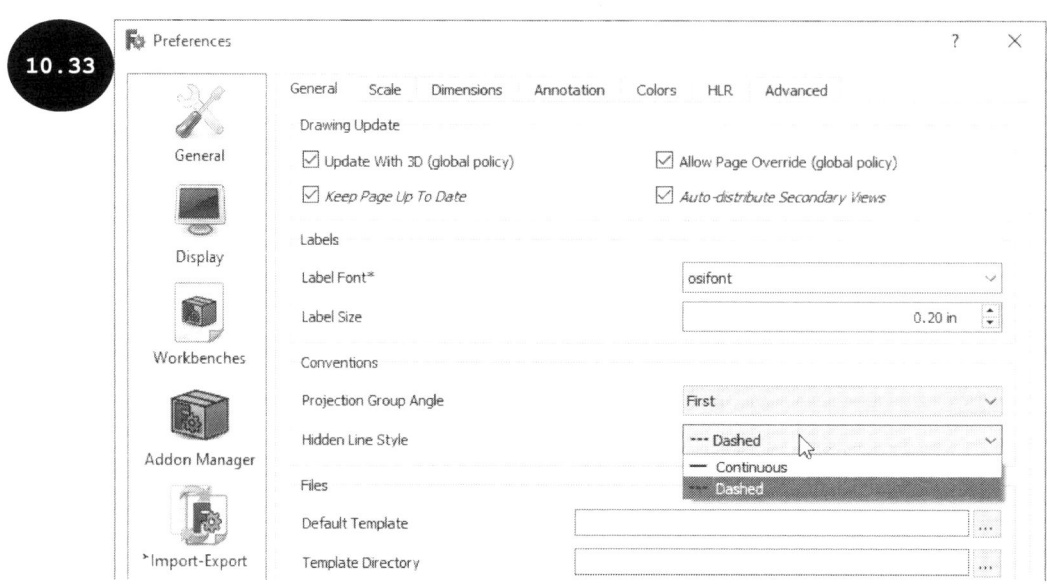

Creating a Section View

A section view is created by cutting a model using a section line and then viewing it from the direction normal to the section line. A section view represents a cross-section of a model for illustrating its internal details. In FreeCAD, you can create a section view by using the **Insert Section View** tool. The method for creating a section view is discussed below:

1. Select an existing view as the parent view in the 3D View area or in the Tree View for creating the section view.

2. After selecting an existing view, click on the **Insert Section View** tool in the **TechDraw Views** toolbar, see Figure 10.34. The **Create Section View** sub-window appears in the **Task Panel**, see Figure 10.35.

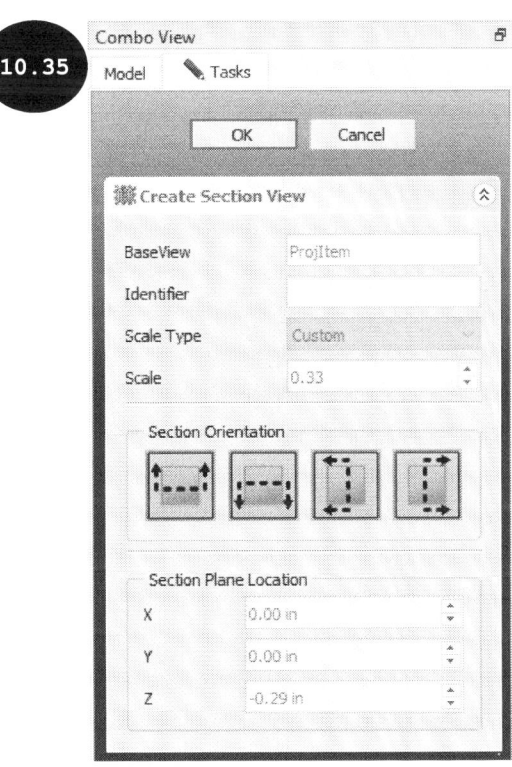

3.   Select the required section line button (**Looking up**, **Looking down**, **Looking left**, or **Looking right**) in the **Section Orientation** area of the **Task Panel**. A preview of the respective section view of the model appears on the sheet, see Figure 10.36. You may need to move the section view to a required location on the sheet by dragging it.

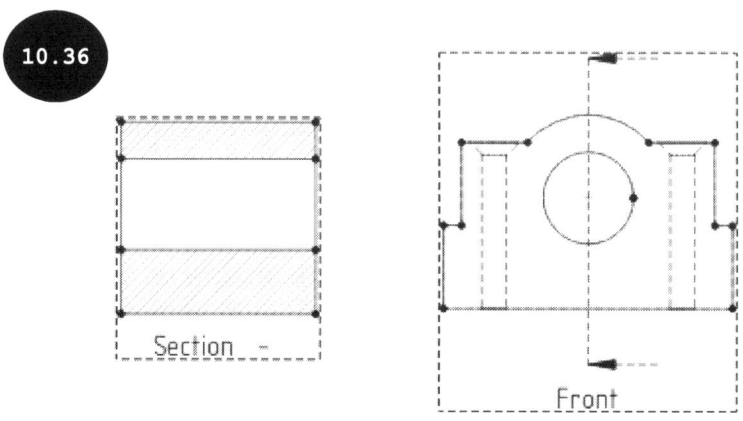

Note: A section view is created by cutting the model using the selected section line and then viewing it from the direction normal to the section line.

The direction of the arrows of the section line represents the viewing direction.

4.   Enter the required name for the section line like A, B, C, or D in the **Identifier** field of the **Task Panel** and then click anywhere on the sheet. The specified identifier name gets assigned to the section line and section view on the sheet, see Figure 10.37. In this figure, A is specified as the identifier name.

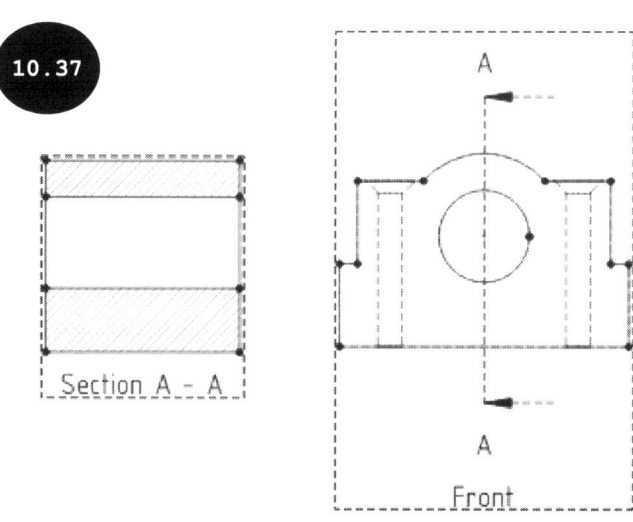

5. Specify the scale of the section view by selecting the required option in the **Scale Type** drop-down list of the **Task Panel**.

6. Enter the required X, Y, and Z distance values in the respective fields of the **Section Plane Location** area to define the location of the section line concerning the center of the view. By default, 0 distance is specified in the **X, Y,** and **Z** fields. As a result, the section line is created such that it passes through the center of the selected view.

7. Click on the **OK** button in the **Task Panel** to confirm the creation of the section view. A section view of the specified section line and parameters gets created. You can move the section view to the required location on the sheet by dragging it after pressing and holding the left mouse button.

Note: If needed, you can control or edit the scale of the hatching lines of the section view. For doing so, select the section view by clicking the left mouse button. The **Property Editor** appears at the lower section of the **Model** tab in the **Combo View** with **View** and **Data** tabs, refer to Figure 10.38. Ensure that the **Data** tab is activated in the **Property Editor** and then scroll down to display the **Hatch Scale** field, see Figure 10.38. Next, enter the required scale value in the **Hatch Scale** field of the **Property Editor** and click anywhere on the sheet. Figure 10.39 shows a section view with its hatch scale modified from 1 to 3.

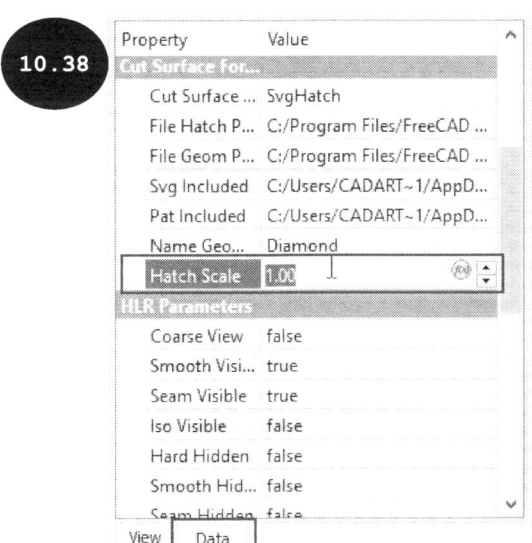

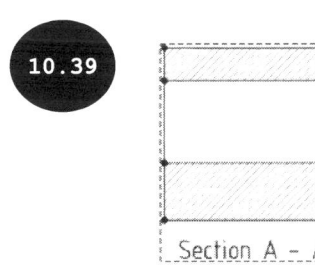

Hatch Scale 1

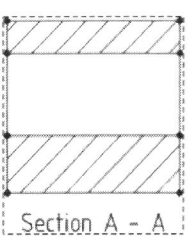

Hatch Scale 3

Creating a Detail View

A detail view is used for showing a portion of an existing drawing view on an enlarged scale. The method for creating a detailed view is discussed below:

1.   Select an existing view as the parent view in the 3D View area or in the **Tree View** to create a detailed view.

2.   After selecting an existing view, click on the **Insert Detail View** tool in the **TechDraw Views** toolbar, see Figure 10.40. The **New Detail View** sub-window appears in the **Task Panel** with default parameters that define a circular portion of the selected view to be detailed, see Figure 10.41. Also, the preview of a detailed view that is enclosed inside the circular portion appears on the sheet, see Figure 10.42.

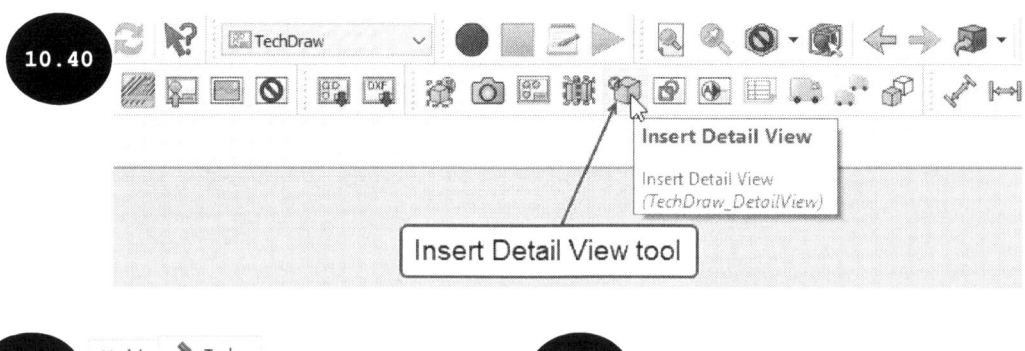

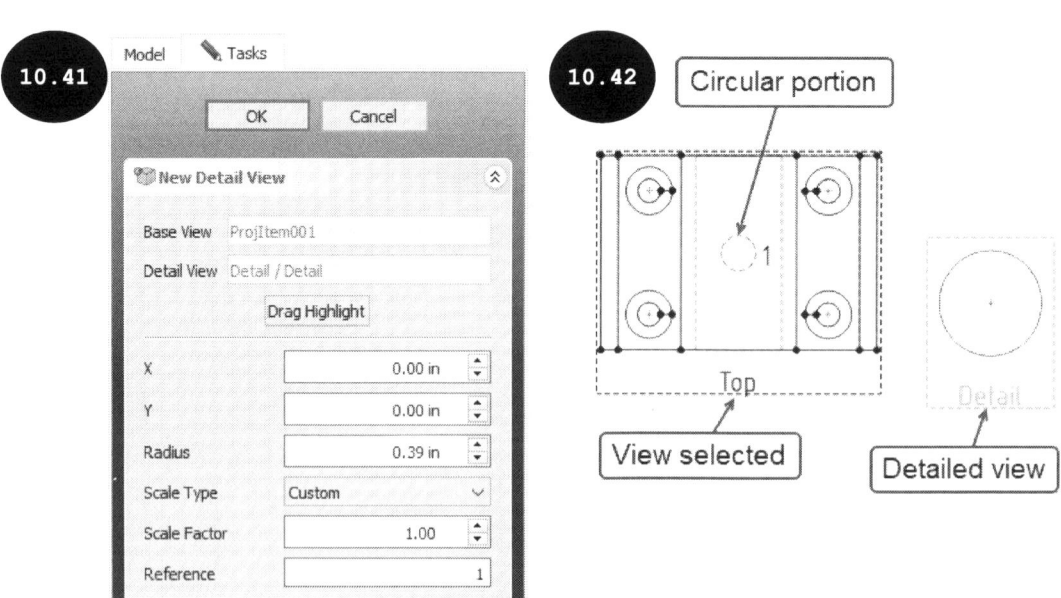

3.   Define a new position for the circular portion on the selected view (see Figure 10.43) by entering X and Y distance values in the respective fields of the **Task Panel**. A preview of the detailed view gets updated, accordingly on the sheet. Note that the X and Y distance values measure from the center of the selected view.

Tip: By default, the circular portion is defined at the center of the selected view, since the X and Y distance values are specified as 0 in the respective fields of the **Task Panel**, refer to Figure 10.41.

Note: You can also define the position of the circular portion of the selected view by dragging it. For doing so, click on the **Drag Highlight** button in the **Task Panel**. The circular portion gets highlighted on the view. Next, drag and drop the circular portion to a required location on the view to be detailed by pressing and holding the left mouse button.

4. Enter the radius of the circular portion to be detailed in the **Radius** field of the **Task Panel**. The preview of the detailed view gets updated, accordingly.

5. Specify a scale of the detailed view by selecting the required option in the **Scale Type** drop-down list of the **Task Panel**. The options in this drop-down list are the same as discussed earlier.

6. Enter a name for the detailed view like A, B, C, D, 1, 2, 3, or 4 in the **Reference** field of the **Task Panel** and then click anywhere on the sheet. The specified name gets assigned to the detailed view on the sheet, see Figure 10.43. In this figure, A is specified as the name of the detailed view.

7. Click on the **OK** button in the **Task Panel**. A detailed view gets created such that a portion of the selected view that is enclosed inside the circular portion gets enlarged, see Figure 10.43. You can move the detail view to the required location on the sheet by dragging it after pressing and holding the left mouse button.

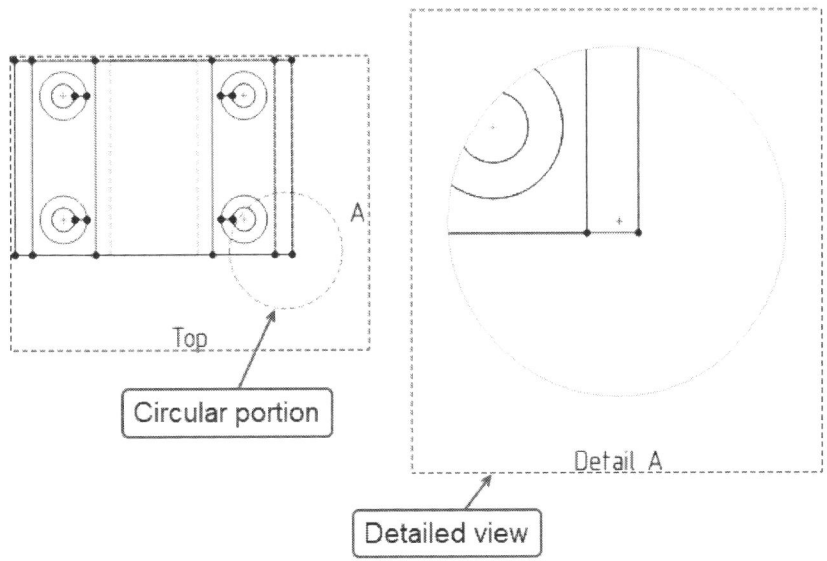

Applying Dimensions

After creating various drawing views of a part or an assembly on a sheet (page), you need to apply dimensions to them. In FreeCAD, you can apply dimensions by using the dimension tools such as **Insert Length Dimension**, **Insert Horizontal Dimension**, **Insert Radius Dimension**, and **Insert Diameter Dimension** available in the **TechDraw Dimensions** toolbar, see Figure 10.44.

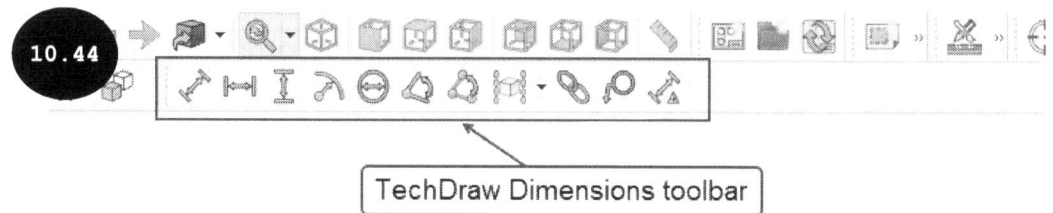

TechDraw Dimensions toolbar

Applying a Length Dimension

You can apply a length dimension to a linear edge/line, between two points/vertices, or between two linear edges/lines of a drawing view by using the **Insert Length Dimension** tool, see Figure 10.45. For doing so, select a linear edge/line, two points/vertices, or two parallel edges/lines of a drawing view. Note that you need to press and hold the CTRL key to select two entities for applying a dimension. Next, click on the **Insert Length Dimension** tool in the **TechDraw Dimensions** toolbar, refer to Figure 10.44. A length dimension gets applied to the selected entity or between the selected entities.

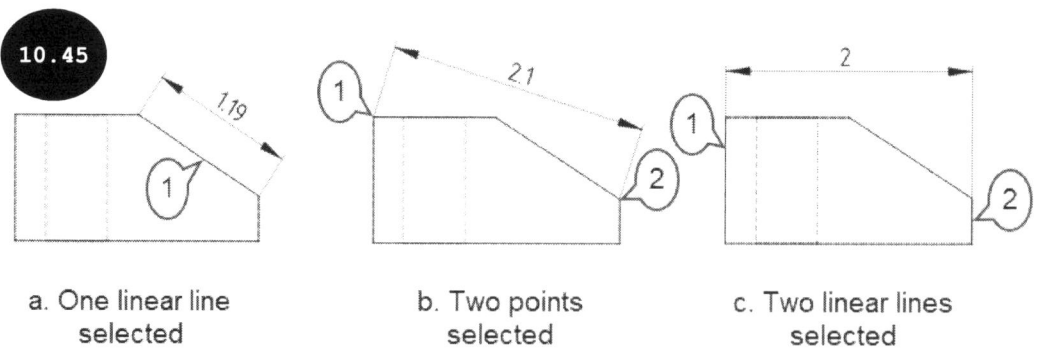

a. One linear line selected

b. Two points selected

c. Two linear lines selected

Note: In Figure 10.45, the display of outer frames/boundaries and labels of the views is turned OFF. You can toggle the display of outer frames and labels of views by clicking on the **Turn View Frames On/Off** tool in the TechDraw Decoration toolbar, see Figure 10.46.

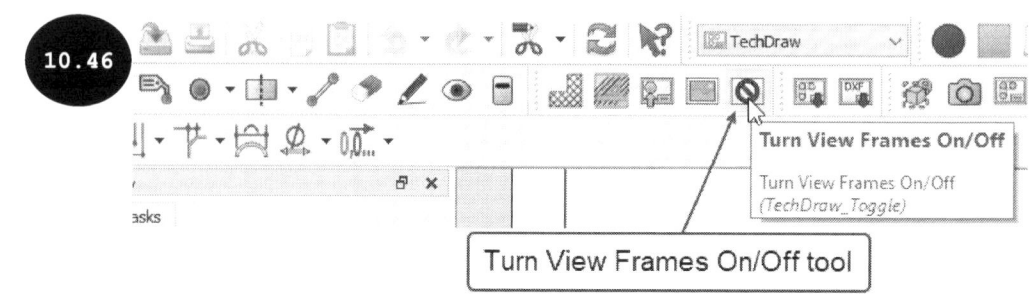

Turn View Frames On/Off tool

Tip: After applying a dimension, you can drag and drop it to the desired location on the sheet, if needed.

Applying a Horizontal Dimension ⊢⊣

You can apply a horizontal dimension to a linear edge/line, between two points/vertices, or between two linear edges/lines of a drawing view by using the **Insert Horizontal Dimension** tool, see Figure 10.47. For doing so, select a linear edge/line, two points/vertices, or two parallel edges/lines of a drawing view and then click on the **Insert Horizontal Dimension** tool ⊢⊣ in the **TechDraw Dimensions** toolbar. A horizontal dimension gets applied to the selected entity or between the selected entities.

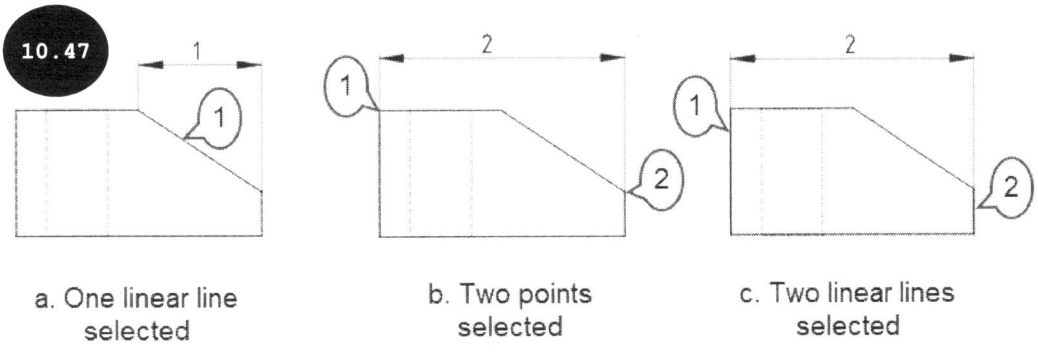

a. One linear line selected

b. Two points selected

c. Two linear lines selected

Applying a Vertical Dimension ⊥

You can apply a vertical dimension to a linear edge/line, between two points/vertices, or between two linear edges/lines of a drawing view by using the **Insert Vertical Dimension** tool, in a similar manner to applying a horizontal dimension.

Applying a Radius Dimension ⋌

You can apply a radius dimension to a circular edge (circle or arc) of a drawing view by using the **Insert Radius Dimension** tool. For doing so, select a circular edge (circle or arc) of a drawing view and then click on the **Insert Radius Dimension** tool in the **TechDraw Dimensions** toolbar. A radius dimension gets applied to the selected circular entity of the view, see Figure 10.48.

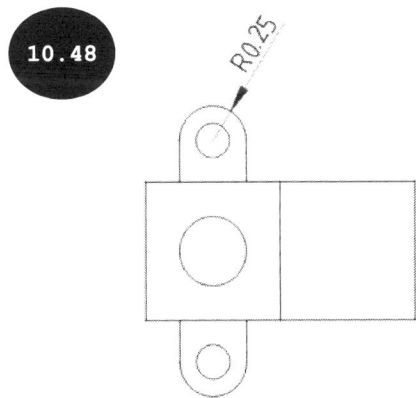

Applying a Diameter Dimension

You can apply a diameter dimension to a circular edge (circle or arc) of a drawing view by using the Insert Diameter Dimension tool, in a similar manner to applying a radius dimension, see Figure 10.49.

Applying an Angle Dimension

You can apply an angular dimension between two linear edges/lines of a drawing view by using the Insert Angle Dimension tool. For doing so, select two linear edges/lines of a drawing view and then click on the Insert Angle Dimension tool in the TechDraw Dimensions toolbar. An angular dimension gets applied between the selected entities, see Figure 10.50.

Applying a 3-Point Angle Dimension

You can apply a 3-point angular dimension by selecting three vertices or points of a drawing view by using the Insert 3-Point Angle Dimension tool. For doing so, select three vertices or points of a drawing view by pressing the CTRL key. Note that the second selected vertex or point should be the apex of the angle. After selecting three vertices or points, click on the Insert 3-Point Angle Dimension tool in the TechDraw Dimensions toolbar. An angular dimension gets applied by selecting three vertices, see Figure 10.51.

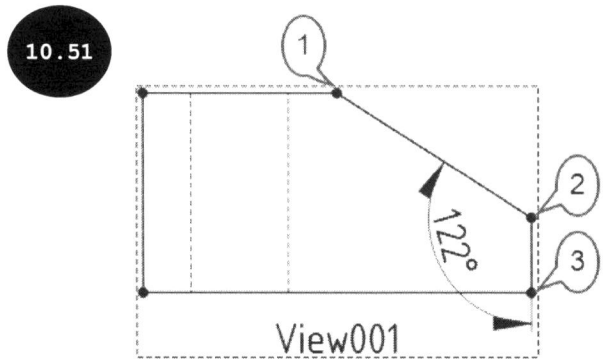

Note: In Figure 10.51, the display of the outer frame and label of the view is turned ON. You can toggle the display of outer frames and labels of the views by clicking on the **Turn View Frames On/Off** tool in the **TechDraw Decoration** toolbar.

Applying a Horizontal Extent Dimension

You can apply a horizontal extent dimension between the leftmost and rightmost points of a selected edge by using the **Insert Horizontal Extent Dimension** tool, see Figure 10.52. For doing so, select an edge (linear, curve, or circular) of a drawing view and then click on the **Insert Horizontal Extent Dimension** tool in the **TechDraw Dimensions** toolbar, see Figure 10.53. A horizontal extent dimension gets applied between the leftmost and rightmost points of the selected edge.

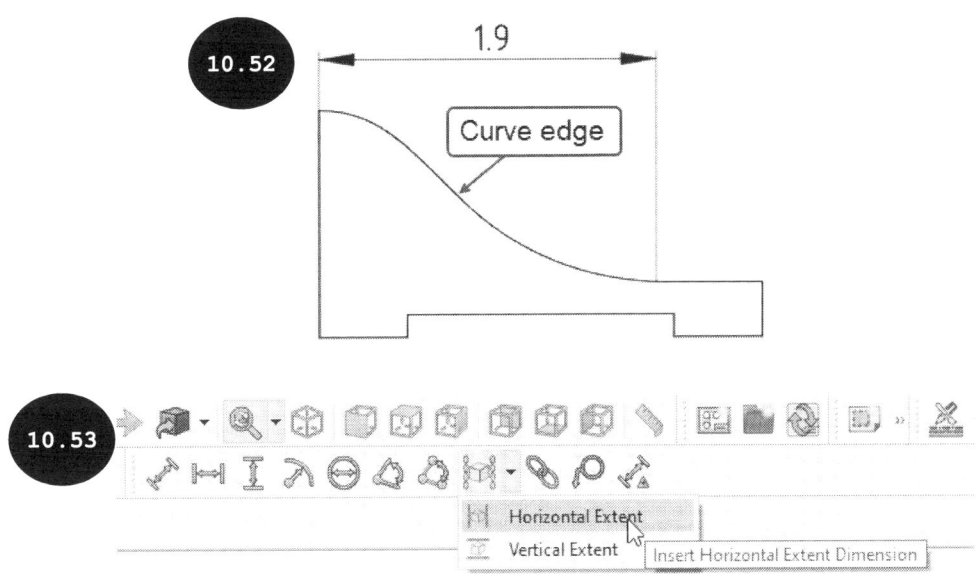

Applying a Vertical Extent Dimension

You can apply a vertical extent dimension between the bottommost and topmost points of a selected edge by using the **Insert Vertical Extent Dimension** tool, similar to applying a horizontal extent dimension, see Figure 10.54.

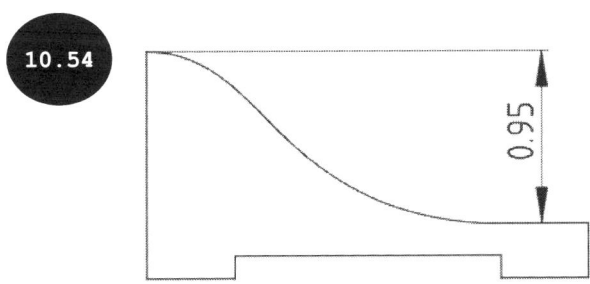

Exporting Drawing as a DXF File

After creating drawing views of a model and applying the required dimensions, you can export the drawing sheet (page) as a DXF file. The method for exporting the current sheet (page) as a DXF file is discussed below:

1. Click on the **Export Page as DXF** tool in the **TechDraw File Access** toolbar, see Figure 10.55. The **Save DXF file** dialog box appears.

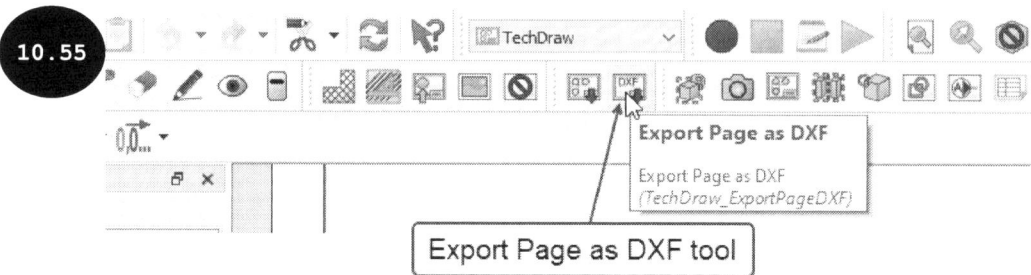

2. In this dialog box, browse to the required location where you want to save the DXF file.

3. Enter the required name of the file in the **File name** field of the dialog box, as required.

4. Click on the **Save** button in the dialog box. The current active drawing sheet (page) gets exported to the DXF file and saved at the specified location.

Exporting Drawing as an SVG File

You can also export the currently active drawing sheet (page) as an SVG file. The method for exporting the current sheet (page) as an SVG file is discussed below:

1. Click on the **Export Page as SVG** tool in the **TechDraw File Access** toolbar, see Figure 10.56. The **Save DXF file** dialog box appears.

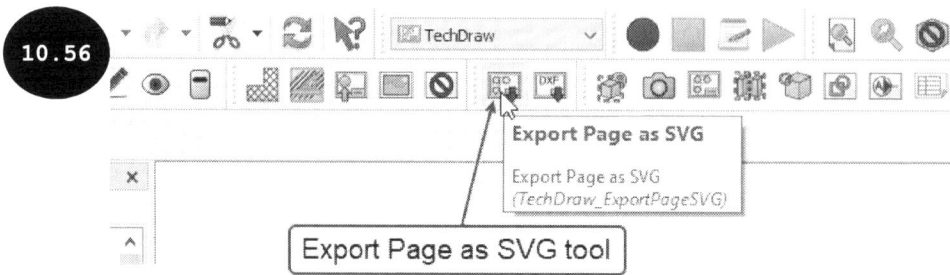

2. In this dialog box, browse to the required location where you want to save the SVG file and then enter the required name of the file in the **File name** field.

3. Click on the **Save** button in the dialog box. The current active drawing sheet (page) gets exported to the SVG file and saved at the specified location.

Tutorial 1

Open the model created in Tutorial 1 of Chapter 5 and then create different drawing views: front, top, right, isometric, and section, as shown in Figure 10.57 in the A4_LandscapeTD sheet template. Also, you need to apply dimensions. Note that the third angle of projection needs to be used for creating drawing views. All dimensions are in mm.

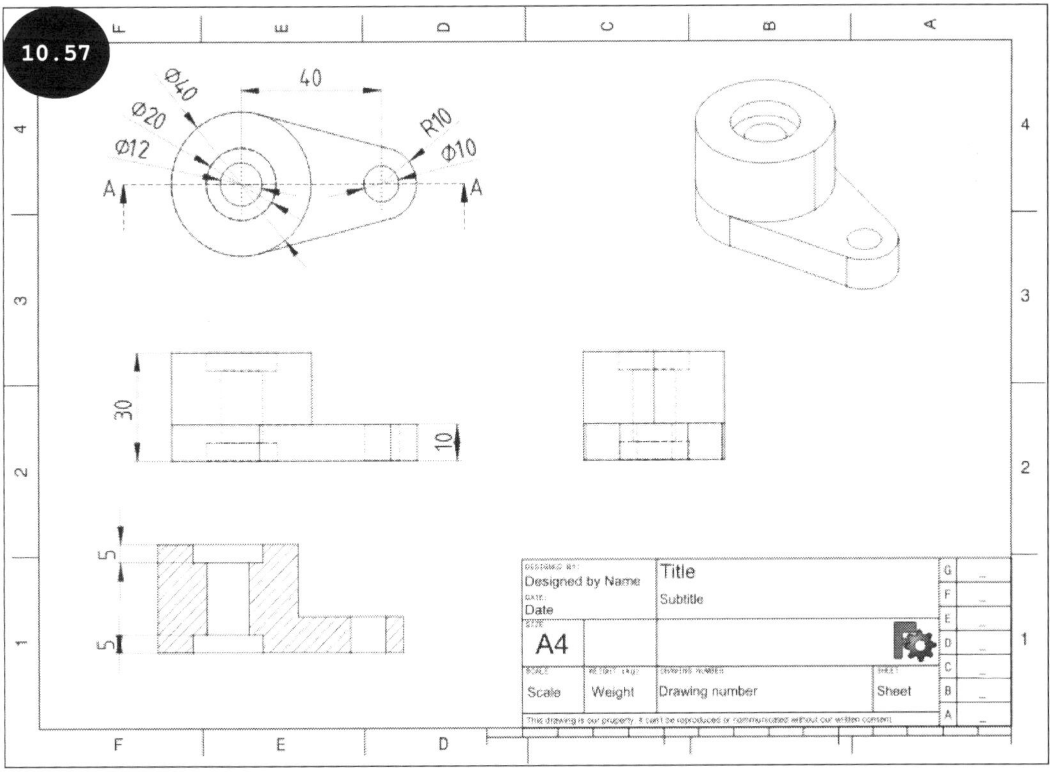

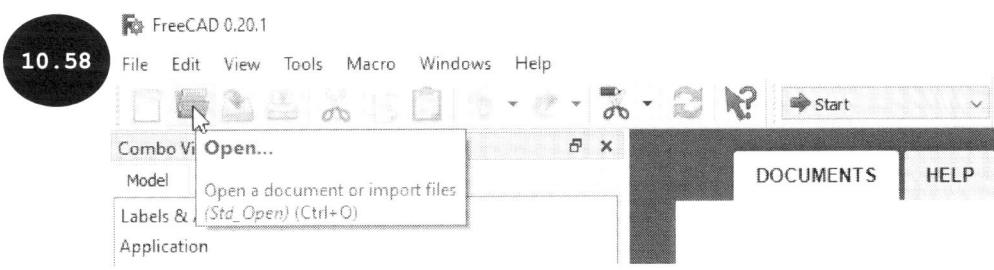

Section 1: Opening Tutorial 1 of Chapter 5

1. Start FreeCAD by double-clicking on the **FreeCAD 0.20** icon on your desktop, if not started already. The startup user interface of FreeCAD appears.

   Now, you need to open the model created in Tutorial 1 of Chapter 5 to create its drawing.

2. Click on the **Open** button in the **File** toolbar, see Figure 10.58. The **Open document** dialog box appears. Alternatively, press the CTRL + O keys to invoke this dialog box.

3. In the **Open document** dialog box, browse to the **Chapter 5** folder and then select the **Ch05-Tutorial 1** model. Note that you need to create this model, if not created in Chapter 5.

4. After selecting the model, click on the **Open** button in the dialog box. The model created in Tutorial 1 of Chapter 5 gets opened in a separate tab and is active, by default, see Figure 10.59.

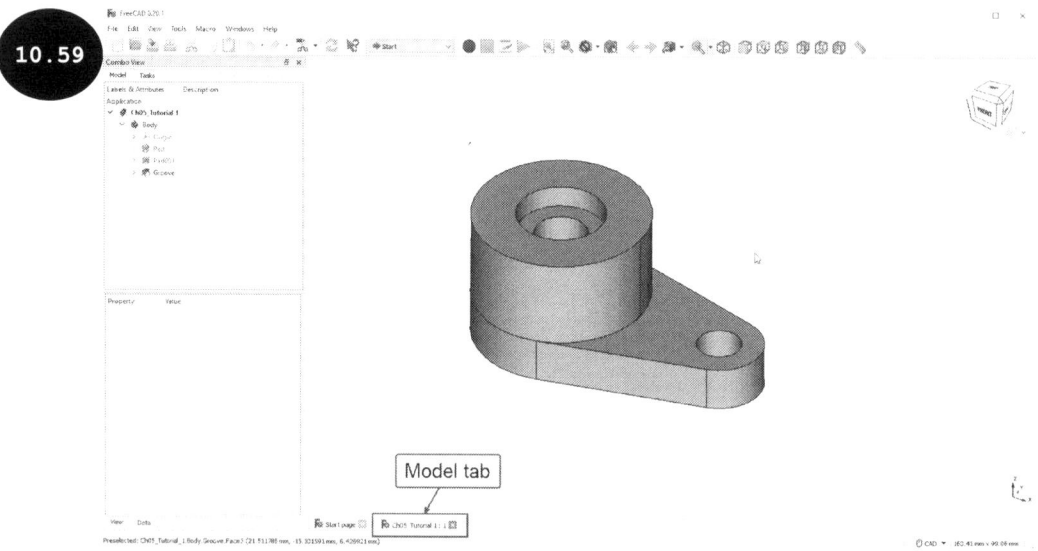

Section 2: Invoking the TechDraw Workspace

Now, you need to invoke the **TechDraw** workspace for creating a 2D drawing of the opened model.

1. Invoke the **Workbench Selector** in the **Workbench** toolbar and then select the **TechDraw** workbench, see Figure 10.60. The **TechDraw** workbench gets invoked.

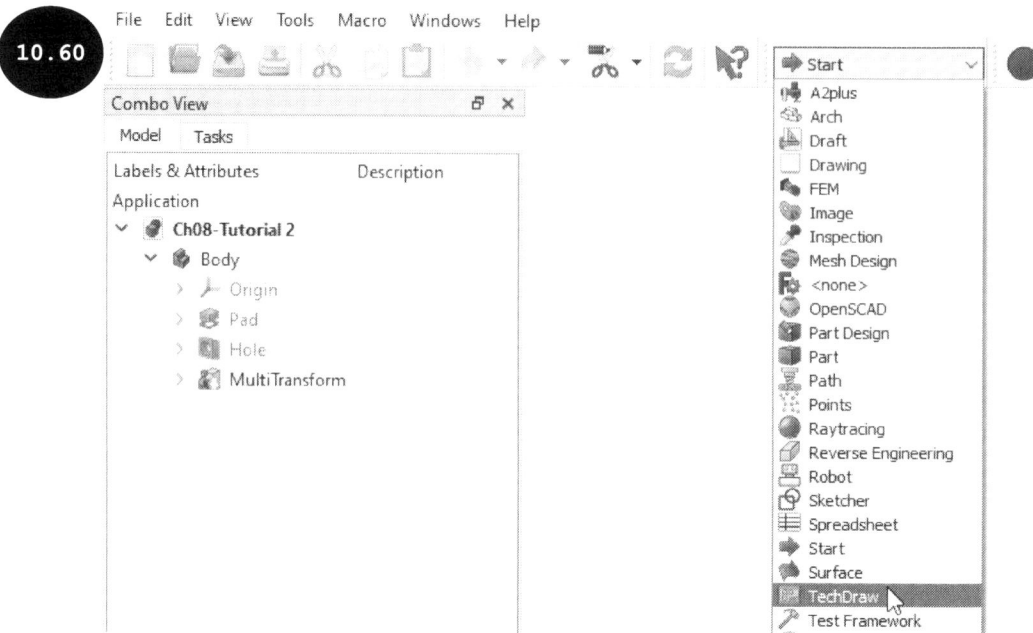

Section 3: Inserting a Drawing Sheet (Page)

Now, you need to insert a drawing sheet (page) of the A4_LandscapeTD sheet template for creating different drawing views of the 3D model.

1. Click on the **Insert Page using Template** tool in the **TechDraw Pages** toolbar, see Figure 10.61. The **Select a Template File** window appears with a list of available drawing templates, see Figure 10.62.

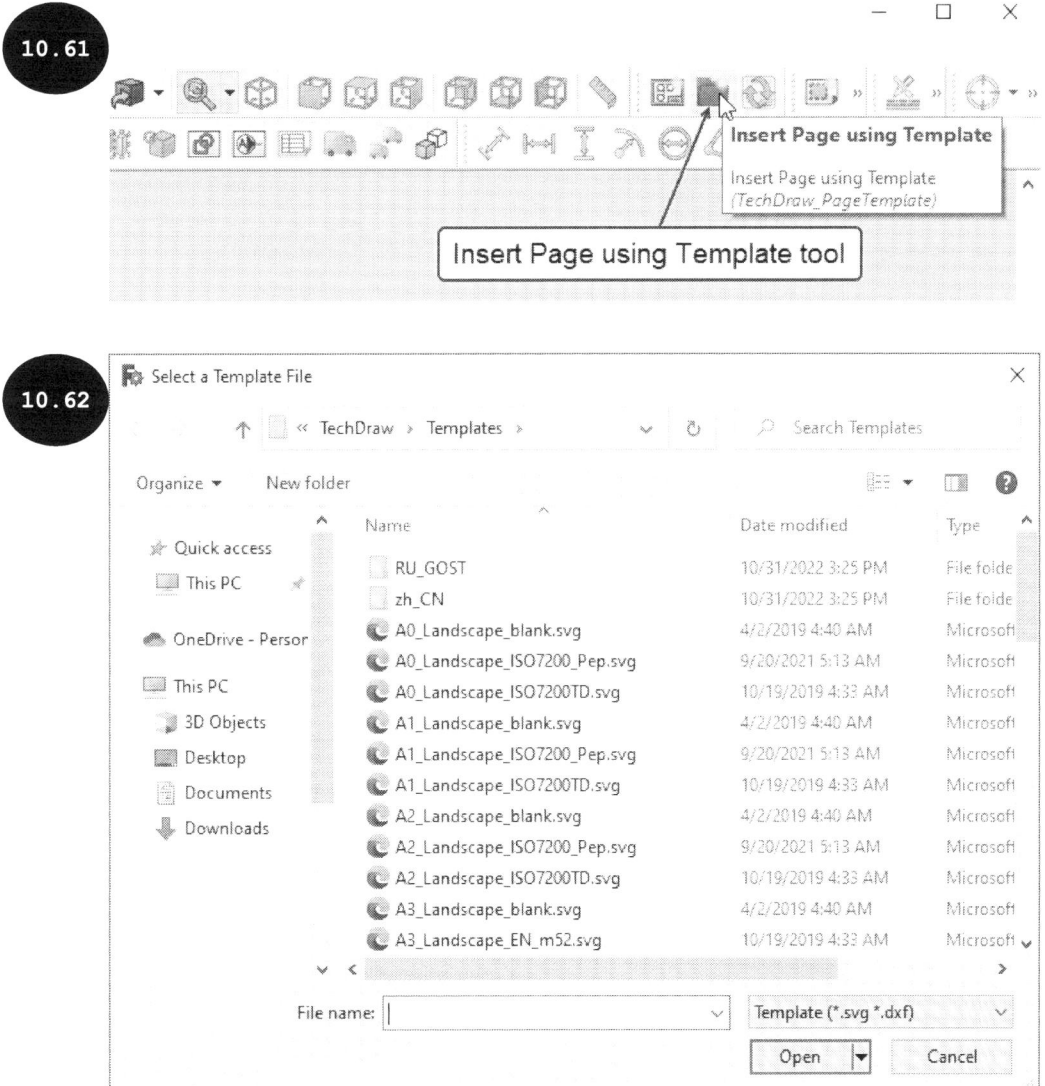

2. In this dialog box, scroll down and select the **A4_LandscapeTD** template. Next, click on the **Open** button. A new drawing sheet (page) of the selected template gets inserted with a default name "*Page*" in a new separate tab and becomes active by default, see Figure 10.63.

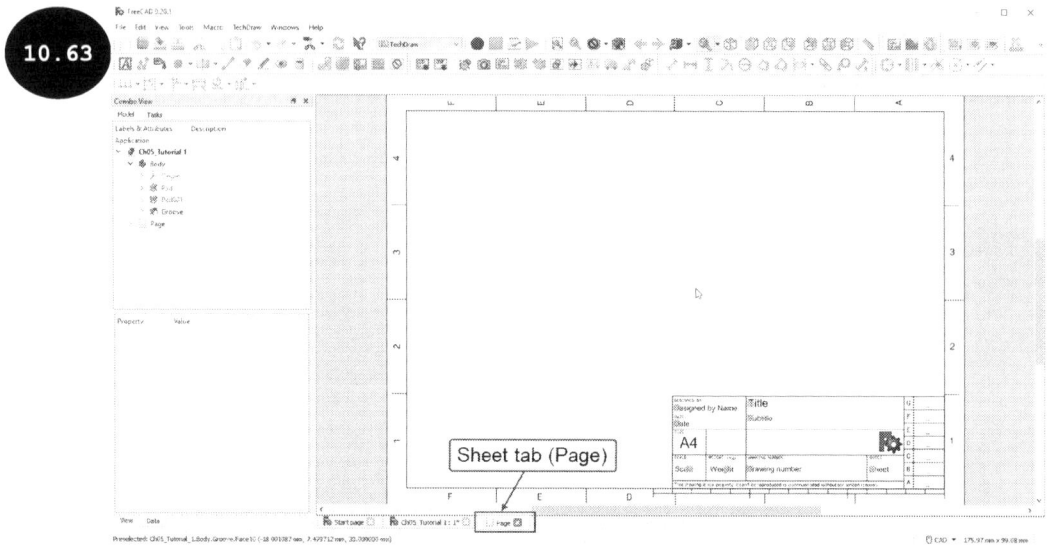

Sheet tab (Page)

Section 4: Specifying Units

Now, you need to specify millimeters (mm) as the measurement units for the document.

1.   Click on **Edit > Preferences** in the **Standard Menu**. The **Preferences** dialog box appears.

2.   Ensure that the **General** section is selected in the left panel of the **Preferences** dialog box and then click on the **Units** tab, refer to Figure 10.64.

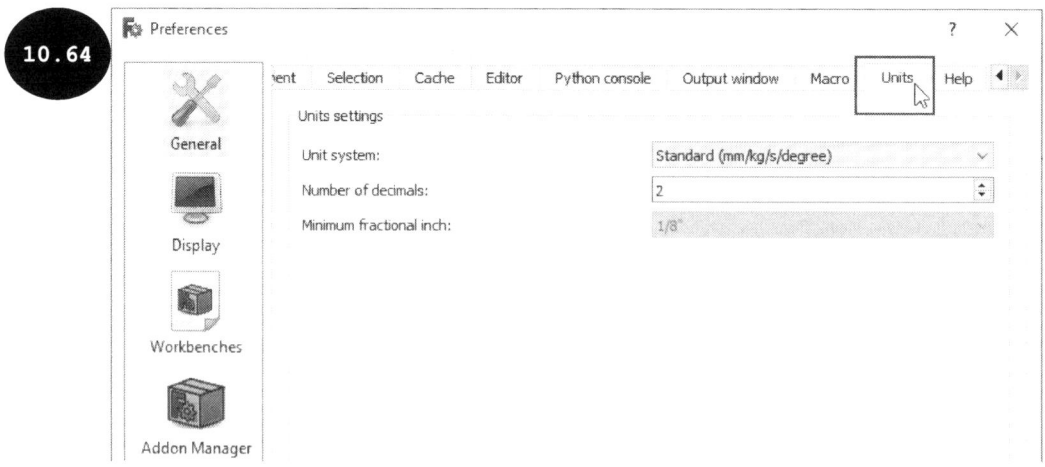

Tip: You may need to click on arrow ▶ at the upper right corner of the **Preferences** dialog box for displaying the **Units** tab.

3.   Ensure that the **Standard (mm/kg/s/degree)** option is selected in the **Unit system** drop-down list of the dialog box as the unit system of the current document.

4. Click on the **Apply** button and then the **OK** button in the **Preferences** dialog box. The selected unit system is defined, and the dialog box is closed.

Section 5: Creating Drawing Views

Now, you need to create multiple linked 2D projection drawing views.

1. Switch to the 3D model by clicking on its tab at the lower left corner of the drawing display area whose drawing views are to be created, see Figure 10.65.

_1.Body.Groove.Edge4 (-14.316083 mm, -13.909728 mm, 10.000000 mm)

2. Set the view orientation of the model to Front by using the **Navigation Cube** as the primary view to be created on the sheet (page), see Figure 10.66.

3. Click on the model "**Body**" in the **Tree View** for creating its view as per its current orientation, see Figure 10.67.

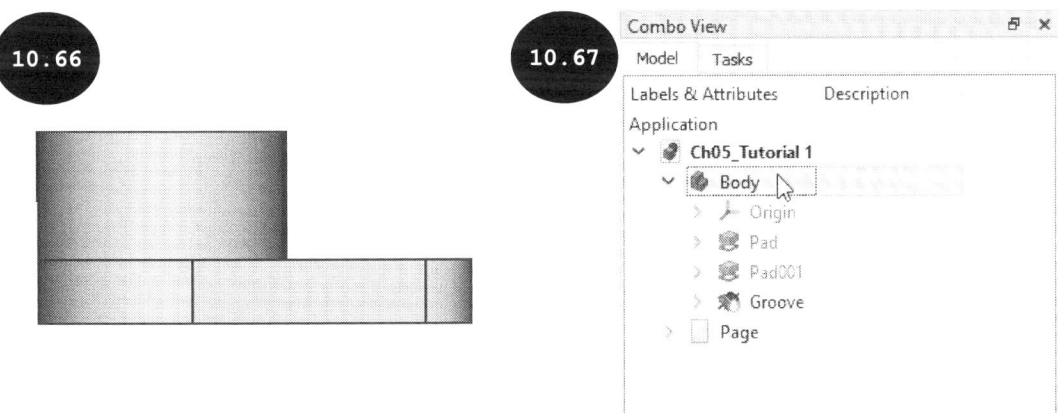

4. Switch to the drawing sheet (page) by clicking on its respective tab "*Page*" for creating the drawing views of the model, see Figure 10.68.

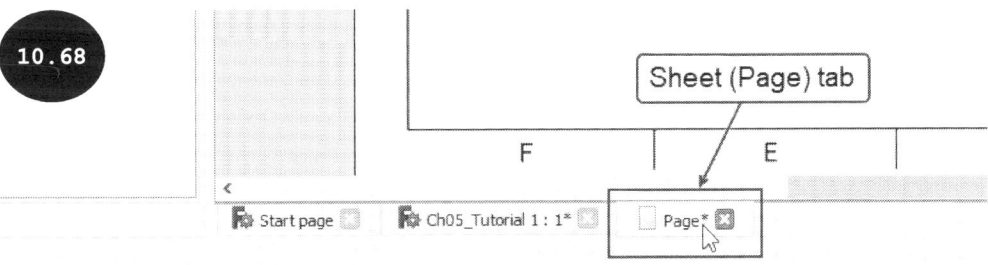

Now, you can create the drawing views of the model.

5. Click on the **Insert Projection Group** tool in the **TechDraw Views** toolbar, see Figure 10.69. The Front view of the model gets created on the sheet (page), see Figure 10.70. Also, the **Projection Group** sub-window appears in the **Task Panel**, see Figure 10.71.

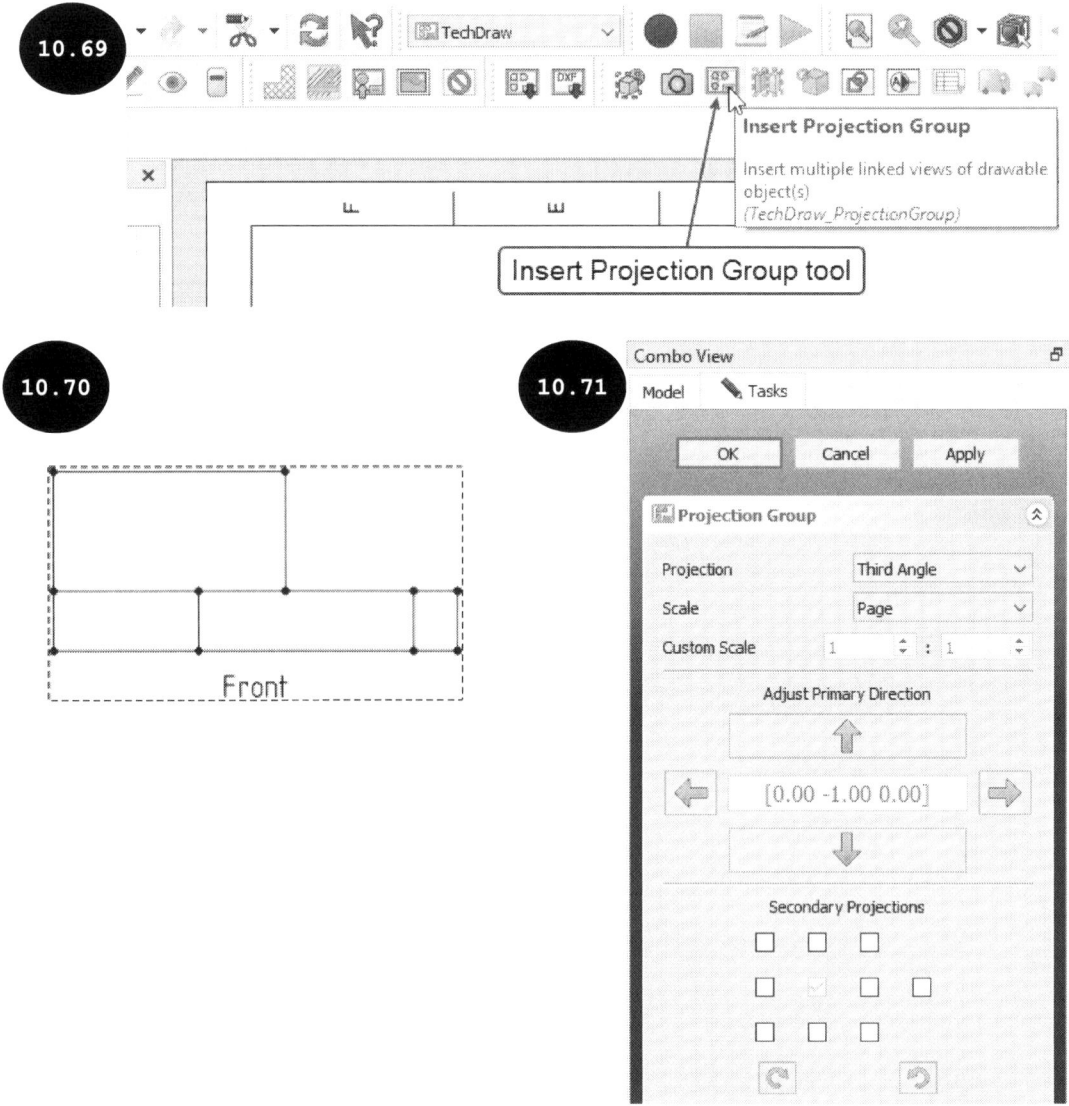

6. Define the third angle of projection for creating the drawing views by selecting the **Third Angle** option in the **Projection** drop-down list of the **Task Panel**.

7. Select the **Custom** option in the **Scale** drop-down list and then set the scale factor to **1:1** in the respective **Custom Scale** fields in the **Task Panel**. Next, press the TAB key and then the F5 key to update the view on the sheet as per the specified scale factor.

8. Select the **Top**, **Right**, and **RightFrontTop** (isometric) check boxes in the **Secondary Projections** area of the **Task Panel**, see Figure 10.72. The respective drawing views get created on the sheet, see Figure 10.73.

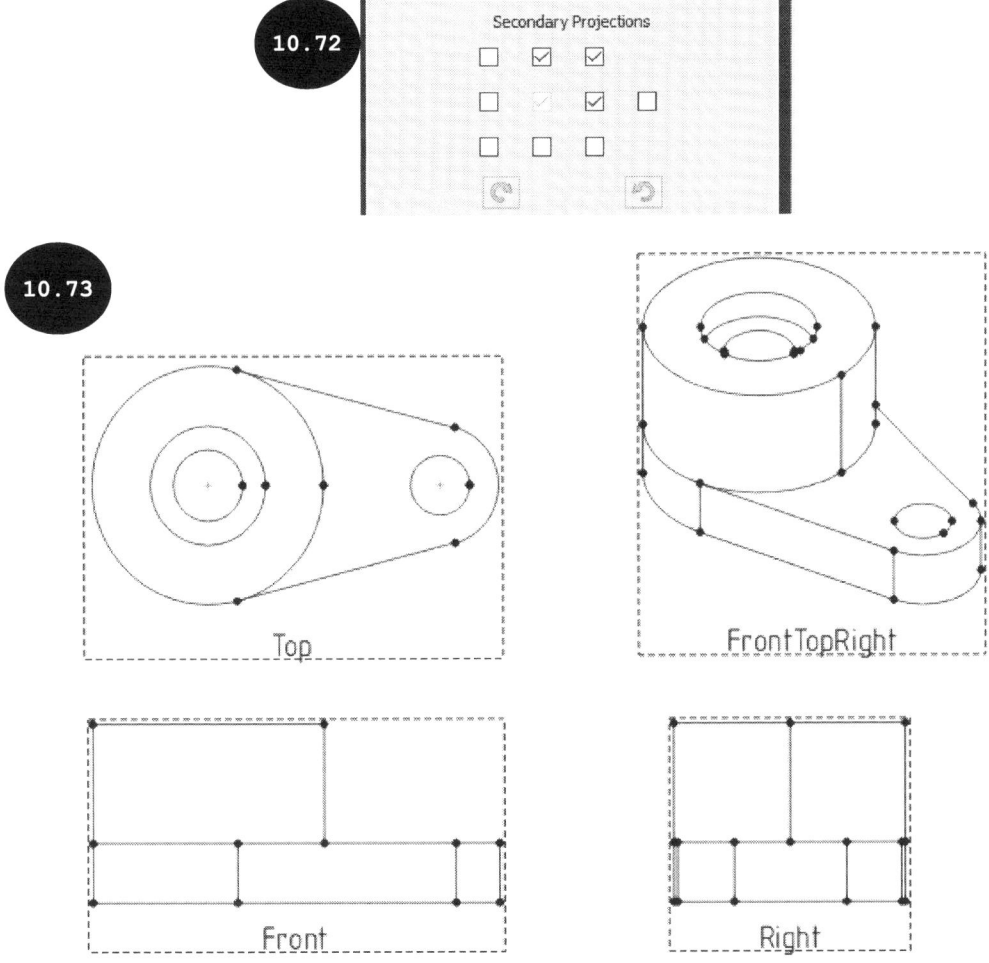

10.72

10.73

Top

FrontTopRight

Front

Right

Note: You may need to move the drawing views of the model to position them on the sheet, as required. For doing so, move the cursor over the outer frame of the view to be moved and then drag it to a new location on the sheet by pressing and holding the left mouse button. Note that when you move the primary view, all its linked projection views will also be moved, accordingly.

9. Click on the **OK** button in the **Task Panel**. The multiple linked 2D projection views get created on the sheet.

10. Define the position of the drawing views like the one shown in Figure 10.74. You can drag the views to define their position on the sheet, as required.

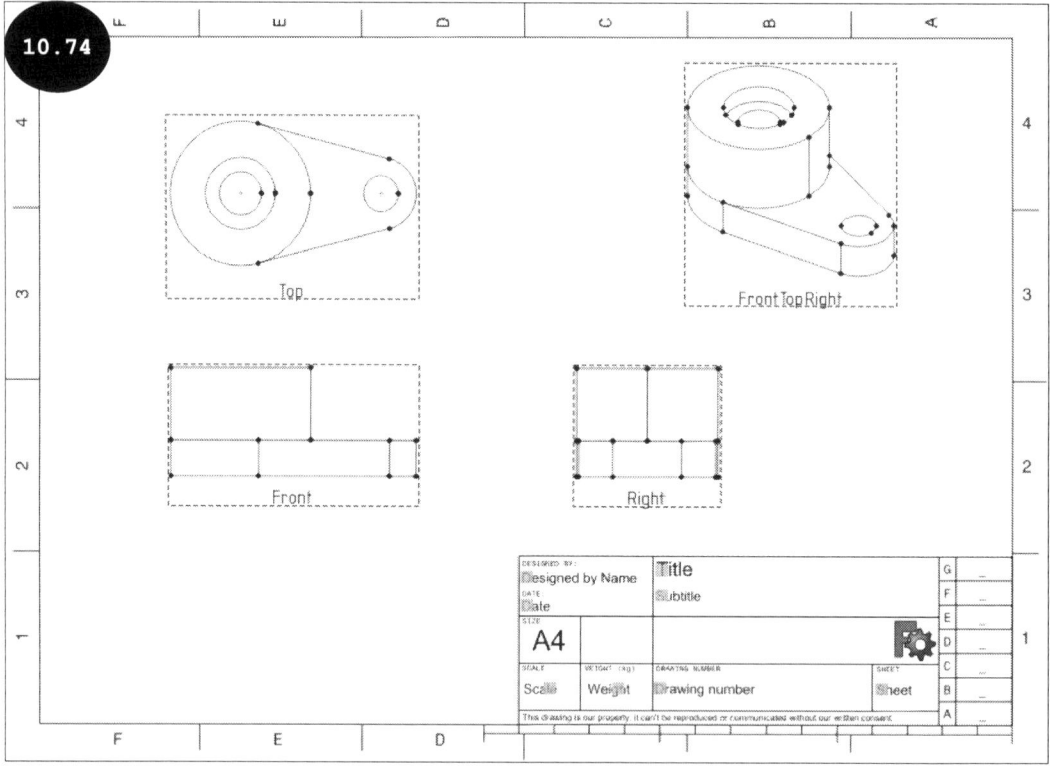

Section 6: Displaying Hidden Edges

Now, you need to turn on the display of hidden edges of the model on the drawing views.

1. Select the Front, Top, and Right views by clicking the left mouse button in **Tree View**. You need to press the CTRL key to select multiple views. The **Property Editor** appears at the lower section of the **Model** tab in the **Combo View** with **View** and **Data** tabs, refer to Figure 10.75.

2. Ensure that the **Data** tab is activated at the bottom of the **Property Editor**, refer to Figure 10.75.

3. Click twice on the **Hard Hidden** field in the **Property Editor** and then select the **true** option in the drop-down list that appears, see Figure 10.75.

Property	Value
X	0.00 mm
Y	0.00 mm
Lock Position	true
Rotation	0.00 °
Caption	
Label	Front
HLR Parameters	
Coarse View	false
Smooth Visi...	true
Seam Visible	true
Iso Visible	false
Hard Hidden	false
Smooth Hid...	false
Seam Hidden	true
Iso Hidden	false

View   Data

4. Click anywhere on the sheet. The display of hidden lines gets turned ON in the selected views with the default hidden line style, see

Figure 10.76. Note that you may need to update the views by clicking on the **Refresh** tool ↻ in the **File** toolbar to display the hidden lines.

10.76

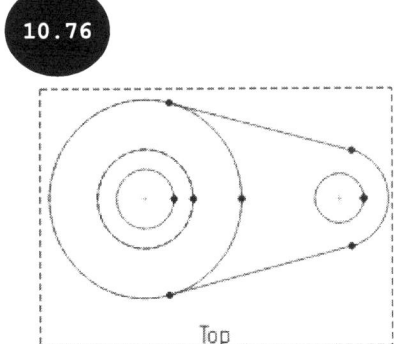

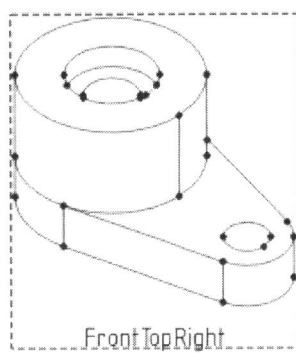

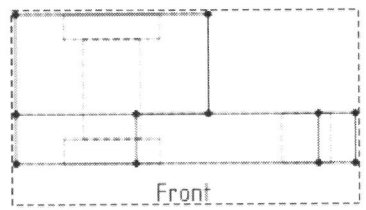

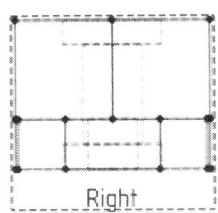

Note: In Figure 10.76, the hidden line style is set to dashed. To set the hidden line style, invoke the **Preferences** dialog box by clicking on **Edit > Preferences** in the **File** toolbar. Next, click on the **TechDraw** section in its left panel of the **Preferences** dialog box and then select the required hidden line style (**Continuous** or **Dashed**) in the **Hidden Line Style** drop-down list, see Figure 10.77. Next, click on **Apply** and then the **OK** button in the dialog box.

10.77

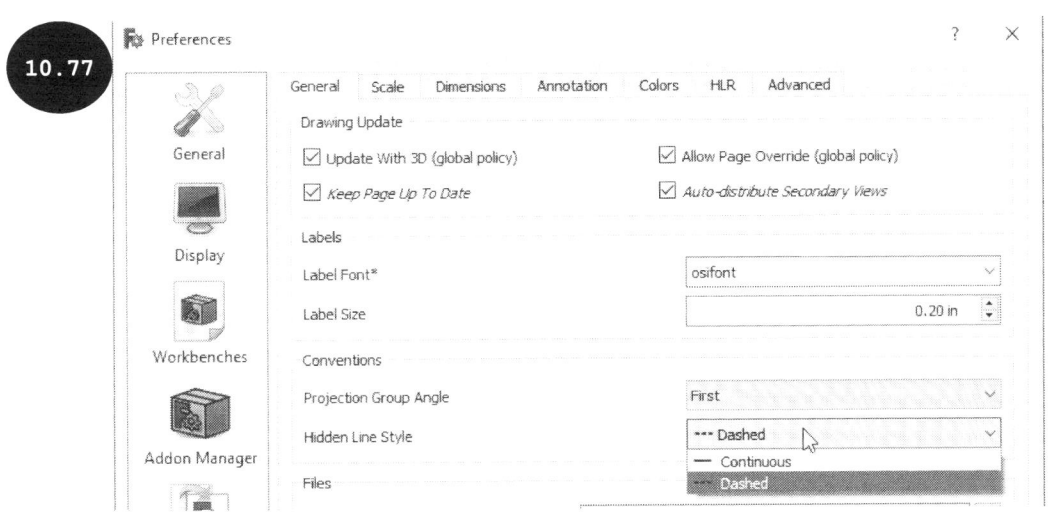

Section 7: Creating the Section View

Now, you need to create a section view.

1. Select the Top view as the parent view for creating the section view.

2. Click on the **Insert Section View** tool in the **TechDraw Views** toolbar, see Figure 10.78. The **Create Section View** sub-window appears in the **Task Panel**, see Figure 10.79.

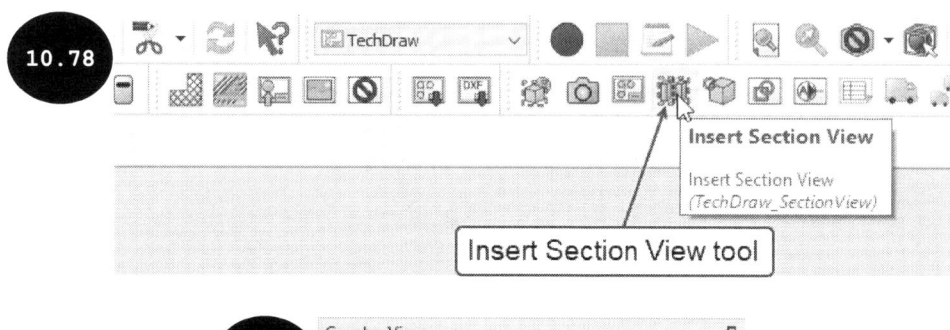

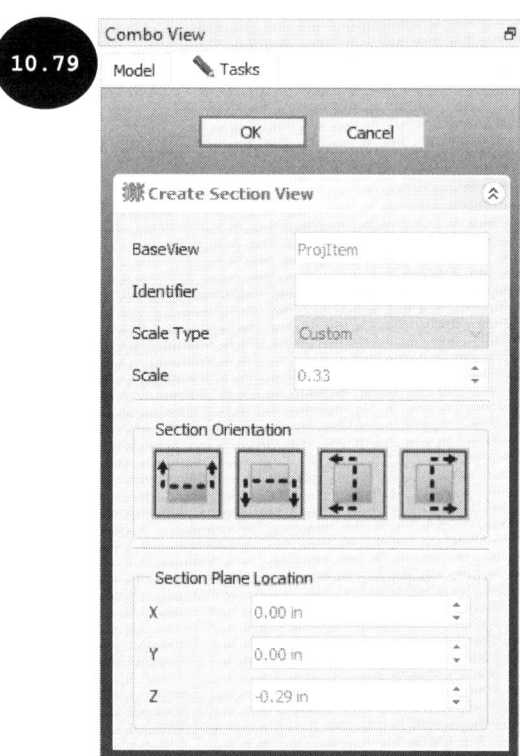

3. Select the **Looking up** section line button in the **Section Orientation** area of the **Task Panel**. A preview of the respective section view of the model appears on the sheet.

4. Move the section view to below the Front view on the sheet by dragging it, refer to Figure 10.80.

5. Enter **A** as the name for the section view in the **Identifier** field of the **Task Panel** and then click anywhere on the sheet. The specified identifier name gets assigned to the section line and section view on the sheet, refer to Figure 10.80.

6. Click on the **OK** button in the **Task Panel** to confirm the creation of the section view. The section view gets created, refer to Figure 10.80.

7. Move the section view as well as the other drawing views to the required locations on the sheet by dragging them after pressing and holding the left mouse button one by one, see Figure 10.80.

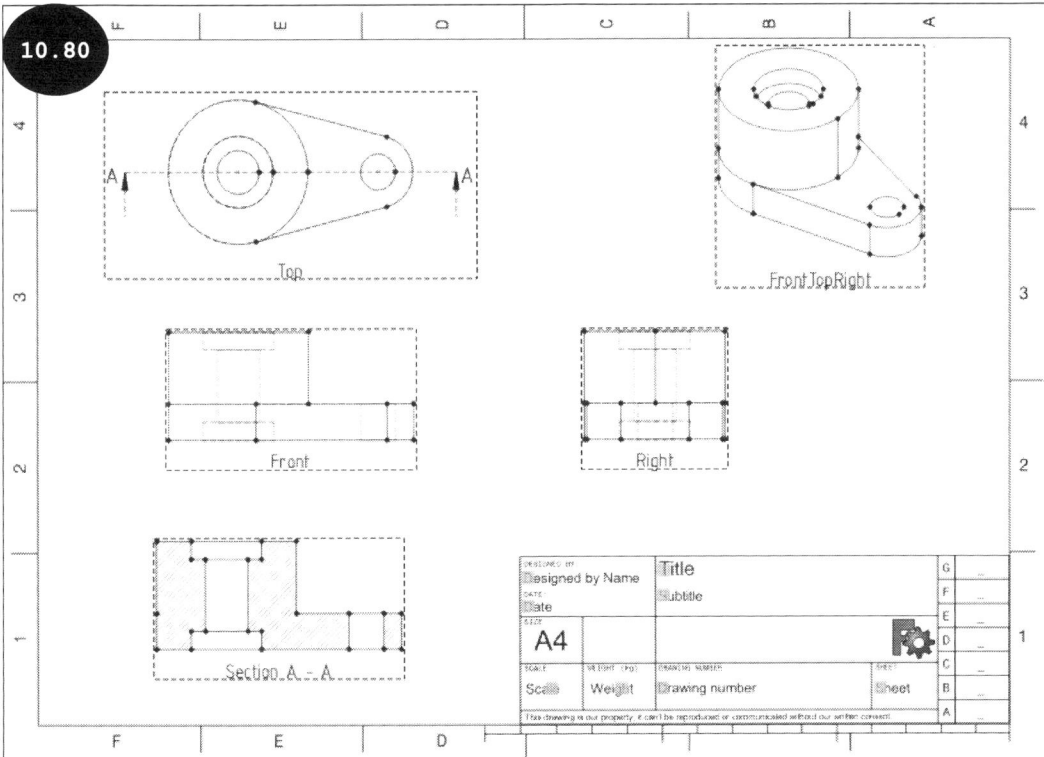

Section 8: Changing the Scale of Hatch Lines
Now, you can change the scale of the hatch lines of the section view.

1. Select the section view by clicking the left mouse button. The **Property Editor** appears at the lower section of the **Model** tab in the **Combo View** with **View** and **Data** tabs, see Figure 10.81.

2. Ensure that the **Data** tab is activated in the **Property Editor** and then scroll down for displaying the **Hatch Scale** field, see Figure 10.81.

3. Enter the **2** in the **Hatch Scale** field of the **Property Editor** (see Figure 10.81) and click anywhere on the sheet. Figure 10.82 shows a section view with its hatch scale set to 2.

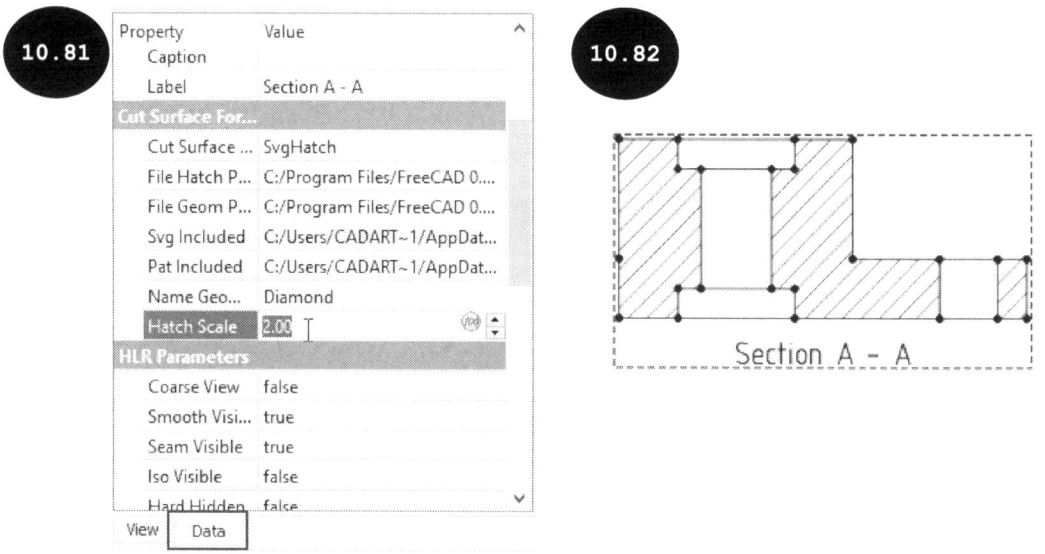

Section 9: Adding CenterMarks

Now, you need to add centermarks to the circular edges of the Top view.

1. Select the left and right inner circular edges of the Top view by pressing the CTRL key, see Figure 10.83.

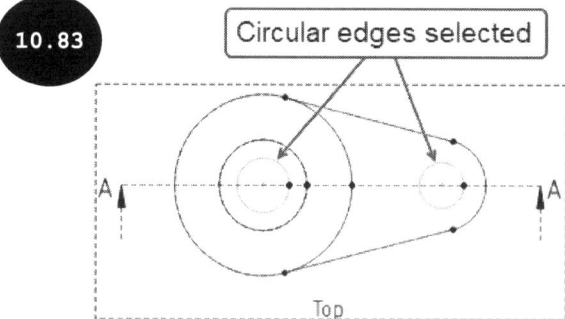

2. Click on the **Add Circle Centerlines** tool in the **TechDraw Centerlines** toolbar, see Figure 10.84. The centermarks get added to the selected circular edges, see Figure 10.85.

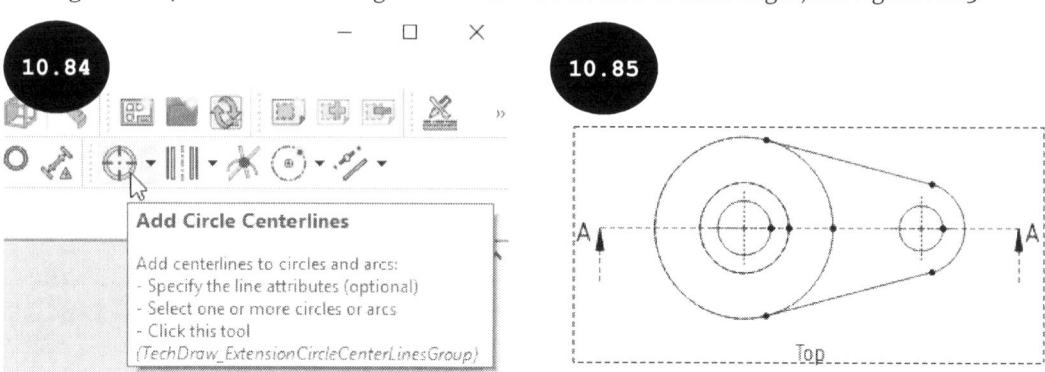

Section 10: Applying Dimensions

Now, you need to apply the required dimensions to the drawing views.

1. Select the vertical centerlines of the centermarks created on the Top view by pressing the CTRL key and then click on the **Insert Horizontal Dimension** tool in the **TechDraw Dimensions** toolbar, see Figure 10.86. A horizontal dimension gets applied between the selected centerlines, see Figure 10.87.

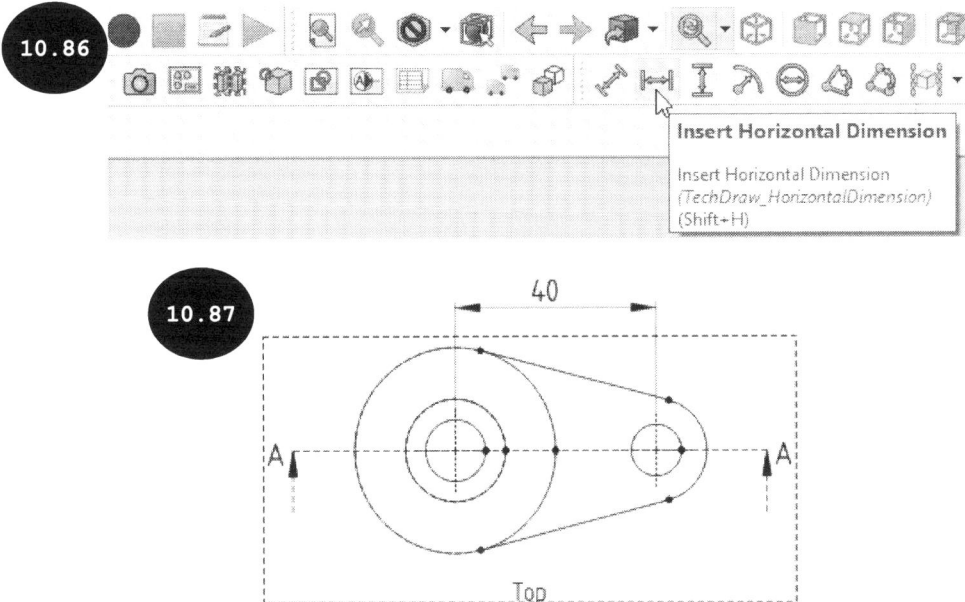

2. Move the dimension vertically upward and place it like the one shown in Figure 10.87. You can move a dimension by dragging it by pressing and holding the left mouse button.

3. Select the left outer circular edge of the Top view and then click on the **Insert Diameter Dimension** tool, see Figure 10.88. A diameter dimension gets applied to the selected circular edge of the Top view, see Figure 10.89. Note that after applying a dimension, you need to define its position on the sheet by dragging it.

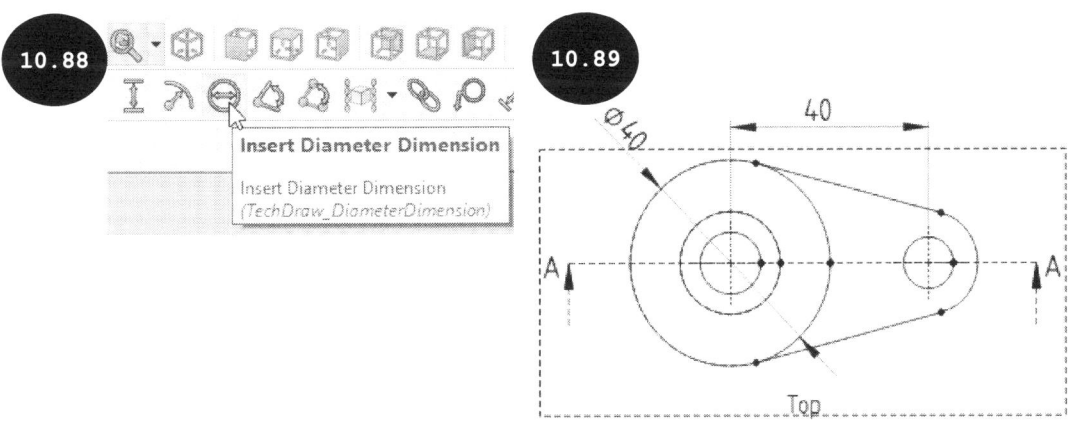

4. Similarly, apply the remaining diameter dimensions on the Top view by using the **Diameter Dimension** tool, see Figure 10.90.

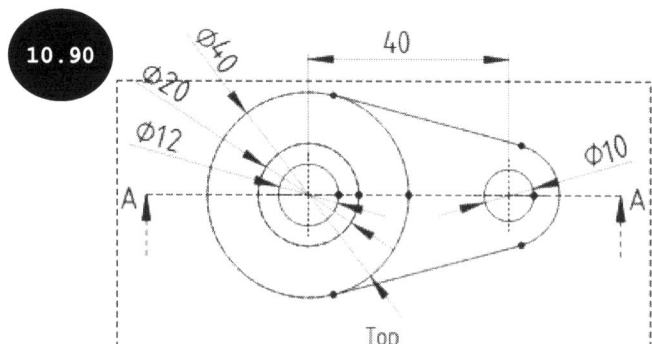

5. Select the right semi-circular (arc) edge of the Top view and then click on the **Insert Radius Dimension** tool. A radius dimension gets applied on the selected edge, see Figure 10.91. After applying a dimension, you need to define its position.

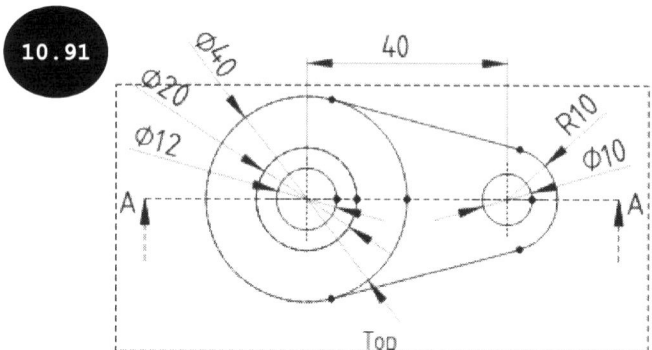

Now, you need to apply the dimensions on the other drawing views.

6. Select the topmost and bottommost horizontal edges of the Front view by pressing the CTRL key and then click on the **Insert Vertical Dimension** tool, see Figure 10.92. A vertical dimension of length 30 mm is applied between the selected edges, see Figure 10.93.

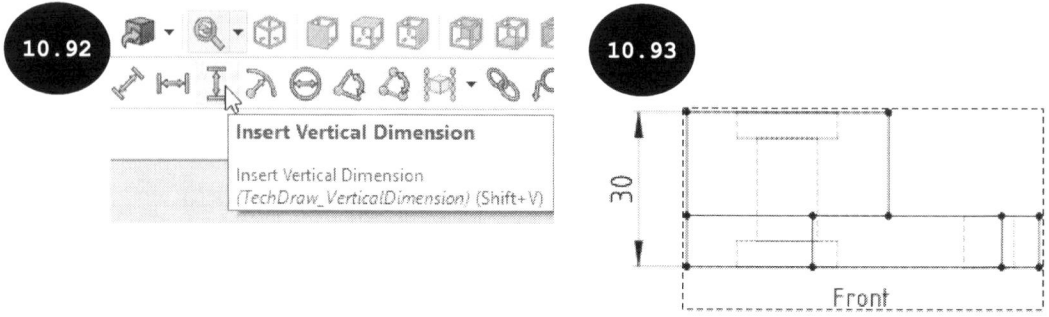

7. Select the rightmost vertical edge of the Front view and then click on the **Insert Vertical Dimension** tool. A vertical dimension of length 10 mm is applied to the selected edge, see Figure 10.94.

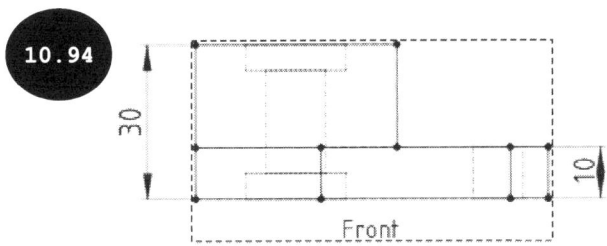

8. Similarly, apply the vertical dimensions to the Section view. Figure 10.95 shows the drawing views after applying all the required dimensions.

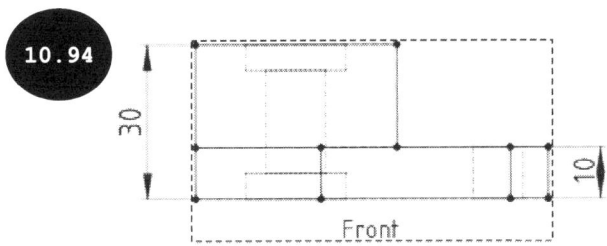

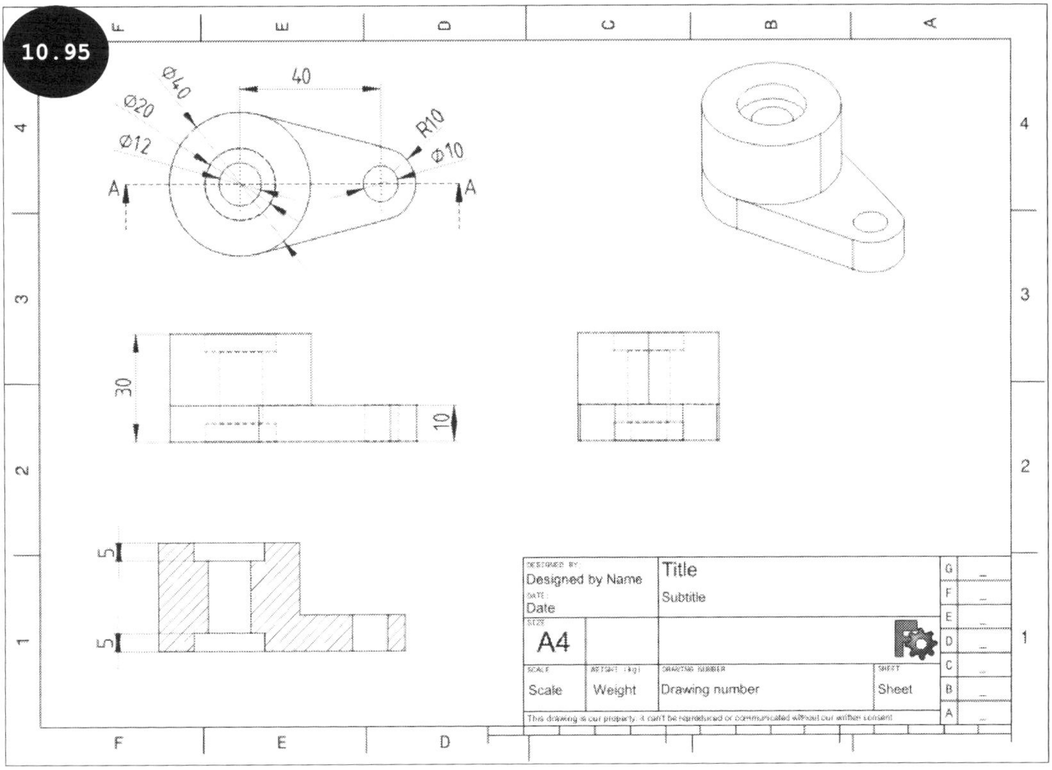

Note: In Figure 10.95, the display of outer frames/boundaries and labels of the views is turned OFF. For doing so, click on the **Turn View Frames On/Off** tool in the **TechDraw Decoration** toolbar, see Figure 10.96. It's a toggle tool.

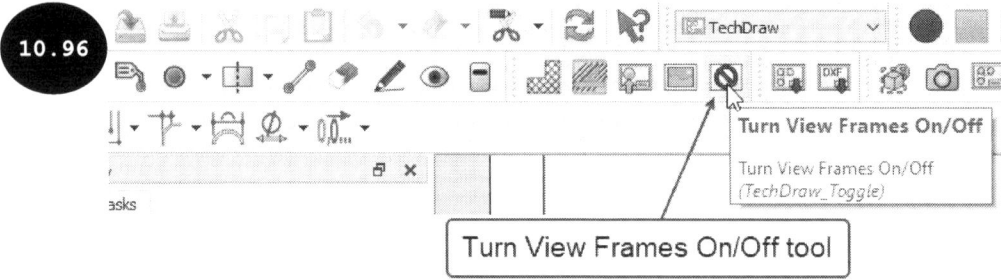

Section 11: Exporting the Drawing File as a DXF File

Now, you can export the current active drawing sheet (page) as a DXF file.

1. Click on the **Export Page as DXF** tool in the **TechDraw File Access** toolbar, see Figure 10.97. The **Save DXF file** dialog box appears.

2. Browse to the required location where you want to save the DXF file.

3. Enter the name of the file in the **File name** field of the dialog box, as required.

4. Click on the **Save** button in the dialog box. The current active drawing sheet (page) gets exported to the DXF file and saved at the specified location.

Section 12: Saving the Drawing File

After creating the drawing, you need to save it. In FreeCAD, a drawing file is saved internally in its 3D model file.

1. Click on the **Save** tool in the **File** toolbar, see Figure 10.98. The drawing file is saved as an internal file to its 3D model.

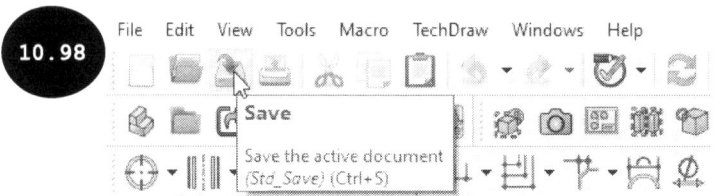

2. Click on **File > Close** in the **Standard Menu** to close the current document.

Hands-on Test Drive 1

Open the model created in Tutorial 2 of Chapter 4 and then create different drawing views: front, top, right, and section, as shown in Figure 10.99 in the A4_Landscape_ISO7200_Pep sheet template. Also, you need to apply dimensions. Note that the third angle of projection needs to be used for creating drawing views. All dimensions are in inches (in).

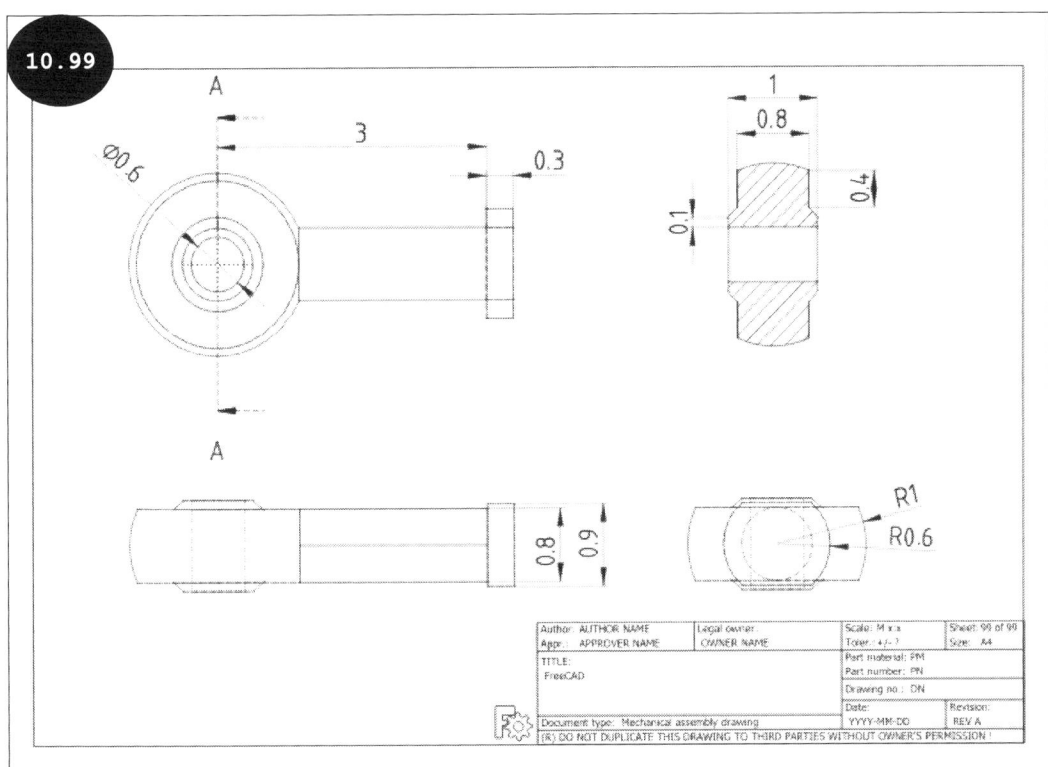

Summary

The chapter discussed how to invoke the TechDraw Workspace for creating a 2D drawing of a part or an assembly. It explained how to insert a drawing sheet, edit the title block text of a sheet, create an independent 2D projection view, modify the scale of a view, create multiple linked 2D projection views of a model, and display hidden lines on the views. It also discussed creating a section view and a detailed view. The methods for applying dimensions and exporting a drawing as DXF and SVG files have also been discussed in this chapter.

Questions

Complete and verify the following sentences:

- In the _____ workbench of FreeCAD, you can create a basic 2D drawing of a 3D model.

- A _____ controls the sheet size, drafting standard, sheet border, etc. of a sheet.

- The _____ tool is used for inserting a new drawing sheet (page) of a default template for creating drawing views.

- The _____ tool is used for creating an independent 2D projection view of a selected model on the drawing sheet (page).

- The _____ option is used for setting the scale of a drawing view as per the default specified scale of the sheet (page).

- The _____ tool is used for creating multiple linked 2D projection views such as the Front, Top, Left, and Right of a 3D model simultaneously on a sheet.

- FreeCAD supports _____ and _____ projection methods for creating drawing views.

- A _____ view represents a cross-section of a model for illustrating its internal details.

- A _____ view is used for showing a portion of an existing drawing view on an enlarged scale.

- The _____ tool is used for applying a radius dimension to a circular edge (circle or arc) of a drawing view.

- The _____ tool is used for applying an angular dimension between two linear edges/lines of a drawing view.

- The _____ tool is used for exporting the currently active drawing sheet (page) as a DXF file.

- A drawing sheet contains the editable text for attributes such as Designed by Name, Date, Title, Subtitle, Scale, and Drawing number in its title block. (True/False)

- After creating a drawing view, you cannot change its scale. (True/False)

- The direction of the arrows of the section line represents the viewing direction of a section view. (True/False)

INDEX

W

Z

Other Publications by CADArtifex
Some of the other Publications by CADArtifex are given below:

AutoCAD Textbooks
AutoCAD 2024: A Power Guide for Beginners and Intermediate Users
AutoCAD 2023: A Power Guide for Beginners and Intermediate Users
AutoCAD 2022: A Power Guide for Beginners and Intermediate Users
AutoCAD 2021: A Power Guide for Beginners and Intermediate Users
AutoCAD 2020: A Power Guide for Beginners and Intermediate Users
AutoCAD 2019: A Power Guide for Beginners and Intermediate Users
AutoCAD 2018: A Power Guide for Beginners and Intermediate Users
AutoCAD 2017: A Power Guide for Beginners and Intermediate Users
AutoCAD 2016: A Power Guide for Beginners and Intermediate Users

AutoCAD For Architectural Design Textbooks
AutoCAD 2023 for Architectural Design: A Power Guide for Beginners and Intermediate Users
AutoCAD 2022 for Architectural Design: A Power Guide for Beginners and Intermediate Users
AutoCAD 2021 for Architectural Design: A Power Guide for Beginners and Intermediate Users
AutoCAD 2020 for Architectural Design: A Power Guide for Beginners and Intermediate Users
AutoCAD 2019 for Architectural Design: A Power Guide for Beginners and Intermediate Users

Autodesk Fusion 360 Textbooks
Autodesk Fusion 360: A Power Guide for Beginners and Intermediate Users (6th Edition)
Autodesk Fusion 360: A Power Guide for Beginners and Intermediate Users (5th Edition)
Autodesk Fusion 360: A Power Guide for Beginners and Intermediate Users (4th Edition)
Autodesk Fusion 360: A Power Guide for Beginners and Intermediate Users (3rd Edition)
Autodesk Fusion 360: A Power Guide for Beginners and Intermediate Users (2nd Edition)
Autodesk Fusion 360: A Power Guide for Beginners and Intermediate Users

Autodesk Fusion 360 Surface and T-Spline Textbooks
Autodesk Fusion 360 Surface Design and Sculpting with T-Spline Surfaces (5th Edition)
Autodesk Fusion 360: Introduction to Surface and T-Spline Modeling

Autodesk Inventor Textbooks
Autodesk Inventor 2024: A Power Guide for Beginners and Intermediate Users
Autodesk Inventor 2023: A Power Guide for Beginners and Intermediate Users
Autodesk Inventor 2022: A Power Guide for Beginners and Intermediate Users
Autodesk Inventor 2021: A Power Guide for Beginners and Intermediate Users
Autodesk Inventor 2020: A Power Guide for Beginners and Intermediate Users

FreeCAD Textbooks
FreeCAD 0.20: A Power Guide for Beginners and Intermediate Users

PTC Creo Parametric Textbooks
Creo Parametric 9.0: A Power Guide for Beginners and Intermediate Users
Creo Parametric 8.0: A Power Guide for Beginners and Intermediate Users
Creo Parametric 7.0: A Power Guide for Beginners and Intermediate Users
Creo Parametric 6.0: A Power Guide for Beginners and Intermediate Users
Creo Parametric 5.0: A Power Guide for Beginners and Intermediate Users

SOLIDWORKS Textbooks
SOLIDWORKS 2023: A Power Guide for Beginners and Intermediate User
SOLIDWORKS 2021: A Power Guide for Beginners and Intermediate User
SOLIDWORKS 2020: A Power Guide for Beginners and Intermediate User
SOLIDWORKS 2019: A Power Guide for Beginners and Intermediate User
SOLIDWORKS 2018: A Power Guide for Beginners and Intermediate User
SOLIDWORKS 2017: A Power Guide for Beginners and Intermediate User
SOLIDWORKS 2016: A Power Guide for Beginners and Intermediate User
SOLIDWORKS 2015: A Power Guide for Beginners and Intermediate User

SOLIDWORKS Sheet Metal and Surface Design Textbooks
SOLIDWORKS Sheet Metal and Surface Design 2023
SOLIDWORKS Sheet Metal Design 2022
SOLIDWORKS Surface Design 2021 for Beginners and Intermediate Users

SOLIDWORKS Simulation Textbooks
SOLIDWORKS Simulation 2023: A Power Guide for Beginners and Intermediate User
SOLIDWORKS Simulation 2022: A Power Guide for Beginners and Intermediate User
SOLIDWORKS Simulation 2021: A Power Guide for Beginners and Intermediate User
SOLIDWORKS Simulation 2020: A Power Guide for Beginners and Intermediate User
SOLIDWORKS Simulation 2019: A Power Guide for Beginners and Intermediate User
SOLIDWORKS Simulation 2018: A Power Guide for Beginners and Intermediate User

Exercises Books
Some of the exercises books are given below:

SOLIDWORKS Exercises Books
SOLIDWORKS Exercises - Learn by Practicing (3 Edition)
SOLIDWORKS Exercises - Learn by Practicing (2 Edition)

AutoCAD Exercises Books
100 AutoCAD Exercises - Learn by Practicing (2 Edition)
100 AutoCAD Exercises - Learn by Practicing (1 Edition)

Printed in Great Britain
by Amazon

53147967R00247